THE LIFE AND LETTERS OF ST. PAUL

THE LIFE AND LETTERS *of* ST. PAUL

By THE REV.

DAVID SMITH, M.A., D.D.

PROFESSOR OF THEOLOGY IN THE MCCREA MAGEE COLLEGE, LONDONDERRY

With a Foreword by

OTTO A. PIPER, Th.D., D.D.

PROFESSOR OF NEW TESTAMENT LITERATURE AND EXEGESIS
PRINCETON THEOLOGICAL SEMINARY

Publishers

HARPER & BROTHERS

NEW YORK · LONDON

TO

MY MOTHER AND SISTERS

Printed in the United States of America

FOREWORD

Though not as universally known as his first work, *In the Days of His Flesh,* Dr. David Smith's *Life and Letters of St. Paul* is long counted among the theological classics. It was written at an opportune time, just when the great period of modern research in the historical background of the New Testament had come to a relative close. The years between 1890 and 1914 were particularly fertile in the field of Pauline scholarship. But though the number of books and articles on Paul is legion, how few are the works that are of more than a historical interest at the present day, or that appeal to any except the specialist and research scholar! Dr. Smith's monumental work has stood the test of time, because in a unique way it combines readability, scholarship and a genuine love for the man of Tarsus and the cause to which Paul had devoted his life. Biblical scholarship passed through a severe crisis, when Dr. Smith composed his work. Modern individualism had misled many a gifted scholar into the belief that a startling and brilliantly presented hypothesis was worth more than the carefully circumscribed presentation of the actual facts. His work continued the glorious tradition of the great British Biblical scholarship of the Alfelds, Lightfoots, Westcotts and Horts. In an unbiased way he acquaints the reader with the whole evidence and tells him candidly what are the established facts, and where differing interpretations are possible or even necessary. His is a very thorough and comprehensive treatment of the subject. But not for a single moment is he dull or pedantic. For in addition to his wide reading and incisive mind, it was his broad familiarity with the ways and problems of human life that enabled him to throw new light upon almost every single word in the Pauline epistles and the pertinent chapters of Acts.

Nor does our author ever lose sight of the fact that the principal documents which tell us of Paul are found in the Bible, and that the primary reason why modern people should be interested in the former Pharisee is his untiring devotion to the cause of Christ and his challenging proclamation of the Word of Life. It is with the Bible as with the great works of art. Anybody who in their presence tries in the first place to assert himself and to criticize the masters instead of approaching them in a spirit of reverence and appreciation, thereby demonstrates his own pettiness. You may not like a certain work of art, or you may not be able to understand it. But that gives you no choice but to leave it alone until you have grown in understanding. Genuine reverence for the greatness and superiority of the Biblical records characterize Dr. Smith's scholarship. The result is a portrayal of the Apostle written with the accuracy of an eyewitness and the naturalness and vividness of an imaginative historian. But with all its simplicity on the one hand, and its erudite footnotes on the other, the book lets you never forget the astounding miracle that the man Paul, the persecutor of the flock, had been called by the risen Christ himself to be his apostle, and that his message is one that addresses itself to us as urgently and pointedly as to the first Christians.

Otto A. Piper

Princeton, N. J.

PREFACE

It is now some thirteen years since, shortly after the appearance of my first book *The Days of His Flesh: the Earthly Life of Our Lord and Saviour Jesus Christ,* I undertook the task of preparing a Life of St. Paul; and during the interval much has happened to delay its execution. When I undertook it, I was minister in the remote Scottish parish of Tulliallan; and presently, toward the close of the year 1907, I was translated to St. Andrew's Church in the Perthshire town of Blairgowrie, where I ministered for two happy years. The employments of that large and delightful charge engrossed my time and taxed my scanty strength, leaving me small leisure; all the less that my service in preaching was widely requisitioned, and I was continually engaged in the ministry of my *British Weekly* Correspondence. Then, quite unexpectedly, I was invited by the General Assembly of the Presbyterian Church in Ireland to occupy the Chair of Theology in the Londonderry College. Reluctant though I was to leave a people whom I loved and a ministry so rich and glad and venture among strangers and untried responsibilities, I could not but recognise the voice of God in an urgent call addressed to me not only without solicitation on my part but despite my express will; and now, as I review my experience, I bless His gracious providence and thankfully acknowledge the goodness and mercy which have attended me and mine since our coming here.

Amid these changes and ever fresh employments, including the production of various lesser books and the delivery of a course of lectures in the United States of America (published under the title *The Historic Jesus*), my preparation of the Life of St. Paul was much retarded. And then, when it was nearing completion, its appearance was arrested by the catastrophe of the war. Perhaps, however, advantage has accrued from the protracted delay. The task has never been absent from my thoughts even when I was not directly engaged upon it. The figure of the Apostle has assumed ever clearer shape in my mind; his surroundings have fallen into truer perspective; and my narrative depicts him more simply as I have seen him, less confused than it might otherwise have been by multitudinous details and less encumbered by elaborate discussions. Its imperfections, as I am painfully conscious, are indeed manifold, but it is the natural outgrowth of long and loving reflection; and with the old historian of the Maccabees I would say: 'If I have written well and to the point, this is what I myself desired; but if meanly and indifferently, this is all I could attain unto.'

The Pauline literature is enormous, and a mere enumeration of the writers who have made me their debtor, would much increase the dimensions of a work already large enough to incur the censure of that aphorism of Callimachus: *μέγα βιβλίον, μέγα κακόν.* There are, however, several whom it were ingratitude to leave unnamed. First, in the ancient Church there is St. Chrysostom, that prince of preachers and master of exegesis; and not unworthy to stand near him is that anonymous Latin scholar of the fourth century who, because his Commentaries on the Pauline Epistles have been preserved among the Works of St. Ambrose of Milan, is known as 'the Ambrosiaster,' and who, on the evidence of St. Augustine (cf. *Contra Duas Epist. Pelag.*, iv. 7), was Hilary, whether St. Hilary of Poictiers or the less celebrated Hilary the Deacon. Of works belonging to the Post-Reformation period there are three which have yielded me continual profit and delight: (1) the *Annotationes* of Hugo Grotius (Huig van Groot), which derives a pathetic interest from the circumstance that it was one of the tasks which employed its brilliant and versatile author during the years of his imprisonment; (2) the *Synopsis Criticorum* of Matthew Poole, that scholar of Emmanuel College, Cambridge, who espoused the cause of Presbyterianism, and composed his monumental work in five folio volumes after his ejectment from his charge for Nonconformity in 1662; and (3) the *Novum Testamentum Græcum* of Johann Jakob Wetstein with its profusion of Classical, Rabbinical, and Patristic illustrations of the sacred text. Of modern literature it were invidious to speak particularly, but I must mention, with peculiar appreciation, those enduring monuments of English scholarship, the works of the late Bishop Lightfoot, especially his editions of the Pauline Epistles; the *Acta Apostolorum* of Dr. Friedrich Blass; the numerous writings of Sir William Ramsay; and Kirsopp Lake's *Earlier Epistles of St. Paul.*

Of late years archæological investigation has revolutionised our conception of the language of the New Testament and disclosed a fresh significance and beauty in the literary monuments of the Christian revelation. The difficulty which the language of the sacred writers has hitherto presented is that it differs widely from that of the 'profane' authors of the period, such as Plutarch and Lucian, whose Greek, apart from various peculiarities, follows the Attic model; and two diverse explanations formerly prevailed. One minimised the peculiarities of the Greek of the New Testament and laboured to prove it excellent Attic; while the other rather emphasised them and alleged that the Greek of the sacred writers was a unique language, formed mainly under the influence of the Hebrew Scriptures and fitly designated, in Rothe's phrase, 'the language of the Holy Ghost.' The truth has been revealed by recent investigation of the ruins of antiquity, especially in Egypt. The rubbish-heap of the buried city of Oxyrhynchus has yielded a multitude of papyrus leaves (published by the Egypt Exploration Fund under the skilful editorship of Dr. Grenfell and Dr.

Hunt). Some are fragments of ancient books, but most are private letters and kindred documents; and it is these that are so instructive (cf. the late Dr. J. H. Moulton's *Prolegomena* to his *Grammar of New Testament Greek*; Dr. Adolf Deissmann's *Light from the Ancient East*; Dr. George Milligan's *Greek Papyri*). They are non-literary; their language is the **Κοινή** or Common Greek, the *lingua franca* of that period; and the significant fact is that the language of the papyri is the language of the New Testament. Hence it appears that there is in reality no such thing as 'New Testament Greek.' What has hitherto borne that appellation is nothing else than the language of common intercourse in use throughout the Roman Empire; and the distinction of the sacred writers is that they first, and indeed they alone, took the spoken language of their day and employed it for literary purposes.

It is a fresh exemplification of that Rabbinical saying which Archbishop Leighton loved to quote: 'The Law of God speaks the tongue of the children of men.' The Gospel is not a philosophy but glad tidings for the world, and therefore it was proclaimed not in the jargon of the schools but in the language of the market and the home. And here is a lesson for the interpreter of the Living Oracles. As these were first delivered in the tongue of the children of men, so must they be rendered to each generation. King James's translators recognised this when they turned the Scriptures into the kindly mother-tongue of their contemporaries; but language is ever changing, and their archaic English is now strange in our ears. It was the fashion with pedants in the later period to disdain the Common Greek and employ the ancient Attic; and the philosopher Demonax was once answered in that strain. 'My friend,' said he, 'my question was put in the present day, and you answer me as if it were the time of Agamemnon.' And it is no less amiss that the Eternal Truth should be spoken to our generation in the language of 'the spacious days of Queen Elizabeth.' It should be clothed in modern speech, the simple, homely speech of daily use. Translation is always a difficult task, as every one who has essayed it is well aware; and no skill could render adequately the rugged, elusive, and impassioned diction of the Apostle. The utmost I dare hope for my attempt is that it may serve to elucidate obscurities and help my readers to a more intelligent comprehension of his arguments.

For information regarding the Pauline world acknowledgment is due primarily to the invaluable work of the ancient geographer Strabo, who flourished in the reign of Tiberius, a native of Amaseia in Pontus and an extensive traveller, ὃς μάλα πολλὰ πλάγχθη, πολλῶν δ' ἀνθρώπων ἴδεν ἄστεα καὶ νόον ἔγνω. Much also is due to the *Naturalis Historia* of the younger Pliny. And Sir William Ramsay's researches have added not a little to our knowledge of Asia Minor in the Apostle's day.

On the vexed question of Pauline chronology I have found Lewin's *Fasti Sacri* incomparably helpful. Its value, to my mind, lies not in its conclusions, which indeed have seldom commanded my consent, but in its large array of collateral evidence. The truth is that there are few fixed points in the record of the Apostle's career. Absolute certainty is unattainable on the available data; and in the scheme which I have presented, I have merely indicated what appears, in my judgment, the probable order of events, stating my reasons and refraining from profitless discussion. It seems to me that my arrangement is, in the main, supported by both internal and external evidence; but I am mindful of Thomas Fuller's admonition: 'Chronology is a surly, churlish cur, and hath bit many a man's fingers. Blame me not therefore, if willing to keep my own hands whole.'

And indeed this has been my constant practice. Controversy is a foolish and futile employment; and I have endeavoured to portray St. Paul simply as I have perceived him during long years of loving and delightful study of the sacred memorials of his life and labour, mentioning the views of others only as they served to illustrate and confirm my own. If ever I have failed in acknowledging any debt, it has been through inadvertence, and I crave forgiveness. And I would fain hope that I have written nothing discourteous, nothing hurtful. This were indeed a grievous offence in the story of one who, amid much provocation, continually bore himself as the very pattern of a Christian gentleman.

D. S.

4, The College,
Londonderry.

CONTENTS

	PAGE
Foreword	v
Preface	vii

BOOK I

SAUL OF TARSUS

His Early Years	17
The Martyrdom of Stephen	34
The Conversion of Saul	45

BOOK II

PAUL THE APOSTLE OF JESUS CHRIST

His Call to the Apostleship of the Gentiles	65
The First Mission:	
i. Ordination of Antioch	78
ii. Evangelisation of Cyprus	81
iii. Evangelisation of Southern Galatia	86
iv. The Homeward Journey	104
The Council at Jerusalem	107
The Second Mission:	
i. Disunion of Paul and Barnabas	116
ii. Progress through Asia Minor	119
iii. The Call of the West	124
iv. Evangelisation of Macedonia	126

THE SECOND MISSION—(*continued*)

PAGE

v. Sojourn at Athens 141

vi. Ministry at Corinth 149

vii. The Homeward Journey 188

DEFECTION IN GALATIA 193

THE THIRD MISSION:

i. The Setting Forth 222

ii. Ministry at Ephesus 224

iii. Trouble at Corinth 234

iv. Retreat to Macedonia 341

v. Sojourn at Corinth 371

vi. The Journey to Jerusalem 459

BOOK III

PAUL THE PRISONER OF JESUS CHRIST

ARREST AT JERUSALEM 471

IMPRISONMENT AT CÆSAREA 480

THE VOYAGE TO ROME 490

THE FIRST IMPRISONMENT AT ROME 502

BOOK IV

THE CLOSING YEARS

THE HISTORICAL PROBLEM 579

THE APOSTLE'S LATER MINISTRY 596

THE SECOND IMPRISONMENT AT ROME 623

THE APOSTLE'S MARTYRDOM 638

APPENDIX

		PAGE
I.	Pauline Chronology	645
II.	The Narratives of Saul's Conversion	662
III.	Paul's Malady	664
IV.	Luke and Antioch	667
V.	The Decree of the Council at Jerusalem	671
VI.	The Sacrament of Baptism	675
VII.	Verbal Peculiarities in the Pauline Letters	681

INDEX

I.	Names and Subjects	697
II.	Greek Words and Phrases	703

MAPS

I.	St. Paul's Travels	1
II.	Asia Minor	222
III.	Ancient Trade Routes	577

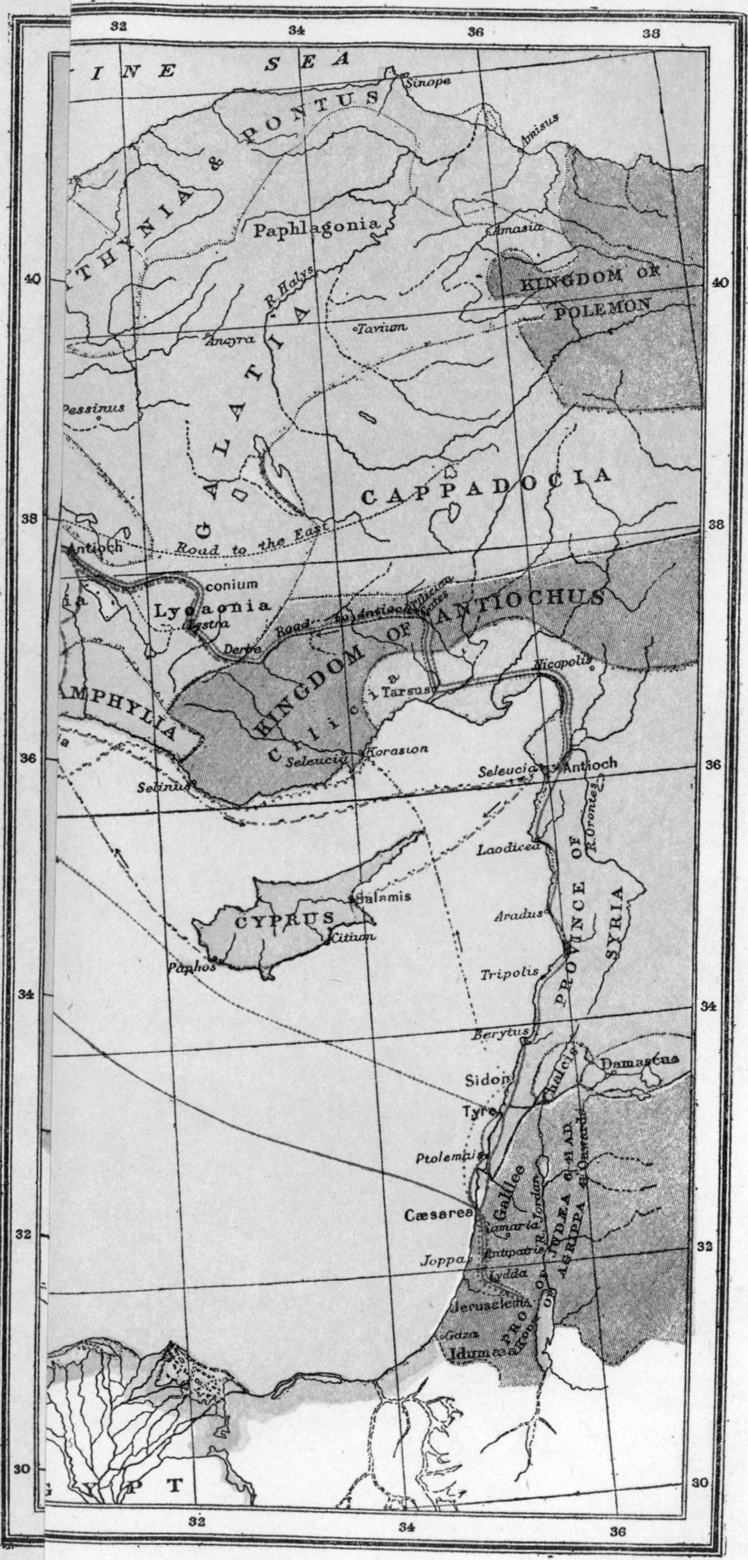

INE SEA
Sinope
PONTUS
Amisus
THYNIA &
Paphlagonia
Amasia
KINGDOM OF
POLEMON
R. Halys
GALATIA
Tavium
Ancyra
Pessinus
CAPPADOCIA
Antioch
Road to the East
conium
Lycaonia
Lystra
Derbe
Road to Antioch
KINGDOM OF ANTIOCHUS
Cilician Gates
Nicopolis
AMPHYLIA
Cilicia
Tarsus
Korasion
Seleucia
Selinus
Seleucia
Antioch
R. Orontes
Laodicea
PROVINCE OF SYRIA
Salamis
CYPRUS
Citium
Paphos
Aradus
Tripolis
Berytus
Chalcis
Damascus
Sidon
Tyre
Ptolemais
Galilee
Cæsarea
Samaria
R. Jordan
Antipatris
Joppa
Lydda
JUDÆA
AGRIPPA
Jerusalem
Gaza
Idumæa
GYPT

THE PREPARATION FOR THE GOSPEL

'Every valley shall be exalted, and every mountain and hill shall be made low; and the crooked shall be made straight, and the rough places plain: and the glory of the Lord shall be revealed, and all flesh shall see it together: for the mouth of the Lord hath spoken it.'

The Prophet Isaiah.

THE PREPARATION FOR THE GOSPEL

Universal destination of the Gospel.

Mt. xxviii. 19; Ac. i. 8.

OUR Blessed Lord, though He was a Jew after the flesh and lived and died in the little land of Palestine, was the Saviour of the World; and His latest charge to His Apostles was that they should 'go and make disciples of all the nations' and be His witnesses 'unto the uttermost part of the earth.' It was a stupendous enterprise, and might seem impossible for that feeble band; but it is an impressive fact, a signal evidence of the overruling providence of Almighty God, that the antecedent history of mankind had been nothing else than a preparation for the work. The storms which for centuries had swept the earth, fraught, as it appeared, with disaster and leaving confusion in their train, had opened a way for the Gospel and facilitated its progress and diffusion.

Providential preparations:

I. The Jewish Dispersion.

The first of those providential preparations was the dispersion of the Jewish people.[1]

Cf. Jo. vii. 35; Ja. i. 1; 1 Pet. i. 1.

Jer. xli-xliv.

This movement began as early as the eighth century B.C. with the transportation of multitudes of the people to the far East by the Assyrian invaders; and it continued during the ensuing centuries, sometimes perforce, as when Pompey carried his Jewish captives to Rome in the year 63 B.C., but more and more by voluntary emigration. In the days of Jeremiah a band of Judæans made insurrection against the governor whom the King of Babylon had set over their devastated land; and, dreading vengeance, the unhappy remnant of the nation migrated southward and settled in Egypt. Subsequently, under the Greek domination, the foundation of new cities and the privileges offered to immigrants attracted adventurous Jews, and the tide of colonists flowed in ever increasing volume to Syria and Egypt, and then to Asia Minor, and westward to Greece, Italy, and Spain.

[1] Cf. Schürer, *The Jewish People in the Time of Jesus Christ*, II. ii. pp. 220 ff.

Its extent. Hence it came to pass that by the beginning of the Christian era the Jewish Dispersion had covered the world, harbouring chiefly in the busy centres of commerce. Its extent appears from the enumeration of the countries represented by the worshippers who had come to the Feast and witnessed the wonders that followed the outpouring of the Holy Spirit on
Ac. ii. 9-11. the Day of Pentecost—Parthia, Media, Elam, and Mesopotamia in the East; Cappadocia, Pontus, Asia, Phrygia, and Pamphylia in Asia Minor; Arabia, Egypt, and Cyrenaica in the South; and Crete and Rome in the West. This is no exaggeration. The geographer Strabo [1] had already affirmed that the Jews 'had invaded every city, and it was not easy to find a place in the world which had not received that race and was not mastered by it.' And, in his letter to the Emperor Caligula, Agrippa mentions Jewish colonies in Egypt, Phœnicia, Cœle-Syria, Pamphylia, and most of Asia Minor as far as Bithynia and Pontus; also in Europe—Thessaly, Bœotia, Macedonia, Anatolia, Attica, Argos, Corinth, and the most and best parts of the Peloponnesus; and, moreover, in the principal islands—Eubœa, Cyprus, and Crete.[2] The evidence remains to this day in the monuments of Jewish life and worship—inscriptions, ostraca, and papyri—which are continually being brought to light in all the countries surrounding the basin of the Mediterranean.

Its magnitude. The Jewish colonies were not only numerous but large. In the vague but expressive phrase of the historian, there were 'infinite myriads' of Jews beyond the Euphrates: 'their number could not be ascertained'; [3] and in the city of Damascus no fewer than ten thousand perished in a massacre during the reign of Nero.[4] Alexandria, the Egyptian capital, was mapped out into five divisions, distinguished by the first five letters of the alphabet; and of these two were designated 'Jewish' since their inhabitants were mainly Jews. There was, moreover, a considerable Jewish admixture in the other divisions; and the total Jewish population of Egypt amounted to no less than a million.[5] Italy also had its Jewish colonies.

[1] Quoted in Jos. *Ant.* XIV. vii. 2.
[2] Phil. *Leg. ad Caium*, 36.
[3] Jos. *Ant.* XI. v. 2.
[4] *De Bell. Jud.* II. xx. 2. In VII. viii. 7 the number is put at 18,000.
[5] Phil. *In Flacc.* 6, 8.

The chief of these was at Rome. Its nucleus was Pompey's captive settlement, whence probably the imperial city derived her apocalyptic title of 'Babylon'; and it is an indication of its growth that in the year 6 B.C., when a Jewish embassy visited Rome to sue for autonomy, it was received on its arrival by over eight thousand resident Jews.[1]

Loyalty of Hellenists to their adopted countries.

Those Hellenists, as the Jews of the Dispersion were styled,[2] remained true to their ancestral faith in the countries of their adoption. They made frequent pilgrimages to Jerusalem, and at the great festivals the sacred capital was thronged with worshippers from afar;[3] and they paid their annual tribute to the Temple, entrusting it to men of good repute appointed in almost every town to receive it and convey it to its destination.[4] None the less were they loyal to their own communities. They accounted the Holy City as their metropolis, but the countries where their lot was cast and where they had been born and nurtured, they regarded as their fatherlands,[5] mindful of the ancient prophet's counsel (Jer. xxix. 7.) to the Babylonian exiles: 'Seek the peace of the city whither I have caused you to be carried away captive, and pray unto the Lord for it: for in the peace thereof shall ye have peace.'[6]

Literary animosity against the Jews.

And thus it came to pass that they exerted a potent influence in the countries of their adoption, and won multitudes of the heathen to their faith. This may indeed seem surprising in view of the prevailing sentiment of the pagan literature of the period. Cicero terms the Jewish religion 'a barbarous superstition';[7] and grave historians impute horrible iniquities to 'the filthy race,' charging them not merely with sloth inasmuch as they did no work each seventh day and devoted each seventh year to idleness, but with the practice (Cf. Ex xxiii. 10, 11; Lev. xxv. 3-5.) of ridiculous and monstrous rites—the worship of an ass's head, and the annual sacrifice of a Gentile stranger.[8] And

[1] Jos. *Ant.* XVII. xi. 1; *De Bell. Jud.* II. vi. 1.

[2] Cf. p. 38.

[3] On the basis of the lambs offered it was estimated that the worshippers at the Passover of A.D. 66 numbered 2,700,200 (Jos. *De Bell. Jud.* VI. ix. 3).

[4] Phil. *De Monarch.* ii. 3. On the enormous tribute of Laodicea, cf. p. 549.

[5] Phil. *De Flacc.* 7.

[6] Cf. the maxim of Bias (Diog. Laert. I. 85).

[7] *Pro Flacc.* 28.

[8] Tac. *Hist.* V. 4, 8. Jos. *Contra Apion.* II. 7 f.; cf. quotation in Suidas (under Δαμόκριτος) from Damocritus the historian's work 'On the Jews.' The charge of worshipping an ass's head was transferred to the Christians, who were

the Roman satirist not only makes merry over their abhorrence of swine's flesh but, like Tacitus, accuses them of hatred of the rest of mankind.[1] All this, however, represents merely the sentiment of the cultured classes; and they knew Judaism only by common report and naturally despised it as an alien thing, the creed of a turbulent race in frequent insurrection against the imperial rule. In truth their animosity was an unwitting tribute; for it was provoked, as they betray in the midst of their revilings,[2] by the successful proselytism of the Jews. 'Among the masses,' says the Jewish historian,[3] 'there has long been much zeal for our religion; nor is there any city, Greek or barbarian, nor a single nation where the custom of our seventh day of rest from labour has not come into vogue; and the fasts and the lamp-lightings[4] and many of our prohibitions regarding food are observed.' Nor is this a mere patriotic boast. 'So far,' says the philosopher Seneca,[5] 'has the usage of the accursed race prevailed that it is now received throughout all lands: the conquered have given laws to the conquerors.' And in the reign of Honorius (A.D. 395-423) the poet Claudius Rutilius Numatianus actually wished that Judæa had never been subdued by Pompey and Titus; for then the pestilence would not have spread so widely, and the conquered nation would not have oppressed its conquerors.[6] Women were especially impressionable, and it is recorded that in the time of Nero the women of Damascus were all, with a few exceptions, captivated by the Jewish religion.[7] It appealed mainly indeed, as Josephus observes, to the lower orders; yet it won not a few ladies of rank even in the imperial capital, like Fulvia, that Roman

Cf. I Th. ii. 15.

An unwitting tribute.

Successful proselytism.

Cf. Ac. xiii. 50; xvii. 4.

thence styled *asinarii*. Cf. Tert. *Apol.* xvi; *Ad Nat.* I. xiv; Min. Fel. *Oct.* ix. 3.

[1] Juv. vi. 160, xiv. 98 ff. Tac. *Hist.* v. 5. Cf. Jos. *Contra Apion.* II. 10.

[2] Cf. Tac. *Hist.* v. 5; Hor. *Sat.* I. iv. 142 f.

[3] Jos. *Contra Apion.* II. 39.

[4] Ex. xxxv. 3. Cf. Sen. *Epist.* xcv; Pers. v. 179-84.

[5] In Aug. *De Civit. Dei*, VI. xi.

[6] *Itinerar.* 395-8:

> 'Atque utinam nunquam Judæa subacta fuisset
> Pompeii bellis imperioque Titi!
> Latius excisae pestis contagia serpunt,
> Victoresque suos natio victa premit.'

[7] Jos. *De Bell. Jud.* II. xx. 2.

lady whose pious generosity was so grossly abused,[1] and Nero's unhappy empress, Poppæa Sabina.[2] Nor were there lacking men of exalted station who embraced the Jewish faith, like the chamberlain of Candace, the Queen of Ethiopia, Azizus, King of Emesa, and Polemo, King of Cilicia.[3]

Ac. viii. 26 ff.

The Gospel's opportunity.

Thus widely were the Jewish people scattered abroad, and their dispersion served to facilitate the diffusion of Christianity. The heralds of the Gospel were themselves Jews, and their mission, like their Lord's, was not to overthrow the ancient faith but to proclaim its fulfilment. It was no small advantage that, wherever they went, they found an audience which could understand their message; and in every town which they visited, they repaired immediately to the Jewish synagogue, and there preached the glad tidings. The Gospel was indeed a message of universal grace, but the providence of God had prescribed the apostolic procedure—'both to the Jew, in the first instance, and to the Greek.'

Cf. Mt. v. 17.

Cf. Ac. ix. 20; xiii. 5, 14 ff.; xiv. 1; xvii. 1-3, 17; xviii. 4, 19 28; xix. 8; xxviii. 17, 23.

Rom. i. 16.

2. A universal language.

Another pathway had been opened by the Greek conquests.[4] Not the least of the difficulties which missionaries in all ages have experienced, has lain in their ignorance of the native languages and the preliminary necessity of laboriously acquiring these; and it has often been supposed that the Apostles were miraculously aided by 'the gift of tongues,' which enabled them, wherever they travelled, to preach in the language of their hearers.[5] The truth, however, is that the difficulty never confronted them. The ambition of Alexander the Great and his successors had been to weld the nations into one world by the universal imposition of Greek usages; and it had been so far achieved that, save in remote regions where the new civilisation had never penetrated, the Greek language was the common speech of all the nations which environed the Mediterranean. The native languages did not indeed perish. Each country retained its own vernacular. Its people were bilingual: they understood the general *lingua franca*, but they clung to their mother-tongues and employed these among themselves, since they were dear

[1] Cf. pp. 389 f. [2] Cf. p. 505.
[3] Jos. *Ant.* XX. vii. 1, 3.
[4] Cf. Legge, *Forerunners and Rivals of Christianity*, chap. i.
[5] Cf. pp. 296 f.

to their hearts and pleasant in their ears.[1] Thus the people
Ac. xiv. 7-11. of Lystra understood the Apostles when the latter addressed them in the Common Greek; but when they witnessed the miracle of the healing of the cripple, in their surprise they lapsed into their vernacular and exclaimed to each other in Lycaonian: 'The gods have come down to us in the likeness
xxi. 37-xxii. 2. of men!' The Common Greek was spoken also at Jerusalem; but when Paul was beset by the mob, he addressed them in Aramaic, and the homely accents arrested their attention and calmed their frenzy. In Egypt, as the papyri which have recently been unearthed so strikingly demonstrate, the Greek language prevailed; and it was spoken freely even at Rome.[2] Plutarch confesses that during his sojourn at the imperial capital in the reign of Trajan (A.D. 98-117) he was entirely ignorant of Latin and had no leisure to acquire it; yet he experienced no difficulty in conducting the negotiations which his native city of Chæronea had entrusted to him, or in discoursing on philosophy to the audiences which waited upon him.[3] In fact Rome, like the other cities of the period, was bilingual; and hence the *Monumentum Ancyranum*, the record of his achievements which the Emperor Augustus designed for erection before his mausoleum, was inscribed both in Latin and in Greek,[4] and Paul's great encyclical on Justification by Faith, though specially destined for the Church at Rome, was written in Greek.

3. The Roman Empire. Nor should it be forgotten how much the imperial constitution furthered the progress of the Gospel. It was a magnificent organisation, created largely by the statesmanship of the Emperor Augustus.[5] He is reported to have boasted that he had found Rome a city of bricks and he left it a city of

[1] Cf. Hieronym. *Procem.*, *Comment. Lib. II in Epist. ad Gal.*: 'Galatas excepto sermone Græco, quo omnis Oriens loquitur, propriam linguam eandem pene habere quam Treviros, nec referre si aliqua exinde corruperint.'

[2] The *graffiti* chalked on the walls in execration of Nero's crimes were in some cases Greek epigrams (cf. Suet. *Ner.* 39). Cf. Juv. iii. 60 f.

[3] *Demosth.* ii. 2.

[4] Suet. *Aug.* 101: 'indicem rerum a se gestarum, quem vellet incidi in aeneis tabulis quæ ante Mausoleum statuerentur.' Cf. Lewin, *Fasti Sacri*, pp. 377 ff.; Schürer, I. i. p. 115. On the Κοινή cf. Moulton, *Gramm. of N. T. Gk.*, vol. 1; Deissmann, *Light from the Ancient East*; Milligan, *Greek Papyri and N. T. Documents*, II.

[5] Cf. Tac. *Ann.* I. 9.

marble;[1] but that was in truth the least of his achievements. His influence reached far beyond the capital and transformed the world. The triumph of the Roman arms had established 'the Roman Peace'[2]—a priceless benefit even to the conquered races which lamented the loss of their independence and chafed under the imperial yoke. Brigandage and piracy had been suppressed, and in the remotest wilds life and property were secure.[3] Civilisation was advanced; commerce flourished; and in its peaceful rivalry ancient hostilities were forgotten.

Romana Pax.

The Empire was the world, and it was all interlinked.[4] From the capital to the farthest frontier ran the Roman roads, those triumphs of engineering skill which have outlasted the decay of nigh two thousand years.[5] Constructed originally for the transit of troops, they served afterwards the happier uses of civilisation and rendered travel easy, uniting the sundered nations and reconciling their estrangement. Asia Minor was traversed from west to east by the great trade route from Ephesus to the Euphrates, and lesser highways intersected the country in every direction; while the famous Egnatian Road stretched from Dyrrachium on the Adriatic through Illyricum, Macedonia, and Thrace to the Hellespont, marked so far as Cypsela on the Hebrus with milestones and measuring thither five hundred and thirty Roman miles.[6] The sea too, cleared of pirates, was a highway betwixt the nations, and, save in the winter season when navigation was suspended,[7] ships laden with merchandise and passengers were

Roman roads.

[1] Suet. *Aug.* 28.

[2] Cf. Sen. *De Prov.* IV. 14; *De Clem.* I. i. 2, iv. 2; Plin. *Nat. Hist.* XXVII. I; Tac. *Ann.* XII. 33.

[3] In the reign of Tiberius Strabo (756) spoke of the happy change which the Roman administration had recently effected by putting down the brigands who had formerly sallied from their fastnesses among the mountains of Arabia and Ituræa near Damascus and plundered merchants from Arabia Felix. And Apollonius of Tyana (cf. *Vit.* I. 20) realised the value of Roman civilisation when he passed beyond its limits.

[4] Cf. Tac. *Ann.* I. 9.

[5] The Latin phrase was not to 'construct' but to 'fortify a road,' *viam munire* (cf. Suet. *Aug.* 30).

[6] Strabo, 322; Cic. *De Prov. Cons.* ii.: 'via illa nostra, quæ per Macedoniam est ad Hellespontum, militaris.' Cf. Tafel, *Via Milit. Rom. Egn.*

[7] Cf. Append. I, p. 648.

continually plying to and fro among the numerous and busy ports on the coasts and islands of the Mediterranean.

Roman Law.

Still more advantageous was the protection which the august authority of Roman Law afforded the heralds of the Gospel.[1] Again and again its strong and impartial hand interposed between Paul and the fury of the populace, pagan and Jewish alike; and it is no wonder that he accounted it a beneficent ordinance of God and charged the Christians to revere it. He recognised in the imperial order a bulwark which restrained the forces of iniquity and averted the impending cataclysm;[2] and it even seemed in his eyes an adumbration of the Heavenly Commonwealth.[3]

Ac. xviii. 12-16; xix. 35-41; xxi. 27 ff. Rom. xiii. 1-7; 1 Tim. ii. 1-4. 2 Th. ii. 6, 7. Eph. ii. 19.

4. Decay of pagan religion.

It constituted the supreme appeal of Christianity that, when it appeared, the pagan religions were dead. The ancient mythology was the basis of the Greek religion, and the poems of Homer and Hesiod were its sacred oracles.[4] It sufficed for centuries, but the rise of philosophy discovered its irrationality; and as early as the sixth century its anthropomorphism was mercilessly ridiculed by Xenophanes, the founder of the Eleatic school.

> 'All things unto the gods have Homer and Hesiod ascribed,
> Whatsoever of men reproaches and blame are accounted,
> Thieving and fornication and cozening one of another.'[5]

From generation to generation the untenability of the ancient religion was ever more clearly recognised; and the situation towards the close of the pre-Christian era was defined by M. Terentius Varro, 'the acutest and most learned of mankind.'[6] There were, he said, three kinds of theology—the mythic, the physical, and the civil. The first was the theology of the poets; and it was a tissue of grotesque and frequently immoral fables, ascribing to the gods everything that belongs not merely to man but to man at his basest. The second was the theology of the philosophers, who traced all things to a natural origin. The first principle, according to Heraclitus, was fire; according to Pythagoras, numbers; according to

[1] Cf. Tac. *Ann.* I. 9: 'jus apud cives, modestiam apud socios.'

[2] Cf. p. 173. [3] Cf. pp. 512, 533. [4] Cf. Herod. II. 53.

[5] Sext. Empir. *Adv. Math.* ix. 193. Cf. Ægid. Menag. on Diog. Laert. ix. 18.

[6] Aug. *De Civ. Dei*, VI. v. ff.

Epicurus, atoms. Finally, there was the theology of the populace—the religious ceremonial decreed, regulated, and maintained by the State. 'This is the kind of theology which the citizens and especially the priests are bound to know and administer; which prescribes what gods, what rites and sacrifices it is right that every man should publicly worship and perform.' Religion had gone, and only ritual remained. As Gibbon has it, 'the various modes of worship which prevailed in the Roman world were all considered by the people as equally true; by the philosopher as equally false; and by the magistrate as equally useful.'[1]

Quest for God.

The ancient faith was dead, but the religious instinct continued indestructible in the human heart which was made for God and is restless until it find rest in Him;[2] and nothing in the annals of that period is more impressive than the confessions which earnest souls have left of their spiritual hunger and their quest for satisfaction. Not the least remarkable is the story of St. Justin Martyr, a pagan though a native of Palestine—how he sought rest successively in each of the philosophic schools, the Stoic, the Peripatetic, the Pythagorean, and the Platonist, and sought it vainly, until at length he found it in Christ.[3]

'Nameless altars.'

His was no singular experience. The world was crying after God, and its religion, even where it was still believed, was unavailing. A striking evidence is furnished by the prevalent custom of erecting altars 'to unknown gods.'[4] Cf. Ac. xvii. 23.
Its origin was generally explained by a curious legend.[5] In the sixth century, it was said, a pestilence had visited Athens, and it continued after the citizens had offered propitiatory sacrifices to all the gods they knew. In their despair they summoned the Cretan poet and prophet, Epimenides; and he drove a flock of sheep, both black and white, to the Areio- Cf. Tit. i. 12.

[1] *Decline and Fall*, chap. ii.

[2] Aug. *Confess.* i. 1: 'Fecisti nos ad Te, et inquietum est cor nostrum, donec requiescat in Te.'

[3] *Dial. cum Tryph.*, *ad init.*

[4] Philostr. *Apoll. Tyan.* vi. 8: 'It is more prudent to speak well of all gods, and that at Athens, where altars even of unknown deities have been set up.' Paus. I. i. 4; Min. Fel. *Oct.* vi. 2; Luc. *Philopatr.* 9, 29.

[5] Diog. Laert. i. 110. Cf. Isid. Pel. *Epist.* iv. 69, where two legends are mentioned.

pagos, and suffered them to stray thence whither they would, and wherever each lay down it was sacrificed 'to the fitting god.' The device proved efficacious, and thenceforward it was the fashion throughout the Greek world [1] to erect 'nameless altars,' bearing the dedication 'to an unknown god' or 'to unknown gods.'

Oriental syncretism.

It was a confession of the insufficiency of the existing religion and the need of a larger revelation; and more and more the heart of the western world turned wistfully toward the mystic faiths of the East as these came within its ken. The worship of Cybele, the Phrygian Mother of the Gods, prevailed in Greece as early as the close of the fifth century B.C., and passed into Rome during the Second Punic War; [2] and other oriental cults soon followed, especially those of the Persian Mithras and the Egyptian Serapis and Isis. It would indeed have been strange had Judaism alone of all the oriental faiths made no appeal to the eager heart of the West; and the fact is that there was no other save the Egyptian that found so much favour. At all events, when in the reign of Tiberius an unsuccessful attempt was made to repress the alien religions which had invaded the capital, it was against the Egyptian and the Jewish rites that it was directed.[3]

Attractiveness of Jewish monotheism.

Its austere ethic and still more its lofty spirituality may indeed have repelled the pagan multitude,[4] but those very characteristics commended the Jewish faith to souls of a nobler order which yearned for purity and shrank alike from the Greek deification of the human and from the Egyptian animal-worship.[5] These welcomed the Jewish monotheism. It was an ideal which at once did no outrage to their intellects and afforded their hearts a satisfaction which they could not find in the cold abstractions of philosophy. Yet they did not for the most part embrace Judaism outright. The ceremonial Law was distasteful to them, and they would not submit to its rites. And so they remained uncircumcised. They revered the One Living and True God and shared in

'The God-fearing.'

[1] At Olympia (cf. Paus. v. xiv. 8); at Pergamum (cf. inscription discovered in 1910 and described by Deissmann, *St. Paul*, pp. 262 ff.).

[2] Cf. Liv. xxix. 11, 14; Ovid. *Fast.* iv. 179 f.; Juv. iii. 137 f.

[3] Cf. Tac. *Ann.* II. 85; Suet. *Tib.* 36; Jos. *Ant.* XVIII. iii. 4.

[4] Juv. xiv. 97; cf. Tac. *Hist.* v. 5.

[5] Cf. Strabo, 760 f.

the worship of Synagogue and Temple, and were frequently conspicuous, like the centurion of Capernaum and that other centurion, Cornelius of Cæsarea, for the lavish generosity of their offerings.[1] But they did not profess themselves Jews, and they were distinguished from the proselytes by the titles of 'the God-fearing' and 'the devout.'[2]

Lk. vii. 4, 5. Ac. x. 1-4.

The Gospel's opportunity.

These men represented a widespread tendency of the period. They were seeking rest for their souls, and they found it after a sort in Judaism. But Judaism was insufficient. It was only a temporary resting-place, a foretaste of a nobler satisfaction. And this is the deepest of all the providential preparations for the Gospel. The world was, if the phrase be pardonable, prospecting for a faith, and its unconscious prayer was answered by the advent of Christianity.

The menace of Judaism.

Cf. Mt. xv. 16, 17; xvi. 8-11, 22, 23; xx. 22; Lk. xviii. 34; xxiv. 25.

The world was thus ready for Christianity; it was waiting for the heralds of the Cross. But the heralds were tardy in appearing. While their Lord was with them, the Apostles had continually grieved Him by their slowness of heart and their imperviousness to the ideals of His Kingdom; and much of their dulness remained after His departure despite the illumination of the Holy Spirit. It is not a little remarkable that for some four years they tarried in Judæa in apparent obliviousness of His farewell charge that they should 'go and make disciples of all the nations'; and it was only the stern compulsion of a fierce persecution that drove them abroad. They were not indeed without excuse. The Lord had bidden them 'begin from Jerusalem,' and it was needful that the Church should be securely established at the centre ere she extended her borders.[3] But the situation presented a graver aspect. The Apostles were not only slow in girding themselves to their mission but they entertained a poor conception of the message which had been entrusted to them. When the persecution was over, Peter went forth on a mission,

Lk. xxiv. 47.

Cf. Ac. ix. 32-xi. 18.

[1] Cf. Jos. *Ant.* XIV. vii. 2; *De Bell. Jud.* VII. iii. 3.

[2] *οἱ φοβούμενοι τὸν Θεόν* (cf. Ac. x. 2, 22; xiii. 16, 26); *οἱ σεβόμενοι τὸν Θεόν* (cf. xviii. 7) or simply *οἱ σεβόμενοι* (cf. xiii. 50; xvii. 4, 17).

[3] Their procrastination was justified in after days by a legend, ascribed to St. Peter, that the Lord had charged them to remain for twelve years at Jerusalem. Cf. Clem. Alex. *Strom.* VI. v. 43: *μετὰ δώδεκα ἔτη ἐξέλθετε εἰς τὸν κόσμον, μή τις εἴπῃ, οὐκ ἠκούσαμεν.* Eus. *H. E.* v. 18.

but it was confined within narrow limits. He never passed beyond the confines of Palestine. His farthest reach was the Plain of Sharon with its cities of Lydda, Joppa, and Cæsarea; and it appears that he addressed himself exclusively to Jews, nor would he ever have thought of preaching to Gentiles had he not received an appeal from Cornelius the centurion of Cæsarea. And Cornelius was not a mere Gentile. He was one of the 'God-fearing.' Yet Peter's action in receiving him and his friends into Christian fellowship and administering to them the Sacrament of Baptism was challenged on his return to Jerusalem by a party of extremists.[1] His offence in their eyes was not that he had admitted Gentiles into the Church, but that he had admitted them uncircumcised. The Mosaic Law, they maintained, was permanently obligatory and its observance was necessary to salvation.

The Church's deliverer.

The thought of those 'champions of circumcision' was that Christianity was simply Judaism *plus* the confession of Jesus as the Christ, the promised Messiah; and had they prevailed, the Church would have degenerated into a mere Jewish sect. She would never have realised her universal mission or grasped her providential opportunities. The hope of the world lay in her emancipation from the past; and the mercy of God did not fail her in that perilous crisis. Out of the very heart of Judaism came a man of large vision and courageous spirit who broke her fetters and led her forth on her world-wide enterprise. And the story of the man and the deliverance which he wrought is now our high theme.

[1] *οἱ ἐκ περιτομῆς* (xi. 2; cf. Gal. ii. 12), 'the champions of circumcision,' more precisely defined as *τινες τῶν ἀπὸ τῆς αἱρέσεως τῶν Φαρισαίων πεπιστευκότες* (xv. 5).

BOOK I

SAUL OF TARSUS

'I will bring the blind by a way that they know not; in paths that they know not will I lead them: I will make darkness light before them, and crooked places straight.'

The Prophet Isaiah.

HIS EARLY YEARS

'He was makin' himsell a' the time; but he didna ken maybe what he was about till years had passed.'—LOCKHART, *Life of Scott*, chap. vii.

TARSUS was pronounced by the greatest of her sons 'no undistinguished city,' and she merited the encomium.[1] She was the metropolis of Cilicia and the western capital, as Antioch was the eastern, of the united Province of Syria-Cilicia. Her origin is lost in the mist of antiquity. According to the mythologists, she had been founded by Triptolemus during the wanderings of the Argives in quest of Io, and her name was derived from the wing (*tarsos*) of Pegasus which had fallen there.[2] She stood, however, in no need of legendary glorification. She owed much to her natural situation, standing as she did on a fair plain, bounded northward by the long range of Taurus and eastward by the ridge of Amanus. This spacious champaign was blessed with luxuriant fertility, albeit it bore one serious disadvantage inasmuch as it was subject to visitations of malaria by reason of its marshes and the sultriness of its climate. Across it flowed the river Cydnus which, issuing from the Taurus and pouring its rapid tide through a deep gorge, emerged close to the city and passed through her midst, occasioning an ill-natured jest which likened the citizens to water-fowl squatted by the stream.[3] Since Tarsus was only three-quarters of a mile from the sea, the course of the Cydnus was very short; yet its stream was navigable, as was proved on one memorable occasion when it floated the gorgeous galley of Cleopatra on her coming from Egypt to Antony's camp in Cilicia.[4] Its waters, cold from the heart of the mountain, were accounted efficacious for the relief of

Tarsus. Ac. xxi. 39

Her situation.

[1] Cf. Strabo, 673-5.

[2] Juv. iii. 118.

[3] Philostr. *Apoll. Tyan.* i. 7.

[4] Plut. *Ant.* xxvi. Cf. Shakespeare's magnificent description in *Ant. and Cleop.* II. ii. 195-223.

swellings of the joints and gouty affections in both men and cattle.

Her prosperity.

At the beginning of the Christian era Tarsus was at the height at once of her prosperity and of her fame. The former was derived partly from the fertility of the neighbouring country and still more from the lucrative commerce which she conducted through her port of Rhegma at the river-mouth. And she enjoyed a yet nobler celebrity. She was at that period the world's principal seat of learning. 'So deeply,' writes the geographer Strabo, 'are the people there imbued with zeal for philosophy that they have surpassed Athens and Alexandria and every other place that can be mentioned.' And she possessed this proud distinction which Alexandria alone shared—that her savants were all natives. Students flocked to her schools from other lands, but she had no need of alien teachers. On the contrary, she had no room for the multitude of her learned sons, and she sent them abroad to enlighten the world. 'Rome especially can learn the multitude of the city's savants; for she is full of Tarsians and Alexandrians.'

Her intellectual fame.

Her famous sons.

This claim is demonstrated by the goodly array of her sons who had attained eminence in every field of intellectual activity. These included the Stoic philosophers Antipater, Archedamus, Nestor, Athenodorus Cordulio, Cato's teacher, and Athenodorus the son of Sandon and the teacher of the Emperor Augustus; also Nestor the Academic, the teacher of Marcellus, the son of Augustus' sister Octavia, and other philosophers; grammarians, too, like Artemidorus and Diodorus; and poets, like Dionysius the tragedian.[1] The neighbouring seaport of Soli, though unenviably immortalised by the term 'solecism,'[2] nevertheless produced not only Chrysippus, the Stoic philosopher, whose father, a native of Tarsus, had migrated thither, but the comic poet Philemon and the natural philosopher Aratus.[3] It is a mere inadvertence when Browning styles Aratus 'a native of Tarsus';[4] but doubtless Aratus, and Chrysippus and Philemon too, would be educated there. And so was another of less happy

[1] There was a school of tragedy known as 'the Tarsian' (Diog. Laert. iv. 58).

[2] Diog. Laert. i. 51. [3] Strabo, 671. [4] *Cleon*, prefatory note.

fame—Apollonius of Tyana.[1] At the age of fourteen his father brought him to Tarsus from his home in Cappadocia to study under the rhetorician Euthydemus, and it is perhaps no reproach to the city that his experience there dissatisfied the future charlatan. His complaint, curiously enough, was that the atmosphere of Tarsus was unfavourable to the study of philosophy, inasmuch as her people were luxurious and dissolute with an unpleasant propensity to scoffing and insolence. It is indeed probable that neither charge was groundless; for Tarsus was a wealthy city, and where there is wealth there is apt to be luxury, and the citizens of the neighbouring capital of Syrian Antioch were notorious for their scurrilous wit.[2] Nevertheless the fact remains that Tarsus was a brilliant city; and if it be true that his city's reputation is the first condition of a man's happiness,[3] it was no small advantage to be born and nurtured in her midst.

But Tarsus had another son greater than all these. There were many Jews in Cilicia, so many that they had a synagogue at Jerusalem where they worshipped when they visited the Holy City not only to celebrate the Feasts but to prosecute their mercantile enterprises. The chief community of those Hellenists would naturally have its home in the busy capital, and it included one household of repute. The father is unknown. His very name is unrecorded, and only a few hints of his character and career remain. These, however, are peculiarly suggestive. It appears from a confused and precarious tradition that he was a late arrival at Tarsus. He was a native of Gischala in northern Galilee, and he had been driven from his home by civil commotion, perhaps the wild insurrection which ensued upon the death of Herod the Great in 4 B.C. and brought the avenging sword of Varus into Galilee.[4] He escaped across the northern frontier with his wife and child, and found an asylum at Tarsus.[5]

The greatest of all. Ac. vi. 9.

His father.

A native of Gischala. Cf. Ac. v. 37.

[1] Philostr. *Apoll. Tyan.* i. 7; cf. vi. 34. [2] Cf. p. 67.

[3] A saying ascribed to Euripides: χρῆναι τῷ εὐδαίμονι πρῶτον ὑπάρξαι τὴν πόλιν εὐδόκιμον (Plut. *Demosth.* i. 1).

[4] Cf. Schürer, I. ii. pp. 4 f.

[5] This tradition is preserved by St. Jerome. Cf. *Catal. Script. Eccl.* (under *Paulus Apostolus*): 'De tribu Benjamin et oppido Judææ Gischalis fuit, quo a Romanis capto cum parentibus suis Tarsum Ciliciæ commigravit, a quibus ob studia legis missus Hierosolymam a Gamaliele viro doctissimo eruditus est.'

A Roman citizen.

It appears from the education which he was able to give his son that he was, if not wealthy, at least well provided; and he occupied an honourable station, since he possessed

Ac. xxii. 28. the hereditary distinction of the Roman citizenship. This was no empty adornment, inasmuch as it conferred the two-

Ac. xvi. 37, 38; xxii. 25, 28; xxv. 10-12. fold privilege of exemption from the degrading punishments of scourging and crucifixion, and the right of appeal to the Emperor's tribunal. It was originally designed as a recognition of conspicuous merit;[1] but more and more under the imperial *régime* it might be obtained by purchase, and thus its lustre was tarnished.[2] A devout Jew, even had he possessed the means, would hardly have stooped to corruption; yet it is unlikely that one who had merited the distinction should have needed to flee into exile. He had probably inherited it; and it is a reasonable surmise that his father or grandfather had been one of the Jews whom Pompey had carried captive to Rome in B.C. 83, and there sold into slavery.[3] Philo relates[4] that they were subsequently emancipated and invested with the Roman citizenship; and many of them returned to their native land.

A true Israelite.

Rom. xi. 1; Phil. iii. 5, 6. Cf. Gen. xlix. 27; Jud. v. 14 (cf. Hos. v. 8), xx.

He possessed, however, a still more honourable distinction and bequeathed a still more precious heritage. He was an Israelite of blameless lineage. He was a son of Benjamin, that martial tribe which, little as it was, had borne itself so gallantly on the battlefields of old. And he represented the noblest type of Jewish piety. He was a zealous adherent of the sect of the Pharisees which, despite too frequent intoler-

Comment. on Philem. 23: 'Talem fabulam accepimus. Aiunt parentes Apostoli Pauli de Gyscalis regione fuisse Judææ, et eos cum tota provincia Romana vastaretur manu et dispergerentur in orbe Judæi, in Tarsum urbem Ciliciæ fuisse translatos, parentum conditionem adulescentulum Paulum secutum.' There are here two errors: (1) Paul is said to have been born at Gischala, whereas on his own testimony (Ac. xxii. 3) he was born at Tarsus; (2) the gross anachronism of assigning the capture of Gischala and the flight apparently to the final death-struggle with Rome in A.D. 70. It would perhaps be unfair to ascribe these glaring inaccuracies to St. Jerome's habitual carelessness. He wrote during his long residence at Bethlehem (A.D. 386-420), and here, professedly, he is merely quoting the local tradition (*talem fabulam accepimus*). It was natural that the Palestinians should desire to make out that the great Apostle was their countryman.

[1] Cf. Suet. *Aug.* 47; Jos. *Vit.* 76.

[2] Cf. Ac. xxii. 28; Dio Cass. lx. 17; Luc. *Dem.* 40.

[3] Cf. p. 3.

[4] *Ad Cai.* II. 568 f.

ance and traditionalism, comprehended most that was godly
and all that was patriotic in the later Judaism. He was a
devout Jew, and in the city of his exile he was true to his
fathers' God and the traditions of their faith.

His wife was like-minded. They had at least two children. His wife.
One was a daughter; and, if it be permissible to suppose that Ac. xxiii. 16.
she was the child whom they carried with them in their flight
from Gischala, she was the elder. And they had also a son. Their son
They called him Saul, that ancient Benjamite name; and Saul. 1 Sam. ix.
since it signifies 'asked for,' it may perhaps be inferred that 1, 2.
he was their only son and was granted them after long desire.
Like Samuel he was the child of many prayers; and ere 1 Sam.
his birth his mother had consecrated him to the service of i. 27.
God.[1] It was the fashion in those days for a Jew to be called Gal. i. 15.
by two names—a Jewish name, which he bore among his own
people, and another which he bore in his intercourse with the
Gentile world.[2] Sometimes the latter was a translation of
the Jewish name, like Didymus, which is the Greek of Thomas, Jo. xi. 16;
'the Twin,' or Dorcas, which is the Greek of Tabitha, 'a Ac. ix. 36.
Gazelle'; sometimes it was quite distinct, like Mark, the Ac. xii. 12,
Latin surname of John the cousin of Barnabas, though 25.
generally it had some resemblance in sound, like the Latin Ac. i. 23;
Justus surnaming Joseph and Jesus. And thus those godly Col. iv. 11.
Jewish parents called their child Saul, and gave him also the
Latin name of Paul, perhaps merely because of the assonance, His Gentile
but it may be because the ancestor who had bequeathed them name of Paul.
the Roman citizenship, had been a freedman of the Æmilian
house, where the cognomen of Paulus was common.[3]

[1] ἀφορίζειν (Gal. i. 15), 'separate' in the sense of 'set apart,' 'consecrate.' Cf. Ac. xiii. 2.

[2] Cf. Lightfoot, *Hor. Hebr.* p. 883 (on 1 Cor. i. 1).

[3] Two other explanations of the double name have been suggested. (1) Since he is called Saul in Acts until his rencontre at Paphos before Sergius Paulus (xiii. 9), it has been supposed that he adopted the name of his distinguished convert, as Scipio after his conquest of Africa was styled 'Africanus' and Metellus after his conquest of Crete 'Creticus' (Hieronym. *Script. Eccl.*; *Comment.* on Phm. 1). So Aug. *Confess.* VIII. 4, and in modern times Beng., Baur, Mey. But the phrase Σαῦλος ὁ καὶ Παῦλος, 'Saul who is also Paul,' implies that he had borne the name all along. Had he only now assumed it, Luke would have written 'Saul who was thenceforth (ἀπὸ τότε) Paul.' (2) *Paulus* means 'little,' and Augustine (*Serm.* cclxxix. 5; *De Spir. et Litt.* 12) supposes that the Apostle assumed it as 'a name of humility' (cf. 1 Cor. xv. 9). Perhaps he might rather

His education.

It was apparently in the year A.D. 1 that Saul was born,[1] and he was thus some five years younger than our Blessed Lord.[2] Since that reference to her pious dedication of her child is the sole mention which is made of his mother, it would seem that she died soon after his birth and he never knew her. But her gracious ambition was not frustrated. It was shared by her husband, and he devoted the child to the honourable career of a Rabbi, 'a teacher of Israel,' and ordered his education to this end.

Parental instruction.

He would faithfully perform his own part at the outset in obedience to that injunction which ranks as the eleventh of the six hundred and thirteen commandments of the Law in Maimonides' *Book of the Precepts* : 'These words which I command thee this day, shall be upon thine heart: and thou shalt teach them diligently unto thy children, and shalt talk of them when thou sittest in thine house, and when thou walkest by the way, and when thou liest down, and when thou risest up.' (Dt. vi. 6, 7.)

'The House of the Book.'

At the age of six or seven [3] the child would be sent to the elementary school. This was connected with the local synagogue, and since the manual of instruction was the Book of the Law, it was known as 'the House of the Book.' [4] The Aramaic vernacular would be the language of his home, and he spoke it in after days as freely as a native of Palestine (Cf. Ac. xxi. 40); and he would learn also the ancient Hebrew, the original language of the Sacred Scriptures. But Greek was the language of a Hellenistic community, and it was the Septuagint version of the Scriptures that the Jews of Tarsus employed.[5]

The Law the lesson-book.

It was the child's lesson-book, and his lifelong familiarity with it is evidenced by his practice of quoting from it in after years.[6] For the first three or four years the

have regarded it as a nickname bestowed on the Apostle by the scurrilous Antiochenes (cf. p. 67) during his sojourn among them. The fact is that both names were given him at his birth, and he dropped his Jewish and went by his Gentile name when he entered on his ministry as the Apostle of the Gentiles.

[1] Cf. Append. I.

[2] Cf. *The Days of His Flesh*, pp. 11 f.

[3] Cf. Schürer, II. ii. p. 49.

[4] בֵּית הַסֵּפֶר.

[5] Cf. Schürer, II. ii. pp. 285 ff.; Swete, *Introd. to O. T. in Greek*, pp. 369-80.

[6] Cf. Swete, *ibid.*, pp. 389 ff., 400 ff.

scholars in the House of the Book were instructed in the rudiments; and then, at the age of ten, they were engaged in learning the Law,[1] and by reason of the scarcity of books in those days when they were transcribed by hand and the difficulty of manipulating the cumbrous rolls, the method was, as it still is in the unchanging East,[2] oral repetition (*mishnah*). *Mishnah.* The teacher read out each sentence, and the pupils recited it in chorus until they had it committed to memory. It was an effective method. One inestimable advantage of it was that every Jew's mind was stored with Holy Writ, and the inaccessibility of the sacred volume thus mattered less. 'From the dawn of understanding,' says the Jewish historian,[3] 'we learn the laws by heart and have them, as it were, engraved on our souls.' It involved, however, obvious disadvantages, not the least being that a Jewish writer was apt to trust to his memory; and this is the main reason of the general laxity and frequent inaccuracy of New Testament quotations from the Old Testament.

The education of a Jewish child was thus essentially religious. Greek Literature. And it was exclusively Jewish. The Sacred Law was the text-book, and heathen literature was ignored. Indeed it was execrated by the more rigid Pharisees. They had a saying: 'Cursed be he who feeds swine: and cursed be he who teaches his son Greek literature';[4] and it is related of R. Judah the Holy that, being asked when a man should teach his son Greek literature, he replied: 'At an hour which belongs neither to the day nor to the night,' since it was written: 'His delight is in the Law of the Lord; and in His Ps. i. 2. Law doth he meditate day and night.'[5] This, however, was an extreme attitude; and though Saul was educated 'after Ac. xxvi. 5. the strictest sect of the Jewish religion,' it is hardly likely that he was indoctrinated with so ungenerous a sentiment.

[1] The curriculum of a child's education from its commencement in the home until manhood was thus defined (*Aboth*, v. 21, appendix): 'At five years old he comes to the reading of Scripture, at ten to *mishnah*, at thirteen to the practice of the commands, at fifteen to *talmud* (doctrine), at eighteen to marriage.' Cf. Schürer, II. ii. p. 52.

[2] Cf. Walter Tyndale, *An Artist in Egypt*, p. 107.

[3] Jos. *Contra Apion.*, II. 18.

[4] Cf. J. H. Ottho, *Hist. Doct. Misn.* pp. 68 ff.

[5] Cf. Wetstein on Ac. vi. 1.

His father was indeed a faithful Jew, but he was also a Roman citizen; and even had he desired it, the intellectual isolation which was practicable at Jerusalem was impossible at Tarsus. He would not educate his son in Greek literature, but the atmosphere which he breathed would colour the lad's mind; and since he spoke Greek, there was no linguistic barrier. He may not indeed have been instructed in all the wisdom of the Greeks, as Moses was in that of the Egyptians; but in after days he exhibited in his writings a flavour especially of the Stoic philosophy,[1] and he could on occasion, as he proved in his speech before the Court of the Areiopagos, employ the intellectual mode of his day. Moreover, he was no stranger to Greek literature. He could quote to good purpose from the philosophers and the poets—his fellow-countryman Aratus, the philosophic poet Epimenides, and the comedian Menander.[2]

Ac. vii. 22.

Ac. xvii. 16-34.

Preparation for Rabbinate:

On attaining his thirteenth year a Jewish boy became 'a son of the commandment.'[3] His childhood was over, and he left the House of the Book and began his preparation for his proper life-work. Saul had been devoted first by his parents' gracious ambition and latterly by his own choice to the career of a Rabbi, but he did not immediately address himself to the sacred studies which were the appointed pathway to that high vocation. A Rabbi's labours were gratuitous. He exacted no fees, and, like the ancient judges, received no

(1) A trade.

Ex. xxiii. 8; Dt. xvi. 19.

[1] Cf. his use of Stoic terms like *αὐτάρκεια* (2 Cor. ix. 8; 1 Tim. vi. 6), *αὐτάρκης* (Phil. iv. 11), *συνείδησις* (Rom. ii. 15, ix. 1, xiii. 5; 1 Cor. viii. 7, 10, 12; etc.).

[2] In Ac. xvii. 28 there are two quotations. (1) *ἐν αὐτῷ γὰρ ζῶμεν καὶ κινούμεθα καὶ ἐσμέν*, a line, as a Syriac fragment discovered by Dr. Rendel Harris (cf. Moulton, *Religions and Religion*, p. 45) proves, from Epimenides. To the same passage belongs the hexameter Κρῆτες *ἀεὶ ψεῦσται, κακὰ θηρία, γαστέρες ἀργαί* (Tit. i. 12). (2) *τοῦ γὰρ καὶ γένος ἐσμέν*, a fragment of a hexameter from the *Phænomena* of Aratus. Cf. Theoph. *ad Autolyc.* II. p. 86 D (ed. Sylburg.), where the beautiful passage is quoted at large. Again, the iambic trimeter *φθείρουσιν ἤθη χρηστὰ ὁμιλίαι κακαί* (1 Cor. xv. 33) belongs, according to Jerome (*Comment.* on Gal. iv. 24), to the *Thais* of Menander. Socrates Scholasticus (iii. 10) ascribes it to Euripides, and possibly Menander borrowed it from the dramatist. There is here a corrective of the present-day disposition to regard the Apostle as 'non-literary,' belonging to 'the artisan non-literary classes' (cf. Deissmann, *Light*, pp. 238 ff.; *St. Paul*, pp. 49 ff.). Much fairer is the judgment of Jerome: 'Scisse autem Paulum, licet non ad perfectum, literas sæculares ipsius verba testantur. . . . Ex quibus et aliis evidens est Paulum non ignorasse literas sæculares.'

[3] Cf. *The Days of His Flesh*, pp. 21 f.

gifts. His ministry was his reward, his disciples were his crown. 'He,' said R. Hillel, 'who serves himself with the crown of the Law perishes.' 'Make not thy disciples,' said R. Zadok, 'a crown, to win glory by them; nor an axe, to live by them.'[1] Hence it was necessary for a Rabbi to earn his livelihood, and he not only 'laboured in the Law' but engaged in some trade. R. Joseph was a miller; R. Oschaja and R. Chanina were shoemakers; R. Abba, R. Chanan, and R. Judah were tailors; another R. Judah was a baker and a third a perfumer; R. Meïr, R. Nahum, and R. Nathan were clerks; R. Jochanan was a sandal-maker; R. Isaac was a smith; R. Nehemiah was a potter; R. Abin was a carpenter.[2] Nor was a Rabbi's craft, however menial, reckoned a degradation; for, unlike the Greeks and Romans who accounted all trades ignoble and relegated them to slaves, the Jews esteemed honest work a sacred obligation. 'Love work,' said R. Shemaiah; and it was a maxim that one who did not teach his son a trade taught him robbery. 'Excellent,' said R. Gamaliel, the son of R. Judah ha-Nasi, 'is the study of the Law together with worldly business, for the practice of them both puts iniquity out of remembrance; and all Law without work must fail at length, and occasion iniquity.' It was a noble ideal, yet it tended to abuse. It was a temptation for a Rabbi to become engrossed in his worldly business to the neglect of his sacred vocation; and the great masters were insistent in their warnings. 'No one,' said R. Hillel, 'that has much traffic is wise.' 'Have little business,' said R. Meïr, 'and be busied in the Law.'[3] Nor were there lacking Rabbis who shamed their high office by covetous and rapacious exaction. Cf. Mk. xii. 40; Lk. xx. 47.

Tent-making.

Since Saul must earn his livelihood in after years, he was put to a trade when his schooldays were over. It was the craft of tent-making; and this was a natural choice, since it was a thriving industry at Tarsus. Cilicia abounded in goats, and their hair was woven into a stout fabric, called *cilicium*, which served for tent-curtains.[4]

[1] Taylor, *Sayings of the Fathers*, I. 14, IV. 9.
[2] Cf. Delitzsch, *Jewish Artisan Life*, V.
[3] Taylor, *ut supra*, I. 11; II. 2, 6; IV. 14.
[4] Plin. *N. H.* VI. 32. Cf. Schürer, II. i. p. 44.

(2) 'The House of Interpretation.

At the age of fifteen[1] he left home to prosecute his studies in the Rabbinical College—'the House of Interpretation'[2] as it was styled—at Jerusalem. It is no evidence of precocity that he began his college career so early. That was the age prescribed by Jewish usage, and it accorded with the narrow range of ancient education. It would seem that the age of pupilarity was even lower among the Greeks, since Apollonius of Tyana was but fourteen when, in A.D. 11, while Saul was still attending the House of the Book, he was brought to Tarsus by his father to study under Euthydemus.[3] John Knox was sixteen when he entered the University of Glasgow in 1521; John Calvin was fourteen when he entered the University of Paris in 1523; and Thomas Chalmers was only half-way through his twelfth year when he matriculated at St. Andrews in 1791.

The Jewish colleges.

There were many Rabbinical colleges. One, which enjoyed considerable reputation, met 'in the vineyard at Jabneh'; and hence it has been inferred that 'a vineyard' was a poetic designation of a school of the wise. The meaning, however, is merely that, whereas a provincial college, like a Christian church in early days, usually assembled in a private house,[4] that at Jabneh, by reason of its numbers, had its meeting-place in a vineyard.[5] The most celebrated

Lk. ii. 46.

of all was naturally the college at Jerusalem, and it met

The teachers.

within the Temple precincts. The teachers were variously

Mk. x. 51; Jo. xx. 16.

denominated. Their commonest designation was Rabbi. Rab meant 'master,' and Rabbi 'my master,' *Monsieur*; and a more honourable form was Rabban or Rabbon, Rabboni.

Mt. xxiii. 9, 10; Ac. v. 34.

Other titles were 'father' (*abba*), 'teacher,' 'lawyers' or 'teachers of the Law,' 'scribes,' that is, 'men of the Scripture,' 'the wise.' In the class-room the Rabbi occupied an

Ac. xxii. 3; cf. Lk. x. 39.

elevated daïs, and the disciples sat round him on the floor; whence they were said to be 'educated at his feet' and to 'powder themselves in the dust of the feet of the wise.'[6]

The study. Cf. Jo. x. 34, xii. 34, xv. 25; Rom. iii. 19.

Their study was the Sacred Law in the large sense of the term, including all the Jewish Scriptures—the Law, the Prophets, and the Hagiographa. The method was *midrash*,

[1] Cf. p. 23, n. 1.

[2] בֵּת הַמִּדְרָשׁ.

[3] Cf. Philostr. *Vit. Apoll.* I. 7.

[4] Taylor, *ut supra*, I. 4.

[5] Cf. Schürer, II. i. pp. 325 f.

[6] Taylor, *ut supra*.

'interpretation,' the investigation of the sacred text; and this comprehended *halachah* and *haggadah*. *Halachah* was the systematisation of the precepts of the Law, the definition, application, and reconciliation of the legal code; and it issued in a vast complexity of casuistical distinctions and vexatious restrictions. *Haggadah*, on the other hand, dealt with the historical and didactic portions of the Scriptures, elaborating and elucidating them by the aid of parable and legend. It pursued the method of allegorical exegesis, recognising in Scripture a fourfold meaning, denoted by the consonants of the word 'Paradise': *peshat*, the simple or literal meaning; *remaz*, the suggested meaning; *derush*, the meaning evolved by investigation; and *sod*, the mystic meaning.[1]

The Rabbinical theology was always subtle and often Saul's
fantastic; and Saul's training in the House of Interpretation Rabbinism.
at Jerusalem left an abiding imprint on his mind. He
handled the Scriptures after the Rabbinical fashion, and
instances abound in his writings. Thus his idea of the 1 Cor. x.
smitten rock which followed the Israelites in their wilderness 1-4.
wanderings is a *haggadic midrash*; while its application to
Christ and his sacramental interpretation of their immersion
in the Red Sea and their overshadowing by the cloud and
their eating of the manna are examples of Rabbinical
allegorising. So also is his interpretation of Sarah and Gal. iv. 21-
Hagar, the free woman and the bond, and their children. 31.
Again, his linguistically impossible argumentation that since
the promise to Abraham speaks of his 'seed' and not his iii. 16.
'seeds,' it refers not to his descendants, the Jewish people,
but to Christ, is a characteristic example of Rabbinical
dialectic, precisely similar to the argument that, since in the
Lord's remonstrance with Cain: 'the voice of thy brother's Gen. iv. 10.
blood crieth unto me from the ground,' the word 'blood'
is in Hebrew plural, the meaning is that in slaying Abel Cain
had slain not only him but all his posterity.[2] And thus in
that argument with his Judaising converts of Galatia the

[1] Cf. Schurer, II. i. pp. 306 ff.; Robertson Smith, *O. T. in Jewish Church*, III. הֲלָכָה (from הָלַךְ, 'go') is properly 'method,' 'rule' directing one's going. הַגָּדָה is 'narrative,' 'legend.'

[2] *Mish. Sanhed.*, IV. 5.

Apostle, perhaps consciously, turned the weapons of his Judaistic adversaries against themselves.

The influence of Gamaliel.

There was, however, a still deeper impression which his training in the House of Interpretation left on the mind of Saul. The glory of the College at that period was the celebrated Rabbi Gamaliel the Elder. He was a grandson of Hillel the Great, who had been distinguished by the gentleness of his disposition and the liberality of his sentiments, presenting herein a marked contrast to his stern and rigid colleague, the Rabbi Shammai. 'A man,' it is written in the Talmud, 'should be gentle like Hillel, and not irritable like Shammai'; and it is related by way of illustration that three Gentiles once visited the two Rabbis successively to discuss the Jewish faith, and afterwards they said: 'The irritability of Shammai sought to drive us from the world: the gentleness of Hillel brought us nigh under the wings of the Shekinah.'[1]

His tolerance. Ac. v. 34-40.

Gamaliel was Hillel's kinsman no less after the spirit than after the flesh. He appears only once in the New Testament, and his behaviour on that occasion reveals his character. The Sanhedrin had arraigned the Apostles and was minded to put them to death; but Gamaliel interposed. 'Refrain from these men,' he pleaded, 'and let them alone; for if this counsel or this work be of men, it will be overthrown; but if it is of God, you will not be able to overthrow them. Perhaps you may be found even to be fighting against God.' It is not surprising that the idea should have arisen that he was actually a Christian,[2] though this is a mere fable born of his truly Christian spirit. The legitimacy of studying Greek literature was one of the articles of controversy between the schools of Hillel and Shammai, and Gamaliel maintained the liberal attitude. His son, the Rabbi Simon, is reported to have said that of the thousand young men who had studied in the House of Interpretation at Jerusalem in his father's time, no fewer than one half had learned Greek wisdom.[3]

His prestige.

Bitterly as he was regarded by the narrower sort of

[1] Taylor, *ut supra*, I. 16, n. 33.
[2] Cf. *Epistola Luciani* in Works of Augustine, VII. pp. 1126 ff. (Migne).
[3] Cf. Wetstein on Ac. vi. 1.

Pharisees in his day, Gamaliel enjoyed the popular esteem. He was one of four Doctors of the Law who were accorded the honourable title of Rabban.[1] And his memory was cherished and revered in after generations. A saying was current that 'from the day when Rabban Gamaliel the Elder died, the glory of the Law ceased, and purity and abstinence died.'[2]

His influence on Saul.

It was no small advantage to Saul that during the most impressionable period of his life he should have been subjected to the gracious influence of this wise and large-hearted teacher; and in after years he gratefully acknowledged how much he owed to his 'education at the feet of Gamaliel.' (Ac. xxii. 3.) The profit, however, did not immediately appear.[3] A dark experience of moral and spiritual conflict lay before the young Rabbi; and in his quest after peace he was betrayed into wild excesses of cruel fanaticism. But the lessons which he had learned in the House of Interpretation were never obliterated from his soul, and they played no small part in his religious and intellectual emancipation.

Saul's Rabbinical ministry at Tarsus.

Despite the liberality of his sentiments Gamaliel was none the less a Pharisee, devoted to the Law and loyal to the national traditions. Under his tuition Saul lost nothing of his early piety, and he left the Rabbinical College with a disciplined and furnished mind, well equipped for the office of 'a teacher of Israel.' Jerusalem was the chief home of Rabbinical wisdom, but there were Rabbis not only in the provinces of the Holy Land but in the great Hellenistic communities. (Cf. Lk. v. 17.) It is proved by inscriptions that there were Rabbis at Rome,[4] and there would be Rabbis also at Tarsus. It appears that his native city remained Saul's home until he broke with his old associations and entered on his career as a Christian Apostle; (Cf. Gal. i. 21; Ac. xi. 25.) and it is probable that he betook himself thither on the completion of his college course, and exercised his ministry in the synagogue which had been the spiritual home of his childhood, plying at the same time his craft of tent-making.

[1] Cf. Schürer, II. i. p. 316.

[2] Taylor, *ut supra*, I. 17, n. 35.

[3] Hence Renan and others have regarded the connection between Gamaliel and Saul as a Lucan fiction.

[4] Cf. Schürer, II. i. pp. 314, 319.

The duty of marriage.

There is no explicit record of his employments during this period; but one event it seems necessary to assume, nor is his own testimony lacking. Among the Jews eighteen was the proper age for marriage;[1] and marriage was accounted a sacred obligation. Its neglect was deemed at once a calamity and a crime. To go childless meant not only that, when the man died, 'his name was blotted out of Israel,'[2] but that he slew his posterity and thus 'lessened the image of God.'[3] Hence marriage was a religious ordinance; and the two hundred and thirteenth commandment in *The Book of the Precepts* is 'to have a wife in purity' in obedience to the Scripture, 'Be fruitful and multiply'; wherefore Maimonides affirmed that if a man passed the age of twenty without marrying, unless it were that he might absolutely devote himself to the study of the Law, he transgressed a positive commandment.[4] It seems likely that Saul, a devout Jew and a strict Pharisee, would marry in due course; and the inference is confirmed by the fact that he was subsequently enrolled in the high court of the Sanhedrin and on at least one memorable occasion participated in its judicial procedure. For it was required, among the qualifications of a Sanhedrist, that he should be not only a married man but a father, inasmuch as one who was softened by domestic affection would be disposed to mercy in his judgments.[5]

Dt. xxv. 6; cf. 2 Sam. xviii. 18.

Gen. i. 28.

Saul's marriage.

Cf. Ac. xxvi. 10.

His widowhood.

It would thus appear that Saul not only married duly but had issue; and the presumption is borne out by his own testimony. It is indeed true that in the days of his apostolic activities he would seem, on his own testimony, to have had no wife; and while recognising the legitimacy of marriage, he held it prudent, in view of the difficulties which then beset the Christians, that they should follow his example

Cf. 1 Cor. ix. 5.

Cf. 1 Cor. vii.

[1] Cf. p. 23, n. 1. Maimonides puts it at sixteen or seventeen. Cf. Lightfoot, *Hor. Hebr.*, on 1 Cor. vii. 6.

[2] Cf. *Shem. Rabb.* lxxiii. 1: 'These four are reckoned as dead—the blind, the leper, the poor, and the childless.' Lightfoot on Lk. ix. 60.

[3] *Jevamoth*, lxiii. 2: 'Whosoever doth not apply himself to begetting and multiplying is even as a homicide. It is as though he lessened the image of God.'

[4] Cf. Lightfoot on 1 Cor. vii. 6.

[5] *Sanhed.* xxxvi. 2. Cf. Selden, *De Synedr.* II. vii. 7.

and shun domestic responsibilities and embarrassments. It does not follow, however, that he had never been married; for his counsel to widows and widowers is that they should remain so, as he had done,[1] and this is an express declaration of his condition. He had married after the Jewish fashion, but his wife was now deceased, and so also was her child, and he had resolved to remain a widower. It is significant that one so affectionate should have maintained an almost unbroken silence regarding this mournful chapter of his life-story; and in view of the sternness of his attitude toward women it would seem as though there were here a hidden tragedy and a bitter memory.[2]

1 Cor. vii. 8.

Cf. 1 Cor. xiv. 34, 35; 1 Tim. ii. 11-15.

Pharisaic method of attaining righteousness.

Those meagre and somewhat precarious suggestions constitute the sole surviving record of Saul's Rabbinical career at Tarsus. It was a period of some fifteen years, and it is no less obscure than the silent years which our Lord passed at Nazareth betwixt His visit to the House of Interpretation at Jerusalem in A.D. 8, and His manifestation unto Israel in A.D. 26. In truth, however, nothing vital is lost; for his real biography during those years is not the record of his outward life, but his inward experience, the working of his mind and soul. And this is plainly evident. He was a

Lk. ii. 41-52.

[1] His words are *λέγω δὲ τοῖς ἀγάμοις καὶ ταῖς χήραις*, 'to widowers and widows.' The masc. *χῆρος* (*viduus*) was very rare, and its place was supplied by *ἄγαμος*. The latter term signified 'unmarried,' and denoted either one whose partner was lost (cf. vers. 11, 34) or one who had never been married. The former is certainly its meaning here. Cf. Euth. Zig.: *'ἀγάμους' γὰρ οὐ τοὺς παρθένους ἐνταῦθά φησιν, ἀλλὰ τοὺς ἀποβαλόντας ὁπωσδήποτε τὰς γαμετάς. καὶ τοῦτο δῆλον ἀπὸ τῶν 'χηρῶν,' ἃς τούτοις συνέταξεν.* The Apostle deals first with widowers and widows (vers. 8, 9), and then with virgins, male and female (vers. 25-28). There are two traditions on this question. One affirms that he was married like the rest of the Apostles (cf. Ignatian *Epist. ad Philad.* iv.: *Πέτρου καὶ Παύλου καὶ τῶν ἄλλων ἀποστόλων τοῖς γάμοις προσομιλησάντων*), but it is weakened by its appeal to the idea (cf. p. 519) that by *γνήσιε σύνζυγε* (Phil. iv. 3) he means 'my true spouse.' Cf. Clem. Alex. *Strom.* III. vi. 53; Eus. *H. E.* III. 30; Orig. *In Epist. ad Rom. Comment.* I. i. On the other hand Tertullian (*De Monogam.* 3) and Jerome (*Epist.* XXII: *Ad Eustochium de Custodia Virginitatis*) represent him as unmarried; but they were biassed by their celibate ideal. For the same reason their opinion prevailed in the mediæval Church. Cf. Chaucer, *The Wife of Bath's Prologue*, 79: 'I woot wel, that th' apostel was a mayde.'

[2] Hence may perhaps have originated the Ebionite slander that the Apostle was not a Jew at all, but a Gentile who with the desire of marrying a priest's daughter became a proselyte, and when she rejected him, turned against the Law. Cf. Epiphan. XXX. 16.

Pharisee; and Pharisaism was in its essence a quest after righteousness. The problem was how a man could be righteous before God; and the answer was: By keeping the Law and fulfilling His commandments. And thus religion was a scrupulous observance not merely of the written Law of Moses but of the unwritten law of the Scribes, that inter-
Mk. vii. 3. minable code of ceremonial regulations and restrictions which was known as 'the tradition of the Elders.'

Its failure. It was a fatal method, and it issued inevitably either in self-righteousness or in despair. Unspiritual men were easily satisfied. When they had performed the prescribed routine of ablution, fasting, and the like, it seemed to them that they had fulfilled God's requirements; and they boasted their perfect righteousness, like the Rabbi Chanina, of whom it is told that he thus challenged the Angel of Death: 'Bring hither the Book of the Law, and see whether there be aught written in it which I have not observed.'[1] Righteousness was with such an affair of external observance; and when they had cleansed the outside of the cup and the
Cf. Mt. xxiii. 25, 26. platter, it seemed to them that all was well though the inside remained foul. The majority were such, and they brought reproach on the whole order. There were, however, Pharisees of a nobler spirit. These had a vision of the infinite
1 Ki. viii. 38. holiness of God and 'the plague of their own hearts'; and ceremonial observances could not satisfy them. They realised their inward estrangement from God, and yearned for reconciliation. They knew no other way than the keeping of the Law, and they addressed themselves to it with eager zeal; but when they had done all, they remained
Mt. xix. 16-22. unsatisfied. Like that young Pharisee in the Gospel-story they had performed every requirement of the Law, but they were still strangers to the peace of God. They had done everything which they knew, and it was insufficient; and their cry was: 'What lack I yet?'

Saul's discovery of its insufficiency. And so it was with Saul of Tarsus. He began his career with unquestioning faith in the efficacy of the Pharisaic way of peace. And it is possible that he might have pursued it to the last without misgiving but for the shock of a stern awakening. In after days he wrote his own spiritual

[1] Cf. Wetstein on Mt. xix. 20.

biography, and told the dark yet blessed story. 'I had never,' he says, 'recognised sin save through law. For I had not known lust had not the Law kept saying: "Thou shalt not lust." And sin got an outlet through the commandment to work out in me every sort of lust; for apart from law sin is dead. I was alive apart from law once; but when the commandment came, sin sprang into life, while as for me, I died; and the commandment which aimed at life—I found it resulted in death. For sin got an outlet through the commandment to "deceive" me and through it to slay me.' Here, with a reticence which evinces the painfulness of the confession, the veil is half lifted from a dark episode of those unrecorded years. What precisely it may have been is unrevealed, and surmise were banal. It is indeed likely that it was no serious transgression; for what might pass with most as a peccadillo would torture a conscience so sensitive. The confession, however, should not be attenuated. In a nature so ardent and impulsive there are ever tragic possibilities; and it is no marvel that his soul should have been swept by a gust of passion and defiled by a deed of impurity. Rom. vii. 7-11.

It was the supreme crisis of his life. It discovered to him 'the plague of his heart'; and he set himself with redoubled devotion to attaining unto righteousness by the only way he knew—the Pharisaic method of ceremonial observance, the performance of 'the works of the Law.' But his labour proved unavailing. He had realised his soul's alienation from God, and external rites never touched the deep-seated malady. Still he entertained as yet no doubt of the efficacy of the method, and its failure only inspired him to more strenuous endeavour. There was no Jew in Tarsus so ardent, no Pharisee so punctilious, no Rabbi so unwearied. A Hellenistic community afforded no adequate arena for his zeal. The Sacred Capital was his fitting sphere, and in due course his opportunity arrived. Redouble devotion. Cf. Ac. xxii. 3; Gal. i. 14.

Ac. vi-viii. 12.

THE MARTYRDOM OF STEPHEN

'Testis tuus est in cœlis,
Testis verax et fidelis
Testis innocentiæ.
Nomen habas coronati,
Te tormenta decet pati
Pro corona gloriæ.

'Pro corona non marcenti
Perfer brevis vim tormenti,
Te manet victoria.
Tibi fiet mors natalis,
Tibi pœna terminalis
Dat vitæ primordia.'

ADAM DE S. VICTORE.

The Lord unknown to Saul in the days of His flesh.

MOMENTOUS events had been transpiring in the Holy Land during Saul's sojourn at Tarsus. When he betook himself to the House of Interpretation in A.D. 15 at the age of fifteen years, our Lord was living obscurely at Nazareth and earning His daily bread in a carpenter's shop. The years passed, and in the spring of A.D. 26 He was manifested at Bethany beyond Jordan as the Messiah, the Promised Saviour, and entered on His public ministry; and in the spring of A.D. 29 He was crucified on Calvary and raised from the dead on the third day. Tidings of that wondrous ministry and its more wondrous consummation must have reached Saul at Tarsus; and, moreover, since he would repair to the great Feasts, he must have been in Jerusalem on each of the occasions when our Lord was there, including the last, the tragic Passion-week. Yet it is remarkable that he never encountered Jesus and never even saw Him. In after years, when his apostleship was challenged on the ground that he lacked
Cf. Ac. i. 21, 22. the essential qualification of fellowship with the Master in the days of His flesh, his only defence was that he had been
Cf. 1 Cor. ix. 1, xv. 8. vouchsafed a vision of the Risen Lord on the road to Damascus. And indeed it is hardly surprising that he should never have encountered Him in Jerusalem. The rulers regarded Jesus with contemptuous disdain and, latterly,
Cf. Mt. xxi. 23 -xxii. with bitter animosity. It was only when they hoped to entangle Him in some damaging controversy, and thus discredit Him in the eyes of the people, that they deigned to

approach Him as He taught in the Temple court ; and they generally dealt with Him through their officers. Saul would share the contempt of his order for the unschooled heretic, and would never cross His path. He would have deemed it an intolerable degradation to mingle with the rude crowd which thronged to hear Him. Cf. Jo. vii. 32, 45.

Progress of the Gospel.

He would share also the satisfaction of the rulers when the Lord was crucified. It appeared as though the trouble were ended and the heresy stamped out ; but this proved a vain hope. The Gospel did not perish. On the contrary, it acquired an unprecedented vitality, and the scene of its victorious operation was no longer remote Galilee but the Sacred Capital. On the Day of Pentecost, little over a month after their seeming triumph, the rulers were startled by the conversion of some three thousand of the populace ; and never a day passed without fresh accessions to the hated community, until presently it numbered over five thousand men, exclusive of women and children, and Jerusalem was ringing with the teaching of the Apostles. Ac. ii. 41, 47. iv. 4. v. 28.

Reasons.

It was indeed an amazing phenomenon, inexplicable save by the facts which the New Testament alleges. The chief of these was the Resurrection of the Lord and the effusion of the Holy Spirit. And it was mainly this that won the people and startled the rulers. If it were indeed true that the Crucified had been raised from the dead and was living and manifesting His heavenly power, then the crucifixion was an impious crime, and in proclaiming the Resurrection the Apostles were laying a terrible indictment against its perpetrators. It accentuated the popular appeal of their message and its terror for the rulers that they believed and proclaimed that the Risen Lord would presently return in His glory to judge the world. Nor should it be forgotten that the primitive Apostles were indubitably endowed with miraculous powers. The evidence is irrefragable. It is no mere legend of a later age, but their own personal and direct testimony. They repeatedly refer to the phenomenon in their letters, and always as a recognised fact, familiar to their readers. It was only temporary, but it did not immediately vanish from the Church on the departure of the Apostles. It gradually diminished until in the fourth century, Cf. iv. 2, v. 28. Cf. iii. 19-28. Cf. Gal. iii. 5; 1 Cor. xii. 9, 10.

as St. Chrysostom certifies,[1] it had quite disappeared; but, on the testimony of St. Justin Martyr and St. Irenæus, it still persisted in the second century and, on the testimony of Tertullian, lingered on into the third.[2] Nor indeed is either the gift or its withdrawal inexplicable. It was a providential dispensation. At its first planting Christianity required special aids, but once it had taken root, these were no longer needed, and it was left to its normal development.[3]

Chagrin of the Jewish Rulers.

Cf. Ac. iv. 1-22; v. 17-42.

Cf. Mt. xxi. 46, xxvi. 5; Lk. xxii. 2.

Cf. Ac. iv. 21, v. 26.

The triumphant progress of the Gospel was galling and disconcerting to the Jewish rulers. They would gladly have taken strong measures with the Apostles and dealt with them as they had dealt with the Lord; and they actually made several ineffectual attempts to intimidate them. But they were restrained by the same prudential consideration which had repeatedly shielded the Lord from their animosity, and postponed the final catastrophe: the Apostles were the heroes of the populace, and their molestation would have excited a dangerous tumult. Thus the Gospel went its way unrestrained, and the Church grew apace.

Primitive communism.

Ac. iv. 32, 34, 35; cf. ii. 45.

But the course of events brought the rulers the opportunity which they desired. There was much poverty in Jerusalem at that period; and since Christianity was a popular movement appealing to 'the common people,' it numbered many poor among its adherents. The spirit of brotherhood was strong in the first believers; and, recognising the obligation of mutual succour, they organised the Church on the principle of communism. 'There was one heart and soul, and not one said that any of his possessions was his own, but everything was common to them. There was not one in need among them; for all that had been owners of lands or houses, would sell them and bring the prices the things fetched and lay them at the feet of the Apostles; and distribution would be made to each as one

[1] *In Epist. II ad Thess. Hom.* IV. *ad init.*

[2] Just. M. *Apol.* I. p. 45 A, B (edit. Sylburg.); Iren. II. xlviii. 2, xlix. 3; Tert. *Apol.* 37.

[3] Cf. Aug. *De Civ. Dei*, XXII. viii. 1: '"Why," say they, "are those miracles which you declared were wrought, not wrought now?" I might indeed answer that they were necessary ere the world believed, to the end that the world might believe. Whoso still seeks for prodigies that he may believe, is himself a great prodigy, in that, while the world believes, he does not.'

Cf. v. 4.

Cf. xii. 12.

had need.' There was no compulsion. If one chose, he might keep his property; and when the first wave of enthusiasm had subsided, there were believers in Jerusalem who, though generous in their hospitality, retained their houses and their wealth. But at the outset communism was the prevailing order; and since men of substance were not lacking, their sacrifice afforded abundant provision and destitution was unknown.

The Essene example.

It was a noble ideal, and consonant with the spirit of the Gospel; yet it was not a Christian invention. Communism was *en l'air* at that period, and it was already practised by the Jewish sect of the Essenes.[1] The latter abjured private property, and each novice surrendered all that he possessed to the superintendents of the order to be employed for the general good.[2] It would seem that the Apostles were here inspired by the example of the Essenes; and though they did not withdraw their followers from the world, they imitated those holy anchorites in one particular. They instituted a common table;

'The daily ministration.'

and just as the common meal of the Essenes was sacramental, being prepared by priests and preceded by ceremonial ablution, so 'the daily ministration' of the believers was hallowed by a eucharistic celebration, either at the commencement[3] or at the conclusion.[4]

Cf. Jud. 12; 2 Pet. ii. 13 R.V.

This common meal was variously denominated 'the Love-feast,' 'the Reception,' or 'the Ministry of Tables';[5] and it was a gracious institution.

Its abuse.

Nevertheless it led to grave abuse. It will appear in due course how it desecrated the Lord's Table among the Gentile converts at Corinth;[6] and it tended also to corrupt the Church by alluring into her ranks unworthy professors who desired only worldly advantage, 'thinking that religion was a source of profit.'[7] It was

[1] Cf. pp. 447, 549 ff.

[2] Cf. Schürer, II. ii. pp. 195 ff. Apollonius is said to have inculcated a similar system. Cf. Philostr. *Vit. Apoll. Tyan.* IV. 13.

[3] Cf. Chrys. *In I Epist. ad. Cor. Hom.* XXVII. 1: τῆς συνάξεως ἀπαρτισθείσης μετὰ τὴν τῶν μυστηρίων κοινωνίαν ἐπὶ κοινὴν πάντες ᾖεσαν εὐωχίαν.

[4] *Didache*, 10: μετὰ δὲ τὸ ἐμπλησθῆναι οὕτως εὐχαριστήσατε.

[5] Cf. Julian (fragment), Loeb Class. Libr. ii. p. 338: διὰ τῆς λεγομένης παρ αὐτοῖς 'ἀγάπης' καὶ 'ὑποδοχῆς' καὶ 'διακονίας τραπεζῶν' (cf. Ac. vi. 2). *Apostol. Constit.* II. 28: τοῖς εἰς ἀγάπην ἤτοι δοχὴν, ὡς ὁ Κύριος ὠνόμασε (Lk. xiv. 13), προαιρουμένοις καλεῖν.

[6] Cf. p. 286.

[7] Cf. Julian, *ut supra*, p. 337.

probably this scandal that soon discredited the fair ideal which was cherished in the enthusiasm of early days. At all events, ere many years had passed, the initial communism was largely abandoned, and 'the poor saints' at Jerusalem needed the succour of Gentile liberality.[1]

Hebrews and Hellenists. At the outset, however, 'the daily ministration' was an institution. It was easily managed at first; but as the numbers multiplied, it grew more and more difficult. And the embarrassment became intolerable when a dissension arose—the Church's earliest controversy. She was indeed as yet exclusively Jewish, yet she was by no means homogeneous. There were two sections in her ranks. One was the Hebrews—the Palestinian Jews, whose pride was that they had always breathed the air of the Holy Land and never been polluted by contact with heathen soil. And the other was the Hellenists,[2] those Jews who had settled or been born abroad, and had returned to the Holy City that they might spend the evening of their lives beneath the shadow of the Temple. These had indeed remained passionately loyal to their ancestral faith, yet they had generally acquired a certain liberality and contracted a Gentile colour of speech and manner; and they were consequently suspect in the eyes of the narrow Hebrews, and were not unnaturally disposed to resentment. How keen the jealousy was appears from the fact that the Hellenists hailing from the various Gentile countries had built synagogues of their own in Jerusalem, where they might meet unmolested when they visited the Holy City or returned thither to reside. (Cf. Ac. vi. 9.)

Hellenist dissatisfaction. The Church included representatives of both these sections of Judaism; and it is not surprising that, rightly or wrongly, a suspicion arose among the Hellenists that their destitute widows were unfairly treated in the daily ministration. And the grievance would be the more acute since the Hellenists, like Barnabas of Cyprus, were the wealthier, and it was their generosity that had mainly provided the common good. (Ac. iv. 36, 37.)

Election of seven Deacons. The administration lay with the Apostles, and the odium fell upon them. It was a perilous situation, inimical to the

[1] Cf. pp. 73 ff.

[2] Ἑλληνισταί, 'Grecians' (A.V.), 'Grecian Jews' (R.V.).

Church's unity and her continued prosperity; and they promptly and effectively redressed it. They convened a general assembly of the Church, and proposed that a board of seven should be elected to superintend 'the ministry of the tables' in order that they might be free to devote themselves to their proper office—'the ministry of the Word.' The procedure exemplifies the democratic constitution of the primitive Church. The Apostles did not issue a decree. They submitted a proposal, and it was approved; and thereafter the assembly proceeded to elect its representatives. The seven men thus called by the Church and ordained by the Apostles were Stephen, Philip, Prochorus, Nicanor, Timon, Parmenas, and Nicolaus. Seven was a sacred number, but it was probably selected for practical reasons. The duties demanded so many for their effective discharge; and doubtless the competing interests were appropriately represented. Three would be Hebrews,[1] three Hellenists, and the seventh, the proselyte Nicolaus, would represent that small though by no means insignificant section—the converts from heathenism who had passed from the Synagogue into the Church.

Their spiritual qualifications.

Cf. 1 Tim. iii. 8-13.

Thus originated the order of the Deacons, literally 'Ministers,' who were charged especially with the care of the poor and afflicted and generally with the supervision of practical affairs.[2] It was indeed a practical office, yet it was in no wise secular; and, like their successors, the seven were chosen not alone for their practical wisdom, but for their spiritual endowments. Of four of them nothing further is recorded, and Nicolaus, though personally blameless, was destined to an unhappy notoriety as the author of a mischievous heresy;[3] but they were all men of godly

[1] The fact that all the seven bore Greek names does not imply that none of them were Hebrews, since every Jew had a Gentile as well as a Jewish name (cf. p. 21).

[2] The Seven are not indeed expressly designated 'Deacons' (διάκονοι), and Chrys. supposes that they were appointed for a merely temporary emergency; but the terms διακονία and διακονεῖν are employed (cf. vers. 1, 2, 4), and their appointment was generally recognised in the early Church as the institution of the permanent office. Thus Irenæus calls Stephen 'the first Deacon' (III. xii. 13), 'the first elected to the Deaconship by the Apostles' (IV. xxvi. 1).

[3] Cf. p. 526.

repute, and two of them attained eminent distinction for service to the Kingdom of Heaven beyond the limits of their special office. Philip was an effective preacher, insomuch that he was known as 'the Evangelist.' And Stephen was no less richly endowed with spiritual and intellectual gifts. Later tradition, after its wont, reckons him as well as Philip among the Seventy Apostles whom our Lord, when setting out on His last journey to Jerusalem, 'sent two and two before His face into every city and place whither He Himself was about to come';[1] but this is unlikely, since he was evidently a Hellenist and, dwelling remote from the Holy Land, he could not have been a companion of the Lord. He may, however, have known Him in the days of His flesh, and he had at all events drunk deep of His grace. He was elected to the Deaconship because he was 'a man full of faith and the Holy Spirit'; and he had already approved himself in 'the ministry of the Word' ere he was called to 'the ministry of the tables.'

Cf. Ac. viii. 5-13, 26-40; xxi. 8.

Lk. x. 1.

Stephen's disputation in Hellenist synagogues.

It seemed as though he were destined to a high career of evangelical enterprise; but another destiny had been ordained for him. He was to glorify the Lord by his death, and thus, as it proved, still more effectively advance the Kingdom of Heaven. It was the spring of the year A.D. 33,[2] and the paschal celebration had brought the customary troops of pilgrims to the Holy City. She was thronged with worshippers from near and far, and the Hellenistic synagogues were crowded with strangers. Here Stephen found a golden opportunity. Himself a Hellenist, he visited the synagogues, and there presented the Gospel. It would have been impossible for each Hellenistic community to maintain a separate synagogue at Jerusalem, and so each synagogue represented a group of adjacent and sympathetic communities. And there were two where Stephen's arguments created an especial stir. One was the synagogue of the North African Jews from Libya with its capital Cyrene and Egypt with its capital Alexandria; and the other the synagogue of the Jews of the Provinces of Asia and Cilicia, comprehending probably all the intervening sweep of

[1] Cf. Epiphan. *Hær.* xx. 4.

[2] Cf. Append. I.

southern Asia Minor along the Eastern Trade Route.[1] It was natural that Stephen should encounter keen discussion in these two synagogues; for in the one there were Jews from the brilliant city of Alexandria, men like Apollos, both learned and eloquent and versed in the Scriptures; while in the other there were Jews not only from Ephesus but from Tarsus, which in those days more than rivalled Alexandria's fame.

Ac. xviii. 24.

Among the latter was Saul. He had come to Jerusalem for the Passover; and he would certainly attend the synagogue of the Cilicians and Asians, and hear Stephen's arguments and bear his part in the disputation. It would be a sharp encounter, but he found himself overmatched. His weapons of Rabbinical dialectic were impotent against his antagonist's wisdom, a wisdom which he had been taught by the Holy Spirit. It was a humiliating experience for the young Rabbi and his fellows, and it exasperated them. Worsted in argument, they would not acknowledge the truth. They raised the cry of blasphemy, and proceeded to indict Stephen before the Sanhedrin. Their charge was that he had announced the overthrow of the Temple and the supersession of the Law; and they produced witnesses to support it.

Saul his protagonist. Cf. Ac. vii. 58.

A charge of blasphemy.

It was a repetition of the scene which had been enacted there just four years previously, when the Lord was arraigned on that self-same charge; and it is no wonder that Stephen's heart was stirred at the thought. It was remarked and

Arraignment before the Sanhedrin. Cf. Mt. xxvi. 59-61.

[1] Cf. Ac. vi. 9—a *crux interpretum.* The problem is twofold: 1. The meaning of *Λιβερτίνων.* Commonly explained as 'Freemen' (*Libertini*), *i.e.* descendants of Pompey's Jewish prisoners (cf. p. 20). Cf. Chrys.: *Λιβερτῖνοι δὲ, οἱ Ῥωμαίων ἀπελεύθεροι οὕτω καλοῦνται.* More probably, however, it is a place-name like *Κυρηναίων* and *Ἀλεξανδρέων*, and there was a town Libertum in N. Africa which sent a bishop (*Episcopus Libertinensis*) to the Synod of Carthage in A.D. 411. Cf. Suid.: *Λιβερτῖνοι· ὄνομα ἔθνους.* Wetstein regards *Λιβερτίνων* as an alternative form of *Λιβυστίνων*, and Vers. Armen. reads 'Libyans' (cf. Ac. ii. 10). 2. The number of synagogues. (1) Only one, 'the Synagogue of the Libertines,' comprehending the four subsequent nationalities (Calv., Beng.). (2) Two, 'the Synagogue of the Libertines, Cyrenæans, and Alexandrians' and 'the Jews of Cilicia and Asia' (Winer-Moulton, p. 160, n. 3). (3) Five, 'the Synagogue of the Libertines, that of the Cyrenæans, that of the Alexandrians, that of the Cilicians, and that of the Asians (Schürer, II. ii. p. 57, n. 44). This, however, would require the reiteration of *τῆς* in each case.

long remembered that, as he stood before the High Priest, his face shone and looked like the face of an angel.[1] After the charge had been laid and the witnesses had given their evidence, the High Priest put the question: 'Is this so?' and he entered upon his defence with the reverential preface which became a loyal Jew in addressing that august court: 'Brethren and fathers, hearken.'

Stephen's defence.

He began with the first count of the indictment—his alleged statement that 'Jesus the Nazarene would overthrow the Holy Place.' He did not deny it; he justified it by demonstrating, in a long *résumé* of the national history, how unessential the Temple was. It had been founded late, and its insufficiency had been proclaimed in the very hour of its institution. The birth of the nation dated from the call of Abraham nigh two thousand years before, and there was no Temple in Abraham's day. He had been a wanderer, and so had all the patriarchs for four centuries. Then in the land of bondage Moses was born. He was ordained of God as the deliverer of His people, yet they did not recognise him. They drove him from their midst, and he betook himself to the land of Midian. It was there, not in a Temple but in a heathen wilderness, that God appeared to him in the burning bush and called him to his task. He led the people forth from Egypt, and again God appeared to him, not in a Temple but in the wilderness of Sinai; and again they turned against Moses and made them a golden calf and worshipped it after the manner of the Egyptians. Still there was no Temple. The Tabernacle was indeed instituted, and they worshipped in it during their wanderings, and brought it with them into the Promised Land. But it was only a temporary institution; and not till the days of Solomon, some four centuries and a half after their settlement in the Promised Land, was the Temple built. Thus for nearly a thousand years Israel had been God's people, and all the while she had no Temple; and when at length the Temple was built, God had proclaimed its insufficiency. 'The Most

[1] Stephen's defence is so remarkable, as Blass observes, that it can be nothing else than an accurate report. Philip would hear it, and Luke may have had it from him at Cæsarea twenty-four years later (cf. Ac. xxi. 8).

High does not dwell in sanctuaries which hands have made; as the prophet says:

'The heaven is My throne, — Is. lxvi. 1.
and the earth My foot-stool:
What manner of house will ye build for Me? saith the Lord;
or what is the place of My rest?
Did not My hand make all these things?'

Angry interruption.

The Sanhedrists had listened complacently to the historical narrative, and even the references to the unfaithfulness of their fathers had given them no offence; but that quotation indicated whither the argument was tending, and they raised a clamour of angry dissent, oblivious that it was the Lord's word that they were reprobating. Their unreasoning fury revealed the hopelessness of persuading them. It was the same spirit which had animated their fathers all down the course of their history. Stephen stood unmoved, and when the storm subsided, he told them the stern truth. '"Stiffnecked" and "uncircumcised in hearts and ears!" you are always opposing the Holy Spirit. Your fathers did it, so do you. Which of the prophets did not your fathers persecute? They killed those who announced beforehand the coming of the Righteous One, and now you have proved His betrayers and murderers.' (Ex. xxxiii. 3; Lev. xxvi. 41; Jer. vi. 10, ix. 26. Cf. Is. lxiii. 10.)

Stoning of Stephen.

Instantly the Sanhedrin was in an uproar. Stephen had dealt thus far only with the first article of the indictment, but he was suffered to proceed no further. The august senators forgot their dignity and 'gnashed their teeth at him' like infuriated beasts. Meanwhile he stood with upturned face, seeing nothing of their menaces, hearing nothing of their clamour; and a vision of the Unseen broke upon him. His surroundings vanished—that circle of angry faces and the enclosing walls and roof of the Hall of Hewn Stone.[1] 'Look you!' he exclaimed, 'I behold the heavens wide opened and the Son of Man standing at the right hand of God'—not sitting on His Judgment-seat but standing as though He had started from His Throne to greet His Martyr and, according to His word, 'receive him unto (Cf. Lk. xxii. 69. Cf. Jo. xiv. 3.)

[1] Cf. *The Days of His Flesh*, p. 468.

Himself.'[1] This sealed his doom. It seemed to them rank blasphemy, and without staying to pronounce sentence they rushed at him and, that the Holy City might not be defiled with his impious blood, dragged him through street and gate, and there outside the city-wall executed on him the blasphemer's horrible doom[2] by stoning him to death. He died with a prayer on his lips. 'Lord Jesus,' he said when the hail of missiles began, 'receive my spirit'; and then he sank, bruised and bleeding, on his knees. 'Lord,' he cried, 'lay not this sin to their charge,' and 'fell asleep.'

Cf. Lev. xxiv. 14; Dt. xxii. 24; 1 Ki. xxi. 13; Heb. xiii. 11-13.

And thus he gained that crown of which his name Stephen, 'the Crown,'[3] had been an unwitting prophecy. He was the leader of 'the noble army of martyrs.'

[1] Cf. Œcum.: ἵνα δείξῃ τὴν ἀντίληψιν τὴν εἰς αὐτόν.

[2] Cf. Lightfoot, *Hor. Hebr.* on Jo. x. 31.

[3] Cf. Aug. *Enarr. in Psalm.* lviii. 5: 'Quod vocabatur accepit. Stephanus enim Corona dicitur.'

THE CONVERSION OF SAUL

Ac. viii. 1b-3, ix. 1-21 (xxii. 4-16, xxvi. 9-20); Gal. i. 17; Ac. ix. 22-25; 2 Cor. xi. 32, 33; Ac. ix. 26-31; Gal. i. 18-24; 2 Cor. xii. 2-4.

'Oh the regret, the struggle and the failing!
Oh the days desolate and useless years!
Vows in the night, so fierce and unavailing!
Stings of my shame and passion of my tears!'

FREDERIC W. H. MYERS.

Illegality of Stephen's doom.

THE execution of Stephen was a flagrant illegality. Judæa was in those days a Roman province; and while the imperial government suffered the Jews to administer their own religious affairs, in capital cases it reserved to itself the ultimate decision. The Sanhedrin might pass the death-sentence, but its execution lay with the Roman procurator. Hence after our Lord had been declared by the High Priest guilty of the capital offence of blasphemy, He was not forthwith sentenced to the Jewish doom of stoning but remitted to the judgment of Pontius Pilate and, after due confirmation of the Jewish court's verdict, sentenced to the Roman penalty of crucifixion.[1] This is the course which should have been followed in the case of Stephen, and his summary execution was an open flouting of the procurator's authority. Nor could the outrage have been committed with impunity had not Pilate during those closing years of his disastrous administration (A.D. 25-35) been reduced to impotence by his long misgovernment.[2]

Cf. Ac. xviii. 12-16.

Persecution in Judæa.

The martyrdom of Stephen was the breaking of a pitiless tempest. The purpose of the rulers was nothing less than the extermination of the Church, and they found in Saul a ready and efficient instrument. He had borne a conspicuous part in the judicial crime. As a member of the Sanhedrin he had recorded his vote against the heretic, and not content therewith he had in the intensity of his zeal so far demeaned himself as to attend the victim to the scene of execution.

Cf. Ac. xxvi. 10.

[1] Cf. *The Days of His Flesh*, p. 463.

[2] *Ibid.* pp. 477 ff.

He took indeed no active share in the brutal work, leaving that to coarser hands. He flung no stone, but when the witnesses who had given evidence in court divested themselves
Cf. Dt. xvii. 7. in order to exercise their statutory prerogative of beginning the bloody business, they laid their cloaks at his feet, and
Cf. Ac. xxii. 20. he stood guard over them—an incident which he remembered in after days with burning shame.[1] And the work thus
Saul's zeal. auspiciously inaugurated was vigorously prosecuted. The rulers appointed Saul their commissioner, and he instituted an energetic inquisition, invading with his minions the homes of the disciples, arresting and imprisoning all who would not abjure their Lord, and arraigning them before the court of the Sanhedrin.[2] The survivors fled from the city, and hid in the fastnesses of Judæa or fled from pursuit across the northern frontier into the territory of despised Samaria.
Cf. Ac. viii. 1. The Apostles alone stood their ground, and it is indeed surprising that they, the leaders of the heresy, should have been able to defy the storm. The reason doubtless was that their miraculous powers had invested them with sanctity in the eyes of the populace, and even in the extremity of their rage the rulers would shrink from molesting them and thus provoking a popular reaction.

His commission to Damascus. After he had purged the Holy City and her environs of the heretical pollution Saul's zeal remained unabated. He
Ac. ix. 1. 'still breathed out threat and slaughter against the disciples of the Lord.' Tidings reached him that some of the fugitives had found an asylum in the old Syrian capital,[3] the far northern city of Damascus; and he resolved to pursue them thither. They were indeed beyond the confines of Palestine, but they were not beyond the jurisdiction of the Sanhedrin, since every Jewish community throughout the Empire was subject in matters of religion to the local synagogue, which

[1] Cf. Aug. *Serm.* ccclxxxii. 4: 'cum sanctus Stephanus lapidaretur, omnium vestimenta servabat, et tanquam manibus omnium lapidabat.'

[2] Ac. xxvi. 11: *αὐτοὺς ἠνάγκαζον βλασφημεῖν*, 'I tried to compel them to blaspheme,' implying that he did not succeed. The process was familiar in after days. Cf. *Martyr. Polyc.* ix: 'When the proconsul insisted and said: "Take the oath, and I release you; revile the Christ," Polycarp answered: "Eighty and six years have I been His servant, and He has done me no wrong; and how can I blaspheme my King, who saved me?"' where *λοιδορεῖν τὸν Χριστὸν* is the Latin *Christo maledicere* (cf. Plin. *Epist.* x. 97).

[3] Cf. Ac. xxii. 5: *τοὺς ἐκεῖσε ὄντας.*

in turn owed allegiance to the supreme court at Jerusalem. So he obtained from Caiaphas the High Priest, as President of the Sanhedrin, *lettres de cachet* to the synagogues of Damascus, empowering him to arrest 'any that were of the Way,[1] whether men or women,' and convey them in bonds to Jerusalem for trial and sentence.

His journey.

He set forth on his journey attended by a band of the Sanhedrin's officers. His route is uncertain, since two were open to him. He might hold northward and, passing through Samaria, cross the Jordan by the ford of Bethshean; or he might cross by the southern ford of Bethany near Jericho and travel northward through Peræa and Batanæa. It was probably the latter route that he adopted, since it was the shorter, making the journey about a hundred and forty miles; and if, as the narrative seems to indicate,[2] he travelled on foot, it would occupy at the customary rate over a week.

His spiritual disquietude.

It was a long march, and it afforded the persecutor ample leisure for reflection. In truth his mind was ill at ease, and the very intensity of his hostility to Christianity is an evidence thereof.

> 'When one so great begins to rage, he 's hunted
> Even to falling.'[3]

A man is never so violent in the assertion of his faith as when he feels it slipping from his grasp; and that was the reason of Saul's 'exceeding madness' against the Church. For years he had been conscious of his alienation from God, and had been labouring to attain peace by the Pharisaic method of legal observance. His labour had been in vain, and his failure had goaded him to ever increased devotion. For

Ac. xxvi. 11.

(1) The futility of Pharisaism.

[1] A designation of the Gospel (cf. Ac. xix. 9, 23, xxii. 4, xxiv. 14, 22); more fully 'The Way of the Lord' or 'The Way of God' (cf. xviii. 25, 26). 'An appellation of the believers, who were generally so named, perhaps,' fancies Chris., 'because they were cutting the way which leads to Heaven.'

[2] The mediæval artists depict him mounted on a caparisoned charger; but, since among the Jews the horse was used only in war, he would ride, if he rode at all, on an ass or a camel (cf. *The Days of His Flesh*, pp. 391 f.). However, (1) the word πορεύεσθαι (ix. 3, xxii. 6) suggests that he travelled on foot; and (2) had he been provided with a beast, his attendants would have set him on its back instead of 'leading him by the hand' (cf. ix. 8, xxii. 11) into Damascus.

[3] Shak. *Ant. and Cleop.* IV. i. 7 f.

long it had never occurred to him that he was on the wrong road, but the suspicion had dawned upon him when he came into personal contact with Christianity. His first introduction to the new faith was probably the controversy with Stephen in the Hellenistic synagogues at Jerusalem.[1] He had then heard from the lips of that masterly exponent the evidence that Jesus was the Messiah, and that He had been raised from the dead and was living and reigning at God's right hand; and the argument had overpowered him. He could not refute it, but he would not accept it; and he had striven to stifle his misgivings and silence the pleadings of the Holy Spirit by engaging in a furious crusade against the heresy.

(2) The teaching of Gamaliel.

Amid the wild tumult the inward voice had been unheard, but in the solitude of his long journey it renewed its importunities, and he was constrained to calm consideration. He would review his past career. He could hardly fail to recall the large-hearted tolerance of his gracious teacher, the wise Rabbi Gamaliel; and the memory of that revered master and his serene faith in Eternal Providence would rebuke his frenzied 'zeal for God.' Could it be, he would ask himself, that he was indeed 'fighting against God'? that, in resisting reason and struggling to suppress his misgivings, he was, in the phrase of a Greek proverb which perhaps he had heard from those honoured lips, 'kicking against the goad,' like a rebellious ox in the traces?[2]

Cf. Ac. xxii. 3; Gal. i. 14; Rom. x. 2.

(3) The testimony of Stephen.

His chief thought, however, would be of the martyr whose blood he had helped to spill. Stephen's arguments would recur to him. He would reconsider them; and the more he considered them, the more inevitable would they appear. Could it be after all that Jesus of Nazareth was indeed the Messiah, and that the Law had been abrogated

[1] Cf. pp. 40 f.

[2] Ac. xxvi. 14. Cf. Pind. *Pyth.* II. 172 ff.: ποτὶ κέντρον δέ τοι / λακτίζεμεν τελέθει / ὀλισθηρὸς οἶμος. Æsch. *Agam.* 1602: πρὸς κέντρα μὴ λακτίζε μὴ παίσας μογῇς. *Prom. Vinct.* 322. Eur. *Bacch.* 794; *Peliad.* (fragm.): πρὸς κέντρα μὴ λάκτιζε τοῖς κρατοῦσί σου. Terent. *Phorm.* I. ii. 27 f.: 'Nam quæ inscitia est / Adversum stimulum calces?' Though so frequent in the classics, the proverb occurs nowhere in Jewish literature, and Saul may have heard it from his liberal teacher. It is included in the Risen Lord's speech in Ac. xxvi. 14, but it is absent from the parallel reports (cf. ix. 5 R.V., xxii. 7), and it is probably an addition by the Apostle, defining the thought of his own heart and the true significance of the Lord's remonstrance.

by a larger revelation? This, he could not but confess, would truly be glad tidings for a soul wearied well-nigh to despair in the quest for righteousness by the hard and futile way of legal observance. And one fact stood before him clear and incontrovertible: not only Stephen but the whole multitude of his fellow-believers had found in Jesus the peace which Saul had so long craved—a glad, triumphant peace which no suffering could shake. And in His name, moreover, the Apostles had wrought wonders which had astonished Jerusalem and which the Sanhedrin durst not dispute. Could it be that the story of the Resurrection was true, and the Crucified was actually reigning at God's right hand? Was it indeed His glory which had irradiated the martyr's face when he stood before the High Priest and when he fell beneath the pelting stones with a prayer to the Lord Jesus on his lips? That spectacle haunted Saul to his dying day, and more than all else it determined the crisis of his life. 'If,' says St. Augustine,[1] 'Stephen had not so prayed, the Church would not have Paul to-day.'

Cf. Ac. xxii. 20.

Damascus.

Such questionings were stirring in Saul's breast during that memorable week as he toiled day after day along the dusty highway or lay by night in his tent tossing on his restless couch. At length he reached the village of Kochaba (*Kaukab*), some ten miles south-west of Damascus,[2] and the fair city opened to his view. She was the ancient Syrian capital, and she holds the distinction of being the oldest city in the world. There was a Jewish legend that she was the home of Adam and Eve after their expulsion from Eden, and that the plain of Damascus was the scene of Abel's murder by Cain.[3] Her origin belongs to the unrecorded past. She

Her antiquity.

[1] *Serm.* ccclxxxii. 11; 'Nam si martyr Stephanus non sic orasset, Ecclesia Paulum hodie non haberet.'

[2] This was the scene of Saul's conversion according to tradition in the times of the Crusades. A later tradition places it about half a mile south-east of the city, where there is now a Christian cemetery.

[3] Cf. Hieron. on Ez. xxxviii. 18: 'Sin autem Damascus interpretatur *sanguinem bibens*, et Hebræorum vera traditio est campum in quo interfectus est Abel a parricida Cain fuisse in Damasco.' Cf. *Travels of Sir John Mandeville*, xiv; Shak. *King Henry VI* (i), I. iii. 39 f.:

'This be Damascus, be thou cursed Cain,
To slay thy brother Abel, if thou wilt.'

The legend originated, as St. Jerome indicates, in the fanciful derivation of the

Cf. Gen. xiv. 15, xv. 2.

already flourished in the days of Abraham, and a later tradition represents his steward, Eliezer of Damascus, as her founder. And she has survived the vicissitudes of four thousand years, a great city still with a population of a quarter of a million when every city of equal antiquity has vanished from the face of the earth or remains only in broken and buried ruins.

Her beauty.

Damascus owes much to her situation. Lying far inland on the margin of the desert, she has escaped the tide of invasion which generation after generation has inundated Palestine; and this is the reason of her long continuance. And, though so near the desert, she enjoys the richest blessings of nature. She occupies the midst of a lovely plain, green and fruitful, watered by the river Barada, the ancient Abana, and bounded westward by Mount Hermon and the long ridge of Anti-Lebanon; and the climate is delightful since the plain is raised some 2300 feet above the level of the Mediterranean. The city was the principal station of caravans from the East, and her markets were thronged with merchants. Her beauty was the admiration of the world. A Hebrew prophet styled her 'the city of praise, the city of my joy'; and to this day the Arabs speak of her as 'pleasant Damascus,' 'honourable,' 'holy,' 'blessed Damascus,' one of the four terrestrial Paradises. And it is told how Mohammed, ere his call to be the prophet of Allah while he was still a camel-driver, surveyed Damascus from the mountain and would not enter her lest, amid her delights, he should forget the glories of Paradise. 'Man,' he said, 'has but one Paradise, and mine is fixed elsewhere.'

Jer. xlix. 25.

Her political connection.

Formerly the capital of Syria, Damascus passed under the dominion of Arabia. Then she was annexed by Pompey to the Roman Empire (62-64 B.C.); but, with that imperial instinct which taught them that an Empire's strength lies in the self-government of its component nationalities, the Romans recognised the subordinate sovereignty of the Arabian king; and thus in the days of Saul, while Damascus belonged to the Roman Empire, she was under the rule of

Cf. 2 Cor. xi. 32, 33.

name from דָּם and שִׁקוּי, 'a draught of blood' (*sanguinis potus*). On Damascus cf. Strabo, 755 f.; G. A. Smith, *Hist. Geogr.*, xxx; Wright, *Palmyra and Zenobia*; Hichens, *Holy Land*, II.

King Aretas, and his representative or 'ethnarch' was guardian of the city. The population was composed mainly of native Syrians, but it included also a considerable colony of Jews who had settled there after their wont to share in the busy and lucrative traffic.[1] They had their synagogues, and it was to these that Saul was commissioned.

A thunder-storm.

When the city came into view, it was a spectacle to gladden the eyes and charm the imagination; yet her beauty made no appeal to Saul. His mental conflict had waxed ever keener as the days passed, and now the decisive hour had arrived. Could he enter the city and, despite his misgivings, prosecute his errand? His future was hanging in the balance, and God interposed and decided the issue. Martin Luther has recorded how it fared with himself at the supreme crisis of his life. His soul had been stirred by his study of the Latin Bible which he had discovered in the College Library at Erfurt, and by a sickness which had brought him to the gates of death; and he was travelling with his friend Alexis through the Thuringian Forest when a terrific storm broke. The thunder rolled and the lightning blazed, and a bolt struck his companion dead by his side and tore up the earth at his feet. It seemed as though the *Dies Iræ* had arrived, and, 'compassed with terror and the agony of death,' he devoted himself to God from that hour.[2] And even such was Saul's experience as he approached Damascus.

A vision of the Risen Lord.

It was the sultry noontide; and in that region thunder-storms of exceeding violence are frequent when the hot breath of the desert smites the snow-capped mountain. Suddenly a dazzling flash enveloped the travellers,[3] and they all fell prostrate. His companions soon recovered from their panic and rose to their feet, but Saul lay still on the ground. The lightning was for him the Lord's minister and the thunder the Lord's voice; and as he lay the Glorified Christ manifested Himself to him. It was no mere subjective phantasm but an actual vision. Of this he never doubted, and he was no irrational enthusiast, no facile dupe of fancy. His

Cf. Pss. xxix; civ. 4; cxlviii. 8.

[1] Cf. p. 4. [2] *Epist.* II. 101.

[3] It is expressly stated that the blaze was a lightning-flash (ἀστραπή). Cf. ix. 3: περιήστραψεν φῶς ἐκ τοῦ οὐρανοῦ. xxii. 6: ἐκ τοῦ οὐρανοῦ περιαστράψαι φῶς ἱκανόν.

subsequent testimony is clear and significant. His apostleship was challenged in after days by the Judaists on the ground that he had never known Jesus or received a commission from Him; and therefore, they alleged, he lacked the authority of the original Apostles. And what was his answer? He asserted that he had indeed seen the Lord and received from Him a direct call to the Apostleship.
1 Cor. ix. 1. 'Am not I an Apostle? Have not I seen Jesus our Lord?' There would have been no cogency in this retort had he not been assured that on the road to Damascus he had a veritable vision of the Lord, not indeed as He had been in His mortal weakness but as He was in His glorified humanity.

His glorified body.

And here lies the distinctive quality of his experience. It was a revelation of the Risen Lord identical with those manifestations which He had vouchsafed to His disciples during the forty days between His Resurrection and His Ascension.[1] He wore the body which He had worn 'all the time that He went in and went out among them,' but it was transfigured; it had undergone the self-same transformation which our mortal bodies shall experience when they are raised incorruptible, qualified for that Kingdom which flesh and blood cannot inherit. It was no longer 'an earthly body' but 'a heavenly body,' no longer 'an animal body' but 'a spiritual body,' no longer 'the body of His humiliation' but 'the body of His glory.' This distinction is receiving surprising illumination from the investigations of physical science. Matter, as it is now known to us, is only in the making, and when the process is complete, it will be a finer stuff. Its evolution keeps pace with our spiritual development; and when the soul is ushered into the domain of the Eternal, 'this muddy vesture of decay' which 'doth grossly close it in,' will experience a corresponding ennoblement. It will not perish, neither will it be left behind; it will be purified and refined. Matter as it is is only matter in the making; and 'the spiritual body' or, in scientific phrase, 'the ethereal body' is 'the animal body' as it shall become in the course of its further evolution.

Cf. 1 Cor. xv. 5-8. Ac. i. 21. Cf. 1 Cor. xv. 50. Cf. 1 Cor. xv. 40, 44; Phil. iii. 21.

Unperceived by physical sense.

And the ethereal body, adapted as it is to the Kingdom which flesh and blood cannot inherit, is superior to the con-

[1] Cf. *The Days of His Flesh*, pp. 521 ff.

ditions of sense. It is, as appears from the records of our Lord's post-resurrection manifestations, invisible to the physical eye and inaudible to the physical ear. The physical eye beholds a physical body, but spiritual vision is needed for the perception of a spiritual body. And hence, when the Lord would manifest Himself to the children of men, there are two ways whereby He may accomplish His gracious purpose. One is that He should submit Himself to their carnal limitations and present Himself before them under their existent conditions; and He took that way at the Incarnation. In this case the miracle was wrought on His own person. The other way is that the miracle should be wrought on them; that the veil of sense should be lifted and their spiritual perceptions unfettered, so that they may behold things which eye cannot see and hear things which ear cannot hear. And this is the way which He took when He manifested Himself to His chosen witnesses during the Forty Days, and again when He manifested Himself to Saul on the road to Damascus.

Cf. Jo. i. 14.

Seen by Saul alone.

See how this is borne out by the sacred narrative. The miracle was wrought upon Saul alone, and thus he alone perceived the manifestation. He saw the Lord and heard His voice, but his attendants saw nothing and heard nothing beyond the physical accompaniments. It was indeed an actual manifestation, yet he did not perceive it with his physical senses. It was not his eyes that 'saw the Lord'; for all the while he was prostrate on his face, blinded by the flash. And he alone experienced it. His companions neither saw the Lord nor heard His voice. They saw the blaze of light, but they did not see the Glorious Form; and they heard a voice, but it was the voice of Saul making reply to the heavenly question, and they wondered at what appeared to them a one-sided conversation.[1]

Cf. Ac. ix. 7.

The Lord's remonstrance.

The Lord's question was a gracious and compassionate remonstrance. He spoke in Hebrew, Saul's kindly mother-tongue, with a pleading iteration of his name: 'Shaûl, Shaûl, why are you persecuting Me?' It was a puzzling inquiry: Saul had never seen Jesus, and he did not recognise Him. He might indeed have guessed who the glorious

xxvi. 14. Cf. Lk. x. 41; xxii. 31.

[1] Cf. Append. II.

stranger was, and had He asked: 'Why are you persecuting My disciples?' he would have had no doubt. But it bewildered him when he was asked: 'Why are you persecuting Me?' He did not yet understand the truth which he learned in after days, that the Glorified Saviour is so truly one with His people, the Head so linked to the members, that their sufferings are His: 'Inasmuch as you did it to one of these My brothers, even these least, you did it to Me.'[1] And so he leaped to the conclusion that his interlocutor was one of the victims of his persecuting zeal. 'Who are you, sir?'[2] he asked. And the answer came: 'I am Jesus, whom you are persecuting.'

Cf. Mt. xxv. 40.

The broken persecutor.

The Lord's errand was not to upbraid. He dismissed the past, and claimed the broken persecutor for a high career of future service. 'I am Jesus,' He said, 'whom you are persecuting. But arise, and enter into the city, and it will be told you what you must do.'[3] Therewith the vision faded, and Saul lay stunned until his attendants raised him. He was in a sorry plight. He had been blinded by the lightning, and they had to lead him by the hand into Damascus—a far different entry than he had contemplated when he set forth from Jerusalem 'breathing out threat and slaughter.' It had been arranged that during his stay in the city as the Sanhedrin's emissary he should reside in the house of a Jew named Judas in Straight Street;[4] and thither they conducted him.

His vision in Damascus.

For three days he lay sightless and oblivious of his surroundings. He tasted nothing, and kept praying until a vision was vouchsafed him. It may have been a dream, 'coming,' as dreams are wont, 'with a multitude of

Eccl. v. 3.

[1] Cf. Aug. *Serm.* cccxlv. 4: 'One whom Paul never saw and never touched, cries in heaven: "Why are you persecuting Me?" He does not ask: "Why are you persecuting My household, My servants, My saints or brothers?" It was none of those things that He said. And what did He say? "Why are you persecuting Me?" He asks, that is, My members. For these, trampled on earth, the Head cried in heaven.'

[2] For this use of *κύριε*, like *domine*, cf. Mt. xiii. 27, xxv. 22, 24; Jo. xx. 15.

[3] In ix. 5, 6 the best authorities omit 'it is hard . . . said unto him.' The true reading is *ἐγώ εἰμι Ἰησοῦς ὅν σὺ διώκεις. ἀλλά ἀνάστηθι. ἀλλά* suggests a pause during which Saul lay mute.

[4] The street still remains, running right across the city. Cf. Hichens, *The Holy Land*, p. 69.

business,' [1] like that which moved the elder Pliny to write his history of the German wars, when, as he lay asleep, the form of Drusus Nero, who had perished in the midst of his victorious career, stood by his couch and prayed him to rescue his memory from oblivion.[2] Nevertheless it was a divine revelation. There was in Damascus a believer of distinction and repute named Ananias, who ere his conversion had been a strict Jew and still remained loyal to the ancient ordinances. Apparently Saul had known him in the past; and in his vision he saw Ananias enter his chamber and lay hands on him and restore his sight. Ananias too had a vision, and it seems to have been no mere dream but a veritable manifestation of the Risen Lord. He had learned from the refugees of Saul's malignant activities in the Holy City and his commission to Damascus, and rumours were current of his experience on the way. But these would be inexplicable to Ananias, and he was fearfully expecting the persecutor's arrival. And thus it surprised him when the Lord told him that the latter was lying stricken in the house of Judas, and bade him repair thither and restore him, silencing his incredulous remonstrance with an intimation of the high part which Saul was destined to play.

Cf. xxii. 12.

Ananias.

Cf. ix. 17.

His visit to Saul.

Ananias obeyed. He betook himself to the house of Judas, and, being admitted to Saul's chamber, he laid his hands on him after the manner of a physician,[3] and addressed him in Hebrew as a fellow-Jew. 'Shaûl,' he said, and added 'brother,' thus claiming him as a fellow-believer, 'the Lord has commissioned me—Jesus who appeared to you on your way hither—that you may recover your sight and be filled with the Holy Spirit.' Forthwith Saul's dark-

[1] Cf. *The Days of His Flesh*, p. 485. Lecky, *Map of Life*, p. 333: 'It has been noticed that often thoughts and judgments, scattered and entangled in our evening hours, seem sifted, clarified, and arranged in sleep; that problems which seemed hopelessly confused when we lay down are at once and easily solved when we awake, "as though a reason more perfect than reason had been at work when we were in our beds."' In Job xxxiii. 14-30 three ways are specified in which God was recognised as speaking to men: (1) by dreams, (2) by sickness, and (3) by prophets.

[2] Plin. *Epist.* iii. 5.

[3] Cf. Senec. *De Benef.* VI. 16: 'Itaque medico, si nihil amplius quam manum tangit et me inter eos quos perambulat ponit, sine ullo affectu facienda vitandaque præcipiens, nihil amplius debeo.'

ness, both physical and spiritual, was dispelled. The purulent incrustation which had seeled his eyes fell off in flakes, and they opened to the light.[1] He rose from his couch and was baptised ; and, taking refreshment, was soon restored to strength.

Saul's testimony in the synagogues.

The first duty which devolved upon him was public confession of his new allegiance, and he hastened to discharge it. Invested with the authority of the Sanhedrin's commission, he visited the synagogues and there, instead of preaching a crusade against the Church, proclaimed his faith in the Lord's Messiahship.[2] It was a startling *volte-face*, and it occasioned amazement. His testimony would in due course have resulted inevitably in a large accession to the Church and a corresponding exasperation of the Jewish authorities, but that issue was meanwhile postponed. His conversion was an upheaval of his life, and it was essential that he should retire for a season and calmly survey the altered conditions and determine his future action. After his conversion in A.D. 386 in his three-and-thirtieth year St. Augustine resigned his professorship of Rhetoric at Milan and repaired to the country-house of his friend Verecundus at Cassiacum, where for a season he 'found rest in God from the fever of the world.'[3] And even our Blessed Lord on receiving His call to enter on His public ministry retired to the wilderness of Judæa and passed forty days in solitary communion and spiritual conflict.[4] And how much more urgent was Saul's need of repose and self-recollection ! He remained only a few days at Damascus, and then he quitted the city and betook himself to a far distant retreat. It was the grim solitude of Mount Sinai in Arabia,[5] where the

His retirement to Arabia.

Cf. Gal. i. 17.

[1] ἀπέπεσαν, λεπίδες, and ἐνίσχυσεν (ix. 18, 19) are medical terms (cf. Hobart, *Med. Lang. of St. Luke*, pp. 38 ff.) exemplifying 'the beloved physician's' accustomed use of professional language.

[2] ὁ Υἱὸς τοῦ Θεοῦ (ix. 20), a Messianic title, synonymous with ὁ Χριστός (ver. 22). Cf. *The Days of His Flesh*, pp. 33, 370.

[3] *Confess.* IX. 2-5.

[4] Cf. *The Days of His Flesh*, chap. IV.

[5] The Arabian retirement has its place in Ac. ix. between ver. 20 and ver. 21. It is omitted by the historian probably because it belonged so peculiarly to Saul's inner life. The locality is indeterminate. 'Arabia' was properly the Sinaitic Peninsula, but at that period it comprehended the region east of the Jordan (cf. Eus. *Onomast.* : Ἰορδάνης ποταμὸς διαιρῶν τὴν Ἰουδαίαν τῆς Ἀραβίας), extending indeed 'from Mount Amanus to the Egyptian coast' (Plin. *H. N.* VI. 32). In

prophet Elijah had met with God in his dark hour ; and none more appropriate could have been chosen. It was there that the Law had been delivered to Moses, and the problem which pressed upon Saul was the value of the ancient revelation and the attitude which he must thenceforth hold to it. In that historic scene, 1 Ki. xix. 8-18.

> 'Where all around on mountain, sand, and sky,
> God's chariot-wheels had left distinctest trace,'[1]

he thought out the question and attained the conviction which he maintained to the last, that the Law was a temporary institution, designed not to cure but to discover the plague of sin. Cf. Gal. iii. 19.

How long his sojourn in Arabia may have continued does not appear. Moses was forty days in the Mount with God, and no less a space would suffice for Saul. It is perhaps foolish to inquire how he sustained himself all the while, but it may be recalled that the desert was peopled by nomad tribes roaming far and wide and pitching their brown tents where they listed, whence, especially in Mesopotamia, they were known as the Scenitæ or Tentmen.[2] Tent-making was Saul's handicraft, and its exercise would win him a ready livelihood among those wanderers, as it did in after days when he visited strange cities in the course of his missionary journeys.[3] His employment there. Cf. Ex. xxiv. 18, xxxiv. 28.

When his season of retirement was over, he returned to His return to Damascus and ministry there.

this large sense Damascus was in Arabia (cf. Strabo, 755 : ἐγγύς πως τῶν 'Αραβίων ὀρῶν τῶν ὑπὲρ τῆς Δαμασκηνῆς. Just. M. *Dial. cum Tryph.*, p. 305A (Sylburg.) : Δαμασκὸς τῆς 'Αῤῥαβικῆς γῆς ἦν καὶ ἔστιν, εἰ καὶ νῦν προσνενέμηται τῇ Συροφοινίκῃ λεγομένῃ) ; and hence it has been supposed that Saul found a retreat at no great distance from the city, in Auranitis (*Hauran*) or Trachonitis. But ἀπῆλθον εἰς 'Αραβίαν, 'I went away into Arabia,' seems to imply a remoter destination ; and it is decisive that in Gal. iv. 25 Arabia signifies the Sinaitic Peninsula. Indeed, if the *midrash* (Gal. iv. 22-31) be indeed, as it seems, an echo of Saul's inward debate during his retirement, it fixes Mount Sinai as the locality. Chrysostom (cf. Theod. Mops., Theodoret.) misses the significance of the retiral into Arabia by regarding it as a missionary expedition : 'See the ardour of his soul. He was eager to occupy the regions which had not yet been tilled but still lay wild. . . . Fervent in spirit, he addressed himself to the instruction of men barbarous and wild, choosing a life of conflict and heavy toil.'

[1] Keble, *Christian Year*, Ninth Sunday after Trinity.

[2] Strabo, 288, 515, 747 f., 765 ; Plin. *H. N.* VI. 32.

[3] Cf. Wetstein on Ac. xviii. 3.

Damascus to resume his testimony. He had thought out the problem of the relation between the Law and the Gospel and attained to assured conviction, and he entered on an active ministry which continued for two full years.[1] His main effort was naturally directed to the task of persuading the Jews of Damascus by appeal to the prophetic Scriptures that Jesus was the Messiah;[2] and he achieved conspicuous and increasing success. He was recognised as the Church's protagonist in the city, and his converts formed a distinct school owning him as its master.[3]

Jewish hostility.

The Jewish authorities were bitterly resentful, and at length they laid a plot for his destruction: so soon was the whilome persecutor menaced with the doom which he had inflicted. They enlisted the sympathy of the ethnarch who governed the city under King Aretas;[4] and he posted guards at the gates to prevent his egress.

Cf. 2 Cor. xi. 32, 33.

Saul, however, was apprised of their intention, and his disciples rallied to his defence and effected his deliverance by an ingenious stratagem.

His escape.

The houses on the city-rampart had windows overhanging the fosse, and they ensconced him in a large basket of woven rope and lowered him from a window under cover of darkness.[5]

Visit to Jerusalem.

On making his escape he betook himself to Jerusalem. It was fitting that he should go thither and confess the faith which he had trampled under foot. And that was doubtless his main errand, but he had another end in view. The Holy City was the home of the original Apostles; and since they were the leaders of the Church, Saul desired to meet them and show them what the Lord had done for him and obtain their benediction upon his future career. There was one in particular to whom his heart turned—the generous Peter, who had played so heroic and devoted a

[1] Cf. Append. I.

[2] ix. 22: *συμβιβαζων ὅτι οὗτός ἐστιν ὁ Χριστός*, quoting Old Testament passages and laying them alongside of their fulfilments in the life of our Lord.

[3] Cf. Ac. ix. 25, where the best authorities read *οἱ μαθηταὶ αὐτοῦ*, 'his disciples.'

[4] Cf. p. 51.

[5] Cf. Wright, *Palmyra and Zenobia*, p. 226: 'As we looked down the walls, in which we recognised pieces of the Roman period, we saw houses on the ramparts, and windows overhanging the ditch. From such a place was Paul let down.' *σπυρίς* (*σφυρίς*) was a large-sized basket (cf. *The Days of His Flesh*, pp. 235, 255). In 2 Cor. xi. 33 it is called *σαργάνη*, which Suidas defines as *πλέγμα τι ἐκ σχοινίου*.

part ever since the Day of Pentecost when the Holy Spirit had descended on the Church. 'To view Cephas' was Saul's ambition, and with this object before him his journey to Jerusalem was, as St. Chrysostom aptly observes, like a pious pilgrimage.[1] Gal. i. 18.

The Church's distrust.

It was in this spirit that he sought the Holy City. He required of the Apostles neither approval nor instruction, since the Lord had spoken to him and called him to His service. But it became him to humble himself before the Church which he had so cruelly injured, and on his arrival he would have taken his place in her ranks. A difficulty, however, emerged. His past clung to him, and his very name was a terror to the disciples. It seemed as though the door of the Church were closed against him; but happily there was one of her members endowed with courage, generosity, and discernment. His proper name was Joseph, and he was a Hellenist, a native of the island of Cyprus, and well born since he had belonged to the priestly caste. Like his kinswoman Mary, the mother of John Mark, he had been richly endowed with worldly goods. He had owned land in his native island, but he had devoted it to the common good. Nor was this generosity his sole title to the Church's esteem. It appears that he was a person of distinguished presence,[2] and it is a testimony to his intellectual qualities that he was credited in after days with the authorship not only of the uncanonical epistle which goes by his name but with that noble work, the anonymous Epistle to the Hebrews.[3] Withal he was distinguished by a winsome graciousness which had earned for him in the Church the designation of Barnabas. It is uncertain what precisely this name signifies, whether 'the son of consolation' or 'the son of exhortation,' but the quality which it betokened appears when it is remembered that the word variously

Barnabas. Cf. Ac. iv. 36, 37. Cf. Col. iv. 10; Ac. xii. 12.

[1] Gal. i. 18: *ἱστορῆσαι Κηφᾶν*. *Κηφᾶς* is Aramaic of *Πέτρος* (cf. Jo. i. 42). *ἱστορεῖν* was used of going to view some great sight, a celebrated place or personage. Cf. Plut. *Pomp.* xl. 1; *Lucull.* ii. 6; *Cic.* ii. 2. Chrys.: *οὐκ εἶπεν 'ἰδεῖν Πέτρον' ἀλλ' 'ἱστορῆσαι Πέτρον,' ὅπερ οἱ τὰς μεγάλας πόλεις καὶ λαμπρὰς καταμανθάνοντες λέγουσιν.*

[2] The people of Lystra took him for Zeus, the King of the Gods (cf. Ac. xiv. 11, 12). *ἐμοὶ δοκεῖ*, says Chrysostom, *καὶ ἀπὸ τῆς ὄψεως ἀξιοπρεπὴς εἶναι ὁ Βαρνάβας.*

[3] Cf. Tert. *De Pudic.* 20.

rendered 'consolation' and 'exhortation' is akin to our Lord's designation of the Holy Spirit, the *Paraclete*, 'the Comforter' or rather 'the Advocate.'[1] And St. Chrysostom has truly defined his disposition by the epithets 'sweetly reasonable, gentle, kindly, accessible.'[2]

His generous championship.

Barnabas came to Saul's aid. With characteristic kindliness he took him by the hand and conducted him to the Apostles. As it chanced, there were only two of the latter in Jerusalem at that time, and these were Peter and James, the Lord's brother, who, though not one of the original Twelve, yet by reason of his sacred kinship and his lofty character enjoyed apostolic prestige.[3] Their colleagues were doubtless absent on circuits among the outlying churches of Judæa,[4] but those two sufficed: their reception of Saul would secure his *entrée*. Barnabas introduced him and told his story, arguing that it became them to receive one who had seen the Lord and so fearlessly confessed Him at Damascus.

Saul's reception by the Apostles.

Cf. Gal. ii. 9.

They accorded him a ready welcome, and Peter took him to his home and entertained him during his sojourn in the Holy City.[5] His errand thither was accomplished once he had been received and had seen the chief 'pillar' of the Church, but he protracted his stay for a fortnight and availed himself of the opportunities which each day brought. His

[1] It is probable (cf. Deissmann, *Bible Studies*, pp. 309 f.) that 'Barnabas' was originally an ancient Semitic name, 'son of Nebo,' the Babylonian deity (cf. Is. xlvi. 1), and the Jews redeemed it from paganism by explaining it as either (1) בַּר נְבוּאָה, 'son of prophecy' or 'exhortation' (cf. Ac. xiii. 1, where Barnabas is called 'a prophet') or (2) בַּר נְוָחָא, 'son of consolation.' Exhortation and consolation were both prophetic functions (cf. 1 Cor. xiv. 3), but the latter belonged more especially to Barnabas. He was at all events less eloquent than Paul (cf. Ac. xiv. 12).

[2] *In Act. Apost. Hom.* XXI: ἐπιεικής τις καὶ ἥμερος ἄνθρωπος ἦν . . . χρηστὸς ἦν σφόδρα καὶ εὐπρόσιτος.

[3] Gal. i. 19; cf. 1 Cor. xv. 7. The title 'Apostle' was somewhat largely employed, being bestowed on others besides the original Twelve; *e.g.*, Barnabas (Ac. xiv. 4, 14; 1 Cor. ix. 5, 6), Silvanus (1 Th. ii. 6). There was in fact no rigid distinction between 'an apostle' and 'an apostolic man.' Thus Clem. Alex. speaks now of 'the Apostle Barnabas' (*Strom.* II. vi. 31, vii. 35) and again of 'the apostolic Barnabas' (II. xx. 116).

[4] Cf. Peter's expedition (Ac. ix. 32 ff.).

[5] Gal. i. 18: ἐπέμεινα πρὸς αὐτόν. Cf. Ac. xxviii. 14; 1 Cor. xvi. 7.

reception by the Apostles had dispelled the suspicions and fears of the disciples, and he moved freely among them. Nor was he content with their fellowship. His desire was to make atonement for the past by confessing the Lord where he had blasphemed His name ; and this he did in a courageous and effective fashion. He visited the Hellenistic synagogues where he had disputed with Stephen, and resumed the controversy, espousing the cause which he had formerly opposed. He was encountered with the weapons which he had himself employed. Worsted in argument, his opponents resorted to 'the syllogism of violence.'[1] They plotted his destruction, and he would have perished had he not been smuggled out of the city under cover of darkness,[2] and conveyed to Cæsarea, whence he took ship and sailed to Tarsus.[3]

His testimony in the Hellenistic synagogues.

Jewish violence.

Flight to Tarsus.

Tarsus was his home, yet it was inevitable that he should be ill received by his former associates, his kinsfolk, and especially his father, that stern old Pharisee. Quarter of a century later, in writing from his prison at Rome to the churches in the Province of Asia, he included among his practical counsels a poignant exhortation. 'Fathers,' he pleads, 'never anger your children, but nurture them in the Lord's instruction and admonition.' 'Fathers, never irritate your children, lest they be discouraged.' There is here a quivering note of personal emotion, and it seems as though the heart of the aged captive had been reverting to the past and recalling the loveless years of his own childhood. Nurtured in the austere atmosphere of traditional orthodoxy, he had experienced scant tenderness and much severity, and had known that 'plague of youth, a broken spirit.'[4] And now on his return home he would seem in the eyes of his father a traitor to the ancestral faith, and would be greeted with a storm of reproaches. It would be a painful encounter —on the one side unmeasured reprobation, and on the other unavailing remonstrance passing into indignant recrimination. It was a desecrating scene. It issued in irremediable

Domestic estrangement.

Eph. vi. 4; Col. iii. 21.

[1] Chrys. on Ac. ix. 23 : ἐπὶ τὸν ἰσχυρὸν συλλογισμὸν ἔρχονται πάλιν οἱ Ἰουδαῖοι.

[2] In Ac. ix. 30 some authorities read εἰς Καισάρειαν διὰ νυκτός.

[3] κατήγαγον, 'brought him down to the coast' ; ἐξαπέστειλαν, 'sent him away out of port.'

[4] Bengel on Col. iii. 21 : 'ἀθυμία, *fractus animus*, pestis juventutis.'

estrangement, and the bitter memory remained with him to the last.

Ministry in Syria-Cilicia.

Cf. Gal. i. 21-24.

Nevertheless he did not flinch. An outcast from home and kindred, he devoted himself for the next nine years [1] to the service of the Gospel in his native city and the surrounding Province of Syria-Cilicia; and he achieved no small success. The fame of his ministry travelled as far as the Province of Judæa, and excited wonder and gladness in the churches there. He was personally unknown to them, but they had heard of his malign activities in the Sacred Capital a few years previously, and on learning that the persecutor was doing the work of an evangelist they praised God for so amazing a transformation.

Spiritual development.

2 Cor. xii. 2-4.

Nor was this his sole employment. It was during that period that he was vouchsafed those two visions which he recounts in a letter to the church at Corinth in the year 55, one a discovery of the righteousness of God and the other a revelation of the glory of the Risen Saviour. It thus appears that his protracted sojourn in his native province was a season not merely of evangelical activity but of inward development, and in either aspect it was a precious discipline for the work which awaited him in the providence of God.

[1] Cf. Append. I.

BOOK II

PAUL THE APOSTLE OF JESUS CHRIST

'Paule doctor egregie,
Tuba clangens ecclesiæ,
Nubes volans ac tonitrum,
Per amplum mundi circulum.

Nobis potenter intona
Ruraque cordis irriga,
Cœlestis imbre gratiæ
Mentes virescant aridæ.'

Latin Hymn.

HIS CALL TO THE APOSTLESHIP OF THE GENTILES

Ac. xi. 19-30; Gal. ii. 1-10; Ac. xxii. 17-21.

The dispersion of the Church and the diffusion of the Faith.

It is an ancient saying which has passed into a proverb, that 'the blood of the martyrs is the seed of the Church';[1] and Saul's conversion was not the sole harvest which sprang from the blood of Stephen. The dispersion of the Church issued in the diffusion of the Faith, since the fugitives played the part of missionaries, proclaiming the glad tidings of Christ wherever they went. Damascus was not the only heathen city where they found an asylum. A little company, mainly Hellenists, passed the northern frontier into Phœnicia, and there doubtless they would visit the cities of Tyre and Sidon and preach in the synagogues; but they did not stay in Phœnicia. They crossed over to the island of Cyprus, and after preaching to the Jews there they returned to the mainland and settled at Antioch.

The city of Antioch.

Now a poor Turkish town of six thousand inhabitants, Antioch was in those days a splendid city. She was the metropolis of Syria, ranking after Rome and Alexandria as the third city of the Roman Empire.[2] Damascus was the Arabian metropolis of Syria, but when the Greeks occupied the country, they desired a capital nearer to the sea for the facilitation of their commerce; and Seleucus Nicator chose a site on the river Orontes fifteen miles from its mouth.[3] The river was navigable, and the passage up the winding stream was only one day's sail,[4] while the port of Seleuceia five miles north of its embouchure opened to the city a still easier access to the sea.

The Greek capital of Syria.

[1] Tert. *Apol.* 50: 'Plures efficimur quoties metimur a vobis: semen est sanguis Christianorum.'

[2] Jos. *De Bell. Jud.* III. ii. 4. The chief ancient authorities on Antioch are Strabo, 749 ff.; Julian, *Misopogon*; Chrysostom, *Homilies to the People of Antioch.* Cf. Gibbon, *Decline and Fall*, chaps. xxiii, xxvi; Renan, *Les Apôtres*, xii.

[3] Jos. *Contra Apion.* II. 4; Strabo, 749.

[4] Strabo, 751.

Her population.

Her population in the days when St. Chrysostom was thrilling her with his matchless eloquence, numbered 200,000,[1] of whom half were Christians; [2] and it comprised four elements. The native Syrians were the primary element. Then there were the invading Greeks. There was also a large colony of Jews, attracted thither at the foundation of the city by the privilege of 'equal citizenship' which Seleucus granted to that race of merchants.[3] Moreover, Pompey had constituted Antioch a free city, the capital of the Province of Syria and the seat of the imperial Legate; [4] and thus there was a Roman element, mainly official, in the population.

Her learning.

She enjoyed, according to Cicero,[5] a high reputation for learning and culture; and this was more than maintained in Christian days when Antioch was the centre of a distinguished school of historical exegesis. Her fair fame, however, was tarnished by another and less honourable reputation. The Antiochenes were characterised by that turbulent disposition which seems inevitable wherever there is a mixture of races; and they were also notorious for their licentiousness. 'The warmth of the climate,' says Gibbon, 'disposed the natives to the most intemperate enjoyment of tranquillity and opulence; and the lively licentiousness of the Greeks was blended with the hereditary softness of the Syrians.' Among the uplands five miles from the city lay

Her turbulence and licentiousness.

'that sweet grove
Of Daphne by Orontes,'

with its umbrageous laurels and cypresses and its gushing fountains, enclosing an inviolate precinct sacred to Apollo and Artemis and giving the city her distinctive title of 'Antioch by Daphne' [6]—a needful distinction inasmuch as there were at least four other Antiochs in Syria, besides

[1] Chrys. *Hom.* XLII, *In S. Ignat. Martyr.*

[2] Chrys. *In Matt. Hom.* LXXXVI, *ad fin.*

[3] Jos. *Ant.* XII. iii. 1.

[4] Plut. *Pomp.* xxxix f.; Plin. *Nat. Hist.* V. 13.

[5] *Pro Arch. Poet.* iii. Philostratus, however, says (*Vit. Apoll. Tyan.* III. 58) that Antioch had no zeal for letters. In any case her enduring literary fame is Christian.

[6] Ἀντιόχεια ἡ ἐπὶ Δάφνῃ.

Antioch in Pisidia and Antioch on the Mæander. The ritual of the grove was a consecration of shame. 'The vigorous youth,' says Gibbon again, 'pursued, like Apollo, the object of his desires; and the blushing maid was warned, by the fate of Daphne, to shun the folly of unreasonable coyness.' 'The morals of Daphne' were proverbial; and so enervating was the abandon that Avidius Cassius, the hardy general of Marcus Aurelius, whose tragic rebellion served only to illustrate the magnanimity of the philosophic Emperor, made it a penal offence for a soldier to visit the place. The corruption of Antioch tainted the whole world, and the Roman satirist deplores the flood of pollution which the Orontes poured into the Tiber.[1]

Antiochene scurrility.

The Antiochenes were further remarkable for a ready wit which was apt to degenerate into scurrility, and which manifested itself particularly in an unamiable trick of coining nicknames.[2] It is related that, when the Emperor Julian the Apostate visited the city in the course of his march to the East, he angered them by injudicious interference with their market, and they avenged themselves by shouting abuse after him in the streets. The long beard which he wore in emulation of his revered philosophers, was an especial object of their ridicule. They termed him 'the Goat,' and exhorted him to 'cut it off and weave it into ropes'; and they styled him also 'the Butcher' because he was continually sacrificing oxen at the altars of his heathen deities.

The nickname 'Christian.' Ac. xi. 26.

This unamiable propensity of the Antiochenes has conferred one lasting benefit. 'The disciples were called Christians first in Antioch.' The name was originally no title of honour; it was a nickname, a derisive epithet wherewith the followers of Christ were branded by the mocking Antiochenes.[3] And its composition betrays its origin. A

[1] Juv. III. 62.

[2] Cf. Julian, *Misopogon*, 338 ff.; Philostr. *Vit. Apoll. Tyan.* III. 58; Socr. *Eccl. Hist.* III. 17. Wetstein on Acts xi. 26.

[3] The evidence is twofold: (1) The name occurs only in two other passages in the New Testament (Ac. xxvi. 28; 1 Pet. iv. 16), and in each it is plainly a term of contempt. (2) χρηματίζειν (Ac. xi. 26) means not merely 'to be named' but 'to be nicknamed.' It signified properly to get a name from one's employment (χρῆμα), one's occupation or conduct. Cf. Rom. vii. 3: a woman μοιχαλις χρηματίσει when she commits μοιχεία. Erasmus: 'Videtur autem inde dicta vox, quod cognomen ex officio quo quis fungitur addi solet. Veluti publicani dicuntur,

literary school or a political party received a designation from the leader's name. Thus, the imitators of Cicero were styled 'Ciceronians'; the partisans of Pompey were styled 'Pompeians'; the attendants of Cæsar, the slaves of the imperial palace, were styled 'Cæsarians'; and later the followers of the heresiarchs Sabellius and Arius were styled 'Sabellians' and 'Arians.' And in like manner, by a felicitous stroke of Antiochene wit, the followers of Christ, that pretender to the throne of Israel who had been crucified under Pontius Pilate, were mockingly designated 'Christians.'

A felicitous appellation.

The nickname was caught up and was carried abroad. It became the general designation of the despised sect of Judaism, and as early as the year 64 it was in vogue among the populace of the imperial capital.[1] It was, however, still a contumelious epithet, and the persecuted folk continued meanwhile to call themselves by their old designations —'the disciples,' 'the believers,' 'the brethren,' 'the saints,' 'the elect'; but ere long it was transfigured by their virtues in the world's estimation, and by the close of the first century they appropriated it and wore it proudly.[2] It was indeed a noble name, nor could a more felicitous appellation have been devised. It blends the three great languages of the ancient world, since 'Christ' is the Greek rendering of the Hebrew 'Messiah,' and the termination is Latin.[3] And thus, like the inscription, JESUS OF NAZARETH THE KING OF THE JEWS, which Pilate put over the cross, in Hebrew and Greek and Latin, the name 'Christian' enshrines the supreme glory of the Gospel and proclaims the universality of its grace. 'Jesting Pilate' and the mocking Antiochenes were unwitting prophets of the Lord.

Jo. xix. 20.

quod publica vectigalia colligunt, ita Christiani, quod Christum profiterentur.' The Jewish designations of the despised sect were 'the Nazarenes' and 'the Galileans.'

[1] Cf. Tac. *Ann.* XV. 44: 'quos per flagitia invisos vulgus Christianos appellabat.'

[2] Both Χριστιανός and Χριστιανισμός are frequent in the epistles of Ignatius. Cf. *ad Magn.* iv.: πρέπον ἐστὶν μὴ μόνον καλεῖσθαι Χριστιανοὺς ἀλλὰ καὶ εἶναι. Lightfoot, *Apost. Fath.* II. i. pp. 415 ff.

[3] This does not prove that the name must have originated at Rome and is unhistorically assigned to Antioch as 'the first Gentile city in which Christians existed' (Baur). Such Latin forms were naturalised in the East. Cf. 'Ηρωδιανοί, 'Αρειανοί, Σαβελλιανοί.

Gentile evangelisation.

The bestowal of a name, however, was not the only service which Antioch rendered to Christianity. She was the scene of a momentous innovation which determined the future of the Faith. Of those Hellenists who after their extensive wandering settled in the city, some were Cypriotes, and they shared the generosity of their countryman Barnabas; while others were Cyrenians, and they had doubtless heard the arguments of Stephen in their synagogue at Jerusalem [1] and caught his spirit. They were thus men of wide sympathies and large ideals. They were Jews, and in the course of their travels through Phœnicia and Cyprus they had addressed themselves exclusively to their co-religionists; but after their settlement at Antioch they took to preaching also to the Gentiles.[2] Their appeal proved effective. They won numerous converts among the heathen populace; and these, strangers as they were to the Jewish Law and its ceremonial rites, were received into the communion of the Church.

Delegation of Barnabas from Jerusalem to Antioch.

It was a novel development, and when a report of it reached Jerusalem, it occasioned no small questioning in the Church. It was decided to despatch a delegate to inquire into it, and Barnabas was appointed. It was a happy choice; for the occasion demanded a man of large sympathy, discernment of God's purpose, and courage to forsake tradition and enter at the divine call on an untrodden path. And such a man was Barnabas—'a good man and full of the Holy Spirit and of faith.'

His approval of the innovation.

He came to Antioch, and he immediately recognised the Lord's hand in the new movement. It was a singular mani-

[1] Cf. p. 40.

[2] Ac. xi. 20: *πρὸς τοὺς Ἕλληνας*. Though the preponderance of MS. authority supports Ἑλληνιστάς (cf. p. 5), the true reading is indubitably Ἕλληνας. (1) There would have been nothing novel in preaching to Hellenists; and in fact all the Jewish residents at Antioch were Hellenists. (2) There is no antithesis between Ἰουδαῖοι and Ἑλληνισταί. The Ἑλληνισταί were Ἰουδαῖοι, and the antithesis of Ἑλληνιστής is Ἑβραῖος (cf. Ac. vi. 1). (3) Ἕλληνας is further attested by *εὐαγγελιζόμενοι τὸν Κύριον Ἰησοῦν*. Preaching to Gentiles, they 'told the glad tidings of the Lord Jesus'; had they been preaching to Jews, whether Hebrews or Hellenists, they would have 'proclaimed and proved from the Scriptures that Jesus was the Son of God, the Messiah' (cf. ix. 20, 22). It is significant that, while reading *τοὺς* Ἑλληνιστάς, Chrys. assumes that it is equivalent to *τοὺς* Ἕλληνας.

festation of grace, and he not merely approved it but lent it his best aid. 'He exhorted them all that with purpose of heart they should abide by the Lord.' He possessed indeed, as his name expresses, the gift of exhortation; but he recognised that more was needed. He would fain have borne an active part in the winning of fresh converts, and since he lacked this aptitude, he considered how he might procure effective reinforcement; and his thoughts turned to Saul. He recalled that memorable fortnight in Jerusalem and the power of the converted persecutor's testimony. Of late, moreover, and especially since his coming to Antioch he had been hearing reports of Saul's evangelical activities in the Province of Syria-Cilicia. Where could a better helper be found? He knew not where in the wide province he might be prosecuting his labours, but he took ship for Tarsus and soon discovered him and brought him to Antioch.

His enlistment of Saul.

Saul's 'bodily presence.'

It was the summer of the year 45 when Saul appeared on the scene,[1] and in his outward aspect there was little suggestion of the distinguished part which he would play. Unchivalrous adversaries in after days sneered at 'the weakness of his bodily presence'; and tradition has preserved a graphic portraiture which is so unflattering that it can hardly be a mere imagination, since the tendency of later generations was rather to idealise the Apostles. It depicts him as 'little in size, bald-headed, bow-legged, well-knit, with contracted brow, somewhat large-nosed.'[2] The phrase 'with contracted brow' seems to denote a short-sighted person's manner of pursing his eyes and wrinkling his forehead;[3] and there is perhaps an evidence that Saul laboured under this infirmity in his habit of 'fastening his eyes' on one whom he addressed.[4]

2 Cor. x. 10.

Cf. Ac. xiii. 9, xiv. 9, xxiii. 1.

[1] Cf. Append. I.

[2] *Act. Paul. et Thecl.* 3: εἶδεν δὲ τὸν Παῦλον ἐρχόμενον, ἄνδρα μικρὸν τῷ μεγέθει, ψιλὸν τῇ κεφαλῇ, ἀγκύλον ταῖς κνήμαις, εὐεκτικὸν, σύνοφρυν, μικρῶς ἐπίρρινον, χάριτος πλήρη. ποτὲ μὲν γὰρ ἐφαίνετο ὡς ἄνθρωπος, ποτὲ δὲ ἀγγέλου πρόσωπον εἶχεν. Cf. Pseudo-Lucian, *Philopat.* 12: Γαλιλαῖος, ἀνακεφαλαντίας, ἐπίρρινος, ἐς τρίτον οὐρανὸν ἀεροβατήσας καὶ τὰ κάλλιστα ἐκμεμαθηκώς.

[3] σύνοφρυς signified also 'with meeting eyebrows,' *junctis superciliis*—a mark of beauty (cf. Theocr. VIII. 75: σύνοφρυς κόρα); but this meaning is inadmissible here.

[4] ἀτενίζειν, one of Luke's medical terms (cf. Hobart, *Med. Lang. of St. Luke*, p. 76), occurring twice in his Gospel and ten times in Acts, and nowhere else in N. T. except 2 Cor. iii. 7, 13, where it denotes a strained gaze.

Possibly it was induced by the blinding flash on the road to Damascus. It is, however, noteworthy that, uncouth as it represents him, the tradition imputes to him no other bodily weakness. On the contrary, it describes him as 'well-knit'; and so he must have been, else he could not have sustained the fatigue of his extensive travel and continual toil in after years. And though thus insignificant in the eyes of the world, he ranks with its greatest. 'Three cubits in stature, he touched the sky'; [1] and discerning souls perceived his spiritual grandeur. And so the tradition adds that he was 'full of grace; for sometimes he showed like a man, but sometimes he had the face of an angel.'

He was well equipped for his task when he came to Antioch. Being forty-five years of age, he was in the full vigour of mature manhood; his mind, so rich in natural endowments, had been disciplined and furnished by education and study; and his soul had been quickened and elevated by singular experiences of heavenly grace. Moreover, during the last nine years he had been doing the work of an evangelist in Tarsus and its environs, and thus he was practised in the art of commending the Gospel and winning men for Christ. It does not appear that he had ever visited Antioch, but the fame of his preaching in the province must have travelled thither, and it would excite lively expectation. For a year he prosecuted his labours among the teeming populace, and they were crowned with abundant success.

His successful ministry at Antioch.

Meanwhile, however, there had been trouble at Jerusalem. Antioch's season of gracious visitation was a time of tribulation for the Church in the Holy City. Herod Agrippa I, King of Judæa (A.D. 37-44) by consent of Imperial Rome, was a gentle and kindly prince,[2] yet he had assumed the rôle of persecutor. His policy was to humour his Jewish subjects, and he addicted himself from the outset of his reign to a scrupulous observance of their religion. 'It was his pleasure,' says the Jewish historian, 'to reside constantly at Jerusalem, and he purely observed the national customs. He lived an undefiled life, nor did a day ever pass with him

Persecution at Jerusalem.

[1] *Orat. Encom.* (ascribed to Chrys.): Παῦλος . . . ὁ τρίπηχυς ἄνθρωπος καὶ τῶν οὐρανῶν ἁπτόμενος.

[2] Jos. *Ant.* XIX. vii. 3.

lacking the legal sacrifice.' His reign was the golden age of Ac. xii. 3. Pharisaism, and it is no wonder that to 'please the Jews' he should have attacked the Church. He executed the Apostle James, the son of Zebedee and brother of John, and cast Peter into prison.

Fugitive prophets at Antioch.

Again the Church was dispersed, and a band of fugitives took refuge at Antioch. They were remarkable personages. They were Prophets, successors of those heroic preachers of old who had been inspired by the Spirit of God to read His 1 Mac. iv. 46, ix. 27, xiv. 41; cf. Ps. lxxiv. 9. purposes and declare His will. The gift of prophecy had ceased in later days. Already in the time of the Maccabees there was no prophet in Israel. Inspiration was lacking, and the prophet's place was supplied by the scribe, the conservator of a dead tradition. With the advent of the Mt. xi. 9-11. Gospel the lost gift was restored. John the Baptist was a prophet of the ancient order; and this is the secret of his mighty power. For centuries the people had been yearning for a living voice, proclaiming with authority the Word of the Living God; and when at length they heard it, they recognised and welcomed it. And the gift remained after Ac. ii. 17, 18. the Lord's departure. It was confirmed on the Day of Pentecost when the Holy Spirit was poured forth; and it continued for generations. In apostolic days it was held in 1 Cor. xii. 28. high honour, and the Prophets ranked next to the Apostles in the Church's esteem.

Famine predicted by Agabus.

It was probably toward the close of the year 44 when that company of prophets appeared at Antioch. They settled there and aided in the work of evangelisation; and presently one of their number, named Agabus, publicly announced the imminence of a widespread famine. It was no groundless alarm. It is recorded that during the reign of Claudius (A.D. 41-54) the Empire was afflicted with 'incessant dearths.'[1] Shortly after his accession there had been a famine at Rome, betokening scarcity in the countries whence her supplies were drawn.[2] Greece suffered in the eighth or ninth year of his reign;[3] and in the eleventh Rome was again visited, and her distress was aggravated by shocks of earthquake and popular tumult.[4]

[1] Suet. *Claud.* 18. [2] Dio Cassius, lx. 11. Cf. Lewin, *Fast. Sac.* 1639.
[3] Eus. *Chron.* Cf. Lewin, 1735. [4] Tac. *Ann.* XII. 43.

It was likely that the wandering calamity would alight nearer home, and probably about the beginning of the year 45, when the prospects of the harvest in the month of March were looking dark, the prophet perceived and announced its approach. His prediction was presently fulfilled. Judæa was ravaged by a sore dearth during the years 45 and 46.[1] The distress of the Jews was alleviated by the munificent generosity of a noble proselyte, Helena Queen of Abdiene, who had visited the Holy City, probably at the Feast of the Passover, to worship and present thank-offerings in the Temple, and was residing in her palace on the Acra[2] when the trouble befell. She despatched some of her officers in hot haste to Alexandria for a supply of corn and others to Cyprus for a cargo of dried figs, and on the arrival of those welcome succours dispensed them among the starving populace.[3] *Fulfilment of the prediction.*

There was no beneficent princess among the Christians in Jerusalem; nevertheless they did not go unrelieved. The prophecy of Agabus had apprised the Antiochenes of the impending calamity; and, though the fertility of their country secured them from personal privation, they were concerned for their co-religionists in the Holy City, and when Saul appeared among them in the course of the summer, he directed their sympathy into a practical channel. His heart was tender toward 'the poor saints' at Jerusalem, inasmuch as some of them would be the widows and orphans of his victims in the first persecution; and he engaged the good offices of the Antiochenes on their behalf. A relief fund was organised. They would doubtless follow the method which subsequently prevailed, contributing each Lord's Day according to their ability; and in course of time the offerings accumulated until, when the famine reached its height on the failure of the harvest in the year 46, there was a sufficient store. And then they purchased supplies and despatched these to Jerusalem. *Antiochene supplies for Jerusalem.* *Cf. Gal. ii. 10.* *1 Cor. xvi. 1, 2.*

Barnabas and Saul were deputed to conduct the transport and present the bounty. Their retinue included a young *Conducted by Barnabas and Saul.*

[1] Cf. Append. I.
[2] Cf. Jos. *De Bell. Jud.* V. vi. 1; VI. vi. 3.
[3] Jos. *Ant.* XX. ii. 5, v. 2; cf. III. xv. 3.

Titus associated with them. Gentile named Titus who was destined to play a meritorious part in after days. For a reason which will emerge in due course, nothing is recorded of his antecedents, but this much is certain, that he was a convert of Saul; *Cf. Tit. i. 4.* and it appears also that he was an Antiochene, inasmuch as he remained uncircumcised, and it was at Antioch that the epoch-making innovation of preaching to the Gentiles and receiving them on the sole ground of faith in Christ first originated. Ere his coming thither Saul had preached in the synagogues and his converts had all been Jews. Evidently Titus had already evinced his worth and won the confidence of Saul; for it was the latter who attached him to the expedition. Nor is his motive obscure. The Antiochene innovation was resented in the Pharisaic section of the Church at Jerusalem; and he would feel that if its legitimacy were challenged, no more effective defence could be offered than the presentation of a believing Gentile who, though uncircumcised, displayed by his gracious endowments an incontrovertible evidence of his acceptance with God.

Conference at Jerusalem. And so it came to pass. It was the summer of 46 when the delegates appeared in the Holy City, and they did not merely deliver the bounty and hasten back to Antioch. They remained in Jerusalem and aided in the distribution.[1] Nor was this their sole employment. Saul was solicitous for the future. He recognised how momentous was the departure from Jewish sentiment involved in his Gospel of salvation by simple faith and its repudiation of the continued obligation of the Law; *Gal. ii. 2.* and, eager to preclude subsequent controversy and embitterment, he held a private conference with the leaders of the Church and submitted his views to them. A heated discussion ensued. There were several members of the conference who belonged to the extreme party of the legalists and who, it appears, eventually reverted to Judaism; *Cf. Gal. ii. 4.* and they condemned the Antiochene innovation. *Judaistic demand that Titus be circumcised.* They affirmed the permanent obligation of the Mosaic Law, and insisted that Titus should forthwith be circumcised. It seems that there was a general disposi-

[1] Cf. Ac. xi. 29 (*εἰs διακονίαν*) and xii. 25 (*πληρώσαντες τὴν διακονίαν*) with vi. 1 (*ἐν τῇ διακονίᾳ τῇ καθημερινῇ*). Barnabas and Saul assisted in 'the daily ministration,' 'the service of tables.' *πληρώσαντες* implies a protracted stay.

tion to accede in the interests of peace; but Saul stoutly resisted the proposal, and eventually he prevailed.[1] The Apostles, particularly James, the Lord's brother, Peter, and John, sided with him. They approved his Gospel, declaring it sufficient and requiring no addition to it in the way of legal observance. And, recognising that 'there are diversities in gifts of grace, but the same Spirit,' and that 'each has his own gift of grace from God, one in this way and another in that,' and 'as the Lord has apportioned to each, as God has called each, so he should comport himself,' they sanctioned his purpose of devoting himself to the evangelisation of the Gentiles. That was manifestly his providential vocation, whereas Peter, on the other hand, was marked out by his peculiar aptitude for the work of evangelising the Jews. And so they allocated to each his separate province and bade each Godspeed.

Saul's refusal.

His Gospel approved.

Cf. Gal. ii. 6.

1 Cor. xii. 4; vii. 7, 17.

It was a wise and magnanimous decision, and the spirit of the apostolic triad is pleasantly evinced by the solitary stipulation which they attached to their approval of Saul's vocation. They desired that, when he and Barnabas went on their mission to the Gentiles, they should still cherish a kindly remembrance of their poor Jewish brethren and continue to relieve their necessities. It was at once a grateful acknowledgment of the generosity of the Antiochene converts and a recognition of the efficacy of such brotherly sympathy in healing the enmity between Jew and Gentile. And they knew well that their desire was granted ere it was preferred, since Saul was eager to make atonement for the past and succour the distress which he had helped to create.

A magnanimous agreement.

Gal. ii. 10.

The conference served a profitable end by establishing Saul in the Church's confidence and legitimising his message. It furnished him with a large opportunity, and it appears that

Its happy effect.

[1] In Gal. ii. 5 the true reading is certainly οὐδὲ πρὸς ὥραν εἴξαμεν, 'not even for an hour did we yield'; but several important authorities (Vet. It., Pesh. Syr., D, Iren., Vict., Tert., Ambrstr.) omit οὐδέ: 'for an hour we yielded.' That is: Titus was circumcised. It was a voluntary concession. He was not *compelled*, but in view of the clamour the point was temporarily conceded in the interests of peace. The variant is probably a mistaken attempt to harmonise Paul's action in the case of Titus with his subsequent action in the case of Timothy (Ac. xvi. 3. Cf. p. 121). It may be remarked that, if Titus were circumcised, this would preclude the idea that the occasion was the Council of 49 (cf. Append. I), since such a concession, while conceivable earlier, was then out of the question.

he zealously availed himself of it. The hearts of the Jewish Christians were, moreover, kindly disposed toward him by the generous subsidy which he had brought them and his sympathetic assistance in the distribution ; and the common distress had drawn all the citizens together. On the occasion
Ac. ix. 29, 30.
of his previous visit to Jerusalem ten years previously he had been driven from the city by Jewish animosity ; [1] but this was now forgotten, and he preached freely and successfully.
Cf. Rom. ix. 1-5, x. 1.
To the last Saul loved his nation and yearned for its salvation; and he would joyfully devote himself to the ministry thus pleasingly presented to him.

Saul's vision in the Temple.

Amid these happy employments the days passed swiftly. Autumn glided into winter, and still he tarried at Jerusalem, oblivious of the call of the Gentile world. Yet he was not without misgivings. It would be about the commencement
Cf. Ac. xxii. 17-21.
of the year 47 when, after the devout Jewish fashion, he one day betook himself to the Temple for a season of solitary prayer.[2] A problem was pressing on his mind, and he would fain know the will of God. The question was whether he should remain in Jerusalem and continue the work which he had so auspiciously begun ; and in the fervour of his supplication he was rapt into unconsciousness of his surroundings.[3] His experience on the road to Damascus was repeated. The Glorified Lord appeared to him, and charged him to leave Jerusalem immediately. Meanwhile indeed the Jews were lending a ready ear to his message ; but their complacence would be short-lived : 'they will not receive your testimony concerning Me.' It reveals the recent trend of Saul's thoughts that he remonstrated and urged that there was reason to anticipate a happier issue. His message was invested with powerful credentials which could hardly fail to conquer the unbelief of the Jews. 'Lord,' he pleaded, 'those very men know that it was I who imprisoned and

[1] Cf. p. 61. [2] Cf. Append. I.

[3] γενέσθαι με ἐν ἐκστάσει, 'fell into an ecstasy.' The idea of ἔκστασις (ἐξίστασθαι) is that one is 'beside oneself,' outwith the control of the ordinary faculties, a condition induced by powerful emotion, as surprise or joy (cf. Mk. v. 42; Lk. v. 26; Ac. ii. 7, iii. 10); hence also of insanity (Mk. iii. 21; 2 Cor. v. 13). Cf. Plut. *Sol.* viii. 1 : ἐσκήψατο ἔκστασιν τῶν λογισμῶν, 'he feigned himself insane.' In his *Paraphr.* Erasmus has here 'raptus extra me.' The antithesis is ἐν ἑαυτῷ γενέσθαι (xii. 11) or εἰς ἑαυτὸν ἐλθεῖν (Lk. xv. 17).

scourged in every synagogue [1] those who believed on Thee; and when the blood of Stephen Thy martyr was being poured out, I am the very man who stood by and approved and watched the garments of his slayers.' Surely his testimony must carry conviction! [2] The Lord ignored the argument and imperiously reiterated His command. The evangelisation of Jerusalem was not Saul's task; his work lay elsewhere. 'Go your way; for I will send you afar as My Apostle [3] to the Gentiles.'

His apostolic commission. Cf. Rom. xi. 13. Cf. Gal. i. 1.

That sentence defined Saul's mission and sealed his ordination. He was thenceforth an Apostle of Jesus Christ—the Apostle of the Gentiles; and his Apostleship was a divine commission.

[1] Scourging was included in the synagogal discipline (cf. Mt. x. 17, xxiii. 34; 2 Cor. xi. 24). Cf. Schürer, II. ii. p. 66; Lightfoot and Wetstein on Mt. x. 17.

[2] Cf. Chrys.: '*A priori* (ἀπὸ λογισμῶν) he must needs suspect that they would certainly receive it.'

[3] ἐξαποστελῶ, cf. Mt. x. 5, 16.

THE FIRST MISSION

'Even with so soft a surge and an increasing,
   Drunk of the sand and thwarted of the clod,
Stilled and astir and checked and never-ceasing
   Spreadeth the great wave of the grace of God;

'Bears to the marishes and bitter places
   Healing for hurt and for their poisons balm,
Isle after isle in infinite embraces
   Floods and enfolds and fringes with the palm.'

FREDERIC W. H. MYERS.

I

ORDINATION OF ANTIOCH

Ac. xii. 25-xiii. 3.

Paul the Apostle of the Gentiles.

HIS call determined Saul's future career. It resolved his perplexity, and he forthwith addressed himself, with a devotion which never flagged, to the work for which God had hitherto been preparing him all unconsciously—the high enterprise of winning the Gentile world for the Faith of Christ. It was a momentous crisis, and he marked it by an eloquent and abiding monument. Hitherto he had gone by his Jewish name of Saul; but from the hour of his vocation to the Apostleship of the Gentiles he disused it and went by his Gentile name of Paul,[1] even in his intercourse with the Jews. (Cf. Ac. xv. 25.)

Return to Antioch.

His path was clear, and he made no delay in entering upon it. Yet he did not embark on his mission from Jerusalem. Antioch was the cradle of Gentile Christianity, the capital of Gentile Christendom, and it was fitting that the Antiochene Church should consecrate and commission him.

[1] Cf. p. 21. In the Received Text the Gentile name is first introduced in Ac. xiii. 9; but in xii. 25 Syr^{p} has 'Saul who was called Paul,' while some minuscs. read 'Paul' and one 'Saul Paul.' Again, in xiii. 1 for 'Saul' several minuscs. read 'Paul.' The probability is that it was after his call in the Temple that he changed his name.

And therefore he left the Holy City, now rejoicing in the near prospect of an abundant harvest, and returned to the Syrian capital.

Accompanied by Barnabas.

He did not return alone. Barnabas accompanied him. His generous soul not only hailed his comrade's call with glad approval but claimed the privilege of sharing in the great enterprise; and, recognising how arduous it would prove, he lent his practical counsel for its effective conduct. It was needful that the Apostle, after the example of the ancient Prophets, should be provided with an attendant—a young disciple who should relieve him of the burden of lesser offices and at the same time learn by his example the art of an evangelist; and it so happened that Barnabas had a young cousin[1] whom he deemed competent. His Jewish name was John, and he bore also, according to the custom of the time, the Latin name of Mark. He resided at Jerusalem with his mother Mary, who was evidently a widow and who was distinguished by her hospitality. Her house was a resort of the Christians in the city; and since her son owed his conversion to Peter, it is no wonder that the great Apostle was held by the household in especial veneration. In after days John Mark served as Peter's attendant, but his chief fame is his authorship of the Gospel which bears his name and which is credibly reputed a report of the Evangelic Tradition as he heard it from his master's lips.[2] Already, in the judgment of his kinsman at all events, he had given evidence of his fitness, and he was attached to the mission in the capacity of attendant. His service would include primarily the business of amanuensis, and probably also the administration of Baptism—an office which Paul seldom discharged with his own hands.[3]

Cf. 2 Ki. iv. 12, vi. 15-17.

Attended by John Mark.

Cf. Ac. xii. 12-17.

Cf. 1 Pet. v. 13.

Cf. Ac. xiii. 5.

Cf. 1 Cor. i. 14-17.

[1] Cf. Col. iv. 10: Μάρκος ὁ ἀνεψιὸς Βαρνάβα. ἀνεψιός was a cousin-german, whether on his father's side (*patruelis*) or on his mother's (*consobrinus*). Cf. Moulton and Milligan, *Vocab.* It is thus uncertain whether Mary, the mother of John Mark, was sister or sister-in-law to Barnabas' father. The use of ἀνεψιός in the sense of ἀδελφιδοῦς, 'nephew' (A.V.), was late.

[2] Cf. Papias in Eus. *Hist. Eccl.* III. 39.

[3] ὑπηρέτης (Ac. xiii. 5), 'attendant,' is used in the classics of the armour-bearer (σκευοφόρος) who acted as squire to a hoplite or heavy-armed soldier (cf. Thuc. III. 17; Xen. *Cyrop.* II. i. 31) and was himself equipped with bow and sling (cf. Aristoph. *Av.* 1186 f.). According to *Act. Barn.* vi, apparently, Mark acted as Paul's amanuensis and reader.

The Antiochene Prophets and Teachers.

The Antiochene Church was predominantly Gentile, and it appears that it had not as yet adopted the synagogal organisation which was subsequently universal in Christian communities. It had no Presbyters or Elders, and its leaders were Prophets and Teachers. The former were doubtless the fugitives who had settled in the city toward the close of the year 44; and though Agabus seems to have taken his departure, three still remained—Symeon Niger,[1] Lucius of Cyrene,[2] and Manaen, an ex-courtier of Herod Antipas, Tetrarch of Galilee and Peræa.[3] And what were the 'Teachers'? In those early days when there were no written Gospels, the story of our Lord's earthly life was preserved after the Jewish manner by oral tradition,[4] and its accurate transmission was a needful and difficult task, demanding not only laborious discipline but scrupulous faithfulness. This was the business of the Teachers;[5] and the importance of their service, as will appear in the sequel,[6] increased with the progress of the years. They were not a distinct order. An Apostle or a Prophet or a Presbyter might be a Teacher; and the transmission of the Evangelic Tradition to his converts was not the least of Paul's apostolic concerns.

Cf. 1 Cor. xi. 23, xv. 1-3.

Dedication and despatch of the missionaries.

On reaching Antioch Barnabas and Paul conferred with the three Prophets, their colleagues in the leadership of the Church, and acquainted them with their purpose. It was

[1] Symeon and Simon were interchangeable forms (cf. Ac. xv. 14), and there is no impossibility in the suggestion that Symeon Niger was Simon of Cyrene (cf. Mt. xxvii. 32). Niger means 'black,' but since it was a common name, it need not imply that he was a negro.

[2] Perhaps Paul's συγγενής, *i.e.*, 'countryman' or 'fellow Jew' (Rom. xvi. 21).

[3] Manaen is the Jewish name Menahem. σύντροφος does not mean 'foster-brother,' *collactaneus* (Vulg.). It was a court title, denoting a member of the prince's personal retinue (cf. Deissmann, *Bib. Stud.*, pp. 310 ff.). Thus Manaen was not a plebeian, the child of Antipas' nurse, but an ex-courtier, one of the few men of worldly rank in the primitive Church. It may be that he was a son of Menahem, the Essene prophet, who during the school-days of Herod the Great predicted his elevation to the Jewish throne, and enjoyed the royal favour on the fulfilment of the prophecy (cf. Jos. *Ant.* XV. x. 5).

[4] Cf. *The Days of His Flesh*, pp. xiii ff.

[5] Ambrstr. on 1 Cor. xii. 28: 'Illos dicit doctores qui in Ecclesia litteris et lectionibus (*v.l.* traditionibus) retinendis pueros imbuebant more Synagogae; quia traditio illorum ad nos transitum fecit.'

[6] Cf. pp. 592 ff.

a momentous departure, and the Prophets durst not lightly lend it their sanction. They sought direction of God, after the accustomed manner, by a season of prayer and fasting; Cf. Ac. xiv. 23. nor did they seek in vain. The Holy Spirit illumined their minds, and they recognised the will of God. They convened the Church,[1] and in name of the congregation ordained the missionaries and sent them forth on their high adventure.

II

EVANGELISATION OF CYPRUS

Ac. xiii. 4-12.

The island of Cyprus.

It was about the beginning of March 47 that Paul and Barnabas, attended by John Mark, took their departure from Antioch.[2] They had chosen the island of Cyprus as the first scene of their missionary labours; and it was a natural choice. Cyprus lay nigh at hand, only seventy miles distant from Seleuceia, the port of Antioch. And since it was the native country of Barnabas, his local Cf. Ac. iv. 36. intimacies would ensure them a welcome and win their message a readier hearing. Moreover, the ground had already been broken by those fugitives from the first Cf. xi. 19. persecution who had subsequently found their way to Antioch and inaugurated the momentous innovation of Gentile evangelisation. It may seem indeed that this should rather have precluded Paul from Cyprus, since his rule, at all events in after days, was never to 'preach the Rom. xv. 20; cf. 2 Cor. x. 15, 16. Gospel where Christ's name was known, lest he should be building on another man's foundation'; but it should be considered that it was to the Jews that his predecessors had Cf. Ac. xi. 19. preached. The Gentiles had never yet heard the Gospel,

[1] Luke's narrative here (vers. 2, 3) is very concise, but it would be clear to readers familiar with the democratic procedure of the primitive Church. Even at Jerusalem questions were not decided by the authority of the Apostles or the Presbyters but by the vote of the brethren, the judgment of the Church, and the Apostles merely gave effect thereto (cf. Ac. i. 15, 16, 21-23; xv. 22). Accordingly in ver. 3 the subject is not 'the Prophets and Teachers' but 'the brethren,' 'the whole Church'; and it is so defined in Cod. Bez. (D) by the insertion of πάντες after προσευξάμενοι.

[2] Cf. Append. I.

and it was to them especially that his mission was directed. Nor was Cyprus his ultimate venue. It was a mere stepping-stone to Asia Minor and the West, and thither his purpose already reached.

Its extent and importance.

Cyprus was a considerable island.[1] Its coast-line measured three hundred and ninety miles, and its length from Cape Dinaretum in the east to Cape Acamas in the west was a hundred and sixty. In ancient days, when it was ruled by tyrants, it contained no fewer than nine kingdoms, and in the time of Pliny its towns numbered fifteen.[2] Nor were its resources inadequate to the maintenance of so large a population. In its midst betwixt the mountain ranges of Olympus and Aoüs stretched a fertile plain, watered by the river Pediæus and clothed not only with vineyards, olive orchards, and corn-fields, but with forests which furnished timber for the shipbuilders of Soli. Its mineral wealth too was abundant. In the very centre of the island at the base of Mount Aoüs lay Tamassus with its mines so rich in copper ore and sulphate of copper for medicinal uses.[3] Citium and Salamis were the seats of a prosperous trade in the manufacture and export of salt.[4]

Intellectual distinction.

Nor was Cyprus destitute of intellectual renown. Salamis was the birthplace of Aristos the historian, and Citium gave to the world Zeno, the founder of the Stoic philosophy, and Apollonius the physician.

A Roman province.

The island was annexed to Rome by Cato Uticensis in 59 B.C., and it was an Imperial Province under a proprætor until A.D. 22 when Augustus made it a Senatorial Province under a proconsul.[5] The latter had his seat at Paphos, a seaport and the Roman capital, situated at the south-west corner of the island. The city was styled New Paphos to distinguish it from Old Paphos, six or seven miles to the south-east, famous for an ancient temple of Aphrodite whither a multitude of worshippers resorted from the other cities to keep festival every year.[6]

[1] Cf. Strabo, 681-85.
[2] Plin. *Nat. Hist.* V. 35.
[3] Strabo, 684; Plin. *Nat. Hist.* XXXIV. 2.
[4] Plin. *Nat. Hist.* XXXI. 39, 41.
[5] Dio Cassius, LIII. 12. Cf. Lightfoot, *Essays on 'Supernatural Religion,'* pp. 292 ff.
[6] Cf. Hom. *Od.* VIII. 362 f.; Hor. *Od.* I. XXX. I f.; Strabo, 683; Tac. *Hist.* II. 2, 3.

A stream of Jewish emigrants had flowed into Cyprus during the hospitable regime of the Ptolemies, and it was reinforced under the early empire when Augustus farmed out the copper mines of the island to Herod the Great.[1] Thus, when Paul and his company landed at Salamis, they found there a large Jewish population, so large that there were several synagogues in the town; and they opened their mission by visiting these and preaching to the congregations. It may seem strange that, though their errand was to the Gentiles, they should have addressed themselves to the Jews; but this was Paul's constant method to the last. In every town which he visited in the course of his travels, he immediately sought out the synagogue and there presented his initial appeal. 'Both to Jew, in the first instance, and to Gentile' was his rule; and it was indeed the fitting procedure. The Law had been a providential preparation for the Gospel; and it was a reasonable expectation that the Jews should welcome the Saviour of whom their Scriptures testified, and recognise it as their vocation to commend Him to the world. The synagogue was everywhere the Gospel's rightful home, its *point d'appui*; and it was only when the Jews had rejected their Messiah that Paul reluctantly turned from them and addressed his appeal to the Gentiles.

Jewish population.

Cf. 1 Mac. xv. 23.

The synagogues of Salamis.

Rom. i. 16; cf. ii. 9, 10.

Cf. Ac. xiii. 46; xxviii. 17-28.

Salamis was only the first station, and after preaching there the missionaries proceeded on their way. They advanced from town to town, turning now southward, now northward, but always pushing westward, until they had traversed the breadth and length of the island.[2] Their labour seems to have accomplished little. Apparently indeed they were courteously received by reason, doubtless, of the esteem wherewith Barnabas was regarded by his fellow-countrymen; at all events, they encountered in their progress through the island none of the hostility which the Gospel elsewhere aroused in Jewish breasts. But while there

Progress through the island.

[1] Jos. *Ant.* XVI. iv. 5.

[2] *διέρχεσθαι* with accus. (ver. 6) is the phrase in the Book of Acts for a missionary progress through a country (cf. xiv. 24; xv. 3, 41; xvi. 6; xviii. 23; xix. 1, 21; xx. 2). It implies constant deviation in order to visit towns lying off the direct route, and this is expressed by the variant in Cod. Bez. (D) *καὶ περιελθόντων δὲ αὐτῶν ὅλην τήν νῆσον.*

is no evidence of opposition, there is none of success either. It is not recorded that they won a single convert in the course of their peregrination.

Paphos.

At length they reached Paphos, and there they achieved their first triumph. Being the administrative capital, the city was the seat of the Roman proconsul, and the office was held in those days by Sergius Paulus. Contemporary history is almost silent regarding him,[1] but the sacred narrative describes him as 'a shrewd man,'[2] evidently, in view of the sequel, with the intention of vindicating his reputation for sanity. At the same time, while practical sagacity was his chief characteristic, it appears that he was in no wise destitute of intellectual distinction. At all events it is probable that he is the Sergius Paulus mentioned by Pliny in the list of authors who had furnished him with information for the second and eighteenth books of his *Natural History*, since both these books contain local and antiquarian memorabilia of the island of Cyprus such as an intelligent resident would be likely to observe and chronicle.[3]

Astrology.

The proconsul was thus at once a man of affairs and a man of letters; nevertheless he was a child of his age and was imbued with its spirit. At that period the idea was universal that the lives of men 'tempered with the stars' and their destinies were legible on the face of the firmament; and the astrologer[4] who professed to decipher the celestial emblazonry was held in boundless reverence. It was not merely in heathendom that the notion prevailed, for many astrologers were Jews;[5] nor was it only by the ignorant multitude that it was entertained, but by statesmen and princes like Pompey, Crassus, and Cæsar,[6] and the Emperors Augustus and Tiberius.[7] The astrologers believed in their

[1] A Cyprian inscription is dated ΕΠΙ ΠΑΥΛΟΥ [ΑΝΘ]ΥΠΑΤΟΥ, 'in the proconsulship of Paulus.' Cf. Lightfoot, *Essays on 'Supernatural Religion,'* p. 294.

[2] *σύνεσις* is knowledge of practical affairs (cf. Suidas under *εἰσβολή* : *σύνεσις, ἐπίληψις τῶν πραγμάτων*) as distinguished from *σοφία*, 'wisdom,' which is intellectual (cf. *Plat. Def.* : *σοφία, ἐπιστήμη ἀνυπόθετος· ἐπιστήμη τῶν ἀεὶ ὄντων· ἐπιστήμη θεωρητικὴ τῆς τῶν ὄντων αἰτίας*). Cf. Mt. xi. 25.

[3] Cf. *Nat. Hist.* II. 90, 97, 112; XVIII. 12, 57.

[4] Variously named *astrologus, magus, mathematicus, Chaldæus*.

[5] Cf. Juv. VI. 542 ff.; Tac. *Ann.* XII. 52.

[6] Cic. *De Div.* II. 87-99.

[7] Suet. *Aug.* 94; *Tib.* 14; Tac. *Ann.* VI. 20 f.

art, and so far they were no impostors; yet they usually turned it to ill account, trading on the credulity of their clients for lust of gold and power. And thus they exerted a baleful influence, insomuch that the Imperial Senate repeatedly decreed their expulsion from Rome,[1] and the Christian Church in after days sternly condemned them, denying them the Sacrament of Baptism and casting them out of her communion.[2] Yet such was the fascination of their mystic art that no severity availed to suppress it, and the superstition lingered until it was dispelled by the progress of scientific knowledge. It was still potent in the fifteenth century. King Louis XI of France held frequent commerce with the stars;[3] and even after 'the new learning' had dissipated the long darkness of the Middle Ages, Philip Melanchthon was 'a believer in judicial astrology, and a caster of horoscopes, and an interpreter of dreams.'

The astrologer Barjesus.

It was the fashion for exalted personages to retain astrologers in their councils; and just as the Emperor Tiberius was attended by his Thrasyllus during his retreat on the island of Capreæ, and King Louis by his Martius Galeotti in the castle of Plessis-les-Tours, so Sergius Paulus had an astrologer in his retinue. He was a Jew; and his proper name was Barjesus, a patronymic like Bartholomew, Bartimæus, and Barsabbas, signifying 'Son of Jesus' or 'Joshua,' while his official title was Elymas, 'the Wizard.'[4] Alert to all that transpired in his province, the Proconsul had heard of the doings of the missionaries in their progress through the island; and on their arrival at Paphos he summoned them before him and, with his astrologer in attendance, inquired into their propaganda.

His jealousy of the missionaries.

It was a golden opportunity, and they gladly embraced it. They expounded the Gospel to him, and he listened with keen interest.[5] Barjesus was standing by; and when

[1] Cf. Tac. *Ann.* II. 32; *Hist.* I. 22; Suet. *Tib.* 36; *Vitell.* 14.

[2] Cf. Bingham, *Antiq.* XI. v. 8; XVI. v. 1.

[3] Cf. Scott, *Quentin Durward*, Note 43.

[4] Ἐλύμας, interpreted in the text ὁ μάγος, 'the Wizard,' is probably akin to Arabic *'alīm*, 'wise' or 'able'; and the variant Ἑτοιμᾶς, 'Ready,' in Cod. Bez. (D) is a Greek rendering of the title.

[5] After πίστεως (ver. 8) Cod. Bez. (D) and several other authorities add **ἐπειδὴ ἥδιστα ἤκουεν αὐτῶν**, 'since he was hearing them very gladly.'

he marked how his master was impressed, he took alarm. His apprehension was lest they should supplant him in the Proconsul's favour and oust him from his lucrative office. And so he kept interrupting them, until Paul lost patience. He looked the charlatan in the face. 'You mass of trickery and rascality! you "Son of the Devil"!' he cried, playing upon his name Barjesus; 'you enemy of all righteousness!

Hos. xiv. 9. will you not stop twisting "the Lord's straight ways"?' There was indeed hot indignation in the Apostle's heart, but there was also shame; for in the Jewish impostor's opposition to the Gospel he recognised the self-same spirit which had once actuated himself. And he denounced against him the very judgment which he had himself suffered: 'Now, look you, the Lord's hand is upon you, and you will be blind, not seeing the sun for a season.' And so it came to pass. A mist fell upon the astrologer's eyes, and like the persecutor on the road to Damascus he had to be 'led away by the hand.'

His doom of blindness.

Cf. Ac. ix. 8.

Conversion of the Proconsul.

It was a temporary visitation, and there was in it a merciful design. Paul's hope was that, resembling himself in his sin and his punishment, Barjesus would resemble him also in his repentance. 'By the sign whereby he had himself been won,' says St. Chrysostom, 'he desired to win him too. And, moreover, "for a season" is not the word of one who would punish, but of one who would convert; for had he meant punishment, he would have made him permanently blind.' The issue is unrecorded,[1] but the miracle was in no wise unavailing. Whether it won the astrologer or no, it won the Proconsul.

Ac. xiii. 13, 14*a*; Gal. iv. 13-15; Ac. xiii. 14*b*-xiv. 21*a*.

III

EVANGELISATION OF SOUTHERN GALATIA

The Province of Pamphylia.

Paphos was the western limit of Cyprus, and now that they had traversed the island, it was time for the missionaries to take their departure and carry the Gospel farther. Their destination was the Province of Pamphylia on the southern

[1] According to the apocryphal *Acts of Barnabas* Barjesus continued obdurate, and persecuted Barnabas and Mark on their second visit to Cyprus (cf. Ac. xv. 39).

coast of Asia Minor, and it presented an attractive and hopeful field. Its population included a considerable Jewish element, and it had been represented in the Holy City on that memorable Day of Pentecost when the Holy Spirit descended on the Apostles and three thousand souls were won to the faith. Thus the Gospel was not unknown in Pamphylia, and the soil was in a measure prepared. It was a fair and fertile country, well watered by the Cestrus, the Eurymedon, and lesser streams which flowed from the Pisidian uplands. The capital was Perga, a sacred city with a famous temple of Artemis on an adjacent eminence; and there were other towns, chiefly Aspendus and the seaports of Attaleia and Sidè.[1]

Cf. Ac. ii. 10.

Paul stricken with malaria.

It would be about the end of June when they set sail from Paphos, and they steered north-westward to the port of Attaleia at the mouth of the Cestrus. The river was navigable, and the ship proceeded six miles up its course to Perga; and there they disembarked, designing probably to make the capital the headquarters of their operations. But, says St. Thomas à Kempis, 'homo proponit sed Deus disponit, nec est in homine via ejus.' Pamphylia is a level crescent, encircling the Pamphylian Sea and backed by the lofty range of the Taurus. In midsummer the climate is warm and enervating, and malaria, the plague of all the southern fringe of Asia Minor, is there especially prevalent. It was early in July when they reached Perga, and the sudden plunge from the free air of Cyprus and the cool sea-breezes into that sweltering caldron was trying for them, particularly for Paul who had borne the chief burden of the work. He was seized with malaria and experienced its peculiar miseries—fever, ague, and racking headache all the more distressing that it affected his eyes, already enfeebled by the blinding flash on the road to Damascus.[2]

A chronic malady.

It was the beginning of a lifelong affliction. The malady clung to him all his days; and whenever his strength ran low, it would grip him and lay him prostrate. It was a grievous embarrassment to his ministry. Again and again, as will appear in the sequel, it frustrated his missionary designs, compelling him to abandon the path which he had

[1] Cf. Strabo, 667.

[2] Cf. Append. III.

2 Cor. xii. 7.

chosen and forgo what seemed precious opportunities; and for a while it fretted his eager spirit. He regarded it, in his own phrase, as 'a messenger of Satan to buffet him': each recurring attack was a disabling stroke of the Adversary, the Enemy of the Gospel. Presently, however, he came to regard it as a heavenly ally. Experience taught him that, when he was restrained from the course which he had meditated, that on which he was driven conducted him to a grander service than he had ever imagined. And thus he recognised his infirmity as, in the language of Scripture, 'a hedge of thorns' fencing in the way which God had marked out for him and preventing him, with gracious severity, from turning aside into paths of his own choosing.

Cf. Job iii. 23, xix. 8; Hos. ii. 6.

Retreat to the Pisidian uplands.

And so it proved at the very outset. It was impossible for the invalid to remain in Pamphylia, and he and Barnabas decided to escape from the enervating climate and travel northward into the uplands of the Province of Galatia, and there prosecute their mission. They were, however, confronted by an unpleasant *dénouement*. It appears that John Mark, softly nurtured in his comfortable home at Jerusalem, had taken unkindly to the hardships of the mission; and Paul's sickness completed his discomfiture. He feared lest he too should sicken, and the proposal to face the toilsome ascent of the Taurus and venture into the unknown territory beyond smote him with consternation. He refused to proceed, and incontinently decamped and returned home.[1] It was sheer pusillanimity. 'John,' it is written, 'withdrew from them and returned to Jerusalem.' The sting of the sentence lies in his designation as 'John.' It was his Jewish name. His Gentile name was 'Mark,' and it had been his while he shared the mission to the Gentiles; but now he had forfeited it by his recreance, and it was restored to him only after he had purged his shame.

Desertion of John Mark.

Cf. Phm. 24; Col. iv. 10; 2 Tim. iv. 11.

The passage of the Taurus.

Abandoned by their attendant, Paul and Barnabas took their departure from Perga. Their route lay across the

[1] Cf. Chrys.: τί δήποτε δὲ 'Ιωάννης ἀναχωρεῖ ἀπ' αὐτῶν; ἅτε ἐπὶ μακροτέραν λοιπὸν στελλομένων ὁδόν· καίτοι γε ὑπηρέτης ἐκεῖνος ἦν, αὐτοὶ δὲ τὸν κίνδυνον εἶχον. There is a happy touch of humour in the comment of *quidam* in Jo. Stephanus Menochius: 'ex affectu erga matrem degentem Ierosolymis.' John was home-sick, and 'either he did not like the work, or he wanted to go see his mother' (Matt. Henry).

steep and rugged range of the Taurus; and it was not merely a toilsome but a dangerous journey, since the mountains were infested by brigands [1] and swept by torrents difficult to ford when they were running full.[2] In midsummer indeed the torrent-beds would be dry, but the 'dangers from brigands' would be all the greater. The journey would be a severe ordeal for a broken invalid, and they would make what haste they could, preaching nowhere by the way.

2 Cor. xi. 26.

Pisidian Antioch.

It would be about the beginning of August when they reached Pisidian Antioch. This important city belonged to the ancient country of Phrygia; but since it was situated close to the border of Pisidia, it was styled 'Antioch toward Pisidia,'[3] in order to distinguish it from other cities of the same name, especially Syrian Antioch and Antioch on the Mæander; and the cumbrous designation was abbreviated to 'Pisidian Antioch.'[4] The ancient delimitation, however, had been obliterated under the imperial regime, and in those days Antioch belonged to the Roman Province of Galatia.[5] This enormous province extended diagonally across Asia Minor from the shore of the Euxine in the north-east until it adjoined the Province of Pamphylia in the south-west. It embraced the ancient kingdom of Pontus, much of Paphlagonia, the ancient country of Galatia, most of Lycaonia and Pisidia, and the south-east corner of

[1] Cf. Strabo, 568, 570.

[2] Cf. Ramsay, *Church in Rom. Emp.*, p. 23.

[3] Ἀντιόχεια ἡ πρὸς Πισιδίᾳ. Cf. Strabo, 557, 569, 577.

[4] Ἀντιόχεια ἡ Πισιδία. Cf. Ac. xiii. 14, where T.R. εἰς Ἀντιόχειαν τῆς Πισιδίας, 'Antioch of Pisidia,' is due to a subsequent extension of the Pisidian frontier (cf. Plin. *Nat. Hist.* v. 24).

[5] It is here assumed that 'Galatia' signifies not, according to the old view maintained by Lightfoot, the ancient kingdom of the Galatæ, a Celtic race, but the Roman Province of Galatia (cf. Ramsay, *Church in Rom. Emp.*, pp. 77 ff.; Lake, *Earlier Epistles of St. Paul*, pp. 254 ff.). The term is thus not ethnographical but political; and 'the Galatians' to whom Paul's letter is addressed were not the northern Galatæ but the Phrygians of Antioch and the Lycaonians of Iconium, Lystra, and Derbe whom he evangelised during his first mission and revisited in the course of his second (cf. Ac. xvi. 6) and third (cf. xviii. 23). The former or North Galatian theory involves the awkward consequence that he engaged in an important ministry which is unrecorded in the Book of Acts and which must be assigned to the second mission. Cf. Ac. xvi. 6, where, however, τὴν Φρυγίαν καὶ Γαλατικὴν χώραν means not 'Phrygia and the country of Galatia' but 'the Phrygian and Galatian District' or 'the Phrygo-Galatic District,' *i.e.*, the part of the Province of Galatia once called Phrygian.

Phrygia; and since it was so large, it was, for the sake of convenience, apportioned into 'Districts' which followed the boundaries of the ancient countries—the Phrygian District, the Isaurian, the Lycaonian, and so forth.[1]

Its population.

Antioch belonged to the Phrygian District, and the population was composed of four elements.[2] There were, first of all, the native Phrygians. The aboriginal race still occupied the surrounding country, but the city was a Greek settlement from Magnesia on the Mæander,[3] founded apparently by Seleucus Nicator, the first of the Seleucid dynasty (312-280 B.C.), who named it after his father Antiochus. It was thus originally a Greek city; but in it, as in all the cities which he founded, Seleucus granted rights of citizenship to Jewish settlers,[4] and so the population included a large and influential Jewish community. Finally, in the year 25 B.C. the country passed under the Roman dominion, and toward 6 B.C. Augustus made Antioch a Roman colony with the designation *Colonia Cæsarea Antiochia*, settling there the veterans of the Legio Alauda with a view to the pacification of the country, particularly the protection of the great Trade Route against the depredations of the brigands who infested the Pisidian mountains.

A kindly reception.

Paul reached Antioch in a piteous plight, enfeebled by sickness and spent by the fatigue of his painful passage of the Taurus; and it was impossible for him to address himself immediately to the work of evangelisation. He was, however, fortunate in his new surroundings. The city stood some three thousand six hundred feet above the sea-level, and the brisk air allayed his fever and repaired his wasted vigour. Nor did he lack the precious succour of human sympathy. He was indeed confined to his lodging, but Barnabas went abroad. He would talk of the Gospel, and his gracious bearing would win him good-will and prompt a kindly interest in his suffering comrade. One friend above

Cf. Gal. iv. 13-15.

[1] Φρυγία Χώρα, Ἰσαυρικὴ Χώρα, Λυκαονικὴ Χώρα, or in full Γαλατικὴ Χώρα τῆς Λυκαονίας, 'the Galatian District of Lycaonia,' as distinguished from Ἀντιοχειανὴ Χώρα, the part of Lycaonia belonging to the *Regnum Antiochi*.

[2] Cf. Ramsay, *Cities of St. Paul*, pp. 245 ff.

[3] Strabo, 577.

[4] Cf. Jos. *Ant.* XII. iii. I.

all was raised up in those dark days; and this was the physician Luke.[1] He was a Greek, and later tradition says that he was a proselyte to Judaism;[2] but this is refuted by the fact that he was uncircumcised, and the probability is that he belonged to that interesting class, the 'God-fearers,' those pious Gentiles who, dissatisfied with their heathen religion and attracted by the pure ideals of the Jewish Faith, attached themselves to the Synagogue and shared its worship without submitting to the ceremonial rites of the Mosaic Law.[3] He was summoned to the invalid's couch; and as he ministered to his bodily infirmity, he heard from his lips the blessed secret which his heart had been craving. Thenceforward he was the Apostle's dearest disciple, and the Church owes him not only the gracious Gospel which bears his name and breathes his master's spirit, but the Book of Acts, that precious record of the heroic ministry in which he bore so large a part.

Luke the physician.

Cf. Col. iv. 11, 14.

Paul made his first public appearance in the Jewish synagogue one Sabbath, probably about a fortnight after his arrival in the city.[4] The congregation was composed not only of Jews but of 'God-fearers,' evidently a numerous and influential section of the community. One of the latter was Luke, and it appears that he was present and witnessed all that passed on this memorable occasion. The missionaries took their places unostentatiously among the worshippers;[5] but their fame had already spread, and the Rulers of the Synagogue had their eyes upon them. The service proceeded after the prescribed order. The Scripture-lessons were read. One was from the Law and the other from the Prophets, and it appears that the passages for the day were the first chapter of the Book of Deuteronomy and the first

Paul's first appearance in the synagogue.

[1] For the evidence that Luke belonged not to Syrian but to Pisidian Antioch see Append. IV.

[2] Cf. Hieron. *Quæst. in Gen.* 46: 'licet plerique tradant Lucam Evangelistam ut proselytum Hebræas literas ignorasse.'

[3] Cf. p. 13.

[4] Cf. Append. I.

[5] When the Rulers of the Synagogue invited them to speak, they 'sent to them' (cf. ver. 15), implying that they sat remote. On the contrary, since sitting was the attitude of a Jewish teacher, Dr. John Lightfoot infers from ἐκάθισαν (ver. 14) that by previous arrangement with the Rulers they occupied the teachers' seat.

chapter of the Book of Isaiah.[1] Then came the event which all had been awaiting. It was the custom that, when a qualified stranger appeared in a synagogue, he should be invited to discourse to the congregation;[2] and accordingly the Rulers sent a message to the visitors inviting them to come forward and speak. Paul accepted the office. He based his discourse on the passages which had just been read and which were still ringing in the worshippers' ears; and Luke has immortalised the scene, not only reproducing the sermon, doubtless from his own notes,[3] but portraying the preacher's bearing—how he adopted the manner of a Greek orator and stood while he spoke instead of sitting like a Jewish teacher, and how, with an instinctive and characteristic gesture, he claimed attention at the outset by a wave of his hand.

Cf. Ac. xxi. 40.

His sermon.

Is. i. 2.

Dt. v. 15, i. 31, vii. 1, i. 38.

xiii. 16 'Israelites,' said he, 'and you God-fearers, listen.
17 'The God of this people Israel elected our fathers and
"brought up"[4] the people during their sojourn in the land
of Egypt, and "with a high arm He led them forth from it,"
18 and for some forty years' time "He carried them like a
19 nurse[5] in the wilderness," and "put down seven nations"
in the land of Canaan and "made their land His people's
20 heritage,"[6] all in the space of some four hundred and fifty
years.[7] And thereafter He gave Judges down to Samuel the

[1] At the present day, doubtless in accordance with ancient usage, these passages are prescribed for the same day in the Jewish Lectionary; and at the commencement of his discourse Paul employs several striking phrases which occur in them (*ὕψωσεν*, *ἐτροφοφόρησεν*, *κατεκληρονόμησεν*). The inference is that the passages had just been read.

[2] Cf. *The Days of His Flesh*, p. 95.

[3] Cf. Append. IV.

[4] *ὕψωσεν*, not 'exalted' but 'brought up,' as in Is. i. 2 LXX: *υἱοὺς ἐγέννησα καὶ ὕψωσα* (cf. li. 18). Israel was not 'exalted' in Egypt; she was 'humbled.' Her bondage was an education.

[5] *ἐτροφοφόρησεν* AC*E. The variant *ἐτροποφόρησεν*, 'bore with their manners,' is more strongly attested (ℵBC²DHLP Vulg.); but the reference to Dt. i. 31 is clear, and there the evidence for *ἐτροφοφόρησεν* and *τροφοφορήσει* is overwhelming.

[6] The only N.T. instance of *κατακληρονομεῖν* in the sense of *κληροδοτεῖν* (T.R.), but the usage is frequent in LXX. Cf. Num. xxxiv. 18; Dt. i. 38, iii. 28; Jud. xi. 24; 2 Sam. vii. 1; Jer. iii. 18.

[7] 400 years of oppression (cf. Gen. xv. 13; Ac. vii. 6), 40 in the wilderness, and the period of conquest—roughly (*ὡς*) ten years. The Received Text puts *ὡς ἔτεσιν τετρ. καὶ πεντ.* after *καὶ μετὰ ταῦτα*, making the time of the Judges 450 years. This differs widely from 1 Ki. vi. 1, but it accords with the traditional Jewish chronology (cf. Jos. *Ant.* VIII. iii. 1): Solomon began the building of the

21 Prophet. And next they requested a King, and God gave them
Saul, the son of Kish, a man of the tribe of Benjamin, for forty
22 years.[1] And He removed him, and raised them up David as
King; and to him He also bore this testimony: "I have Ps. lxxxix.
found David," the son of Jesse, "a man according to My 20; 1 Sam. xiii. 14.
heart," who "will perform all My pleasure." Is. xliv. 28.
23 'From this man's seed according to promise God has brought
24 Israel a Saviour—Jesus. Ere His appearance on the scene John
had proclaimed a baptism of repentance to all the people of
25 Israel. And while John was accomplishing his career, he would
say: "What you suppose me to be, I am not.[2] No, look you, Cf. Jo. i.
One is coming after me whose sandal I am not worthy to loose." 19-28.
26 'Brothers, sons of Abraham's race and the God-fearers among
you, to you[3] has "the word" of this salvation "been sent forth." Ps. cvii. 20.
27 For the dwellers in Jerusalem and their rulers by ignoring this
word fulfilled also by their judgment the voices of the Prophets
28 which are read every Sabbath;[4] and, though they found no
reason for death, they requested Pilate that He should be
29 executed. And when they had carried out everything that is
written of Him, they took Him down from the Tree and
30 laid Him in a tomb. But God raised Him from the dead.
31 And He appeared in the course of a good many days to those who
had gone up with Him from Galilee to Jerusalem; and these are
32 at this hour His witnesses to the people. And we are telling you
33 good tidings of the promise made to the fathers—that God has
fulfilled this for our children[5] by raising Jesus, as it is written
also in the second Psalm: "Thou art My Son: this day have I
34 begotten Thee." And that He raised Him from the dead never
more to turn to corruption, He has thus declared: "I will give Is. lv. 3.
35 Thee the holy promises to David, the faithful promises." And
therefore also in another Psalm He says: "Thou wilt not give Ps. xvi. 10.

Temple in the fourth year of his reign, 592 years after the Exodus. Deduct (1) 40 years in the wilderness, (2) 25 of Joshua's leadership (cf. Jos. *Ant.* v. i. 29), (3) 40 of Saul's reign (cf. Ac. xiii. 21), (4) 40 of David's (cf. 1 Ki. ii. 11), and (5) the first four of Solomon's; and there remain, as the period of the Judges, 443 or 'some 450' years.

[1] Cf. Jos. *Ant.* VI. xiv. 9. The duration of Saul's reign is nowhere stated in O. T.

[2] Reading τί ἐμὲ ὑπονοεῖτε εἶναι, οὐκ εἰμὶ ἐγώ and taking τί in the sense of ὅ (cf. Mk. xiv. 36).

[3] ὑμῖν CEHLP Vulg., 'you Hellenists and Gentiles.'

[4] Otherwise: 'by ignoring it and the voices of the prophets they condemned Him and fulfilled them.'

[5] τοῖς τέκνοις ἡμῶν ℵABC*D Vulg. Observe the Apostle's solicitude to include both sections of His audience, Jews and Gentiles equally. He says 'the (not "our") fathers' and 'our (not "their") children.' The promise was a common heritage.

1 Ki. ii. 10.

36 Thine Holy One to see corruption." For David in his own
generation served the will of God and fell asleep,[1] and was laid
37 to his fathers and saw corruption ; but He whom God raised
did not see corruption.

38 'Therefore be it recognised by you, brothers, that through
39 Him is remission of sins being announced to you, and from all
the unrighteousness from which you could not be absolved in
terms of the Law of Moses, every one who has faith is absolved
in Him.'

An interruption.

Here, like Stephen in his defence before the Sanhedrin, he was interrupted. The historical review at the outset of his discourse would gratify the patriotic sentiment of his Jewish hearers, and he was careful from time to time to appeal also to the God-fearers in the congregation. And thus for a while his argument commanded unanimous approval ; but when he came to speak of the crime of the rulers and people of the Holy City and its condemnation by the Resurrection, the narrower sort of his Jewish hearers, already suspicious, took offence. He marked their frowns and their mutterings, and closed with a solemn warning :

40 'Beware, therefore, lest the sequel be what is written in the
prophets :

Hab. i. 5.

41 "See, ye despisers, and wonder, and vanish away ;
for that I am working a work in your days,
a work which ye will in no wise believe if one declare it
to you."'

Breach with the synagogue.

Silence ensued.[2] The congregation sat awe-stricken, until Paul and Barnabas, desirous evidently of avoiding a rencontre with the Rulers, rose to take their departure ; and then from all sides came entreaties that they would return the next Sabbath and resume the argument.[3] The proposal was

[1] So Vulg., Bez., R.V. Others (Calv., A.V.) take *γενεᾷ* as object of *ὑπηρετήσας* ('having served his own generation') and construe *τῇ τοῦ Θεοῦ βουλῇ* either with *ὑπηρετήσας* ('having served by the will of God') or with *ἐκοιμήθη* ('by the will of God fell asleep').

[2] After ver. 41 Cod. Bez. (D) has *καὶ ἐσίγησαν*, 'and they kept silence.'

[3] ℵABCDEI Vulg., Chrys. : *ἐξιόντων δὲ αὐτῶν παρεκάλουν*, 'and as they (Paul and Barnabas) were going out, they (the congregation) besought.' If *μεταξύ* has here its ordinary signification 'between,' then *εἰς τὸ μεταξὺ σάββατον* means 'on the intervening Sabbath.' Two explanations have been suggested. (1) Since *σάββατον* or *σάββατα* denoted not only 'Sabbath' but 'week' (cf. Lk. xviii. 12), Dr. John Lightfoot understands that they were requested to attend the weekday

distasteful to the Rulers, and they abruptly dismissed the assemblage. But they could not thus stifle the interest which had been evoked, and a number of the Jews and the God-fearers [1] followed the missionaries and professed their faith. With the impulsiveness which characterised not only the Antiochenes but their neighbours of southern Galatia, and which was demonstrated alike by their initial enthusiasm and their subsequent defection, they would fain have been baptised forthwith ; [2] but Paul and Barnabas restrained their impetuosity, and meanwhile 'talked with them and urged them to continue in the grace of God.' And the event justified their caution. Throughout the week the Gospel was the general talk,[3] and the interest even of the Gentile populace was excited. The whole city was eager to hear it, and on the ensuing Sabbath the synagogue was besieged by an enormous crowd. The jealousy of the Jews was aroused. Even those who had been favourably disposed resented the idea of the Gentiles being put on an equality with themselves; and when the Apostle resumed his discourse, he was greeted with interruptions. Objections were raised, and when these were answered, ribaldries against the Crucified succeeded, until the missionaries could endure it no longer and took their predetermined course. They had, as was fit, presented the Gospel in the first instance to the Jews, and since these had rejected it, they abandoned them and turned to the Gentiles.

Cf. Gal. i. 6, iii. 1-4, iv. 14, 15.

Successful ministry among the Gentile populace.

They quitted the synagogue, and thenceforth addressed themselves to the general populace. And their message was cordially received. It pleased the Gentiles that their

meetings on Monday and Thursday (cf. *The Days of His Flesh*, p. 94). Similarly (2) Grotius, who would read *σαββάτων* for *σάββατον*, *medio tempore inter duo sabbata*, 'in the interval between the two Sabbaths.' *μεταξύ*, however, meant also 'next after.' Cf. Jos. *De Bell. Jud.* v. iv. 2: *Δαυίδου τε καὶ Σολομῶνος, ἔτι δὲ τῶν μεταξὺ τούτων βασιλέων*. *Contra Apion.* i. 21. Thus *τὸ μεταξὺ σάββατον* is 'the next Sabbath,' and so Cod. Bez. (D) reads *ἑξῆς* and one cursive *ἐπιόν*.

[1] *τῶν σεβομένων προσηλύτων* (ver. 43) is impossible. It combines two distinct classes—the God-fearers or worshippers (cf. p. 13) and the proselytes. The distinction was forgotten, and *προσηλύτων* is manifestly an erroneous gloss on *τῶν σεβομένων*.

[2] After Βαρνάβᾳ (ver. 43) 137 Syr^p c* add *ἀξιοῦντες βαπτισθῆναι*, 'claiming to be baptised.'

[3] After ver. 43 Cod. Bez. (D) and Syr. Vers. add: 'And it came to pass that the Word of God spread all over the city.'

cause had been espoused against Jewish insolence, and there were not a few who were animated by a holier sentiment. Their hearts had been touched, and they welcomed the Saviour's grace. Nor was the work confined to the city. Visitors from the surrounding country heard the message of salvation, and they carried the glad tidings with them to their homes until all the Phrygian District had shared the benediction.

Expulsion of the missionaries from Antioch.

So signal a triumph exasperated the Jews, and they resorted to violence. Among the 'God-fearers' who had made the synagogue their spiritual home were some ladies of good station. They were apparently the wives of magistrates, and they lent themselves to the malignant designs of the Jewish leaders. The latter instigated an attack upon Paul and Barnabas, and those ladies prejudiced their husbands' minds and procured the condemnation of the missionaries and their expulsion from the District as disturbers of the peace.

Iconium.

It would be about the end of October when they were driven from Antioch;[1] and, quitting the Phrygian District, they journeyed to Iconium, the metropolis of the Lycaonian District, upwards of eighty miles east by south of Antioch. Formerly the frontier town of Phrygia,[2] it had for administrative convenience been included by the Romans in Lycaonia;[3] but the citizens retained their ancient language and clung to their ancient traditions, and persisted in regarding themselves as Phrygians.[4] And indeed they had reason for historic pride. Iconium was, like Damascus, a city of immemorial antiquity. It was associated with the name of the Phrygian king Nannacus, who was reputed to have reigned before the Flood and was immortalised by the Greek proverb 'since Nannacus,' denoting extreme age.[5] Though

[1] Cf. Append. I.

[2] Xen. *Anab.* I. ii. 19: εἰς Ἰκόνιον, τῆς Φρυγίας πόλιν ἐσχάτην.

[3] Cf. Strabo, 568; Cic. *Ad Fam.* XV. iv. 2; Plin. *Nat. Hist.* V. 25.

[4] Cf. Ramsay, *Church in Rom. Emp.*, p. 39.

[5] Suid.: τὰ ἀπὸ Ναννάκου· ἐπὶ τῶν ἐπὶ παλαιότητι θαυμαζομένων. Νάννακος γὰρ Φρυγῶν βασιλεὺς πρὸ τῶν τοῦ Δευκαλίωνος χρόνων. Another proverb was 'the tears of Nannacus,' τὰ Ναννάκου κλαύσομαι (Suid.), referring to his unavailing lamentation and supplication on learning of the approaching disaster of the Flood.

fallen from its traditional greatness in the Apostle's day, it remained a fine and prosperous city. It lay on the southern margin of a wilderness, the dreary upland of the Axylus, cold and barren, and so waterless that its only inhabitants were wild asses and a breed of rough-haired sheep which throve there surprisingly and yielded a rich profit to their keepers, who obtained water by sinking wells, accounted the deepest in the world, and occupied the few towns in the country, the chief being Sovatra, where water was so scarce that it was bought and sold. But nature had dealt more kindly with Iconium. Behind it to the west lay the highlands which reached up to the ridge of the Taurus; and thence flowed a multitude of streams which fertilised the environs of the town and, having no outlet to the sea, lost themselves in a vast expanse of marshes.[1]

Successful ministry.

The Royal Road, constructed by Augustus, ran from Antioch to Lystra, passing through Misthia and skirting Lake Caralis; and Paul and Barnabas would travel by that easy highway for some five and thirty miles, and then, at a point two or three miles beyond Misthia, they would diverge from it and follow the less commodious road which led thence to Iconium.[2] On their arrival they proceeded precisely as they had done at Antioch,[3] and they had a much similar experience. They visited the synagogue, and Paul's preaching [4] evoked an immediate response, winning a large number both of the Jews and of their Gentile adherents. So striking a success displeased the Jewish leaders, and they set themselves to counteract it. They would naturally, like their *confrères* at Antioch, have raised opposition in the synagogue, and thus have driven the missionaries to withdraw from it and devote themselves exclusively to the Gentiles; but this was impracticable by reason of the number of the Jewish converts. And so a conference was held between the religious and civil authorities of the Jewish community, the Rulers of the Synagogue and the Archons, as they were

Machinations of the Jewish rulers.

[1] Strabo, 568.

[2] Cf. *Act. Paul. et Thecl.* 3.

[3] Ac. xiv. 1: κατὰ τὸ αὐτό, not *simul*, 'at the same time,' 'together' (Wetst., A.V., R.V.), but *similiter*, 'in the same manner' (Blass).

[4] In xiv. 1 for 'they' (αὐτούς) Cod. Bez. (D) has 'he' (αὐτόν). Paul was always foremost, and the preaching was his office.

designated—the chiefs of the senate or civil court which had been established by Augustus in each Hellenistic community for the administration of its internal affairs.[1] The issue was that they succeeded in poisoning the minds of the Gentiles and exciting them against the missionaries and their followers.[2] The animosity, however, was short-lived. 'The Lord quickly gave peace,' and they continued their ministry throughout the winter [3] with undaunted courage, reinforced by miraculous tokens of the Lord's presence and co-operation.

Assault by the rabble.

All the while, however, they were harassed by the machinations of the Jewish authorities, and a dangerous situation gradually developed. The citizens were ranged in two hostile factions according as their sympathies lay with the Jewish rulers or with the missionaries. It would have mattered little at Antioch, a Roman colony where just laws prevailed and order was resolutely maintained; but at Iconium with its native magistracy that security was lacking, and at length, probably in the early summer, the partisan animosity flared up, and a mob of Jews and Gentiles, instigated by the Jewish Archons, made a savage assault on Paul and Barnabas, shouting abuse and pelting them with stones.

Flight from Iconium.

They escaped and fled from the town, accompanied

[1] Phil. *In Flacc.* 10. Cf. Schürer, II. ii. pp. 63 ff., 243 ff.

[2] The narrative here (xiv. 1-6) is somewhat perplexing. Ver. 3 seems an interruption, introducing an extended and successful ministry in the midst of a fierce persecution, between its outbreak and its violent consummation. It is tempting to conjecture either that the verse is an interpolation or that it has been misplaced and should stand between ver. 1 and ver. 2; but the reading of ver. 2 in Cod. Bez. (D) and Syriac Version elucidates the passage: *οἱ δὲ ἀρχισυνάγωγοι τῶν Ἰουδαίων καὶ οἱ ἄρχοντες τῆς συναγωγῆς* (Syr. om. *τῆς συναγ.*) *ἐπήγαγον αὐτοῖς* (Syr. om. *αὐτοῖς*) *διωγμὸν κατὰ τῶν δικαίων* (Syr. om. *κ. τ. δικ.*) *καὶ ἐκάκωσαν τὰς ψυχὰς τῶν ἐθνῶν κατὰ τῶν ἀδελφῶν· ὁ δὲ Κύριος ἔδωκεν ταχὺ εἰρήνην*, 'But the Jews' Rulers of the Synagogue and the Archons brought on a persecution and made the souls of the Gentiles evil affected against the brethren; but the Lord quickly gave peace.' Thus the course of events was: an unsuccessful attempt by the Jewish religious and civil authorities to rouse the Gentiles against the Apostles (ver. 2); prosecution by the latter of a successful ministry despite the persistent animosity of the Jewish authorities (ver. 3); creation of two parties in the town through Jewish machinations (ver. 4); their collision, achieving the end which the Jewish authorities had been seeking all the while (vers. 5, 6).

[3] Cf. Append. I.

by some of their supporters, who were, no less than themselves, objects of resentment.[1] It was a magisterial judgment which had expelled them from Antioch, and it had excluded them not merely from the city but from the Phrygian District. Now, however, they were fugitives from a riot, and they were safe so soon as they were clear of the town. The Lycaonian District remained open to them, and they were free to settle where they would within its bounds. This determined their course. The Iconian fugitives dispersed over the District and preached the Gospel, but this was impracticable for Paul and Barnabas. It was only in the towns that the common Greek was spoken, and since the rural peasantry knew only their Lycaonian vernacular, they would not have understood the missionaries.[2] And thus it was necessary that the latter on their flight from Iconium should betake themselves to another town, and they naturally turned to the nearest.

Lystra.

This was Lystra, which lay fully twenty miles to the south, occupying an eminence some 3780 feet above sea-level on the northern bank of a stream which flows through a pleasant valley and loses itself in the marshes eastward.[3] Originally a place of small importance, it had acquired some consequence under the imperial regime, inasmuch as it was the terminus of the Royal Road from Antioch and, like Antioch, a military colony, the eastmost of the chain of fortified towns which Augustus had established for the repression of the brigands of Pisidia and Isauria. Lystra was proud of her new position,[4] nevertheless she remained undistinguished. She had little commerce, and conse-

[1] Cod. Bez. (D) illuminates the situation by amplifying ver. 7 thus: *κἀκεῖ εὐαγγελιζόμενοι ἦσαν, καὶ ἐκινήθη ὅλον τὸ πλῆθος ἐπὶ τῇ διδαχῇ· ὁ δὲ Παῦλος καὶ Βαρνάβας διέτριβον ἐν Λύστροις*, 'and there they were preaching the Gospel, and the whole populace (*i.e.* of the District) was moved at the teaching; but Paul and Barnabas were employed at Lystra.' Here two distinct ministries are implied, that of the Apostles at Lystra and that of their followers in the surrounding District.

[2] Cf. p. 7.

[3] The site was identified in 1885 close to the modern *Khatyn Serai* on the evidence of a marble pedestal dedicated to Augustus and inscribed DIVUM AUG(USTUM)/COLONIA JUL(IA) FELIX GEMINA/LUSTRA/CONSECRAVIT/D(ECRETO) D(ECURIONUM).

[4] Cf. Ramsay, *Church in Rom. Emp.*, p. 50.

Cf. Ac. xiv. 19.

Cf. vers. 11-13.

quently she had no Jewish community and no synagogue. Her populace was composed of the Roman garrison and the aboriginal Lycaonians who preserved their native language and worship, though they spoke also the Common Greek and could understand the preaching of the missionaries.

A pious home.

Cf. 2 Tim. i. 5, iii. 15.

Cf. Ac. xvi. 3.

Though there was no Jewish community, there was at least one Jewish family at Lystra. The mother was a widow [1] named Eunice, and she had a son named Timothy, a mere lad.[2] Her husband, apparently long deceased, had been a Gentile, and had remained a Gentile all his days, since the boy had never been circumcised ; yet, despite her loyal acquiescence in the conditions which her marriage imposed, she was a devout Jewess, and her hereditary piety was confirmed by the gracious presence in the home of her aged mother Lois,[3] who aided her in the religious nurture of the child and his instruction from his earliest days in the Jewish Scriptures. The missionaries would speedily make their acquaintance, and it may be that they lodged in that peaceful and pious house during their stay at Lystra. In any case all the three were won to the Faith, and Timothy proved in after years a trusted and efficient coadjutor of Paul.

Healing of a cripple.

Cf. Ac. xvii. 17.

Since there was no synagogue in the town, they addressed themselves forthwith to the heathen populace. It was difficult to commend the Gospel to pagan hearts, ignorant of the hopes and promises which it fulfilled, and it seems to have fallen at the outset upon deaf ears. One day, however, an opportunity presented itself. Paul was preaching, perhaps in the market-place, and he observed one eager listener amid the listless throng. He was a helpless cripple,

[1] In Ac. xvi. 1 one cursive has Ἰουδαίας χήρας, while the imperf. ὑπῆρχεν (ver. 3), 'used to be,' 'had been,' implies, according to Greek usage, that he was dead. Had he been still alive, the pres. (ὑπάρχει) would have been used. Cf. iv. 13. That Timothy belonged to Lystra appears from xvi. 1, where ἐκεῖ must refer to Λύστραν and not to the remoter Δέρβην. In xx. 4 Τιμόθεος, being so well known, receives no local designation, but the Syriac and Armenian Versions have 'Timothy of Lystra.'

[2] Some fifteen years later his 'youth' still handicapped him in his ministry (cf. 1 Tim. iv. 12).

[3] μάμμη (2 Tim. i. 5) denoted either a paternal or maternal grandmother (cf. Suid. under τήθη : ἡ πατρὸς ἢ μητρὸς μήτηρ), but their mutual sympathy seems to indicate that Lois and Eunice were not only mother and daughter but co-religionists.

and he sat drinking in the good tidings. The wistful face appealed to the Apostle, and he recognised an opportunity of at once befriending the sufferer and moving the crowd. He looked hard at the man and, speaking out that every one might hear, he bade him 'stand upright on his feet.' Never in his life had the cripple stood or walked, but he instinctively obeyed. He sprang up, and not merely stood but walked about.

The Apostles taken for Zeus and Hermes in human form.

Instantly the bystanders awoke from their apathy. An amazing thing had happened before their eyes, and they drew their own conclusion. In those days it was generally believed in the heathen world that the gods, when they pleased, descended from heaven and walked the earth in human form, conversing with men;[1] and that very country was the scene where, according to a pleasant fable, such a theophany had been vouchsafed. It was told how Zeus and Hermes had appeared in the guise of needy strangers and, repulsed from a thousand doors, had been welcomed in their poor hut by a couple of aged peasants, Philemon and Baucis, at the village of Tyriæum on the borders of Phrygia and Lycaonia.[2] Hence it was perhaps that the worship of Zeus and Hermes prevailed in Lycaonia: they were pre-eminently 'the gods' of the country.[3] The story would be familiar to the people of Lystra, and it was very natural that on witnessing the miracle they should leap to the conclusion that the wonder had recurred. The cry was raised in their vernacular: 'The gods are come down to us in the likeness of men!' and they took the silent and benevolent Barnabas for Zeus, 'the King of gods and men,' and Paul the preacher for Hermes, 'the Interpreter and Prophet of the Gods.'[4]

Prepara- for sacrifice.

Mindful of the reproach which their ancestors had unwittingly incurred, they incontinently dispersed to publish the wonderful tidings and prepare a fitting welcome for the

[1] Cf. Hom. *Od.* XVII. 485-7; Cic. *De Harusp.*, 28.

[2] Cf. Ovid, *Met.* VIII. 611 ff. *Tyaneius*, the common reading in l. 719, is impossible, since Tyana was in Cappadocia. The MSS. vary (*Trimeius*, *Thineyus*, *Thyrneius*, etc.), and *Tyrieius* or *Tyriaius* is probable.

[3] Cf. Deissmann, *Light from the Ancient East*, p. 280, n. 1.

[4] Cf. Lucian, *Somn.* 2: Ἑρμοῦ λαλιστάτου καὶ λογιωτάτου θεῶν ἁπάντων. *Pseudolog.* 24: ὁ λόγιος Ἑρμῆς. Iamblich. *De Myster. Ægypt.* (*ad init.*): θεὸς ὁ τῶν λόγων ἡγεμὼν ὁ Ἑρμῆς. Hor. *Od.* I. x. 1.

celestial visitors. Ignorant of the Lycaonian speech, the missionaries had not understood the outcry, and would wonder what the commotion meant; and when they were left standing alone, they betook themselves to their abode. Meanwhile the people hurried to the Temple of Zeus, which, according to custom,[1] was situated outside the city; and when the priest learned what had transpired, he hastened to celebrate the occasion. He summoned his attendants,[2] and they brought oxen and wreathed the victims' horns with garlands,[3] and drove them into the city until they reached the gateway of the house where the divine visitants had their abode.[4] There they erected an altar and prepared to offer sacrifice.

The Apostles' protest.

Cf. Gen. xxxvii. 29; Mt. xxvi. 65.

It was only then that the missionaries realised what was afoot. They were aghast and, expressing their abhorrence of the blasphemy in oriental fashion by rending their garments, they rushed out and vigorously protested. They assured the priests and the deluded crowd that they were not gods but mere mortals, and their errand was nothing else than to rescue them from the vanity of idolatry and turn their hearts to the Living God. And they implored them to desist from their wild purpose and return home.[5]

Popular resentment.

The remonstrance succeeded. There was no sacrifice, and the crowd dispersed crestfallen. The incident, however, had an untoward result. Enthusiasm gave place to resentment. The protest against idolatry angered the priesthood, and the populace were aggrieved at the exposure of their superstitious delusion. The situation was not only discouraging but dangerous. A mere spark would suffice to enkindle a conflagration, and this was supplied when a company of Jews from Antioch and Iconium appeared on

Fanned by Jewish visitors.

[1] Cf. Wetstein.

[2] Cod. Bez. (D) has (ver. 13) *οἱ δὲ ἱερεῖς . . . ἐνέγκαντες . . . ἤθελον*.

[3] Cf. Plut. *Æmil. Paul.* xxxiii. 1. Lucian, *De Sacrif.* 12; *De Syr. Dea*, 58. Eur. *Heracl.* 529. Aristoph. *Pac.* 913; *Av.* 893. Plin. *Nat. Hist.* XVI. 4. Verg. *Æn.* v. 366.

[4] ἐπὶ τοὺς πυλῶνας (ver. 13), neither the gates of the city (Blass) nor those of the temple (Ramsay) but the gateway of the house (cf. xii. 13)—*ante fores ædium in quibus Paulus et Barnabas diversabatur* (Grotius).

[5] To ver. 18 numerous authorities add ἀλλὰ πορεύεσθαι ἕκαστον εἰς τὰ ἴδια (cf. Jo. xix. 27).

the scene.[1] To the present day at the season of harvest, which on those cool uplands falls about the end of August, merchants from the neighbouring towns visit Lystra in order to purchase grain; [2] and that was probably the errand of those Jews from Iconium and Antioch. They found Paul discoursing in the market-place, and recognised him. Their animosity was unabated, and they denounced him as an impostor and asserted that his teaching was 'all lies.' The bystanders were easily roused, and they pelted him with stones. When a similar assault was made upon him at Iconium, he had evaded it; but now he was hemmed in by the crowd and there was no escape.[3] He was struck down and lay senseless, to all appearance dead. It was a lawless outrage, and when the perpetrators saw what they had done and considered the penal consequences, they took alarm, and in the hope of concealing their crime they dragged away their victim's body and deposited it outside the town and left it there.

Paul stoned.

It was now evening,[4] and the Apostle's friends sought the place; and as they mournfully surrounded his lifeless form, they received a joyful surprise. It proved that he was not dead but merely stunned, and he presently revived.[5] He had sustained no mortal injury, but he was sorely bruised, and indeed he bore the scars all his days. Flight was impossible for him: nor indeed was it necessary, since his assailants were apprehensive of being called to account by the magistrates

His resuscitation.

Cf. Gal. vi. 17.

[1] The text of ver. 19 is thus amplified by several authorities: *διατριβόντων δὲ αὐτῶν καὶ διδασκόντων ἐκεῖ ἐπῆλθάν τινες Ἰουδαῖοι ἀπὸ Ἰκονίου καὶ Ἀντιοχείας· καὶ διαλεγομένων αὐτῶν παρρησίᾳ ἔπεισαν τοὺς ὄχλους ἀποστῆναι ἀπ' αὐτῶν, λέγοντες ὅτι οὐδὲν ἀληθὲς λέγουσιν ἀλλὰ πάντα ψεύδονται· καὶ λιθάσαντες, κ.τ.λ.*, 'And while they stayed and were teaching there, some Jews arrived from Iconium and Antioch; and while they were reasoning boldly, they persuaded the multitudes to withdraw from them, saying that nothing they said was true but all lies. And having stoned,' etc.

[2] Ramsay, *Church in Rom. Emp.*, p. 69.

[3] He was actually stoned (λιθάσαντες), whereas at Iconium the rabble had merely 'flung stones' (λιθοβολῆσαι). Hence in his subsequent catalogue of 'hair-breadth escapes' he enumerates only one stoning (2 Cor. xi. 25).

[4] In ver. 20 the Sahidic Version has, 'and when the disciples surrounded him and evening was come.'

[5] A legend-monger would inevitably have represented his resuscitation as a miraculous resurrection, and Luke's sobriety here accredits the previous narrative of the healing of the cripple.

and would not venture to molest him further. And so under cover of the darkness he painfully made his way back to the town and crept home to his lodging.

Derbe.

Refreshed by the night's repose he was able on the morrow to set forth with Barnabas from the unfriendly town. They directed their steps south-eastward and travelled to Derbe. The precise site of this town has never been identified, but it lay at much the same elevation as Iconium 'on the flanks of Isauria,' near the Kingdom of Antiochus.[1] It was the frontier town of the Province of Galatia, and this constituted its chief if not its sole importance. It was a customs station, a receiving house for merchandise, and a resting place for travellers.

A peaceful and successful ministry.

It appears from the meagreness of the record that their sojourn at Derbe was uneventful, yet it was neither unpleasant nor unprofitable. They encountered no enmity and suffered no persecution. The town must have seemed a quiet haven

Cf. 2 Tim. iii. 11.

after their turbulent experiences at Antioch, Iconium, and Lystra ; but, peaceful as it was, their ministry was crowned with large success. The record is brief but eloquent : 'they evangelised the city, and they won numerous disciples.'

Cf. Ac. xx. 4.

And one of these was Gaius, who in after days proved a serviceable comrade of the Apostle.

IV

Ac. xiv. 21*b*-26.

THE HOMEWARD JOURNEY

Return through Galatia.

It was in the month of September that the missionaries had come to Derbe, and it would be midwinter ere they had accomplished so large a ministry. They had reached the eastern limit of the Province, and it was now time that they should turn homeward. The direct route to Syrian Antioch ran through the Kingdom of Antiochus and crossed the Taurus by the Cilician Gates ; but it was impracticable at that season when the snow blocked the mountain-passage. Nor is it likely that, even had it been practicable, they

[1] Strabo, 569. Cf. Ramsay, *Hist. Comm. on Gal.*, pp. 228 ff. ; *Cities of St. Paul*, pp. 385 ff.

would have followed it. In each of the three cities where they had preached in the course of their eastward progress, their ministry had been abruptly terminated. They had been violently expelled, and had left their converts not merely discouraged but uninstructed and unconsolidated; and there was imminent danger of their falling away from the Faith. It was imperative that this peril should be averted. Wherever in the course of his ministry the Apostle preached and planted the Gospel, he never counted his work complete until he had organised a Church and ordained Presbyters charged with the offices of administration and instruction. And therefore he determined to return with Barnabas by the way they had come, and revisit the converts in each city. They ran little risk in readventuring on those scenes of violence; for they would engage in no public propaganda. The Christian communities were now their exclusive concern; and even if the popular resentment still survived, it would receive no provocation.

Cf. Tit. i. 5.

Revisitation of the converts.

And so it came to pass. They retraced their steps through Southern Galatia and revisited successively the towns of Lystra, Iconium, and Antioch. In each they counselled their converts and confirmed them in the faith, exhorting them to steadfastness whatever trials they might encounter; and finally they had Presbyters elected and solemnly ordained them to the sacred office.[1] At Antioch they had the gladness of meeting again with Luke, 'the beloved physician' and the future historian; and he has betrayed his presence at this point by introducing a personal touch into the narrative. The missionaries, he says, 'confirmed the souls of the disciples, exhorting to continuance in the Faith, and that *we* must through many afflictions enter into the Kingdom of God.'[2]

Col. iv. 14.

Progress to the coast.

Antioch was their last station in the Province of Galatia, and their route thence ran southward to the coast. It was

[1] *χειροτονεῖν* (ver. 23), properly 'elect by show of hands,' accurately defines the democratic procedure of the Apostolic Church (cf. 2 Cor. viii. 19). The term, however, was also used vaguely in the sense of 'elect,' 'appoint.' Cf. Ac. x. 41; Æsop. *Fab.* 200ᵇ: *τοῦ δὲ Διὸς μέλλοντος χειροτονῆσαι αὐτοῖς τὸν βασιλέα.* In *Fab.* 44 it has its proper sense of 'popular election': *ἐν συνόδῳ τῶν ἀλόγων ζώων πίθηκος ὀρχησάμενος καὶ εὐδοκιμήσας βασιλεὺς ὑπ' αὐτῶν ἐχειροτονήθη.*

[2] Cf. Append. IV.

the road they had travelled so painfully on their upward journey about a year and a half previously. They had then made what haste they could, preaching nowhere by the way; but now they retrieved the lost opportunity. They preached as they went.[1] The chief town which they touched in their

Adada.

passage through Pisidia, was Adada,[2] and it appears that they evangelised it. At all events its modern representative is named after the Apostle *Kara Bavlo*, and about a mile to the south of it stand the ruins of an ancient church. Proceeding thence, they addressed themselves to the passage of

Passage of the Taurus.

the Taurus; and this was no slight ordeal. It was springtime, and the torrents, fed by the melting snow, would be running in full flood; and it was doubtless a reminiscence of that grim adventure when, in recounting his 'hair-breadth

2 Cor. xi. 25.

'scapes' some six years later, Paul mentioned 'dangers from rivers.' Achieving the perilous passage, they descended

Perga.

into the Province of Pamphylia and reached the city of Perga. It was there that Paul had sickened in the midsummer of 47; and now they effect the design which had been so painfully yet, as they had discovered, so wisely overruled: they 'spoke the word at Perga.' They made no long stay; for, warned by experience, they would be anxious to escape from Pamphylia ere the heat of summer. The river Cestrus was navigable as high as Perga, and as it had been the destination of the ship which conveyed them from Cyprus, so they might have sailed thence on their homeward voyage; but they were fain to lose no opportunity. And

Attaleia.

therefore they travelled to the seaport of Attaleia; and after preaching there[3] they embarked for Syrian Antioch, not later than the month of June in the year 49.

[1] On διελθόντες τὴν Πισιδίαν (ver. 24), cf. p. 83.

[2] Ἄδαδα (Ptol. v. v. 8), Ἀδαδάτη (Strabo, 570).

[3] After Ἀττάλειαν (ver. 25) Cod. Bez. (D) and several other authorities add εὐαγγελιζόμενοι αὐτούς.

THE COUNCIL AT JERUSALEM

Ac. xiv. 27, 28; Gal. ii. 11-16; Ac. xv. 1-32.

'How can the Lord call Egypt his people, and Assyria the work of his hands, and all the Gentiles (who for number are as the flocks of Kedar, and the abundance of the sea) the kingdoms of our Lord, and of his Christ, if you number all such as your charity cannot judge converts among Heathens and Pagans, who have not a visible claim and interest in Christ? We look upon this visible Church, though black and spotted, as the hospital and guest-house of sick, halt, maimed and withered, over which Christ is Lord-physician and Master; and we would wait upon those that are not yet in Christ, as our Lord waited upon us and you both.'

SAMUEL RUTHERFURD, *Lett.* II. 68.

Back at Antioch.

IT was midsummer of the year 49 when Paul and Barnabas reached Antioch, and they at once reported at a general assembly of the Church how they had fared in the prosecution of their mission. They had not come to stay; for the world was wide, and they had only begun the task of winning the Gentiles, and they contemplated a second mission. It was, however, impossible for them to embark upon it immediately. They needed a season of repose after their labours, especially Paul who, despite his sickness, had borne the chief burden. The summer would be gone ere he was restored to vigour, and travel was difficult in the winter.

The feeling at Jerusalem.

Thus it came to pass that they 'wore away no little time' at Antioch. Nor was it idly spent; for they found themselves involved in a grave and bitter controversy. A report of their mission had been conveyed to Jerusalem. Indeed intelligence of their doings in South Galatia must already have travelled thither. Jews from Pisidian Antioch would attend the Passover in the spring of 48, and they would publish the story of the rupture between the Apostles and the Synagogue; and at each succeeding feast Galatian worshippers would bring tidings in no friendly spirit. Their activities would be the talk of the city, and the accounts would be eagerly canvassed in the Church. The Twelve and most of their followers recognised that the Galatian movement was a legitimate issue of the agreement in the summer of 46;[1] and on the return of the missionaries they followed their accustomed procedure by appointing a deputy to visit Antioch and investigate the situation.[2]

Cf. viii. 14; xi. 22.

Peter's friendly visit to Antioch.

The deputy was Peter; and on reaching the Gentile capital and conferring with Paul and Barnabas he not only approved of their work but associated unreservedly with the Church. The Antiochene Christians were mostly Gentiles. They were uncircumcised, and they disregarded the Jewish rite of ceremonial ablution of the hands before eating;[3] yet the Jewish Apostle joined them at table, oblivious of the intolerable pollution which, in Jewish eyes, he thereby contracted.

Judaistic dissatisfaction.

Meanwhile the Pharisaic party in the Church at Jerusalem were grievously dissatisfied. They still cherished the dislike which they had expressed at the Conference in 46 to the admission of the Gentiles without the imposition of the Mosaic Law; and they were shocked by the report of the Galatian mission. They would have had it condemned, and in view of his declared attitude the appointment of Peter as deputy to the Antiochene Church accentuated their disquietude. It appears that there was one of their number who took the lead and organised an active opposition;[4] and it was resolved that representatives of the party should proceed to Antioch. They went on their own authority, but they professed to represent James, the Lord's brother. It was indeed true that he was the head of Jewish Christianity, and he had a natural tenderness for Jewish scrupulosity; but when they claimed his approval in their present action, they did him wrong, and he subsequently repudiated the imputation.

Deputation to Antioch.

Cf. Gal. ii. 12.

Cf. Ac. xv. 24.

Insistence on circumcision.

On reaching Antioch they promptly threw down the gauntlet, and startled the Church by the declaration:

[1] Cf. p. 75.

[2] On the historical position of Gal. ii. 11 ff. cf. Append. I.

[3] Cf. *The Days of His Flesh*, p. 244.

[4] In Gal. ii. 12 for πρὸ τοῦ γὰρ ἐλθεῖν τινας some Latin MSS. have *prius enim quam venisset quidam*, 'before a certain man had come,' while for ἦλθον ℵBD*FG read ἦλθεν, 'he came,' which Origen refers to James, supposing him to have visited Antioch.

'Unless you be circumcised after the custom of Moses, you cannot be saved.' It was a blunt denial of the Christianity of the Antiochenes. Most of them were converts from heathenism, and they had been admitted to the Church's fellowship on the sole ground of faith in Christ. They had never been required to accept the Jewish Law and observe its ceremonies. They were uncircumcised, and therefore they were still heathen and still unsaved.

Plausible arguments.

The visitors maintained their position stoutly, and they would have no difficulty in adducing arguments which seemed *prima facie* incontrovertible. The question was whether the Lord had ever abrogated the ancient Law; and they would appeal to His studious adherence to it in the days of His flesh—His insistence on submitting to the Baptism of John Mt. iii. 15.
in order that He might 'fulfil all righteousness'; His declara-
tion that He 'had not come to pull down the Law but to v. 17, 18.
complete it,' and that 'until heaven and earth passed away, no jot or tittle would pass away from the Law until everything came to pass'; and His direction to the young Ruler
that 'if he would enter into life, he must keep the command- xix. 17.
ments.' And hence they would conclude triumphantly that so far from abrogating the Law He had asserted its permanent obligation. It was indeed an illegitimate inference, proceeding on a narrow interpretation; yet it would seem irrefragable. And the zeal of its advocates would carry conviction. They were bigots, but they were honestly persuaded that the historic faith was at stake; and they would taunt Peter and Paul and Barnabas with disowning the traditions of their fathers and bartering away their sacred heritage.

Vacillation of Peter and Barnabas. Cf. Lk. xxii. 54-62.

It had always been a foible of Peter, an infirmity of his impulsive and generous nature, that he was easily overborne and shrank from ridicule; and he was intimidated by those blustering Judaists. He remained indeed unconvinced, but in the interests of peace he was disposed to compromise. The observance of the Law was, as even Paul allowed, a matter of no moment; and why not acquiesce in the contention of those sticklers and let them have their way? And so he bowed to the storm, and withdrew from fellowship with the Gentile converts and would no longer share their meals. His example was contagious, and it was followed by all the Hellenist Christians, even by Barnabas.

Paul's stout resistance.

It was a serious situation, threatening a cleavage in the Church; and the disaster was averted by the prompt and steadfast courage of Paul. He publicly challenged Peter, and charged him with 'play-acting,' assuming a rôle which was not his real character.[1] It was indeed true that legal observance was a matter of no moment; and so long as a Jewish Christian recognised that salvation was by faith in Christ alone, he might, if he would, continue to practise the old rites. But when it was claimed that these were essential to salvation, then their repudiation was an imperative duty; and thus Peter's action was disloyalty at once to Christ, to himself, and to his Gentile brethren. From every point of view he stood condemned. The protest was unanswerable, and Peter responded with his accustomed impetuosity. He ceased his 'play-acting' and came out in his proper character, and his example rallied Barnabas and the rest of the Jewish Christians.

Reference to Jerusalem.

Thus the Judaists were foiled, but they would not accept defeat. Antioch was the capital of Gentile Christendom, and its judgment was, in their view, no impartial verdict; and so they urged that the question should be submitted to the Apostles and Elders at Jerusalem, and that an Antiochene deputation, consisting of Paul and Barnabas and several others, should proceed thither.[2] The challenge was accepted by the Church, and it was not unwelcome to Paul. It was no absolute reference to the decision of the Twelve and their colleagues at Jerusalem. In view of the agreement at the Conference in 46 he entertained no doubt what their verdict would be; but even had they decided against him, he would still have maintained his position and

[1] Gal. ii. 13. *ὑποκριτής*, the epithet wherewith our Lord constantly branded the Pharisees, signified properly not 'a hypocrite' but 'an actor' on the stage. Cf. *The Days of His Flesh*, p. 102.

[2] In Ac. xv. 2 the subject of *ἔταξαν* is *οἱ ἀδελφοί* (cf. xiii. 3), but according to Cod. Bez. (D) supported by Syriac Version, they were impelled by the insistence of the Judaists: *ἔλεγεν γὰρ ὁ Παῦλος μένειν οὕτως καθὼς ἐπίστευσαν διισχυριζόμενος· οἱ δὲ ἐληλυθότες ἀπὸ Ἱερουσαλὴμ παρήγγειλαν αὐτοῖς τῷ Παύλῳ καὶ Βαρνάβᾳ καί τισιν ἄλλοις ἀναβαίνειν πρὸς τοὺς ἀποστόλους, κ.τ.λ.*, 'for Paul stoutly contended that they should so remain as they had believed; but those who had come from Jerusalem urged them, Paul and Barnabas and some others, to go up to the Apostles, etc.'

proclaimed a free Gospel of salvation by faith alone. He went up to Jerusalem, not to learn what he must preach, but to have the issue between Jewish and Gentile Christianity defined and obtain a final settlement of the vexatious controversy. The question was already determined in his mind, and this is proved by his procedure. The route from Antioch to Tarsus led through Phœnicia and Samaria, and Christianity had already been introduced into those countries. There was a church in every town where the travellers halted, and they visited each and told the glad story of 'the conversion of the Gentiles'—the cause which they were going to Jerusalem not to debate but to vindicate.

Cf. viii. 1-25; xi. 19.

Arrival and reception of the delegates.

In view of all that had transpired the winter must have been well advanced ere they left Antioch, and their progress through Phœnicia and Samaria would occupy a considerable time. Thus it was probably about the beginning of the year 50 when they reached Jerusalem. The Judaists had hastened thither, and the Church was apprised of the approach of the Antiochene deputies and accorded them a gracious reception. No immediate mention was made of the controversy which had arisen at Antioch. The ostensible errand of Paul and Barnabas was to report upon their mission; and it was only after they had told the story at an ordinary meeting of the Church that the true issue emerged. Several representatives of the Pharisaic party[1] rose and took objection to the procedure of the missionaries, and insisted on the necessity of circumcising Gentile converts and requiring them to observe the Mosaic Law.

The Council.

This raised the vital question, and a general assembly was convened for its consideration.[2] It appears that here, as on the occasion of Paul's first visit to Jerusalem after his conversion,[3] all the Twelve except Peter, who had just returned from Antioch, were absent from the city, doubtless

[1] According to Cod. Bez. (D) and Syr. Vers. these were the Judaists who had created the trouble at Antioch and had come to Jerusalem to prosecute their complaint: οἱ δὲ παραγγείλαντες αὐτοῖς ἀναβαίνειν πρὸς τοὺς πρεσβυτέρους ἐξανέστησαν λέγοντες.

[2] It was a democratic assemblage. After πρεσβύτεροι (ver. 6) 137 Syr^{p} add σὺν τῷ πλήθει (cf. ver. 12). The question was decided by 'the Apostles and the Elders *with the whole Church*' (ver. 22).

[3] Cf. p. 60.

in the prosecution of their apostolic enterprises.[1] James, the Lord's brother, however, who ranked with the Twelve in apostolic honour, was present, and he, as the acknowledged head of Jewish Christianity, presided over the assembly and was supported by the Elders of the Church.

A keen discussion.

Cf. Ac. x-xi. 18.

The proceedings commenced with the hearing of the objection, and thereafter a keen and protracted discussion ensued. It was an open debate, and feeling ran high until at length Peter intervened. He reminded the excited assembly of a decisive fact. Some ten years previously, while still dominated by Jewish prepossessions, he had gone upon a missionary circuit, and had been summoned from Joppa to Cæsarea by Cornelius the Centurion, a 'God-fearer,' and had been led by the incontrovertible evidence of the Holy Spirit's operation to admit him and his household into Christian fellowship, though they were uncircumcised Gentiles; and his action had been approved by the Church. That was now 'ancient history,' and it had never been challenged. The question of the admission of the Gentiles was already settled. They had been released from ceremonial obligation, and the Church could not now reimpose upon them a yoke which even the Jews had found intolerable.

Statements of Paul and Barnabas.

The Elders intimated their concurrence, and the controversy ceased. A hush fell upon the tumultuous assembly, and when Paul and Barnabas arose they had no need to defend their cause. They simply recounted amid breathless attention the wonders which God had wrought through them among the Gentiles.

James's motion.

When they concluded, it only remained that the assembly should pronounce its judgment, and it devolved upon James to formulate and submit the motion. He was invested with unique authority in the Jewish Church by reason not alone of his sacred kinship[2] but of his personal character.

[1] The evidence is twofold: (1) Had any others of the Twelve been present, they would surely have taken part in the discussion. (2) In ver. 12 Cod. Bez. (D), with Syr^{p} c*, reads *συγκατατιθεμένων δὲ τῶν πρεσβυτέρων τοῖς ὑπὸ τοῦ Πέτρου εἰρημένοις ἐσίγησεν πᾶν τὸ πλῆθος*, 'and, the Elders assenting to what had been said by Peter, all the multitude kept silence.' Had the rest of the Twelve been present, they would have been mentioned as assenting.

[2] On the prestige of the *δεσπόσυνοι*, 'the Lord's kindred,' cf. letter of Africanus in Eus. *Hist. Eccl.* I. 7.

His ascetic austerity had earned him the appellation of 'the Righteous,'[1] and thus he was free from every suspicion of laxity. He was the very exemplar of Jewish piety, and his espousal of the cause of the Gentile Christians constituted an emphatic refutation of Judaistic scrupulosity. In a speech fragrant with the spirit of the ancient faith he submitted his judgment. 'My judgment,' he said, 'is that we should not harass the Gentile converts to God, but should send them a letter that they abstain from the pollutions of idols, and fornication, and bloodshed.'[2]

The Council's decree.

It was a courageous and indeed revolutionary proposal. It absolutely released the Gentile converts from the ceremonial Law, and imposed upon them three simple and indisputable obligations: that they should renounce the unholy rites of idolatry and worship the one living and true God; that they should practise chastity;[3] and that they should recognise the sanctity of human life. It was probably only the authority of James that reconciled the Council to so startling and sweeping an innovation. It was indeed, as the event proved, profoundly distasteful to the extremer Judaists; yet they durst not openly dissent, and the resolution was accepted without opposition and registered as a decree of the Church.

Message of reassurance to Syria-Cilicia.

The Council's business did not end here. The controversy so wantonly excited at Antioch had occasioned grave disquietude not only in the Gentile capital but in the dependent churches throughout the Province of Syria-Cilicia; and in order to restore peace it was resolved to embody the decree in a circular letter. This was to be conveyed by Paul and Barnabas; and, still further to reassure the Gentile Christians, two representatives of the Church at Jerusalem

[1] Cf. Hegesippus' account of his Nazirite asceticism, his piety, and his martyrdom in Eus. *Hist. Eccl.* II. 23.

[2] On the text of the Council's decree cf. Append. V.

[3] On the ceremonial interpretation of the decree the introduction of 'fornication' seems incongruous, and two remedies have been suggested. 1. Dr. John Lightfoot understood by πορνεία either bigamy and polygamy or marriage within the prohibited degrees (so Ramsay). 2. πορνείας has been conjecturally emended into χοιρείας (Bentley quoted by Wetstein), 'swine's flesh,' or πορκείας (cf. Scrivener, *Introd.*, p. 491), 'pork,' from Latin *porcus*. But both words are unexampled. 'Swine's flesh' is χοίρειον (sc. κρέας).

Deputation of Judas and Silas.

Cf. Ac. i. 23.

1 Th. i. 1; 2 Th. i. 1; 2 Cor. i. 19; cf. 1 Pet. v. 12.

Ac. xvi. 37, 38.

Cf. xv. 32.

were deputed to accompany them. One was Judas Barsabbas, probably, in view of the common patronymic, a brother of Joseph Barsabbas who had been nominated with Matthias some twenty years previously to the vacancy in the ranks of the Twelve. The other was Silas; and he is introduced without more explicit designation inasmuch as he was afterwards so well known. Silas, the name which he bears in the Book of Acts, is the familiar abbreviation of Silvanus, the more ceremonious designation which he bears in the Apostle's letters. He was apparently a man of good condition, since he was, like Paul, a Roman citizen. Both deputies were prominent in the Church of Jerusalem; and they were well qualified for the office, since they both belonged to the prophetic order. Their message to Antioch would be a living word of God.

The letter ran thus:[1]

Encyclical letter.

'The Apostles and the Presbyters, your brothers,[2] to the Gentile brothers in Antioch and Syria and Cilicia: greeting. Whereas we heard that some of our number[3] had troubled you with arguments to the unsettlement of your souls—to whom we gave no instructions—it was our unanimous decision to choose delegates and send them to you with our beloved Barnabas and Paul, men who have surrendered their lives for the name of our Lord Jesus Christ. We have therefore commissioned Judas and Silas, who will themselves also deliver the same message verbally. It was the Holy Spirit's decision and ours[4] to impose upon you no further burden beyond these essentials—abstinence from things sacrificed to idols and bloodshed and fornication. From these you will do well to keep yourselves.[5] Farewell.'

[1] Doubtless an authentic copy, since the letter was an important document, and not only would the original remain for future reference (cf. Ac. xxi. 25) but Paul would preserve his copy and each Church the copy it received. It would thus be easily accessible, and so painstaking a historian as Luke would not neglect so ready an opportunity.

[2] Not *καὶ οἱ ἀδελφοὶ* (ℵ^cEHLP) but *ἀδελφοὶ* (ℵ*ABCD), 'the Apostles and the Presbyters, themselves brothers' (cf. 1 Tim. ii. 5). They wrote in name of the whole Church (cf. vers. 22, 25), and they disown hierarchical pretension by writing as 'brothers to brothers.'

[3] Omitting *ἐξελθόντες* with ℵ*B.

[4] A characteristically primitive expression. The voice of the Spirit-guided Church was the Spirit's will articulate.

[5] The v.l. *πράξατε* ($CD^{gr}HL$), 'from these you have done well in keeping yourselves,' would be a generous recognition that the Gentile converts had hitherto been irreproachable.

Armed with this gracious communication, Paul and Barnabas, with their fellow-deputies from Antioch and the two delegates of the Council, took their departure from Jerusalem. On the way thither their progress had been leisurely, broken by visits to the Christian communities *en route*; but now they were eager to report the happy issue, and they made such haste that they reached Antioch 'in a few days.'[1] The Church assembled, and its heart was gladdened by the Council's letter and the kindly discourse of Judas and Silas.

Return to Antioch.

[1] Cod. Bez. (D) ἐν ἡμέραις ὀλίγαις κατῆλθον.

THE SECOND MISSION

'She heard it, the victorious West,
In crown and sword array'd!
She felt the void which mined her breast,
She shiver'd and obey'd.

'She veil'd her eagles, snapp'd her sword,
And laid her sceptre down;
Her stately purple she abhorr'd,
And her imperial crown.'

MATT. ARNOLD.

I

Ac. xv. 33-40.

DISUNION OF PAUL AND BARNABAS

Ministry of Judas and Silas in Syria-Cilicia.

JUDAS and Silas remained a while at Antioch. They had come to undo the mischief which the controversy had wrought and heal the rankling sore which it had left. The work demanded time and patience; and since the Council's letter was addressed not alone to the Church of Antioch but to all the churches of Syria-Cilicia, it is likely that the delegates would make a circuit of the province. And thus their mission would occupy a considerable time, probably at least a month. At length it was successfully accomplished; and the Church formally recognised the service which they had rendered and gave them their discharge.[1]

Alienation of Paul and Barnabas.

They were now free to take their departure, and Judas forthwith returned to Jerusalem. Silas, however, remained behind. It appears that there had grown up betwixt him

[1] ἀπελύθησαν μετ' εἰρήνης (cf. xvi. 36) denotes their formal discharge by the Church on the accomplishment of their commission, and does not necessarily imply their departure from the city. Silas remained (cf. ver. 40); and the situation is elucidated in CD(Cod. Bez.) Vulg. by the gloss (ver. 34): ἔδοξε δὲ τῷ Σίλᾳ ἐπιμεῖναι αὐτοῦ, 'but it seemed good to Silas to remain there,' D Vulg. adding μόνος δὲ Ἰούδας ἐπορεύθη, 'but Judas went his way alone.'

and Paul a warm sympathy, and the Apostle detained him in view of an untoward eventuality which had of late presented itself to his mind. The vacillation of Barnabas in the trouble with the Judaists would rankle in his memory, and his distrust of his old friend and comrade had been strengthened during their visit to Jerusalem. They had found John Mark there at home with his mother Mary. He was ashamed of the part which he had played in Pamphylia and desirous to retrieve his character; and Barnabas, with his wonted generosity and perhaps a natural partiality for his kinsman, would have condoned the past, and he contemplated the association of Mark with the next mission and his reinstatement in the office of attendant. To Paul, however, such lenience was displeasing, and he viewed the deserter with unabated disapprobation.

Dissension regarding John Mark.

In due course the question was brought to a direct and open issue. It was now springtime and travel was once more practicable, and Paul proposed that they should address themselves to a second expedition and revisit the churches which they had founded in Cyprus, Pamphylia, and Galatia. Barnabas agreed, but when he intimated his desire that John Mark should again attend them, Paul stoutly objected. 'The man who deserted from us in Pamphylia and went not with us to the work! I refuse to take him with us.'[1] Barnabas insisted, and a sharp altercation ensued. It was a collision of temperaments and ideals: on the one side, the passionate enthusiasm which sacrifices all for a sacred cause and accounts faltering a treason meriting measureless condemnation and eternal contempt; and, on the other, that sweet reasonableness which 'is always trustful, always hopeful, always patient,' 'despairing of no man.' Agreement was impossible, and the dispute ended in a rupture betwixt the two.

1 Cor. xiii. 7; Lk. vi. 35 R.V. marg.

Dissociation.

It was a tragic *dénouement*. 'Which,' says St. Chrysostom, 'was the better counselled it is not for us to show'; and it were perhaps well to leave it there. Yet one cannot but think how different the issue might have been

[1] The stinging sentence (Ac. xv. 38) is plainly an echo of Paul's indignant protest. ἀποστάντα (A, ἀποστατήσαντα), 'played the apostate' (cf. 2 Th. ii. 3), replaces the gentler ἀποχωρήσας of the historian (xiii. 13).

Cf. Ac. ix. 26, 27. had Paul remembered how much he owed to the charity of Barnabas, who had believed in him when no one else would, and by his generous faith in the humbled persecutor had won for him an opportunity of redeeming his shameful past. By the subsequent course of events God adjudged the controversy, and His judgment was a vindication of Barnabas. His kinsman's generosity afforded John Mark an opportunity of purging his disgrace; and that he right Cf. 2 Tim. iv. 11. nobly availed himself of it Paul at the long last ungrudgingly recognised. Meanwhile, however, the alienation was complete. It seems indeed that the old comrades parted in charity, since they divided the field between them, Barnabas taking Cyprus and Paul Galatia. But their parting was final. It would appear that they held each other in friendly Cf. 1 Cor. ix. 6. remembrance; for there is a kindly though obscure reference to Barnabas in a letter of Paul some five years later. But there is no evidence that they ever resumed the old fellowship; probably they never saw each other's face again. This is the last appearance of Barnabas in the sacred narrative; and tradition, whatever it may be worth, affirms that he died a martyr's death in Cyprus. The Jews burned him at the stake outside the gate of Salamis and threw his ashes into the sea.[1]

Alliance of Paul and Silas. Ac. xv. 40. Barnabas gone, Paul turned to Silas and adopted him as his comrade. It is written that he 'made choice of him,' suggesting that there were others who would willingly have accompanied him. And indeed there was no lack of competent and devoted men in the Church of Antioch; but the fitness of Silas was pre-eminent. It was proved by the distinction he had won at Jerusalem and by his recent service in the Gentile capital. And he possessed two especial qualifications. One was that he was a Jew and at the same time an ardent champion of Gentile liberties; and the other that he was a Roman citizen with the wide outlook which that dignity implied and the prestige and immunity which it ensured wherever Roman Law prevailed. And thus he was fitted at once to disarm Jewish prejudice and to win Gentile confidence.

[1] *Act. Barn.* xxiii.

II

PROGRESS THROUGH ASIA MINOR

Ac. xv. 41-xvi. 8.

The Church bade the missionaries Godspeed and they set forth. The original design had been that Paul and Barnabas should, at all events in the first instance, revisit the converts whom they had already won; and they would then have retraced their former route, taking ship to Cyprus and proceeding thence by Pamphylia to Southern Galatia. But now that they have parted company, they go their separate ways. Barnabas betook himself to Cyprus, and Paul with his new colleague travelled overland direct to Galatia. The change of programme presented a double advantage. Since the overland route led through the Province of Syria-Cilicia, it afforded the missionaries an opportunity of visiting the disquieted churches by the way and reiterating the assurances which Silas and Judas had already addressed to them in their hasty circuit for the delivery of the Council's letter. Moreover, the time which would have been consumed in revisiting Cyprus was now at their disposal; and their purpose was that after traversing Southern Galatia from east to west they should continue their progress westward from Pisidian Antioch into the Province of Asia and, travelling through the populous valley of the Lycus and Mæander by the great Trade Route, evangelise the cities which lay along it—Apameia, Colossæ, Laodiceia, Hierapolis, Tralles, and Magnesia—until they reached its western terminus, Ephesus, the brilliant capital of the province.

Departure of the missionaries.

Their projected itinerary.

Nothing is recorded of their doings in the course of their journey through Syria-Cilicia save that they 'confirmed the Churches'; but it would be a pleasant and profitable ministry. After his recent circuit of the province Silas was no stranger; and as for Paul, it was he who, some ten years previously, had founded those churches, and he would be received by his spiritual children with affectionate gladness. Their progress would thus be slow, and they would doubtless be detained longest at Tarsus, where Paul had ancient

Progress through Syria-Cilicia.

Cf. Gal. i. 21.

associations and numerous friends. Nor indeed, if they had set out from Antioch in the spring, was haste necessary; for the Taurus lay betwixt them and Galatia, and the crossing by that famous pass, the Gates of Cilicia,[1] was impracticable ere the close of May.[2]

Across *Regnum Antiochi.*

Through the Gates of Cilicia they entered the Kingdom of Antiochus; and it is remarkable that they seem to have preached nowhere within its borders. Already the Roman Empire had captivated the Apostle's imagination. He was dreaming of its transfiguration into a Commonwealth of God, and he hastened across the intervening territory until he had passed the frontier and gained the town of Derbe.

Revisitation of the Galatian Churches.

There he began his course of revisitation. His chief trouble in South Galatia had been the hostility of the Jews, and in order to assuage it and save his converts from further molestation he brought with him a copy of the Council's decree. The Council's letter indeed had been addressed particularly to the churches of Syria-Cilicia, but the decree which it embodied was an authoritative judgment on the vexed question of the relation of Gentile Christians to the Jewish Law, and thus it had a general import. It constituted the charter of Gentile liberty, and therefore he would present it to the Galatian churches. His hope was that it would not merely silence the clamour of the Jews but bring them to a juster appreciation of his Gospel. They had misconstrued it. His attitude was that the ancient Law had served its end, and now that it had been fulfilled in Christ, its ordinances were no longer obligatory. They belonged to the category of 'things indifferent'; and so long as a Jew recognised that salvation was by faith alone, he was free, if he would, to observe the ancient rites which long usage had endeared to him. The Apostle insisted on Gentile freedom, but he would not needlessly wound Jewish sentiment. And he was anxious to make this clear.

Cf. 1 Cor. vii. 18, 19; ix. 20.

Association of Timothy.

An effective opportunity presented itself when he reached Lystra. He found there his friends, the widow Eunice and her mother Lois and her son Timothy. They had proved true to the faith which they had professed; and

[1] Cf. Strabo, 537.

[2] Cf. Ramsay, *Church in Rom. Emp.*, pp. 84 f.

Timothy, young as he was, had attested his devotion not only in Lystra but in the neighbouring town of Iconium. Paul recognised in the lad the promise of future usefulness, and he decided to engage him in the service of the Gospel by associating him with the mission in the room of John Mark. His mother was a devout Jewess, but his father had been a Gentile and the lad had never been circumcised. Here Paul perceived an opportunity of defining his attitude toward the Law and correcting misapprehension. Circumcision was indeed a thing indifferent, but it was sacred in Jewish eyes; and since Timothy was half a Jew, he circumcised him.[1] His action here stands in significant contrast with his stout refusal of the Jewish demand four years previously that Titus should be circumcised.[2] Titus was a Gentile, and his circumcision had been required as necessary to salvation; but Timothy was half a Jew, and his circumcision was a recognition of Jewish liberty in 'things indifferent.' It was a gracious and conciliatory action, none the less wise that it was misinterpreted and afterwards employed by his ungenerous enemies as a controversial weapon against the large-hearted Apostle.[3]

Cf. 1 Tim. iv. 14.

His circumcision.

Thus they travelled westward from town to town and church to church until they reached Pisidian Antioch;[4] and there Paul would be affectionately greeted by his old friends, particularly the physician Luke. Their intention was to proceed westward into the Province of Asia, and there break fresh soil; but it was providentially frustrated.

A providential interposition at Pisidian Antioch.

[1] Evidently with his own hand. The operation did not require a priest: any Jew might perform it after the example of Abraham (cf. Gen. xvii. 23).

[2] Cf. p. 75. The contrast between Paul's refusal to circumcise Titus (cf. Gal. ii. 3) and his voluntary circumcision of Timothy served Baur (cf. *Paul*, I. pp. 129 f.) as an argument for his theory that the Book of Acts is a *Tendenzschrift* with an irenical purpose.

[3] Cf. p. 201.

[4] τὴν Φρυγίαν καὶ Γαλατικὴν χώραν, 'the Phrygo-Galatic District,' *i.e.*, the Phrygian District of the Province of Galatia, to which Antioch belonged. Cf. p. 90. διῆλθον κωλυθέντες would seem to imply that the hindrance preceded: 'they passed through the Phrygo-Galatic District because they had been hindered.' Hence the variant διελθόντες (HLP), dependent like κωλυθέντες and ἐλθόντες on ἐπείραζον. But κωλυθέντες is a 'timeless aorist' (cf. Moulton, *Proleg.* pp. 134 f.). Cf. xxiii. 35: ἔφη . . . κελεύσας, 'said he and commanded'; xxv. 13: κατήντησαν εἰς Καισαρείαν ἀσπασάμενοι τὸν Φῆστον, 'arrived and greeted.' Heb. ii. 10; ix. 12.

'They were hindered,' it is written, 'by the Holy Spirit from speaking the Word in Asia.' What precisely the hindrance may have been is matter of conjecture; but this much is certain—that it was no supernatural revelation; it

Ac. xx. 3.

was a providential dispensation. An apt illustration occurs later in the narrative, where it is related that Paul, at the conclusion of his third mission, was on the point of taking ship at Corinth when he learned that a plot was on foot among his Jewish fellow-passengers to assassinate him in the course of the voyage; and he abandoned his purpose and travelled overland. There is here nothing supernatural; and some pious scribe, taking it amiss that God should be thus, as it seemed to him, left out of account, has refashioned the sentence and written: 'He purposed to set sail for Syria, but the Spirit told him to return through Macedonia.'[1] And indeed the emendation, needless though it be, is after the general manner of the Holy Scriptures. They recognise God's will and God's hand in everything that befalls, and they ignore 'secondary causes.' These indeed are never lacking, but they never stand alone. The hand of God is always behind them. They are His providential dispensations, revelations of His will and leadings of His Holy Spirit.

The plan of evangelising Asia overruled.

And so it was that the missionaries 'were hindered by the Holy Spirit from speaking the Word in Asia.' Their purpose was providentially overruled; nor is it difficult, in view of their circumstances, to surmise with reasonable probability what it was that befell. It would be midsummer when they reached Antioch, the very season when Paul, three years before, had arrived there in the grip of the malaria which had stricken him in Pamphylia and which permanently afflicted him, recurring whenever he was overtoiled. And now he was exhausted by his long travel afoot and his incessant labours by the way. Symptoms of his malady appeared, and the physician Luke forbade him to prosecute his purpose of advancing into Asia. The rich, alluvial valley of the Lycus and Mæander, with its warm springs and its sultry climate,[2] was, especially at that season,

[1] Cod. Bez., Syr$^{p\ mg}$: ἠθέλησεν ἀναχθῆναι εἰς Συρίαν· εἶπεν δὲ τὸ Πνεῦμα αὐτῷ ὑποστρέφειν διὰ τῆς Μακεδονίας.

[2] Cf. p. 548.

a hotbed of malaria; and to adventure himself there would have been perilous for the Apostle; it would inevitably have involved a disastrous and probably fatal sickness.

Quest for a new field.

In this warning Paul recognised the guiding voice of the Holy Spirit. Asia was providentially closed against him, and he must turn elsewhere for a field of operation. Whither should he betake himself? The south was impracticable, since in the coastal lowlands, as his experience in Pamphylia had taught him, he would have been exposed to the same peril; and he had already preached in the east. The north alone remained, and he set out from Pisidian Antioch accompanied not only by Silas and Timothy but by Luke. He was ailing, and 'the beloved physician,' with kindly solicitude, would attend him on his way and see him settled on his next field of operation.[1]

Travelling northward.

They set their faces northward and travelled through the Phrygian uplands. It was a healthful and invigorating region, but it was sparsely peopled and had few towns and no cities, and nowhere did Paul find what he sought. Like the Master's in the days of His flesh, his heart ever yearned toward the multitude; and his constant venue was some busy centre where need abounded, and where, moreover, the Common Greek was spoken and men's minds were alert and receptive. It was such a scene that he sought; and he wandered on with his company in fruitless quest until they found themselves abreast of Mysia, the north-western corner of Asia Minor. It presented no fitting field, and their thoughts turned toward the extensive Province of Bithynia and Pontus which stretched from the borders of the Kingdom of Polemo a little eastward of Amisos to the shores of the Propontis. As they approached it, however, it proved less

Cf. Mt. ix. 35, 36; Mk. vi. 34.

[1] The evidence is that from this point Luke tells the story in the first person (cf. ver. 10). It is remarkable that at the beginning of the paragraph (vers. 6-10), where he indicates with extreme brevity the course of the northward wandering, he employs the third person (διῆλθον, ἐπείραζον, αὐτούς), and then suddenly after the arrival at Troas passes into the first. On the assumption that he belonged to Pisidian Antioch (cf. Append. IV) two explanations suggest themselves: either that he set out after Paul and his two colleagues and overtook them at Troas; or, as seems more probable, that he set out with them and it was only at Troas that he determined to cast in his lot with them. Not till he had become a participator in the work did he introduce himself into the narrative.

and less alluring. It lay remote, an outskirt of the Empire, a mere backwater of the tide of the world's life. Its cities were few, and even the chief of them, Nicæa and Nicomedia, were of small importance. 'The spirit of Jesus,'[1] the passion for souls, warned them that their work did not lie there; and on reaching the frontier they turned back and entered Mysia and travelled through it, preaching nowhere,[2] until they reached Troas on the western coast.

III

THE CALL OF THE WEST

Ac. xvi. 9-11.

The city of Troas.

Troas was an illustrious city.[3] It was founded by Antigonus, and was originally named after him Antigonia. Subsequently it was named Alexandria after Alexander the Great; and to distinguish it from the Egyptian Alexandria it was designated Alexandria Troas, that is, Alexandria in the Troad.[4] It was a Roman colony,[5] and it is a striking evidence of its prestige that Julius Cæsar was credited with the design of transferring thither the seat of the imperial government.[6]

Glimpses of the West.

It was by no purpose of their own that the missionaries found themselves at Troas. They had been carried thither, as it seemed, like driftwood by the tide; yet, as the event proved, that tide was the will of God, and His hand had been guiding them all the while to unsuspected issues. The city presented a hopeful arena for evangelical enterprise, and Paul may have contemplated settling there for a season. It had, however, been otherwise ordained, and, ere he could commence operations, God's larger purpose was discovered to him. On his arrival he would view his surroundings with

[1] τὸ πνεῦμα Ἰησοῦ ℵABC[2]DE.

[2] παρελθόντες δὲ τὴν Μυσίαν, *præterita Mysia*, *prætergressi Mysiam* (Wetstein). They travelled through the country, passing along without stopping anywhere.

[3] Strabo, 581.

[4] Ἀλεξάνδρεια ἡ Τρῳάς. Strabo, 593.

[5] Strabo, 593; Plin. *Nat. Hist.* v. 33.

[6] Suet. *Jul. Cæs.* 79.

curious interest. Troas was a busy seaport, situated on the western verge of the Orient; and she was frequented by European merchants who thronged her markets and traversed her streets, presenting in their western attire novel figures to Jewish eyes. Especially noticeable were the Macedonians with their Greek mantles and the broad hats which served at once as a shelter from the summer heat and as helmets in their frequent affrays.[1] The spectacle would stir his mind, and his imagination would reach afar over the blue Ægean to the lands beyond the golden sunset—Greece, the home of art, poetry, and philosophy, and Rome, the Imperial City, the mistress of the world. Could it be that God was calling him thither, and that it was for this end that his purpose of preaching in the Province of Asia had been overruled and he had in his ignorance been conducted to Troas?

Call to Macedonia. He would communicate his musings to his companions, and after he had lain down to rest his waking meditations shaped themselves into a dream. A man stood before him in the Macedonian attire which he had remarked in the streets of Troas, and addressed to him the appeal: 'Cross over to Macedonia, and succour us.'[2] In the morning he related the dream to his companions; and, chiming as it did with their surmises, they took it as a divine revelation[3] and resolved to obey it. Luke was with them. He had accompanied Paul from Pisidian Antioch, and the Holy Spirit had been inclining his heart to the service of the Kingdom of Heaven. He recognised in this new departure, this high enterprise, a personal appeal; and he responded to it. He cast in his lot with the missionaries, and thenceforth he was a devoted comrade of the Apostle.

The voyage. Next day[4] they set sail for Macedonia. It was now the

[1] The Greek mantle (*χλαμύς*) was originally a Macedonian garment. Cf. Becker, *Charicles*, p. 421. On the sun-hat (*καυσίη*) cf. quotation in Suidas: *καυσίη, ἡ τοπάροιθε Μακηδόσιν εὔκολον ὅπλον,/καὶ σκέπας ἐν νιφετῷ καὶ κόρυς ἐν πολέμῳ.*

[2] *βοήθησον ἡμῖν*, cf. Mt. xv. 25; Mk. ix. 22, 24; Heb. ii. 18.

[3] Cod. Bez. (D) reads (ver. 10) *διεγερθεὶς οὖν διηγήσατο τὸ ὅραμα ἡμῖν, καὶ ἐνοήσαμεν ὅτι προσκέκληται, κ.τ.λ.*, 'on waking he related the vision to us, and we perceived that,' etc.

[4] Cod. Bez. (D), Syr$^{p\ mg}$, 137: *τῇ δὲ ἐπαύριον ἀναχθέντες.*

month of August, and the Etesian Winds were blowing steadily from the north-west;[1] but, aided by the current which bore down from the Hellespont,[2] the ship was able to lay a straight course as far as the island of Samothrace. There she harboured for the night; and next morning she held across to the Thracian coast and, working westward with the aid of tides and land-breezes, ere nightfall made the port of Neapolis in Macedonia.

Ac. xvi. 12-xvii. 4; 1 Th. ii. 9; Phil. iv. 15, 16; Ac. xvii. 5-15.

IV

EVANGELISATION OF MACEDONIA

Philippi.

Ten to twelve miles inland[3] on the river Gangites,[4] a tributary of the Strymon, lay the town of Philippi; and thither they betook themselves. It was a fitting scene for the inauguration of their European ministry. The town was named after Alexander the Great's father, Philip of Macedon, who had founded it on the site of the ancient Crenides or 'Wells' for the working of the gold and silver mines which at that period constituted the main wealth of the district.[5] Hard by was the field of the famous battle which determined the imperial destiny of Rome, and in memory of his victory Augustus had made the town a military colony with the high-sounding title, preserved to this day on coins, COLONIA JULIA AUGUSTA PHILIPPENSIUM. A Roman colony was a miniature of the Imperial City,[6] reproducing her institutions and aping her dignity with an often ridiculous punctiliousness; and Philippi exhibited this foible in full measure Her chief magistrates, properly 'duumvirs,' assumed the lofty designation of 'prætors,'[7] and their officers went by

[1] Cf. Append. I, p. 648. [2] Plin. *Nat. Hist.* II. 100.

[3] ἀπὸ ἑβδομήκοντα σταδίων (Appian, *Civil Wars*, IV. 106).

[4] The name varies: Gangas or Gangites (Appian, *ibid.*), Angites (Herod. VII. 113).

[5] Strabo, 330.

[6] Cf. Gellius, XVI. 13: 'Ex civitate propagatæ . . . Populi Romani, cujus istæ coloniæ effigies parvæ simulacraque esse quædam videntur.'

[7] στρατηγοί. Cf. vers. 20, 22, 35, 36, 38.

the name of 'lictors.'[1] Nor was she content with this petty vanity. When Macedonia fell under the dominion of the Romans after its conquest in 168 B.C., it was divided into four districts,[2] and Amphipolis was the capital of the eastern district; but Philippi in her pride appropriated this pre-eminence.[3] Despite her small arrogance the city contained a rich and varied life, and afforded the heralds of the Gospel a rare opportunity. The population was composed of three main elements. First, there were the Roman colonists, the dominant caste; then there were the native Macedonians, numerically the strongest section; and finally there was a considerable admixture of Orientals, though, inasmuch doubtless as the city in those days engaged little in commerce, this included few Jews. Philippi was in truth a meeting-place of East and West, and she was daily visited by strangers from all lands, situated as she was on the Egnatian Road, that magnificent highway which stretched from Dyrrachium on the Adriatic to the Hellespont.[4]

The Jewish place of prayer.

The missionaries entered on their work without delay, and Paul pursued the method which he had followed in the East, addressing his first appeal to the Jews. These were indeed few at Philippi, so few that they had no synagogue; yet they maintained their religious usages, and they had a 'place of prayer' which, after the manner of Jewish worship, was situated outside the town by the riverside, that they might have water for the purposes of ceremonial ablution.[5]

[1] *ῥαβδοῦχοι*. Cf. vers. 35, 38.

[2] Liv. XLV. 29. Cf. Wetstein on Acts xvi. 12.

[3] Cf. ver. 12: *ἥτις ἐστὶν πρώτη τῆς μερίδος Μακεδονίας πόλις*, 'which is the chief city of its division of Macedonia'—a touch of local colouring. *πρώτη* is otherwise taken as denoting not the *dignity* but the *situation* of Philippi—the first Macedonian city which the Apostles visited—on the ground that Neapolis was not in Macedonia but in Thrace. The geographical connection of Neapolis, however, varied. It was indeed once in Thrace, but it was now reckoned in Macedonia (cf. Strabo, 330; Ptol. III. xiii. 9). It is true that Pliny (*Nat. Hist.* IV. 18) connects it with Thrace, but he assigns Philippi to Thrace as well.

[4] Cf. p. 9.

[5] Ver. 13: *ἐνομίζομεν προσευχὴν εἶναι*, ℵABC, 'we supposed there was a place of prayer.' *προσευχή* was a general term, and while it might be applied to a synagogue (cf. Jos. *Vit.* 54; Juv. III. 226), it generally denoted a mere meeting-place, sometimes in the open. Cf. Schürer, II. ii. pp. 68 ff. On the ablutionary necessity cf. Jos. *Ant.* XIV. x. 23; *Letter of Aristeas*: *ὡς δὲ ἔθος ἐστὶ πᾶσι τοῖς*

It was probably not a building but a secluded nook on the river-bank. On the Sabbath after their arrival Paul and his companions repaired thither. It was a curious feature of the social life of Macedonia that women were there accorded singular freedom and exercised an exceptional authority;[1] and this no less than the paucity of the Jewish population may be the reason of the remarkable circumstance that, when the missionaries reached the place of prayer, they found a little assemblage of women-folk. They seated themselves and opened a conversation. Paul bore the principal part, and at the very outset he won a notable

Lydia.

convert. Her name was Lydia; and though it was a common name in those days,[2] it had probably in her case a local reference. For she was not a Philippian. She belonged to the city of Thyatira, a Macedonian colony in the ancient country of Lydia, then included in the Province of Asia.[3] Thyatira was a seat of the celebrated Lydian industry of purple-dyeing,[4] and Lydia was prosperously engaged at Philippi in the sale of purple fabrics. She was not a Jewess but 'a God-fearer,'[5] and she had doubtless learned the Jewish faith in her native country, where there was a considerable Jewish population.[6] It is plain that she was well-to-do, since she had a commodious residence; moreover, she had a family, and, since she was absolute mistress, she was presumably a widow.

Cf. ver. 15.

Her conversion.

Being a God-fearer, Lydia was a seeker after the truth. She had recognised the insufficiency of paganism, and had found a measure of contentment in Judaism's pure and lofty monotheism; but its ceremonial was distasteful to her, and her heart remained unsatisfied. The Gospel appealed to her need, and she listened day by day with ever fuller conviction, until at length she professed her faith[7] and she and her family were admitted to the fellow-

Ἰουδαίοις, ἀπονιψάμενοι τῇ θαλάσσῃ τὰς χεῖρας, ὡς ἂν ηὔξαντο πρὸς τὸν Θεόν, ἐτρέποντο πρὸς τὴν ἀνάγνωσιν.

[1] Cf. p. 136, n. 5.

[2] Hor. *Od.* I. viii. I.

[3] Strabo, 625.

[4] Plin. *Nat. Hist.* VII. 57.

[5] Cf. p. 13.

[6] Cf. Jos. *Ant.* XII. iii. 4.

[7] Her conversion did not occur immediately on the first Sabbath. The imperfs. ἐλαλοῦμεν and ἤκουεν imply repeated conversations and audiences.

ship of the Church and received the sacramental seal of Baptism.[1]

Lydia was Europe's first convert, and she was richly endowed with the Christian graces. At the very outset she exhibited that generous kindness which distinguished the Philippian Church and won for it, some ten years later, the Apostle's grateful praise. No sooner had she been baptised than she invited Paul and his three companions to make her house their abode during their sojourn in the town. And she couched her invitation in terms of exquisite delicacy, representing their acceptance of it as a personal favour, an attestation of their confidence in the sincerity of her faith and her worthiness of the Holy Sacrament which had just been administered to her. 'If,' she pleaded, 'you have judged that I am faithful to the Lord, come into my house and stay.' And when they demurred, she would take no denial. 'She constrained us,' says Luke, employing the self-same word wherewith he describes the hospitable importunities of the two disciples at Emmaus when the Stranger who had joined them by the way 'made as though He would go further,' and 'they *constrained* Him, saying, "Stay with us; for it is toward evening, and the day is now far spent."'[2]

Her hospitality.

Cf. Phil. iv. 15.

Cf. Lk. xxiv. 29.

Lydia's house was thenceforward the abode of the missionaries and the meeting-place of their converts. Her conversion was the first-fruits of a successful ministry which extended beyond the narrow limits of the Jewish community and moved the whole city. The lack of a synagogue with its jealous rulers proved thus far advantageous, that there was no outbreak of Jewish hostility, and the Apostles continued to resort to the place of prayer and there discoursed to the townsfolk who followed them to hear the Word. The days passed prosperously and peacefully, and it can hardly have been earlier than the close of the year when an incident befell which interrupted their activities and brought their Philippian sojourn to an abrupt termination.

A successful ministry.

Cf. ver. 40.

Cf. ver. 21.

The pagan mind was tolerant of new ideas and hospitable to alien religions, and the Apostles encountered in Gentile

A crazed slave-girl, a fortune-teller.

[1] Cf. Append. VI.

[2] These are the only instances of παραβιάζεσθαι in the New Testament.

communities nothing of that fierce resentment which their doctrinal innovations excited in Jewish breasts. Nevertheless the Gospel was an offence to the Gentiles no less than to the Jews, and whenever it touched their worldly interests, they were up in arms. So it happened at Philippi. It chanced one day that the missionaries were passing through the town on their way to the place of prayer when they encountered an unhappy creature—a slave-girl belonging to a company of charlatans[1] who employed her in fortune-telling and traded with her on the credulity of the populace. She was a ventriloquist, and in those days that faculty was regarded as a form of possession: the inhabiting spirit, it was supposed, spoke through the adept, using his lips and voice as its instruments.[2] The girl was also insane, and this only confirmed the popular faith in her declarations, since in the East a peculiar reverence attaches to a *hamako*, 'whom Heaven hath deprived of ordinary reason, in order to endow him with the spirit of prophecy.'

Healed by Paul.

Like every one else in Philippi, the poor girl had heard the fame of the missionaries and apparently she had listened to their preaching and caught some of their phrases; and when she spied them, she reverentially approached and followed in their train, crying aloud: 'These men are slaves of the Most High God. They proclaim to you "the way of salvation,"' as though they were exalted visitants and she their herald announcing their advent and mission.[3] The

[1] 'There might be several masters of a single slave, *e.g.* two brothers' (Blass).

[2] A ventriloquist (ἐγγαστρίμυθος) was dominated 'a Eurykles' after a celebrated ventriloquist of that name (cf. Aristoph. *Vesp.* 1019), and also, as here, 'a Python' (ℵABC*D* παιδίσκην τινὰ ἔχουσαν πνεῦμα Πύθωνα, 'a certain damsel having a spirit, a Python,' where Πύθωνα is in apposition to παιδίσκην). Python is probably derived from Pytho, the oracle of the Pythian Apollo at Delphi. Cf. Plut. *De Defact. Orac.* 414 E: εὔηθες γάρ ἐστι καὶ παιδικὸν κομιδῇ τὸ οἴεσθαι τὸν Θεὸν αὐτὸν ὥσπερ τοὺς ἐγγαστριμύθους, Εὐρυκλέας πάλαι νυνὶ δὲ Πύθωνας προσαγορευομένους, ἐνδυόμενον εἰς τὰ σώματα τῶν προφητῶν ὑποφθέγγεσθαι, τοῖς ἐκείνων στόμασι καὶ φωναῖς χρώμενον ὀργάνοις.

[3] The MSS. (ver. 16) vary between ὑπαντῆσαι (ℵBCE) and ἀπαντῆσαι (ADHLP). Both verbs, with their nouns ὑπάντησις and ἀπάντησις, are used of the public ovation on the arrival of a distinguished personage. Cf. *Teb. Pap.* 43 (of a magistrate's arrival): παρεγενήθημεν εἰς ἀπάντησιν. 1 Th. iv. 17; Mt. xxv. 6; Ac. xxviii. 15; Mt. viii. 34; Jo. xii. 13; Lk. xvii. 12; Mt. viii. 28; Jo. iv. 51, xi. 20, xii. 18. The only other instance of κατακολουθεῖν in the New Testament is Lk. xxiii. 55—a significant parallel.

contretemps recurred daily until it became intolerable, and Paul, sharing the prevalent idea,[1] turned and, in the Lord's name, bade the spirit depart from the girl. Instantly her frenzy ceased, and she was restored to sanity.

Arraignment of the Apostles by her masters.

It was a merciful work, yet it was ill received, especially by the girl's owners. She was useless now for fortune-telling, and their lucrative traffic was destroyed. They seized Paul and Silas and dragged them to the market-place where the law-court was situated,[2] and there arraigned them before the magistrates. They were cunning rascals, and they proceeded cleverly. Their real grievance was the loss of their profits, but that would never have been entertained. And so they gave the case a political colour, and indicted the Apostles as disturbers of the peace: they were Jews, and they were engaging in a Jewish propaganda in contravention of Roman law. And the rabble which had trooped into the court loudly applauded.

Their summary condemnation.

It was a dexterous indictment, and it powerfully appealed to the Philippian magistrates. Infringement of Roman institutions would in any case have been a serious offence in the eyes of those petty magnates with their pompous pretensions to imperial dignity;[3] and it happened that just then the Jews were in particularly evil odour and had been expelled by the Emperor Claudius from the capital.[4] Cf. Ac. xviii. 2. Therefore, when a couple of itinerant Jews were brought before them on such a charge, the prætors made short work with them. Investigation was needless, and they pronounced instant sentence. They ordered their lictors to remove the culprits and strip and scourge them: SUMMOVETE, LICTORES, DESPOLIATE, VERBERATE.[5]

[1] Cf. *The Days of His Flesh*, pp. 105 ff.

[2] At Athens several law-courts were situated in the market-place. Cf. Antiphon (Jebb's *Selections from the Attic Orators*, 7. § 10): ἐνταυθοῖ πεποιήκασι τὴν κρίσιν ἐν τῇ ἀγορᾷ. Lys. *De bon. Aristoph.* § 55: ἐγγὺς οἰκῶν τῆς ἀγορᾶς οὔτε πρὸς δικαστηρίῳ οὔτε πρὸς βουλευτηρίῳ ὤφθην οὐδεπώποτε.

[3] Cf. Horace's ridicule of the prætor at Fundi (*Sat.* I. v. 34-36).

[4] Cf. Suet. *Claud.* 25. Dion Cass. lx. 6. Orosius (VII. vi. 15) assigns the edict of banishment to the ninth year of Claudius, *i.e.* 49; but since he antedates the Claudian history by a year (cf. p. 646), the date is 50, the very year which was just closing when the Apostles were arrested.

[5] Cf. Sen. *Controv.* xxv. περιρήξαντες αὐτῶν τὰ ἱμάτια, not 'rent their own garments' in token of horror—a Jewish fashion (cf. p. 102), but 'tore off the

Scourged, though Roman citizens.

It was, though they did not know it, a grave outrage. Paul and Silas were both Roman citizens, and a Roman citizen's person was sacrosanct. It was illegal, indeed it was accounted nothing less than *lèse-majesté,* to scourge him; and thus, when they subjected the Apostles to the lictors' rods, the prætors were perpetrating a flagrant violation of the Roman law which they were so zealous in vindicating. The outrage was executed in full severity; and it may seem strange that Paul should have submitted to it on this and two other unrecorded occasions. The remedy was easy. He had merely to inform the lictors that he was a Roman citizen, and they durst proceed no further. So he did at Jerusalem some seven years later when he was bound to the whipping-post by the order of Claudius Lysias, the military commander; and his protest was instantly effective. And no doubt a like protest would be made by both the prisoners in this instance, but they had to deal at Philippi with another sort of men than Lysias and his centurion. Even if it were heard amid the clamour of the rabble, their claim would be laughed to scorn by the stupid and insolent minions; and thereafter they would hold their peace, disdaining entreaty, unlike Verres' victim in the forum of Messana, who kept shrieking above the hiss of the lash *Civis Romanus sum.*[1]

Cf. 2 Cor. xi. 25.

Cf. Ac. xxii. 24-29.

Their imprisonment.

After enduring the cruel ignominy they were conveyed, faint and bleeding, to prison. The gaoler was ordered to confine them closely, and he placed them in the innermost cell of the dungeon underground, and not merely secured them by fetters chained to the wall but put their feet in the stocks.[2] When night fell, the smarting of their wounds and the uneasiness of their posture held them sleepless, and they kept a holy vigil. At midnight they were singing a hymn,

Cf ver. 34.

prisoners' garments,' *i.e.* ordered them to be stripped for scourging. Cf. Wetstein's array of illustrative passages.

[1] Cic. *In Verr.* v. 62.

[2] *τὸ ξύλον*, *nervus*, termed also *ποδοκάκη* and *ποδοστράβη*, was a wooden frame with five apertures for feet and hands and neck (cf. schol. on Aristoph. *Equit.* 1046). Generally, however, only the feet were secured. Cf. Plut. *De Gen. Socr.* 598 B: *οἱ δὲ τοὺς πόδας ἐν τῷ ξύλῳ δεδεμένοι τὰς χεῖρας ὀρέγοντες ἐβόων δεόμενοι μὴ ἀπολειφθῆναι.* Luc. *Tox.* 29: *οὐδὲ ἀποτείνειν τὰ σκέλη δυνάμενοι ἐν τῷ ξύλῳ κατακεκλεισμένα.*

and the prisoners in the neighbouring cells were listening wonderingly to the unaccustomed sound, when suddenly—a rumble and a crash! It was an earthquake—no infrequent occurrence in that region, but none the less an interposition of God, a stroke of His delivering hand; and as the prison rocked on its foundations, the doors burst open and the chains dropped from the gaping masonry. The gaoler, asleep in his house overhead, was rudely awakened; and on rushing down and finding the cell-doors open, he naturally concluded that the inmates had fled. And indeed they would presently have seized the opportunity, but meanwhile they were huddling terror-stricken in their cells. Their escape would have involved dire consequences for the gaoler, since by the Roman law a warder was responsible for his charge, and in case of his disappearance must take his place and suffer his penalty.[1] The prospect appalled him, and like a true Roman, preferring death to disgrace, he was about to plunge his sword into his breast when his hand was stayed. Paul had heard his exclamation of despair, and he shouted: 'Do yourself no harm; for we are all here.'

An earthquake at midnight.

It was good news for the gaoler, and he called for lights that he might verify it. The pause afforded him leisure for reflection. The doings of the missionaries were common knowledge in Philippi, and doubtless he had listened to their preaching. He had been impressed by their message of salvation, and had been pondering over it; and the happenings of that night of terror brought him to decision. When the lights arrived, he first of all had the other prisoners secured;[2] and then he bounded into the Apostles' cell and after a reverent greeting he conducted them out to the vestibule and there addressed to them the question which had long been stirring in his anxious breast: 'Sirs, what must I do to be saved?' They told him that the way was faith in the Lord Jesus; and there in the dimly lighted vestibule they discoursed of the Saviour to the gaoler and his assembled household—his officers and his wife and

Conversion of the gaoler and his household.

[1] Cf. Wetstein.

[2] In ver. 30 Cod. Bez. (D) has *καὶ προήγαγεν αὐτοὺς ἔξω τοὺς λοιποὺς ἀσφαλισάμενος καὶ εἶπεν αὐτοῖς*, 'and brought them forth after securing the rest, and said to them.'

children.[1] Every heart was won; and only then were earthly concernments remembered. He washed the wounds of the Apostles, and they baptised him and his household. They were still his prisoners, and he must detain them at the pleasure of the magistrates; but he would not recommit them to their cell. He brought them upstairs to his house and entertained them there. They had tasted nothing since their arrest, and, late as it was, a meal was spread before them, and the gladness of the converted household made it a very festival.

Alarm of the magistrates.

Meanwhile the magistrates were ill at ease. They could hardly review their high-handed procedure without compunction; and the earthquake, breaking their restless slumbers, smote them with superstitious alarms.[2] Was it, they asked themselves, a wrathful visitation of the god whom those two Jews had proclaimed? The Roman law-courts opened at the early hour of 8 A.M.;[3] and when the panic-stricken magistrates met, they hastily agreed to repair the wrong. They despatched their lictors to the prison with an order for their release.

Their apology to the prisoners.

The gaoler received the mandate, and joyfully informed them that they were at liberty to take their departure; but Paul scornfully declined. He was minded to teach the magistrates a lesson and ensure his converts in Philippi against future molestation. 'They scourged us publicly,' said he, 'without a trial, Romans though we are, and cast us into prison; and are they now for casting us out privily? No indeed; let them come in person and bring us out.' The gaoler repeated his answer to the lictors, and they reported it to the magistrates. It increased their alarm. It was the first intimation they had that the men they had abused were Roman citizens, and they realised the gravity of their position. They hastened to the prison and humbled themselves before the missionaries. They

[1] In ver. 33 several lesser authorities have *οἱ υἱοὶ αὐτοῦ*, 'his children.'

[2] In ver. 35 Cod. Bez. (D) and Syr. Vers. read *συνῆλθον οἱ στρατηγοὶ ἐπὶ τὸ αὐτὸ εἰς τὴν ἀγορὰν καὶ ἀναμνησθέντες τὸν σεισμὸν τὸν γεγονότα ἐφοβήθησαν καὶ ἀπέστειλαν τοὺς ῥαβδούχους*, 'the prætors assembled in the forum, and in remembrance of the earthquake which had happened were affrighted, and commissioned the lictors.'

[3] Cf. *The Days of His Flesh*, p. 477.

brought them out and, representing to them the risk they ran of fresh annoyance from their prosecutors and the rabble, besought them to quit the city.[1] Their profession of solicitude on this score was a feeble attempt to shift the blame from themselves, and their actual concern was to be rid of the troublesome affair.

Departure from Philippi.

The Apostles were content with their vindication. They betook themselves to the house of Lydia, and there met with their converts and bade them farewell. Paul and Silas and Timothy then took their departure, but they left Luke behind. He remained at Philippi, and laboured there until the spring of 57, when he rejoined Paul on his way to Jerusalem at the close of his third mission, never more to leave him until his ministry ended with his martyrdom at Rome.[2]

Thessalonica.

The missionaries proceeded westward by the Egnatian Road. They passed through the towns of Amphipolis, an Athenian colony on the Strymon, thirty-three miles from Philippi,[3] and Apollonia Mygdoniæ, near the eastern extremity of Lake Bolbe and thirty miles distant from Amphipolis;[4] but they stayed at neither, and the reason was that there was no considerable Jewish population in either and consequently no synagogue,[5] and where there was no synagogue it was difficult to win a hearing for the Gospel. And so they held on to Thessalonica (*Salonika*), which was

[1] In ver. 39 Cod. Bez. (D) has *καὶ παραγενόμενοι μετὰ φίλων πολλῶν εἰς τὴν φυλακήν, παρεκάλεσαν αὐτοὺς ἐξελθεῖν εἰπόντες· ἠγνοήσαμεν τὰ καθ' ὑμᾶς ὅτι ἐστὲ ἄνδρες δίκαιοι. καὶ ἐξαγαγόντες παρεκάλεσαν αὐτοὺς λέγοντες· ἐκ τῆς πόλεως ταύτης ἐξέλθατε μήποτε πάλιν συνστραφῶσιν ἡμῖν ἐπικράζοντες καθ' ὑμῶν*, 'and they came with many friends to the prison and besought them to go out, saying, "We were ignorant of your case, that you are righteous men." And they brought them out and besought them, saying, "Go out from this city, lest they again gather about us, clamouring against you."'

[2] The first-personal narration (cf. xvi. 17) is here interrupted and resumed at xx. 5.

[3] Originally *Ἐννέα Ὁδοί* or 'Nine Ways'; renamed Amphipolis by the Athenian colonists because it was almost encircled by a winding of the river, *ἐπ' ἀμφότερα περιρρέοντος τοῦ Στρυμόνος* (Thuc. I. 100; IV. 102).

[4] Ptolem. *Geogr.* III. iii. 33; Plin. *Nat. Hist.* IV. 17.

[5] The reason why they settled at Thessalonica was *ὅπου ἦν συναγωγὴ τῶν Ἰουδαίων*, which (since *ὅπου* differs from *οὗ* as *ὅστις*, *quippe qui*, from *ὅς*) signifies 'since there was a synagogue of the Jews there,' implying that there was none at Amphipolis or Apollonia.

not only the capital of the second of the Roman districts but the chief city of all Macedonia alike in population and in prestige.[1] It occupied the site of the ancient Therma, whence the Thermaic Gulf, at the head of which the city stood, derived its name;[2] and it was founded about 315 B.C. by Cassander, who merged the neighbouring townships in it and named it after his wife Thessalonica, the half-sister of Alexander the Great.[3] It was a free city, a self-governing democracy;[4] and its magistrates were designated Politarchs.[5] The distance between Philippi and Thessalonica was a hundred miles, and if the missionaries travelled afoot, the journey, at the customary rate, would occupy five or six days.[6]

Ministry in the synagogue.

There was a large and influential community of Jews in Thessalonica, and their activity is indicated by the number of 'God-fearers' who frequented their synagogue. The missionaries found a lodging in the house of a Jew who bore the name of Jason, the Hellenistic substitute for Jesus or Joshua;[7] and Paul started his ministry after his wont by visiting the synagogue and demonstrating from the Scriptures that the Messiah was to suffer and rise from the dead, and that their prophecies had been fulfilled in Jesus. And he added urgency to his appeal by proclaiming the Lord's Second Advent and the Final Judgment—a consummation

Cf. 1 Th. i. 9, 10; 2 Th. ii. 5.

[1] Strabo, 323; Luc. *Asin.* 46.

[2] Herod. VII. 121.

[3] Strabo, 330.

[4] Plin. *Nat. Hist.* IV. 17. Cf. Ac. xvii. 5: αὐτοὺς προαγαγεῖν εἰς τὸν δῆμον.

[5] Cf. Ac. xvii. 6, 8. Boeckh, *Corp. Inscript.* 1967 (a Thessalonian inscription): πολιταρχούντων Σωπάτρου τοῦ Κλεοπάτρας καὶ Δουκίου Ποντίου Σεκούνδου Πουβλίου Φλαυίου Σαβείνου Δημητρίου τοῦ Φαύστου Δημητρίου τοῦ Νικοπόλεως Σωίλου τοῦ Παρμενιῶνος τοῦ καὶ Μενίσκου Γαίου Ἀγιλληίου Ποτείτου· ταμίου τῆς πόλεως Ταύρου τοῦ Ἀμμίας τοῦ καὶ Ῥήγλου. The metronymics here illustrate the independent status of Macedonian women (cf. p. 128). It is noteworthy that several of the names of the inscription were borne by Thessalonian converts—Secundus (cf. Ac. xx. 4), Demetrius in its shortened form of Demas (cf. Col. iv. 14; Phm. 24; 2 Tim. iv. 10), Gaius (cf. Ac. xix. 29). The title 'politarch' was not peculiar to Thessalonica, since it occurs in an Egyptian papyrus. Cf. *Oxyrh. Pap.* 745.

[6] The supposition that Amphipolis and Apollonia were the stations where they halted overnight, implies that they indulged in the expensive luxury of carriage and thus accomplished the journey in three stages of over thirty miles each.

[7] Cf. p. 21. Jos. *Ant.* xii. v. 1: ὁ μὲν οὖν Ἰησοῦς Ἰάσωνα ἑαυτὸν μετωνόμασεν.

which, in common with the rest of the primitive Christians, he regarded as imminent.[1] For three weeks[2] he continued his argumentation, and he achieved no small success. Some of the Jews were won, including Aristarchus who afterwards proved so true and helpful a comrade to him, and also his host Jason, if indeed he be identical with the Jason who was with him at Corinth some five or six years later; but most of the converts belonged to the order of 'the God-fearers,' and it accords with the independence which women enjoyed in Macedonian society, that not a few of these were ladies, the wives of leading citizens.[3]

Cf. Ac. xxvii. 2; Col. iv. 10, 11. Rom. xvi. 21.

Jewish hostility.

This success enkindled Jewish resentment, and after the three weeks' reasoning in the synagogue the missionaries found its doors closed against them and betook themselves with the converts they had won to an active ministry among the Gentile population.[4] This must have continued for a considerable time, since ere they left the city they had established an organised congregation; and during its course they endured no small hardship. It was necessary, at all events until the Church was organised, that they should earn their daily bread. More than once indeed they received welcome supplies from their friends at Philippi, but these were insufficient, and Paul resorted to his craft of tent-making, toiling far into the night that he might be free for his ministry during the day.

Cf. 1 Th. v. 12, 13.

Cf. Phil. iv. 15, 16.

Cf. 1 Th. ii. 9.

A cry of treason.

The Jews meanwhile were observing the progress of the Gospel with jealous eyes; and, exasperated by its success, they had recourse to ignoble tactics. The market-place of the city was the haunt of a gang of loafers and rascals who

[1] Cf. p. 153.

[2] *σάββατα τρία*, either 'three Sabbaths' or 'three weeks' (cf. Lk. xviii. 2). In the latter case Paul attended the weekday as well as the Sabbath assemblies (cf. p. 94, n. 3).

[3] *γυναικῶν τε τῶν πρώτων*, not 'of the chief women,' which would be *τῶν τε γυναικῶν τῶν πρώτων*, but 'of the wives of the chief men.' So Cod. Bez. (D): *καὶ γυναῖκες τῶν πρώτων*.

[4] A distinct Gentile ministry is implied by the reading of Cod. Bez. (D) in ver. 4: *καί τινες ἐξ αὐτῶν ἐπείσθησαν. καὶ προσεκληρώθησαν τῷ Παύλῳ καὶ Σίλᾳ (τῇ διδαχῇ) πολλοὶ τῶν σεβομένων καὶ Ἑλλήνων πλῆθος πολὺ καὶ γυναῖκες τῶν πρώτων οὐκ ὀλίγαι*, 'And some of them were persuaded. And there cast in their lot with Paul and Silas many of the Worshippers and a great multitude of Gentiles and wives of the chief men not a few.'

lounged about ready for any mischief;[1] and the Jewish traders got hold of them and incited them against the missionaries, playing upon their political prejudices, telling them what had happened at Philippi, and representing the Gospel as a treasonable propaganda. It was the Apostle's preaching of the Second Advent that specially served their turn; and they construed it as a prediction of the imminent overthrow of the Roman Empire and the enthronement of Jesus. This is the first appearance of a perversion which persisted for generations and brought no small trouble on the Church. It is told that during the reign of Domitian (A.D. 81-96), in view of the Messianic dreams of the Jews, an imperial edict was issued, ordering the execution of the descendants of King David. Information was laid against several peaceable Jewish husbandmen who were honoured as grandsons of Judas the Lord's brother, and they were cited before the Emperor. He was alarmed, like Herod the Great, when he heard of the birth of the King of the Jews, and he examined those supposed aspirants to his throne. On learning what humble folk they were and what the Kingdom of the Christ really was—'not a worldly or earthly kingdom but a heavenly and angelic, which would come into being at the consummation of the age when He should come in glory to judge living and dead,' he recognised the baselessness of his apprehension, and dismissed them and revoked the edict.[2]

Securities for good behaviour.

It was thus a dangerous cry that the Jews of Thessalonica

[1] *τῶν ἀγοραίων ἄνδρας τινὰς πονηρούς*, 'certain evil men of the *habitués* of the market-place,' 'the hangman boys in the market-place' (Shak. *Two Gentlemen of Verona*, IV. iv. 60). *ἀγοραῖος* is defined by Theophrastus in his sketch of 'The Reckless Man,' *ὁ ἀπονενοημένος*, *Char.* XVI. (VI.), as *τῷ ἤθει ἀγοραῖός τις καὶ ἀνασεσυρμένος καὶ παντοποιός*, 'in character a coarse fellow, defiant of decency, ready to do anything' (Jebb); and then further on: *καὶ οὐκ ἀποδοκιμάζειν δὲ οὐδ' ἅμα πολλῶν ἀγοραίων στρατηγεῖν*, 'he does not disdain to be leader of a gang of *ἀγοραῖοι*'—an allusion to the turbulence of the hangers-on of the market-place. Cf. Plut. *Æmil. Paul.* 38. 3: *ἀνθρώπους ἀγεννεῖς καὶ δεδουλευκότας, ἀγοραίους δὲ καὶ δυναμένους ὄχλον συναγαγεῖν καὶ σπουδαρχίᾳ καὶ κραυγῇ πάντα πράγματα βιάσασθαι.* The Latin term is *forensis*. Cf. Hor. *A. P.* 245. Suidas defines *ἀγοραῖος νοῦς* as *ὁ πανευτελὴς καὶ συρφετώδης καὶ ἀπόρρητος οὐδὲ πεφροντισμένος*. Cf. Plat. *Protag.* 347 E: *τοῖς συμποσίοις τοῖς τῶν φαύλων καὶ ἀγοραίων ἀνθρώπων*, contrasted presently with *καλοὶ κἀγαθοὶ συμπόται καὶ πεπαιδευμένοι*.

[2] Hegesippus in Eus. *Eccl. Hist.* III. 20. Cf. Just. M. *Apol.* II. pp. 58 f. (ed. Sylburg.).

raised, and their rascals took it up and presently had the city in an uproar. The rabble beset the house of Jason, intending to seize the missionaries and deal with them after the lawless fashion of 'a free democracy.' Happily their victims were abroad, but they got hold of Jason and several other Christians, and dragged them before the Politarchs, vociferating their charge of treason. It was an ugly charge, and no Roman magistrate durst treat it lightly. The Politarchs doubtless knew something of the Gospel from those ladies of their circle who had embraced it. At all events they were plainly well-disposed toward the missionaries and rated the charge at its proper worth. They durst not set it aside, but they adopted the mildest possible course and exacted security from Jason and his fellow-victims for the good behaviour of themselves and the accused.[1]

Departure from Thessalonica.

It was a shrewd settlement. It inflicted no injury on the missionaries or their sureties, and at the same time it satisfied the accusers and safeguarded the Politarchs from the suspicion of misprision of treason. It would indeed disappoint the Jews that their troublers had come off so lightly; yet they were thus far gratified that their annoyance was ended. It was impossible for the missionaries to remain in the city and expose Jason and his fellow-sponsors to the penalty which they would incur in the certain event of a fresh outbreak of Jewish animosity. They must forthwith take their departure, and their converts readily acquiesced. They waited only until nightfall, and under covert of darkness, that they might escape observation and molestation, they quitted Thessalonica.

At Berœa.

It was about the beginning of the year 51 when they arrived at Thessalonica, and, in view of all that had transpired, it would be about the month of May when they took their departure. Diverging from the Egnatian Road, they travelled some forty miles westward to Berœa, an important and populous town at the base of Mount Bermius.[2] Immediately

[1] λαβόντες τὸ ἱκανόν, *satisdatione accepta*, a Latin phrase. Cf. Mk. xv. 15. Chrysostom (*In I Epist. ad Thess.* 1) supposes that Jason and the others were pledged for the appearance of the Apostles to stand their trial; but in that case the latter would not have stolen away and left their friends to suffer in their stead.

[2] Strabo, 330; Luc. *Asin.* 34.

on their arrival they repaired on the Sabbath Day to the synagogue, and their experience there was a pleasing surprise. Whatever the reason, the Jews of Berœa exhibited a singular reasonableness.[1] They listened to Paul's demonstration of the Messiahship of Jesus, and so deeply were they impressed that they daily examined the Scriptures in order to verify his contention. Their study carried conviction to their minds, and many of them professed faith. Here as at Thessalonica not a few ladies of rank were numbered among 'the God-fearers,' and not only did they join the ranks of the converts themselves but they brought their husbands with them.[2] It was a gracious and unique experience. The Jews were keenly interested in the Gospel, and diligently investigated its scriptural evidence; and even where conviction was lacking, there was no hostility, and the missionaries continued in the fellowship of the synagogue.

Reasonableness of the Jews.

It was a peaceful and prosperous ministry, and it must have lasted some time, probably two or three months at the least. Suddenly, however, it was rudely interrupted. Tidings of the missionaries' doings reached Thessalonica and roused the indignation of the Jews there. They hastened to Berœa and repeated the tactics which had proved so successful in their own city, raising the cry of treason and exciting the fury of the mob. Paul was the special object of their resentment, and it would have gone hardly with him had he been arraigned a second time on that perilous charge. His one chance lay in immediate flight; but he was narrowly watched, and it was only by a ruse that he effected his escape. His friends supplied him with an escort, and sent him away from the city in the direction of the coast as though he intended taking ship at Methone or Pydna. His enemies would observe his movement, and they could easily have overtaken him and arrested him ere he set sail; but, once clear of the city, his guides turned southward and conducted him overland through Thessaly until they brought him to Athens.[3] There he was secure from molestation, and

Enemies from Thessalonica.

Paul's escape to Athens.

[1] Chrysostom explains εὐγενέστεροι as ἐπιεικέστεροι, 'more sweetly reasonable.'

[2] ἀνδρῶν, not merely 'men' but, after the analogy of ver. 4, 'husbands.'

[3] According to the reading ἕως ἐπὶ τὴν θάλασσαν (ℵABE), *usque ad mare*, 'as far as the sea,' there was no stratagem: they actually took ship and sailed to

they left him and returned home. His destination had been unknown when he fled from Berœa, but his guides carried a message to Silas and Timothy, informing them where he was and bidding them join him with all speed.

V

SOJOURN AT ATHENS

1 Thes. ii. 17-iii. 5; Ac. xvii. 16-34; 1 Cor. i. 16, xvi. 15.

Persecution in Macedonia.

Paul had been driven from Macedonia, but he still regarded that country as his appointed sphere. He had been providentially summoned thither, and his labours had proved abundantly successful. Much remained to be accomplished, and his hope was that, when Silas and Timothy arrived, they might report that the storm had blown over and he was free to return and resume his interrupted ministry. In due course they appeared, but they brought disappointing tidings. The animosity of those Thessalonian Jews who had pursued him to Berœa, was unabated; indeed it had rather increased. They had returned to their own city, and they were harassing his converts there, rivalling the malignity of their Judæan *confrères* in the days of the first persecution which had begun with the martyrdom of Stephen and which, as he would recall with crimson shame, he had himself inspired and directed. (Cf. 1 Th. ii. 14-16.)

Return of Silas and Timothy to Macedonia.

It was impossible for him meanwhile to return, since his appearance in Macedonia would have exasperated his enemies and aggravated the distress of his friends. But his heart was anxious for the latter. They were beset by ruthless and unscrupulous adversaries, bent on detaching

Athens. But most probably ἕως is an assimilation to ἕως Ἀθηνῶν in the following verse, and the true reading is ὡς ἐπὶ τὴν θάλασσαν (HLP), 'to go ostensibly to the sea' (cf. Moulton's Winer, p. 771). (1) ἤγαγον ἕως Ἀθηνῶν, 'they led him as far as Athens,' suggests not a sea-voyage but an overland journey. (2) In ver. 15 Cod. Bez. (D) after ἕως Ἀθηνῶν has παρῆλθεν (cf. xvi. 8) δὲ τὴν Θεσσαλίαν· ἐκωλύθη γὰρ εἰς αὐτοὺς κηρύξαι τὸν λόγον, 'and he passed over Thessaly; for he was hindered from preaching the Word among them,' *i.e.*, he hurried through the country without staying to preach at any of the towns *en route*, as Larissa and Pharsalus. So Beza, Grotius, Bengel, Neander.

them from the Faith either by terrorism or by cajolery; and his sympathy was accentuated by the dread of seeing his work undone. He could not abandon them to their fate without an effort to save them; and he and Silas decided that, loath as they were to part with him, Timothy should repair to Thessalonica in order to encourage the persecuted Christians and hold them steadfast in the face alike of threats and of blandishments. It was a heavy charge for a mere lad, and Silas would more fittingly have undertaken it; but it would have been impolitic for him to appear at Thessalonica, since he had borne a leading part in the mission and was hardly less obnoxious to the persecutors than Paul. So they despatched Timothy, whether overland through Thessaly or by a coasting vessel. Meanwhile indeed the trouble had its seat at Thessalonica, but it was likely to spread; and presently Silas also took his departure for Macedonia. His destination is not expressly stated, but it can hardly have been other than Philippi; and this probability is confirmed by the speedy arrival from the ever generous Philippians of a welcome contribution to Paul's necessities.[1]

Cf. Phil. iv. 15.

Paul alone at Athens.

Thus the Apostle was left alone at Athens. He had no thought of preaching there, since Macedonia was his field and he was waiting anxiously for his recall thither. It proved, however, that the seeming interruption of his purpose was in truth a providential dispensation, the constraint of an unseen Hand conducting him to a larger ministry. Athens, pre-eminent in literature, art, and philosophy, was pre-eminent also in religion.[2] She rivalled Rome in her hospitality to alien cults.[3] The beautiful city was crowded with temples, shrines, altars, and images, which met the Apostle's eye at every turn as he strayed in street and market-place yearning wistfully for Macedonia. His soul was stirred. He was touched by the pity of it all, and one spectacle especially moved him—an altar bearing the in-

The hungry heart of heathendom.

[1] Cf. Append. I.

[2] Cf. Soph. *Œd. Col.* 260: *εἰ τάς γ' Ἀθήνας φασὶ θεοσεβεστάτας / εἶναι.* Lycurg. *adv. Leocrat.*: *εὖ γὰρ ἴστε, ὦ Ἀθηναῖοι, ὅτι πλεῖστον διαφέρετε τῶν ἄλλων ἀνθρώπων τῷ πρός τε τοὺς θεοὺς εὐσεβῶς ἔχειν.*

[3] Strabo, 471: *Ἀθηναῖοι δ' ὥσπερ περὶ τὰ ἄλλα φιλοξενοῦντες διατελοῦσιν, οὕτω καὶ περὶ τοὺς θεούς.* On Roman syncretism cf. p. 12.

scription TO AN UNKNOWN GOD. Such altars were common in the Greek world,[1] but this was the first he had encountered, and it spoke to him of the heathen heart's yearning after the Living and True God. He could not resist the mute appeal. He knew the blessed secret which would satisfy that blind desire, and he must proclaim it.

Reasoning in synagogue and market-place.

Nor was opportunity lacking. There were Jews at Athens, and he visited the synagogue and reasoned with the congregation, which as usual included 'God-fearers.' It was, however, the general need that had stirred his compassion and that he would fain satisfy ; and at Athens there was a peculiar facility in appealing to the populace. It was the historic fashion of the philosophers to discourse in the market-place, and Paul followed their example and conversed with the citizens who daily frequented that intellectual exchange, less intent on business than on the discussion of the latest political or metaphysical question.[2] Cf. Ac. xvii. 21.

Jealousy of the philosophers. Cf. 1 Th. i. 7-9.

A novel doctrine was always welcome, and the Apostle's message excited keen interest, all the more that tidings of the stir which it had occasioned in Macedonia had reached the city. His popularity, however, quickly involved him in embarrassment. The chief schools of philosophy at that period were the Epicurean and the Stoic, and their professors viewed him as an unauthorised invader of their province and, forgetting for the moment their mutual jealousy, made common cause against him. Some of them sneered at him and affected to regard him as an unintelligible quack. 'What,' they asked, 'would this charlatan[3] like to make

[1] Cf. p. 11.

[2] This disposition was the bane of Athens. Cf. Demosth. *Phil.* I. 10.

[3] σπερμολόγος, 'seed-picker,' was properly a little bird which picked up the seed as it fell from the hand of the sower (cf. Mt. xiii. 4), and it had two metaphorical uses : (1) a thief who lived by what he could pick up, like Shakespeare's Autolycus, 'a snapper-up of unconsidered trifles' (*Winter's Tale*, IV. iii. 26) ; so a worthless rascal ; (2) an intellectual charlatan whose learning was second-hand and undigested ; cf. Browning, *An Epistle* : 'Karshish, the picker-up of learning's crumbs.' The latter is the meaning here. Cf. Eustath. on Hom. *Od.* v. 490 : οὕτω τέτραπται καὶ τὸ σπερμολογεῖν ἐπὶ τῶν ἀλαζονευομένων ἀμεθόδως ἐπὶ μαθήμασιν ἔκ τινων παρακουσμάτων. . . . ὁ δὲ κυρίως, φασί, σπερμολόγος καὶ σπερμονόμος εἶδός ἐστιν ὀρνέου λωβώμενον τὰ σπέρματα, ἐξ οὗ 'Αττικοὶ σπερμολόγους ἐκάλουν τοὺς περὶ ἐμπόρια καὶ ἀγορὰς διατρίβοντας διὰ τὸ ἀναλέγεσθαι τὰ ἐκ τῶν φορτίων, φασὶν, ἀπορρέοντα καὶ διαζῆν. ἐκ τούτου τὴν αὐτὴν ἐλάγχανον κλῆσιν καὶ οἱ οὐδενὸς λόγου ἄξιοι.

out?' Others took a more serious view. The burden of the Apostle's discourse had been the Lord's Passion, Resurrection, and Return to judgment; and, philosophers as they were, they grossly misconstrued his language. 'Resurrection' is in Greek *Anastasis*, and they took this for a proper noun. They supposed it was the name of a goddess, and when Paul spoke of 'Jesus and Anastasis,' they fancied that he meant, after the heathen fashion, a couple of deities.[1] 'He seems,' was their conclusion, 'to be a proclaimer of strange divinities.'

Charge of introducing strange divinities.

The Court of the Areiopagos.

And this would have been a grave offence—the very offence which had proved fatal to Socrates, who was arraigned on the charge of 'corrupting the young men and not recognising the gods whom the city recognised, but other novel divinities.'[2] The court which took cognisance of such cases was the Council of the Areiopagos. This ancient and august tribunal, though it existed long ere his time, received its historic constitution from Solon. Its chief function was the investigation and adjudication of cases of homicide, but its jurisdiction extended also to such lesser offences as sacrilege, treason, and conspiracy; and it exercised a censorial supervision of the civic life, reprimanding and punishing immorality, indolence, and prodigality.[3] It regulated the education of the young and controlled the introduction of novel forms of worship;[4] and thus it had jurisdiction in the case of Paul, who was charged with 'proclaiming strange divinities.'

Arraignment of Paul.

The prestige and emolument of the philosophers were menaced, and in their resentment dignity and courtesy alike were forgotten. They accosted him with a sneering affectation of deference and humility. 'Can we,' they inquired

[1] Chrys.: *καὶ γὰρ 'τὴν ἀνάστασιν' θεόν τινα εἶναι ἐνόμιζον, ἅτε εἰωθότες καὶ θηλείας σέβειν.*

[2] Plat. *Apol.* 24 B; Xen. *Mem.* I. i. 1; Diog. Laert. II. 40.

[3] Cf. Demosth. *adv. Aristocr.*; Isid. *Areop.* 149.

[4] *ἐπίθετα* as distinguished from *πάτρια*, the ancient rites of the state. Cf. Suidas under *ἐπιθέτους ἑορτάς*: *ἐλέγετο δὲ παρ' αὐτοῖς καὶ ἄλλα ἐπίθετά τινα, ὅσα μὴ πάτρια ὄντα ἡ ἐξ ἀρείου πάγου βουλὴ ἐδίκαζε.* Just. M. (*Ad Græc. Cohort.*, ed. Sylburg. p. 20 C) quotes a tradition that Plato learned the doctrine of the unity of God from the Jewish Law, but fear of the Areiopagos prevented his mentioning the name of Moses.

'understand what this novel teaching is that you are talking of? They are strange matters that you are introducing to our ears; so we wish to understand what these mean.' And they took hold of him and brought him into the court.

His defence. The seat of the Council was the Areiopagos or Hill of Ares to the west of the Acropolis.[1] Its proceedings were open,[2] and thus, when Paul rose to answer the charge which had been preferred against him, he was confronted not merely by the judges but by a throng of curious spectators. He availed himself of the opportunity, and his defence was really a *concio ad populum*, a commendation of the Gospel to the hungry heart of heathendom.

xvii. 22 'Athenians,' he said, 'at every turn your exceptional
23 religiousness[3] is before my eyes. I was passing through
your city and inspecting your sacred institutions, and I
found among them an altar bearing the inscription TO AN

[1] *ὁ ἄρειος πάγος* meant properly the hill where the court had its seat (cf. Luc. *Anach.* 19), but it was used also to denote the court itself, *ἡ βουλὴ ἡ ἐξ ἀρείου πάγου*, or the judges, *οἱ Ἀρειοπαγῖται* (cf. Alciphr. *Ep.* III. 72: *εἰς αὐτὸν ὁ ἄρειος πάγος ἀποβλέπουσιν*. Cic. *ad Attic. Ep.* I. 14: 'Senatus *ἄρειος πάγος*. Nihil constantius, nihil severius, nihil fortius.' Sen. *De Tranquill. Anim.* 3: 'Ariopagus, religiosissimum judicium'). When it is said that Paul 'stood *ἐν μέσῳ τοῦ ἀρείου πάγου*,' it is meant that he stood, not 'in the midst of the hill' but 'in the midst of the court,' *ἐν μέσῳ τῆς βουλῆς τῆς ἐξ ἀρείου πάγου*.

[2] This is proved by a law prohibiting interruption of the proceedings by laughter or applause.

[3] In classical Greek *δεισιδαίμων* means 'religious.' Cf. Arist. *Pol.* v. 11: A ruler should be conspicuously diligent in his duties toward the gods, since his subjects have less fear of unjust treatment *ἐὰν δεισιδαίμονα νομίζωσιν εἶναι τὸν ἄρχοντα καὶ φροντίζειν τῶν θεῶν*. Xen. *Cyrop.* III. iii. 58. In later Greek it acquired the bad sense of 'superstitious,' already found in Theophr. *Char.* XXVIII (XVI): *ἡ δεισιδαιμονία δόξειεν ἂν εἶναι δειλία πρὸς τὸ δαιμόνιον*. Cf. Plut. *De Superstit.* 1: Ignorance regarding the gods divides at its source into two channels, engendering in the hard soil of refractory natures atheism (*ἀθεότης*) and in the moist soil of softer natures superstition (*δεισιδαιμονία*). Phil. *Quod Deus sit Immut.* 35: As fortitude (*ἀνδρεία*) is the mean between audacity (*θράσος*) and cowardice (*δειλία*), temperance (*σωφροσύνη*) between luxury (*ῥᾳθυμία*) and parsimony (*φειδωλία*), prudence (*φρόνησις*) between craft (*πανουργία*) and folly (*μωρία*), so piety (*εὐσέβεια*) is the mean between superstition (*δεισιδαιμονία*) and impiety (*ἀσέβεια*). Max. Tyr. xx. 6: *ὁ μὲν εὐσέβης φίλος θεῷ, ὁ δὲ δεισιδαίμων κόλαξ θεοῦ*. The term, however, still retained a neutral sense (cf. Moulton and Milligan, *Vocab.*); and so it is employed here and in xxv. 19—the only N. T. instances. It is inconceivable that the Apostle should have opened his conciliatory speech with an insulting epithet.

UNKNOWN GOD. What, then, you are worshipping without
Cf. ver. 18. knowing it, this it is that I am "proclaiming" to you.
24 'The God who made the world and everything that is in
it, He is Lord of heaven and earth; and He does not dwell
25 in sanctuaries which hands have made, nor is He ministered
to by human hands "as though He needed anything,"[1] since
it is He who gives every one life and breath and everything.
26 And He made of one stuff[2] every nation of men to dwell
everywhere on the face of the earth, ordaining fixed seasons
27 and the boundaries wherein they should dwell, that they
might seek God if so be they might grope for Him[3] and
find Him, although He is all the while not far from each one
28 of us. "For it is in Him that we live and move and are," as
indeed some of your poets have said; "for we are indeed
29 His offspring."[4] Since then we are God's offspring, we
ought not to suppose that the Deity is like a thing of gold or
silver[5] or a stone, a carving of man's art and imagination.
30 'Now though God overlooked the times when they knew
no better, His present charge to men is that every one every-
31 where should repent, inasmuch as He has set a day on which
He will soon judge the world in righteousness before the
tribunal of a Man whom He has ordained; and He has given
proof of it to every one by raising Him from the dead.'

Derisive interruption.

Here the Apostle's argument has reached its goal, and he is about to proclaim the Christian message. All that he has hitherto said is a mere paving of the way, and it is indeed a skilful prelude. The charge against him was religious innovation, and he meets it by claiming that, as St. Chrysostom puts it, he was 'introducing nothing strange, nothing novel,' but simply asserting the truth which, on their own confession, his hearers had been blindly groping after. His attitude is at once generous and tactful. He does not, after the Jewish fashion, denounce the pagan religion as an unholy thing; rather, in the spirit of his large-hearted

[1] Paul here quotes the Epicurean doctrine (Lucr. II. 644-51). Cf. the Pythagorean dictum: *ὅστις τιμᾷ τὸν θεὸν ὡς προσδεόμενον, οὗτος λέληθεν οἰόμενος ἑαυτὸν τοῦ θεοῦ εἶναι κρείττονα.* Similarly the Eclectic Demonax excused himself for not sacrificing to Athene, *οὐδὲ γὰρ δεῖσθαι αὐτὴν τῶν παρ' ἐμοῦ θυσιῶν ὑπελάμβανον* (Luc. *Dem.* 11).

[2] *ἐξ ἑνός* ℵAB, 'of one common material' (cf. Gen. ii. 7). No definition is required—*αἵματος* (DEHLP) or *ἀνθρώπου* (Blass). Cf. Heb. ii. 11.

[3] *ψηλαφᾶν*, of a blind man feeling a thing to make out what it was (cf. Æsop. *Fab.* 57, ed. Halm) or groping his way (cf. Dt. xxviii. 29 LXX.).

[4] Cf. p. 24.

[5] ℵAE *χρυσίῳ ἢ ἀργυρίῳ*.

master, the Rabbi Gamaliel,[1] he recognises the germ of truth which it contained. It was a veritable *præparatio evangelica* ; and he seeks to persuade his hearers by appealing not only to the familiar testimonies of their poets, Epimenides and Aratus, but to the distinctive doctrines of the Epicurean and Stoic philosophies—the Epicurean doctrine of the divine remoteness and independence of human ministration and the Stoic doctrine of Providence.[2] Just as in the synagogue of Pisidian Antioch he had sought to conciliate the Jews by an historical review, proving that the Gospel was the consummation of their ancestral faith,[3] so now in the Court of the Areiopagos he seeks to commend it to the Greeks by proving it the fulfilment of their agelong yearning after God. The historical argument was appreciatively received in both instances, but its application was displeasing. When he pointed to the conclusion that their ceremonial Law was superseded, the Jews caught fire ; and when he indicated what he meant by *anastasis,* the Athenians were moved to derision. To their minds the idea of the Resurrection was preposterous,[4] and some of them greeted it with scoffs, while others, more courteous but no less contemptuous, told him that they would hear him on some other occasion. They had no leisure for such folly. *Solvuntur risu tabulæ.*

Cf. vers. 25, 26.

It was an ignominious *dénouement,* but it was so far satisfactory that it ended the proceedings and relieved the Apostle from further legal annoyance. The case was laughed out of court, and he was set at liberty. Ridicule is fatal to a cause, and now that he was the jest of the keen-witted city, he could preach there no longer. His ministry had been brief, lasting perhaps about a month,[5] and it had achieved little. Yet it was not entirely fruitless. His converts were few, but one of them at least was a personage of importance —Dionysius, a member of the Council of the Areiopagos.[6]

Termination of Paul's ministry at Athens.

His converts.

[1] Cf. p. 28.
[2] Cf. Epict. I. V : περὶ προνοίας ; Sen. *De Providentia.*
[3] Cf. pp. 92 ff. [4] Cf. p. 311. [5] Cf. Append. I.
[6] Tradition makes Dionysius the first bishop of Athens. Cf. Eus. *Hist. Eccl.* III. 4 ; IV. 23. His name is invested with a fictitious celebrity by the ascription to him of those remarkable works, *The Heavenly Hierarchy* and *The Divine Names,* whence St. Thomas Aquinas derived so much of his theology. Cf. Westcott's essay on *Dionysius the Areopagite* in his *Religious Thought in the West.*

Of the others only one is named—a woman called Damaris. The name is apparently a variant of Damalis, which signifies 'a heifer'; and since it is the sort of designation which was commonly borne by Athenian courtesans, and women of good fame lived in close seclusion,[1] it is probable that she belonged to that numerous and unhappy order; and it may be taken as an evidence of her subsequent devotion that she was counted worthy of particular mention.

Stephanas of Corinth.

It appears that Paul won at Athens another convert who has left an honourable name, though, since he was not an Athenian, it does not appear in the record of the Athenian ministry. Four years later, in his correspondence with the

1 Cor. xvi. 15.

Church at Corinth, he mentions one of its leading members, Stephanas, and terms him and his household 'the first-fruits' of his labours in the Province of Achaia. Stephanas was a Corinthian, but evidently he had been sojourning at Athens and had there encountered the Apostle and been won for Christ. It happened after the departure of Silas

Cf. 1 Cor. i. 16.

and Timothy when Paul was at Athens alone, since he had baptised Stephanas with his own hands—an office which,

Cf. Jo. iv. 2.

like the Master, he was not accustomed to discharge.

Cf. 1 Cor. i. 17.

Preaching was his business, and he left the administration of baptism to his colleagues, especially, it seems,[2] to his attendant.

Reasons for departure.

Cf. 1 Cor. xvi. 15-17.

Stephanas proved a loyal and generous friend in after years, and it was a merciful providence which had brought him into the Apostle's life at this juncture. Athens was no longer endurable; and there were two special reasons which

(1) *Faux pas* of his defence.

constrained Paul to take his departure.[3] One was the shame of his ignominious failure, aggravated by bitter self-reproach. In his speech before the Council of the Areiopagos he had committed what he now recognised as a fatal error. His

Cf. 2 Cor. xi. 3.

mind had been 'corrupted from its simplicity toward Christ.' He had forgotten that faith's best array is 'not

Cf. 1 Cor. ii. 1-5.

men's wisdom but God's power,' and had attempted to meet philosophy with philosophy and win his hearers by 'per-

[1] Cf. Becker, *Charicles*, pp. 405 ff., 248 f.

[2] Cf. p. 79.

[3] It is significant that the same word (χωρίζεσθαι) is used of Paul's departure from Athens and the expulsion of the Jews from Rome (cf. xviii. 1, 2).

suasive words of wisdom.' It had proved a disastrous blunder, and he determined that he would never repeat it. Thenceforward he would eschew 'lofty speech and wisdom' and 'announce God's testimony,' 'knowing nothing except Jesus as Christ and that a crucified Christ,' and relying on the 'demonstration of the Spirit and of power.' He would fain quit the scene of his failure and make a new beginning elsewhere. And he had another motive. He had been exhausted by those eager months of travel and preaching and controversy and alarm; and as he fretted his heart at Athens with anxiety for his converts in Macedonia, he fell sick. It was a recurrence of his chronic malady; and while he languished alone and despised in the gay city, 'in weakness and fear and much trembling,' his thoughts turned to Stephanas, and he resolved to betake himself to Corinth and cast himself on the care of that kindly friend. It was a convenient retreat, no farther remote than Athens from Macedonia, which he still regarded as his appointed sphere and whence he was eagerly expecting the return of his colleagues with the welcome tidings that tranquillity had been restored and he was free to resume his interrupted ministry. Thither therefore he repaired, probably, in his enfeebled condition, taking ship across the Saronic Gulf and landing at the port of Cenchreæ.

(2) Sickness.

Cf. 1 Cor. ii. 3.

VI

MINISTRY AT CORINTH

Ac. xviii. 1-4; 1 Th.; Ac. xviii. 5-10; 2 Th.; Ac. xviii. 11-18*a*.

Corinth.

Corinth was the commercial and political capital of the Roman Province of Achaia, and her prosperity was largely due to her position on the narrow isthmus between the Corinthian and Saronic Gulfs. The rounding of Cape Malea, the southernmost promontory of Greece, was a perilous adventure. 'When you round Malea,' ran the proverb,[1] 'forget your home.' Hence ships making the voyage between Italy and Asia were accustomed to shun the cruel

[1] Strabo, 378: Μαλέαν δὲ κάμψας ἐπιλάθου των οἴκαδε.

headland with its treacherous tides and restless billows by steering up the Corinthian Gulf and putting in at the harbour of Lechæum, where they either unloaded or, if they were small enough, were hauled on rollers across the Isthmus to Schœnus and there relaunched.[1] This brought Corinth an enormous commerce, and her revenue was not a little augmented by the crowds which frequented the Isthmian Games.[2] From the earliest days she was distinguished as 'the wealthy Corinth';[3] but this unhappily was not her sole notoriety. On the adjacent Acrocorinthus stood the famous temple of Aphrodite with upwards of a thousand courtesan votaries, who plied their traffic in the city, chiefly with the shipmasters, enriching the temple by the ruin of their victims and occasioning a proverb that 'it was not every man who could afford the voyage to Corinth.'[4] Though surpassed in literary and philosophic fame by her brilliant neighbour Athens, she was by no means barren in intellectual renown; and she was distinguished in statecraft and still more in art, especially, like the adjacent town of Sicyon, in painting, statuary, and bronze-work.[5]

A heavy calamity had befallen Corinth in the year 146 B.C., when she was plundered and burned to the ground by the Roman army under Lucius Mummius; but she had been restored in 44 B.C. by Julius Cæsar, who made her a Roman colony with the title COLONIA LAUS JULIA CORINTHUS and settled in her a large body of Roman freemen.[6] Her natural advantages had facilitated the recovery of her former prosperity, and in the Apostle's day she was once more the emporium of Greece. The Roman colonists were the pre-

[1] Strabo, 369, 378, 380.

[2] Strabo, 378. Cf. note on 1 Cor. ix. 24, p. 275.

[3] Cf. Hom. *Il.* II. 570: ἀφνειόν τε Κόρινθον. Pind. *Ol.* XIII. 4: τὰν ὀλβίαν Κόρινθον. Thuc. I. 13.

[4] Strabo, 378: οὐ παντὸς ἀνδρὸς ἐς Κόρινθον ἔσθ' ὁ πλοῦς. Hor. *Epist.* I. xvii. 36: 'Non cuivis homini contingit adire Corinthum.' κορινθιάζεσθαι was synonymous with ἑταιρεῖν, 'play the harlot'; and in Shakespeare's day 'a Corinthian' meant a roysterer—'a lad of mettle, a good boy, by the Lord' (1 *King Henry IV*, II. iv. 12).

[5] Strabo, 382; Verg. *Georg.* II. 464.

[6] Strabo, 381. The victory of Mummius was disgraced by atrocious vandalism. Polybius (XL. 7) tells how he saw priceless pictures flung on the ground and soldiers using them as dice-boards.

dominant element in her population;[1] but the majority of the citizens were Greeks, and there was also, as in every commercial centre, a considerable community of Jews.

Association with Aquila and Priscilla.

Cf. 2 Cor. xi. 9.

On his arrival at Corinth the Apostle would be kindly welcomed by Stephanas, but, with that delicacy which always characterised him, he would not trespass on his grateful convert's hospitality. Despite his weakness he presently addressed himself to the winning of his livelihood, and it was his good fortune to encounter a Jewish fellow-craftsman. This was the tent-maker Aquila. He was a native of Pontus on the Euxine, but he had migrated thence to Rome, and the previous year had been driven from the Imperial Capital by the anti-Jewish edict of the Emperor Claudius.[2] Quite recently he and his wife Priscilla[3] had settled at Corinth, which, as the capital of Achaia and the headquarters of the military administration in the Province, afforded abundant employment for practitioners of his craft. Christianity was already established at Rome,[4] and since there is no suggestion of their conversion by Paul, it is probable that Aquila and Priscilla were already Christians. Community of race and faith and calling drew them to each other, and the Apostle took a lodging in their house[5] and worked with Aquila.

Evangelical inactivity.

He had neither time nor strength for the prosecution of an active ministry; nevertheless he did what he could. Each Sabbath he attended the synagogue and addressed the congregation; but he studiously refrained from opening a serious discussion.[6] That, as it seemed to him, would have

[1] It is noteworthy how many of the Corinthian converts had Roman names. Cf. Crispus and Gaius (1 Cor. i. 14), Fortunatus (xvi. 17), Tertius and Quartus (Rom. xvi. 22, 23), Titius Justus (Ac. xviii. 7).

[2] Cf. p. 131.

[3] A diminutive of Prisca (cf. Rom. xvi. 3; 1 Cor. xvi. 19; 2 Tim. iv. 19). Cf. Drusa and Drusilla, Livia and Livilla, Claudia and Claudilla, Tertia and Tertulla, Quarta and Quartilla.

[4] Cf. p. 506. The language of Suetonius (*Claud.* 25: 'Judæos impulsore Chresto,' a common spelling of 'Christo') seems to imply that it was Messianic fermentation that occasioned the expulsion, and this may have been occasioned by controversy between Jews and Christians. The Christians were in Roman eyes merely a Jewish sect, and they would share the expulsion.

[5] *ἔμενεν παρ' αὐτοῖς*, cf. *The Days of His Flesh*, p. 449.

[6] In ver. 4 Cod. Bez. (D) has *εἰσπορευόμενος δὲ εἰς τὴν συναγωγὴν κατὰ πᾶν σάββατον διελέγετο καὶ ἐντιθεὶς τὸ ὄνομα τοῦ* Κυρίου Ἰησοῦ, *ἔπειθεν δὲ οὐ μόνον* Ἰουδαίους *ἀλλὰ καὶ* Ἕλληνας, 'And going into the synagogue every Sabbath, he would

been futile, since he was expecting the arrival of Silas and Timothy with tidings that the way was open for his return to Macedonia. He was only a temporary sojourner at Corinth, and he would not engage there in an enterprise which he must presently abandon. He contented himself therefore with seeking quietly to influence all whom he encountered, Jews and Gentiles alike, as opportunity presented itself.

Arrival of Silas with deputies and a contribution from Philippi.

Cf. 2 Cor. xi. 9.

So he continued for several weeks,[1] and then the situation changed. His colleagues arrived from Macedonia. Silas came from Philippi, and it seems that he did not come alone. Several deputies of the Philippian Church accompanied him, conveying not only its greetings to the Apostle but a generous contribution. This was both welcome and opportune. It not only assured him of the undiminished affection of his friends but relieved him in his weakness from the burden of daily toil and set him free for the prosecution of his proper vocation, the ministry of the Word.

Timothy's arrival from Thessalonica with a letter.

Cf. 1 Th. ii. 14-16.

Cf. iii. 6-8.

Timothy also arrived from Thessalonica. He came alone, but he brought a letter from the Thessalonian Presbyters, informing the Apostle of the progress of events in their midst and craving his counsel.[2] It was indeed a distressful communication. The persecution not merely continued but had waxed so fierce that it matched the cruel tragedies which had been enacted in Judæa. It was grievous intelligence for the Apostle, dashing his fond hope of an immediate return to Macedonia; yet it was accompanied by a gladdening assurance: the Church had stood firm, loyal to the Faith and constant in her affection for him and his colleagues.

Troubles at Thessalonica:

Had this been all, there would have been no need for a letter. Timothy, young and inexperienced though he was, could have told the Apostle of the sufferings of the Thessalonians and conveyed to him the assurance of their steadfastness. But difficult and perplexing questions had arisen requiring his counsel; and that he might understand these

reason, introducing also the name of the Lord Jesus; and he would persuade not only Jews but also Gentiles.' The imperf. ἔπειθεν signifies merely 'sought to persuade,' whether he succeeded or not.

[1] Cf. κατὰ πᾶν σάββατον, 'Sabbath after Sabbath.'

[2] The evidence lies in the Apostle's frequent references in the course of his letter to the Thessalonian communication. Cf. Rendel Harris, *A Study in Letter-writing*, in *Expositor*, September 1898.

and handle them effectively, it seemed fit to the embarrassed Presbyters that they should be expressly formulated and clearly defined. And so they wrote him a letter.

(1) Jewish calumniation.

The trouble had two sources. One was Jewish calumniation of the Apostle's doctrine and conduct. It was alleged that his Gospel was not merely heretical but immoral. It was antinomian. Its proclamation of salvation by faith in Christ apart from the works of the Law was a relaxation of moral obligation. His character too was assailed. In the course of his ministry at Thessalonica he had repeatedly received monetary aid from the generous Philippians;[1] and his enemies fastened upon this circumstance and, notwithstanding that he had toiled among them for his daily bread, they accused him of preying upon his dupes and making a trade of religion. These—'error, uncleanness, and trickery' —were the odious offences which were laid to his charge. Cf. ii. 3.

(2) Expectation of the Lord's immediate Return.

And there was another trouble which was still more serious, inasmuch as its source lay within the Church. It was a universal persuasion of the primitive Christians that the Lord's Return was imminent and He would appear in glory ere that generation had passed away;[2] and the Apostle shared it. In his preaching at Thessalonica he had proclaimed the impending consummation, and when the storm of persecution broke upon them, his converts consoled themselves with the prospect of a speedy deliverance.

An historic parallel.

The issue was disastrous, and it has repeatedly recurred. One instance is especially conspicuous. The course of history was viewed as a succession of 'ages,' and the early Christian imagination, proceeding on the Jewish notion that the world was only some five thousand years old when the Saviour came, saw in the story of Creation a programme of the future and recognised six ages corresponding to the six days of creation. The first, according to St. Augustine,[3] extended form Adam to the Flood, the second from Noah to Abraham, the third from Abraham to David, the fourth from David to the Babylonian Captivity, the fifth from the Captivity to the Saviour's Birth, and the sixth from the Saviour's

[1] Cf. p. 137.

[2] Cf. *The Days of His Flesh*, pp. xxix f.

[3] *Quæst in Jud.* xlix; *Enarr. in Psalm. XCII*, 1.

Birth to the end of the world. And just as the six days of creation were succeeded by a Day of Rest, so the six ages will be followed by the Millennium, a thousand years of peace. By and by the idea arose that each of the past ages had lasted a thousand years; and hence it was reckoned that the year 1000 A.D. would terminate the current age and witness the Lord's Advent and the Final Judgment. The awful consummation was solemnly announced in 909 by the Council of Trosly; and as the fateful date approached, Europe was strangely moved. The end of all things was at hand, and men abandoned their worldly pursuits and ambitions. Buildings were suffered to fall into decay or pulled down since they would be no longer needed. The wealthy assigned their possessions to the Church, and the deeds of gift which still survive are generally prefaced with the formula *appropinquante mundi termino*, 'the end of the world drawing nigh.' Every mischance—an eclipse, an earthquake, or a pestilence—was accounted a premonition of the impending catastrophe according to the prophetic scriptures, and the terrified people would seek refuge in caves and fastnesses. Many bound themselves in villainage to religious houses, and such as could went on pilgrimage to the Holy Land, the supposed scene of the Lord's visible appearing.[1]

Cf. Rev. xx. 1-7.

Similar, though on a lesser scale, was the situation at Thessalonica. The Church was seething with excitement. Enthusiasm and fanaticism were rampant; confusion prevailed; discipline was defied, and controversy raged. The Presbyters were impotent, and they communicated their difficulties to the Apostle and besought his counsel.

The First Letter to Thessalonica

The Apostle's reply.

He immediately responded to their appeal, and his reply is invested with a peculiar interest as the earliest of his extant letters. He did not write it with his own hand, but dictated it to an amanuensis. This was the fashion at that period in consequence largely of the prevalence of illiteracy;

[1] Cf. Mosheim, *Eccl. Hist.* III. ii., chap. III. 3; Milman, *Latin Christianity*, v. xiii.

and it still obtains in the East, where the public scribe, seated at his table with inkstand and pen in readiness, is a familiar figure on every city-street.[1] Illiteracy, however, was not the only reason for the employment of an amanuensis. 'Writing fair,' as Shakespeare observes, is a rare accomplishment, and it was peculiarly difficult for the Apostle. Not only was his sight defective,[2] but his hands were coarsened by the rough toil of tent-making, and penmanship would be no easy task for his cramped and indurated fingers. This is no mere surmise; for in an interesting passage where he is writing with his own hand, he playfully alludes to his large, sprawling characters. And here lay a further reason for his employment of an amanuensis, since papyrus, though the least expensive of writing materials, was at the cheapest very costly.[3] It was sparingly used, and this appears not only in the custom of including in a letter greetings from mutual friends [4] but in the close and minute penmanship of extant manuscripts. A letter written by a scribe was authenticated by an autograph signature;[5] and the Apostle's practice was to take the pen from his amanuensis at the close and write the final benediction with his own hand in his characteristic and unmistakable style.

Gal. vi. 11.

Cf. Rom. xvi. 3-16, 21-23.

Cf. 2 Th. iii. 17, 18; 1 Cor. xvi. 21; Col. iv. 18.

His amanuensis.

In the present instance the amanuensis would be either Silas or Timothy. The former was well qualified for the task, and he subsequently discharged it for the Apostle Peter; but it seems probable that it was rather performed by Timothy, since he was attached to the mission in the capacity of attendant, and the business of scribe belonged to his office.[6] In any case it was no menial function. The letter was the Apostle's, but he associates himself with both

Cf. 1 Pet. v. 12.

[1] Cf. Hichens, *The Near East*, p. 209. [2] Cf. p. 70.

[3] The price varied with the quality. The sheets measured 9 to 11 inches by 5 to $5\frac{1}{2}$; and a single sheet is quoted as selling now at a drachma and three obols or fully 1/-, again at three obols or about $4\frac{1}{2}$d., and again at two obols or about 3d. Cf. Milligan, *N. T. Documents*, pp. 11 f.

[4] In a 2nd c. papyrus with thirty-one lines no fewer than thirteen are occupied with greetings. Cf. Milligan, *ibid.* p. 12.

[5] Cf. Chrys. *In Epist. II ad Thess.* 1: καθάπερ καὶ νῦν ἐφ' ἡμῶν ἐστίν. ἀπὸ γὰρ τῆς ὑπογραφῆς δῆλα γίνεται τὰ γράμματα τῶν πεμπόντων. Plat. *Epist.* XIII begins Πλάτων Διονυσίῳ τυράννῳ Συρακουσῶν εὖ πράττειν and proceeds ἀρχή σοι τῆς ἐπιστολῆς ἔστω καὶ ἅμα σύμβολον ὅτι παρ' ἐμοῦ ἐστί. For interesting examples cf. *Oxyrh. Pap.* 246, 275, 497.

[6] Cf. p. 79.

his companions at the very outset and maintains the association throughout: '*we* thank God,' '*our* Gospel,' 'what sort of men *we* proved among you,' 'what a reception *we* had when *we* appeared among you.'[1] They had shared his ministry at Thessalonica, and they shared also his present solicitude; and with characteristic generosity he would honour them in the eyes of the Church.

i. 1. Paul and Silvanus and Timothy to the Church of the Thessalonians in God the Father and the Lord Jesus Christ. Grace to you and peace.

Grateful acknowledgment of the Church's faith.

The letter from Thessalonica had assured the Apostle of the Church's affectionate loyalty to himself and his colleagues despite the calumnies of his Jewish enemies. 'We know,' it had said, 'what sort of men you proved among us for our sakes'; and he prefaces his reply with a warm reciprocation. He assures them that he and his colleagues on their part cherished a constant and grateful remembrance of all that the Thessalonians had been and done; and he tells them how it had gratified him to find that the fame of their faith and devotion had travelled beyond their own country of Macedonia. It had preceded him to Athens and Corinth and was the talk of the Province of Achaia.

2 We thank God always for you all, making mention of you in
3 our prayers with an unceasing remembrance of the work of
your faith and the toil of your love and the endurance of your
hope in our Lord Jesus Christ before our God and Father.
4 We know, brothers beloved by God, that He has chosen you,
5 because our Gospel went not home to you in word only but
also in power and in the Holy Spirit and much assurance,
just as you know what sort of men we proved among you for
6 your sakes. And you followed our example and the Lord's by
welcoming the Word amid much distress with the joy of the
7 Holy Spirit, so that you proved a pattern to all who hold the
8 Faith[2] in Macedonia and in Achaia. For from you the Word

[1] That this is not *pluralis majestaticus* is proved by the introduction of first per. sing. when the Apostle refers particularly to himself (cf. ii. 18, iii. 5). There is no clear instance of 'the editorial *we*' in the Pauline writings.

[2] τοῖς πιστεύουσι. πιστεύειν is the cognate verb of πίστις, 'faith,' and it is a disadvantage in translation that the old English use of 'faith' as a verb (cf. Shak. *King Lear*, II. i. 72: 'make thy words faith'd') is now obsolete.

of God has pealed forth,[1] not only in Macedonia and Achaia;
no, in every place your faith toward God has gone forth, so
9 that we have no need to say anything; for they are telling
their own story of us—what a reception we had when we
appeared among you, and how you turned to God from your
10 idols to serve a living and true God and await His Son from
Heaven whom He raised from the dead—Jesus our Rescuer
from the coming wrath.

Refutation of Jewish calumnies.

And now the Apostle turns to the calumnies of his Jewish enemies. In reporting these the Presbyters had assured him of their unshaken confidence. 'We know,' they had written, 'that your appearance among us has proved no empty thing.' And this generous testimony made the task of refutation easy for him. His teaching was condemned as erroneous and immoral, and he points in reply to its gracious influence upon his converts. And he was accused of cowardly and selfish trickery. He had been, in the stinging phrase of a later generation, 'a trafficker on Christ,'[2] and had sought to ingratiate himself with his dupes by soft and flattering speech. There was indeed a show of reason in the taunt; for he had always behaved at Thessalonica with exceeding tenderness. But it was the tenderness of a loving heart. He had never played the Apostle or stood upon his dignity. He had treated his converts as a father treats his children, nay, as a nurse treats her charge with

> 'a simple, merry, tender knack
> Of stringing pretty words that make no sense,
> And kissing full sense into empty words.'[3]

When his calumniators represented this as flattery, they were flying in the face of facts. He had come to Thessalonica with the wounds of his scourging at Philippi yet unhealed, but his spirit was unbroken, and he had boldly proclaimed the Gospel at the risk of provoking fresh outrage. And so far from 'trafficking on Christ' he had toiled early and late at his craft of tent-making that he might earn his daily bread.

[1] ἐξήχηται, like a peal of thunder (cf. Ecclus. xl. 13) or a clear, ringing trumpet (Chrys.).

[2] χριστέμπορος. Cf. *Didache*, xii.

[3] E. B. Browning, *Aurora Leigh*, I.

ii. 1 You know yourselves, brothers, that our appearance among
2 you has proved no empty thing. No, though we had previously
been subjected to suffering and outrage, as you know, at
Philippi, we had the boldness in our God to tell you the Gospel
3 of God in the midst of a great conflict. For our appeal is not
inspired by error or uncleanness, nor is there trickery behind
4 it; no, as we have been proved by God ere being entrusted with
the Gospel, so we speak with the design of pleasing not men
Jer. xi. 20. 5 but God, 'the Prover of our hearts.' For we never resorted
to flattering speech, as you know, or a fair pretext for greedy
6 ends, God is witness ; nor did we ever seek glory of men either
from you or from others, though we might have stood upon our
7 dignity as Christ's Apostles. No, we played the babe among
8 you like a nurse fondling her children.[1] Thus yearning for
you, we were well pleased to impart to you not only the Gospel
of God but our own lives also, because you were so endeared
9 to us. For you remember, brothers, our toil and moil. Working
night and day that we might be no burden upon any of you,
10 we preached to you the Gospel of God. You are our witnesses,
and so is God, how holy and righteous and blameless was our
11 relation with you who hold the Faith, even as you know how
we dealt with each one of you like a father with his own
children, exhorting you and cheering you and solemnly charg-
12 ing you to comport yourselves worthily of the God who is
calling you into His own Kingdom and Glory.

Congratulation of the Thessalonians on their steadfastness.

The Presbyters had written that they 'thanked God' for all that Paul and his colleagues had done for them ; and he responds by assuring them that they had inspired himself and his colleagues with a like gratitude : 'We too thank God unceasingly.' And the reason of their gratitude was the heroic steadfastness of the Thessalonians in face of a cruel persecution. It seems that some of them had actually sealed their testimony with their blood ; and thus the Thessalonian Church had won a place with the churches of

[1] Reading νήπιοι, 'babes' (cf. 1 Cor. iii. 1 ; xiii. 11) with ℵ*BC*D*FG Vulg. What was called by the calumniators 'flattering speech' was in truth the language of affection, like a nurse's blandishments. So Orig. (*In Matt. Ev.* xv. 7 : ἐγένετο νήπιος καὶ παραπλήσιος τρόφῳ θαλπούσῃ τὸ ἑαυτῆς παιδίον καὶ λαλούσῃ λόγους ὡς παιδίον διὰ τὸ παιδίον), Aug. (*De Catech. Rud.* 15 : 'Hinc ergo factus est parvulus in medio nostrum tanquam nutrix fovens filios suos. Num enim delectat, nisi amor invitet, decurtata et mutilata verba immurmurare ?'), Hieronym. Hence the verb συννηπιάζειν, *coinfantiari*, denoting our Lord's adaptation of Himself to human childishness by the Incarnation (Iren. IV. lxiii. 1). The variant ἤπιοι, 'gentle,' is a dull smoothing away of the bold metaphor, facilitated by the preceding ν.

Judæa in 'the noble army of martyrs,' God's faithful witnesses in all ages from the ancient Prophets to the Lord and His Apostles.

13 And therefore we too thank God unceasingly that on receiving the Word of God from our lips you welcomed it as no
word of men but as what it truly is—the Word of God which is
14 set in active operation in you who hold the Faith.[1] For you
followed the example, brothers, of the churches of God which
are in Judæa in Christ Jesus, in that you also experienced at
the hands of your fellow-countrymen the same sufferings which
15 they experienced at the hands of the Jews—the men who slew
the Lord and the Prophets and hunted us forth. God they
16 never please, and all men they oppose, seeking to prevent us
from speaking to the Gentiles that they may be saved, to 'fill Gen. xv.
up the measure of their sins' always. 'But the wrath of God 16.
has fallen upon them to the uttermost.'[2]

Review of the recent course of events.

A mere assurance of his abiding interest in his converts was insufficient, since they might naturally doubt it. Indeed it may be that his enemies had charged him with cowardly desertion in fleeing from the storm and seeking a secure asylum in Achaia. And so to disabuse their minds he reviews the course of events since his departure from Thessalonica. His first destination had been Athens, and there he had eagerly awaited the arrival of his colleagues, hoping that they would tell him that the way was clear for his return. But, to his bitter disappointment, they had reported that the persecution was still raging, and that his reappearance at Thessalonica would not merely involve the sacrifice of his own life but aggravate the sufferings of his converts by provoking fiercer hostility. So keen was his solicitude that he could not leave them unsuccoured and allow his work to be undone; and it was agreed that Timothy, who by reason of the subordinate part which he had played would be less obnoxious, should venture back,

[1] ἐνεργεῖται, not middle, 'operates,' but passive, 'is set in operation.' So most probably in every instance (cf. Mayor on Ja. v. 16). God and spiritual powers, whether good or evil, are said ἐνεργεῖν, 'to operate' (cf. 1 Cor. xii. 6, 11; Gal. ii. 8, iii. 5; Eph. i. 11, 20, ii. 2; Phil. ii. 13); their instruments are said ἐνεργεῖσθαι, 'to be set in operation' (cf. 2 Cor. iv. 12; Eph. iii. 20; Col. i. 29). The Word is in itself ἐνεργής (Heb. iv. 12), potentially 'operative,' and it becomes actually 'operative' where there is faith: it 'is set in operation in believers' by the Holy Spirit. And faith, again, 'is set in operation through love' (Gal. v. 6).

[2] A stock phrase of Jewish eschatology. Cf. *Test. XII Patriarch.* vi. 11.

and nerve them to stand fast against the fury of their persecutors and the subtler risk of seduction from their allegiance by insidious misrepresentations. And now that Timothy had returned to Corinth the Apostle was gladdened by his report of their heroic steadfastness and by the letter which he had brought and which told him that they remembered how he had warned them during his ministry amorg them to expect persecution for the Gospel's sake. And he reassures them of his constant affection and solicitude and his eager and prayerful longing to return and renew his ministry among them.

17 And as for us, brothers, in the desolation of our temporary
separation from you—in presence, not in heart—we were
the more intensely eager, with much longing, to see your
18 face; because we wished to go to you—I Paul indeed once
19 and again—and Satan closed the way. For what is our
hope or joy or crown of boasting—is it not even you?—
20 before our Lord Jesus at His Advent?[1] Yes, you are our
iii. 1 glory and our joy. And so, when we could endure[2] no longer,
2 we made up our minds to be left alone at Athens, and sent
Timothy, our brother and a minister of God in the Gospel
of Christ, to establish you and exhort you in the interest
3 of your faith, that no one might be cajoled amid these distresses. You know yourselves that this is our appointed
4 lot. For while we were with you, we foretold you that distress was in store for us; and so it came to pass, and you
5 know it. It was for this reason that I on my part, when I
could endure no longer, sent to ascertain your faith for fear
lest the Tempter had tempted you and your toil should
issue in emptiness.

6 And now that Timothy has come to us from you and told
us the good tidings of your faith and love and that you have
always a kindly remembrance of us, longing to see us just
7 as we are longing to see you, we have on this score been
comforted, brothers, about you, above all our constraint
8 and distress, through your faith, because 'now we live if

[1] The sentence is broken by the Apostle's emotion. He intended to say: 'What is our hope or joy or crown before the Lord? Is it not our converts?' But he breaks off in his haste to assure the Thessalonians that they are included. 'Therefore he added ἢ οὐχὶ καὶ ὑμεῖς; For he did not say "you" simply but "you also" with the others' (Chrys.).

[2] *στέγειν*, properly 'cover.' Hence (1) 'keep out,' cf. Thuc. II. 94: *νῆες οὐ στέγουσαι*, 'leaky ships'; (2) 'keep in,' cf. Plat. *Rep.* 621 A: *οὗ τὸ ὕδωρ ἀγγεῖον οὐδὲν στέγειν*, 'a leaky vessel.' Here either 'contain our longing' or 'keep out anxiety.'

9 you stand fast in the Lord.'[1] For what thanks can we
render to God regarding you for all the joy which we experi-
10 ence on your account before our God, while night and day
we pray with exceeding earnestness that we may see your
face and repair the defects of your faith ?[2]
11 Now may He, our God and Father and our Lord Jesus
12 Christ,[3] direct our way to you. And may the Lord make
you increase and overflow in love for one another and for
13 all men like our love for you, that He may establish your
hearts blameless in holiness before our God and Father at
the Advent of our Lord Jesus 'with all His holy ones.' Zech. xiv. 5.

An exhortation to holiness.

It was a grief and an embarrassment to the Apostle throughout his ministry, that when the Judaists alleged that his Gospel of salvation by Faith issued in antinomianism, they could adduce what seemed a damning evidence of their contention. His Gentile converts too often retained the low ideals of their old heathen ethic and disgraced their Christian profession by moral laxity. So it had happened at Thessalonica, and he now introduces a call to consecration.

iv. 1 To proceed: brothers, we beg and exhort you in the Lord
Jesus that, as you received from us directions how you should
comport yourselves and please God—and so indeed you are
2 comporting yourselves—that you do it more fully. You know
3 what charges we gave you through the Lord Jesus.[4] For this
is the will of God—your sanctification. He would have you
4 abstain from fornication; He would have each of you know
how to master his own vessel[5] in sanctification and honour,

[1] Bornemann, chiefly on account of 'das ganz deutliche Metrum,' regards this as an adapted verse from a Christian or Jewish hymn, suggesting as the original *ζῶμεν ἐὰν ἡμεῖς/στήκομεν ἐν* Κυρίῳ, 'we live if we stand fast in the Lord.'

[2] *καταρτίζειν*, 'join together.' (1) In a political connection, 'reconcile contending factions' (cf. 1 Cor. i. 10). An umpire was called *καταρτιστήρ* (cf. Herod. v. 28). (2) As a medical term, 'replace a dislocated joint' or 'set a broken bone.' Cf. Galen, *Opera*, XIX. p. 461 (Kühn): *καταρτισμός ἐστι μεταγωγὴ ὀστοῦ ἢ ὀστῶν ἐκ τοῦ παρὰ φύσιν τόπου εἰς τὸν κατὰ φύσιν.* (3) 'Repair a torn fabric,' *e.g.*, a net (cf. Mt. iv. 21).

[3] Cf. the co-ordination of God and Christ in i. 1. Observe how the Apostle's sense of their oneness is expressed by the sing. *κατευθύναι*. Cf. 2 Th. ii. 16, 17.

[4] Particularly in delivering the decree of the Council of Jerusalem (cf. Ac. xvi. 4).

[5] *σκεῦος* signifies the body (cf. 2 Cor. iv. 7) as the vessel containing (1) the soul (cf Lucr. III. 440; Cic. *Tusc. Disput.* I. 52: 'Corpus quidem quasi vas est aut aliquod animi receptaculum'; Phil. *Quod Deterius Potiori insidiari soleat*, p. 223: *τὸ τῆς ψυχῆς ἀγγεῖον τὸ σῶμα*), (2) the Holy Spirit (cf. ver. 8; 1 Cor. vi. 19; Barn. *Epist.* vii. 3, xi. 9; Herm. *Mand.* v. 2). So Tert. (*De Resurr. Carn.* 16),

Jer. x. 25; Ps. lxxix. 6. Ps. xciv. 1.

5 not in the passion of lust like 'the Gentiles who know not God,'
6 and never transgress or take advantage of a brother in the
matter, because 'the Lord is an avenger' in all these cases,
7 as we formerly told you and solemnly testified. For when God
called us, He did not mean us to be unclean; no, the con-
8 dition was sanctification. Therefore, when one disregards it,
it is not man that he disregards but God who 'puts His Holy
Spirit in you.'

Ez. xxxvii. 14.

The eschatological difficulty.

And now the Apostle addresses himself to the eschatological question which was disturbing the Thessalonian Church, and deals with three vexing problems which it had raised and which the Presbyters had submitted to him in their letter. The first concerned the maintenance of 'brotherly friendship,' and it had been occasioned by the extravagance of a number of enthusiasts. Anticipating the immediate end of the age, they had abandoned their worldly employments and were idly scanning the heavens to catch the first flash of the Lord's appearing. They had been reduced to penury and were dependent on charity for their daily bread, with the natural result that a spirit of resentment had been aroused in the minds of sober Christians who were burdened with their support. Thus the Church's peace was broken, and her enemies were moved to derision. 'If,' says St. Chrysostom, referring to a like scandal in his own day, 'this is an offence to those who are with us, it is a far worse offence to the outsiders. They find ten thousand accusations and handles when they see a man in good health and well able to provide for himself begging and needing help from his neighbours. This is why they call us "traffickers on Christ."'

(1) Idle expectance of the Lord's Return.

Is. liv. 13.

9 Regarding brotherly friendship you have no need that one
should write you. For you are yourselves 'taught of God'
10 to love one another; indeed you are performing the duty

Chrys., Theodrt., Ambrstr., and the Fathers generally. 'To win one's vessel' (τὸ ἑαυτοῦ σκεῦος κτᾶσθαι) means to get the mastery over one's body and deliver it from the desecration of lust. Cf. Shak. *Oth.* IV. ii. 83: 'To preserve this vessel for my lord.' According to another interpretation σκεῦος signifies 'wife' (cf. 1 Pet. iii. 7). So Theod. Mops.; Aug. (*Contra Julian. Pelag.* IV. 56; *Serm.* cclxxviii. 9). Thus the Apostle would mean that as a safeguard against illicit indulgence each man should 'get his own wife' (cf. 1 Cor. vii. 2). But what would be the force of εἰδέναι then?

toward all the brothers throughout Macedonia. But we
11 exhort you, brothers, to perform it more fully, and make it
your ambition to live peacefully and busy yourselves with
your own affairs and work with your hands as we charged you,
12 that you may comport yourselves decorously before those outside and be dependent on no one.[1]

(2) Anxiety for the departed.

The second problem concerned 'those who were falling asleep.' Death had been busy at its ceaseless work since the introduction of the Christian Faith into Thessalonica; and as one and another passed away and the promise of the Lord's Return remained still unfulfilled, the mourners, uninstructed as yet in the blessed hope of the Resurrection, wondered how it would fare with their beloved at His appearing. Would they be absent on that great Day and miss its gladness and glory?

13 And we would not have you miss the truth,[2] brothers, regarding those who are falling asleep, lest you grieve like the rest
14 who have no hope. If we hold the faith that Jesus died and
rose, so too will God bring with Jesus those whom He has laid
15 to sleep.[3] For this we tell you in a word of the Lord[4] that we,
the living, the survivors until the Advent of the Lord, shall
have no precedence of those who have been laid to sleep;
16 because the Lord in His own person, heralded by a cry of
command, by an archangel's voice, and by the trumpet of
God, will descend from heaven, and the dead in Christ will
17 rise in the first instance;[5] then we, the living, the survivors,

[1] Or, taking *μηδενός* as neut., 'have need of nothing.'

[2] *ἀγνοεῖν*, not simply 'to be ignorant' but 'to be ignorant where one might and should have known.' It was used, *e.g.*, in the Common Greek of making a wrong return in an assessment schedule (cf. Moulton and Milligan, *Vocab.*). Hence under the Levitical economy 'a sin of ignorance' (*ἀγνόημα*) was held culpable and required expiation.

[3] *τοὺς κοιμηθέντας διὰ τοῦ* 'Ιησοῦ, 'those who have been laid to sleep by Jesus,' a true passive (cf. Moulton, *Proleg.*, p. 162). Another construction connects *δια τοῦ* 'Ιησοῦ with *ἄξει*, 'God will through Jesus bring with Him,' *i.e.*, in His train, or perhaps prolept., 'to be with Him (in His glory).' So Theod. Mops. Chrys., while approving the former, mentions both interpretations. The latter obliterates the double parallelism—*τοὺς κοιμ. διὰ τοῦ* 'Ιησοῦ with 'Ιησοῦς *ἀπέθανεν* and *ἄξει σὺν αὐτῷ* with *ἀνέστη*.

[4] Referring either to our Lord's general teaching (cf. Jo. vi. 39, 40) or to an unrecorded *logion*.

[5] *πρῶτον* ℵABD^cEKL, 'in the first instance,' balanced by *ἔπειτα*. The resurrection will be the first act in the drama. The variant *πρῶτοι* D*FG, 'first,' means that the dead in Christ will be raised before the ungodly (cf. Rev. xx. 4, 5).

will in their company be rapt away amid clouds to meet the
Lord [1] in the air. And thus shall we be always with the Lord.
18 Therefore comfort one another with these words.

(3) The time of the Lord's Return.

The third inquiry concerned the time of the Lord's Return; and it was a bewildered appeal for some definite pronouncement which might calm the prevailing unrest. The Apostle answers that he has none to offer, and recalls how the Lord in the hour of His departure had censured that very inquiry as an illegitimate intrusion into the Father's secret council. The one certainty was that the Lord's Return would be a sudden surprise; and here he takes occasion to reiterate his admonition against moral laxity. It was impossible to foretell when the Lord would appear; but all would be well if only they remembered His word: 'In whatsoever employments I may surprise you, in these will I also judge you,'[2] and held themselves in constant readiness to meet Him without shame.

Cf. Ac. i. 6, 7.

Cf. Ac. i. 7.

v. 1 Regarding 'the periods and the crises,' brothers, you have
2 no need that anything be written to you. For you yourselves
know perfectly well that the Day of the Lord comes like a
3 thief in the night.[3] When they are saying 'Peace and
safety,' then all of a sudden ruin swoops upon them like her
pangs upon a woman with child; and they shall not escape.
4 But you, brothers, are not in darkness that the Day should
5 surprise you like a thief; for you are all sons of light and sons
6 of day. We belong neither to night nor to darkness; so then
let us not slumber like the rest but be wakeful and sober.
7 It is by night that slumberers slumber, and it is by night that
8 drunkards get drunken. But as for us, since we belong to the

Cf. Mt. xxiv. 43.

Cf. Jo. xii. 36.

Cf. Jo. iii. 19-21; Ac. ii. 15.

But the apocalyptic idea of two resurrections (*ἀνάστασις καθολικὴ καὶ μερική*) is foreign to Paul's thought. He contemplates only one—that of 'the dead in Christ'; and when he says that they will rise 'in the first instance,' he means that they will be raised before the living are 'rapt away,' and both will go home together. Moreover, the apocalyptic 'first resurrection' is not a general resurrection of believers, but a resurrection of the martyrs who had fallen in the Domitian persecution. The cause for which they had died would triumph, and they would share its triumph.

[1] *εἰς ἀπάντησιν*, cf. p. 130, n. 3.

[2] *ἐν οἷς ἂν ὑμᾶς καταλάβω, ἐν τούτοις καὶ κρινῶ.* Cf. *Unwritten Sayings of Our Lord*, 11.

[3] The Jews inferred from Ex. xii. 29 that the Messiah would come at midnight, and the early Christians inferred from Mt. xxv. 6 that the Lord would return at midnight. Cf. Hieronym. on the latter passage.

day, let us be sober, 'wearing a cuirass,' that of faith and love, Is. lix. 17.
9 and 'a helmet,' the hope 'of salvation'; forasmuch as God
did not ordain us to wrath but to win salvation through our
10 Lord Jesus Christ, who died for us that, whether we wake or
11 slumber, we may share His life. And therefore exhort each
other and build one another up, as indeed you are doing.

Not the least serious aspect of the Thessalonian situation was the disorganisation of the Church. The prophets of the approaching Advent were irresponsible enthusiasts, and they pursued their propaganda regardless and indeed contemptuous of the judgment of the Presbyters. Authority was flouted and discipline defied. Their wild excesses occasioned resentment, reprobation, and recrimination; and, what was still worse, they excited ridicule. Their prophecies discredited even the legitimate operations of the Spirit. Reasonable men looked askance upon all enthusiasm, forgetting the Lord's precept: 'Show yourselves approved bankers'[1] and the duty which it inculcates of distinguishing betwixt genuine coins and base counterfeits. Practical admonitions.

12 And we beg you, brothers, to appreciate those who toil
among you and rule over you in the Lord and admonish
13 you, and to hold them in very high and loving esteem for their
14 work's sake. 'Be at peace among yourselves.' And we Mk. ix. 50.
exhort you, brothers, admonish the disorderly, cheer the
faint-hearted, lend a helping hand to the weak, be long-
15 suffering toward all. See that no one ever repays evil with
evil, but always pursue the kindly course with one another
16, 17 and with all men. Always rejoice.[2] Pray unceasingly.
18 In every situation be thankful; for this is God's will in
19, 20 Christ Jesus for you. Do not quench the Spirit; do not set
21 prophecies at naught; but prove everything, retain the Job i. 1, 8,
22 genuine,[3] 'eschew every evil' sort.[4] ii. 3.

[1] γίνεσθε τραπεζῖται δόκιμοι. Cf. *Unwritten Sayings of Our Lord*, VI.

[2] πάντοτε χαίρετε, the shortest verse in the Greek Testament. 'No literary production has ever so often repeated the word "joy" as the New Testament' (Renan, *Les Apôtres*, v).

[3] Like bankers (τραπεζῖται) who tested coins (νομίσματα) to ascertain whether they were genuine (καλά) or counterfeit (κίβδηλα). To 'test' or 'prove' was δοκιμάζειν; the process was δοκιμή; a coin which stood the test was δόκιμον, one which did not stand it was ἀδόκιμον.

[4] Or 'every sort of evil.' εἶδος, (1) 'appearance' (cf. Lk. ix. 29; 2 Cor. v. 7); (2) 'form,' 'shape' (cf. Lk. iii. 22); (3) 'sort,' 'kind'; as a philosophical term, 'species.'

23 Now may He, the God of peace, make you entirely and
perfectly holy, and may your spirit and soul and body in
entire completeness be kept beyond blame at the Advent of
24 our Lord Jesus Christ.[1] Faithful is He who is calling you;
and 'He will also bring it to pass.'

Num. xxiii. 19; Ps. xxxvii. 5.

The Apostle's sign-manual.

And now after his wont the Apostle puts his sign-manual to the letter. It is no mere signature but an unbaring of his heart. He bespeaks the prayers of the Presbyters for himself and his colleagues. And he extends his affection to the whole Christian community, and bids them 'greet all the brothers with a holy kiss.' It was the Oriental fashion with kinsfolk and brothers, when they met, to embrace and kiss each other on cheek or forehead; and it prevailed in the Christian Brotherhood. And it was the fashion, moreover, with a Jewish Rabbi, when a disciple pleased him, to embrace him and kiss his forehead in token of commendation.[2] It is the latter usage that the Apostle intends here. The kiss which he bids the Presbyters bestow on his behalf was his recognition of the faith which his Thessalonian converts had displayed in those days of trial. The letter was addressed to the Presbyters, but it was a message for the Church, and he insists on its being read in public assembly.

Cf. Gen. xxxiii. 4, xiv. 14, 15; Lk. xv. 20. Cf. Rom. xvi. 16; 1 Cor. xvi. 20; 2 Cor. xiii. 12; 1 Pet. v. 14.

25,26 BROTHERS, PRAY FOR US. GREET ALL THE BROTHERS
27 WITH A HOLY KISS. I ADJURE YOU BY THE LORD THAT THE
28 LETTER BE READ TO ALL THE BROTHERS. THE GRACE OF
OUR LORD JESUS CHRIST BE WITH YOU.

Timothy the bearer of the letter.

The transmission of letters was in those days no light matter. There was indeed an imperial post instituted by Augustus on the model of the Persian *angaria*;[3] but this was a state service, and private despatches were conveyed

[1] The idea of ὁλοτελής is *complete perfection*; that of ὁλόκληρος (cf. Ja. i. 4) *unmutilated entirety*. ὁλοκληρία (Ac. iii. 16) is *entire soundness of body*. The Apostle prays, in view of the ἀταξία (cf. ver. 14) of the Thessalonians, that they may be ὁλοτελεῖς; in view of their ἀκαθαρσία (cf. iv. 7), that they may be ὁλόκληροι, sanctified in their entire nature, not only their spiritual nature (πνεῦμα) or their intellectual (ψυχή) but their physical (σῶμα). The tripartite division of human nature was a Stoic conception. Cf. M. Aur. xii. 3: τρία ἐστίν ἐξ ὧν συνέστηκας· σωμάτιον, πνευμάτιον, νοῦς.

[2] Cf. *The Days of His Flesh*, p. 361.

[3] Cf. Suet. *Aug.* 49.

by private messengers.[1] It was common for a wealthy man to maintain a staff of couriers,[2] but the less affluent hired messengers as occasion arose, while the poor were dependent on the service of a friend or the favour of a casual traveller, and it was thus that the Apostle's letters were conveyed. In the present instance it appears that Timothy acted as his courier.[3] It was an important office. For Paul's couriers were no mere posts. Not only were they entrusted with the communication of personal tidings, but they were charged with the amplification and enforcement of the written message.

Cf. Rom. xvi. 1, 2.

Cf. Eph. vi. 21, 22; Col. iv. 7, 8.

Active ministry at Corinth.

It was in the month of September that Paul had come to Corinth, and he had no intention of remaining there. His hope was that peace would be restored in Macedonia, and he would be free to return thither and resume his interrupted ministry. Corinth was merely a temporary asylum, and it seemed useless to inaugurate there an enterprise which he must presently abandon. He passed several weeks in anxious expectancy, busy at his tent-making and availing himself of such opportunities as presented themselves for testifying of Christ. At length in the month of October Timothy arrived from Thessalonica; and his report, grievous as it was, terminated the Apostle's suspense. The persecution still continued, and there was nothing for it but that he should remain at Corinth. And so, after he had written and despatched his letter to Thessalonica, he addressed himself to an energetic ministry in the Achaian capital.

Rupture with the synagogue.

The liberality of his Philippian friends had relieved him of the necessity of earning his daily bread, and he abandoned his tent-making and devoted his full time and strength to his evangelical activities.[4] The synagogue was his arena, and he no longer contented himself with tentatively 'introducing the name of Jesus'[5] but 'solemnly testified that

[1] *Cursores* or *tabellarii*. Cf. Cic. *Phil.* II. 31; Mart. *Epigr.* III. 100; Plin. *Epist.* VII. 12; Tac. *Agric.* xliii.

[2] The luxurious Ælius Verus, Hadrian's adopted son, called his *cursores* by the names of the winds and adorned them with Cupid's wings.

[3] His departure from Corinth is proved by the fact that Crispus and Gaius were baptised by Paul.

[4] *συνείχετο τῷ λόγῳ* ℵABDE Vulg., 'was in the grip of,' *i.e.*, 'closely occupied with the Word.' *συν. τῷ Πνεύματι* HLP, 'was in the grip of,' *i.e.*, 'constrained by the Spirit.'

[5] Cf. p. 151, n. 6.

the Messiah was Jesus.' A keen and protracted controversy ensued, and after his wont he supported his contention by appealing to the Scriptures.[1] His reasoning was incontrovertible, but his opponents were impervious to argument. Exasperated by their dialectical discomfiture, they resorted to threats and blasphemies. Persistence was futile, and he 'shook out his garments,' signifying after the symbolic fashion still practised in the East that he abandoned them and would hold no further intercourse with them.[2] They had rejected the Gospel, and he would thenceforward make his appeal to the Gentiles.

Cf. Neh. v. 13.

His adherents.

He quitted the synagogue, but he did not go alone. Stephanas, whom he had won to the Faith at Athens ere coming to Corinth,[3] would accompany him; and he carried with him also several prominent members of the Jewish congregation. One was no less a personage than Crispus, one of the Rulers of the Synagogue;[4] and the other Titius Justus.[5] The latter was not a Jew. His Latin name suggests that he was a Roman colonist, but he was a 'God-fearer,'[6] and thus like Crispus he had doubtless been present during those heated discussions in the synagogue and had been persuaded by the Apostle's arguments. Another bore the Latin name of Gaius, and he also was probably a Roman colonist and a 'God-fearer.' He was a man of substance, and he proved in after days a right worthy member of the Corinthian Church, winning praise for his generous hospitality. He and Crispus were the only Corinthians besides Stephanas and his household whom Paul baptised with his own hands; and the reason was that Timothy, on whom in his capacity

Cf. Rom. xvi. 23.

Cf. 1 Cor. i. 14.

[1] Cod. Bez. (D) supported by Syr. Vers.: *πολλοῦ δὲ λόγου γινομένου καὶ γραφῶν διερμηνευομένων ἀντιτασσομένων αὐτῶν, κ.τ.λ.*

[2] *ἐκτινάξασθαι τὰ ἱμάτια*, distinct from (1) *διαρήσσειν τὰ ἱμάτια*, 'rend one's garments' (cf. Mt. xxvi. 65; Ac. xiv. 14), a protest against blasphemy, and (2) *ἐκτινάσσειν τὸν κονιορτὸν τῶν ποδῶν*, 'shake off the dust of one's feet' (cf. Mt. x. 14; Ac. xiii. 51), the custom of a Jew on leaving unclean Gentile soil and passing into the Holy Land (cf. *The Days of His Flesh*, p. 218). *P. E. F. Q. St.*, July 1906, p. 191: 'Taking the open part of the dress in the right hand and shaking it means, "I have nothing to do with it."'

[3] Cf. p. 148.

[4] Cf. *The Days of His Flesh*, p. 94.

[5] B*D^{gr2} Syr^{p} Vulg. *Τιτίου Ἰούστου.* ℵE *Τίτου Ἰούστου.* $AB^{3}D^{*}HLP$ *Ἰούστου.*

[6] Cf. 13.

of attendant the administration of the Sacrament properly devolved, had gone on his errand to Thessalonica at the time of their conversion. From Paul's explicit statement that these were the only Corinthians whom he baptised, it may be inferred that Titius Justus received the Sacrament from the hands of Silas.

Jewish animosity.

Few though the converts may have been, they were numerous enough to require a meeting-place now that the doors of the synagogue were closed against them; and Justus supplied their need. He was well-to-do, and he placed at their service an apartment of his commodious house.[1] It proved an unfortunate arrangement. The house adjoined the synagogue, and the assembling of the Christians in such close proximity would be construed as a deliberate defiance. Their numbers quickly increased by the accession of Gentile converts, and this further exasperated the Jews. They naturally regarded Paul with special animosity, and so menacing became their attitude that his life was endangered. He was in continual apprehension of a murderous assault. It was an alarming situation, and it is no wonder that his heart failed him. Cf. Ac. xviii. 10; 2 Th. iii. 2.

Evil tidings from Thessalonica.

In the midst of his disquietude Timothy returned with unhappy tidings. The trouble at Thessalonica had increased. Not only was the persecution still raging, but the eschatological frenzy was wilder than ever. It had been fostered by several enthusiasts who recognised in the distress of the Christians the beginning of the storm and announced that 'the Day of the Lord was upon them.' The Church was panic-stricken, and the Apostle's letter had proved ineffectual. His counsels were nullified by the fervour of the enthusiasts, who not only claimed prophetic inspiration but recalled how he had preached the imminence of the Lord's Advent while he was among them and alleged his authority for their affirmations. Moreover, they produced a letter which he was credited with having written. Perhaps it was a forgery, but more probably it was a personal (Cf. 2 Th. i. 4-7. Cf. iii. 11. Cf. ii. 2.)

[1] The variant μεταβὰς ἀπὸ τοῦ 'Ακύλα, 'having removed from the house of Aquila' (D* 137), represents Paul as leaving his lodging in the house of Aquila and Priscilla (cf. ver. 3) and taking up his abode with Titius Justus—a violation of the Lord's injunction (Lk. x. 7). Cf. *The Days of His Flesh*, p. 218.

communication which he had written ere the controversy arose, and which now lent itself to an interpretation which he had never contemplated.

A reassuring vision.

It happened that, when the report of the situation at Thessalonica reached him, Paul was menaced by an outbreak of Jewish hostility, and the accumulation of trouble overwhelmed him. It seemed as though his ministry at Corinth were doomed, and he must again seek safety in flight. In his despondency he turned to the Holy Scriptures, and he found there the message which he so much needed. Apparently he had lighted on that passage in the ancient Prophet: 'Fear not, for I am with thee; be not dismayed, for I am thy God: I will strengthen thee; yea, I will uphold thee with the right hand of My righteousness. Behold, all they that are incensed against thee shall be ashamed and confounded; they that strive with thee shall be as nothing, and shall perish.' The brave words rang in his ears, and when he went to rest, they shaped his dreams. In a vision the Glorified Lord spoke to his troubled heart. '"Fear not,"' was His command, 'but speak and keep not silence; "for I am with thee"; and no man will set upon you to do you evil; because I have much folk in this city.'

Is. xli. 10, 11.

The mischievous expectation of an immediate Advent.

The vision rallied the Apostle, and he resumed the conflict with fresh fortitude. His first step was the writing of another letter to the distracted Church at Thessalonica, and it was a delicate and difficult task. His embarrassment was that he shared the universal belief in the imminence of the Second Advent. During his Macedonian ministry he had proclaimed that the Lord would certainly appear within the lifetime of that generation, and he had reaffirmed it in his first letter. Indeed it was his proclamation of this doctrine that had occasioned all the trouble; and the only effective remedy lay in a clear recognition of its absolute erroneousness and a return to the explicit teaching of the Lord. He had represented the progress of His Kingdom as no sudden catastrophe but a gradual and protracted development, like the ripening of the harvest—'first the blade, then the ear, then the full corn in the ear,' or the operation of leaven, slowly permeating the mass of dough. And He had spoken of the Bridegroom 'tarrying' and the

Cf. iv. 15-17.

Mk. iv. 28; Mt. xiii. 33.

Mt. xxv. 5, 14, 19.

Master 'travelling into a far country' and returning 'after a long time.' It was human impatience of the divine long-suffering that had introduced the idea of an immediate Advent; and it would have been well not only for Thessalonica but for Christendom in succeeding generations had the Apostle recognised the mischievous error and boldly repudiated it. But herein he was the child of his time. It was only the stern logic of events that exposed the error, and meanwhile he clung to it.

The Apostle's corrective.

Hence the difficulty which he experienced in dealing with the Thessalonian situation. Blind to the truth which would have calmed the wild frenzy and restored the Church to sanity, he had recourse, though not without a latent misgiving which betrays itself in frequent hesitation, eager emphasis, and confused expression, to an ingenious theory which in very deed amounts to a denial of his postulate of the imminence of the final consummation. He insists that it is no innovation and no recantation. He had advanced it in his (Cf. II. 5.) personal teaching during his sojourn at Thessalonica. But his statement of it can hardly have been very precise, else it would not have been so entirely ignored. Probably it had been obscure in his own thought, and it was only now in the stress of controversial necessity that it was distinctly envisaged.

Jewish idea of pre-Messianic confederacy of lawlessness.

His argument is summarised by St. Jerome in the epigram that 'Christ would not come unless Antichrist had preceded';[1] and it is based on a doctrine which figures largely in the later Jewish theology, and which finds its earliest expression in the second Psalm—that the world's hostility to God would wax ever worse until it attained its height in a confederacy of the heathen nations against Him; and then the Messiah would appear, and 'break them with a rod of iron, and dash them in pieces like a potter's vessel,' and inaugurate His triumphant and glorious reign.[2] The idea

[1] *Algas. Quæst.* xi: 'Christum non esse venturum nisi præcessisset Antichristus.' Cf. Pelagius on 2 Th. ii. (in his commentary on the Pauline Epistles preserved among the works of St. Jerome): 'Nisi Antichristus venerit, non veniet Christus.'

[2] On the history and development of the idea cf. Bousset, *Der Antichrist* (Engl. transl. *The Antichrist Legend*); Schürer, *Hist. of Jew. People*, II. ii. pp. 164 ff.; art. *Antichrist* in *Encycl. Bibl.*

was shaped and elaborated by the national experience in succeeding generations, especially by the atrocities which were perpetrated by Antiochus Epiphanes and which roused the Maccabees to their heroic struggle. Antiochus is that enemy of God and His saints depicted in the Book of Daniel—the king who 'should do according to his will, and exalt himself and magnify himself above every god, and speak marvellous things against the God of gods, and prosper till the indignation should be accomplished.' The oppressed Jews recognised in him an incarnation of the world's enmity against God, and thenceforward that furious blasphemer stood in their minds as the image of the Messiah's protagonist in the final conflict. On that tragic Day of Atonement in the year 63 B.C., when Cneius Pompeius after long besiegement captured Mount Sion, and not only massacred twelve thousand Jews, but hewed down the priests at the altar and intruded into the Holy of Holies, where no foot save the High Priest's had ever trod,[1] it seemed as though the dread consummation had arrived; and the insulting foe was styled 'the Sinner,' 'the Lawless One.'[2]

Dan. xi. 36.

Cf. 2 Th. ii. 8.

Christian idea of the Antichrist.

It was natural that the Jewish doctrine should be retained in Christian theology with the necessary modification that the consummation was no longer the Advent of the Messiah but the Return of the Lord Jesus Christ; and it is in Paul's second letter to the Thessalonians that it makes its earliest appearance in Christian literature. Toward the close of the first century a new and significant title was coined for the enemy who should lead the forces of evil in the final conflict. He was called 'Antichrist,'[3] which signifies a rival Christ, an impostor arrogating to himself the true Christ's powers and offices and claiming the homage which is His prerogative.[4] Paul does not employ the title, but the idea

[1] Cf. Jos. *Ant.* XIV. iv. 2-4; *De Bell. Jud.* I. vii. 3-5.

[2] Cf. *Psalm. Sol.* ii. 1: ἐν τῷ ὑπερηφανεύεσθαι τὸν ἁμαρτωλὸν ἐν κριῷ κατέβαλλε τείχη ὀχυρά. xvii. 13: ἠρήμωσεν ὁ ἄνομος ἐπὶ τὴν γῆν ἡμῶν ἀπὸ ἐνοικούντων αὐτήν.

[3] St John is the first writer and the only N. T. writer who uses the appellation. Cf. 1 Jo. ii. 18, 22, iv. 3; 2 Jo. 7.

[4] Cf. ἀντιβασιλεύς, ἀνθύπατος (*proconsul*), 'antipope.' Chrys.: οὐ γὰρ εἰδωλολατρείαν ἄξει ἐκεῖνος ἀλλ' ἀντίθεός τις ἔσται καὶ πάντας καταλύσει τοὺς θεοὺς καὶ κελεύσει προσκυνεῖν αὐτὸν ἀντὶ τοῦ Θεοῦ. Theod. Mops.: 'Temptat enim ille per omnia illa quæ Christi sunt imitari, utpote et Christum se esse dicens.'

is his; for, according to his conception, the final apostasy will issue not from heathendom but from unbelieving Israel.[1] Cf. ii. 4. The Enemy, 'the Man of Lawlessness,' 'the Lawless One,' will be a false Messiah, an incarnation of Satan even as Cf. ii. 9. Christ was an incarnation of God,[2] enthroning himself in the Sanctuary, claiming divine attributes, and in the power of Satan exhibiting delusive signs and wonders.

The appearance of the Man of Lawlessness the prelude of the Second Advent.

Such is the conception which Paul here introduces; and it effectively served his immediate purpose. The Thessalonian enthusiasts believed that the Day of the Lord was imminent, and they were looking for His appearance, oblivious of the tremendous prelude. The order of events was, first, the revelation of Antichrist, and then, and not till then, the revelation of Christ.[3] Nor would that preliminary be immediately fulfilled. Already indeed the forces of lawlessness were gathering and seething beneath the surface like volcanic throbbings which will presently burst forth in ruinous convulsion; but meanwhile there was a restraining barrier, and until this was removed, the storm would not break.

The imperial 'restraint.'

What this barrier was the Apostle does not explicitly define. He speaks of it with studious reserve, designating it now 'the restraint' and again 'the restrainer,' and referring his readers to the teaching which they had heard from his lips during his ministry among them. And the reason appears when it is understood that the restraining barrier against the forces of lawlessness was the strong and beneficent authority of the Roman Empire, which maintained universal order and administered impartial justice.[4] Already, par- Cf. Ac. ticularly at Thessalonica, he had experienced its protection, xvii. 5-9. and it was his security amid the dangers which menaced him at Corinth even while he wrote. It is no wonder that he Cf. Rom. accounted it 'an ordinance of God,' and counselled his xiii. 1-3; converts to reverence and obey it; and so late as the close 1 Tim. ii. 1-3. of the second century Tertullian recognised it as the prin-

[1] Cf. Iren. v. xxx. 2, where the Antichrist's descent is reckoned from the tribe of Dan in accordance with Jer. viii. 16.

[2] Cf. Ambrstr.: 'Imitabitur enim Deum, ut sicut Filius Dei divinitatem suam homo natus vel factus signis ac virtutibus demonstravit; ita et Satanas in homine apparebit, ut virtutibus mendacii ostendat se Deum.'

[3] Cf. the apocalyptic programme in *Didache*, xvi.

[4] Cf. p. 10.

cipal reason why the Christians should pray for the peace of the Roman Empire that it delayed the impending horrors of the End of the World.[1]

The imperial authority, then, was the barrier, and until it was destroyed the storm would not break; and when this is understood, the Apostle's cryptic language becomes luminous. By 'the restraint' he means the Roman rule, and by 'the restrainer' the Roman Emperor. Nor is it strange that he should have spoken thus vaguely. If the preaching of the Kingdom of Heaven was construed as treason,[2] the least whisper of the impending dissolution of the Empire would have exposed him and his followers to condign punishment.[3]

Antichrist a person.

It hardly admits of question that the Antichrist was, in the Apostle's thought, no mere impersonation of the principle of evil[4] but an actual person. Not only does he style him 'the Man of Lawlessness,' 'the Son of Ruin,' 'the Lawless One,' but he represents his appearing as 'a revelation' and 'an advent' in precise analogy with the revelation and advent of the Lord. Here, however, his definition ceases. Who the Antichrist would be he neither indicates nor professes to know. His identification was reserved for later generations, and each recognised him as a present enemy of God and the Gospel.

Cf. 2 Th. ii. 3, 6, 8, 9.

Historical identifications:

(1) Nero *redivivus.*

The earliest identification is found in the Book of Revelation some forty years later. Much had transpired during the interval—not only the destruction of Jerusalem, sacred and dear to Christian as well as Jewish hearts, but the persecutions

[1] *Apol.* 32.

[2] Cf. pp. 131, 138.

[3] Cf. Chrys.: *εἰ γὰρ εἶπεν ὅτι μικρὸν ὕστερον καταλυθήσεται ἡ Ῥωμαίων ἀρχὴ, ἤδη εὐθέως ἂν αὐτὸν καὶ κατώρυξαν ὡς λυμεῶνα καὶ τοὺς πιστοὺς ἅπαντας ὡς ἐπὶ τούτῳ ζῶντας καὶ στρατευομένους.* Hieronym. *Algas. Quæst.* xi: 'Nec vult aperte dicere Romanum imperium destruendum, quod ipsi qui imperant æternum putant.' The Fathers generally understand 'the restraint' as the Roman authority (*τὴν Ῥωμαϊκὴν ἀρχήν*), but there were at least two other interpretations: 1. The miraculous grace of the Holy Spirit. Cf. Severianus (Cramer, *Cat.* vi. 388): '*τὸ κατέχον,*' *φησί, τὴν τοῦ Ἁγίου Πνεύματος χάριν.* This Chrys. rejects because (1) Paul would then have spoken explicitly: there would have been no occasion for reticence; and (2) the *charisms* of the Holy Spirit had then ceased, yet Antichrist had not appeared. 2. The decree of God, *τοῦ Θεοῦ τὸν ὅρον* (Theod. Mops.). It rules out both that in neither case could Paul have contemplated 'the restrainer' being 'removed.'

[4] So Lightfoot.

of Nero and Domitian. Rome, once the guardian of justice and the refuge of the oppressed, was now the murderess of the saints, and the name of Nero was execrated. Such was the horror which his cruelties had inspired in the minds of his outraged subjects that, when he died, they could scarce believe it; and a wild legend arose and persisted long that he was still alive, lurking among the Parthians and biding his time to swoop upon Rome and wreak vengeance upon his enemies.[1] It evinces the strength of the belief that there are on record no fewer than three instances of impostors presenting themselves in his name. The year after his death, in the reign of Galba, a slave, who resembled the tyrant in his turn for harping and singing, gathered an armed following in the island of Cythnos and occasioned a widespread panic, which subsided only when, not without difficulty, he was slain and his head exhibited in Asia and Rome.[2] The second appeared in the East during the reign of Titus, escaping on the dispersion of his followers into Parthia;[3] and the third in the reign of Domitian thirty years after Nero's death.[4] The legend that he was still alive persisted early in the second century, and it was hoped by the Christians in those days that he would return and usher in the end.[5]

It was thus natural that the Christians should recognise Nero as the Enemy of God and expect that he would reappear and inaugurate the final conflict; and this is St. John's doctrine of the Antichrist in the Book of Revelation. 'The wild beast which you saw was, and is not, and will presently
ascend from the abyss and go his way to ruin. And the xvii. 8.
inhabitants of the earth will be amazed, they whose name has not been written on the Book of Life from the foundation of the world, when they see the wild beast, that he was and is not and will come.' This is the Antichrist—Nero
redivivus—a baleful counterpart of Him 'who is and who i. 8, 18.
was and who is coming,' 'the Living' who 'became dead and is living for evermore.'[6]

[1] Cf. Suet. *Ner.* 57.

[2] Cf. Tac. *Hist.* II. 8, 9.

[3] Zonar. XI. 18.

[4] Suet. *Ner.* 57.

[5] Dion. *Chrys. Orat.* xxi.

[6] Chrys. commits the anachronism of identifying the Pauline 'Man of Lawlessness' with Nero *redivivus*; and Baur and Weizsäcker, accepting the identification, find in it an argument against the Pauline authorship of the epistle.

(2) The Huns.

The legend gradually ceased as time ran its course and the advent of the Antichrist was still delayed; and another reading of the prophecy came into vogue in the latter half of the fourth century. The Huns were pressing upon the Empire from the East, and in this new peril Ephrem Syrus perceived a premonition of the impending catastrophe.[1] And again in the seventh century, when Christendom was

(3) Islam.

menaced by Islam, this fresh terror was interpreted as the approach of the Antichrist.[2]

(4) The Universal Bishop.

As strife and confusion increased within the borders of the Church, a new possibility was discerned; and so early as the close of the sixth century, when John, the Patriarch of Constantinople, the rival of the Bishop of Rome, assumed the style of Universal Bishop, St. Gregory the Great indignantly denounced 'the haughty and pompous title.' He called upon all Christian hearts to reject 'the blasphemous name.' And he recognised in the presumption which usurped 'this uncanonical dignity,' a sign of the coming of Antichrist and compared it to the pride of Satan in aspiring to be higher than all the angels.[3]

(5) The Pope.

The growing corruption of the Church stirred the hearts of her nobler sons, and it inflamed the indignant zeal of the Spirituals, those stern enthusiasts of the Franciscan Order.[4] Toward the close of the twelfth century Joachim, Abbot of Floris in the Kingdom of Naples, identified the apocalyptic

Rev. xvii. 5

'Babylon the Great, the Mother of the harlots and of the abominations of the earth,' not with pagan Rome but with the worldly and vice-laden Rome of his day; and in the thirteenth century Peter John Oliva dared to affirm not only that the Scarlet Woman 'stood for the Roman nation and Empire as it was once in the state of paganism and as it was afterwards in the faith of Christ' but that 'in the opinion of some Antichrist would be a false Pope.' It was but a step further to John Wycliffe's assertion that the Pope was not the Vicar of Christ but the Vicar of Antichrist.[5]

[1] Homilies on the Antichrist. Cf. Pseudo-Hippolytus, περὶ τῆς συντελείας τοῦ κόσμου, and Philip Solitarius, *Dioptr.* iii. 10 ff. (Migne, *Pat. Gr.* 127).

[2] Apocalypse of Pseudo-Methodius (*Orthodoxographa*).

[3] *Epist.* IV. 32, 33.

[4] Milman, *Lat. Chr.* XII. vi.

[5] *Dial.* xxxi. 73.

And Luther had no hesitation in declaring that 'the Pope is the Antichrist' and identifying him with 'the Man of Lawlessness.' This became an article of the Reformed Creed,[1] and the Romanists naturally retaliated and declared that the Reformation was the Apostasy and Luther and his accomplices the precursors of Antichrist.[2] And indeed to peaceable men it might reasonably seem as though the Reformation were nothing else than the mustering of the forces of evil against the Church of God. The state of the world, as they viewed it, is thus depicted in a Colloquy of Erasmus written in 1525 amid the confusions which culminated two years later in the sack of Rome:[3] 'A financial famine is pressing hard on every court; the peasants are exciting perilous commotions, undeterred from their purpose by so many massacres; the populace is studying anarchy; the house of the Church is being shaken by perilous factions; this way and that the seamless robe of Jesus is being torn asunder. The Lord's Vineyard is being wasted no longer by a single boar, and at the same time the authority of the priests is in peril and their tithes withal, the dignity of the theologians, the majesty of the monks; confession is tottering, vows are wavering, the pontifical laws are slipping away, the Eucharist is called in question, Antichrist is expected; the whole world is in travail with I know not what great evil.'

(6) The Reformers.

An unchristian invention.

Thus it appears that each successive age has recognised a contemporary fulfilment of the prophecy of the Antichrist, and has taken those commotions which, appalling as they seem to faithless hearts, are ever the birth-pangs of a nobler order, for mutterings of the approaching storm,

[1] In their address to King James his translators express their contentment with his *Argumentum pro Juramento Fidelitatis*, 'which hath given such a blow unto that man of sin, as will not be healed.' Cf. *Westminster Confession*, XXV. vi: 'The Pope of Rome . . . is that antichrist, that man of sin, and son of perdition, that exalteth himself in the church against Christ, and all that is called God.'

[2] Cf. Erasm. *Epist.* XV. 17 (London, 1642), *Ludovico Episc. Torracensi*, June 18, 1521: 'Ex amicorum litteris didici monachum quendam apud Christianissimum Galliarum Regem in concione magis etiam insanisse: qui dixerit jam adventurum antichristum, cum extiterint quatuor præcursores, Minorita nescio quis in Italia, Lutherus in Germania, Jacobus Faber in Gallia, Erasmus in Brabantia.'

[3] *Colloq. Puerp.*

harbingers of the end of all things. Those pages of history enforce the warning which our Lord gave His disciples on the eve of His departure: 'See to it that no one lead you astray. You will presently hear of wars and rumours of wars: look you, be not alarmed. All this is but the beginning of travail-pangs. It must come to pass, but the end is not yet. And of that day and hour no one knows, neither the angels of heaven nor the Son, but the Father alone.' It is a grievous fault of the Apostolic Church that she was deaf to her Lord's admonition and clung to her impatient expectation of an immediate Advent, involving herself, as the years passed, in ever deeper embarrassment and bewilderment; and it must be confessed that the prime responsibility rests with Paul. It was he who imported into Christian theology that Rabbinical notion which has persisted to this day and has so often served the unhallowed uses of controversial warfare. It is alien from the teaching of our Blessed Lord. He foretold indeed the rise of false Christs and false prophets amid the confusion of the Jewish state as the already inevitable catastrophe of her destruction by the Romans approached;[1] but the eschatological programme of a final apostasy and a scenic triumph is a picturesque fiction of the later Jewish theology. And it is instructive that, though the Apostle John accepted it in the Book of Revelation and recognised the Antichrist as Nero *redivivus*, he presently abandoned the wild dream. In his First Epistle, the latest of his writings, where he deals with the Cerinthian heresy, he defines the Antichrist as a spirit or principle—the Doketic denial of the reality of the Incarnation; and since that principle found various expressions, he recognised many Antichrists in his day. This rendering of the idea won a measure of acceptance, and it still had its advocates in St. Augustine's day;[2] but unfortunately the cruder notion maintained its ground and prevailed.

Mt. xxiv. 4, 6, 36; Mk. xiii. 8.

Mt. xxiv. 24.

ii. 18, 22, iv. 3; cf. 2 Jo. 7.

The Apostle's use of the idea.

That imagination of Jewish eschatology was familiar to Paul's mind, and it furnished him with a cogent argument against the excesses of the Thessalonian enthusiasts. The Second Advent was indeed imminent. The glorious con-

[1] Cf. *The Days of His Flesh*, pp. 423 f.

[2] Cf. *De Civ. Dei*, xx. xix. 3.

summation was at hand, but it would not immediately arrive. It would be heralded by two world-shaking preliminaries—the dissolution of the Roman Empire and the appearance of the Antichrist;[1] and neither of these had yet come to pass. The argument was indeed an effective antidote to the Thessalonian unrest; but it was a stark contradiction of the admonition which the Lord had left with His disciples and which the Apostle had quoted in his first letter, that they should refrain from curious inquiry regarding 'the periods and the crises.' And it seems that he presently recognised the illegitimacy of the argument. At all events he never repeated it; nor is there any record of the effect which it produced on the distracted Church at Thessalonica.

Cf. v. 1.

The Second Letter to Thessalonica

The address.

The letter begins with the customary address:

i. 1 Paul and Silvanus and Timothy to the Church of the Thessa-
2 lonians in God our Father and the Lord Jesus Christ. Grace to
you and peace from God the Father and the Lord Jesus Christ.

Commendation and encouragement.

Ere entering on his argument the Apostle pays a deserved tribute to the constant and increasing faith and love of the Thessalonians, and assures them of his pride in their heroic steadfastness amid the storm of persecution. And he bids them recognise what the ordeal meant. God's righteousness demanded the vindication of His cause; and thus their sufferings were an evidence of His speedy intervention. The day of reckoning could not be long delayed. It appears that the tidings of the Church's unhappy plight had been conveyed to the Apostle not merely by Timothy's report but by a letter from the Presbyters; and he expressly acknowledges it. In response to his request for their prayers they had assured him that they 'were always praying' for him and his colleagues, and he reciprocates: 'we also are always praying for you.'

Cf. 1 Th. v. 25.

[1] Cf. Hieronym. *Algas. Quæst.* xi: 'Nisi, inquit, fuerit Romanum imperium ante desolatum et Antichristus præcesserit, Christus non veniet: qui ideo ita venturus est ut Antichristum destruat.'

3 It is our duty to be thanking God always for you, brothers;
and indeed it is well deserved, because your faith is growing so
largely and the love which you all without exception bear to
4 one another is so increasing that we on our part boast of
you among the Churches of God for your endurance and faith
amid all your persecutions and the distresses which you are so
5 stoutly supporting—a demonstration of the righteous judgment
of God, that you may be accounted worthy of the Kingdom
6 of God for which you are indeed suffering, since it is righteous in
God's sight to repay distress to those who are distressing you,
7 and relief to you who are distressed—to you and us too—
when the Lord Jesus is revealed from heaven with His mighty
Is. lxvi. 15.
8 angels 'in a flame of fire,' taking vengeance on 'those who
Jer. x. 25; Ps. lxxix. 6.
know not God' and those who hearken not to the Gospel of
9 our Lord Jesus. These will pay the penalty—the ruin of
Is. ii. 10, 19, 21.
eternal [1] banishment 'from the face of the Lord and from the
10 glory of His strength,' when He comes to be 'glorified in His
holy ones' and 'admired' in all who have held the Faith—
11 for our testimony was confirmed on you [2]—on that Day. And
with this end in view we also are always praying for you,
that our God may count you worthy of your calling [3] and fulfil
by His power your every desire for goodness and every work
Is. xxiv. 15, lxvi. 5.
12 of faith, that 'the name of our Lord' Jesus 'may be glorified
in you' and you in Him, according to the grace of our God and
the Lord Jesus Christ.

The eschatological programme.

And now the Apostle plunges into his argument. He begins with a warning. The source of the trouble at Thessalonica was threefold: the confident predictions of the enthusiasts, their plausible argumentation, and their appeal to a letter

[1] It is illegitimate to build on this phrase a dogma of 'everlasting punishment.' The idea of αἰώνιος is *quality*, not *duration*. In the *Book of Enoch* εἰς τὸν αἰῶνα denotes a period of seventy generations (x. 5, 12), and a period of 500 years is called ζωὴ αἰώνιος, 'an eternal life.' Eternity excludes the idea of time. 'Eternity (αἰών),' says Philo (*Quod Deus sit Immutabilis*, p. 277), 'is the life of God; and in Eternity there is neither past nor future.'

[2] The MS. reading ἐπιστεύθη is difficult. The choice lies between connecting ἐφ' ἡμᾶς with τὸ μαρτύριον, 'our testimony unto you,' though ἐπὶ here would rather mean 'against' (cf. Lk. ix. 5), and referring it, notwithstanding the order, to ἐπιστεύθη, 'our testimony was believed as far as you,' *ad vos usque, in occidente* (Beng.). Two minuscs. (31, 139) have ἐπιστώθη, 'was confirmed' (cf. 2 Tim. iii. 14), and this probably is the original reading. The phrase occurs in LXX (Ps. xciii. 5; 2 Chr. i. 9). Cf. W. H., *Notes*.

[3] Our calling is probation. God calls us not because we are worthy but that we may prove worthy. Cf. Aug. *Lib. de Prædest. Sanct.* 37: 'Elegit ergo nos Deus in Christo ante mundi constitutionem, prædestinans nos in adoptionem filiorum: non quia per nos sancti et immaculati futuri eramus, sed elegit prædestinavitque ut essemus.'

which professed to have emanated from him and his colleagues and which, they claimed, supported their eschatological contentions. It is hardly likely that this was a deliberate forgery; and the probability is that it was a private communication which he had written ere the controversy emerged and which lent itself to misconstruction. These were the influences which had done the mischief, and he begs the Thessalonians to disregard them and turn a deaf ear to the cry: 'The Day of the Lord is upon us!' The time was not yet ripe for the Second Advent, and the evidence was twofold. First, according to the eschatological programme the final consummation would be preceded by the inauguration of the Great Apostasy and the appearance of the Man of Lawlessness. The Apostle portrays this impious Adversary in the Jewish fashion after the pattern of his historic prototype Antiochus Epiphanes, who, like all the Seleucid kings, had assumed the title of God and, in his attempt to extirpate the Jewish religion, 'polluted the Sanctuary in Jerusalem' by building over the Altar an altar to Zeus Olympius.[1] The Man of Lawlessness was a veritable Antichrist, a rival of Christ, usurping His prerogatives. His appearance would precede the Second Advent, and he had not yet been revealed. The forces of evil were indeed already gathering, but they were still restrained by the strong barrier of the imperial order; and until that barrier was broken down, the catastrophe would be averted. The continued existence of the Roman Empire was thus an evidence that the time for the Lord's Return had not yet arrived.

Cf. 1 Mac. i. 54-59; 2 Mac. vi. 2.

[1] The Fathers, taking the Apostle's language as a literal prediction, found its interpretation difficult after the destruction of the Temple, when the Sanctuary no longer existed. Irenæus (V. xxx. 4) says merely 'he will sit in the Temple at Jerusalem,' ignoring the difficulty; but his successors proposed two explanations. 1. Pelagius conceived of a restored Temple ('Templum Hierusalem reficere tentabit omnesque legis ceremonias restaurare'). 2. The Antiochene interpreters took 'the Sanctuary' as meaning 'the Churches'—εἰς τὰς πανταχοῦ ἐκκλησίας (Chrys.), *in domibus orationum* (Theod. Mops.). Hieronym. mentions both views and prefers the latter, substituting 'the Church' for 'the Churches' (cf. *Algas. Quæst.* xi: 'in Templo Dei, vel Hierosolymis, ut quidam putant, vel in Ecclesia, ut verius arbitramur'). Aug. (cf. *De Civ. Dei*, XX. xix. 2) cannot decide ('ego prorsus quid dixerit me fateor ignorare'); but he justly observes that the Apostle cannot have meant a heathen temple, and mentions approvingly another opinion—that it is not Antichrist himself that is intended but the whole body of his followers, and εἰς τὸν ναὸν means 'as the Sanctuary' ('tanquam ipse sit Templum Dei').

ii. 1 But we beg you, brothers, as regards the Advent of our Lord
2 Jesus Christ and our gathering home to Him,[1] that you be not
Mt. xxiv. 6. hastily swept from your judgment or 'alarmed' either by prophetic inspiration or by argument [2] or by a letter purporting
to be from us [3] to the effect that the Day of the Lord is upon
3 us. Let no man lead you astray in any manner, inasmuch as
1 Mac. ii. 15. 'the Apostasy' must come in the first instance, and the Man
of Lawlessness,[4] 'the Son of Ruin,' be revealed, the Adversary
Cf. Jo. xvii. 12. 4 who so 'exalts himself above every' so called 'god' or object
Dan. xi. 36; cf. Ez. xxviii. 2. of worship as to take his seat in the Sanctuary of God, pro-
5 claiming himself God.[5] Do you not remember that, while
6 I was still among you, I used to tell you all this? And for
the present you know what is the restraint, that he may be
7 revealed at his own season. For the mystery of lawlessness [6]
is already being set in operation, pending only the removal of
Ps. Sol. xvii. 13. 8 the temporary restrainer. And then will 'the Lawless One'
be revealed, whom the Lord Jesus 'will sweep away with the
breath of His mouth' and annihilate with the apparition of
9 His Advent.[7] And his advent according to the operation of
Mt. xxiv. 24. Satan is accompanied with every sort of power and 'signs and
10 portents' of falsehood and with every sort of error of unrighteousness for those who are doomed to ruin; forasmuch as
they did not welcome the love of the Truth [8] that they might
11 be saved. And it is for this reason that God is sending them
12 the operation of error, that they may put faith in the lie, in

[1] In the only other N. T. passage where ἐπισυναγωγή occurs (Heb. x. 25), it denotes the assembling of the Church. Our gathering in Church is prophetic of our final home-gathering. It is a kindly word. Cf. our Lord's use of the verb (Mt. xxiii. 37).

[2] Chrys.: διὰ πιθανολογίας (cf. Col. ii. 4).

[3] One 9th c. MS. (P) has ὡς παρ' ἡμῶν. Cf. Theod. Mops.: 'quasi ex nobis'; Ambrstr.: 'tanquam a nobis missam.' δι' ἡμῶν is perhaps an assimilation to the preceding clauses.

[4] ὁ ἄνθρωπος τῆς ἀνομίας ℵB. τῆς ἁμαρτίας (ADEFGKLP) is probably an interpretative gloss. Cf. 1 Jo. iii. 4.

[5] ἀποδεικνύναι was used of the proclamation of a king. Cf. Strabo, 540: βασιλέα δ' ἠξίουν αὐτοῖς ἀποδειχθῆναι. 547: καὶ τούτων ἀπέδειξεν αὐτὸν βασιλέα. Jos. *Ant.* VI. iii. 3; VI. xiv. 2.

[6] An impious counterpart of τὸ τῆς εὐσεβείας μυστήριον (1 Tim. iii. 16).

[7] Cf. Hieronym. *Algas. Quæst.* xi: 'et quomodo tenebræ solis fugantur adventu, sic illustratione adventus sui eum Dominus destruet atque delebit.' ἐπιφανεία denoted the breaking of day (cf. Polyb. III. xciv. 3), the sudden appearance of an enemy (cf. I. liv. 2), the apparition of a deity (cf. Plut. *Them.* xxx. 3). Hence 'the appearing of Christ' either at the Incarnation (cf. 2 Tim. i. 10) or at the Second Advent (cf. 1 Tim. vi. 14).

[8] Not simply 'truth' as opposed to 'falsehood' but 'the truth of the Gospel' (cf. Rom. ii. 8; 2 Cor. iv. 2, vi. 7, xiii. 8; Gal. ii. 5, 14; Eph. i. 13; Col. i. 5) or 'Him who is the Truth' (cf. Jo. xiv. 6). Chrys.: ἀγάπην δὲ ἀληθείας τὸν

order that all may be judged who have not put faith in the
Truth but consented to unrighteousness.

Exhortation to steadfastness.

It was a dark prospect, and the Apostle expresses his thankfulness that the Thessalonians would have no part in the impending Apostasy. And he charges them meanwhile to abide by his teaching, and prays for their comfort and confirmation.

13 But it is our duty to be thanking God always for you,
brothers 'beloved of the Lord,' that God chose you from the Dt. xxxiii.
beginning [1] to be saved by sanctification of the Spirit and faith 12.
14 in the Truth. And to this He also called you through our
Gospel, that you may win the glory of our Lord Jesus Christ.
15 So then, brothers, stand firm, and hold fast the traditions
which you were taught whether by word or by letter of ours.
16 And may He, our Lord Jesus Christ and God our Father, who Cf. 1 Th.
loved us and gave us eternal comfort and a good hope in grace, iii. 11.
17 comfort your hearts and establish them in every good work
and word.

Request for the Thessalonians' prayers. Cf. Ac. xviii. 10.

The Apostle has now completed his argument, but ere closing the letter he introduces two practical concerns. One is his own situation at Corinth, where even as he wrote he was menaced by Jewish hostility; and he bespeaks the prayers of the Thessalonians not merely for his personal safety but for the success of his ministry.

iii. 1 To conclude: pray, brothers, for us, that 'the Word of the Ps. cxlvi.
Lord may run its course' and be glorified, as it is indeed 15.
2 among you, and that we may be rescued from the outrageous [2]
3 and evil men; for it is not every one that has faith. But
faithful is the Lord, and He will establish you and guard you

Χριστὸν καλεῖ. They were doomed because they had not welcomed the love of Christ. It favours this interpretation that, except in Lk. xi. 42, ἡ ἀγάπη τοῦ Θεοῦ is always subjective ('God's love for us'), not objective ('our love for God').

[1] ἀπ' ἀρχῆς, either 'from all eternity' (cf. 1 Jo. i. 1, ii. 13, 14) or 'from the beginning of your Christian life' (cf. 1 Jo. ii. 7, 24, iii. 11). The phrase occurs nowhere else in the Pauline writings, and the variant ἀπαρχήν BFGP Vulg. ('chose you as the first-fruits') may be authentic. Cf. Rom. xvi. 5; 1 Cor. xvi. 15. Strictly the Philippians were 'the first-fruits of Macedonia,' but as converts of the same mission the Thessalonians might fairly share the designation.

[2] ἄτοπος (cf. Lk. xxiii. 41) denotes *lawless violence*. Cf. *Oxyrh. Pap.* 904, where a police official complains of ἀτοπήματα inflicted upon him in the discharge of his duty—'being suspended by ropes and belaboured with blows on the body.'

4 from the Evil One. And we have, in the Lord, every confidence in you[1] that what we charge you both are doing and
5 will do. And may the Lord direct your hearts into the love
of God and into the endurance of Christ.

Rebuke of pious idlers.

His other concern was the restoration of order in the Thessalonian Church. The prime offenders were the enthusiasts who, anticipating the Lord's immediate Return, had abandoned their industries and were living on charity; and he reminds them of his own example during his ministry at Thessalonica—how he had toiled late and early at his craft of tent-making that he might earn his daily bread.

6 And we charge you, brothers, in the name of our Lord Jesus
Christ, that you withdraw from every brother who is comporting himself in a disorderly fashion and not according to the
7 tradition which you received from us. You yourselves know
how you must follow our example. We were never disorderly
8 among you and never owed the bread we ate to any one's
charity. No, toiling and moiling night and day, we worked
9 hard that we might not be a burden upon any of you. Not
because we have no authority, but that we might present
10 ourselves to you as a pattern for your imitation. For, when we
were among you, we used to give you this charge: 'If one will
11 not work, neither let him eat.'[2] We hear of some comporting
themselves among you in a disorderly fashion, plying no busi-
12 ness but playing the busybody.[3] And such persons we charge
and exhort in the Lord Jesus that they peaceably do their work
13 and eat their own bread. And as for you, brothers, do the
14 honourable thing and never lose heart. And if any one does
not hearken to what we are saying in our letter,[4] mark the man

Cf. 1 Cor. ix. 4-10.

[1] Cf. Gal. v. 10. Since, however, πεποιθέναι is construed with either ἐν (cf. Phil. ii. 24, iii. 3, 4) or ἐπί with accus. (cf. Mt. xxvii. 43; 2 Cor. ii. 3) or dat. (cf. Lk. xi. 22; 2 Cor. i. 9; Heb. ii. 13), ἐν Κυρίῳ may here be the direct object: 'we have confidence in the Lord regarding you.'

[2] A proverbial maxim. Wetstein quotes Rabbinical parallels. Cf. a monk's saying (Socr. *Eccl. Hist.* IV. 23): ὁ μοναχὸς εἰ μὴ ἐργάζοιτο, ἐπίσης τῷ πλεονεκτεῖ κρίνεται.

[3] On the word-play cf. 1 Cor. vii. 31; 2 Cor. vi. 10. περιεργάζεσθαι, 'play the περίεργος' (cf. 1 Tim. v. 13). Cf. Plat. *Apol.* 19 B: Σωκράτης ἀδικεῖ καὶ περιεργάζεται ζητῶν τά τε ὑπὸ γῆς καὶ οὐράνια. M. Aur. x. 2; Ecclus. iii. 23.

[4] Since the Apostle apprehends that his written message may carry less weight than a personal address (cf. 2 Cor. x. 11), it is plain that neither he nor his readers regarded his letters as inspired oracles. By 'the letter' (τῆς ἐπιστολῆς) he means the present letter (cf. 1 Th. v. 27); but Grot., Beng., and others connect διὰ τῆς ἐπιστολῆς with σημειοῦσθε, 'signify him in your letter,' meaning that he expected an answer.

and have no intercourse with him, that he may feel ashamed.
15 And do not count him as an enemy but admonish him as a
16 brother. And may He, the Lord of Peace, give you peace at
every moment wherever you may be. The Lord be with you
all.

And now he takes the pen and signs the letter with his own hand; and in view of the mischievous use which had been made of that letter professing to be his, he calls attention to his characteristic autograph and intimates that no letter is his which does not bear it. **The Apostle's sign-manual.** Cf. ii. 2.

17 THE GREETING WITH MY OWN—PAUL'S—HAND. THIS IS
18 THE TOKEN IN EVERY LETTER: THUS I WRITE. THE GRACE
OF OUR LORD JESUS CHRIST BE WITH YOU ALL.

It would be the month of November when the letter was written; and after its despatch, doubtless by Timothy, Paul addressed himself with undivided energy to the work of evangelising Corinth. He was not unaided. Silas had been with him ever since his return from Macedonia;[1] nor would Timothy's errand to Thessalonica occupy long. He would soon return and resume his office as attendant. For a while no difficulty was encountered. The Jews would indeed watch the progress of the Gospel with jealous eyes, but they refrained from overt opposition. It was not that their hostility was abated, but rather that they were held in check by 'the restraint' of the Roman law and durst not venture on molestation. **Peaceful ministry at Corinth.**

Thus peacefully passed the winter and the spring, but midsummer brought trouble. Achaia was a senatorial province, and it was governed by a Proconsul who held office, as a rule, for a single year. The proconsular year began on July 1,[2] and in the inauguration of the new administration the Jews recognised their opportunity.[3] **Accession of new Proconsul.**

The new Proconsul was L. Junius Annæus Gallio, the elder brother of the celebrated L. Annæus Seneca and uncle of the poet Lucan. His original name was M. Annæus Novatus,[4] **L. Junius Annæus Gallio.**

[1] Cf. p. 152. [2] Cf. Append. I.

[3] Cf. the Sanhedrin's renewed activity against Paul on the accession of Festus to the procuratorship of Judæa (p. 484).

[4] He is the Novatus of the dedication of Sen. *De Ira*.

but he was adopted by the distinguished rhetorician L. Junius Gallio and assumed his name. The gracious qualities which won him this good fortune, he retained throughout his career; and his famous brother, who dedicated to him his works on 'Anger' and 'The Happy Life,' has pleasantly portrayed his character[1]—his gentleness, his frugality, his courtesy, his tact, his truthfulness, and withal his modesty and amiability. 'Other vices he knew not, but flattery he hated': 'to love him to the utmost was to love him all too little': 'no mortal was so sweet to one as he was to all.'

Arraignment of Paul. Mistaking gentleness for weakness, the Jews conceived that they might bend Gallio to their purposes. Soon after his accession they let loose the animosity which they had so long been harbouring, and, swooping upon the Apostle, probably while he was preaching in the market-place, they brought him into the Proconsul's court. They displayed none of the astuteness which had characterised the procedure of their Thessalonian co-religionists. The latter had (Ac. xvii. 7.) cunningly twisted the proclamation of the Kingdom of Heaven into a seditious propaganda, thus at once enlisting the sympathy of the Greek populace and compelling the attention of the Roman magistrates; but it was a purely Jewish grievance that the Corinthian Jews preferred. 'This man,' ran their indictment, 'is persuading people to worship God contrary to the Law.'

The case dismissed. They quickly discovered that they had misconceived the character of the Proconsul. The fury of the howling fanatics[2] was odious to the cultured and tolerant Roman gentleman. Had their complaint been valid, he would indeed have entertained it and adjudicated it on its merits; but it had no *locus standi* in his court. It was a Jewish case, and since the Jews enjoyed autonomy in the regulation of their religious affairs,[3] it fell under the jurisdiction of the local synagogue. Paul was essaying to speak in his defence, but Gallio interrupted him and contemptuously stopped the proceedings. 'If,' he said, 'it had been some injustice or wicked knavery,

[1] *Nat. Quæst.* IV, *Præfat.*

[2] In Ac. xviii. 13 Cod. Bez. (D) has καταβοῶντες καὶ λέγοντες, 'shouting and saying.'

[3] Cf. p. 45.

you Jews, it would have been reasonable that I should have patience with you; but if it be questions about a word and names and your own law, you will see to it yourselves. I refuse to be a judge of these things.' Therewith he dismissed the case and ordered his lictors to remove the complainants from the bar.

Popular demonstration of anti-Jewish sentiment.

The court was thronged with spectators, the rabble of the city, who had seen Paul arrested and had followed to learn what was ado; and the issue delighted them by reason alike of the popularity which his ministry had won him and of the prevailing antipathy to the Jews. As the discomfited prosecutors were retiring from the court, they pressed about them and hustled them, and, not content with a hostile demonstration, they proceeded to actual violence. They laid hold on Sosthenes, who held the office of Ruler of the Synagogue, being probably the successor of Crispus, and in virtue of his office had taken a leading part in the prosecution, and fell to belabouring him.[1] It was the sort of horse-play which a mob loves, and, though it was done in full view of his tribunal, Gallio ignored it. He was disgusted with the Jews, and he regarded their rough handling as rude justice.[2]

Peaceful prosecution of Corinthian ministry.

This attempt to arrest the progress of the Gospel in Corinth served rather to further it. The Jews had invoked the Roman law, and it had declared against them; and thenceforth not only was Paul secure from their molestation, but the popular sympathy was engaged on his behalf. It was early in August, A.D. 52, that he was arraigned before the

[1] In Ac. xviii. 17 the chief authorities (ℵAB Vulg.) have simply πάντες, 'they all,' and the question is who are meant. 1. On the supposition that Sosthenes the Ruler of the Synagogue is identical with 'Sosthenes the brother' (1 Cor. i. 1) and that, like Crispus, he was already a Christian (so Lightfoot), the Jews are meant; and a few insignificant MSS. read πάντες οἱ Ἰουδαῖοι. The idea is that in their discomfiture they vented their spleen on their apostate ruler. But they would hardly have ventured so far after their repulse. 2. DEHLP read πάντες οἱ Ἕλληνες, 'all the Greeks,' and, though only a gloss, this rightly defines the situation. If this Sosthenes be the Sosthenes of the epistle, he was converted subsequently; and indeed the identification is precarious, since the name was quite common.

[2] It is an entire misunderstanding of the narrative that has made the name of Gallio a byword for religious indifference—'a lukewarm Laodicean or an indifferent Gallio' (Scott, *Old Mort.* chap. XXI). His conduct is a conspicuous example of the Roman justice which so often befriended the Apostle.

Proconsul, and he prosecuted his ministry undisturbed until the close of February, A.D. 53.[1]

VII

THE HOMEWARD JOURNEY

Ac. xviii. 18*b*-22.

Departure from Corinth.

It was time that the Apostle should take his departure from Corinth and turn his face homeward. His mission had lasted three years, and now that he had evangelised Macedonia and Achaia, he must carry the Gospel elsewhere and win yet other lands for Christ. And his resolution was precipitated by an untoward necessity. It appears that Corinth was somewhat insalubrious for strangers. Seneca mentions in one of his letters that his brother Gallio during his residence there was stricken with fever and, ascribing his ailment to local conditions, immediately quitted the city and made a sea-voyage.[2] The malady which afflicted the Proconsul, would find a ready victim in the Apostle, liable as he was to recurring attacks of ague [3] and exhausted by toil, peril, and anxiety; and like Gallio he left the city and betook himself to the port of Cenchreæ with the intention of embarking immediately on the homeward voyage.

The Apostle's company.

It is remarkable how, as the narrative proceeds, the Apostle bulks ever more largely in the historian's eyes; and from this stage onward the interest centres exclusively in him. He is the sole *persona dramatis*, and his companions figure unobtrusively in the background. No mention is made of his colleagues, Silas and Timothy, at his departure from Corinth; but it must be assumed that they accompanied him. The latter certainly did, since he attended him on his next mission; and so, it may be concluded, did Silas, though his participation in the second letter to Thessalonica is the last express record of his association with Paul, and

Cf. Ac. xix. 22.

[1] Cf. Append. I.

[2] Sen. *Epist.* civ: 'Illud mihi in ore domini mei Gallionis, qui cum in Achaia febrem habere cœpisset, protinus navem ascendit, clamitans non corporis esse sed loci morbum.'

[3] Cf. Append. III.

on the next and only occasion when he appears in the sacred narrative he is associated with the Apostle Peter, if he be indeed the Silvanus who served as the latter's amanuensis in the writing of his first letter. Nor were these his sole companions. His friends Aquila and Priscilla, whose house had been his abode during the eighteen months of his sojourn at Corinth, were minded to try their fortune elsewhere. Ephesus, the capital of the Province of Asia, had attracted them, and they would accompany the Apostle so far on his journey.

Cf. 1 Pet. v. 12.

Illness at Cenchreæ.

Syrian Antioch was his destination, and his purpose was to sail from Cenchreæ to Ephesus and thence to Seleuceia; but it was unpleasantly overruled. It seems that his indisposition increased, and ere he could embark he was prostrated by his malady. It happened fortunately that there resided at Cenchreæ a deaconess named Phœbe, who had doubtless been won by his preaching in the adjacent capital and who played a conspicuous and honourable part in the Church which presently grew up at the seaport. The care of the sick was a special office of the order of Deaconesses in the Apostolic Church; and it would appear that Phœbe had compassion on the invalid and tended him in his sickness. At all events, in a letter which he wrote four years later, he mentions her with affectionate commendation, and gratefully recalls how he, like many another, had experienced her kindly ministration; and it is reasonable to recognise here a reminiscence of the present crisis.[1]

Cf. Rom. xvi. 1, 2.

Nazirite vow.

It was a timely succour; for he was eager to press forward on his journey and address himself to fresh enterprise; and his anxiety is revealed by his behaviour. He was a Jew, and though he recognised that the Mosaic Law had fulfilled its end and was superseded by a nobler order, he clung to

[1] The evidence of Paul's sickness at Cenchreæ is threefold: 1. His vow (cf. Ac. xviii. 18). 2. The imperf. ἐξέπλει (Ac. xviii. 18), implying that his embarkation was delayed. 3. The term προστάτις (Rom. xvi. 2), which had two significant uses: (1) The patron of a resident alien at Athens was styled his προστάτης. (2) 'A succourer *from disease.*' Cf. Soph. *O. T.* 303 f.; Eur. *Andr.* 220 f. Thus Phœbe earned the title of προστάτις (1) by befriending a helpless stranger, and (2) by performing the womanly office of 'succouring his sickness' (προΐστασθαι τῆς νόσου). In Plin. *Epist.* x. 97 nursing is specified as an office of the Christian deaconesses (*ministræ*). Cf. Bingham, *Antiq.* II. xxii. 10.

the ancient pieties. It was customary for a Jew in sickness or any other distress not only to pray for deliverance but to assume the old Nazirite vow with such modifications as the altered conditions of the national life necessitated. The primitive observances were abstinence from wine and letting the hair grow during 'the days of separation,' and then on their accomplishment the presentation of a peace offering in the Temple at Jerusalem and the cropping of the hair and the burning of it in the fire on the altar. In later times, however, when so many of the Jews dwelt in other lands remote from the Temple, it would have been unseemly to travel unkempt to the Holy City, and it sufficed that the votary should shear his head ere setting forth and convey the hair to the Temple.[1] In the eagerness of his desire that God would restore him and suffer him to continue his labours, Paul assumed the Nazirite vow; and when his prayer was granted, he shaved his head and set forth on his voyage across the Ægean.[2]

Cf. Num. vi. 1-21.

Stay at Ephesus.

His destination was still Syrian Antioch, but it was necessary for the fulfilment of his vow that he should visit Jerusalem by the way; and so he took his passage by a ship bound for Cæsarea. She did not sail thither direct, but steered her course across the Ægean and put in at Ephesus; and there Aquila and Priscilla disembarked and established themselves in their new abode. The business of her lading detained the vessel some time in harbour; and the delay was in no wise unwelcome to Paul, since it afforded him an opportunity of acquainting himself with the Asian capital which he had intended visiting in the course of his second mission[3] and which, though his purpose had been overruled,

[1] Cf. Jos. *De Bell. Jud.* II. xv. 1.

[2] In Ac. xviii. 18 it is grammatically indeterminate whether *κειράμενος* relates to Paul or Aquila. It is generally referred to Paul; but some (as Chrys., Grot., Mey., Blass) connect it with Aquila, thus absolving the Apostle of a quite gratuitous suspicion of Judaism. The suggestion that the order of the names Πρίσκιλλα καὶ Ἀκύλας is designed to connect *κειράμενος* with the latter is untenable, since this is, with a single exception (1 Cor. xvi. 19), the constant order (cf. Ac. xviii. 26; Rom. xvi. 3; 2 Tim. iv. 19), marking doubtless the wife's superior distinction in the Church. It is decisive that Aquila stayed at Ephesus, whereas, had the vow been his, he must have proceeded to Jerusalem for its fulfilment. The construction of the sentence is plain when *καὶ σὺν αὐτῷ* Π. *καὶ* Ἀ. is taken as parenthetical.

[3] Cf. p. 119.

he still designed to win for Christ. It happened opportunely that the day of his arrival was the Sabbath,[1] and he betook himself to the Jewish synagogue and discoursed to the worshippers. His reception was a happy augury of future success. It seems that he gained at least one convert in Epænatus, whom he subsequently designated 'the first-fruits of Asia for Christ'; and so keen was their interest in his discourse that his hearers begged him to continue a while in their midst. It was impossible for him to comply, since he must proceed to Jerusalem for the discharge of his vow, and he would fain arrive in time for the approaching Feast of Pentecost. He must therefore take his departure and prosecute his journey; but he promised that, if it were God's will—a proviso which experience had taught him to emphasise—he would soon return.

Rom. xvi. 5.

Cf. Rom. i 10; 1 Cor. iv. 19.

Timothy's mission to Galatia.

Ephesus was the western terminus of the great Trade Route which led through the valley of the Mæander and the Lycus into Southern Galatia, the scene of the Apostle's previous labours; and his thoughts would go out to his churches there. Indeed there was reason for anxiety; for since his visitation of them in the early summer of the year 50 they had been grievously disturbed, and it may be that disquieting rumours had reached his ears. He would fain ascertain the truth; and it seems that he commissioned Timothy to travel thither from Ephesus, and revisit his home at Lystra, and rejoin him at Syrian Antioch with a report of the Galatian situation.[2]

Visit to Jerusalem and arrival at Antioch.

Setting sail from Ephesus, the ship arrived at Cæsarea, and there Paul disembarked and repaired to Jerusalem.[3]

[1] In Ac. xviii. 19 Syr. Vers. and several other authorities insert τῷ ἐπιόντι σαββάτῳ, 'on the following Sabbath,' after Ἔφεσον.

[2] This is conjectural (cf. Ramsay, *St. Paul the Traveller*, pp. 182 ff.), but it is by no means gratuitous. It is a reasonable explanation of the intimate knowledge which the Apostle's letter to the Galatian Churches evinces of the Galatian situation.

[3] Cf. Ac. xviii. 22: ἀναβάς, 'having gone up (to Jerusalem).' ἀναβαίνειν was the technical term for 'going up to the sacred capital' (cf. Lk. ii. 42; Jo. xii. 20). Conversely καταβαίνειν, 'go down from the capital to the provinces' (cf. κατέβη εἰς 'Αντιόχειαν). In view of the fact that in ver. 21 the chief authorities read ἀλλὰ ἀποταξάμενος καὶ εἰπών· πάλιν ἀνακάμψω, κ.τ.λ., omitting δεῖ με πάντως τὴν ἑορτὴν τὴν ἐρχομένην ποιῆσαι εἰς Ἱεροσόλυμα, some interpreters entirely eliminate the visit to Jerusalem and understand by ἀναβάς 'having gone up from

It was his fourth visit to the Holy City since his conversion, and it would extend over the sacred week. The time was spent in fellowship with the Church and the discharge of his devout offices in the Temple ; and then he took his departure, and travelled northward to Syrian Antioch, thus bringing his second mission to a close.

the harbour (of Cæsarea) to the town,' and by *κατέβη εἰς Ἀντιόχειαν* 'went down by ship from Cæsarea to Seleuceia, and thence on foot to Antioch' (Blass)—an amazing construction. Even if the clause in ver. 21 be abandoned, *ἀναβάς* and *κατέβη*, in view of their accustomed use, clearly indicate the visit to Jerusalem. Probably the clause was omitted in consequence of a misunderstanding of these terms ; but in any case it accurately defines the situation.

DEFECTION IN GALATIA

Ac. xviii. 22*b*, 23*a*; Gal.

'Paul, who walked in the Master's steps, diversified his discourse to suit his scholars' need, now burning and cutting, anon applying gentle salves.'

ST. CHRYSOSTOM.

Evil tidings from Galatia.

SYRIAN ANTIOCH was the capital of Gentile Christendom, and the Apostle's first duty on his arrival would be to lay before the Church which had sent him forth on his mission, a report of his achievements during those three eventful years. It was a stirring narrative, and it would inspire his hearers with gratitude to Almighty God and a resolution to prosecute still further the heroic enterprise of winning the world for Christ. Presently, however, his gladness was overclouded by evil tidings. Timothy had left him at Ephesus and travelled inland to Southern Galatia to ascertain how the churches there were faring; and now he arrives at Antioch with a distressful story.

Apparent settlement of the Judaistic controversy.

The decision of the Council at Jerusalem in the beginning of the year 50 had seemed to the Apostle a final settlement of the Judaist controversy; and it was with a sense of relief that he set forth on his second mission in the spring. He had betaken himself to Galatia, and had communicated the Council's resolution to each of his churches. It was a happy issue of a dissension which had threatened the disruption of Christendom. Henceforth Jew and Gentile would be 'one in Christ Jesus,' tolerant of mutual differences in the larger unity of a common faith. As the champion of Gentile liberty Paul was solicitous to define his attitude toward Jewish tradition. Ceremonial rites belonged to the category of 'things indifferent.' The one essential was faith in Christ, and they were not necessary to salvation; nevertheless they were endeared to the Jewish heart by long use, and there was no harm and there might be profit in their continued observance, so long as the solitary efficacy of faith

Cf. Ac. xvi. 4.

Gal. iii. 28.

was recognised. It was therefore, in his judgment, legitimate for Jewish Christians, if they would, to maintain those sacred and venerable institutions; and at Lystra he had furnished an impressive demonstration of his attitude. He adopted Timothy as his attendant, and since the lad was half Jewish, he circumcised him in token of his consideration for Jewish sensibilities.

Its recrudescence in Galatia.

It seemed a happy settlement, and he left his Galatian converts and passed over to Europe with a thankful heart. His confidence, however, was quickly put to shame. The question had indeed been decided by the Council at Jerusalem, but the extremists, though overborne at the moment, remained obdurate and resolved to prosecute their contention. They were doubtless the same men who had invaded Syrian Antioch and excited dissension there; and they conceived the base design of dogging the Apostle's steps and disseminating their doctrines in his churches. Under their energetic leader,[1] they had followed him to Galatia and engaged in a vigorous propaganda. (Cf. Gal. v. 10.)

A mischievous propaganda. Cf. v. 9.

They were indeed a little company, yet, like the 'little leaven leavening the whole mass,' they wrought much mischief; and the secret of their success was twofold. On the one hand, they were uncompromising extremists, and zeal is always impressive. They had thrown off all disguise. Hitherto, at the conference at Jerusalem in the year 46, in the disputation at Antioch, and again at the Council, they had professed themselves Christians, and had required merely the imposition of the rite of circumcision upon the Gentile converts. (Cf. ii. 4.) They had, however, been 'false brothers' all the while; and now that they had defied the Council's decision, they were done with compromise and displayed their true colours. (Cf. iv. 10.) They had reverted outright to Judaism; and insisted not merely on circumcision but on the full round of ceremonial observance. And, on the other hand, the Galatians were easily captivated. They were a singularly impressionable people, and they had shown it by their behaviour when Paul and Barnabas first appeared in their midst. (Cf. iv. 13-15.) They had received the strangers with open arms. They had lavished their sympathy on the ailing Apostle

[1] Cp. p. 108.

and enthusiastically embraced his message. And then, when the Judaists appeared, they lent to their representations a no less facile ear, and incontinently abjured the cause which they had so rapturously espoused.

A threefold indictment.

The procedure of the Judaists was base and unchivalrous. It was a personal campaign, an envenomed and unscrupulous attack upon the Apostle. There were three counts in their indictment. Like their Macedonian *confrères* they assailed his conduct and his Gospel. They charged him with unprincipled plausibility, and they fastened particularly on his gracious concession to Jewish sentiment in circumcising Timothy, representing it as a shameless inconsistency, a 'rebuilding of what he had pulled down.' And they assailed his Gospel of Justification by Faith apart from the Works of the Law, insisting that it issued in antinomianism, and adducing in evidence the moral laxity which, in Galatia as in Macedonia, the Gentile Christians too often displayed. Their chief attack, however, was directed against his Apostleship. They did not indeed absolutely deny it, but they alleged that he had received it from the original Apostles, the men who had known the Lord in the days of His flesh and had been called and commissioned by Him. These were the true 'pillars' of the Church, and Paul's claim to equal authority with them was an audacious usurpation.

Cf. ii. 18.

The Apostle's distress.

It was a heavy grief to him when the tidings of the Galatian defection reached his ears. He could not believe that it was deliberate or final; and, remembering the devotion of his converts, he was sure that, if only he could hasten to them and reason with them, all would yet be well. Meantime this was impracticable, since he must remain a while at Antioch. As soon as he might he would visit them and disabuse their minds; but the situation was serious and demanded prompt intervention, and so he immediately addressed himself to the writing of a letter, probably employing Timothy as his amanuensis.

Cf. iii. 4; v. 10.
Cf. iv. 19, 20.

The Letter to the Galatians

The address.

The letter is the impassioned outpouring of a wounded and troubled heart, a swift and indignant protest against an unexpected and intolerable wrong. He plunges straightway *in medias res* without his accustomed greeting and commendation. Commendation indeed was impossible, and in its stead he substitutes a pained and astonished remonstrance. In the very first sentence he introduces the question of his Apostleship. His Gospel, he asserts, was no human tradition but a divine revelation, and his ordination was a direct commission from the Risen Lord.

i. 1 Paul, an Apostle not from men nor through a man but
through Jesus Christ and God the Father who raised Him
2 from the dead, and all the brothers who are with me, to the
3 churches of Galatia. Grace to you and peace from God
4 our Father and the Lord Jesus Christ, who gave Himself
for our sins that He might pluck us from the present evil age
5 according to the will of our God and Father, to whom be
the glory for ever and ever. Amen.

An indignant remonstrance.

He opens his argument with a pained and indignant remonstrance: 'I wonder that you are so quickly deserting'; and there is, as St. Chrysostom remarks, a note of reassurance in the words. He does not say that they 'had deserted' but that they 'were deserting'; suggesting that their apostasy was not yet a *fait accompli* and might even now, as he fondly believed, be arrested. (Cf. v. 10.) The reason of his surprise was their misapprehension of the situation. There was in truth no difference between himself and the original Apostles. Their Gospel and his, as he presently demonstrates, were identical, and it was only Judaist perversion that made them out different. He and Silas had made this plain when they delivered the decree of the Council to the Galatian Churches. They had strongly warned them then against accepting any other Gospel, and now he reiterates the warning.

6 I wonder that you are so quickly deserting[1] from Him who
7 called you in Christ's grace, to a different Gospel, which is not
really other than mine save that there are certain men who
are disturbing you and desiring to pervert the Gospel of the

[1] *μετατίθεσθαι* denoted primarily military desertion (cf. App. *Iber.* 17: *σοι δι' αὐτους ἐς 'Ρωμαίους μετέθεντο*), then change of opinion. Thus Dionysius of Heracleia, who left the Stoics for the Epicureans, was termed *ὁ μεταθεμένος*, 'the Turncoat' (Diog. Laert. vii. 166).

8 Christ.[1] But if any one—even we or an angel from heaven—
preach to you another Gospel than we preached to you, let him
9 be accursed. As we have previously said, I now repeat:
If any one preaches another Gospel than you received, let him
be accursed.

This is strong language, and he glances contemptuously at the Judaist calumny which construed his gracious and conciliatory attitude as smooth-tongued plausibility and charged him with caring more for man's approbation than for God's. **An aside.**

10 Am I now 'persuading men rather than God'? or seeking
to 'please men'? Had I still been 'pleasing men,' I would
not have been Christ's slave.

And now he deals with the attack upon his Apostleship and his Gospel; and he refutes it by an appeal to historical facts. It was true that he had never known the Master in the days of His flesh, but he had seen Him, the Risen and Glorified Lord, on the road to Damascus. That experience, as the Galatians knew, had revolutionised his life; and the reason was that the Saviour had then been revealed to him and had called him to preach His Gospel among the Gentiles. It was a divine revelation and a divine commission, and it had received no human confirmation. He did not repair to the Apostles at Jerusalem for approval or instruction, but retired to Arabia and after a season of solitary meditation returned to Damascus and proclaimed the Gospel which the Lord had taught him and commissioned him to preach. **A divine revelation and a divine commission.**

11 Now as regards the Gospel which was preached by me, I
would have you know, brothers, that it is not a Gospel accord-
12 ing to man. For it was not from man that I received it or
was taught it; no, it was through a revelation of Jesus Christ.
13 You have heard of my career once in Judaism—that I passed
all bounds in persecuting the Church of God and devastating it,
14 and outstripped in Judaism many contemporaries among my
people in the exuberance of my initial zeal [2] for the traditions
15 of my forefathers. But when it was the good pleasure of Him
who set me apart 'from my mother's womb' and called me Cf. Jer. i. 5.

[1] Cf. Ramsay, *Hist. Comm. on Gal.*, pp. 260 ff.

[2] Cf. n. on ii. 14.

16 through His grace, to reveal His Son in me[1] that I might
preach His Gospel among the Gentiles, I held no immediate
17 communication with flesh and blood, nor did I go up to
Jerusalem to the men who were Apostles before me. No, I
went away to Arabia, and returned again to Damascus.

Subsequent relations with the Twelve:

(1) First visit to Jerusalem.

It thus appeared that neither his Gospel nor his Apostleship was in the first instance derived from the Twelve; and his independence of their instruction and authority was demonstrated by his subsequent relations with them. It was not till the summer of the year 36, three years after his conversion, that he paid his first visit to Jerusalem.[2] Meanwhile he had been preaching his Gospel at Damascus, and during his brief stay of a fortnight at the sacred capital he saw only Peter and James, the Lord's brother. It was a purely personal visit, devoted to friendly intercourse. He was not presented to the Church; he neither sought nor received official recognition; and the evidence was that on his departure he was still a stranger to the churches of Judæa. He betook himself to Tarsus, and busied himself for the next nine years in evangelising the Province of Syria-Cilicia; and it surprised the Judæan Christians when they heard how their whilome persecutor was employed. It would have been no surprise to them had he carried from Jerusalem the seal of apostolic sanction.

18 Then three years after I went up to Jerusalem to view
19 Cephas,[3] and I stayed with him for fifteen days. And no
other of the Apostles did I see except James the brother of the
20 Lord. Now in what I am writing to you, look you, before God
21 I am not lying. Then I went away to the regions of Syria
22 and Cilicia. And I was personally unknown to the Christian
23 Churches of Judæa; only they were always hearing: 'The
man who was our persecutor once, now is preaching the Gospel
24 of the Faith which he once devastated!' And they glorified
God in me.

(2) The Conference at Jerusalem.

His next interview with the Apostles was the Conference at Jerusalem in the autumn of 46, the fourteenth year after his conversion;[4] and what then transpired was decisive.

[1] *I.e.*, 'in my person,' as the scene or arena of the revelation. Cf. ver. 24; Phil. i. 30; 1 Tim. i. 16; Mt. xiv. 2.

[2] Cf. pp. 58 ff.

[3] Cf. p. 59.

[4] Cf. pp. 73 ff.

The question of the permanence of the Law had been raised by the Judaists. They demanded the circumcision of Titus, the young Gentile convert who had accompanied him from Antioch; but he had stoutly refused, and he had won the support of the Twelve, whom the Galatian propagandists lauded in his disparagement as 'the reputed men,' the 'pillars' of the Faith. They had approved his Gospel and recognised his call to evangelise the Gentiles.

ii. 1 Then after an interval of fourteen years[1] I again went up
to Jerusalem, accompanied by Barnabas; and I took Titus
2 also with me. It was in pursuance of a revelation that I
went up; and I communicated to them the Gospel which
I am proclaiming among the Gentiles, but privately to 'the
reputed men': perhaps, methought, the course I am
3 running or have run may have an empty issue.[2] Yet neither
was Titus my companion, Greek as he was, compelled to
4 be circumcised. The suggestion, however, was made in
deference to the false brothers who had been smuggled into
the conference. They had stolen in to spy upon our freedom
which we have in Christ Jesus, that they might reduce us
5 to slavery. But not for an hour did we yield in submission,
that the truth of the Gospel might still remain with you.[3]
6 Now from 'the men reputed to be something'—whatever
they once were makes no difference to me: God does not
accept any man's person[4]—to me 'the reputed men' com-
7 municated nothing. On the contrary, when they saw that
I had been entrusted with the Gospel for the Uncircumcision
8 as Peter had been entrusted with it for the Circumcision—for
He who had operated in Peter's heart to make him an Apostle
to the Circumcision, had operated in mine also for the
9 Gentiles—and when they recognised the grace which had
been given me, James and Cephas and John, 'the men Cf. Rev. iii.
reputed to be pillars,' plighted fellowship with Barnabas and 12.

[1] Cf. Append. I.

[2] Cf. Moulton, *Gram. of Gk. Test.*, *Proleg.*, p. 193.

[3] On the text, involving the question whether Paul resisted or conceded the Judaist claim, cf. p. 75.

[4] Cf. Rom. ii. 11. *πρόσωπον λαμβάνειν* is a Hebrew phrase, פָּנִים נָשָׂא (cf. Job xiii. 10), signifying 'take at face-value,' regard a man for his outward appearance or external circumstances (wealth, rank, and the like) without considering his character, his intrinsic worth. By *ὁποῖοί ποτε ἦσαν* Paul means their knowledge of the Lord in the days of His flesh; and he dismisses as *προσωπολημψία* the Judaistic insistence upon this accidental circumstance.

me [1] on the understanding that the Gentiles should be our
10 province and the Circumcision theirs; stipulating only that
we should remember the poor. And this was indeed the very
thing that I was anxious to do.

(3) The rencontre at Antioch.

Three years later at the close of 49 the legitimacy of Paul's Gospel was again challenged by the Judaists when they visited Antioch in pursuance of their propaganda.[2] It chanced that Peter was there, and he, the chief 'pillar,' stultified himself by weakly bowing before the storm of their invective. But Paul's fearless steadfastness rallied him, and he acknowledged his fault.

11 But when Cephas came to Antioch, I opposed him to his
12 face because he stood condemned.[3] For ere certain men had
come from James, he would eat with the Gentiles; but when
they came, he drew off and kept himself apart for fear of the
13 champions of circumcision. And the rest of the Jews also
joined in his masquerading, insomuch that even Barnabas was
14 carried away by it. But when I saw that they were not keeping
by the straight path of the truth of the Gospel, I said to Cephas
in presence of all: 'If you, being originally a Jew,[4] live after the
Gentile and not after the Jewish fashion, how is it that you
are compelling the Gentiles to judaise?'

Justification by Faith attested by experience.

Now that he has, by an appeal to incontrovertible and acknowledged facts, vindicated the divine authority of his Apostleship and the legitimacy of his Gospel, Paul addresses himself to the vital issue. In opposition to the Judaist

[1] δεξιά, 'right hand,' bore the general signification of 'pledge.' Suid.: δεξιάς· συνθήκας. Cf. 1 Mac. xi. 50, 62; xiii. 50, where a single person is spoken of as giving δεξιάς, not δεξιάν.

[2] Cf. pp. 108 ff.

[3] Some of the Fathers, particularly Chrys. and Hieronym., conceived that the contention at Antioch was simulated. There was really no difference between Paul and Peter, and they got up the dispute and carried it through that the Judaists might be admonished by the latter's submission. *οὐ μάχης ἦν τὰ ῥήματα ἀλλ' οἰκονομίας.* This would have been *ὑπόκρισις*, 'play-acting' (cf. *The Days of His Flesh*, p. 102), but not the sort Paul charges Peter with.

[4] *ὑπάρχειν*, 'be at the outset,' 'exist to begin with,' denoting an antecedent condition which essentially affects the situation. Suid.: *τὸ ὑπάρχειν οὐχ ἁπλῶς 'τὸ εἶναι' σημαίνει ἀλλὰ 'τὸ πάλαι εἶναι,' καὶ 'προεῖναι,' 'φθανειν.'* Plat. *Tim.* 30 C: *τούτου δ' ὑπάρχοντος*, *his positis*, 'this granted,' 'assuming this.' *Rep.* 458 A: *θέντες ὡς ὑπάρχον*, 'assume,' 'take for granted.' Diog. Laert. iii. 99: *ᾧ δὲ ὑπάρχει πάντα ταῦτα, οὗτός ἐστιν εὐδαίμων τελέως*, 'the possession of all these things is the antecedent condition of perfect happiness.' Cf. Ac. xxvii. 34: 'this is an essential condition of your preservation.' Phil. ii. 6.

insistence on the permanent obligation of the ceremonial Law and the necessity of its observance by Gentile converts, he demonstrates his doctrine of Justification by Faith in Christ; and he introduces the argument in a passage which is intelligible only when it is recognised as a personal soliloquy, an autobiographical retrospect, a review of his spiritual progress from the Law to Faith.[1] The starting-point is the discovery of the insufficiency of legal observance and the necessity of faith in Christ. This is followed by a discomfiting experience. Faith does not bring immediate deliverance. Sin still dwells in the believer and exerts its unhallowed tyranny. Indeed it is only when one is 'in Christ' that one realises what sin is and how hard is the attainment of holiness. It seems as though Christ were a minister not of righteousness but of sin; and two temptations present themselves. One is to acquiesce in moral imperfection, and conclude that holiness is no evangelical concern. Faith is sufficient for salvation, and works matter nothing. This is the antinomian attitude, and too many of the Apostle's converts adopted it. But where the spiritual instinct is keen, the temptation is rather to despair of the efficacy of faith and revert to the Law. This is the attitude which the Judaists imputed to Paul. They pointed particularly to his circumcision of Timothy and construed it as a confession of the necessity of legal observance, and they sneered at him for 'rebuilding what he had pulled down.' His reply is that if this were his attitude, he would indeed prove himself a transgressor, not against the Law but against something holier. He would be 'setting aside the grace of God.' For faith brings a high and sure deliverance through mystic union with Christ. This is a thought which his experience revealed to Paul ever more clearly. The believer is identified with Christ at each successive stage of His redemptive career—His Death, His Burial, His Resurrection, and His Risen Life.

[1] The passage is not a continuation of the remonstrance with Peter. At ver. 14 the historical review ends, and ver. 15 begins the doctrinal discussion (Theod. Mops., Calv., Grot.). Galatians is a hasty sketch of the argument subsequently elaborated in Romans, and this passage is a forecast of the Apostle's spiritual autobiography in the latter (vii.).

15 We, Jews by nature and not 'sinners of the Gentiles'
16 yet knowing that a man is not accounted righteous on the
score of works of the Law unless accompanied by faith in
Christ Jesus, even we had faith in Christ Jesus, that we
might be accounted righteous on the score of faith in Christ
and not on the score of works of Law, because on the score
of works of Law 'no flesh will be accounted righteous.'
Ps. cxliii. 2. 17 Now if in seeking to be accounted righteous in Christ[1] we
were ourselves also found sinners, is Christ then a minister
18 of sin? Away with the idea![2] For if I am 'building
again what I pulled down,' I am proving myself a trans-
19 gressor. For through Law I died to Law that I might live
20 to God. I have been crucified with Christ; and it is no
longer I that live but Christ that lives in me; and the life
which I now live in the flesh, I live in faith—faith in the
Son of God who loved me and surrendered Himself for me.
21 I do not set aside the grace of God; for if righteousness be
through Law, then Christ died for naught.

The Galatian defection a denial of experience.

Thus experience attests faith as the only pathway to righteousness; and here lay the marvel of the Galatians' defection. They had abandoned the Gospel of Faith and adopted the old futile method of ceremonial observance; and it was a denial of their own blessed experience. It was inexplicable; it seemed as though an evil eye had bewitched them.

[1] ἐν Χριστῷ, a formula expressing succinctly the believer's relation to Christ and all that flows therefrom; never in Synoptics and in Fourth Gospel only in connection with 'abide,' 'be one.' It is distinctively Pauline, and refers exclusively to the Risen Lord and the relation of believers to Him (cf. 2 Cor. v. 16). The idea is illustrated by various analogies: a man must be *in the air* to breathe, a fish *in the water* to live, a plant *in the soil* to grow. Observe the Pauline nexus of Christian experience: (1) Χριστὸς ὑπὲρ ἡμῶν, 'Christ for us'—Substitution (cf. 2 Cor. v. 21). (2) ἡμεῖς ἐν Χριστῷ, 'we in Christ'—Justification (cf. 2 Cor. v. 17; Rom. vi. 11). He died for all (cf. 2 Cor. v. 14, 15; Jo. iii. 16); therefore all saved *in posse*, but none *in esse* unless 'in Christ,' resting on Him by personal, appropriating faith. (3) Χριστὸς ἐν ἡμῖν, 'Christ in us'—Sanctification (cf. Gal. ii. 20; 2 Cor. xiii. 5; Rom. viii. 10). Not only is an animal *in the air* but the air *in the animal*. (4) ἡμεῖς ὑπὲρ Χριστοῦ—Consecration (cf. 2 Cor. v. 20).

[2] μὴ γένοιτο, an emphatic repudiation of an untenable suggestion. In N. T. peculiarly Pauline—fourteen times in Epp. and once in Pauline Gospel (Lk. xx. 16); but a common Jewish phrase, being negative of ἀμήν, which is rendered γένοιτο, 'so be it' in LXX (cf. Num. v. 22; Dt. xxvii. 15; 1 Ki. i. 36; Pss. xli. 13, lxxii. 19, lxxxix. 52, cvi. 48). Cf. *Protev. Jac.* vi: καὶ εἶπε πᾶς ὁ λαός· γένοιτο, γένοιτο, ἀμήν (response to the priestly prayer at the presentation of Mary).

iii. 1 You witless Galatians! who is it that cast a spell on you?[1]
—you before whose eyes Jesus Christ was placarded on the
2 Cross.[2] This only I desire to learn from you: Was it on
the score of works of Law that you received the Spirit or on
3 the score of the hearing of faith? Are you so witless?
After being initiated by the Spirit are you now attaining
4 perfection by the flesh? Did you suffer so much all to no Cf. Ac.
5 purpose?—if it be indeed all to no purpose. He therefore xiii. 45-52;
who is lavishing the Spirit upon you[3] and putting powers xiv. 4-6, 19, 20.
in operation within you—is it on the score of works of Law
6 or on the score of the hearing of faith, as Abraham 'had Gen. xv. 6.
faith in God, and it was reckoned to him as righteousness'?

Faith the condition of the promise to Abraham.

This quotation introduces a further development of the argument. Not only is the doctrine of Justification by Faith demonstrated by experience but it is the doctrine of the ancient Scripture. It was on the score of his faith that Abraham was pronounced righteous; and the blessing was not his alone: it was the heritage of his sons for evermore. And who are the sons of Abraham? They are those who share his faith, and not merely believing Jews but believing Gentiles as well, as the Scripture expressly declares; for was not this the promise to Abraham: 'All the Gentiles shall be blessed in thee'? Indeed there is no other way; for according to the Scripture the Law brings to erring men not a blessing but a curse, and Christ has redeemed us from its curse in order that we may by faith receive the promised blessing.

[1] The superstition of the malign influence of 'an evil eye' (ὀφθαλμὸς βάσκανος), still prevalent in the East (cf. *P. E. F. Q. St.*, July 1918, pp. 112 ff.), was universal in ancient days. Its special victims were flocks, plants, and children. Cf. Verg. *Ecl.* III. 103; Plin. *Nat. Hist.* VII. 2; Plut. *Symp.* v. 7.

[2] προγράφειν, like *proscribere* (cf. Suet. *Ner.* 39), was used of a public intimation posted up by authority of the magistrates. Cf. ἀ[ξιοῦμεν π]ρογραφῆναι in a notice placarded by the strategus of Hermopolis Magna at the request of the parents of a spendthrift, intimating that they will not be responsible for his debts (Milligan, *Gk. Pap.* 27). ἐσταυρωμένος (cf. Mt. xxviii. 5; Mk. xvi. 6) represents the crucifixion not as a mere historic incident (σταυρωθεὶς) but as an abiding and eternal fact (cf. Jo. xx. 27; Rev. v. 6, xiii. 8). The chief authorities omit τῇ ἀληθείᾳ μὴ πείθεσθαι and ἐν ὑμῖν.

[3] ἐπιχορηγεῖν, 'furnish with lavish generosity.' A χορηγός at Athens was a wealthy citizen charged with the provision and equipment of a chorus for the performance of a drama in the theatre—a costly public service. Cf. 2 Cor. ix. 10; Col. ii. 19; 2 Pet. i. 5, 11.

7 You perceive, then, that it is those who hold by faith that
8 are sons of Abraham. And since the Scripture foresaw that
God accounts the Gentiles righteous on the score of faith, it
Gen. xii. 3. preached the Gospel to Abraham beforehand: 'All the
9 Gentiles will be blessed in thee.' And so it is those who hold
10 by faith that are blessed with faithful Abraham. For all who
hold by works of Law are under a curse; for it is written:
Dt. xxvii. 'Cursed is every one who continues not in all the things which
26. 11 are written in the Book of the Law to do them.' Now that in
Law no one is accounted righteous in God's judgment is plain,
Hab. ii. 4. because 'the righteous man on the score of faith shall live.'
Lev. xviii. 12 But faith is not the principle of the Law; no, 'he who does
5. 13 them will live in them.' Christ redeemed us from the curse of
the Law by submitting Himself to cursing on our behalf [1]—
Dt. xxi. 23. because it is written: 'Cursed is every one who is hanged on
14 a tree'—that the blessing of Abraham might reach to the
Gentiles in Jesus Christ, that we might through faith receive
the promise of the Spirit.

Unaltered by the Law. Faith, then, was the original condition of justification; and the Apostle proceeds to demonstrate that it is the condition still. The promise to Abraham had remained unfulfilled until the Advent of Christ; for it had been made to Abraham 'and to his seed,' and, he says, deftly employing against his Judaist assailants the fanciful method of Rabbinical interpretation, 'his seed' here signifies not the multitude of his descendants but his one descendant, Christ. And that the promise might be sure all down the expectant ages, it was confirmed by a covenant. The initial condition of the covenant was faith; and since a covenant, even a human covenant, is inviolate and, once it has been ratified, none of its terms may be set aside or modified, it is impossible that when the Law was given four hundred and thirty years later, it should have altered the covenant with Abraham and his Seed and substituted Works as the condition instead of Faith. That would have been an invalidation of the promise; it would have eliminated the very idea of promise,

[1] *γενόμενος ὑπὲρ ἡμῶν κατάρα*, 'having become a curse' (cf. 2 Cor. v. 21). He did not become 'cursed' (*κατάρατος*) or 'a sinner' (*ἁμαρτωλός*). He identified Himself vicariously with accursed sinners. Only personal sin makes one accursed. 'Ideo non dixit: *Factus pro nobis maledictus* sed *maledictum;* is enim qui propter peccatum morti offerebatur, maledictus fiebat, in sua enim causa moriebatur' (Ambrstr.).

since a promise implies grace, and what is earned by works is not a free gift but a legal right.

15 Brothers, I take an example from human affairs.[1] A
covenant, though but a human covenant, once it has been
16 ratified no one sets aside or adds new terms to it. Now to Gen. xii. 7,
Abraham were the promises spoken 'and to his seed.' It xiii. 15,
is not said [2] 'and to his seeds' in the plural, but in the singular xvii. 7, xxii. 18,
17 'and to thy seed'; and this is Christ.[3] Here is what I mean: xxiv. 7.
A covenant ratified beforehand by God the Law, which has Ex. xii. 40
come into being four hundred and thirty years later, does not LXX.
18 irratify to the invalidation of the promise. For if the inheritance be dependent on law, it is no longer dependent on
promise; whereas it is God's free gift to Abraham through
promise.

Here the Apostle pauses to consider two objections which a Jew might urge against his argument and which had presented themselves to his own mind when he was thinking out the problem of the relation between the Law and the Gospel. (Judaist objections:) The first is: What is the use of the Law? If salvation be God's free gift, and we are saved by faith in Christ as Abraham was saved by faith in the Promise, why was the Law ever given? (1) What is the use of the Law? What purpose does it serve? His answer, which he subsequently elaborates in his great encyclical on Justification by Faith, is that the function of the Law was not to achieve salvation but to discover sin. (Rom. vii. 7-13: cf. iii. 20, iv. 15, v. 20.) It did not justify; it condemned and revealed the need of a Saviour and drove men back in faith upon the Promise. And, he adds, it was in its very nature less gracious and sacred than the Promise. For the Promise was a direct word of God; but in the giving of the Law Moses served as a mediator between God and the people. (Cf. Ex. xx. 19.) And neither did Moses receive the Law directly from God; for, according to the Rabbinical

[1] Chrys.: τί ἐστι 'κατὰ ἄνθρωπον λεγω'; ἐξ ἀνθρωπίνων παραδειγμάτων.

[2] On this indefinite use of λέγει or φησί (sc. Θεός or ἡ γραφή) introducing a quotation cf. Rom. xv. 10; Eph. iv. 8, v. 14; 1 Cor. vi. 16.

[3] A specimen of Rabbinical exegesis (cf. p. 27). Of course the argumentation is impossible, since σπέρμα in the sense of 'offspring' is, like זֶרַע, a collective noun, and the plur. could mean only 'seeds of grain'; nor does Paul employ it seriously. He is here speaking, as he proposed, κατὰ ἄνθρωπον (Hieronym.). He borrows the method of his opponents, thus cleverly 'turning the tables' against them.

Cf. Ac. vii. 53; Heb. ii. 2.

theology, it was delivered to him on Mount Sinai by the ministration of angels.[1] Thus in the Law God is twice removed; in the Promise it is with Him alone that we have to do.

19 What, then, is the use of the Law? It was added to
accentuate transgressions until the coming of the Seed to
whom the Promise had been made; and it was ordered through
20 angels in the hand of a mediator. And where there is a
mediator, there is not only one party; but God is one.[2]

(2) Is the Law in opposition to the Promise?

But, it may be further objected, on this view the Law is in opposition to the Promise. It does not justify; it condemns, and thus extinguishes the hope which the Promise had inspired. No, answers the Apostle, the purpose of the Law was the ultimate and complete fulfilment of the Promise. It condemned the sinner in order that he might realise the impossibility of attaining righteousness by observance of its requirements and might welcome the Gospel of Justification by Faith in Christ.

21 Is the Law, then, in opposition to the promises of God?
Away with the idea! For had there been given a Law which
could impart life, righteousness would have been indeed on
22 the score of law; but the Scripture has shut up the whole
race in the prison of sin, that the Promise may be given, on
the score of faith in Jesus Christ, to those who have faith.

The Law a preparation for Faith.

It were, however, a poor account of the Law's function to represent it as merely a gaoler holding the condemned in durance until they were delivered by faith in Christ. The old dispensation was more than a term of imprisonment: it was a period of education. And the Law was more than a gaoler: it was, says the Apostle, employing a phrase which has no modern equivalent, 'a pedagogue,' which signifies literally 'a boy-leader' and is perhaps most nearly repre-

[1] Cf Jos. *Ant.* XV. v. 3; Schürer, II. i. p. 344.

[2] It would be alike wearisome and unprofitable to adduce all the various interpretations of this passage (cf. Poole, *Synops. Crit.*, and Alford). The meaning is plain when it is recognised that the 'mediator' here is not Christ (cf. 1 Tim. ii. 5; Heb. viii. 6, ix. 15, xii. 24)—a notion originated apparently by Origen (cf. Lommatzsch, V. p. 273) and adopted by Chrys., Aug., Hieronym., Ambrstr.—but Moses (Basil., Greg. Nyss., Theod. Mops., Theodt.).

sented by 'tutor.' The pedagogue was not a teacher. He was a superior slave whose office was not merely to conduct the boy to his teacher but to superintend his manners and morals.[1] He was the boy's guide, and his office ceased when his charge attained maturity and, imbued with right principles, no longer needed dictation and control. And this was the function of the Law. It was the stern tutor of our wayward boyhood; but now that we have attained spiritual manhood, 'the measure of the stature of Christ's fulness,' Eph. iv. 13.
we are ruled not by Law but by Faith. In Christ we are no longer children but full-grown sons; for He is the Eternal Son, the Archetype of Sonship, and Faith conforms us to Him and imbues us with His Spirit. It 'clothes us with Him,' says the Apostle, employing an Old Testament figure. When the Spirit of the Lord took possession of a man, it Cf. Jud. vi.
was said that 'the Spirit clothed him.' The man was, as 34; 1 Chr. xii. 18; 2
it were, an incarnation of the Spirit; and our Lord employed Chr. xxiv.
the ancient language in His last command to His disciples: 20 in marg.
'Tarry in the city, until you clothe yourselves with power Lk. xxiv.
from on high.' And so by Faith's loving and adoring self- 49.
surrender we 'clothe ourselves with Christ.' It is Faith that effects the transformation; and it obliterates all accidental distinctions, and by conforming humanity to its Divine Ideal restores its primal unity. It reconciles the long antagonism between Jew and Gentile; for since it was by Faith that Abraham was accounted righteous, we are his children and his heirs as we share his Faith.

23 Ere the coming of faith we were shut up under Law's
wardenship, awaiting the faith which should by and by be
24 revealed. And so the Law served as our tutor until Christ's
advent,[2] in order that we may be accounted righteous on
25 the score of faith; but now that faith has come, we are no
26 longer under a tutor. For you are all through faith sons
27 of God in Christ Jesus; for as many of you as were baptised Cf. Rom.
28 into Christ clothed yourselves with Christ. The distinctions xiii. 14;
of Jew and Greek, slave and free man, male and female Eph. iv. 24; Col. iii. 10.

[1] Cf. Plat. *Lys.* 208 C.

[2] εἰς Χριστόν, not 'to bring us unto Christ, the Teacher,' which would require πρὸς Χριστόν, but 'with a view to Christ,' *i.e.*, the attainment of spiritual maturity (cf. Eph. iv. 13).

29 disappear; for you are all one in Christ Jesus.[1] And if
you are Christ's, then are you Abraham's seed, heirs
according to promise.

Tutelage and sonship.

Hence emerges the truth that Faith inaugurates a higher and nobler condition; and this the Apostle enforces by another illustration. He has likened our state under the Law to that of a boy under his pedagogue; and now he likens it to that of an orphan minor who, according to the Syrian law which obtained in Southern Galatia, was placed by his father's will, for such term as the latter judged necessary,[2] under the tutelage of guardians and trustees responsible respectively for his person and his property. He was indeed a son and the heir of the estate; but throughout his minority he was no freer than a slave, and only when the appointed term expired did he enter on his birthright and enjoy the privileges of sonship. That was our condition under the Law. We were indeed sons all the while, for we had been created in the image of the Eternal Son; but we had forfeited the status of sonship, and we were no better than slaves with darkened hearts, until the Eternal Son appeared and by putting His Spirit into our hearts taught us to recognise our Father and restored us to our original and proper status.

iv. 1 Here is my meaning: All the time the heir is a minor,[3]
he differs in no respect from a slave, though he is lord of all,
2 but is under guardians and trustees during the term appointed
3 by his father. So we also, when we were minors, were
4 enslaved under the world's dim lights;[4] but when the time-

[1] Christ, the new Head of humanity, restores the lost unity which it had τῷ λόγῳ τῆς φύσεως (Theod. Mops.) in Adam. In Him we are no longer scattered and alien fragments but a living unity (εἷς), as the branches, while distinct, are all one in the living vine.

[2] According to Roman law the ward was free from his guardians (*tutores*, ἐπίτροποι) when he reached the age of fourteen, and from his trustees (*curatores*, οἰκόνομοι) at twenty-five. Cf. Ramsay, *Hist. Comm. on Gal.*, pp. 391 ff.

[3] νήπιος, properly 'an infant,' generally 'one under age.' Tertullian (*De Virg. Vel.* 1) distinguishes four stages in the historical development of religion: (1) *rudimenta*—natural religion; (2) *infantia*—the Law and the Prophets; (3) *juventus*—the Gospel; (4) *maturitas*—the Paraclete.

[4] στοιχεῖον, from στοῖχος, 'a row,' 'line,' or 'rank,' bore three meanings. 1. A letter. Cf. τὰ στοιχεῖα, 'the Alphabet.' Hence στοιχεῖα signified 'rudiments.' Cf. Heb. v. 12. Euclid's στοιχεῖα, 'the Rudiments of Geometry.' 2. The rudiments of the universe, the four 'elements' of fire, water, air, and

limit expired, God sent forth His Son, born of woman, born
5 under Law, to redeem those who were under Law, that we
6 might recover the status of sonship.[1] And because you are
sons, God sent forth the Spirit of His Son into our hearts,
7 crying, '*Abba!* Our Father!'[2] And so you are no longer
a slave but a son. And if you are a son, you are also an
heir; and it is God's doing.

A pained remonstrance.

Here lay the marvel of the Galatians' defection. They were converts from heathenism, and their old idolatry had been a degrading bondage; yet after tasting the sweetness of the liberty of sonship they had reverted to bondage, exchanging the clear light of the Gospel for the dim lights of Judaism. Could it be that the Apostle's labour on their behalf had been lost? He refuses to believe it, and he appeals to their chivalry. He was a Jew, yet that he might win the Gentiles he had identified himself with them and incurred obloquy and persecution: should not they be true to him?

earth. Cf Wisd. of Sol. vii. 17; 2 Pet. iii. 10, 12. Suid.: *στοιχεῖόν ἐστιν ἐξ οὗ πρώτου γίνεται τὰ γινόμενα καὶ εἰς ὃ ἔσχατον ἀναλύεται.* Hence, as an astronomical term, 'the heavenly bodies.' Cf. Just. M., *Apol.* I. p. 44 A (ed. Sylburg.): *τὰ οὐράνια στοιχεῖα.* Metaphorically 'great luminaries,' distinguished personages. Cf. Polycrates in Eus. *H. E.* III. 31: *κατὰ τὴν Ἀσίαν μέγαλα στοιχεῖα κεκοίμηται.* 3. A 'spirit' or 'demon,' since each element had its genius or tutelary spirit. Cf. Rev. vii. 1 (the angels of the winds), xiv. 18 (the angel of fire), xvi. 5 (the angel of the waters). By *τὰ στοιχεῖα τοῦ κόσμου* (cf. Col. ii. 8, 20) the Apostle means Judaistic observances, and the phrase was explained in two ways by the Fathers. (1) The Jewish 'days, months, seasons, and years' (ver. 10), which were regulated by 'the luminaries of the world.' Chrys. (cf. Theod. Mops., Ambrstr.): '*τὰ στοιχεῖα τοῦ κόσμου*, that is, new moons and Sabbaths; for these days arise for us from the course of moon and sun.' (2) 'The rudiments,' the crude ideas of the Jewish Law, were an elementary stage in the world's religious education, *quasi initia et exordia literarum* (Hieronym.). The former interpretation is near the mark. The Jewish ordinances were 'the lights of the world,' because they were the best illumination that the world had in those days, and, though divinely appointed, they were dim compared with the light of the Christian revelation.

[1] *υἱοθεσία* is literally 'setting in the place of a son,' and Paul always uses the term in accordance with this its proper signification. 'Adoption' in his conception is not the introduction of aliens into God's family but the reinstatement of sons in their birthright (cf. ver. 6). *ἀπολαμβάνειν* is not simply 'receive' but 'get back'; and so *τὴν υἱοθεσίαν ἀπολάβωμεν* means 'recover our lost status of sonship.' Cf. *The Atonement in the Light of History and the Modern Spirit*, pp. 147 ff.

[2] This combination of the Hebrew address (אַבָּא) and its Greek equivalent (ὁ Πατήρ) was apparently a liturgical formula. Cf. Mk. xiv. 36; Rom. viii. 15.

He was confident that they would : for he remembered their overflowing kindness to him at his first appearance among them. And it was precisely this that made him wonder at their present attitude. The blame did not lie with him ; for he had loved them all along even in his sternest remonstrances. Nor did it lie with them : they had done him no wrong. It lay with the men who had misled them and alienated their affection from him by insidious calumnies. They must not imagine that in saying this he was jealous of the influence which the Judaists had won over them in his absence. He could not always be with them, and it pleased him that others should visit them and pay them the attentions which he would fain pay them himself. But this was his complaint—that the attentions of the Judaists were dishonourable. It was not the good of the Galatians that they had in view, but the vindication of their own prestige. The end of their blandishments was to oust the Gentile Christians from their position of equality in the Church and oblige them to sue for recognition on the Judaistic terms.

8 But in those days, not knowing God, you were enslaved to
9 gods which were by nature no gods at all ; now, however, that
you have recognised God or rather have been recognised by
God, how is it that you are turning back again to the dim
lights, so feeble and poor, and consenting to be again enslaved
10 to them anew ? You are scrupulously observing days and
11 months and seasons and years.[1] I am apprehensive about
12 you : perhaps I have laboured on you to no purpose.[2] Cast
in your lot with me, because I have cast in mine with you,[3]
13 brothers, I pray you. You have done me no wrong. You
know that it was by reason of a physical infirmity that I
14 preached the Gospel to you on the former of my visits ; [4] and
what was trying to you in my physical condition you did not
scorn or loathe. No, as though I had been an angel of God

[1] Sabbaths, new moons, feasts, Sabbatical years. Cf. Col. ii. 16.

[2] Cf. n. on ii. 2.

[3] *γίνεσθε ὡς ἐγώ, ὅτι κἀγὼ ὡς ὑμεῖς*, 'become as I am, because I became as you are,' *i.e.*, 'I, originally a Jew, abjured Judaism and put myself in the position of you Gentiles' (Theod. Mops.). Chrys. supposes that Paul is addressing Jewish converts (*τοὺς ἐξ Ἰουδαίων*) and appealing to them to follow his example in abandoning Judaism : 'become as I am, because I was once as you—zealous for the Law' (cf. i. 14). 'I had this zeal long ago, but see how I have changed' (Theodrt.).

[4] Cf. Append. III.

15 you welcomed me, as though I had been Christ Jesus. What,
then, has become of your reason for counting yourselves so
happy? For I bear you witness that, if possible, you would
16 have dug out your eyes and given them to me. And so I
17 have turned your enemy by dealing truly with you?[1] They
are paying court to you—not honourably; no, they wish to
18 exclude you that you may pay court to them. But it is an
honourable thing to be courted in an honourable cause—always,
19 and not only when I am present among you, my children, who
are costing me fresh travail-pangs until Christ be formed in
20 you.[2] And I find myself wishing[3] to be present among you
at this moment and change my tone: I am so perplexed
about you.

Allegory of the slave-girl and the free woman.

The Apostle's heart was overflowing with tender pity for his misguided converts; and, as though anxious to soften whatever severity might, in his vexation, have escaped his lips, he introduces an affectionate, almost playful appeal in the tone of a father remonstrating with his foolish children. 'Come, my children!' he says, 'I will tell you a story.' It is the old story of Hagar and Ishmael, and he spiritualises it after the manner of Rabbinical exegesis[4] and turns it into a parable of the relation between Law and Faith.

Cf. ver. 19.

Gen. xvi, xxi. 1-21.

21 Tell me, you who are wishing to be under Law, do you
22 not hear the Law? It is written that Abraham had two
sons, one by the slave-girl and one by the free woman.
23 But the child of the slave-girl is born according to the
flesh, while the child of the free woman is born through the
24 promise. And the story is allegorical. The mothers are
two covenants. One is from Mount Sinai and bears a
25 race of slaves; and this is Hagar. Sinai is a mountain in
Arabia, and corresponds to the present Jerusalem; for
26 she is in slavery with her children.[5] But the Jerusalem

[1] ἀληθεύειν (cf. Eph. iv. 15), not merely 'speak the truth' but 'deal truly.' Cf. Æsop. *Fab.* 349 (Halm), *The Boy and his Father:* φοβηθεὶς δὲ μή πως ὁ ὄνειρος ἀληθεύσῃ, 'afraid lest the dream should prove true.'

[2] As the embryo is formed in the womb. The process of their spiritual birth must begin afresh.

[3] ἤθελον, 'I was wishing all the time.' Cf. Rom. ix. 3; Ac. xxv. 22.

[4] Cf. p. 27.

[5] There is here a perplexing variety of readings. 1. ℵCFG, Vet. It., Vulg., Arm., Æth.: τὸ γὰρ Σινᾶ ὄρος ἐστὶν ἐν τῇ Ἀραβίᾳ, 'for Sinai is a mountain in Arabia.' 2. KLP, Syr., Chrys. and Gk. commentators generally: τὸ γὰρ Ἄγαρ Σινᾶ ὄρος ἐστὶν ἐν τῇ Ἀραβίᾳ, 'for Hagar is Mount Sinai in Arabia.' 3. ABDE, Ambrstr.: τὸ δὲ Ἄγαρ Σινᾶ ὄρος ἐστὶν ἐν τῃ Ἀραβίᾳ, 'now Hagar is

27 above is free, and she it is that is our mother. For it is
written:
Is. liv. 1. 'Rejoice, thou barren one who bearest not:
Break forth and shout, thou who travailest not:
For many are children of the desolate, more than hers
who hath her husband.'
28 Now you, brothers, like Isaac, are children of promise;
29 but just as then the son according to the flesh persecuted
Gen. xxi. 10. 30 the son according to the spirit, so is it now also. But what
says the Scripture? 'Cast out the slave-girl and her
son; for the son of the slave-girl shall not share the
31 inheritance with the son of the free woman.' Wherefore,
brothers, we are not a slave-girl's children but the free
v. 1 woman's. It was for freedom that Christ freed us:[1]
stand firm, then, and do not again get into the grip of a
yoke of slavery.

A decisive issue.

Cf. Ac. xv. 1.

The controversy turned on the rite of circumcision. The Judaists maintained that it was necessary to salvation, and insisted that the Gentile converts should submit to it. And they found a powerful reinforcement of their contention in Paul's generous deference to Jewish sentiment in circumcising Timothy. They represented this as a disavowal of his doctrine of the sole necessity of faith and a confession of the necessity of circumcision; and he meets their allegation with a direct and emphatic contradiction. It was a perversion of his action. 'I Paul,' he says, 'I who am charged with admitting the necessity of circumcision, tell you on the contrary that, if you be circumcised, Christ will profit you nothing.' And the reason is that the admission of the necessity of circumcision in order to salvation would be a confession of the insufficiency of faith; and there would then be nothing for it but to fall back on the old futile method of legal observance. It was thus a choice between Christ and the Law, Circumcision and Grace.

Mount Sinai in Arabia.' The first is most strongly attested, and the others are probably transcriptional variations. *τὸ γὰρ Ἄγαρ* is dittographic; and in the case of *τὸ δὲ Ἄγαρ* a hasty copyist, with *ἥτις ἐστὶν Ἄγαρ* fresh in his mind, mistook *γάρ* for *Ἄγαρ*, and the conj. *δέ* was added. Once the corruption was established, *τὸ Ἄγαρ* (for *ἡ Ἄγαρ*) required explanation; whence the notion that *Ἄγαρ* was the Arabian name for Sinai. Cf. Chrys.: *Ἄγαρ ἐλέγετο ἡ δούλη· τὸ δὲ Σινᾶ ὄρος οὕτω μεθερμηνεύεται τῇ ἐπιχωρίῳ αὐτῶν γλώττῃ.* This is a pleasant fancy, but it lacks evidence; and it discredits Chrys.'s topographical reliability that he places the mountain adjacent to Jerusalem, explaining *συνστοιχεῖ* by *γειτνιάζει, ἅπτεται.*

[1] Cf. p. 265.

The defection of the Galatians was an inexpressible amazement to the Apostle; it had so falsified the promise of their early career. The only explanation was that it was not their own doing. They had been misled. The Judaists accused him of plausibility, unscrupulous persuasiveness, Cf. i. 10.
and he retorts the charge. It was their 'persuasion' that had wrought the mischief, and it was a wicked persuasion: it was not God that had inspired it. The Judaists were a little coterie; indeed it was all the doing of one man, that energetic organiser of the propaganda, and the success of his machinations exemplified the proverb that 'a little leaven leavens the whole mass.' The responsibility rested with him, and the Apostle not only exonerated his converts but confidently anticipated that they would see reason. How preposterous the situation was! The Judaists on the one hand were persecuting him for preaching salvation by faith in Christ and thus ruling out circumcision, and on the other hand they charged him with admitting and proclaiming the necessity of circumcision. It was past patience; and the Apostle is here betrayed by his exasperation into the one coarse sentence in all his extant correspondence. 'Would,' he cries, 'that those sticklers for circumcision would go the whole length in the way of mutilating the flesh!'

2 Look you, I Paul tell you that, if you be circumcised,
3 Christ will profit you nothing. And I testify again to every
man who is submitting to circumcision, that he is bound to
4 do the whole Law. You are removed from Christ's sphere
of operation[1] inasmuch as you are being accounted righteous
5 in that of Law; you are banished from Grace. As for us,
it is by the Spirit on the score of faith that we are expecting
6 the fulfilment of the hope of righteousness. For in Christ
Jesus it is neither circumcision that is of any avail, nor uncircumcision, but faith operative through love.

7 You were running honourably: who has checked you in
8 your course of obedience to the truth?[2] The 'persuasion'

[1] κατηργήθητε ἀπὸ τοῦ Χριστοῦ, *constructio prægnans*, 'invalidated by being separated from Christ.' Cf. Rom. vii. 2, 6.

[2] The Apostle's favourite metaphor of the foot-race in the stadium. Cf. ii. 2; 1 Cor. ix. 24-29; Phil. iii. 13, 14; 2 Tim. iv. 7, 8. ἐνκόπτειν, a military term, 'cut up a road' to render it impassable (cf. 1 Th. ii. 18). The variant ἀνέκοψεν, though supported only by a few minuscs., is very attractive, since ἀνακόπτειν was used of the warders of the course (ῥαβδοῦχοι, μαστιγοφόροι) 'beating back' a runner who violated the rules (cf. 2 Tim. ii. 5) and expelling him from the lists.

Cf. 1 Cor. v. 6.
9 did not come from Him who is calling you. 'A little leaven
10 leavens the whole mass.' I have confidence in you in the
Lord that you will take no other view; and your disturber
11 will bear the condemnation, whoever he may be. And as
for me, brothers, if I am still proclaiming circumcision, why
am I still being persecuted? In that case the stumbling-
12 block of the Cross[1] is invalidated. Would that your
unsettlers would mutilate themselves outright![2]

The ethical question.

In the churches of Galatia as in those of Macedonia and indeed all the Gentile communities which the Apostle evangelised,[3] the Judaists found a specious argument in the persistence among his converts of the low standard of heathen ethic. They adduced it as an evidence of their allegation that the Gospel of Justification by Faith apart from Works issued in antinomianism. And so he concludes his letter with an inculcation of moral purity. It was indeed a blessed truth that the Gospel had emancipated believers (Cf. v. 1.) from the bondage of the Law and freed them from its intolerable yoke; but their liberty was not licence. The Galatians had grievous need of this warning. They were a passionate and impulsive people, and the controversy had excited their animosities. It had banished love, and they were at each other's throats like quarrelsome dogs. It is (Prov. xvii. 14.) written that 'the beginning of strife is as when one letteth out water'; and so it proved in Galatia. When the barrier of love was broken down, the full flood of evil passions was let loose and poured forth its devastating tide.

And what was the remedy? In our complex nature there are two domains—the flesh, which in fallen man is the seat of sinful passions; and the spirit, the side of our nature which is akin to God and which is dominated by His Holy Spirit. And the secret of holiness lies in resolutely eschewing the former and dwelling in the latter and responding to its

[1] A twofold *σκάνδαλον*: (1) the idea of a crucified Messiah, since the Jews were expecting a victorious King; (2) the necessity of an atonement, since on their view the Law—repentance and ceremonial observance—sufficed.

[2] *ἀναστατοῦν*, 'disturb by political commotion' (cf. Ac. xvii. 6; xxi. 38). Colloquially in Common Greek 'drive out of house and home,' 'upset.' Cf. Moulton and Milligan, *Vocab.* *ἀποκόψονται*, like the emasculated priests of Cybele (Suid.: Γάλλοι· οἱ ἀπόκοποι). Chrys.: *εἰ βούλονται, μὴ περιτεμνέσθωσαν μόνον ἀλλὰ καὶ περικοπτέσθωσαν.*

[3] Cf. p. 161.

hallowed instincts. It is against the works of the flesh that the Law is directed ; and if we yield to the spirit's impulses, then the restraint of Law is unnecessary.

13 It was with a view to freedom, brothers, that you were called ;
only do not make your freedom an outlet for the flesh.[1] No,
14 through love be one another's slaves. For all the Law is fulfilled
in a single precept : ' Thou shalt love thy neighbour as thyself.' Lev. xix.
15 But if you snarl and snap at one another, beware lest you be 18.
consumed by one another.
16 Here is my meaning : Comport yourselves by the spirit, and
17 no desire of the flesh will you ever perform. For the desire of
the flesh is so against the spirit's and the spirit's so against
that of the flesh—for these are mutually antagonistic—that
18 whatever things you will you may not do. But if you are led
by the spirit, you are not under Law.

The works of the flesh and the fruit of the spirit.

That there may be no misunderstanding and no evasion the Apostle descends to particulars and specifies the evils which belong to the domain of the flesh and the graces which grow in the soil of the spirit. The former he designates ' the works of the flesh ' and the latter ' the fruit of the spirit,' since the former are the unaided operations of our sinful nature, while the latter are nourished by heavenly grace as the harvest is nourished by the sunshine and the rain. ' Why,' says St. Chrysostom, ' does he call them " the fruit of the spirit " ? Because the evil works arise from ourselves alone. Wherefore he calls them " works " ; whereas the good need not only our own diligence but also the philanthropy of God.' The works of the flesh are a dark chaos, but the fruit of the spirit is a vital growth, an organic development. They fall into a triple triad : ' love, joy, peace '—love yielding joy and joy peace ; ' long-suffering, kindness, goodness '—kindness being more than long-suffering, and goodness, the inward character, more than kindness, its outward expression ; ' fidelity, meekness, self-restraint '—fidelity being possible without meekness, and

[1] ἀφορμή (cf. Rom. vii. 8, 11 ; 2 Cor. v. 12, xi. 12) is used in a 4th c. papyrus letter of the efflux or escape of water : μὴ θελήσῃς οὖν, κύριε, μῖνε [μεῖναι] ἐκτὸς ἡμῶν αὔριον διὰ τὴν ἀφορμὴν τοῦ ὕδατος εἵνα δυνηθῶμεν ποτίσαι τὸν μέγαν κλῆρον, ' please then, sir, do not stay away from us to-morrow because of the outflow of the water, that we may be able to irrigate the large holding.' Moulton and Milligan, *Voc.*

meekness being weakness unless it flows from self-restraint. And union with Christ ensures all these graces, since we are then crucified with Him, raised with Him, and live with Him.

19 Now the works of the flesh are manifest. And these are
20 fornication, uncleanness, indecency, idolatry, sorcery,[1] en-
mities, strife, jealousy, frenzies, intrigues, divisions, factions,
21 envies, drunken bouts, revelries, and so forth—things of which
I warn you, as I have already done, that those who practise
22 the like will not inherit the Kingdom of God. But the fruit
of the spirit is love, joy, peace; long-suffering, kindness,
23 goodness; fidelity,[2] meekness, self-restraint. Against the
24 like there is no law. And those who belong to Christ Jesus
have crucified the flesh with its passions and its desires.

The duty of charity.

Cf. ver. 16.

A holy life is in the first instance personal, but it exhibits itself in one's social relations; and so after bidding his readers 'comport themselves by the spirit,' referring to their individual behaviour, the Apostle now further exhorts them to 'march by the spirit,' referring to their mutual intercourse. It is a military term, and it expresses the duty of loyalty to one's comrades, especially in this instance the duty of befriending the weak and raising the fallen. It was a needful counsel; for in their zeal against the alleged antinomianism of the Gospel the Judaists had dealt ruthlessly with moral delinquencies, and it appears that there was a particular case where the offender had been mercilessly handled and expelled from the Church's communion. This, in the Apostle's judgment, was a violation of Christian charity. Discipline is indeed a necessary office of the Church, but its aim is not the destruction but the restoration of the sinner. He is an erring brother, and the Church's concern is not to condemn but to 'restore' him, even as a physician knits a broken limb or a fisherman repairs a torn net. Severity is the spirit of Pharisaism, not the law of Christ. It is un-

[1] Traffic with astrologers, fortune-tellers, and the like. Cf. Chrys. *In Cap. I. Epist. ad Gal.* 7: 'Many Greek customs are kept among some of our people—omens and auguries, and tokens, and observations of days, and the casting of horoscopes, and the scripts full of all manner of impiety which, as soon as their children are born, they put together to avert evil from their head.' Cf. Milligan, *Gk. Pap.* 47—a 3rd c. specimen of those magical incantations.

[2] πίστις, cf. Mt. xxiii. 23; Rom. iii. 3; Tit. ii. 10.

becoming in the truly 'spiritual'; and the Apostle reprobates it by two trenchant considerations. One is the liability of the best of men to fall and find themselves in sore need of charity. And the other is the imperfection even of the highest achievement. It is easy to be proud and censorious if we compare ourselves with others and exalt ourselves at their expense; but it humbles us when we consider how far at the best we have fallen short of our possibilities and opportunities. And this is the ultimate test. 'Each will bear his own load.' We are like ships homeward bound. What counts is the cargo which each is bringing, and it were a sorry boast that one has a better cargo than another. It may still be a poor cargo, and the just boast is not that one's cargo is better than another's but that it is full and precious.

25 If we live by the spirit, let us also march by the spirit.[1]
26 Let us not turn vain-glorious, provoking one another,
vi. 1 envying one another. Brothers, if a man be detected in some
trespass, you, the spiritual, restore [2] the offender in a spirit
of meekness. Have an eye to yourself, lest you also be
2 tempted. Bear one another's burdens, and thus you will
3 fulfil the Law of Christ.[3] For if one fancies he is something
4 while he is nothing, he is deluding himself. But let each
prove his own work,[4] and then what he is himself will be his
only ground of boasting and not what his neighbour is.
5 For each will bear his own load.[5]

It is characteristic of impulsive natures that their generous impulses quickly flag; and so it was with the Galatians. They started bravely on the Christian race, but they soon tired; they were lavish in their generosity to the Apostle when he first came among them, but their affection presently cooled and they turned against him; and recently they had evinced their disposition in a somewhat sordid fashion. In

The duty of honourable dealing.

Cf. v. 7.

Cf. iv. 15.

[1] στοιχεῖν, 'walk in line,' 'keep step in the ranks'—a military term (cf. Xen. *Cyrop.* VI. iii. 34). Cf. Phil. iii. 16.

[2] καταρτίζετε, cf. n. on 1 Th. iii. 10, p. 161.

[3] These are your burdens, this your law—not ceremonial observances (cf. Lk. xi. 46; Ac. xv. 10, 28) but one another's infirmities; not the Law of Moses but the Law of Christ (cf. Jo. xiii. 34).

[4] Cf. n. on 1 Th. v. 21, p. 165.

[5] βάρη (ver. 2), the grievous burdens of sorrow and sin; φορτίον, a 'load,' *e.g.* a ship's 'cargo' (cf. Ac. xxvii. 10).

those days when as yet there was no written Gospel, the record of the Lord's ministry and teaching was an oral tradition, and there was an order of 'teachers' or 'catechists' who had it by heart and, after the Jewish manner, drilled the churches in it by dint of repetition.[1] It was laborious work, and the catechist was entitled to remuneration. It was a debt of honour, and in the first flush of their enthusiasm the Galatians would gladly render it; but as their ardour abated, they fretted and begrudged it. It was indeed a base dereliction, and the Apostle might justly have assailed it with indignant reprobation; but he deals with it after his wont in a large spirit and unfolds the lofty principle which it involved. He quotes the ancient proverb: 'Whatever a man sows, this will he also reap.'[2] The harvest is determined by two conditions. One is the sort of seed which is sown: sow wheat, and you reap wheat; sow tares, and you reap tares. And the other is the quality of the soil: a poor soil, a poor harvest. This is a law of Nature, and it is inexorable: Nature is not mocked. And the law holds equally in the moral domain. Here there are two soils—the perishing flesh and the immortal spirit; and each yields an appropriate harvest. The harvest of the flesh is, like itself, corruptible: it decays and perishes. But the spirit is immortal, and the harvest which it yields is eternal. And here lay the misery of the Galatians' ungenerous behaviour. They were sowing perishable seed in perishable soil. They might indeed reap the harvest of a little worldly enrichment, but it would profit them at the longest only for a brief space. Generosity, on the other hand, is sowing in the soil of the spirit, and it yields an eternal harvest of peace and joy: spiritual enrichment endures for ever. Selfishness is a short-sighted policy. It means grasping at the poor profit of the moment and letting slip the enduring prize. 'Honourable things,' says the proverb, 'are difficult';[3] but it always pays to 'do the

Cf. Mt. xiii. 3-8.

[1] Cf. p. 80.

[2] Cf. Job iv. 8. Schol. on Plat. *Phædr.* 260 D: *ἐπὶ τῶν τοιαῦτα πασχόντων οἷα ἔδρασαν. παρῆκται δὲ ἀπὸ τοῦ στίχου· 'εἰ δὲ κακὰ σπείρεις, κακά κεν ἀμήσαιο,' καὶ πάλιν· 'ὃς δὲ κακὰ σπείρει, θεριεῖ κακὰ κήδεα παισίν.'* Cic. *De Orat.* II. 261: 'Ut sementem feceris, ita metes.'

[3] Cf. Plat. *Rep.* IV. 435: *ἴσως γάρ, ὦ Σώκρατες, τὸ λεγόμενον ἀληθές, ὅτι χαλεπὰ τὰ καλά.* The maxim is ascribed to Solon.

honourable thing,' and the difficulty is a challenge to our faith and courage.

6 And let one who is being taught the Word by rote give his
7 teacher a share in all his goods. Be not deceived: God is not
mocked. 'Whatever a man sows, this will he also reap.'
8 For one who sows in the soil of his own flesh, of the flesh will
reap corruption; while one who sows in the soil of the spirit
9 will reap a life eternal. And let us do the honourable thing and
never lose heart; for at the proper season we shall reap if
10 we do not faint. So then, while the season is ours, let us be
doing the work of goodness by all, especially by the household
of the Faith.

The argument is now complete, and the Apostle, after his wont,[1] takes the pen from his amanuensis that he may authenticate the letter by his autograph. As a rule the autograph was merely a benediction, but in his affectionate solicitude for his erring converts he expands it into a personal message. Fatigue and anxiety had unnerved him, and as his trembling hand shaped the words with more than the accustomed uncouthness, he playfully apologised for the ungainly scrawl. 'See,' he says, 'with what large letters I am writing to you with my own hand.'[2] Yet he persists. It seems that there were pusillanimous souls among the Gentile converts in Galatia who had been intimidated by Jewish violence and, though they cared nothing for the Law, professed zeal for it and sought to prove it by active proselytism. All their concern was to escape persecution for the Cross; and thus, as the Apostle could testify, they missed the supreme benediction. The Cross was his only boast. The Galatians remembered how he had been stoned by the Jews at Lystra. He still bore the scars on his body and the stripes of the lictors' scourge, and these were no disfiguring mutilation; they were a sacred seal, more sacred by far than the boasted circumcision of the Judaists. Even

The sign-manual.

Ac. xiv. 19.

Cf. 2 Cor. xi. 24, 25.

[1] Cf. p. 155.

[2] ἔγραψα, epistolary aorist (cf. Moulton's Winer, p. 347). Taking it as an ordinary aorist ('I have written'), Chrys. regards the sentence as retrospective, referring to the entire letter, and supposes that in this instance the Apostle did not employ an amanuensis, since it was a stern letter and he would have no third party hear his reproofs; 'which was a token of much generosity.' But in fact he observed no such secrecy (cf. i. 2).

as heathen votaries branded the symbols of their deities on their arms and necks, so his scars were 'the brands of Jesus,' and he wore them proudly before the world. His person was sacrosanct.

11 SEE WITH WHAT LARGE LETTERS I AM WRITING TO YOU
12 WITH MY OWN HAND. AS MANY AS WISH TO SHOW A FAIR
FACE IN THE FLESH, THEY IT IS THAT ARE COMPELLING YOU
TO SUBMIT TO CIRCUMCISION, ALL TO ESCAPE BEING PERSE-
13 CUTED FOR THE CROSS OF CHRIST. FOR THOSE WHO ARE
SUBMITTING TO CIRCUMCISION DO NOT EVEN KEEP THE LAW
THEMSELVES; NO, THEY WISH YOU TO SUBMIT TO IT THAT
14 THEY MAY BOAST IN YOUR FLESH. BUT FAR BE IT FROM
ME TO BOAST EXCEPT IN THE CROSS OF OUR LORD JESUS
CHRIST, THROUGH WHICH [1] THE WORLD HAS BEEN CRUCIFIED
15 TO ME AND I TO THE WORLD. FOR NEITHER CIRCUMCISION
NOR UNCIRCUMCISION IS ANYTHING, BUT A NEW CREATION.[2]
16 AND AS MANY AS MARCH BY THIS RULE, 'PEACE' BE UPON
THEM AND MERCY, EVEN 'UPON THE ISRAEL' OF GOD.
17 HENCEFORTH LET NO ONE ANNOY ME; FOR I BEAR ON MY
BODY THE BRANDS OF JESUS.[3]
18 THE GRACE OF OUR LORD JESUS CHRIST BE WITH YOUR
SPIRIT, BROTHERS. AMEN.

Pss. cxxv. 5, cxxviii. 6.

The despatch of the letter. Cf. iv. 20.

The letter would be despatched immediately; for the situation demanded prompt intervention. If he might, the Apostle would have hastened in person to Galatia and reasoned with his deluded converts face to face; but this

[1] The antecedent of δι' οὗ is probably τῷ σταυρῷ. If it were Ἰησοῦ Χριστῷ, ἐν ᾧ would be more natural.

[2] κτίσις, (1) the act of creating (cf. Rom. i. 20); (2) the creation, the totality of created things (cf. Rom. viii. 22); (3) a creature, a single created thing (cf. Heb. iv. 13).

[3] στίγμα occurs in various connections. Cf. Wetstein. A thievish or runaway slave was branded on the forehead with the letter F (*fur* or *fugitivus*), whence he was designated a στιγματιάς, *litteratus*, *notatus*, *inscriptus* (cf. Becker, *Gallus*, p. 222); criminals were similarly branded; and soldiers sometimes tattooed their commander's name on their arms. None of these references, however, is suitable here, not even the last, since the soldier's στίγμα was merely occasional. The religious custom of branding symbols of a heathen deity on the body is exemplified in the action of Ptolemy Philopator when he compelled the Jews to be branded with an ivy-leaf, the emblem of Dionysus (cf. 3 Macc. ii. 29). This is probably the Apostle's reference: the Lord's *sacræ notæ* were on his body, and these made his person sacrosanct. It is an unfortunate suggestion that he playfully represents himself as protected by a charm (Deissmann, *Bibl. Stud.*, pp. 349 ff.).

was meanwhile impossible. He was needed at Antioch, and writing was the only way. He would despatch the letter without delay, and he would doubtless entrust it not to a mere courier but to some 'beloved brother and faithful minister and fellow-slave in the Lord' who could, in some measure, supply his place and reinforce his written argument. Perhaps it was Silas. He was well qualified for the office alike by his personal character and by his acquaintance with the Galatian churches.

Cf. Col. iv. 7, 8.

THE THIRD MISSION

'Micantis more lampadis
Perfundit orbem radiis,
Fugat errorum tenebras
Ut sola regnet veritas.'

LATIN HYMN.

I

THE SETTING FORTH

Ac. xviii. 23.

Sojourn at Antioch.

PAUL must have required a season of repose after the labour and anxiety of his second mission, but this was denied him. The world's need of Christ was like an importunate voice in his ears, and the unhappy plight of his Galatian churches was a heavy burden on his heart. He must straightway gird himself for another mission, and hasten first of all to Galatia and reinforce his letter by personal ministration. His stay at Syrian Antioch was therefore brief. He 'put in some time,' says the historian, indicating a season of impatient detention by mechanical though necessary employments;[1] and from the subsequent narrative it appears what the chief of these was.

Organisation of Gentile charity to the poor in Jerusalem.

There was always much poverty in Jerusalem, and it would seem that these were hard times in the city, and the humbler sort of the Jewish Christians were in sore straits. Paul had observed their destitution during his recent visit, and he recognised here at once a duty and an opportunity. Already the Antiochene Christians had generously succoured the distress of their Jewish fellow-Christians, and they had pledged themselves to continue their benefaction as occasion arose;[2] but the need was great and ever increasing with the growth of the Church. The bounty of Antioch was in-

Cf. Gal. ii. 10.

[1] *ποιήσας χρόνον τινά*, cf. Mt. xx. 12 (where *μίαν ὥραν ποιεῖν* is contemptuously contrasted with *βαστάζειν τὸ βάρος τῆς ἡμέρας*); Ac. xv. 33, xx. 3; Ja. iv. 13.

[2] Cf. p. 73.

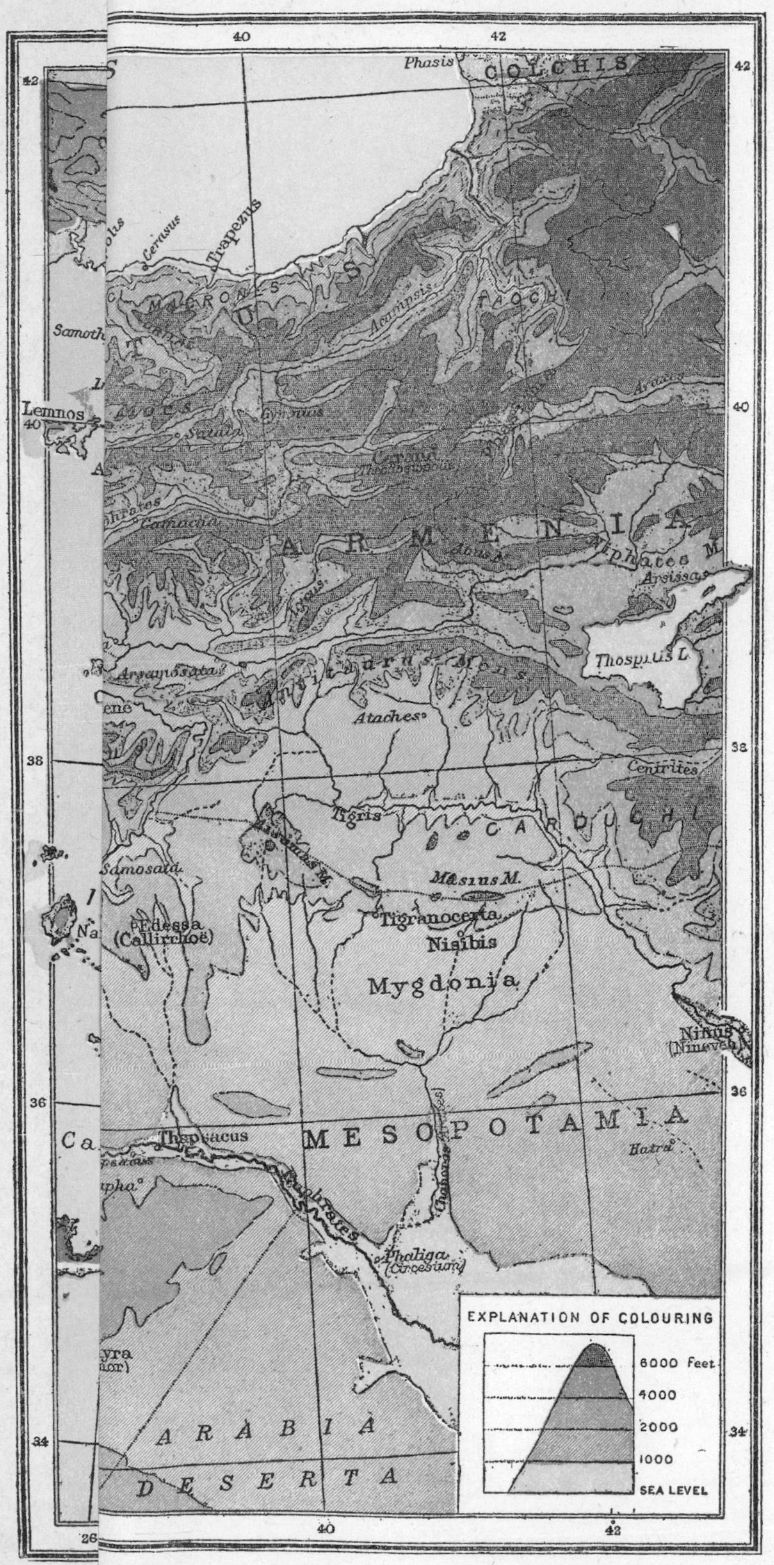

Phasis
COLCHIS
Trapezus
Cerasus
MACRONES
Samoth
Lemnos
Acampsis
TAOCHI
ARMENIA
Arsissa
Thospitis L.
Arsamosata
Antitaurus Mons
Atachès
Centrites
Tigris
CARDUCHI
Samosata
Masius M.
Tigranocerta
Nisibis
Edessa
(Callirrhoë)
Mygdonia
Ninus
(Nineveh)
MESOPOTAMIA
Thapsacus
Hatra
Phaliga
(Circesium)
ARABIA
DESERTA
EXPLANATION OF COLOURING
6000 Feet
4000
2000
1000
SEA LEVEL

sufficient, and Paul proposed that the Antiochene Church, as the mother of Gentile Christendom, should call upon her daughters to share the responsibility, and should authorise him to organise in every Gentile community a contribution for the relief of 'the poor among the saints at Jerusalem.' His proposal was heartily approved. The Church not only furnished him with the authority he desired, but associated with him, apparently, two of its members as his coadjutors in the enterprise. One of these was Titus, that young Antiochene who had attended Paul and Barnabas on their errand of charity to Jerusalem seven years previously; and his appointment was a felicitous, perhaps an intentional, stroke of policy. The association in the Apostle's company of the Gentile whom he had refused to circumcise at the bidding of the Judaists,[1] and of Timothy whom he had afterwards circumcised in consideration of his Jewish antecedents, was an impressive demonstration of his attitude toward the Law and an effective rejoinder to his Judaist calumniators.

Cf. Rom. xv. 26; 1 Cor. xvi. 1.

Cf. 2 Cor. viii. 6, 16-19; xii. 17, 18.

A healing ordinance.

It was pure charity that dictated the organisation of the relief fund, yet it promised at the same time to serve an ulterior end. So practical a demonstration of Christian brotherhood could hardly fail in commending the Gentile converts to the Jewish Church and in putting the Judaists to shame. Paul recognised in it the possibility of beneficent and far-reaching results. He anticipated the healing of the disastrous breach in the East, and he foresaw that this would facilitate his farther ministry in the West and especially in the imperial capital which was already the goal of his desire.

Cf. 2 Cor. x. 12-14.

Cf. Rom. xv. 28, 29.

Departure on third mission.

It was probably in the month of July that he set forth with his companions on his third mission. Galatia was his immediate destination, and he would travel hastily by the overland route through the Cilician Gates.[2] He would visit the Galatian churches in succession—at Derbe, Lystra, Iconium, and Pisidian Antioch. The historian intimates merely that 'he made an orderly progress through the country, and confirmed all the disciples'; but, brief as it is, the record is significant. It shows that the Apostle's purpose

Visitation of Galatian Churches.

Ac. xviii. 23.

[1] Cf. p. 74.

[2] Cf. p. 104.

was achieved. His letter and the ministration of Silas—if he was indeed its bearer—had turned the tide of disaffection and won back the ever impetuous Galatians to their allegiance; and his visit completed the good work. He had the happiness of seeing his converts re-established in the Faith, and they gave practical assurance of their sincerity. Not only did they adopt the financial proposal and pledge themselves to its support, but they furnished a fresh recruit to his little band of fellow-workers in the person of Gaius of Derbe. At all events Gaius was with him at Ephesus and accompanied him thence to Achaia; and the probability is that he joined the Apostle in his progress through Galatia.

Cf. 1 Cor. xvi. 1.

Cf. Ac. xix. 29; xx. 4.

II

MINISTRY AT EPHESUS

Ac. xviii. 24-xix. 20.

Journey to Ephesus.

Ac. xviii. 20, 21.

His destination on quitting Galatia was already fixed. He had promised the Ephesians when he visited them on his way to Jerusalem, that he would return and gratify their desire to hear more of his doctrine; and now he hastens to redeem his pledge. If two full months be allowed for his ministry in Galatia, it would be about the beginning of October when he took his departure from Pisidian Antioch and turned his steps westward. The ordinary route was the busy highway along the valley of the Lycus and the Mæander, but this he avoided and, holding to the north, travelled across the sparsely peopled uplands. His reason was twofold—not only his old dread of venturing into that sweltering pass in the heat of autumn,[1] but a desire to expedite his arrival at Ephesus. Had he followed the trade route, he must have lingered by the way to preach at Colossæ, Laodicea, and other cities; and meanwhile he had a larger design. Ephesus was his goal, and if he won her, he would win Asia.[2]

[1] Cf. p. 122.

[2] In his *Life of Polycarp* (ii) Pionius represents Paul as visiting Smyrna in the course, apparently, of this journey from Galatia to Ephesus and staying there with Strataeas, a son of Eunice the daughter of Lois and thus a brother of Timothy. The passage so abounds in palpable inaccuracies as to possess no historical value. Smyrna was remote from his route, and in any case he was in haste to reach Ephesus and would linger nowhere.

The capital of Asia.

The Asiarchate.

Cf. Ac. xix. 31.

For Ephesus was justly styled 'the Light of Asia.'[1] She was the capital of that magnificent Province, the seat of the imperial Proconsul, and moreover the centre of that important confederation, the Asiarchate.[2] It was ever the wise policy of Rome to reconcile her subject peoples to her dominion by respecting their *amour propre* and according them the utmost measure of autonomy compatible with their imperial relationship; and a conspicuous example is the organisation of the chief cities of each province into a confederation or union.[3] These unions were mainly religious. They fostered the imperial idea by establishing the worship of the Emperor and erecting temples in his honour. Each city had its temple and priesthood, and the provincial High Priest was termed 'the Ruler' of the Province. Thus, Galatia had its Galatarch, Bithynia its Bithyniarch, Pamphylia its Pamphyliarch, and Asia its Asiarch. His principal function was the supervision of the cult of the Emperor throughout the province, but he was charged also with the presidency of games and festivals and the erection of monuments. The chief of these provincial unions was that of Asia; and the Asiarch was, next to the Proconsul, the most important personage in the Province. He held office only for a term, whether a single year or, as seems more probable, a quinquennium; and since, like the Jewish High Priest,[4] he retained his title after the expiry of his term, there was a college of Asiarchs at Ephesus—the acting Asiarch and the Asiarchs *emeriti*. Combining national sympathy and imperial allegiance, they exerted a healing influence in the State, and served the cause of order on occasions of popular tumult.

Commercial prosperity.

Ephesus was not only the capital of the Province of Asia, but the leading city of Asia Minor; and she owed her abounding prosperity, in the first instance, to her geographical position.[5] Situated close to the mouth of the river Caÿstros, she was a busy seaport with extensive docks despite the

[1] Plin. *Nat. Hist.* v. 31: 'lumen Asiæ.'

[2] Cf. Lightfoot, *Apost. Fath.* II. iii. pp. 404-415.

[3] κοινόν, *commune.*

[4] Cf. *The Days of His Flesh*, p. 464.

[5] On the city of Ephesus cf. Strabo, 639-42.

troublesome accumulation of alluvial deposit; and it assured her an enormous commerce that she was the western terminus of the important trade route to the Euphrates.

Intellectual distinction.

She was famous also in literature and art. The catalogue of her distinguished sons includes the names of the philosopher Heracleitos and his friend Hermodoros who so provoked the jealousy of the citizens that they banished him, bidding him, if he would surpass his fellows, surpass them elsewhere,[1] and who acted as interpreter to the Roman Decemvirs when they drew up their Twelve Tables, the foundation of Roman jurisprudence, after the model of the laws of Solon;[2] the poet Hipponax; the painters Parrhasios and Apelles; and in later times Alexander, who was styled 'the Lamp' for his many-sided brilliance as an orator, a statesman, an historian, a poet, an astronomer, and a geographer.

The Temple of Artemis.

Her principal glory, however, was her Temple of Artemis, which ranked as one of the Seven Wonders of the ancient world.[3] The original temple had been burned to the ground on the night when Alexander the Great was born, having been fired by Herostratos, an ambitious madman who, since he could not achieve fame, coveted notoriety.[4] It was, however, rebuilt on a larger scale and in greater magnificence. Its walls and pillars were gleaming marble, and the interior was fitted with ivory, cypress, and cedar.[5] Its length was four hundred and twenty-five feet, and its breadth two hundred and twenty; while its stately columns, numbering a hundred and twenty-seven and each erected by a king, were sixty feet in height.[6] It was two hundred and twenty years in building, and the enormous cost was defrayed by the whole of Asia with a splendid devotion like Israel's at the making of the Tabernacle in the Wilderness, even the women contributing their jewels and ornaments.[7]

Cf. Ex. xxxv. 20-29.

[1] Strabo, 642: *φάντες· ἡμέων μηδεὶς ὀνήϊστος ἔστω· εἰ δὲ μή, ἄλλῃ τε καὶ μετ' ἄλλων.* Cf. Cic. *Tusc. Quæst.* v. 36.

[2] Strabo, 642.

[3] Cf. Phil. Byzant. *De Sept. Orb. Spect.*

[4] Cf. Strabo, 640; Plut. *Alex.* 3; Cic. *De Nat. Deor.* II. 27; Val. Max. VIII. 14.

[5] Plin. *Nat. Hist.* XVI. 79.

[6] *Ibid.* XXXVI. 21.

[7] Strabo, 640.

The image of the goddess.

The chief treasure of the temple was an image of the goddess—a pedestal surmounted by a bust which was studded with breasts symbolising fecundity. So worn and blackened with age that it was impossible to determine whether the material was ivory or ivy-wood,[1] it accorded ill with the magnificence of its surroundings; nevertheless it was hallowed by antiquity and by the tradition that, like other sacred images, it had fallen from heaven. (Cf. Ac. xix. 35.)

The privilege of asylum.

Her temple conferred many advantages on Ephesus. One, though of doubtful value, was the privilege of asylum. The sacrosanct area varied in extent from time to time. It had originally been limited to the sacred precincts, but Alexander the Great increased it to a radius of two hundred yards,[2] and Mithridates still farther to the length of a bow-shot, which again was doubled by Mark Antony, so that a portion of the city was included. This, however, proved mischievous inasmuch as it afforded impunity to criminals, and it was reduced by the Emperor Augustus.[3]

The silversmiths.

A more profitable advantage was the prosperity which accrued to the city from the presence of the temple in her midst. 'The Great Goddess Artemis' was the supreme deity of the Province; (Cf. Ac. xix. 27.) and, since the temple at Ephesus was her chief shrine, multitudes of worshippers trooped thither, especially in the month named after her Artemisios, when solemn assemblies and festivals were held in her honour. These brought wealth to the city. They naturally desired to carry home memorials of their visits, and to meet this requirement silver models of the temple were manufactured.[4] It was a lucrative industry, and the silversmiths of Ephesus were an influential guild. (Cf. Ac. xix. 24-27.) The city owed much to her temple, and it is no wonder that she gloried in it and styled herself 'the Sacristan of the Great Goddess Artemis,' engraving the title on her coins and accounting it her proudest boast. (Cf. Ac. xix. 35.)

Ephesian Magic.

The religion of Ephesus had a viler side. Gross darkness covered even 'the Light of Asia.'

[1] Plin. *Nat. Hist.* XVI. 79.
[2] Precisely, a stadium, *i.e.* 606¾ foot.
[3] Strabo, 641.
[4] Cf. Herod. II. 63; Diod. Sic. I. 97, XX. 14.

'They say this town is full of cozenage;
As, nimble jugglers that deceive the eye,
Dark-working sorcerers that change the mind,
Soul-killing witches that deform the body,
Disguised cheaters, prating mountebanks,
And many such-like liberties of sin.'[1]

She was the chief home of oriental magic, and 'the Ephesian Letters' were famous all over the world—charms and incantations credited with sovereign efficacy in averting evil and procuring good luck. An anecdote is told of an Ephesian wrestler who encountered a Milesian at the Olympic Games and proved victorious until it was observed that he wore a charm on his ankle; and when this was removed he was worsted in thirty bouts.[2]

Apollos of Alexandria.

Ac. xx. 34; 1 Cor. iv. 12; cf. Ac. xviii. 3.

On his arrival at Ephesus the Apostle found a lodging in the house of his friends Aquila and Priscilla, whom he had left there on his way to Jerusalem;[3] and he resumed, doubtless in company with Aquila, his old craft of tent-making. They had not been idle in the service of the Gospel during the interval, and they had an interesting experience to relate. A remarkable personage had appeared at Ephesus. This was Apollos, a native of Alexandria, distinguished, as became one nurtured in that brilliant city, for his learning and eloquence.[4] He was a Jew, but he belonged to the school of John the Baptist. It was only a few of John's disciples who had recognised Jesus as the Messiah. The majority of them remained outside the Church, and continued their master's mission after his death, preaching his message and administering his baptism. They were distinguished from the Jews by their persuasion of the imminence of the Messiah's Advent and their incul-

A Jewish disciple of John the Baptist.

Cf. Mt. ix. 14.

[1] Shak. *Com. of Err.* I. ii. 97-102.

[2] Suidas under Ἐφέσια γράμματα. Cf. Plut. *Sympos.* vii. 5; Clem. Alex. *Strom.* I. xv. 73, V. viii. 45; Erasm. *Adag.* See a specimen of those magical papyri in Deissmann's *Light from the Ancient East*, pp. 249 ff.

[3] Cf. 1 Cor. xvi. 19, where (according to DEFG) Paul, writing at Ephesus, says: 'Aquila and Prisca with whom I lodge (παρ' οἷς καὶ ξενίζομαι).' Vulg. *apud quos et hospitor.*

[4] λόγιος (Ac. xviii. 24) combined the ideas of *eloquence* and *learning.* It was an epithet of Hermes, the god of eloquence (cf. Luc. *Gall.* 2). Aristotle styled Theophrastus 'the most learned (λογιώτατον) of his disciples' (Strabo, 618).

cation of the duty of repentance in preparation for that consummation; and they differed from the Christians in that they regarded His Advent as still future, whereas the latter believed that He had come and that He was Jesus.

His preaching in the synagogue.

The sect had established itself at Alexandria, and it possessed in Apollos an ardent and effective advocate. On arriving in Ephesus he preached in the Jewish synagogue his gospel of the Coming Messiah, adducing in its support the testimony of the Prophetic Scriptures. This was the method of the Apostles and their successors in their reasonings with the Jews. They compiled collections of prophetic 'testimonics' like Melito's *Selections from the Law and the Prophets regarding the Saviour and All Our Faith*;[1] and it seems that the disciples of the Baptist had anticipated the method. Their collection of 'testimonies' was appropriately entitled *The Way of the Lord*, referring to their master's definition of his office, and Apollos had mastered it: he had it by heart.[2] He accurately portrayed the Messiah as the prophets had foretold Him.[3]

Jo. i. 23; cf. Mt. iii. 3; Mk. i. 2, 3; Lk. iii. 4-6.

Instructed by Aquila and Priscilla.

Aquila and Priscilla were among his hearers, and they interviewed him and showed him wherein his message was lacking. It was indeed all true: it was the very Gospel which they preached; but they had recognised a further truth which made a momentous difference: *the Messiah had come, and He was Jesus.*[4] They showed how the story of Jesus answered, line by line, to the prophetic picture of the Messiah. The evidence was clear, and Apollos could not resist it. It did not contradict his faith; it rather confirmed and completed it, and he forthwith embraced Christianity.

[1] ἐκλογὰς ἔκ τε τοῦ νόμου καὶ τῶν προφητῶν περὶ τοῦ σωτῆρος καὶ πάσης τῆς πίστεως ἡμῶν (Eus. *Hist. Eccl.* IV. 26). Cf. Hatch, *Ess. in Bibl. Gk.*, pp. 203 ff.; Burkitt, *The Gospel Hist. and its Transmission*, pp. 126 ff. 'The testimony of the Christ' (I Cor. i. 6) is a designation of the Gospel.

[2] κατηχούμενος τὴν Ὁδὸν τοῦ Κυρίου. Cf. *The Days of His Flesh*, p. xvii.

[3] Ac. xviii. 25. For τὰ περὶ τοῦ Ἰησοῦ (ℵABDEL, Vulg.), 'the story of Jesus' (Cf. Lk. xxiv. 19), one would expect rather τὰ περὶ τοῦ Χριστοῦ, 'the things regarding the Messiah'; but the phrase is employed from the Christian point of view. Though Apollos did not perceive it, the prophetic picture of the Messiah was a picture of Jesus (cf. Lk. xxiv. 27).

[4] εἶναι τὸν Χριστὸν Ἰησοῦν (cf. Ac. xviii. 5), not 'Jesus was the Christ' (A.V., R.V.), but 'the Christ was Jesus.' They began with the prophetic picture of the Messiah, and then showed how the history of Jesus answered to it.

Called to Corinth.

It happened that several Corinthians visited Ephesus at that juncture; and, charmed by the gifts of Apollos, they invited him to accompany them on their return home. He consented, and the little brotherhood of Ephesian Christians —Aquila, Priscilla, Epænetus, and the converts they had won—furnished him with a letter of commendation to the Church at Corinth.[1] He proved conspicuously successful in Achaia alike in edifying the believers and in arguing with the Jews; nevertheless, as presently appeared, his ministry had, through no fault of his, an unfortunate issue, fostering a spirit which wrought no small mischief in the Corinthian Church.

Paul and the Baptist's disciples.

Ere Paul arrived at Ephesus Apollos had taken his departure; but he encountered there a little company of John's disciples, about a dozen in number. Their position was different from that of Apollos. There were two sections in the Baptist's school; the majority who still maintained his original attitude of expectation, and others who shared his subsequent recognition of the Messiahship of Jesus. Apollos belonged to the former. Of the latter some, like Andrew and John, had cast in their lot with Jesus and had witnessed the progress of His revelation; but others dwelt remote and had no knowledge of the later developments; and this immature type—a sort of backwater of religious thought—persisted in the Hellenistic world. It had its representatives at Ephesus. These were 'disciples,' believing in Jesus, and this differentiated them from the Jews; but on the other hand it differentiated them from the Christians that they were ignorant of the Resurrection of the Lord and the Advent of the Holy Spirit. They had been baptised with John's baptism of repentance, but they were strangers to the baptism of the Holy Spirit and the rich grace which it conveyed. Paul encountered this little community, isolated alike from the Synagogue and

Cf. Jo. i. 35-37.

Cf. Ac. xix. 1, 2.

[1] According to the amplification of Ac. xviii. 27 in Cod. Bez. (D): *ἐν δὲ τῇ Ἐφέσῳ, ἐπιδημοῦντές τινες Κορίνθιοι καὶ ἀκούσαντες αὐτοῦ παρεκάλουν διελθεῖν σὺν αὐτοῖς εἰς τὴν πατρίδα αὐτῶν· συγκατανεύσαντος δὲ αὐτοῦ οἱ Ἐφέσιοι ἔγραψαν τοῖς ἐν Κορίνθῳ μαθηταῖς ὅπως ἀποδέξωνται τὸν ἄνδρα· ὃς ἐπιδημήσας εἰς τὴν Ἀχαίαν πολὺ συνεβάλετο ταῖς ἐκκλησίαις*, 'Now certain Corinthian visitors in Ephesus heard him and besought him to cross over with them to their country; and on his consenting the Ephesians wrote to the disciples at Corinth that they might welcome the man; and he on visiting Achaia greatly helped the Churches.'

the Church; and he acquainted them with the later development of the Christian revelation. They welcomed it, and entered into the full gladness of the Faith.

His Ephesian ministry.

The Apostle began his ministry at Ephesus after his accustomed method. He addressed his first appeal to the Jews, preaching and reasoning in the synagogue amid ever increasing hostility until after three months he was forced to desist. There is little reference in the Book of Acts to the persecutions which he suffered at this crisis or indeed throughout his sojourn in the city; but how fierce these were appears from incidental allusions in his correspondence. His life was in daily peril from the fury of that 'wild beast,' the mob; and it would seem that he was haled before the magistrates and sentenced to scourging and imprisonment. He quitted the synagogue with the disciples whom he had won; and, hiring the lecture-hall of a rhetorician named Tyrannos, discoursed there daily betwixt 11 A.M. and 4 P.M.[1] These were the only possible hours. The rhetorician lectured in the morning,[2] and it was only when his class was over that his hall was available. Moreover the Apostle had to earn his daily bread, and since the working-day began at sunrise and ended an hour before the sultry noon-tide, it was only in the afternoon that he was free to preach and the populace to hear.

Cf. 1 Cor. xv. 32; 2 Cor. i. 8, xi. 23.

The embarrassment of popular superstition.

Such was the beginning of his ministry at Ephesus; and a stirring and fruitful ministry it proved, lasting for two years and pervading the entire Province of Asia. It was the general populace of the city that he addressed after his rupture with the synagogue, and its character presented at once peculiar opportunities and peculiar difficulties. Since Ephesus was the home of Eastern magic, it was steeped in superstition. It was infested with charlatans who professed to avert ill luck and dispel diseases by their charms and incantations. The theory in those days was that all distempers were due to demonic possession, and the cure lay in the exorcism of the evil spirit.[3] The gift of healing was

[1] In Ac. xix. 9 Cod. Bez. (D) has ἀπὸ ὥρας πέμπτης ἕως δεκάτης.

[2] Aug. *Conf.* VI. 11: 'Dubitamus pulsare quo aperiantur cætera? Antemeridianis horis discipuli occupant; cæteris quid facimus? cur non id agimus?'

[3] Cf. *The Days of His Flesh*, pp. 105 ff.

one of the miraculous endowments of the Apostolic Church,[1] and Paul's exercise of it at Ephesus at once promoted and embarrassed his ministry. It won him indeed a hearing and demonstrated that God was with him; but at the same time it identified him in the eyes of the populace with the heathen adepts and excited the jealousy of the latter.

The Apostle a magical personage.

The enthusiasm which his miracles aroused was boundless, and it was exhibited in a pathetic fashion. He was regarded as a magical personage. There was a miraculous efficacy in the touch of his hand and even in contact with his belongings; and he could not lay aside his napkin or the apron which he wore at his work without its being filched and carried to sick-rooms. It was indeed gross superstition, but it was natural in those heathen folk and there was faith behind it. Faith never misses its reward; and the blind faith of those Ephesians was honoured like that of the poor woman at Capernaum who was persuaded that, if only she might touch the Master's clothes, she would be healed of her hemorrhage. There was healing in the Apostle's napkin even as in the tassel of the Lord's robe. (Mt. ix. 20.)

Discomfiture of two exorcists.

Nor did the superstition go uncorrected. The difference between Paul and the heathen adepts was attested by at least one notorious incident. Recognising the potency of the name of Jesus on his lips, they introduced it as an *onomasticon sacrum* into their incantations. It chanced that two itinerant exorcists visited the city. They were brothers, and, like so many practitioners of black art in those days, they were Jews,[2] sons of a priest named Sceva.[3] There was an unhappy creature in the city, evidently a madman, subject (Cf. Ac. xiii. 6; Mt. xii. 27.)

[1] Cf. pp. 35 f.

[2] The Jewish Essenes seem to have practised exorcism (cf. Lightfoot, *Coloss.*, p. 89).

[3] Luke tells the story just as he had heard it, and after the manner of popular tales it is somewhat confused. As it stands (Ac. xix. 13-16), it presents two difficulties. (1) It begins by speaking of seven exorcists (ver. 14), and presently of only two (vers. 16), the former number being perhaps a confusion with the demoniac's 'sevenfold' possession (cf. *The Days of His Flesh*, p. 207). (2) Sceva is styled a High Priest. Both are removed in the revised text of Cod. Bez. (D): 'among whom also the sons of one Sceva, a priest, wished to do the same: they had a custom of exorcising such persons; and they came in to the demoniac and began to invoke the Name, saying, "We charge you by Jesus, whom Paul preaches, to come forth."'

to fits of violence. Insanity was accounted a phase, indeed the worst phase, of demonic possession; and the two exorcists were summoned to deal with the case. If the man was a Jew, as he appears to have been, it was natural that his friends should resort to the Jewish practitioners. Aware of the difficulty of their task, the latter employed the novel incantation which had of late proved so efficacious. Their adjuration irritated the patient. He had heard in his normal condition of Paul and his preaching of Jesus, and the familiar names excited his disordered mind. He broke into a frenzy. 'Jesus,' he cried, 'I recognise, and Paul I know; but you—who are you?' and he sprang upon them like a wild beast. They were overpowered by his insane fury. Ere he was mastered their clothes were torn to shreds, and they escaped from the house severely mauled.

Cf. Ac. xix. 17.

Salutary result.

The incident had important consequences. It had happened in a Jewish house, and thus it touched the Jewish community no less than the Gentile populace. The whole city was impressed, and the issue proves how justly the situation was appreciated. The inference was not that the magicians had been worsted by the Apostle in their own art but that magic was an unholy thing. The Ephesian Letters were discredited and contemned; and the Christians who had clung to the superstition confessed their error and abjured it, and such of them as possessed magical papyri made a public bonfire of them. It was like the Florentine Holocaust of Vanities in the Piazza della Signoria in the days of Savonarola, and it involved no trifling sacrifice. The magicians sold their charms dear, and the value of the parchments which were cast into the flames was estimated at nigh £2000.[1]

Spread of the Gospel throughout the Province. Cf. Ac. xix. 10, 26; 1 Cor. xvi. 19. Cf. Col. ii. 1.

It is an evidence of the hold which the Gospel had taken of the city, and the conquest of Ephesus proved a far-reaching triumph. She was the metropolis of Asia, and tidings of her gracious visitation quickly spread throughout the Province. Paul remained within her gates, but his message travelled where his voice had never been heard, and churches grew up which had never seen his face, not alone that little

[1] 50,000 *drachmæ*. A *drachma* was worth some 8½d. Cf. *The Days of His Flesh*, p. 310.

group in the Lycus valley—at Colossæ, Laodiceia, and Hierapolis—which he had occasion to counsel by letter some seven years later when he was a prisoner at Rome, but those at Smyrna, Pergamos, Thyatira, Sardes, and Philadelphia which St. John addresses in the Book of Revelation, and those at Magnesia, Tralles, and Miletus which St. Ignatius afterwards addressed. His companions, especially Timothy and Titus, would be active in this missionary enterprise, and Ephesian converts like Erastus would bear their part; but the work was doubtless done chiefly by representatives of the various cities, like Epaphras and Philemon of Colossæ and Nympha of Laodiceia, who visited Ephesus, and there heard the Gospel from his lips and carried it home.

Rev. ii. 8-iii. 13.

Cf. Ac. xix. 22.

Cf. Phm. 1, 2, 19; Col. iv. 15.

III

TROUBLE AT CORINTH

1 Cor. vi. 12-20; 2 Cor. vi. 14-vii. 1; 1 Cor. i-vi. 11; Ac. xix. 21, 22; 1 Cor. vii-xvi; 2 Cor. ii. 1, xiii. 2; x-xiii. 10.

Evil tidings of Corinthian Church.

Thus prosperous was the Ephesian ministry, yet amid its manifold engrossments the Apostle was not neglectful of the interests of the Gospel elsewhere, nor unmindful of the churches which he had already established. That of Corinth engaged his special solicitude. It was an important community, and soon after his arrival at Ephesus he had despatched Titus and the colleague whom the Antiochene Church had associated with him,[1] to acquaint the Corinthians with his scheme for the relief of the poor at Jerusalem and enlist their sympathy and support. They had at the moment espoused it with enthusiastic alacrity, and the two deputies had returned to Ephesus with a pleasing report; but in the autumn of the year 54 [2] the Apostle was troubled by the arrival of painful intelligence.

Cf. 2 Cor. xii. 18.

Cf. 2 Cor. viii. 10-12, ix. 2.

Asceticism and libertinism.

That licentious city, where the chief shrine was the Temple of Aphrodite and immorality was not a vice but a cult, was a perilous abode for the new faith. It was difficult

[1] Cf. p. 223. [2] Cf. Append. I.

for the Corinthian converts to break with their past and dissociate themselves from their environment; and the inevitable issue was the emergence of two opposite tendencies, two antagonistic attitudes. One was asceticism; and this was the natural resort of resolute souls touched by the ethical appeal of the Gospel. They accounted the flesh essentially evil, and insisted on its mortification. They practised abstinence in eating and drinking, and not merely censured illicit intercourse between the sexes but condemned the institution of marriage and enjoined celibacy. The other tendency was more congenial to the natural mind, and it was the more dangerous since it was disguised by an affectation of superior spirituality. It agreed that the flesh was evil but accounted it as evanescent.[1] The immortal spirit was the arena of religion, and the mortal flesh had no religious value. Hence it mattered nothing what a man did with his body. He might indulge it as he would without damage to his spiritual life. The maxim was: 'Everything is allowable for me. Foods for the belly, and the belly for foods: God will do away with both it and them.'

Cf. 1 Cor. viii, ix.

Cf. 1 Cor. vii.

1 Cor. vi. 12, 13.

A case of incest.

It was rank libertinism; and it was boldly practised by a section of the Church at Corinth. The scandal came to a head in a flagrant and shocking case. A member of the Church had formed an incestuous alliance with his step-mother[2]—an iniquity not only contrary to the Scriptures but abhorrent even to pagan sentiment. The offender was a Gentile convert, and the partner of his sin was evidently still a heathen, since she is not included in the Apostle's censure. This, in the case of a legitimate union, would have been accounted an indiscretion, but it was merely a trivial aggravation of so monstrous a transgression.

Cf. 1 Cor. v.

Cf. Lev. xviii. 7, 8.

Cf. 2 Cor. vi. 14; 1 Cor. vii. 10-16.

A lost letter of admonition.

Tidings of the scandal reached the Apostle's ears. It would be hotly resented by the ascetic section of the Corinthian Church, and it is likely that, when their remonstrances proved unavailing, they reported the situation to him and solicited his intervention. In any case he heard of it, and

Cf. 1 Cor. v. 9-11.

[1] Cf. Iren. I. xx. 2; Epiphan. *Hær.* XXVII. 5: φασὶ γὰρ εἶναι τὴν φυλακὴν τὸ σῶμα.

[2] Theodrt. infers from 2 Cor. vii. 12 that the father was dead: καὶ τεθνεὼς ἠδίκητο, τῆς εὐνῆς ὑβρισθείσης.

he straightway wrote a letter of admonition. Like many others which he wrote in the course of his ministry, this letter has no place in his extant correspondence; nor indeed is its disappearance surprising, since a document which was a memorial of her shame, would hardly be preserved in the archives of the Corinthian Church, or, if it were, it would be jealously kept secret; all the more that its publication was unnecessary inasmuch as it dealt with a purely local concern. It is, however, from the Apostle's testimony indubitable that the letter was actually written, and his allusions indicate its trend; and, moreover, by a happy chance in nowise uncommon at least two considerable fragments of it have been incorporated in his extant correspondence with the Corinthian Church.[1]

Surviving fragments.

Fragments of the First Letter to Corinth

(1 Cor. vi. 12-20)

12 'Everything is allowable for me': yes, but it is not everything that is profitable. 'Everything is allowable for me':
13 yes, but I will not allow anything to master me. 'Foods for
the belly, and the belly for foods: God will do away with both
it and them.' The body, however, is not for fornication, but
14 for the Lord, and the Lord for the body. And God both raised
15 the Lord and will raise us up through His power. Do you not
know that your bodies are members of Christ? Shall I, then,
take the members of Christ and make them a harlot's members?
16 Away with the idea! Or do you not know that, when one is
united with a harlot, they are one body? For 'the two,' it is
17 said, 'shall become one flesh.' But, when one is united to the
Lord, they are one spirit.
18 Flee from fornication. Every other sin which man commits
is outside of the body; but the fornicator sins against his own
19 body. Do you not know that your body is a sanctuary of the
Holy Spirit who is within you and whom you have from God?
20 And you are not your own; for you were bought at a price.
Glorify God, then, in your body. . . .

Gen. ii. 24.

(2 Cor. vi. 14-vii. 1)

14 Do not yoke yourselves incongruously with strangers to
the Faith.[2] For what participation have righteousness and

Dt. xxii. 10.

[1] Cf. Append. I.

[2] ἑτεροζυγοῦντες, a LXX word (cf. Lev. xix. 19); only here in N. T. It denotes not merely intermarriage but all manner of intimacy with heathen.

lawlessness? Or what fellowship has light with darkness?
15 And what concord is there between Christ and Beliar?[1] Or
what portion has one who holds the Faith with a stranger to
16 it? And what agreement has a sanctuary of God with
idols? For we are a sanctuary of the Living God, even as
God has said:

'I will dwell in them and walk in them, Ez. xxxvii.
And I will be their God and they shall be My people. 27; Lev. xxvi. 12.
17 Wherefore come forth from the midst of them Jer. li. 45;
And be separated, saith the Lord, Is. lii. 11.
And touch no unclean thing;
And I will receive you; Ez. xx. 41.
18 And I will be to you as a father, 2 Sam. vii.
And ye shall be to Me as sons and daughters, 14; Is. xliii. 6;
Saith the Lord Almighty.' Hos. i. 10;

vii. 1 Since, then, we have promises like these, beloved, let us Am. iv.
cleanse ourselves from all pollution[2] of flesh and spirit, 13 LXX.
perfecting holiness in God's fear.

Contents of the letter: (1) Disciplinary mandate. Cf. 1 Cor. v. 3-5.

From these fragments and the Apostle's references to it the drift of the lost letter may be gathered. First it dealt with the particular case, and in virtue of his apostolic authority Paul directed that the Church should convene and pronounce upon the offender a solemn sentence of excommunication, not indeed excluding him absolutely and irrevocably but debarring him meanwhile from Christian fellowship and intercourse until he should repent and crave restitution. The Church's discipline was always remedial, and the ultimate end of that stern sentence was the sinner's restoration.

Cf. Gal. vi. 1.

(2) Ethical admonition. Cf. 1 Cor. v. 9-13.

From the particular case he passed to the general question, and addressed to the Corinthians a warning against the prevalent sin of fornication. Their heathen environment exposed them to constant danger. In the midst of abounding

[1] Βελίαρ (Βελίαλ), Heb. בְּלִיַּעַל, 'worthlessness.' Cf. Jud. xix. 22: 'sons of belial,' *i.e.*, 'worthless fellows.' Later (frequently in *Test. of XII Patr.*) a proper name, a title of Satan.

[2] The verb μολύνειν occurs thrice in N. T. (1 Cor. viii. 7; Rev. iii. 4, xiv. 4); the noun μολυσμός only here. The term is appropriate to the Apostle's argument, since it denoted the pollution of fornication, either literal fornication (Rev. xiv. 4) or the whoredom of idolatry, the pollution of heathen intercourse (cf. 1 Esdr. viii. 83; 1 Cor. viii. 7).

and unabashed impurity it was difficult for them to escape its foul contagion, and they ran an especial risk when, like that miserable offender, they allied themselves in marriage, even legitimate marriage, with their heathen neighbours. They had need of peculiar vigilance; and unhappily they had been lulled to security by a false philosophy. He quotes two pleas which were much on their lips in extenuation of their moral delinquencies. One was the antinomian maxim: 'Everything is allowable,' meaning that, since the spirit was the domain of religion, the flesh mattered nothing to the spiritual man: it belonged to the category of 'things indifferent.'[1] Yes, is his answer, but nothing is allowable for the spiritual man which injures his spiritual life and brings his soul into bondage. The other maxim was: 'Foods for the belly, and the belly for foods: God will do away with both it and them.' That is, the body is mortal; it is only the soul's temporary prison-house, and when it decays, the soul will soar unfettered. Nay, is his answer, the body is no perishing thing. It is destined to share the soul's immortality. God will not do away with it. He will raise it to incorruption and glory; and meanwhile it is the Holy Spirit's Sanctuary.

Further evil tidings.

1 Cor. i. 11.

He would anxiously expect a reply to his letter, but none arrived. Early, however, in the year 55 tidings reached him which aggravated his distress. His informants were 'the people of Chloe,' but who these may have been is somewhat of a puzzle. Chloe, which signifies in Greek 'a tender shoot,' occurs as a woman's name;[2] and thus Chloe may have been a Christian lady engaged, like Lydia of Philippi,

[1] Cf. the attitude not only of the Nicolaitans (cf. p. 526) but of 'the Spirituals' at the time of the Reformation. One of the latter was Johann Agricola, *Magister Islebius*, b. at Eisleben in 1492, died at Berlin in 1566. He studied under Luther, and caused the latter much vexation by his doctrinal excesses in after days. He taught, in common with the rest of his sect, that 'whatever a man's life may be and however impure, still he is justified if only he believes the promises of the Gospel' (cf. Jortin, *Erasm.* I. p. 356). If only he has faith, he may do what he will. Good works are legalism. The believer is above the Law. As Agricola said, 'all who had anything to do with Moses would go to the Devil, for Moses ought to be hanged.' This sect had its adherents in England, where they went by the name of 'the Ranters' and practised open libertinism. Cf. *Reliq. Baxter.* I. i. § 122.

[2] Cf. Hor. *Od.* III. ix.

in some extensive trade, and 'the people of Chloe' might then be her sons or her employees who travelled hither and thither on mercantile errands and had brought to Ephesus a report of the situation at Corinth. It would still remain uncertain which of these cities was her place of abode, though from the simplicity of the Apostle's reference it might be inferred that she was a Corinthian well known to his readers. On the other hand, while names borrowed from natural objects were common, they were usually borne by slaves; and there is perhaps probability in an ancient suggestion that Chloe is here the name not of a woman but of a place, some forgotten town which had received the Gospel.[1] Thus 'the people of Chloe' would be Christian traders who trafficked with the various cities and had passed from Corinth to Ephesus.

Recalcitrancy of the Corinthians.

Whoever they may have been, they brought the Apostle distressing intelligence. The situation at Corinth had gone from bad to worse. His mandate regarding that shameful case had been openly flouted. Indeed some went the length of charging him with cowardice because he had written instead of paying them a personal visit and meeting them face to face. The offender had never been called to account. He still remained in the fellowship of the Church uncondemned and unrebuked, at all events by the majority of the members; and it was a painful feature of the situation that, so far from realising the shame of it, they were swollen with spiritual and intellectual pride and were indulging their characteristic disposition to strife.

Cf. 1 Cor. iv. 18-21. *Cf. 1 Cor. v.*

Their contentious disposition.

They were indeed a contentious people. Some forty years later St. Clement of Rome had occasion to write them, and he speaks of 'the matters in dispute among them, the accursed and unholy sedition, so alien and strange to the elect of God, which a few persons in their rashness and self-will had kindled to such a pitch of madness that their name, once august and renowned and universally beloved, had been

[1] Cf. Ambrstr. on 1 Cor. i. 11, where three current explanations are mentioned: 'Aliquibus videntur homines esse manentes et fructificantes in fide Dei (hence 'the men of tender growth'): aliquibus videntur locus esse, ut puta si dicatur: Ab iis qui sunt Antiochiæ: aliquibus autem videtur feminam fuisse Deo devotam, cum qua multi essent colentes Deum.'

greatly reviled.' And he rebukes their 'arrogance and pride and folly and anger,' their rebellious contempt of authority, their 'strifes and wraths and divisions and cleavages among themselves.'[1]

Parties in the Church.

Precisely similar was the situation unfolded to the Apostle. The Corinthian Church was an arena of unholy contention, and the quarrel was peculiarly painful to him inasmuch as he was personally involved. It was the old Judaist controversy, but it had been vexatiously complicated. Each party was agitated by a cross-current. In Galatia it had been a clear issue between those who held by his Gospel of the equal privileges of Jew and Gentile and the justification of both by faith in Christ, and those who insisted on the permanent obligation of the Jewish Law and assailed his apostolic authority; but at Corinth there was a

The party of Paul and the party of Apollos.

cleavage on this side and on that. For over a year the learned and eloquent Apollos had been teaching in the city, and his ministry had created a situation which, being Paul's friend in all loyalty and affection, he had never designed and indignantly resented. His brilliance had charmed those of his hearers who had been accustomed to the dazzling oratory and ingenious dialectic of the Greek sophists;[2] and they contrasted his manner with Paul's, much to the latter's disparagement. The contrast was indeed extreme; for the Apostle, though superior in intellect and erudition, had

Cf. 2 Cor. x. 10.

none of the outward graces of Apollos. His person was uncouth and his delivery unimpressive; and these natural disadvantages had been specially apparent during his ministry at Corinth. When he came thither from Athens, not only was he suffering from a recurrence of his chronic malady but, with the humiliating failure of his attempt at philosophic disquisition in the Court of the Areiopagos fresh in his memory, he studiously eschewed the arts of rhetoric

Cf. 1 Cor. ii. 1-5.

and preached simply and plainly in reliance on the power of the Holy Spirit.[3] The Corinthians contrasted him with the brilliant Alexandrian; and though it was the self-same Gospel that both preached, each had his admirers who

[1] Clem. Rom. *Epist. ad Cor. I*, i, xiii, xlvi.

[2] Cf. Hatch, *Influence of Greek Ideas*, pp. 94 ff.

[3] Cf. pp. 148 f.

pitted one against the other, 'windily bragging in praise of the one to the other's disparagement.' Some said, 'I hold by Paul,' others 'I hold by Apollos'; and the preference developed into unseemly partisanship. It was an unpleasant position for the loyal-hearted Apollos, and it became so intolerable that he presently quitted Corinth and joined Paul at Ephesus. Cf. iv. 6. Cf. xvi. 12.

Judaist propaganda.

On the other side there was a corresponding cleavage. The Judaists had their emissaries at Corinth, perhaps the very men who had done the mischief in Galatia, and they adapted their vexatious propaganda to the situation. In Galatia they had insisted on the necessity of circumcision; but at Corinth the Church contained few Jewish converts and an appeal to Jewish prejudice would have fallen unheeded. And so they appealed to the Corinthian instinct for contention, and assailed the authority of Paul. Hence it is that in his reasonings with the Church he never touches on the controversy regarding the Jewish Law. It was a question of personal claims and partisan contentions that he had to deal with, and his argument is a personal apologia, an assertion and vindication of his apostolic authority. Cf. 2 Cor. x. 7, xi. 22, 23, xii. 11, 12.

The party of Cephas and the party of Christ.

The Judaists had come to Corinth armed with credentials from the Church at Jerusalem. Just as Apollos had brought a commendatory letter from the Christians of Ephesus, so they had brought one from the Church at Jerusalem. It was endorsed by Peter, and they paraded his pre-eminent dignity and represented Paul's exercise of apostolic functions as an illegitimate usurpation. They won adherents, and thus a party arose which abjured Paul and asserted the supremacy of Peter. Hence the cry 'I hold by Cephas.' Furthermore, the criterion of apostleship, they alleged, was personal contact with the Lord in the days of His flesh; and since Paul lacked this he was no Apostle. Hence the cry 'I hold by Christ.' Just as there was no essential distinction between the admirers of Paul and the admirers of Apollos, so neither did these cries denote separate parties. There was only this difference—that the profession of allegiance to Cephas was inspired by a spirit of pure partisanship, the preference of one teacher to another; whereas Cf. Ac. xviii. 27. Cf. 2 Cor. iii. 1. Cf. 2 Cor. v. 16.

the claim of adherence to Christ defined the reason of that preference.[1]

The scandal of litigation.

Nor were these the only contentions which were devastating the Corinthian Church. Since the Jews were permitted under the imperial government to administer their own affairs except in capital cases,[2] every synagogue had its court of justice. The Jewish Synagogue was the model of the primitive Church, and every Christian community had its court which adjudicated not merely *quoad spiritualia* but *quoad temporalia*. This, however, did not content the Corinthians. They referred their disputes to the civil tribunals, and dishonoured their Christian profession in the eyes of their heathen neighbours. That horrible case of immorality and the quarrels which it had engendered would furnish abundant occasion for litigation ; and it may be that the foul scandal had figured in the common courts to the Church's unspeakable shame.

SECOND LETTER TO CORINTH

The address.

On hearing this evil report of his Corinthian converts the Apostle immediately addressed himself to the composition

[1] So this difficult passage (1 Cor. i. 12) is interpreted by F. C. Baur (*Paul*, I. pp. 261 ff.). Opinion is much divided, and there are two main alternatives. 1. Four distinct parties are recognised : (1) *οἱ Παύλου*, (2) *οἱ* Ἀπολλώ, (3) *οἱ* Κηφᾶ, (4) *οἱ Χριστοῦ*. The question then is who the last may have been. Storr (*Einleit.* III. 107) took them as the party of James the brother of Christ (cf. 1 Cor. ix. 5), supposing that they claimed superiority to the party of Cephas. Neander, again, regarded them as a professedly neutral party, refusing allegiance to any human teacher, whether Paul or Apollos or Cephas, and 'professing to adhere to Christ alone, to acknowledge Him only as their teacher, and to receive what He announced as truth from Himself without the intervention of any other person' (*Plant. of Chr.*, I. p. 236), really making the Sacred Name a partisan badge. 2. An ancient interpretation (cf. Poole, *Synops. Crit.*), recently revived (cf. Lake, *Earlier Epistles of St. Paul*, pp. 127 f.), punctuates after Κηφᾶ : '"I am of Paul," and "I am of Apollos," and "I am of Cephas." But I am of Christ.' There were thus only three parties—*οἱ Παύλου*, *οἱ* Ἀπολλῶ, and *οἱ* Κηφᾶ, and the Apostle repudiates them all. 'Be Christ's,' he says, 'and then you have everything (cf. 1 Cor. iii. 22, 23).' This yields an excellent sense, and it is somewhat countenanced by the circumstance that Clem. Rom., referring to the passage enumerates only those three parties. Cf. *Epist. ad Cor. I*, xlvii : *πνευματικῶς ἐπέστειλεν ὑμῖν περὶ αὐτοῦ τε καὶ* Κηφᾶ *τε καὶ* Ἀπολλώ, *διὰ τὸ καὶ τότε προσκλίσεις ὑμᾶς πεποιῆσθαι.* There is, however, a twofold objection : (1) This interpretation would require *ἐγὼ μέντοι* (or *ἀλλ' ἐγὼ*) Χριστοῦ. The *δέ* clauses are plainly co-ordinate. (2) In 2 Cor. x. 7 Paul evidently refers to a separate 'Christ-party.'

[2] Cf. p. 45.

of a second letter.[1] He employed as his amanuensis one Sosthenes, probably an Ephesian convert; [2] and he begins with the customary address, skilfully interweaving suggestions of the subsequent argument. He affirms his own apostolic vocation; and he greets his readers as 'the Church of God at Corinth'—*lætum et ingens paradoxon*—'men sanctified in Christ Jesus, by calling saints,' tacitly contrasting their shameful actual with their heavenly ideal, and rebukes their dissension by reminding them of their catholic fellowship.

i. 1 Paul, by calling an Apostle of Christ Jesus through God's
2 will, and Sosthenes the brother, to the Church of God which is
at Corinth, men sanctified in Christ Jesus, by calling saints,
in fellowship with all who call upon the name of our Lord Jesus
3 Christ in every place, their Lord and ours. Grace to you and
peace from God our Father and the Lord Jesus Christ.

Appreciation of the Corinthian gifts.

With all their faults the Corinthians were not lacking in distinguished and precious endowments. They were an intellectual community, delighting in eloquence and wisdom, 'speech' and 'knowledge'; and though it had proved a snare to them, this was an excellent quality, and the Apostle, in view of the hard things which he must presently say, begins with a sentence of warm appreciation and generous confidence.

4 I thank God always regarding you for the grace of God
5 which is given you in Christ Jesus, that in everything you are
so enriched in Him, in every sort of 'speech' and every sort of
6 'knowledge,' as the testimony of the Christ was confirmed in
7 you, that you are not lacking in any gift of grace, while you
8 await the revelation of our Lord Jesus Christ, who will also
confirm you to the very end, unchargeable on the Day of our
9 Lord Jesus Christ. Faithful is God, through whom you were
called into fellowship with His Son, Jesus Christ our Lord.

The Corinthian scandal.

And now the Apostle addresses himself to his painful task

[1] ἐδηλώθη γάρ μοι (i. 11), 'it has just been shown me,' aor. of immediate past. Cf. Lk. xv. 24, xxiv. 34; Jo. xii. 19, xiii. 1, xxi. 10. Chrys. *In Ep. I ad Cor. Hom.* XIII. 3 (where the preacher rebukes an outburst of applause): ἐκροτήσατε ἐνταῦθα: 'You applaud here?'

[2] Cf. p. 187.

of dealing with the scandal which, as he had learned by credible report, was disgracing the Corinthian Church. It was a threefold scandal—partisanship, fornication, and litigation.

1. Partisanship.

The partisan spirit which was rampant in the Church and had rent it into bitter factions, first engages his attention, since he was personally implicated. He had been doubly assailed. One party was pitting him against Apollos. These were Gentile converts who had been nurtured in the atmosphere of Greek culture. They were intellectuals, and they contrasted the rude simplicity of his teaching with the eloquence of the brilliant Alexandrian. Another party was composed of Jewish converts, and these, inspired by the Judaist propagandists, challenged his apostleship and exalted the authority of the original Apostles, especially Peter; and it seems that, on the ground that he had never known Christ in the flesh, they insisted that he had never been ordained and his administration of the Sacrament of Baptism was invalid. He meets both with indignant scorn. That spirit of partisanship was a denial of Christ's supremacy. He was the only Lord, and Paul and Apollos and Peter were all alike His poor ministers. For himself he laid no claim to authority; and he was thankful to remember that so few of them had received Baptism at his hands. His apostolic function was far higher. It was not baptising but preaching the Gospel, and preaching it not 'in wisdom of speech' but in all simplicity.

10 Now I beseech you, brothers, by the name of our Lord Jesus
Christ, that you all speak in accord and that there be no
cleavages among you, but that you be all knit[1] together in
11 mind and judgment. For it has just been shown me regarding
you, my brothers, by the people of Chloe that there are strifes
12 among you. This is my meaning—that each of you is saying
'I hold by Paul' or 'I hold by Apollos' or 'I hold by Cephas'
13 or 'I hold by Christ.' Has Christ been portioned? Was Paul
14 crucified for you, or were you baptised into Paul's name? I
am thankful that I baptised none of you except Crispus and
15 Gaius, lest some one should say that it was into my name that
16 you were baptised. (And I baptised also the household of
Stephanas: for the rest I know not whether I baptised any

[1] κατηρτισμένοι, cf. n. on 1 Th. iii. 10, p. 161.

17 other.)[1] For it was not to baptise that Christ made me an
apostle; no, it was to preach the Gospel, not in wisdom of
speech, lest the Cross of the Christ should be made an empty
thing.

His answer to the intellectuals.

The question of his apostleship was comparatively unimportant at Corinth, where the Judaists were an insignificant party; and so he reserves it for subsequent discussion, and meanwhile addresses himself to the contemptuous indictment of the dominant intellectuals, giving free play to his vein of sarcasm, that keen weapon which he could on occasion employ so effectively. At every turn he deals them a shrewd thrust: now stigmatising their vaunted 'wisdom' as 'folly,' and telling them that what they deemed 'folly' was a divine 'wisdom' which they were
incapable of receiving; now jeering at their colossal self- iv. 8.
complacency, and crying shame on a pravity which could v. 1, 2.
flaunt its spiritual pretensions in the midst of unblushing
immorality. Again and again he brands them with the iv. 6, 18,
stinging epithet of 'windy braggarts' and plies them with 19; v. 2.
the contemptuous interrogation 'Do you not know?' iii. 16; v. 6; vi. 2, 3, 9.

The wisdom of God's folly.

They disdained the unadorned simplicity of his preaching and termed it 'folly'; and he pleads guilty to the charge. His preaching had not indeed been characterised by the wisdom which they desiderated; but that was no reproach. The Gospel was not a philosophy. It was God's message of salvation, and it appealed to the poor and lowly. Its very simplicity was its glory, and it was stripped of its power when it was tricked out in the gaudy dress of human wisdom, like that reeden flute in the Rabbinical legend which lay in the Temple and yielded music of surpassing sweetness until they covered it with gold and studded it with gems, and then its music was gone.

18 For the speech of the Cross is indeed for those who are on
the way to destruction, 'folly'; but for us who are on the way
19 to salvation, it is God's power. For it is written:

[1] A marginal note added by the Apostle on reading over the letter after dictating it to his amanuensis (cf. Milligan, *N. T. Documents*, p. 14). It is an explanation, not a correction: Stephanas, though a Corinthian, had been baptised at Athens. Cf. p. 148.

Is. xxix. 14.

'I will destroy the wisdom of the wise,
And the shrewdness of the shrewd will I set aside.'

Is. xix. 12; xxxiii. 18. Is. xix. 11.

20 'Where is the wise man?' 'Where is the scribe?' Where is
the questioner of this age?[1] Has not God 'turned to folly
21 the wisdom' of the world? For, since in the wisdom of God
the world did not through its wisdom recognise God, it was
God's good pleasure through the folly of the message we pro-
22 claim to save those who have faith; since Jews ask signs and
23 Greeks seek wisdom, but we proclaim a crucified Christ,[2]
24 to Jews a stumbling-block and to Gentiles folly, but to the
called on their part, both Jews and Greeks, Christ God's power
25 and God's wisdom; forasmuch as God's 'foolish' is wiser than
men and God's 'weak' stronger than men.

The strength of God's weakness.

This truth is written on every page of experience and history. God's way in grace is His way in providence. His mighty works are ever wrought by feeble instruments. 'When Philip the Good, in the full blaze of his power, and flushed with the triumphs of territorial aggrandisement, was instituting at Bruges the order of the Golden Fleece, "to the glory of God, of the blessed Virgin, and of the holy Andrew, patron saint of the Burgundian family," and enrolling the names of the kings and princes who were to be honoured with its symbols, at that very moment an obscure citizen of Harlem, one Lorenz Coster, or Lawrence the Sexton, succeeded in printing a little grammar, by means of moveable types. His invention sent no thrill of admiration throughout Christendom, and yet, what was the good Philip of Burgundy, with his Knights of the Golden Fleece, and all their effulgent trumpery, in the eye of humanity and civilisation, compared with the poor sexton and his wooden types?'[3]

26 For look at your calling, brothers: not many wise men
after the flesh, not many powerful, not many high-born.
27 No, it is the foolish things of the world that God chose to

[1] *σοφός*, the Greek philosopher; *γραμματεύς*, the Jewish Rabbi; *συνζητητὴς τοῦ αἰῶνος τούτου*, the sceptic lacking heavenly illumination—a general term but specially appropriate to the unbelieving Jews who are frequently said *συνζητεῖν* (cf. Mk. i. 27, viii. 11, ix. 14, 16; Ac. vi. 9, xxviii. 29). The verb is used also of the disciples 'questioning' about the Betrayal (Lk. xxii. 23) and the Resurrection (Mk. ix. 10; Lk. xxiv. 15).

[2] *Χριστὸν ἐσταυρωμένον*, cf. n. on Gal. iii. 1, p. 203.

[3] Motley, *Dutch Republic*, Hist. Introd. vii.

put the wise men to shame; and it is the weak things of
the world that God chose to put the strong things to shame;
28 and it is the low-born things of the world and the things
which are naught accounted that God chose, the things
29 which have no being to invalidate those which have, that
30 no flesh may boast before God. And from Him it is that
you have your being in Christ Jesus, who was made wisdom
to us by God's appointment, righteousness and sanctifica-
31 tion and redemption, that it may be as the Scripture says:
'Let him that boasts boast in the Lord.' Jer. ix. 23, 24.

Reason for the simplicity of Paul's preaching at Corinth.

It was indeed no wonder that the Corinthians should have remarked the simplicity of Paul's preaching during his ministry among them; for it was specially conspicuous on that occasion. He had come straight from Athens, humbled by the failure of his attempt at philosophical disquisition in the Court of the Areiopagos.[1] He had determined that never again would he repeat the disastrous experiment, and in his teaching at Corinth he had eschewed the arts of oratory.

ii. 1 And as for me, when I came to you, brothers, it was not with
lofty speech or wisdom that I came, announcing to you the
2 testimony of God.[2] For my determination was to know
nothing among you except Jesus as Christ and that a crucified
3 Christ. And it was in weakness and fear and much trembling
4 that I was brought among you; and my speech and my message were not arrayed in persuasive words of wisdom but
5 in demonstration of the Spirit and of power, that your faith
might be arrayed not in men's wisdom but in God's power.

The divine wisdom of the Gospel.

And this was his constant method; yet in his unadorned Gospel there was a high wisdom beyond the range of childish intellects. It was the revelation of God's agelong purpose of grace; and it had ushered in a new era and antiquated the pretentious philosophies of the past. It was hidden from the merely intellectual man, but it was recognised by the spiritual; for it was a revelation of the Spirit, and only by the teaching of the Spirit could it be comprehended, only by the language which the Spirit inspired could

[1] Cf. p. 148.

[2] ℵ^cBDEFGLP *τὸ μαρτύριον τοῦ Θεοῦ*. The Gospel is either *τὸ μαρτύριον τοῦ Χριστοῦ* (cf. i. 6), 'the testimony which the Apostles bore to Christ' (cf. Jo. xv. 27; Lk. xxiv. 48; Ac. i. 8, 22, iii. 15, v. 32, x. 39, 41), or *τὸ μαρτύριον τοῦ Θεοῦ*, 'the testimony which God bore in Christ' (cf. 1 Jo. v. 9-11). ℵ* AC *τὸ μυστήριον τοῦ Θεοῦ*, 'the mystery of God' (cf. ver. 7).

it be expressed. 'To evil persons the whole system of this wisdom is insipid and flat, dull as the foot of a rock, and unlearned as the elements of our mother tongue; but so are mathematics to a Scythian boor, and music to a camel.'[1]

6 Yet it is wisdom that we talk in the judgment of the mature[2]
—a wisdom, however, not of this age nor of this age's decadent
7 leaders. No, it is God's wisdom in a mystery[3] that we talk—
the hidden wisdom which God foreordained ere the ages for
8 our glory. And none of this age's leaders has recognised it;
for if they had recognised it, they would not have crucified
9 the Lord of Glory. But, as it is written:

Is. lxiv. 4; lxv. 16, 17.

'Things which eye never saw and ear never heard,
And the heart of man never dreamed,[4]
All the things which God prepared for those who love Him.'

10 To us, however, God revealed it through the Spirit; for the
11 Spirit searches all things, even the depths of God. For who
is there among men that knows the things of the man except
the man's spirit which is within him? Thus also the things
12 of God none has recognised except God's Spirit. And we—
it is not the spirit of the world that we have received, but the
Spirit which issues from God, that we may know the things
13 which have been graciously bestowed on us by God. And
these things we also talk, not in words taught by human
wisdom but in words taught by the Spirit, combining
14 spiritual things with spiritual.[5] But a merely intellectual

Cf. Prov. xiv. 10.

[1] Jeremy Taylor, *The Great Exemplar*, Pref. 43.

[2] *τέλειος* denoted what had attained its end (*τέλος*) and so, generally 'perfect.' More particularly: (1) a full-grown man, one who has attained mature age and the perfection of his powers (cf. 1 Cor. xiii. 10, 11, xiv. 20; Heb. v. 14). (2) In connection with the Greek Mysteries, 'initiated' into the secret lore, the perfect knowledge. Of this use there is no clear instance in N. T. Here (cf. iii. 1, 2) 'full-grown,' 'mature,' said sarcastically of the boastful intellectuals. Cf. *τῶν καταργουμένων*, 'who are being invalidated' (cf. 2 Cor. iii. 7, 11): a new era had dawned and the vaunted 'wisdom of this age' was out of date.

[3] Cf. p. 320.

[4] *ἐπὶ τὴν καρδίαν ἀνθρώπου οὐκ ἀνέβη* (cf. Ac. vii. 23), a LXX phrase (cf. Jer. iii. 16, xliv. 21, li. 50).

[5] As the wisdom of men is fitly expressed by words of human wisdom, so the wisdom of God must be matched with words taught by His Spirit. *συνκρίνειν*, 'combine,' the correlative of *διακρίνειν*, 'separate.' Cf. Plat. *Phæd.* 72 C: *κἂν εἰ ξυγκρίνοιτο μὲν πάντα διακρίνοιτο δὲ μή, ταχὺ ἂν τὸ τοῦ Ἀναξαγόρου γεγονὸς εἴη· ὁμοῦ πάντα χρήματα.* The word meant also (1) 'compare' (cf. 2 Cor. x. 12) and (2) 'interpret,' especially a dream (cf. Gen. xl. 8, xli. 12; Dan. v. 12); and hence two other interpretations of the text: (1) 'comparing spiritual things with spiritual,' *spiritualibus spiritualia comparantes* (Vulg.), *i.e.*, illustrating spiritual truths by O. T. types (Chrys.); (2) 'interpreting spiritual things by spiritual' or 'interpreting spiritual things to spiritual men' (Ambrstr., Theophyl.).

man[1] does not receive the things of God's Spirit, for they are
folly to him ;and he cannot recognise them, because they are
15 spiritually examined.[2] But the spiritual man examines every-
16 thing, while he is himself examined by none. For 'who is so Is. xl. 13.
acquainted with the Lord's mind that he may instruct Him ?'
But we have Christ's mind.

And now he delivers a sharp home-thrust. His critics sneered at the simplicity of his teaching during his ministry at Corinth ; and he retorts that it was nothing else than an accommodation to their incapacity. He had found them so dull. It was impossible for him to address them as spiritual men. They were not even 'carnal'; they were simply 'carneous'—creatures of flesh. They were very babes in Christ, and babes' food was all that they could receive. And it was all that they could even yet receive. For they had made no progress toward spirituality. They remained carnal, swayed by the passions which dominate human hearts where God has no place ; and they proved it by their unhallowed contentions. For what else did their pitting of one teacher against another mean but that they left God out of account ? Paul and Apollos were merely His ministers, each doing his appointed task. Paul had planted the good seed, and Apollos, his successor, had watered it ; but it was God that had made it grow. And His was all the praise. An unspiritual contention.

iii. 1 And I, brothers, could not talk to you as spiritual men but
2 only as carneous, as babes in Christ.[3] I fed you with milk,

[1] Corresponding to the trichotomy πνεῦμα, ψυχή, σῶμα (cf. n. on 1 Th. v. 23, p. 166), there are three classes of men according as one or other of these elements predominates: ὁ πνευματικός, ὁ ψυχικός, ὁ σωματικός or σαρκικός. The ψυχή was twofold—ψυχὴ ἄλογος, 'their rational soul,' the merely sentient life, and ψυχὴ λογική, 'the reasonable soul,' the intellectual life, the νοῦς. Hence ψυχικός was either 'sensuous' or 'intellectual.' Here ψυχικὸς ἄνθρωπος is a merely intellectual man, possessing only 'the wisdom of this age,' not 'the wisdom of God' revealed 'through the Spirit.'

[2] Cf. pp. 252 f.

[3] The weight of authority supports σαρκίνοις in ver. 1 and σαρκικοί in ver. 3. Since the termination -ινος (Engl. '-en', cf. 'wooden') denotes the material of which a thing is made (cf. Mt. iii. 4: ζώνη δερματίνη, Mk. xv. 17: ἀκάνθινος στέφανος), σάρκινος is *carneus*, 'made of flesh' (cf. 2 Cor. iii. 3). On the other hand, σαρκικός is *carnalis*, denoting carnal tastes and inclinations, τὸ φρόνημα τῆς σαρκός (Rom. viii. 6). The Corinthians were not really 'intellectual' (ψυχικοί); they were not even 'carnal' (σαρκικοί); they were just 'carneous' (σάρκινοι), creatures of flesh, mere 'babes' with the intellect undeveloped.

not with meat ; for it was all you were yet able for. Indeed
3 even now it is still all you are able for ; for you are still carnal.
For where there are jealousy and strife among you, are you
not carnal and comporting yourselves after the fashion of
4 mere man ? When one says 'I hold by Paul' and another
5 'I hold by Apollos,' are you not mere men ? What, then, is
Apollos ? and what is Paul ? Ministers through whom you
were won to faith ; and each ministered as the Lord granted
6 him. I planted, Apollos watered ; but all the while it was
7 God that made it grow.[1] And so neither the planter is any-
8 thing nor the waterer, but only God the growth-giver. The
planter and the waterer are one, yet each will receive his
9 proper wage according to his proper toil. For we are God's
fellow-workers ; you are God's tilth, God's building.[2]

The foundation and the building.

The Apostle has passed abruptly from the metaphor of husbandry to that of building, and now he proceeds to develop the latter. He was employed in the erection of God's spiritual Sanctuary, and he had done his part at Corinth. He had laid the foundation, and he had left Apollos to build up the walls. The foundation was essential, and he had laid it firm and clear. It was Jesus Christ, and the supreme test of his successors' work was : Were they building on that foundation ? The Judaists, in rejecting the Gospel of salvation by faith in Christ and substituting the old method of legal observance, were building on another foundation, and their work was condemned. But it was possible for a man to be building on the one and only foundation and yet be building in vain, erecting a worthless and unenduring structure. Here the question is whether a man's work will stand the fiery test of the Final Judgment. The Apostle may have been thinking of the burning of the city of Corinth by the Roman conqueror [3] or the burning of the Temple of Artemis at Ephesus,[4] and how in each instance the marble and gems had survived the ordeal. And the Greek historian [5] tells how in the time of Darius the Athenians invaded Asia and, landing at Ephesus, proceeded to Sardes and took the city. It was a poor place in those days. Most

[1] Cf. the saying of Ambroise Paré, the father of modern surgery : 'I dressed his wounds, but God healed him.'

[2] Cf. a similar transition from husbandry to building in Mt. xxi. 33-44.

[3] Cf. p. 150.

[4] Cf. p. 226.

[5] Herod. v. 101.

of the houses were constructed of reeds and some of bricks with reeden roofs; and when one of them was set ablaze, the conflagration passed from house to house and spread all over the city. Perhaps the Apostle had this local history before his mind when he spoke of building with 'wood, hay, stubble.' It is not enough to build on the one foundation; we must see to it how we are building and what we are building. There must be no perishable stuff in the fabric of God's Sanctuary but only precious and enduring materials; and this was the fatal error of the Corinthian intellectuals. They held indeed the doctrine of salvation by faith in Christ, which Apollos preached no less than Paul. They were building on the one foundation, but they were building sorry stuff. It ensured their salvation that they were building on Christ, but it would be a bare salvation. Their work would perish, and they would be saved like 'brands plucked out of the fire.'

Cf. Rev. xxi. 18-21.

10 According to the grace of God which was given me, as a wise
master-builder I laid the foundation, and another is building
11 on it. But let each see to it how he is building on it. For
another foundation can none lay beside that already in
12 place; and this is Jesus Christ. And if one is building on
the foundation gold, silver, precious stones, wood, hay, stubble,
13 the work of each will become manifest; for the Day will show
it, because the Day is being revealed in fire,[1] and the fire is the
14 thing that will test the quality of each man's work. If one's
work which he built on the foundation shall remain, he will
15 receive a wage; if one's work shall be consumed, he will suffer
the loss of it; yet he will himself be saved, but only as 'through
16 fire.'[2] Do you not know that you are God's Sanctuary, and
17 the Spirit of God dwells in you? If one is spoiling the Sanctuary
of God, God will spoil him. For the Sanctuary of God is holy;
and so are you.[3]

[1] ἀποκαλύπτεται, pres., because the Day was conceived as imminent. Cf. I Th. v. 2.

[2] A proverbial phrase. Cf. Ps. lxvi. 12; Am. iv. 11; Zech. iii. 2; Jud. 23. Equally alien from the Apostle's thought are (1) Chrys.'s interpretation that, while his work will be consumed, the man himself will live on in the torment of eternal fire, and (2) the mediæval reference to Purgatory (cf. Aquin. *Summ. Theol.*, Suppl. XCIX. iv. 3).

[3] οἵτινες, relat. attracted into agreement with subj. of its own clause (cf. Gal. iii. 16; I Tim. iii. 15). Not 'and this Sanctuary you are,' which would be a superfluous repetition of ver. 16, but 'and this (*i.e.*, 'holy') you are.'

The folly of intellectual conceit.

And more than this. The intellectuals were not merely preparing disaster for themselves on the Day of Judgment; they were incurring present loss. The conceit of wisdom is always folly, and God always puts it to shame. And the spirit of partisanship is a narrowing of religion. When the Corinthians attached themselves to a particular teacher, they enjoyed only so much profit as he could impart. But every teacher is merely an interpreter of the Lord, and his interpretation is at the best but partial. Hold by Paul, and you receive only what Paul can give; hold by Apollos, and you receive only what Apollos can give; hold by Cephas, and you receive only what Cephas can give. But all that each has is in Christ; and if you hold by Him, then you have all that His interpreters can supply, and infinitely more.

18 Let no one deceive himself. If any one fancies he is wise
among you in this age, let him become foolish that he may
19 become wise. For the wisdom of this world is folly in God's
judgment; for it is written: 'He catches the wise in their
20 craftiness,'[1] and again: 'The Lord recognises the reasonings
21 of the wise that they are futile.' And so let no one boast in
22 men. For all things are yours, whether Paul or Apollos or
23 world or life or death: all are yours, and you are Christ's,
and Christ is God's.

Job v. 13.
Ps. xciv. 11.

The illegitimacy of human judgment.

Christian teachers are 'stewards of God's mysteries,' and of course they are responsible for their discharge of their stewardship. But they are responsible to their Heavenly Master, and to Him alone; and not till the Great Day will they be called to account. According to the legal procedure of those days the accused was subjected to a precognition or preliminary examination and committed for trial if 'a true bill' were found against him.[2] And here lay the audacious blunder of the Corinthians. They were anticipating the Final Assize and usurping the office of the Divine Judge. At the best human criticism is a mere precognition, a preliminary examination; and, as the Apostle has already protested, a mere intellectual's examination of spiritual questions is worthless. He recognised no human 'day'

Cf. Ac. xxv. 26.
Cf. ii. 14, 15.

[1] Paul does follow LXX (ὁ καταλαμβάνων σοφοὺς ἐν τῇ φρονήσει) but translates directly and more accurately.

[2] Cf. Lightfoot, *Fresh Revision of N. T.*, pp. 62 ff.

and no human 'judgment.' There was no day but 'the Day of Jesus Christ' and no judgment but His; and meanwhile the only 'examination' which he acknowledged was neither man's criticism nor his own estimate but the Lord's approval. Cf. i. 8.

iv. 1 Let a man reckon us as officers of Christ and stewards of
2 God's mysteries. On these terms of course it is required in
3 stewards that one should be found faithful; but to me it
matters very little that I should be examined by you or by a
4 human day. Nay, I do not even examine myself. For I am
conscious of no fault,[1] yet I am not on this score proved
5 righteous; my examiner is the Lord. And so pass no judgment prematurely, until the Lord comes, who will illumine
the secrets of darkness and manifest the purposes of our
hearts; and then will each get his praise from God.

The self-complacency of the Corinthians and the ignominy of the Apostles.

It might be that the Corinthians would sneer at this brave speech. If Paul had indeed so little regard for human judgment, why had he taken such pains to answer their criticisms and define the relations between himself and Apollos? He answers that in all his references to Apollos and himself he had the Corinthians in view, and was censuring their vanity and seeking to recall them to sane and scriptural views. Their boasted excellences were God's gifts, and they were reasons for thankfulness rather than for pride. Their conceit was boundless. They had, in their own esteem, attained the very summit of perfection, and with scathing sarcasm he contrasts their self-complacency with the hard estate of the Apostles, scorned and persecuted for Christ's sake.

6 Now, brothers, in these references of mine to Apollos and
myself there is a covert allusion.[2] It is meant for you, that
you may learn by our example the precept 'Abide by what is
written,' so that none of you may brag windily in praise of

[1] *οὐδὲν ἐμαυτῷ σύνοιδα*, *nihil mihi conscius sum*, 'I am aware of nothing,' *i.e.*, no guilt. Cf. Plat. *Apol.* 21 B: *ἐγὼ γὰρ δὴ οὔτε μέγα οὔτε σμικρὸν σύνοιδα ἐμαυτῷ σοφὸς ὤν.* Hor. *Epist.* I. i. 61: 'nil conscire sibi, nulla pallescere culpa.'

[2] *μετασχηματίζειν*, (1) 'change the *σχῆμα*, outward form' (cf. 2 Cor. xi. 13-15; Phil. iii. 21); so 'disguise' (cf. 1 Sam. xxviii. 8 Sym.; 1 Ki. xiv. 2 Theod.). (2) *σχῆμα*, *figura*, as a grammatical term denoted 'a veiled allusion.' Cf. Quintil. IX. 2; Mart. *Epigr.* III. lxviii. 7; Suet. *Dom.* 10; *Juv. Vit.*: 'Venit ergo Juvenalis in suspicionem quasi tempora figurate notasset.' Hence *μετασχηματίζειν*, 'have a covert allusion beyond the immediate reference.'

7 one to his neighbour's disparagement. For who is it that
distinguishes any of you? And what has any of you which he
did not receive? And if he did receive it, why is he boasting
Cf. Rev. iii. 17. 8 as though he had not received it? Already you are satiated!
Already you have waxed rich! You have come to your
kingdom and left us behind! Ah, would that you had come
9 to your kingdom, that we might share it with you! For, I
fancy, God has exhibited us, the Apostles, at the last as condemned criminals,[1] because we have been made a spectacle to
10 the world, both to angels and to men. We are foolish for
Christ's sake, but you are shrewd in Christ; we are weak, but
11 you are strong; your lot is glory, but ours dishonour. To
this very hour we are hungry and thirsty, ill clad, buffeted,
12 homeless; we toil, working with our own hands; we meet
13 reviling with blessing, persecution with patience, calumny with
entreaty; we are made as the offscouring of the world, the
scapegoat of all,[2] to this very day.

[1] A metaphor from the circus. The sated appetite of the spectators was stimulated at the close by a piquant entertainment: condemned criminals, ἐπιθανάτιοι (cf. Chrys.: 'ὡς ἐπιθανατίους,' τουτέστιν, ὡς καταδίκους), were introduced to fight unarmed with wild beasts (cf. xv. 32)—the final event of the performance (ἐσχάτους). These were the *bestiarii*. Cf. Tert. *De Pudic.* 14: 'Et puto, nos Deus apostolos novissimos elegit velut bestiarios.'

[2] περίψημα, literally 'scrapings,' denoted (1), like κάθαρμα and περικάθαρμα, the refuse or scum of society, a rascal. Cf. *purgamentum*. (2) It acquired a nobler signification from a custom which obtained at Athens, where, especially in time of plague or famine, a criminal, the vilest that could be procured, was thrown into the sea to propitiate the wrath of Poseidon. Cf. Phot. *Lex.*: οὕτως ἐπέλεγον τῷ κατ' ἐνιαυτὸν ἐμβαλλομένῳ νεανίᾳ ἐπὶ ἀπαλλαγῇ τῶν συνεχόντων κακῶν. 'περίψημα ἡμῶν γενοῦ', ἤτοι σωτηρία καὶ ἀπολύτρωσις, καὶ οὕτως ἐνέβαλον τῇ θαλάσσῃ ὡσανεὶ τῷ Ποσειδῶνι θυσίαν ἀποκτίννυντες. Hence περίψημα and περικάθαρμα came to signify *a piacular offering*. Cf. Tob. v. 18: ἀργύριον . . . περίψημα τοῦ παιδίου ἡμῶν γένοιτο. Prov. xxi. 18: περικάθαρμα δὲ δικαίου ἄνομος. So in his interpretation of the prophecy of Caiaphas (Jo. xi. 49, 50) Origen 'makes bold to say' that our Lord, more than the Apostles, was πάντων περίψημα, comparing 2 Cor. v. 21 (*In Evang. Joan.* xxviii. 14). (3) The word was used in the general sense of 'a devoted servant,' especially in the epistolary formula ἐγώ εἰμι περίψημά σου. Cf. Ignat. *Ad Eph.* viii: περίψημα ὑμῶν, καὶ ἁγνίζομαι ὑπὲρ ὑμῶν. Barn. *Ep.* iv. 9; vi. 5. This use is well exemplified in the Paschal Epistle of Dionysius the Great (Eus. *Hist. Eccl.* VII. 22), where, speaking of the plague at Alexandria, he describes how the Christians tended the sufferers with unselfish devotion, in many instances catching the fatal infection and thus 'practically fulfilling the common phrase, which always seems a mere formula of courtesy, by dying "the devoted servants" of them all (αὐτῶν πάντων περίψημα).' Thus πάντων περίψημα denotes 'homines non solum abjectissimi, sed piaculares' (Beng.); and the Apostle means that the humiliation of himself and his comrades was a redemptive ministry (cf. Col. i. 24). Perhaps the nearest equivalent in modern speech is 'scapegoat'; but the term is untranslatable, and the Vulg. simply transliterates it (*omnium peripsema*).

These were bitter words, and no sooner had they passed his lips than the Apostle's heart smote him, and he concludes with an affectionate remonstrance. The Corinthians were his converts, his spiritual children. He was their 'father in Christ,' and thus he stood to them in a relation which none of his successors, however faithful and devoted, could occupy. There was love in his severity; his rebukes were the admonitions of a father. It grieved him that they had so slighted his example; and—such was then his intention—he was despatching Timothy, another of his spiritual children, to Corinth, not merely to deliver the letter but to recall him and his teaching to their remembrance. Why did he not rather visit them in person? It was not, as his adversaries alleged, because he durst not confront them. He would visit them ere long; and his hope was that his letter and Timothy's appeal would meanwhile restore order and make his visit a pleasure and not a pain.

An affectionate remonstrance.

14 I am not putting you to shame in writing all this; no,
15 I am admonishing you as my beloved children. For,
though you have ten thousand tutors[1] in Christ, still you
have not many fathers; it was I who begat you in Christ
16 Jesus through the Gospel. Therefore, I beseech you, follow
17 my example. It is for this very reason that I am sending[2]
you Timothy. He is my child, beloved and faithful in
the Lord; and he will remind you of my ways in Christ
Jesus—my manner of teaching everywhere in every church.
18 With the notion that I am not coming to you some of you
19 have taken to windy bragging. But I shall come to you
soon, if the Lord will, and I shall discover not what those
20 windy braggarts are saying but what power they have;
for it is not in 'saying' that the Kingdom of God lies but
21 in 'power.' Which do you wish? Is it 'with a rod' that
I am to come to you, or in love and a spirit of meekness?

Cf. 2 Sam. vii. 14; Pss. ii. 9, lxxxix. 32.

The Apostle next passes on to the second of the scandals which were disgracing the Corinthian Church—that shameful case of immorality. It was now a thing of long standing. Several months ago it had reached his ears, and he had promptly written to them, charging them to deal with the offender and dictating the sentence which they should

2. Fornication.

[1] Cf. pp. 206 f. [2] ἔπεμψα, epistolary aorist. Cf. p. 219.

pronounce. But his mandate had been disregarded. The scandal continued, and they were unabashed and unashamed. He reiterates his mandate. They might in their unspiritual self-complacency think it a little matter; but even a little matter might work much evil. Was it not a proverb that 'a little leaven leavens the whole mass'?[1] The Feast of the Passover was approaching,[2] when the Law required that the Israelites should purge their houses of leaven; and he bids them celebrate the holy season by purging this evil leaven out of their midst.

Insistence on discipline.

v. 1 There is a consistent report[3] of fornication among you,
and fornication of a sort which is unknown even among the
2 Gentiles; some one[4] has his father's wife. And you are swollen
with windy pride, and did not rather mourn, that the doer of
3 this work might be removed from your midst. For I, absent
in the body but present in the spirit, have already passed
judgment as though present on him who thus wrought this
4 thing: 'In the name of the Lord Jesus: assembled—you and
5 my spirit with the power of our Lord Jesus: deliver such a
man to Satan for the destruction of the flesh, that the spirit
6 may be saved on the Day of the Lord.'[5] It is nothing honour-

[1] Cf. p. 213.

[2] Cf. Append. I.

[3] ὅλως, all the reports agreed—a solid consensus.

[4] τινα, 'a certain one,' well known, though the Apostle refrains from naming him. Cf. Col. ii. 8.

[5] Here he quotes the formal resolution which in his first letter he had directed the Corinthian Church to adopt. First (ver. 4), the constitution of the judicial assembly: (1) its authority—'in the name of the Lord Jesus' (cf. Mt. xviii. 20; Col. iii. 17); and (2) the sederunt: (*a*) the members of the Church (ὑμῶν), (*b*) the spirit of the absent Apostle (cf. ver. 3), who communicated his judgment, and (*c*) 'the power of the Lord Jesus' (cf. Lk. v. 17). So Chrys., Calv., Grot. Otherwise: 1. Construe 'with the power of the Lord Jesus' with 'deliver' (Beza). 2. 'In the name of the Lord Jesus' with 'deliver,' 'assembled . . . Jesus' being parenthetical (Luth., Beng. Mey., Alford). 3. Both 'in the name of the Lord Jesus' and 'with the power of our Lord Jesus' with 'deliver' (Mosheim). 4. Connect 'in the name of the Lord Jesus' with ver. 3: 'him who thus wrought this thing in the sacred name,' *i.e.*, while professing to be a Christian (a view mentioned by Chrys.). Then follows the sentence (ver. 5). This has been interpreted in two ways (cf. Aug. *Contra Epist. Parmen.* III. 3): 1. The miraculous infliction of some bodily punishment, perhaps even death—the view of Chrys., whose advocacy of it is responsible for its general acceptance. He supposes that the offender was to be stricken judicially with 'an evil ulcer or other disease,' comparing Job's trial by Satan (Job ii. 7) and the doom incurred by certain Corinthians for sacrilegious observance of the Holy Supper (xi. 30-33). Cf. Baur, *St. Paul*, I. pp. 299 ff. The cases of Ananias and Sapphira (Ac. v.

able, this boast of yours. Do you not know that 'a little
7 leaven leavens the whole mass'? Clear out the stale leaven,
that you may be a fresh mass, unleavened as indeed you are.
8 For our Passover was sacrificed, even Christ; and so let us
keep the Feast not with stale leaven nor with leaven of malice
and wickedness but with unleavened bread of sincerity and
truth.

A misunderstanding corrected.

2 Cor. vi. 14.

In his first letter the Apostle had strenuously enjoined on the Corinthians the avoidance of contaminating intercourse. 'For,' he asks in a surviving fragment of the letter, 'what participation have righteousness and lawlessness? Or what fellowship has light with darkness?' His counsel had been misconstrued, partly, perhaps, in all good faith by the ascetic party in their zeal for moral purity, and partly also by the libertines in their resentment of moral restraint. It had been represented as an injunction to have dealings only with the morally irreproachable, and this was denounced as an impossible requirement. It would necessitate separation from the world and the conversion of the Church into a community of recluses. The perversion of his counsel had reached the Apostle's ears, and he now corrects it and

1-11) and Elymas (xiii. 8-11) are generally adduced. 2. The sentence signifies merely exclusion from the fellowship of the Church (ver. 11; cf. Mt. xviii. 17) and from participation in her ordinances in order that the offender might recognise the heinousness of his sin and be moved to repentance (Ambrstr.). It may seem as though a bodily chastisement were implied by 'the destruction of the flesh'; but in Paul's thought 'the flesh' denotes not the body merely but the body corrupted by sin, the seat of evil passions. The body (σῶμα) is a sacred thing destined to incorruption at the Resurrection; and its destruction would not be the salvation of the man but his mutilation, as Chrys. recognises ('if the soul is saved, beyond all contradiction the body will share its salvation'). It is the sinful flesh that is to be destroyed through repentance, that the man himself, soul and body, may be saved. 'Deliver to Satan' is the converse of 'baptise into Christ' (cf. Gal. iii. 27; Rom. vi. 3). As one 'baptised into Christ' is 'in Christ,' so one 'delivered to Satan' is 'in the Evil One' (cf. 1 Jo. v. 19). The sentence was that the offender, who claimed to be 'in Christ,' should be relegated to his true position, 'in Satan,' in order that he might realise the misery and shame of it. The phrase recurs in 1 Tim. i. 20. It is not the regular phrase for 'excommunicate,' which was ἀποσυνάγωγον ποιεῖν (cf. Jo. ix. 22, xii. 42, xvi. 2) or ἀφορίζειν (cf. Lk. vi. 22); and apparently the Apostle here employs the Greek formula of execration, which runs thus on one of the Magical Papyri in British Museum: νεκυδαίμων, παραδίδωμί σοι τὸν δ(εῖνα), ὅπως . . .', 'Spirit of the Dead, I deliver to thee X, in order that . . .' This formula would be familiar to the Corinthians.

explains that he had not referred to the inevitable intercourse of human society but to the fellowship of the Church.

9 I wrote to you in my letter that you should not associate
10 with fornicators; not, certainly, the fornicators of this world
or the greedy and extortioners or idolaters, since you would
11 then have to quit the world. And now I write[1] to you that
you should not associate with any one bearing the name of
'brother' who is a fornicator or greedy or an idolater or a
reviler or a drunkard or an extortioner—that with a person
12 of this sort you should not even eat. For what have I to do
with judging those outside? Is it not of those within that
Dt. xxii. 24. 13 you are judges? Those without God will judge. 'Remove
the evil man from your own company.'

3. Litigation.

And now the Apostle passes to the third scandal. The Corinthians were naturally a contentious people; and that deplorable case of immorality had enkindled their animosities. They bandied accusations and recriminations, and they carried their quarrels before the heathen magistrates. It was a pitiful exposure of the Church's shame; and it is no wonder that it should have moved the Apostle to indignant protest. First, he points out that it was unnecessary, since the Church, like her model, the Jewish Synagogue, had a judicature of her own, and if one Christian had a grievance against another, it was before the Church's court that he should bring it and not before a heathen tribunal. It is written that 'judgment is given to the saints': they will judge the world, both men and angels; and surely, he argues with keen irony, they are competent for the adjudication of petty grievances—an office which demanded no high spirituality and was fitly entrusted to the Church's lesser rulers. Indeed, he continues, there should be no litigation between Christians. It is always a losing fight, and the winner has the worst of it. For the only true victory lies in the sufferance of wrong.

Dan. vii. 22; cf. Mt. xix. 28; Lk. xxii. 30; Rev. iii. 21, xx. 4.

vi. 1 Has any of you the effrontery, when he has an affair with
his neighbour, to go to law before the unrighteous and not
2 before the saints? Or do you not know that the saints will
judge the world? And if the world is judged at your bar,
3 are you unfit for petty tribunals? Do you not know that

[1] νῦν δὲ ἔγραψα, epistolary aorist. Cf. p. 219.

4 we shall judge angels, let alone secular affairs?[1] Rather,
if you have secular tribunals, place them that are naught
5 accounted in the Church—place these on the bench.[2] I say
it to move you to shame. Has it come to this, that there
is no one among you wise enough to be able to intervene and
6 decide his brother's case, but brother goes to law with
7 brother, and that before strangers to the Faith? To go no
farther, the fact is that you are absolutely the losers in having
lawsuits with one another. Why not rather be wronged?
8 Why not rather be defrauded? Nay, it is you that do the
9 wronging and defrauding, and that to brothers. Or do you
not know that wrong-doers shall not inherit God's Kingdom?
Be not deceived. Neither fornicators nor idolaters nor
10 adulterers nor sodomites nor thieves nor greedy persons,
no drunkards, no revilers, no extortioners shall inherit
11 God's Kingdom. And all this some of you used to be;
but you washed yourselves clean, you were sanctified, you
were accounted righteous in the name of the Lord Jesus
Christ and in the Spirit of our God.[3]

Arrival of Corinthian delegates.

At this point the progress of the letter was arrested by a welcome interruption—the arrival of three delegates from Corinth, Stephanas, Fortunatus, and Achaicus, bearing a communication from their Church. It was the long expected answer to the Apostle's first letter, and it necessitated an extensive alteration of his plans. His intention had been that on the completion of the present letter Timothy should convey it to its destination, and not only reinforce its argument but refute the allegation that Paul was afraid to visit Corinth and face his critics by explaining the true reason of his protracted sojourn at Ephesus. And indeed an explanation was needed; for his original intention had been to make but a brief stay in the Asian capital, and proceed thence to Corinth and, save for an excursion to Macedonia, remain there until the close of his mission, thus affording

Cf. xvi. 17.

Cf. iv. 17, 18.

Cf. 2 Cor. i. 15, 16.

[1] βιωτικός was used like the mediæval *sæcularis* in contrast with *religiosus*. Cf. Chrys. on Rom. xiii. 1: ταῦτα διατάττεται καὶ ἱερεῦσι καὶ μοναχοῖς, οὐχὶ τοῖς βιωτικοῖς μόνον.

[2] τοὺς ἐξουθενημένους ἐν ἐκκλησίᾳ, not Apostles or Prophets or Teachers but such as were endowed with the humbler gifts of administrative capacity (cf. xii. 28). Otherwise: 'Do you place on the bench those who are set at naught in the Church (*i.e.*, heathen magistrates)?' This, however, ignores μὲν οὖν, *immo vero* (cf. Lk. xi. 28).

[3] Vers. 12-20, a fragment of the first letter. Cf. p. 236.

Cf. 1 Cor. xvi. 8, 9.

the Corinthians the privilege of a second ministry in their midst. This promise he had been unable to fulfil, for he had been detained at Ephesus by the unexpected emergence of precious opportunities and imperative claims; and he reckoned that he must remain a full year longer. His present intention was to leave Ephesus after Pentecost, 56.[1] Nor would he even then proceed direct to Corinth. Trouble had arisen in the north. It seems that the Judaist propagandists, in their passage from Galatia to Achaia, had travelled through Macedonia and had prosecuted their mischievous enterprise *en route*; and thus the Macedonian churches, so lately convulsed by eschatological excitement, were in the throes of another and more bitter controversy. And therefore his intention was that on his departure from

Cf. 1 Cor. xvi. 5, 6.

Ephesus in May, 56, he should betake himself in the first instance to Macedonia, and, after allaying the trouble, proceed to Corinth and there perhaps pass the ensuing winter.

Mission of Timothy to Macedonia and Corinth.

All this it was expedient that the Corinthians should understand, in order that their minds might be disabused of the suspicion that he had played them false; and Timothy would have explained it on delivering the letter. But now the letter was delayed. It must be extended to cover the questions raised by the Corinthian communication; and since these were numerous and difficult, it would be some time ere it was completed. And since the delegates would convey it on their return, Timothy was relieved of that office, and he was meanwhile available for another and most urgent service. He would still indeed visit Corinth as Paul's deputy, but he would travel thither by the overland route and visit the distracted churches of Macedonia

Ac. xix. 22; cf. 1 Cor. xvi. 11, 12.

by the way. It was a difficult mission, and the Apostle associated with him several of his Ephesian company, particularly Erastus. He calculated that they would reach Corinth soon after the delivery of the letter by the three delegates, and they would reinforce its argument by their personal appeal.

[1] In the year 56 the Day of Pentecost was May 9. Cf. Lewin, *Fast. Sac.*, p. 307.

And now he resumes his interrupted task and proceeds to discuss the problems which the Corinthian rescript propounded. That document has of course perished,[1] but the course of the Apostle's argument discloses its general purport. It was a statement of the controversy which had arisen out of that disgraceful scandal—a Corinthian Christian's union with his stepmother. That was the original *casus belli* between the ascetics and the libertines, but the controversy had travelled beyond it. Fresh issues had emerged, and these it had been decided to submit to the Apostle's consideration. They concerned sexual relations: things sacrificed to idols: abuses in public worship: spiritual gifts: the resurrection of the body: the collection for the poor at Jerusalem. The statement would be drawn up by the Elders of the Church, and they deputed three of their number to convey it to Ephesus and expound it to the Apostle. Probably these were representatives of the conflicting parties. Stephanas, the earliest of his converts in Achaia and his tried friend,[2] would represent Paul's supporters, while Achaicus and Fortunatus would appear on behalf of the ascetics and the libertines.[3]

The Corinthian rescript.

Disappointing though it was, the Corinthian communication afforded the Apostle no small gratification. It explained the long delay in replying to his first letter. His disciplinary mandate had not indeed been executed, but it had been seriously considered and the rescript invited discussion of large and important problems. It was a precious opportunity, and he gladly embraced it in the hope of effecting a complete and enduring settlement. His gratification appears in the kindlier tone which characterises the remainder of his letter. He desists from sarcasm, and addresses himself to high and serious argument, and labours to resolve the perplexities of his friends.

The Apostle's Answer. Cf. xvi. 17.

[1] The canon of the Armenian Church contains two brief and absolutely worthless letters, purporting to be the Corinthian communication and Paul's reply. Cf. Fabricius, *Cod. Apocr. N. T.*, pp. 918 sq.; Giles, *Cod. Apocr. N. T.*, II. pp. 509 sq.

[2] Cf. p. 148.

[3] Since tradition, after its wont, makes Achaicus one of the Seventy Apostles, it may perhaps be inferred that he was a Jewish Christian and the representative of the ascetic party.

I. Sexual relations.

(1) The legitimacy of marriage.

The rescript submitted a group of problems connected with the relation of the sexes. The first of these was the question of the legitimacy of marriage, which the ascetics contemned. If they did not prohibit it outright, they at all events counselled celibacy as the more honourable estate. The Apostle's decision is that marriage is not merely legitimate but, as a rule, expedient. He would rather indeed that his own example were followed. He was a widower,[1] and he had remained unmarried; but the grace of continence was not granted to all, and his concession was absolute. In every case 'marriage is better than the fever of desire.'

vii. 1 Regarding the doctrine you write about, that 'it is
2 honourable for a man never to touch a woman': Since
fornication is so frequent, let each man have his own wife
3 and each woman her proper husband. Let the husband
pay the wife her due, and the wife pay the husband his.
4 It is not the wife that has authority over her own body,
but the husband; and likewise it is not the husband that
5 has authority over his own body, but the wife. Never defraud
one another, unless it be by agreement for a season, that
you may devote yourselves to prayer[2] and then resume your
relationship, lest Satan tempt you since you lack self-control.
6, 7 I say this by way of concession, not of injunction; and I
wish that all men were like myself. But each has his own
gift of grace from God, one in this way and another in that.
8 And I say to widowers and widows,[3] it is honourable for
9 them if they remain like me; yet if they be lacking in self-
control, let them marry; for marriage is better than the
fever of desire.[4]

(2) Divorce

Then he turns to the question of divorce; and here there is no need for argument. The Lord had delivered His verdict, and that was final. Divorce is illegitimate except for adultery; and a divorced woman must remain unmarried or else be reconciled to her husband.

[1] Cf. p. 31.

[2] T. R. 'fasting and prayer.' א*ABCDEFGP om. τῇ νηστείᾳ καί. A similar ascetic interpolation occurs in Mk. ix. 29. Cf. *The Historic Jesus*, p. 73.

[3] Cf. p. 31, n. 1.

[4] πυροῦσθαι, 'be consumed with the fire of lust' (cf. Rom. i. 27), not 'be burned in Gehenna for their sin' (Cypr. *Epist. XII ad Pompon.* iv).

10 To the married my charge—not mine but the Lord's—is that
11 a wife should not be divorced from a husband; but if she be Cf. Mt. v.
divorced, let her remain unmarried, or else let her be reconciled 32.
to her husband; and that a husband should not put away his
wife.

Here the question presents itself whether unbelief is a legitimate reason for divorce. Since, according to the Scriptures, idolatry is spiritual whoredom, it was maintained that a convert whose spouse remained a heathen should seek divorce; and the idea, it appears, had been encouraged by the Apostle's warning in his first letter against being 'incongruously yoked with strangers to the Faith.'

(3) Mixed marriages.

2 Cor. vi. 14.

On this question there was no express decision of the Lord, yet he answers it with absolute confidence. A mixed marriage should not be dissolved where there was mutual contentment. It was not an unholy union, since, by the law of imputation, the believer sanctified the unbeliever; and, moreover, there was always the hope that the believer might win the unbeliever. Where, however, contentment was lacking, it was legitimate to sever the union in the interest of peace.

12 To the rest I say—I, not the Lord: If any brother has a wife
who is a stranger to the Faith, and she is well pleased to dwell
13 with him, let him not put her away; and a wife—if she has a
husband who is a stranger to the Faith, and he is well pleased
14 to dwell with her, let her not put her husband away. For the
husband who is a stranger to the Faith has been hallowed by
fellowship with his wife, and the wife who is a stranger to the
Faith has been hallowed by fellowship with the brother; else
15 your children are unclean, but as it is they are holy. If,
however, the stranger to the Faith seeks divorce, let him have
it: the brother or the sister is not enslaved in such cases.
16 It is in peace that God has called you. For how do you know,
wife, but that you will save your husband? Or how do you
know, husband, but that you will save your wife?

The grand principle was that 'it is in peace that God has called us.' Christianity destroys nothing; it transfigures everything. It takes our lives as it finds them, and enters graciously into them, blessing and enriching them. Hence it follows that, whatever be a man's condition at his conversion, he should maintain it and live the new life amid the

Godly contentment.

old surroundings. For example, a Jew should not undo his circumcision ; nor need a slave fret that he must remain a slave. Slavery was indeed a grievous condition, and if an opportunity of emancipation offered, it should be welcomed. But the rule was that ' where each was called, there he should remain in God's company.' A believer, though he was a slave, was ' the Lord's freedman ' ; and though he was free, he was still ' Christ's slave.'

17 Only, as the Lord has apportioned to each, as God has
called each, so let him comport himself. And so I am giving
18 order in all the churches. Had one been circumcised when
he was called? Let him not undo the operation.[1] Has
one been called in uncircumcision? Let him not be cir-
19 cumcised. Circumcision is nothing, and uncircumcision is
20 nothing: keeping God's commandments is everything. In
21 the calling wherein each was called, let him remain. Were
you a slave when you were called? Never mind; but if
you can gain your freedom, avail yourself of the opportunity.[2]
22 For one who was a slave when he was called in the Lord is
the Lord's freedman; similarly, one who was free when he was
23 called is a slave of Christ. 'You were bought at a price':
24 become not slaves of men. Where each was called, brothers,
there let him remain in God's company.

' Christ's slave.'

vi. 20.

The Apostle had a special reason for thus introducing the question of slavery and enlarging upon it. In his first letter, by way of inculcating the moral obligation of redemption,

[1] This was sometimes done by Jews to escape Gentile taunts in the baths and gymnasia (cf. Schürer, I. i. p. 203). On the method cf. Wetstein.

[2] *μᾶλλον χρῆσαι* admits of two interpretations. 1. Supply *τῇ δουλείᾳ* : 'although (cf. Lk. xi. 8) you can gain your freedom, rather remain in slavery' (*μᾶλλον δούλευε*). So Chrys. : *θέλων δεῖξαι ὅτι οὐδὲν βλάπτει ἡ δουλεία ἀλλὰ καὶ ὠφελεῖ.* Similarly Ambrstr. (who regards the precept as corrective of a possible misunderstanding: 'lest perhaps, on hearing, "Were you a slave when you were called? Never mind," one should be more negligent in good service of his master after the flesh, and thus the doctrine of Christ should be blasphemed'), Beng., Meyer, Alford. 2. Supply *τῇ ἐλευθερίᾳ* : 'if indeed (cf. Lk. xi. 18) you can gain your freedom, avail yourself of it,' *εἰ δύνασαι ἐλευθερωθῆναι, ἐλευθερώθητι* (Chrys., who quotes this interpretation disapprovingly). So Luth., Beza, Calv., Grot., Lightfoot. This is preferable, since it is natural to supply *τῇ ἐλευθερίᾳ* from *ἐλεύθερος*. On *χρῆσθαι* in the sense of 'avail oneself of an opportunity within one's reach,' cf. ix. 12, 15. The Apostle does not mean that slavery is actually the preferable condition but only that it should be accepted when it is one's appointed lot.

he had written: ‘You are not your own; for you were bought at a price. Glorify God, then, in your body’; and it seems that the Corinthians had asked what redemption was worth if it was only a new bondage. Paul answers with that paradox: ‘The Lord's freedman, Christ's slave.’ Here is a magnificent conception which had captivated his imagination and colours all his thought of redemption. It was based upon a merciful Greek usage. When a slave was hardly treated, he might take refuge in a temple, particularly the Temple of Theseus or the Temple of the Erinnyes at Athens, and claim the privilege of being sold to the deity.[1] He had previously brought thither his purchase-price, the hoarding of his poor *peculium*, and when this was handed over to his master in the presence of witnesses, he forthwith passed into the god's possession, and thenceforth he was unassailably and irrevocably free. He did not pass into the service of the temple. He had been ‘bought for freedom.’ He was the god's property, and it would have been sacrilege for any mortal to claim dominion over him.[2]

And here the Apostle recognised an image of the Christian
Redemption. The sinner is ‘a slave of sin,’ and the legalist Rom. vi.
is ‘a slave of the Law’; but when he ‘entrusts himself to 17, 20. Gal. iv.
Christ for freedom,’ he is ‘bought at a price,’ and thenceforth 1-7, v. 1.
he is ‘called for freedom.’ He is ‘Christ's slave,’ and it 1 Cor. vi. 20, vii. 23;
were sacrilege that he should ever again ‘become a slave of Gal. v. 13.
man’ or ‘again get into the grip of a yoke of slavery.’ His 1 Cor. vii. 23; Gal.
slavery to Christ is a sacred freedom, a complete and irre- v. 1.
vocable emancipation. And hence, when Paul styled himself Cf. Rom.
‘a slave of Jesus Christ,’ it was no epithet of self-abasement i. 1; Phil. i. 1.

[1] Cf. schol. on Aristoph. *Equit.* 1308; Suidas under Θησεῖον; Plut. *Thes.* 36; Pollux, VII. 13.

[2] The usage is exemplified by an inscription recently discovered at Delphi (cf. Deissmann, *Light from the Ancient East*, pp. 327 ff.). It is dated the first year of 2nd c. B.C. ἐπρίατο ὁ Ἀπόλλων ὁ Πύθιος παρὰ Σωσιβίου Ἀμφισσέος ἐπ' ἐλευθερίᾳ σῶμα γυναικεῖον ᾇ ὄνομα Νίκαια, τὸ γένος Ῥωμαίαν, τιμᾶς ἀργυρίου μνᾶν τριῶν καὶ ἡμιμναίου. προαποδότας κατὰ τὸν νόμον Εὔμναστος Ἀμφισσεύς. τὰν τιμὰν ἀπέχει. τὰν δὲ ὠνὰν ἐπίστευσε Νίκαια τῷ Ἀπόλλωνι ἐπ' ἐλευθερίᾳ, ‘The Pythian Apollo bought from Sosibius of Amphissa for freedom a woman slave named Nicæa, by race a Roman, at a price of three and a half minæ of silver. Previous vendor according to the law, Eumnastus of Amphissa. The price received. And the purchase (*i.e.*, herself) Nicæa entrusted to Apollo for freedom.’ Then follow the signatures of the witnesses.

but a title of supreme honour, his proudest boast. Because he was 'Christ's slave,' he was 'the Lord's freedman.'

(4) Virginity. The next question related to the practice of virginity which already prevailed among the Jewish sect of the Essenes,[1] and which by and by came into high repute in the Christian Church. It was thus early advocated by the ascetic party at Corinth as a special merit in both sexes.

Here again the Apostle confesses that the Lord had left no decision, and he propounds his own judgment with unconcealed diffidence. It follows from the legitimacy of marriage that there is no essential excellence in virginity. This he allows; nevertheless there was a consideration which weighed with him and disposed him, in existing circumstances, to concede the ascetic contention. The Day of the Lord, according to the confident though mistaken expectation of the Apostolic Church, was at hand; and in view of that imminent consummation and its disastrous prelude it were well that a Christian, as he valued his own peace and desired to acquit himself worthily, should refrain from worldly entanglements. The Lord's cause claimed his entire devotion, and domestic cares would distract his mind. Michelangelo never married, alleging that 'art is a sufficiently exacting mistress'; and are the claims of the Kingdom of Heaven less engrossing or less imperative?

Hence, in existing circumstances, it seemed to the Apostle that celibacy was not merely a counsel of prudence but a Christian duty. Nevertheless he would leave it an open question, and he recognises a situation where marriage was expedient. Evidently he is dealing here with an actual case which had been submitted to his judgment—that of a Christian who had plighted his troth and had since been persuaded of the excellence of virginity yet shrank from doing his *fiancée* a wrong.

His handling of the case is well illustrated by the story of Ammon, the Egyptian monk.[2] He found himself in that very position; and in deference to his kinsfolk's importunities he kept his troth, but on bringing his bride home he read to her the Apostle's counsel in this passage and

[1] Cf. p. 447. [2] Cf. Socr. *Eccl. Hist.* IV. 23.

enlarged upon it, setting forth the ills of marriage and the advantages of virginity. His arguments prevailed, and the wedded yet virgin pair betook themselves to a hut in the Nitrian Desert and lived there for a while in pure companionship, until at her proposal they took up their abodes in separate huts and practised the ascetic life to the end of their days.

It is such 'spiritual marriage' that the Apostle recommends where troth has been plighted and cannot without cruelty be broken; and the relationship must in nowise be confounded with that perilous intimacy which clerics and monks maintained in after days with 'sisters' and 'beloved,' and which was justly stigmatised as a scandal in the case of Paul of Samosata.[1] The virginity which is here contemplated is a triumph of heroic self-abnegation, a voluntary abstinence from legitimate indulgence; and the Apostle recognises the extreme difficulty of the achievement, and while recommending it does not enjoin it. It is marriage that he has in view; and while he suggests abstinence from its privileges, he freely permits their exercise. He distinctly reaffirms the permanence of the marriage-bond. Abstinence must be by mutual consent, and the refusal of nuptial rights would be an injustice.

25 Regarding virgins:[2] I have no injunction of the Lord, but
I give my judgment as one whose experience of the Lord's
26 mercy entitles him to trust. I think, then, this is as a general
principle[3] the honourable course in view of the present con-
27 straint—it is honourable for a man to be in this estate. Are
you bound to a wife? Do not seek release. Have you no
28 wife to be released from?[4] Do not seek one. If, however,
you do marry, you have committed no sin; and if your

[1] Cf. Eus. *Hist. Eccl.* VII. 30. It was in the course of this unhappy case that the ἀδελφαί or ἀγαπηταί were stigmatised by the Antiochenes, with their knack of coining epithets (cf. p. 67), as *συνείσακτοι*, *virgines subintroductæ*. Cf. Heinichen on Eus. *l.c.*, Exc. XIII.; Bingham, *Ant.* VI. ii. 13.

[2] παρθένος was both masc. and fem. Cf. Rev. xiv. 4. ὁ παρθένος was a title of the Apostle John.

[3] καλὸν ὑπάρχειν, cf. n. on Gal. ii. 14, p. 200.

[4] λέλυσαι does not imply that the man has been bound. Cf. Ignat. *Ad Magn.* xii: εἰ γὰρ καὶ δέδεμαι, πρὸς ἕνα τῶν λελυμένων ὑμῶν οὐκ εἰμί, 'though I am bound, I am not comparable with one of you who are free.'

virgin marry, she has committed no sin. But such persons
will have distress in the flesh, and I am for sparing you.
29 This, however, I admit,[1] brothers: Our opportunity is
abridged; henceforth those who have wives must be as
30 though they had none,[2] and those who weep as though they
did not weep, and those who rejoice as though they did not
rejoice, and those who buy as though they possessed nothing,
31 and those who use the world as though they refrained from its
full use; for the world as it is now constituted is passing away.
32 And I wish you to be free from anxiety.[3] The unmarried man
is anxious about the Lord's affairs—how he may please the
33 Lord; while one who is married is anxious about the world's
34 affairs—how he may please his wife; and so his interests are
divided. Also the woman—the widow and the virgin[4]—is
anxious about the Lord's affairs, that she may be holy both in
body and in spirit; but one who is married is anxious about
35 the world's affairs—how she may please her husband. This
I say for your profit, not that I may cast a halter round your
necks; no, the end in view is seemliness and attendance on
the Lord without distraction.[5]
36 But if one thinks he is behaving unseemly toward his virgin,
in case he be over-lusty, and there is no help for it, let him do
37 what he desires; he is not sinning; let them marry. But one
who stands steadfast in his heart and has no constraint but has
authority where his own will is concerned, and has decided in
his own heart to keep his virgin intact, will do honourably.
38 And so, while one who puts his virgin to the use of marriage
does honourably, one who refrains will do better.[6]

[1] *φημι*, cf. x. 15, 19; xv. 50.

[2] *τὸ λοιπὸν ἵνα*, ellipt., 'henceforth (see to it) that.' Cf. 2 Cor. viii. 7; Mk. v. 23. Tertullian's 'superest ut' (*Ad Uxor.* I. 5) and Vulg. 'reliquum est ut' import a Latin idiom.

[3] Epict. III. xxii. 45-49 is an interesting parallel to this passage.

[4] Reading *μεμέρισται. καὶ ἡ γυνὴ ἡ ἄγαμος καὶ ἡ παρθένος μεριμνᾷ* (W. H., Nestle). Tisch.: *τῇ γυναικί. καὶ μεμέρισται καὶ ἡ γυνὴ καὶ ἡ παρθένος· ἡ ἄγαμος μεριμνᾷ*, 'and there is a difference between the wife and the virgin: the unmarried woman is anxious.'

[5] *ἀπερισπάστως*, cf. Lk. x. 40: *περιεσπᾶτο περὶ πολλὴν διακονίαν*, 'distracted about much service,' the only other instance of the phrase in N. T.—a significant parallel.

[6] The situation here has been conceived in two ways. The prevailing idea, as old as Chrys. (cf. *De Virg.* 78), is that the Apostle is dealing with the case of a father who, recognising the excellence of virginity, would keep his daughter unmarried but fears he is dealing hardly with her when he sees her youth fading (*ἐὰν ᾖ ὑπέρακμος*, 'if she be past the flower of her age'). This is supported by (1) *ὑπέρακμος*, if it mean 'past the flower of youth,' and (2) *γαμίζειν*, if it must be understood as 'give in marriage.' On the other hand, it is irreconcilable with *γαμείτωσαν*, which can hardly mean anything else than 'let them (*i.e.*, the *τις* and

39 A woman is bound all her husband's life-time ; but if he be
gone to his rest, she is free to marry whom she will, provided
40 it be in the Lord. But she is more blessed if she remain as she
is, according to my judgment ; and I fancy too I have God's
Spirit.

2. Things sacrificed to idols.

The second problem which the Corinthian rescript submitted to the Apostle was the legitimacy of eating things sacrificed to idols ; and this was a problem which inevitably confronted a Christian community in a heathen city. It was only a portion of a sacrificial victim that was consumed on the altar, sometimes only a few hairs ; and the remainder was used as food. The sacrifices were numerous, insomuch that the meat-market was largely furnished from the temples. And thus the likelihood was that the meat which a Christian purchased was the flesh of an idol-sacrifice. It may indeed have been possible for him, ere he made his purchase, to inquire and ascertain its origin ; but there was no such remedy when he was invited to the table of a heathen friend. It was the fashion for a devout heathen, by way of thanksgiving for good fortune, to hold a feast in the temple of his deity and invite his acquaintances to share it.[1] It was a religious celebration, and participation was impossible for a Christian. His presence at the banquet would have been open idolatry, an act of homage to the heathen deity. It was, however, another matter when a Christian was invited by a heathen neighbour to visit his house and enjoy his hospitality. It was simply a social

his *παρθένος*) marry.' It is thus not a father but a lover that is in question, nor are the objections to this view valid. (1) *ὑπέρακμος* occurs only here, and while it might mean 'past the flower of youth,' it may rather mean 'exceedingly lusty.' Cf. *ὑπερακμάζειν*, 'excel in youthful vigour' (Athen. 657 D). (2) *γαμίζειν* is found only in N. T. (cf. Mt. xxii. 30 ; xxiv. 38) ; and on the analogy of similar formations (cf. *πελεκίζειν*, *ἱματίζειν*, *σαββατίζειν*, *ἰουδαΐζειν*) it should denote, not 'give in marriage,' but rather 'practise marriage,' 'put to the marriage-use.' Moreover, neither *ἀσχημονεῖν* nor *ἔχων ἀνάγκην* is appropriate to mere paternal severity. The former implies *gross indecency* (cf. Rom. i. 27 ; Rev. xvi. 15), and *ἀνάγκη* can only signify the constraint of passion overpowering *ἐξουσίαν περὶ τοῦ ἰδίου θελήματος*.

[1] Specimens of such invitations have been unearthed at Oxyrhynchus. *Oxyrh. Pap.* 110 : *ἐρωτᾷ σε Χαιρήμων δειπνῆσαι εἰς κλείνην τοῦ κυρίου Σαράπιδος ἐν τῷ Σαραπείῳ αὔριον, ἥτις ἐστιν ιε̄, ἀπὸ ὥρας θ*, 'Chæremon invites you to dine at the table of the Lord Sarapis in the Temple of Sarapis to-morrow, the 15th, at 3 o'clock.' Cf. No. 523.

occasion ; and why should a Christian refuse the invitation, and thus not merely exclude himself from kindly human intercourse but miss the opportunity for leavening the world ? Still a difficulty remained. The flesh of victims sacrificed in the heathen temples would be served without scruple at a heathen table ; and was it legitimate for a Christian to partake of it ?

Conflicting opinions.

The question was agitating the Corinthian Church, and two opinions were hotly maintained. There was a scrupulous party which absolutely condemned the eating of things sacrificed to idols, and there was a liberal party which regarded it as an affair of no moment ; and after the manner of controversialists each had run to an extreme. It appears that the advocates of liberalism were in so far the worse offenders that they had sinned against the law of charity by assuming an air of superiority and regarding their opponents with supercilious contempt. At all events it is to them that the Apostle addresses his remonstrances and reproofs.

Arrogant liberalism.

He begins by quoting a series of sentences from their statement of the controversy, and he dismisses each with a curt and incisive criticism.

viii. 1 Regarding things sacrificed to idols : 'We are aware that
we all have knowledge.'

Here speaks the self-complacent intellectual who has never learned the Socratic lesson that the beginning of knowledge is the recognition of one's ignorance,[1] still less the Christian truth of the supremacy of love. And so the Apostle answers :

Knowledge breeds windy conceit ; it is love that builds
2 up. If any one fancies he has attained any knowledge, he
3 has no such knowledge yet as he should have ; but if any one
loves God, he it is that is known by Him.

Cf. Dt. xxxii. 17; Ps. cvi. 37; Rev. ix. 20.

The prevalent notion alike of the later Jews and of the primitive Christians regarding the gods of heathendom was that they were demons ; and though they were subsequently accounted as merely dead men superstitiously deified, yet

[1] Plat. *Apol.* 21 D.

it was maintained that the demons worked in their names.[1] Hence the danger of participation in heathen rites. It involved the risk of demonic possession; and this is the reason which the scrupulous party alleged for abstinence from meat which had been sacrificed to idols. The intellectuals had adopted what seemed to them a more rational attitude. They regarded the heathen gods as mere fictions of superstition, and they argued that, since an idol was 'nothing in the world,' it could inflict no injury. The fear of exposure to the malign operation of demons by eating things sacrificed to idols was a baseless apprehension.

4 Regarding, then, the eating of things sacrificed to idols:
'We are aware that an idol is nothing in the world, and that
5 there is no God but One. For, though there are so-called
"gods," whether in heaven or on earth, as there are many
6 "gods" and many "lords,"[2] yet for us there is one God, the
Father, who is the source of all things, and it is to Him that
we tend; and one Lord, Jesus Christ, through whom are all
things, and through Him are we.'

It may be so, answers the Apostle; but it is not every one who has attained so enlightened a view. Some cling to the old notion, and their scruples are entitled to consideration.

7 But your knowledge dwells not in all. Some, retaining to this hour the old notion about the idol, eat the food as an idol-sacrifice, and their conscience, being weak, is polluted.

8 'Food,' said the liberals again, 'will not recommend us to God. We are neither the worse off by not eating nor the better off by eating.'

True, answers the Apostle, but here again consideration is a duty. It is spiritually injurious to do what one's conscience disapproves; and if your example induces a weak

[1] Cf. Theophil. *Ad Autol.* I. p. 75 B (Sylburg.): *καὶ τὰ μὲν ὀνόματα ὧν φῂς σέβεσθαι θεῶν ὀνόματά ἐστι νεκρῶν ἀνθρώπων.* Tert. *De Spect.* 10: 'Scimus nihil esse nomina mortuorum, sicut nec ipsa simulacra eorum: sed non ignoramus qui sub istis nominibus et institutis simulacris operentur et gaudeant et divinitatem mentiantur, nequam spiritus scilicet dæmones.'

[2] *κύριος* was a title not only of the heathen deities (cf. p. 269, n. 1) but of the Roman Emperors. Cf. the refusal of the Egyptian Jews to call Cæsar 'Lord,' since they 'held that God alone was the Lord' (Jos. *De Bell. Jud.* VII. x. 1).

brother to violate his conscience, you are wronging not merely him but Christ who died for him. It is sacrilege to esteem lightly the purchase of the Saviour's precious blood.

9 Beware, however, lest this authority of yours prove a
10 stumbling-block to the weak. For if some one see you, the
man with knowledge, at table in an idol-temple, will not his
conscience, in case he is weak, be built up to the pitch of eating
11 the things sacrificed to idols? Your knowledge is the ruin of
12 the weak man, the brother for whom Christ died. And thus,
in sinning against the brothers and smiting their conscience,
13 weak as it is, it is against Christ that you are sinning. Wherefore, if food ensnares [1] my brother, I will eat flesh never more,
lest I ensnare my brother.

The liberal defence: (1) The plea of Christian liberty.

And now he proceeds to examine two pleas which the liberals urged in defence of their attitude. One was the plea of Christian liberty. They had a grievance, and indeed a serious grievance. Whatever scorn they might have felt, they would have suffered their opponents to practise their scrupulosity; but this did not suffice the latter. Not content with personal abstinence, they insisted that their practice should be the Church's law. It was a denial of Christian liberty, and the liberals naturally resented so intolerable a tyranny.

A larger concern.

The Apostle's answer is that, while Christian liberty is indeed a sacred right, it is a Christian duty to forgo one's rights when larger interests are at stake. And by way of illustration he adduces his own example, in no spirit of self-glorification but with the double purpose of resolving the immediate perplexity and at the same time repelling the Judaist attack on his own apostolic authority.

Paul's apostleship.

He has just affirmed his willingness to abstain from flesh rather than injure a weak brother. Was that a dereliction either of his Christian liberty or of his apostolic authority? His apostleship, he deftly remarks, needed no vindication with the Corinthians. For they owed him their conversion, and this constituted an incontrovertible attestation of his divine commission; it was his sufficient answer to his critics.

ix. 1 Am I not free? Am I not an Apostle? Have I not seen
2 Jesus our Lord? Are not you my work in the Lord? If to

[1] Cf. *The Days of His Flesh*, p. 99.

others I am not an Apostle, yet to you at least I am ; for you
3 are the seal of my apostleship in the Lord. My defence to
my critics [1] is just this.

He was an Apostle, and he was entitled to apostolic privileges. The other Apostles had wives who accompanied them on their missionary travels ; and wherever they sojourned, they were maintained at the Church's expense. These privileges belonged to him, yet he had never exercised them. He had remained unwed that he might the more freely devote himself to his ministry ; and it was notorious that he and his former colleague Barnabas had never exacted maintenance from the Church. The Corinthians knew how, during his ministry among them, he had earned his daily bread by plying his craft of tent-making, and how ill he would at times have fared but for the generosity of his Macedonian friends.[2] That was his constant practice ; he was pursuing it even then at Ephesus.

His apostolic rights.

Cf. vii. 29-35.

4, 5 Are we not entitled to food and drink? Are we not
entitled to travel about with a sister, a wife, like the rest of
6 the Apostles and the Lord's brothers [3] and Cephas? Or is
it only Barnabas and I that are bound to work for our daily
bread?

Cf. Mt. xiii. 55=Mk. vi. 3.

And what was the reason? He had a right to remuneration. It is a principle of common equity that a man should be paid for his service and live by the fruit of his labour ; and it is recognised by the Scriptures. The Sacred Law enjoins that the very oxen should be allowed their mouthfuls of the grain which they tread out on the threshing-floor ; and a man is more in God's sight than an ox. And if the rule held in common work, it held much more in spiritual service. If the ploughman and the thresher were entitled to their wage, should the sowers of the heavenly seed go unrequited? And who had so strong a claim on the Corinthians as Paul and his companions who had won them to the Faith? Yet he had waived his right. And the reason was his solicitude

Why he did not exercise these.

[1] τοῖς ἐμὲ ἀνακρίνουσιν, 'those who examine me.' Cf. pp. 252 f.

[2] Cf. p. 152.

[3] Cf. *The Days of His Flesh*, p. 18.

for the advancement of the Gospel. He would suffer any privation rather than put a hindrance in its way.

7 Who ever goes a-soldiering at his own expense? Who plants
a vineyard, and does not eat its fruit? Or who tends a herd,
8 and never tastes the milk of the herd? Is this mere human
9 reasoning? Is it not also the teaching of the Law? For in
Dt. xxv. 4. the Law of Moses it is written: 'Thou shalt not muzzle the
ox while it is treading out the grain.' Is it for the oxen that
10 God is concerned? Or is it entirely on our account that He
says it? Yes, it is on our account that it was written that the
plougher has a right in doing his work and the thresher has a
11 right in doing his to the hope of getting a share. If we sowed
for you the spiritual seed, is it a great thing if we shall reap
12 your material harvest? If others share the claim upon you,
do not we still more? But we did not exercise this claim.
No, we put up with [1] everything that we may occasion no
hindrance to the Gospel of Christ.

His imperious call.

Here the Apostle was trenching on painful ground. It was a shame to the Corinthians that they had withheld his remuneration while he ministered among them, in face, too, of the generous example of their Macedonian fellow-converts. They knew the ordinance of the Law in this matter and the Lord's reaffirmation of it. His maintenance was their duty, and it in nowise absolved them that he had uncomplainingly suffered their neglect. Nor was he complaining now. Self-respect restrained him, and a higher motive still. His preaching of the Gospel was no voluntary office. It had been thrust upon him. He had reluctantly undertaken it at the Lord's behest, conscious of his unfitness; and his *nolo episcopari* had defined the conditions of his ministry. It was not a voluntary service; else he would have been at liberty to bargain for remuneration. It was a divine stewardship, a sacred trust, an imperious obligation; and therefore the arrangement of terms did not lie with him: he must do the work and fare as he might. He was indeed entitled to his wage; but, wage or no wage, he must dreach the Gospel. That was his sole concern.

Cf. Ac. xxii. 17-21.

Cf. Num. xviii. 8, 31;

13 Do you not know that those who do the Temple's work, eat
of the Temple's provision; those who attend the altar, share

[1] Cf. n. on 1 Th. iii. 1, p. 160.

14 the altar's portion? So also the Lord gave order for those Dt. xviii. 1-5.
who proclaim the Gospel to get their livelihood from the Cf. Mt. x. 10; Lk. x, 7.
15 Gospel. But I have exercised none of these rights. And I
am not writing this in order that it may be so done in my case;
for it is a point of honour for me to die rather than——[1] No
16 one will make my boast an empty thing. For, if I preach the
Gospel, it is nothing for me to boast of; for necessity is imposed
17 upon me; ay, woe is me if I do not preach it! For if it be
by choice that I am engaged in this business, I have a wage;
but if it be by compulsion, I am entrusted with a stewardship.

The winning of men his sole interest. The preaching of the Gospel was his sole concern, and its triumph his only reward; and therefore he sacrificed his personal interests and abjured his rights. His one concern was the winning of men for Christ, and he would not contemn their prepossessions and prejudices but, where no principle was at stake, would defer to these and always treat them gently and patiently and sympathetically.

18 What, then, is the wage which induces me in preaching the
Gospel to set no charge upon it, refraining from the exercise of
19 my full right in the Gospel's service? Being free from all
men, I made myself a slave to all that I might gain the greater
20 number. And I became to the Jews as a Jew that I might
gain Jews; to those under Law as under Law, though I am
not myself under Law, that I might gain those under Law;
21 to those without Law as one without Law—though I am not
without God's Law; no, I am within Christ's Law—that I Cf. Gal. vi. 2.
22 might gain those without Law; to the weak I became weak
that I might gain the weak; to every one I have become
23 everything that I might in every case save some. And every- Cf. 1 Jo. i. 3.
thing I do on account of the Gospel, that I may share its
fellowship with others.

His self-discipline. And thus he proved his Christian liberty by freely relinquishing it, and he commends his attitude to the Corinthian liberals by a familiar example—the Isthmian Games which every fifth year drew eager multitudes to their city.[2] The

[1] An aposiopesis. He is about to say 'I had rather starve, ἀποθανεῖν λιμῷ (Chrys.), than accept grudging remuneration,' when he repents of the harshness.

[2] Cf. p. 150. [Clem. Rom.] *Ad Cor.* II. vii: ἀγωνισώμεθα, εἰδότες ὅτι ἐν χερσὶν ὁ ἀγὼν καὶ ὅτι εἰς τοὺς φθαρτοὺς ἀγῶνας καταπλέουσιν πολλοί, ἀλλ' οὐ πάντες στεφανοῦνται εἰ μὴ οἱ πολλὰ κοπιάσαντες καὶ καλῶς ἀγωνισάμενοι, 'let us contend, knowing that the contest is at hand, and that many voyage hither to the corruptible contests, yet it is not all that are crowned but only those that have toiled much and contended honourably.'

prize was a poor chaplet of parsley-leaves, and the victor wore it proudly; but he would never have won it by the effort of the hour unless he had subjected himself to a long and strenuous preparatory discipline. And self-discipline is needful for our nobler contest if we would win the unfading crown.

Cf. 2 Tim. iv. 8.

24 Do you not know that the runners in the race-course all run
but only one wins the prize? Run like him that you may
25 succeed in winning it. And every one who enters the contest
practises self-control in every particular—they to win a fading
26 crown, but we an unfading. For my part, then, it is thus that
I run—with a clear end in view; it is thus that I box—as no
27 'striker of the air.'[1] No, I bruise[2] my body and enslave it,
lest perchance, after acting as herald of the game for others,
I should myself fail in the ordeal.[3]

(2) The plea of sacramental security.

It was not merely, however, as a violation of Christian liberty that the intolerance of the scrupulous party in the Corinthian Church was resented. It was maintained that there was no danger in the eating of things sacrificed to idols inasmuch as the Christian Sacraments provided an efficacious prophylactic. The idea was natural to minds familiar with the ritual of the Greek Mysteries, and it persisted in the Church and persists to this day.[4] The Mysteries were 'a medicine of immortality.' Their aim was the communication of the divine life, and this was achieved by the ceremonial of initiation, especially the purificatory lustration and the sacrificial feast which followed it and which was designated 'Salvation.' It was supposed that the deity was present in the consecrated food, and in eating it the worshippers ate the deity and thus participated in the divine life. It was a purely physical process, and it was an offence to the moral instinct. Thus it is told of Diogenes the Cynic that, when the Athenians urged him to be initiated,

[1] ἀέρα δέρειν, *aerem verberare*, a common proverb, denoting *futile endeavour*. The metaphor is a boxer missing his antagonist and striking the empty air. Eustathius derives the proverb from Hom. *Il.* xx. 446: τρὶς δ' ἀέρα τύψε βαθεῖαν. Cf. Verg. *Æn.* v. 377: 'verberat ictibus auras.'

[2] ὑπωπιάζω, cf. *The Days of His Flesh*, p. 322.

[3] ἀδόκιμος γένωμαι, cf. n. on 1 Th. v. 21, p. 165.

[4] Cf. Hatch, *Influence of Greek Ideas and Usages*, Lect. x; Legge, *Forerunners and Rivals of Christianity*, I. pp. 130 f.

since the initiated were awarded the first place in the Unseen World, he answered: 'It is absurd if Agesilaus and Epaminondas are to drag it out in the mire, and any worthless creatures through their having been initiated are to inhabit the Islands of the Blessed.' 'What mean you?' he said again. 'Will Patæcion the thief have a better fate after death than Epaminondas, because he has been initiated?'[1]

To the Greek mind the Sacraments of Baptism and the Eucharist were the Christian Mysteries, and accordingly the intellectual Corinthians argued that, since they were sharers in the divine life through the sacramental lustration and the sacramental feast, they were immune from danger. They were possessed by the Divine Spirit, and they were therefore secure against demonic invasion and ran no risk through eating things sacrificed to idols. So they reasoned; and the Apostle, following up his insistence on the necessity of strenuous self-discipline, proceeds to demonstrate the vanity of their dream of sacramental security. A vain confidence.

He adduces an historical parallel. The Israelites had their Sacraments in the Wilderness. They were besprinkled by the Shekinah, the overshadowing Cloud of the Lord's Presence; and they passed through the waters of the Red Sea. This was their Baptism, their sacramental lustration after the twofold symbolism of effusion and immersion.[2] And they had also their Eucharist, since the manna and the water from the stricken rock were their sacramental meat and drink. All the forty years of their pilgrimage they not only ate that heavenly bread but drank that heavenly drink; for, according to a Jewish legend, the rock of Horeb followed their march, and wherever they encamped, it stood at the entrance of the Tabernacle and poured forth its abundant stream.[3] An historical parallel. Cf. Ex. xiii. 21, 22; xiv. 19-31. Cf. Ex. xvi-xvii. 7.

x. 1 For I do not wish you to ignore the fact,[4] brothers, that our
fathers were all under the Cloud and all passed through the
2 Sea, and all pledged themselves to Moses by baptism in the
3 Cloud and in the Sea; and they all ate the same spiritual food

[1] Diog. Laert. VI. 39; Plut. *De Aud. Poet.* IV. 76.
[2] Cf. Append. VI.
[3] Cf. Lightfoot, *Hor. Heb.*, and Wetstein on 1 Cor. x. 4.
[4] Cf. n. on 1 Th. iv. 13, p. 163.

4 and all drank the same spiritual drink; for they drank all the
while of a spiritual rock as it followed them, and the rock was
5 the Christ. Yet with the greater number of them God was
not well pleased; for 'they were laid low in the wilderness.'

Num. xiv. 16.

A warning to ourselves.

After the spiritualising method of exegesis which he had learned in the Rabbinical school,[1] the Apostle sees in the ancient story a foreshadowing of the Christian order and a condemnation of the fond delusion of sacramental security. The Cloud and the Sea signified Baptism, and the bread from heaven and the water from the rock the Eucharist. 'The rock was the Christ.' He was with the Israelites all unknown, ministering to them the grace which is now revealed in His Holy Sacraments. Yet it proved unavailing. They were seduced into idolatry, fornication, rebellion, and discontent. And their experience is an abiding admonition. There is no security in sacramental ritual. Temptation is ever present, and the one protection is God's aid—not the *opus operatum* of a sacramental rite but the grace which the rite expresses and seals, and which is ever accessible to humble and believing souls.

6 And all this constitutes a warning to us, that we may not
7 lust after evil things as they did. Do not turn idolaters like
some of them, as it is written: 'The people sat down to eat
8 and drink, and arose to frolic.' And let us not commit fornication as some of them did, and there fell in a single day twenty-
9 three thousand.[2] And let us not try the Lord's patience too
far, as some of them tried it, and they were destroyed by the
10 serpents. And do not murmur as some of them did, and they
11 were destroyed by the destroying angel. All this happened to
them by way of warning; and it was written for the admonition
12 of us to whom the tribute of the ages has accrued.[3] And so
13 let him who fancies he stands firm look to it lest he fall. No
temptation has seized you but such as is the common lot of
man; and God is faithful: He will not allow you to be tempted

Ex. xxxii. 6.
Num. xxv. 1-9.
xxi. 5, 6.
xvi. 41-50; cf. Ex. xii. 23; 2 Sam. xxiv. 16, 17.

[1] Cf. p. 27.

[2] According to Num. xxv. 9, 'twenty-four thousand.' A mere slip of memory, the variant 'twenty-four thousand' (Arm.) being a copyist's emendation.

[3] We are 'the heirs of all the ages'—the experience of the past and the wisdom it teaches. τέλη, 'taxes,' 'tribute,' 'toll' (cf. Mt. xvii. 25; Rom. xiii. 7). τελώνης, 'a tax-gatherer'; τελώνιον, 'the receipt of custom,' 'the place of toll' (cf. Mt. ix. 9).

beyond your ability, but along with the temptation He will make also the way of escape, that you may be able to bear up.

The peril of complicity with idolatry.

And now the Apostle points the lesson as regards the vexed question of eating things sacrificed to idols: Eschew idolatry; have no complicity with it. There was reason in the scrupulosity of the narrow party; and he demonstrates this with gentle irony by a dexterous manipulation of the confident contention of the intellectuals. For the sake of argument, not that he approved it, as, he observes, they were shrewd enough to perceive, he accepts their pagan theory of the Eucharist—that, as in the sacrificial feast of the Greek Mysteries the initiate fed on the deity and thus participated in the divine life, so in the Holy Supper the communicants drink Christ's blood and eat His flesh, and thus they all participate in His life. This crude notion, he remarks, was the primitive idea of sacrifice, and it appears in the sacrificial ritual of the Old Testament.[1] It was not the Apostle's view, but it was the view of the Corinthian intellectuals, and the consequence was obvious: if the principle held alike of the feast of the Lord's Table and of the feasts of the Jewish altar, then it held of the heathen sacrifices, and by eating things sacrificed to idols we participate in the idol's life. Ah, but, exclaim the intellectuals, you are admitting too much! An idol is not a reality; there is no actual personality behind it. True, answers the Apostle, but the Scriptures affirm that the heathen sacrifices are offered to demons; and so indeed they are. There may be no such deity as Aphrodite or Bacchus; but the demons of lust and drunkenness are grim realities, and heathenism is their worship. Idolatry is the cult of uncleanness, and you cannot participate in it without pollution. Resolutely eschew it, and beware of provoking the righteous displeasure of Almighty God.

14, 15 Wherefore, my beloved, flee away from idolatry. I am
16 speaking as to shrewd men: judge you of my admission. The
Cup of Blessing[2] which we bless—is it not a participation
in the blood of Christ? The bread which we break—is it

[1] Cf. *The Atonement in the Light of History and the Modern Spirit*, pp. 33 ff.
[2] The Sacramental Cup. Cf. *The Days of His Flesh*, p. 446.

17 not a participation in the body of Christ? Because there
is one bread, we, many as we be, are one body; [1] for we all
18 have a share of the one bread. Look at historic Israel:
are not they that eat the sacrifices participants of the altar?
19 What, then, is my admission? Is it that meat sacrificed
20 to an idol is anything? or that an idol is anything? No,
Dt. xxxii. 17. but that the things which they sacrifice, 'they sacrifice
to demons and to a God who is no God'; and I do not
21 wish you to participate with demons. You cannot drink
the Lord's Cup and a cup of demons; you cannot share
22 in the Lord's Table and a table of demons. Or are we
Dt. xxxii. 21. 'provoking the Lord to jealousy'? Are we stronger than
He?

The law of expediency.

There was, however, a larger consideration than personal risk. It was the duty of Christian expediency, and this the Apostle now presents. He quotes the libertine maxim 'Everything is allowable' (Cf. vi. 12.) which he has already treated in his first letter to Corinth,[2] and which had apparently been repeated by the liberals in their plea for Christian liberty. And his answer is that the proper consideration is not whether a thing be *allowable* but whether it be *profitable*, since, as William Penn has it, 'it is not enough that a thing be Right, if it be not fit to be done.' And nothing is 'fit to be done' which, however innocent in itself, is hurtful to one's neighbour or liable to misconstruction. And he illustrates the application of the principle. When you go to market, it is unnecessary, it were mere morbid scrupulosity, to investigate the source of the meat which is offered for the sale. That does not concern you. And in the event of your accepting heathen hospitality, eat your host's provision without demur. You know nothing of its origin, and it were discourtesy to inquire. Suppose, however, one of your fellow-guests is a Christian of the narrow sort, and he warns you that a particular dish contains sacrificial flesh: then quietly abstain from it. You have indeed no personal scruple, but if you ate it, your neighbour would be shocked. Your innocent action would appear to him unfaithfulness, and why should you expose yourself to needless calumniation? Seek always

[1] So Calv., Beng. According to the ancient idea of the sacrificial meal, the common food established a common life. Otherwise: 'because we, the many, are one bread, one body.'

[2] Cf. p. 236.

the glory of God, and give no occasion, if you can help it, for aspersion of your Christian profession.

23 'Everything is allowable': yes, but it is not everything
that is profitable. 'Everything is allowable': yes, but
24 it is not everything that builds up. Let none seek his
25 own interest—rather, his neighbour's. Everything that
is sold in the meat-market eat, examining nothing in defer-
26 ence to conscience; for 'to the Lord the earth belongs Ps. xxiv. 1.
27 and all that it contains.' If some stranger to the Faith
invites you and you choose to go, eat everything that is set
before you, examining nothing in deference to conscience.
28 But if some one[1] say to you, 'This is a thing sacrificed in
29 the Temple,'[2] do not eat it in deference to that person, your
informant, and to conscience (by 'conscience' I mean not
your own conscience but your neighbour's); for what is
the use of my liberty being judged by another conscience?[3]
30 If I partake with thankfulness, why am I calumniated for
31 a thing which I give thanks for? Whether, then, you eat
or drink or whatever you do, do everything for God's
32 glory. Put no difficulty in the way of Jews, Greeks, or
33 the Church of God, as I on my part pleasure every one in
everything, not seeking my own profit but that of the
xi. 1 generality of men, that they may be saved. Follow my
example, as I follow Christ's.

The administration of the primitive Church, following as it did the model of the Jewish Synagogue, was both familiar and congenial to Jewish Christians; but it was novel to Gentile converts, and it is no surprise that, though the Apostle had, after his wont, been careful to instruct the Corinthians in the proper usages, difficulties should have arisen. Two in particular had proved so serious that they were referred to his consideration.

3. Abuses in public worship.

Cf. 2 Th. ii. 15.

[1] (1) A heathen fellow-guest (Chrys.), perhaps mischievously to annoy you; (2) the host, *nempe convivator* (Grot.); (3) a Christian fellow-guest of the scrupulous order (Alford, Meyer). The last is attested by the sequel, since only with a Christian would it be a matter of conscience.

[2] ἱερόθυτον ('sacrificed in the Temple') or θεόθυτον ('sacrificed to the god') is the heathen term, used out of courtesy at a heathen table rather than the opprobrious Christian term εἰδωλόθυτον ('sacrificed to an idol').

[3] ἵνα τί (γένηται), 'that what may come to pass?' *i.e.*, to what good purpose, for what good end? Better forgo one's liberty than expose one's conduct to misconstruction and one's profession to calumniation. So Chrys.

Unveiled women.

One had to do with the position of women in the Church, and it had probably been occasioned by the Apostle's doctrine that in Christ 'the distinctions of Jew and Greek, slave and free man, male and female disappear.' (Gal. iii. 28.) Certain enthusiasts among the Corinthian women-folk had applied the principle in a startling fashion. Spurning the old restrictions, not merely had they claimed and exercised the right to pray and prophesy in the assemblies of the Church, but they had, by necessary consequence, discarded the custom which required that a woman should wear a veil when she appeared in public. It was a Jewish custom. (Cf. Gen. xxiv. 65.) The veil was the mark of a modest woman, and its forcible removal by a rude hand was reckoned an outrage and the perpetrator was liable to a heavy penalty.[1] The regulation was approved by the Christian Church and was imposed on Gentile communities; and thus the action of those Corinthian women was a violation of canonical order.

The significance of the veil.

It raised a double question: on the one hand, whether a woman might speak in the Church, and, on the other, whether she might appear unveiled in a public assembly. It was the latter that was agitating the Corinthians, and the Apostle meanwhile deals with it exclusively. He begins by enunciating a large principle—the law of subordination. The woman is the head of the home, but she rules it in her husband's name: he is her head. His head, again, is Christ, and he rules his wife in Christ's name. Nor does the subordination end here. God is the head of Christ. (Cf. Phil. ii. 8; Heb. v. 8; Jo. viii. 29.) The Father is supreme in the Godhead, and the Son, who was obedient to the Father in the days of His flesh and did always the things that were pleasing to Him, is subject to Him eternally. (Cf. 1 Cor. xv. 27, 28.) There is thus a chain of subordination: woman's head is man, man's head is Christ, and Christ's head is God; and it is a violation of the divine order of the Universe when woman disowns her subordination and departs from her degree.

2 I commend you for 'your remembrance of me in everything
and your firm adherence to the traditions as I delivered them
3 to you.'[2] And I wish you to know that every man's Head

[1] Cf. Grotius and Wetstein on 1 Cor. xi. 5.

[2] He quotes the rescript's protestation of loyalty.

is Christ, and woman's head is the man, and Christ's Head is God.

The Christian usage.

This principle, the Apostle argues, determines the question of the veil. It was indeed right that a man should pray or prophesy with uncovered head. And here emerges a Christian idea. The ancient usage was that priests in offering sacrifice and worshippers in the exercise of prayer should be veiled in token of reverence and acknowledgment of their unworthiness to approach the Divine Presence;[1] but the Christians prayed with uncovered head in recognition of their privilege of free access to the Throne of Grace.[2] They honoured Christ by entering with boldness into the Holy Place; and therefore the Apostle declares that 'every man praying or prophesying with his head covered shames his Head.' It was otherwise, however, with a woman. She was subordinate, and she must maintain her degree. The veil was a token of subordination, a symbol of subjection to man, her head; and by discarding it she shamed him. Her unveiling was a partial uncovering of her head, and why, he argues, should she be content with that? Why not uncover it entirely by cutting off her hair, and thus complete her husband's dishonour and her own disgrace? See what this means. The cutting off of a women's hair had a twofold significance. It was a sign of mourning: a widow cut off her hair and deposited it in her husband's tomb;[3] and it was also a token of connubial unfaithfulness: an adulteress was shaved.[4] If, argues the Apostle, you will cast off your veil, then go all the way: cut off your hair, and proclaim yourself a widow; shave your head, and proclaim yourself an adulteress.

Cf. Heb. iv. 15, 16, x. 19-22.

Is. xv. 2; Jer. vii. 29, xvi. 6; Ez. vii. 18; Am. viii. 10.

4 Every man praying or prophesying with his head covered
5 shames his Head; and every woman praying or prophesying
with her head unveiled shames her head, for she is one and

[1] Cf. Lightfoot, *Hor. Heb.* on 1 Cor. xi. 4. This was the general custom also with the heathen. Cf. Grotius.

[2] Cf. Tert. *Apol.* 30: 'Illuc suspicientes Christiani manibus expansis, quia innocuis; capite nudo, quia non erubescimus; denique sine monitore, quia de pectore oramus.'

[3] Cf. Robertson Smith, *Religion of Semites*, p. 306.

[4] In some quarters at all events. Cf. Tac. *Germ.* 19

6 the same thing as the shaved adulteress. If a woman is not to
be veiled, let her also cut off her hair; but if it be disgraceful
for a woman to cut off her hair or shave her head, let her be
veiled.

Appeal to Scripture.

Thus far he has merely appealed to the Christian usage, but now he clinches his argument by a double sanction. First, he appeals to the Scriptures. The ancient story of Creation teaches woman's subordination to man. Man was created first, 'in the image of God'; and then woman was 'taken out of man.' Man, the crown of His creation, is the glory of God; but woman, since she was derived from him, is the glory of man. Her glory is to his as the moon's light to the sun's.[1] And even as the Sabbath was made for man, and not man for the Sabbath, so man was not created for woman but woman for man. She was made for his help, and this is her office evermore. It is in subordination to him that she fulfils the end of her being; and therefore it is fitting that she should wear a symbol of subjection on her head. The disuse is more than a dishonouring of man. We are encompassed continually, and especially in the place of prayer, by an invisible multitude, an innumerable company of holy angels; and it becomes us to comport ourselves worthily in their presence. 'If,' reasons the Apostle, 'you despise your husband, reverence the angels.'[2]

Cf. Gen. i. 26, 27; ii. 18-23. Cf. Mk. ii. 27. Cf. 1 Cor. iv. 9; Heb. xii. 22; 1 Tim. v. 21.

Gen. i. 26, 27, v. 1. Gen. ii. 23. Gen. ii. 18.

7 For a man ought not to have his head veiled, since he is
primally 'the image' and glory 'of God'; whereas the woman
8 is man's glory. For it was not man that was 'taken out of'
9 woman but woman that was 'taken out of' man; yes, and
it was not man that was created for the woman but woman

[1] 'Minus aliquid viro, ut Luna lumen minus Sole' (Grot.).

[2] Chrys.: εἰ γὰρ τοῦ ἀνδρὸς καταφρονεῖς, φησί, τοὺς ἀγγέλους αἰδέσθητι. Of other interpretations of διὰ τοὺς ἀγγέλους (ver. 10) these may be mentioned: (1) The two guardian angels who, according to a beautiful Jewish belief, accompany every one, on the right side and the left. Cf. Hieronym. on Mt. xviii. 10. (2) The leaders of the Church (Ambrstr., Euth. Zig.). Cf. Rev. ii. 1, etc.; Socr. *Eccl. Hist.* IV. 23, where Evagrius terms Serapion, bishop of Thmuis, ὁ τῆς Θμουϊτῶν ἐκκλησίας ἄγγελος. (3) Evil angels who, according to a repulsive Jewish notion, were themselves incited to wantonness by the sight of an unveiled woman and would incite her. Cf. Tert. *Contra Marc.* V. 8; *De Virg. Vel.* 7; Wetstein's Rabbinical quotations.

10 that was created for the man. Therefore the woman ought
to have a symbol of subjection [1] on her head in reverence for
the angels.

This subordination is no depreciation of woman. On the contrary, her honour lies in its due observance. Man and woman are sharers alike in the Lord's grace, and the sacred office of motherhood is her supreme service to humanity. Her subordination to man does not mean that she is inferior to him, but only that each has a peculiar position in the universal economy. She is subordinate to man, even as Christ is subordinate to God; and even as the Son has equal honour with the Father, so woman has equal honour with man.

Woman's rightful honour.

Cf. 1 Tim. ii. 15.

Cf. Jo. v. 23.

11 Nevertheless neither is woman apart from man nor man
12 apart from woman in the Lord. For just as the woman was
taken out of the man, so also the man is propagated by the
woman; but all things spring from God.

And, further, the Apostle appeals to the instinct of propriety. By almost universal agreement, by that custom which is 'second nature,' [2] it was recognised as seemly that men should crop their hair and women wear theirs long.[3] Long hair was accounted effeminate foppery in a man,[4] and short hair was a woman's shame. And what modesty demanded before men, reverence demanded in the presence of God.

The instinct of propriety.

13 Determine it by your own judgment: is it fitting that a
14 woman should pray to God unveiled? Does not Nature
herself teach you that, if a man have long hair, it is a dishonour
15 to him; while, if a woman have long hair, it is a glory to her,
because her hair has been given her for a covering?

[1] ἐξουσίαν, 'a symbol of authority,' *i.e.*, the man's authority over the woman. 'μετωνυμία frequens Hebræis, ubi signum rei significatæ nomen accipit' (Grot.). The variant κάλυμμα (cf. Iren. I. i. 16) is an interpretative gloss. The 'veil' was the symbol of the 'authority.'

[2] Cf. Galen. *De Tuend. Val.* I.: ἐπίκτητοι φύσεις τὰ ἤθη.

[3] Cf. Plut. *Quæst. Rom.* 84: συνηθέστερον δὲ ταῖς γυναιξὶν ἐγκεκαλυμμέναις τοῖς δὲ ἀνδράσιν ἀκαλύπτοις εἰς τὸ δημόσιον προϊέναι· καὶ γὰρ παρ' Ἕλλησιν, ὅταν δυστυχία τις γίνεται, κείρουσι μὲν αἱ γύναικες κομῶσι δὲ οἱ ἄνδρες, ὅτι τοῖς μὲν τὸ κείρεσθαι ταῖς δὲ τὸ κομᾶν σύνηθές ἐστι.

[4] Cf. Eustath. on Hom. *Il.* (III. p. 288): κόμην δὲ ἔχειν καὶ εὔκομον εἶναι γυναικικώτερόν ἐστιν. Mart. *Epigr.* X. 65.

Dismissal of the question.

It were injustice to the Apostle to take his quaint reasoning here as serious argument. He treats those obtrusive women with appropriate badinage; and this appears in his closing sentence where he drops the mask of gravity and declines to debate the question. All that need be said is that their behaviour is a violation of Christian usage as sanctioned by the Apostles and observed in all the churches. At the same time his condemnation is unqualified and emphatic; and the true reason of his hostility to the innovation lay in the moral laxity which prevailed at Corinth and which rendered womanly restraint peculiarly expedient.

16 If, however, any one has a fancy for disputing the question, we have no such custom nor have the churches of God.[1]

Profanation of the Love-feast.

The other problem concerned the Sacrament of the Lord's Supper, and it had arisen from the association of the holy ordinance with the kindly institution of the Love-feast.[2] The custom was that all should assemble, bringing provision according to their ability. The poor brought little and the destitute nothing; but the rich brought much, and thus there was no lack.[3] All shared alike, and the common meal was sacramental. Sometimes at the close but generally at the outset it was sanctified by prayer and the breaking of bread in the name of the Lord Jesus Christ. 'Ere the feast begins,' says Tertullian, 'it is whetted by prayer to God'; and 'after the communion of the mysteries,' says St. Chrysostom, 'they all betook themselves to the common banquet.' The Corinthians, however, were sundered by fierce animosities, and they introduced their feuds into the very Love-feast. Besides their partisanship it appears that the spirit of social caste prevailed. The rich disdained the poor and would not associate with them. They kept apart, and consumed their abundance, regardless of their neighbours who had little to eat and drink. It was a hideous contrast—here hunger, and there surfeit and drunkenness;

[1] This is all that the Apostle has to say: the discarding of the veil is contrary to Christian usage. Chrys. understands: 'disputation is not our custom.'

[2] Cf. p. 37.

[3] Cf. Tert. *Apol.* 39.

and the Apostle cries shame upon it. If they would have revelry, let them have it at home, and not flaunt it in the faces of the poor.

17 But in my next charge I do not commend you, because your
18 meetings are not for the better but for the worse. For, in the
first place,[1] at your meetings in Church I hear cleavages exist
19 among you; and to some extent I believe it. For there must
indeed be parties among you that it may become manifest
20 who are the men of sterling worth among you.[2] At your
meetings together, then, there is no possibility of eating the
21 Lord's Supper. For each of you is in haste to get his own
supper at the eating; and one is hungry while another is
22 drunken. Why, have you not homes to eat and drink in?
Or are you despising the Church and shaming the homeless?

The Institution of the Supper.

It was a horrible scandal, and the worst feature of it was its desecration of the Holy Supper. In such an assembly there was nothing sacramental. The Corinthians had assured the Apostle of their remembrance of the traditions which he had delivered to them, and in the matter of the women's veil he had accepted their assurance and commended their loyalty. But here it was impossible for him to commend them. Had they remembered the Evangelic Tradition of the Institution in the Upper Room, the scandal would never have arisen; and so he reiterates the Tradition and bids them henceforth bear it in mind and realise the sacredness of the ordinance.

What am I to say to you? Shall I commend you? In this
23 matter I do not commend you. For I received from the Lord[3]
the tradition which I delivered to you: 'The Lord Jesus,
24 on the night of His betrayal, took a loaf, and after giving thanks
He broke it and said: "This is My body sacrificed for you.

[1] πρῶτον μέν should be balanced by ἔπειτα δέ: 'in the first place cleavages, in the next profanation of the Supper.' But the parenthesis (ver. 19) disturbs the sequence.

[2] δόκιμοι, cf. n. on. 1 Th. v. 21, p. 165.

[3] On the sanctity of the Evangelic Tradition cf. *The Days of His Flesh*, pp. xvf. Paul does not mean that his account of the Institution was a special revelation to himself. He would then probably (cf., however, Lightfoot on Gal. I. 10) have said not ἀπό but παρὰ τοῦ Κυρίου, since ἀπό denotes merely the source; while παρά implies that the gift is immediate and direct. Thus ἀπὸ τίνων λαμβάνουσι τέλη; (Mt. xvii. 25), since kings receive tribute through their tax-gatherers. Cf. Moulton's Winer, p. 463.

25 This do in memory of Me." And so too with the cup at the
close of the Supper.[1] "This cup," He said, "is the New
Covenant sealed with My blood. This do, every time you
26 drink it, in memory of Me."' For every time you eat this
bread and drink this cup, it is the Lord's death that you are
27 proclaiming until He come. And so whoever eats the bread
or drinks the cup of the Lord unworthily, will be answerable for
28 the body and blood of the Lord. And let a man prove himself
29 and thus eat of the bread and drink of the cup. For one who
eats and drinks brings a judgment on himself by eating and
drinking, if he does not discern the Body.[2]

Cf. Ex. xxiv. 8.

Cf. Heb. vi. 6, x. 29.

A divine judgment.

Unworthy communication was a fearful sacrilege, bringing heavy condemnation; and of this evidence was not lacking. It seems that in those days Corinth had been visited by a pestilence, and the Christians were sharing in the general calamity; and here the Apostle sees a divine judgment. It betokened the Lord's displeasure; yet, he recognises, there was mercy in it. For it was no mere judgment; it was a chastisement. Despite their grievous offence the Corinthians were God's children, and it was as His children that He was dealing with them; 'for what son is there whom a father does not chastise?' Their affliction was His stern call to repentance.

Cf. Heb. xii. 7.

30 It is for this reason that many among you are weak and sick
31 and not a few are falling asleep.[3] If we had dealt discerningly
32 with ourselves, we would not have suffered judgment; yet in
suffering the judgment it is chastisement at the Lord's hand
that we are undergoing, that we may not share the world's
condemnation.

The Apostle's charge.

Accordingly he charges them to lay the lesson to heart and realise the ideal of the Love-feast. It was called also 'the Reception'; and this name defined its true character. Each guest should be a kindly host.

33 And so, my brothers, in meeting to eat hospitably receive[4]

[1] Cf. *The Days of His Flesh*, p. 446; *The Feast of the Covenant*, p. 16.

[2] Chrys.: *τουτέστι, μὴ ἐξετάζων, μὴ ἐννοῶν, ὡς χρὴ, τὸ μέγεθος τῶν προκειμένων, μὴ λογιζόμενος τὸν ὄγκον τῆς δωρεᾶς.*

[3] *κοιμῶνται*, only of Christian death (cf. pp. 405 f).

[4] *ἐκδέχεσθε*, not 'wait for' but 'receive,' 'hospitably entertain' (cf. Moulton and Milligan, *Vocab.*), as befitted the occasion—a *δοχή* or 'Reception' (cf. p. 37).

34 one another. If one be hungry, let him eat at home, that your
meeting may not bring a judgment upon you. And as for the
rest of the business, whenever I come, I shall set it in order.

The next question in the rescript concerned Spiritual Gifts; and the difficulty was occasioned by the presence in the Corinthian Church of persons distinguished by special endowments. These were known as 'the Spirituals,'[1] and their endowments were designated 'spiritual gifts' or 'gifts of grace.'[2] In modern parlance 'a spiritual man' is merely one who is spiritually minded, but in ancient days, among Pagans, Jews, and Christians alike, the phrase denoted one possessed by a spirit other than his own, which had entered into him and used him as its instrument, operating through his various faculties. Hence, since there were both good spirits and evil, there were two kinds of possession; and it was not enough that a man should be 'spiritual': it was necessary, especially in a heathen community, to ascertain whether the spirit which inhabited him were an evil spirit or the Spirit of God. 4. Spiritual Gifts.

The Apostle furnishes two criteria. The first is sanity. The Greeks had their prophets, their soothsayers and diviners; and their inspiration was a wild frenzy. The god possessed them, and they uttered his oracles, like the Pythian prophetess, with streaming hair and foaming lips. It was the spirit that spoke, and they knew not what they were saying.[3] It was otherwise with the Christian prophet. Like his Hebrew prototype, he was not the mouthpiece but the messenger of God. The inspiration of the Holy Spirit illumined his mind and quickened his vision. 'The spirit of the prophet was subject to the prophet,' and he declared soberly and sanely[4] the revelation vouchsafed to him. The second test is the ascription of due honour to Jesus. The formula of faith was JESUS IS LORD; and the formula A twofold test. xiv. 32.

[1] *οἱ πνευματικοί*, cf. xiv. 37.

[2] *τὰ πνευματικά*, cf. xiv. 1; *χαρίσματα*, cf. xii. 4, 9, 28, 30, 31.

[3] Cf. Chrys. *In I Ep. ad Cor. Hom.* XXIX. 1, 2, where he quotes Plat. *Apol.* 22 C: *ὥσπερ οἱ θεομάντεις καὶ οἱ χρησμῳδοί· καὶ γὰρ οὗτοι λέγουσι μὲν πολλὰ καὶ καλά, ἴσασι δὲ οὐδὲν ὧν λέγουσι.*

[4] *μετὰ διανοίας νηφούσης καὶ σωφρονούσης καταστάσεως* (Chrys.).

of abjuration, both Jewish and Pagan, JESUS IS ACCURSED;[1] and the Apostle recognises here a test of 'the spirituals.' One who confessed the Lordship of Jesus was inspired by the Holy Spirit; and one who denied it in his frenzied ecstasy was possessed by an evil spirit.[2]

xii. 1 Regarding spiritual gifts, brothers, I do not wish you to
2 ignore the facts. You know that you were once Gentiles,
3 led blindly away to dumb idols.[3] Wherefore I would have
you recognise that no one talking in God's Spirit says JESUS
IS ACCURSED; and no one can say JESUS IS LORD unless in
the Holy Spirit.

Disparity of spiritual gifts.

It was not here, however, that the Corinthian trouble mainly lay, but in the abundance of the gifts of the Spirit and their manifold diversity. Some were high and rare, conferring on their possessors a peculiar prestige, while others, being lowly and commonplace, were little esteemed; and the disparity had provoked arrogance, rivalry, jealousy, and discontent. To this scandal the Apostle addresses himself, and he administers a twofold corrective.

All equally sacred.

First he reminds the Corinthians that all spiritual endowments are gifts of God and operations of His Spirit, and therefore all, whether greater or less, are alike sacred.

4 There are diversities in gifts of grace, but the same Spirit;
5 and there are diversities in ministries, and the same Lord;
6 and there are diversities in operations, but it is the same God
7 that in all cases sets all of them in operation. To each is
8 given the Spirit's manifestation for the general profit. For
to one through the Spirit is given speech of wisdom; to
another speech of knowledge according to the same Spirit;[4]

[1] The test of a Christian in time of persecution was that he should (1) swear by the genius of the Emperor (ὅμοσον τὴν Καίσαρος τύχην) and (2) curse Christ (λοιδόρησον τὸν Χρίστόν). Cf. p. 46, n. 2.

[2] With St. John at Ephesus, in view of the Doketic heresy of Cerinthus, the criterion was recognition of the reality of the Incarnation, the oneness of the human Jesus and the Divine Christ (cf. 1 Jo. iv. 1-3). In the *Didache* it is the Christlikeness of the prophet's behaviour. Cf. ix: οὐ πᾶς δὲ ὁ λαλων ἐν πνεύματι προφήτης ἐστίν, ἀλλ' ἐὰν ἔχῃ τοὺς τρόπους Κυρίου.

[3] This sentence is manifestly corrupt. For ὅτι ὅτε W. H. suggest ὅτι ποτέ (cf. Eph. ii. 11)—a simple and satisfactory emendation.

[4] σοφία, knowledge acquired by discursive reasoning; cf. i. 20, 21, where σοφία is heathen philosophy. γνῶσις, knowledge acquired intuitively by perception of a revelation; cf. Rom. i. 19, 22, where τὸ γνωστὸν τοῦ Θεοῦ is the revelation in Nature which the σοφοί missed. Hence προφητεία, μυστήρια, and γνῶσις are coupled (xiii. 2).

9 to his neighbour, in the same Spirit, faith; to another gifts
10 of healing, all in the one Spirit; to another operations of
miraculous powers; to another prophecy; to another dis-
cernings of spirits; to another various kinds of tongues;[1]
11 and to another interpretation of tongues. But all these are
set in operation by the one and self-same Spirit, diversely
endowing each individual just as He will.

And, furthermore, not only are all spiritual gifts sacred, but all are precious; all are necessary, the least as well as the greatest. All equally necessary.

> 'All service ranks the same with God:
> If now, as formerly he trod
> Paradise, his presence fills
> Our earth, each only as God wills
> Can work—God's puppets, best and worst,
> Are we; there is no last nor first.'[2]

This lesson the Apostle illustrates and enforces by a parable which political philosophers had frequently employed.[3] As the latter had represented the State, so he represents the Church as a corporate unity. She is the Body of Christ, and each Christian is a member. All the members are necessary to the body, and the lack of one, even the humblest, would involve its mutilation. They all share a common life, and if one is injured, its suffering too is common.

12 For, as the body is one and has many members, while all
the members of the body, many as they are, are one body,
13 so also is the Christ. For in one Spirit were we all baptised
into one body, whether Jews or Greeks, whether slaves or
14 free men, and were all given to drink of one Spirit. For
15 the body is not one member but many. If the foot say
'Because I am not a hand, I do not belong to the body,'
16 it does not on this account not belong to the body. And
if the ear say 'Because I am not an eye, I do not belong to
the body,' it does not on this account not belong to the body.
17 If the whole body were an eye, where were the hearing?
18 If the whole were hearing, where were the smelling? But,
as it is, God has placed the members, each one of them,

[1] *E.g.*, prayer, praise, adoration. Cf. xiv. 15, 16.

[2] Browning, *Pippa Passes*.

[3] Cf. the famous instance from Plutarch (*Cor.* 6) in Shak. *Cor.* I. i. 99 ff.

19 in the body as He chose. And if they had all been one
20 member, where had been the body? As it is, there are
21 many members but one body. And the eye cannot say to
the hand 'I have no need of you,' or again the head to the
22 feet 'I have no need of you.' No, much rather it is the
members of the body which are deemed to be naturally
23 the weaker, that are necessary; and what we deem the
more dishonourable members of the body, it is these that
we invest with a fuller honour, and our unseemly members
24 have a fuller seemliness, while our seemly members have
no need of it. Ay, God blended the body by giving a fuller
25 honour to the part which lacks it, that there may be no
cleavage in the body but that the members may be alike
26 concerned for one another. And if one member suffers,
all the members suffer with it; if a member is glorified, all
27 the members rejoice with it. And you are Christ's Body,
and its members individually.

Enumeration of spiritual gifts.

The fact, then, is that, just as there are various functions in the body, so there are various ministries in the Church; and the Apostle enumerates these. First and supreme is Apostleship, which rested on the direct commission of the Lord Jesus Christ; second, Prophecy, which was an inspiration of the Holy Spirit;[1] and third, Teaching, the laborious office of conserving and transmitting the Evangelic Tradition, the yet unwritten record of the Saviour's earthly ministry.[2] Besides these there were lesser ministries; miracle-working,[3] especially healing in the name of the Lord; 'helpings'[4]—the relief of the distressed in soul or body; 'administrations'—the diaconal business of managing the Church's affairs and probably also the judicial office in the Christian law-courts;[5] and finally 'talking with tongues' and the companion office of their interpretation. All these were distinct gifts of grace, and though several might be conjoined, as in the case of Paul himself who was an Apostle and also a Prophet and a Teacher and a worker of miracles, it was impossible that one man should possess them all. And hence it was each man's duty to accept the gift which was bestowed upon him, whether greater or less, and employ it loyally in the service of the Church.

[1] Cf. p. 72. [2] Cf. p. 80. [3] Cf. p. 35.
[4] ἀντιλήμψεις, cf. Ac. xx. 35: δεῖ ἀντιλαμβάνεσθαι τῶν ἀσθενούντων.
[5] Cf. p. 258.

28 And God has placed us all in the Church—first Apostles,
second Prophets, third Teachers; then miraculous powers,
then gifts of healing, helpings, administrations, various kinds
29 of tongues. Are all Apostles? Are all Prophets? Are all
30 Teachers? Have all miraculous powers? Have all gifts of
healing? Do all talk with tongues? Do all interpret?

Yet this in nowise excluded ambition for the higher gifts; indeed, loyalty lay no less in strenuous qualification of oneself for a higher trust than in faithful exercise of one's actual endowments. There was, however, no room for discontent. That was fatal, and there was one sovereign remedy for all the ills which were rife in the unhappy Church of Corinth. Spiritual gifts are precious, but there is a still nobler grace—the grace of Love. Love is best of all—better than tongues, better than prophecy, better than revelation, better than faith, better than miracles. All these belong to the present, and they have no place in Eternity. But Love will endure. Without it all spiritual gifts are poor, and its presence would banish discontent, strife, and jealousy. And so, ere dealing more particularly with the Corinthian situation, the Apostle chants a hymn in praise of Love, 'the Sovereign Way.'[1] The Sovereign Way.

31 Strive zealously for the greater gifts of grace; and
furthermore I point out to you a sovereign way:

xiii. 1 If I talk with the tongues of men, ay, and of angels,[2]
Yet have not Love,
I am become resounding brass or a clanging cymbal.[3]
2 And if I have prophecy
And be acquainted with all the mysteries and all knowledge,
And if I have all faith,
Enough to 'remove mountains,'[4] Cf. Mt. xvii. 20.

[1] Cf. St. Thomas à Kempis' praise of Love (*De Imit. Chr.* III. v. 3-8).

[2] Cf. *Test. of Job*, xlvii, where Job shows his three daughters his miraculous girdle which would carry them into Heaven. When they put it on, the first spoke 'the angelic dialect' (ἀγγελίκῃ διαλέκτῳ), the second that of the principalities (ἀρχῶν), and the third that of the cherubim (τῶν ἐν ὕψει).

[3] A reference to the noisy instruments—tabrets, cymbals, and rattles—employed at heathen festivals. 'A clanging cymbal' was proverbial. Tiberius used to term Apion the grammarian *cymbalum mundi* (Plin. *Nat. Hist.* I, *Epist. Nuncup.*).

[4] A proverb of achieving impossibilities. Cf. *The Days of His Flesh*, p. 397.

Yet have not Love,
I am naught.
3 And if I dole out all my possessions,
And if I surrender my body to be burned,[1]
Yet have not Love,
In nothing am I profited.

4 Love is long-suffering, kind is Love;
There is no jealousy in Love, no vaunting, no windy
5 pride, no unseemliness;
Zech. viii. 17 LXX. She never seeks her own, is never irritated,[2] never 'reckons
her ill';
6 She rejoices not over unrighteousness but rejoices with the
truth;
7 She always keeps counsel,[3] is always trustful, always
hopeful, always patient.

8 Love never fails;
But if there be prophecies, they will be disused,
Or tongues, they will cease,[4]
Or knowledge, it will be disused.
9 For it is but partially that we can know
And partially that we prophesy;
10 But when the perfect is come,
The partial will be disused.

11 When I was a child,
I talked as a child,
I felt as a child,

[1] *ἵνα καυθήσο(ω)μαι* (cf. Dan. iii. 28 LXX; Heb. xi. 34; Sen. *Epist.* XIV), the traditional fate of Barnabas (cf. p. 118). The variant *ἵνα καυχήσωμαι* (approved by W. H.), 'that I may boast,' *i.e.*, in a spirit of ostentation, is probably a copyist's emendation in view of the fact that burning was not the actual manner of the Apostle's martyrdom; and it would be facilitated by his fondness for the verb *καυχᾶσθαι* (cf. i. 29, 31; iii. 21; iv. 7).

[2] *οὐ παροξύνεται*, perhaps a reminiscence of the *παροξυσμός* between Barnabas and himself (cf. Ac. xv. 39).

[3] *πάντα στέγει*, according to the double signification of the verb (cf. n. on 1 Th. iii. 1, p. 160), either (1) 'is proof against everything,' every annoyance (so R.V. marg. 'covereth all things'); or (2) 'keeps in everything,' never betrays a confidence, is not *rimosa*, 'leaky-minded.' Most probably the latter. Cf. Ecclus. viii. 17: *μετὰ μωροῦ μὴ συμβουλεύου, οὐ γὰρ δυνήσεται λόγον στέξαι*, 'Take not counsel with a fool; for he will not be able to conceal the matter.' Luc. *Nav.* 11: *καίτοι ἐτελέσθημεν, ὡς οἶσθα, καὶ στέγειν μεμαθήκαμεν*, 'we were initiated and have learned to keep counsel.' Proverb (cf. Alciphr. *Epist.* I. 13): *Ἀρεοπαγίτου στεγανώτερος*, 'closer than an Areopagite.' 'Areopagita taciturnior dicebatur qui commissum arcanum optime contineret' (Erasm.).

[4] Prophecies and tongues are for the advancement of the Faith, and when it is universal (*ταύτης πανταχοῦ διασπαρείσης*), they will be no longer needed (Chrys.).

I reckoned as a child ;
But now that I have become a man,
I have disused childish things.
12 For meanwhile we look in a mirror and guess at what we see,
But then—face to face ; [1]
Meanwhile it is but partially that I can know,
But then shall I know as fully as I am known.

13 At present there remain Faith, Hope, Love—these three ;
But the greatest of these is Love.

The gift of tongues.

The trouble which had arisen in the Corinthian Church in connection with Spiritual Gifts, had specially to do with 'the gift of tongues' ; and here emerges a problem which is singularly perplexing, and that for two reasons. One is that the gift was a temporary phenomenon. It abounded in the Apostolic Church, and it still lingered, on the testimony of St. Irenæus,[2] in the second century and revived early in the third amid the wild excesses of the Montanist prophets ; [3] but toward the close of the fourth, as St. Chrysostom expressly asserts, it had quite vanished, and the Apostle's allusions to the Corinthian situation puzzled even that master of exegesis. 'The whole passage,' he observes, 'is exceedingly obscure ; and the obscurity is occasioned by our ignorance of the facts and the cessation of happenings which were common in those days but unexampled in our own.' And, moreover, the evidence of the New Testament is extremely bewildering. For one thing, it is surprisingly meagre. The phenomenon was extensively diffused in apostolic days, appearing at Jerusalem, at Cæsarea Stratonis,

Perplexity of the problem: A temporary phenomenon.

Meagreness of the evidence.

Ac. ii. 1-13 ; x. 46 ; xix. 6.

[1] δι' ἐσόπτρου, 'in a mirror.' 'According to the popular conception, a man looks *through* a mirror, inasmuch as he imagines that the form he sees is behind the mirror' (Moulton's Winer, p. 476). The seen and temporal is only the shadow of the Unseen and Eternal, and in our present condition we see only God's reflection in His works (cf. Rom. i. 20) : even in Christ, 'the Visible Image of the Invisible God,' He is 'to our mortal eyes subdued, flesh-veiled.' Hereafter, however, we shall see Him 'face to face,' 'even as He is' (1 Jo. iii. 2) —not His reflection but Himself. Wetstein understands 'through a window of dim glass,' quoting the Rabbinical saying : 'All the prophets saw through dim glass, but Moses through clear glass' (*Jevam.* 49). An attractive interpretation but impossible, since ἔσοπτρον never means anything but 'a mirror' (cf. Ja. i. 23).

[2] V. vi. 1.

[3] Tert. *Adv. Marc.* v. 8 ; Eus. *Hist. Eccl.* v. 16-19.

at Ephesus, and at Corinth; yet it is mentioned by Luke and Paul alone of the sacred writers.[1] Nor is the scantiness of the evidence the sole or the main difficulty. The principal passages are the historian's narrative of the happenings at Jerusalem on the Day of Pentecost and the Apostle's discussion of the Corinthian situation; and these present widely divergent accounts of the nature of the phenomenon.

Its inconsistency.

Luke's account: talking foreign languages. Ac. ii. 4.

According to the former, it was a miraculous faculty of speaking foreign languages; and this gift was bestowed on the Apostles and their companions after their Baptism with the Holy Spirit. 'They began to talk with other tongues as the Spirit gave them utterance'; and the listening multitude, representing no fewer than fifteen diverse nationalities, were amazed to hear a band of Galileans discoursing in their various languages.

The general notion.

If this narrative stood alone, there would be little doubt what the gift of tongues was: it was a miraculous endowment, vouchsafed by the Holy Spirit to those who received Him, whereby they were able to speak strange languages which they had never learned. So it was understood by the sacred historian, and his account was generally accepted by the Christian Fathers[2] and succeeding interpreters. Thus conceiving it, they enlarge upon the practical utility and the spiritual significance of the endowment. It was, they represent, no small furtherance of the Gospel that its first preachers were able, by the grace of the Holy Spirit, to proclaim it to all nations in their own native languages. And it served, moreover, as a prophecy of the unity of the Catholic Church, the gathering together of the scattered children of God into one family. It was indeed nothing less than the undoing of the ancient curse of Babel. 'The punishment of tongues,' says Hugo Grotius, 'scattered men abroad; the gift of tongues regathered the scattered into one people.'

Cf. Gen. xi. 1-9.

[1] The promise that after His departure His disciples would 'talk with new tongues' is ascribed to our Lord in the spurious conclusion of the Second Gospel (Mk. xvi. 17).

[2] Cf. Orig. *In Epist. ad Rom.* I. 13; Chrys. *In I Epist. ad Cor. Hom.* XXIX. 1; Aug. *Enarr. in Ps.* XVIII. 10, *De Civ. Dei*, XVIII. 1; Ambrstr. on 1 Cor. xiv. 14.

This, however, is a doubtful representation, and even in the historian's narrative evidences of its untenability are not lacking. First, that multitude of strangers in Jerusalem at the Feast of Pentecost was composed of Hellenists, devout Jews who had come to worship in the Holy City; and they had no need to be addressed in the languages of their adopted countries. They would probably understand Aramaic, and they would certainly understand the Common Greek, the *lingua franca* of that period.[1] Hence, if the gift of tongues was a linguistic endowment, it was, so far as they were concerned, an unnecessary miracle. And again, it is difficult to conceive how that promiscuous multitude could have been addressed simultaneously in so many languages. There is no indication that the various nationalities formed distinct groups, and the speech of one nationality would have been unintelligible to all the others. There seems no evasion of the difficulty save the theory of St. Gregory of Nazianzus[2] that it was a miracle not of speech but of hearing. The Apostles spoke in their own language, and by the grace of the Holy Spirit their discourse was intelligible to all their diverse audience. So the legend has it that the Spanish missionary, St. Vincent Ferrer, was understood by Greeks, Germans, Sardinians, Hungarians, and other races when he preached to them in Latin or in his mother-tongue as spoken at Valentia.[3] It is, moreover, significant that, on the historian's testimony, the preaching of the Apostles on the Day of Pentecost occasioned not merely perplexity but mockery. It seemed to some of their hearers that they were intoxicated; and this suspicion could hardly have arisen had they merely talked in foreign languages. It would indeed have been natural that their audience should marvel at their proficiency, but it would have been impossible to mistake their speech for drunken babbling. What was unintelligible to one would have been intelligible to others by his side. And, finally, when Peter addressed the astonished assemblage, what was his explanation of the miracle? He declared it a fulfilment of the ancient prophecy: 'I will pour forth of My Spirit upon all flesh; and your sons and your daughters shall

Its untenability.

Joel ii. 28-32.

[1] Cf. p. 7. [2] *Orat.* xli. 15.
[3] Alban Butler, *Lives of the Saints*, Apr. 5.

prophesy, and your young men shall see visions, and your old men shall dream dreams.' This defines the phenomenon: it was not talking foreign languages; it was prophecy—revelation and ecstasy.[1]

Paul's account.

And this accords with our Apostle's references to the situation at Corinth. Here there is no suggestion of speaking foreign languages; indeed the idea is positively precluded.
1 Cor. xiv. 10, 11. When languages are in question, they are termed 'voices.' The word 'tongue' had been appropriated to a special use, and another was required. Again, the Apostle's phrase is 'talking with a tongue' or 'with tongues,' and the historian
Ac. ii. 4. had to amplify this into 'talking with *other* tongues' in order to express the idea of 'talking in foreign languages' as
Vers. 6, 11. distinguished from 'talking in one's own dialect' or 'tongue.' Moreover, the purpose of the gift of tongues, according to the historian, was to render the message intelligible to the audience, and there was no such necessity at Corinth. There indeed the gift of tongues rendered the speakers unintelligible. They needed an interpreter, and his qualification was not knowledge of foreign languages but spiritual understanding.
Cf. xii. 30. Interpretation was not a natural acquirement but a spiritual gift.

The basis of investigation.

This representation must be unreservedly accepted. Not only was it written earlier, but Paul had personal contact with the phenomenon; and his account of it is unintentionally corroborated by the inherent inconsistency of the historian's narrative. The latter's misconception of the gift of tongues evinces how short-lived the phenomenon was. Though it lingered here and there for generations, it was generally no more than a vague memory ere the close of the first century. Its entire disappearance in St. Chrysostom's day rendered it obscure to that master of sacred interpretation; and perhaps our best advantage over him and his

[1] It in nowise impairs the historical trustworthiness of the Book of Acts that it represents the 'tongues' as foreign languages, since this was apparently the prevailing belief, shared even by the gifted persons themselves. At all events it was the idea of the Irvingite prophets. 'Mary Campbell herself expressed her conviction that the tongue given to her was that of the Pelew Islands, which, indeed, was a safe statement, and little likely to be authoritatively disputed: while some other conjectures pointed to the Turkish and Chinese languages as those thus miraculously bestowed' (Oliphant's *Life of Edward Irving*, p. 328).

contemporaries lies in the recognition of the fact that the Pauline references are the surest date for investigation. At the same time we have this further advantage that, since St. Chrysostom's day, the phenomenon has occasionally reappeared; and consideration of these more recent manifestations is helpful toward a just solution of the problem.

Modern instances of the gift of tongues.

The most striking instances of the gift of tongues in modern times are 'the little prophets of the Cevennes' at the close of the seventeenth century and the Irvingites early in the nineteenth; and it is remarkable that these exhibited respectively the phenomenon of the Day of Pentecost as portrayed in the Book of Acts and the ecstasies which convulsed the Corinthian Church.

'The little prophets of the Cevennes.'

The story in the former instance is that among the persecuted Huguenots who found an asylum amid the mountains of the Cevennes after the Revocation of the Edict of Nantes, the spiritual gifts of the Apostolic Church reappeared—miracles of healing, prophecy, and talking with tongues. The last was bestowed mainly on young children, who were stricken with convulsions rendering them insensible to pain. During their seizures they preached and exhorted, not in the Romance patois of their native mountains, but in good French.[1] This instance, however, is hardly apposite. French was no strange language to the 'little prophets.' Their patois was indeed their habitual language, but French was the language of the Huguenot Bible and of Huguenot devotion; and their exhortations were probably nothing else than passages of Scripture and of sermons. Nor is their repetition of these psychologically inexplicable. The words which they had heard and forgotten, lay dormant in their 'subliminal consciousness' and awakened when their 'supraliminal consciousness' was paralysed by sickness. It is a like phenomenon when the forgotten but imperishable past recurs in seasons of mental aberration and is uttered in ravings. Coleridge furnishes a remarkable instance in the case of a young woman some five and twenty years of age and quite illiterate, unable either to read or to write, who, in the delirium of a nervous fever, poured forth Hebrew and

[1] Cf. Heath in *Contemp. Rev.*, Jan. 1886; Bruey, *Histoire du fanatisme*, i. pp. 148 ff.

Greek and Latin in a pompous tone and with such distinct and accurate enunciation that pages of her utterances were taken down. The explanation subsequently emerged. She had been for several years in the service of a clergyman who was accustomed to pace to and fro in a corridor adjoining the kitchen reciting favourite passages of the Scriptures and the Fathers.

The Irvingite movement.

The movement associated with the name of Edward Irving had its origin on the shores of the Firth of Clyde. It too was a revival of the spiritual gifts which abounded in the Apostolic Church, and it began simultaneously, in the month of March 1830, in two humble dwellings—the cottage of Fernicarry at the head of the Gareloch, where Mary Campbell, a young woman of saintly character, lay wasting with consumption; and the home of two unlearned but devout brothers, James and George Macdonald, at Port-Glasgow on the other side of the Firth. It was a time of spiritual awakening and unrest. A persuasion of the imminence of Christ's Return to establish His Millennial Reign had taken possession of a group of prophetic enthusiasts, and had been widely diffused by the apostolic zeal of their leader, Edward Irving; and it was believed that the consummation would be heralded by a recurrence of the spiritual gifts which had accompanied His First Advent. The wild hope had reached the peaceful shores of the Gareloch; and one Sunday evening a company of friends had gathered round Mary Campbell's couch and were praying for the restoration of the gifts, when suddenly she received the gift of tongues and 'broke forth in loud, ecstatic utterances,' continuing for upwards of an hour.

The gift of tongues.

The gift of healing.

It was the gift of healing that was first bestowed on the Macdonalds. Their sister was lying sick, and she prayed for the Baptism of the Spirit. Her request was granted: her weakness was forgotten, and for several hours she poured forth her soul in praise, prayer, and exhortation. She interceded for her brother James, that he too might be endued with power from on high. This request also was granted, and at his command she arose from her couch, healed of her sickness. He wrote to Mary Campbell, informing her what the Lord had done and charging her also to 'rise up and walk.' She obeyed; her disease left her; the gift of tongues remained with her, and she entered on the career of an inspired prophetess.

Erskine of Linlathen's testimony.

The gifts, especially prophecy and tongues, continued and increased; and the fame of so marvellous a manifestation spread abroad and the two dwellings were frequented by curious visitors from near and far. One of these was the wise and saintly Thomas Erskine of Linlathen, who after sojourning six weeks with the Macdonalds published this testimony: 'Whilst I see nothing in Scripture against the reappearance, or rather the continuance, of miraculous gifts in the Church, but a great deal for it, I must further say that I see a great deal of internal evidence in the west country to prove their genuine miraculous character, especially in the speaking with tongues. . . . After witnessing what I have witnessed among these people, I cannot think of any person decidedly condemning them as impostors, without a feeling of great alarm. It is certainly not a thing to be lightly or rashly believed, but neither is it a thing to be lightly or rashly rejected. I believe that it is of God.' [1]

Nature of the gift of tongues: (1) Actual 'possession.'

It is the gift of tongues that is our immediate concern, and the accounts which Erskine and other witnesses have left, are very instructive. Three facts emerge. (1) The experience was regarded by the subjects as an actual possession. 'They declare,' wrote a London solicitor, who visited Port-Glasgow to investigate the phenomenon,[2] 'that their organs of speech are made use of by the Spirit of God; and that they utter that which is given them, and not the expressions of their own conceptions, or their own intention.' 'The voices,' says Erskine,[3] 'struck me very much, perhaps more than the tongues. It was not their loudness, although they were very loud, but they did not sound to me as if they were the voices of the persons speaking; they seemed to be uttered through them by another power.'

(2) A true language.

(2) The tongues were not mere babbling. 'The languages,' says Erskine,[4] 'are distinct, well-inflected, well-compacted languages; they are not random collections of sounds; they are composed of words of various length, with the natural variety,

[1] Erskine, *Letters*, pp. 182 ff.
[2] *Ibid.*, p. 181.
[3] *Ibid.*, p. 186.
[4] *Ibid.*, Appendix VIII, pp. 392 f.

and yet possessing that commonness of character which marks them to be one distinct language. I have heard many people speak gibberish, but this is not gibberish, it is decidedly well-compacted language.' Specimens have been preserved as they were written down by hearers, and one of these runs: 'O Pinitos, Elelastino Halimangotos Dantita, Hampooteni, Farini, Aristos, Ekampros.' (3) The tongues were unintelligible to the speakers unless the additional gift of interpretation was vouchsafed. Erskine relates how on one occasion, after James Macdonald 'had prayed a considerable time, first in English and then in a tongue, the command to pray for an interpretation was brought to his mind, and he repeated "It is written, 'Let him that speaketh in a tongue pray that he may interpret.'" He then prayed for interpretation with great urgency, until he felt that he had secured the answer, and when repeating over the concluding words of what he had spoken in the tongue, which were "*disco capito*," he said, "And this is the interpretation: the shout of a King is among them."'[1]

(3) Unintelligible even to the speakers without interpretation.

Similarity of the Corinthian tongues.

Precisely these are the characteristics of this singular phenomenon as it presented itself in the Corinthian Church. Its reality is attested by its persistence and its spontaneous recurrence in seasons of spiritual excitation; and the question is whether it be possible to ascertain its actual nature and define the principles underlying it.

The gift of prophecy and the gift of tongues.

It is an illuminating fact that the gift of tongues was closely related to the gift of prophecy, and both were con-

[1] *Ibid.*, p. 186. The gift of tongues is claimed by 'the Pentecostal Brethren,' and this testimony has been communicated by a Welsh correspondent (April 10, 1911): 'I have recently heard "the gift of tongues"; and some time ago in Swansea Pentecostal Brethren from Bournemouth held special meetings. They claim to speak and pray in "unknown tongues." During the meeting I heard several of the congregation pray, with the "gift of tongues," in a language unknown to themselves; but, as soon as they ceased praying thus, one of the Pentecostals interpreted. I have heard even some Welshmen in my own district speak with "the gift of tongues." One friend of mine, a Welshman, said that he went to his room one afternoon to pray for a special blessing, and the blessing asked for was "the gift of tongues." Before leaving the room he had the "gift." I have heard the strange language, the pronunciation similar to this:—"*Sacra cara me a prori prori prori*, etc." This friend told me there was no connection whatever between him and the "Pentecostals," and I have every reason to believe his statements.'

comitants of the Baptism of the Spirit. 'When Paul had laid his hands on them, the Holy Spirit came upon them, and they began to talk with tongues and to prophesy.' And what was the difference between prophesying and talking with tongues? It was a difference not of kind but of degree. In its scriptural sense prophecy was not prediction. It was the proclamation of a divine message, the telling of a vision, the glowing testimony of a heart moved by the Holy Spirit. 'One who prophesies,' says the Apostle, 'talks to men edification and encouragement and consolation.' A 'teacher' repeated and expounded the sacred tradition;[1] a 'prophet' uttered a revelation, he preached the word which God had spoken to his own soul. Prophecy was a rapturous outpouring of mingled exhortation, adoration, prayer, and praise; and it would frequently happen that the prophet was overwhelmed by the fulness of his vision of God. The glory was ineffable; language failed him, and, like the Apostle, he could utter nothing but 'inarticulate groanings.' This was 'talking with tongues'—the crying of a surcharged soul.[2] And here lies the difference between 'prophesying' and 'talking with tongues.' Both were the utterance of souls possessed by the Holy Spirit, but in the one case the language was intelligible, in the other it was unintelligible.

Ac. xix. 6; cf. x. 44-46.

1 Cor. xiv. 3.

Rom. viii. 26.

Abuse of spiritual gifts.

'Talking with tongues' was an actual experience, and the Apostle knew it well. 'Thank God,' he says, 'I talk with tongues more than any of you.' It was not the experience that was objectionable in his eyes and that created the scandal at Corinth; it was the abuse of it. His attitude is identical with that of Erskine of Linlathen. Erskine was profoundly impressed by the revival of spiritual gifts in his day. In its initial stage he recognised it as indubitably a divine operation. Yet he never identified himself with the movement. He maintained an attitude of critical though

1 Cor. xiv. 18.

[1] Cf. p. 80.

[2] 'Most frequently,' says Irving (Oliphant's *Life*, p. 329), 'the silence is broken by utterance in a tongue, and this continues for a longer or a shorter period, sometimes occupying only a few words, as it were filling the first gust of sound; sometimes extending to five minutes, or even more, of earnest and deeply-felt discourse, with which the heart and soul of the speaker is manifestly much moved to tears, and sighs, and unutterable groanings, to joy, and mirth, and exultation, and even laughter of the heart.'

reverent observation; and while he never questioned the possibility or the desirability of the restoration of spiritual gifts to the Church, yet in view of subsequent developments, especially in the community which gathered round Edward Irving, he saw reason to revise his judgment of the actual situation. 'We have had great trial,' he wrote at the beginning of the year 1834,[1] 'about the spiritual gifts. The spirit which has been manifested has not been a spirit of union, but of discord. I do not believe that the introduction of these gifts, whatever they may be, has been to draw men simply to God. I think the effect has rather been to lead men to take God, as it were, on trust from others; to be satisfied with God having declared something to another, and not to expect the true fulfilment of the promise, "They shall all be taught of the Lord."' 'God,' he had written a month previously,[2] 'is our all, and having God, we have lost nothing. These gifts are but signs and means of grace; they are not grounds of confidence; they are not necessarily intercourse with God; they are not holiness, nor love, nor patience; they are not Jesus. But surely they shall yet appear, when God has prepared men to receive them.'

Prophecy the best gift.

Precisely similar was the situation which had emerged at Corinth. Emulation had created discord; and the reason was that in their zeal for gifts of grace the Corinthians had forgotten the highest gift of all—the grace of Love. And so the Apostle recalls them to this sovereign way. It would not lessen their zeal for spiritual gifts; it would rather aid them in attaining these. And so in counselling them to pursue Love he bids them also not only strive for spiritual gifts but strive for the highest within their reach. And that
Cf. xii. 28. was the gift of Prophecy. There was indeed, according to the Apostle's classification, one still higher—the grace of Apostleship; but it was a divine vocation beyond the grasp of human ambition, and the gift of Prophecy was the loftiest goal of legitimate aspiration.

xiv. 1 Pursue Love; but strive zealously for spiritual gifts, most of all that you may prophesy.

Limitation

And now he proceeds to deal with that troublous business

[1] *Letters*, p. 206. [2] *Ibid.*, p. 204.

—'talking with tongues.' It was a phase of the gift of Prophecy. It was prophetic rapture, and it was indeed a sacred and solemn experience to be highly and reverently prized. Yet it was subject to this practical limitation, that it was talking to God, and it was unintelligible to men, and thus it could not serve that precious use of Prophecy—the edification of the Church. And therefore Prophecy was a better gift and more to be desired. **of the gift of tongues.**

2 For one who talks with a tongue talks not to men but to
God; for no one understands,[1] but in spirit he talks mysteries;
3 whereas one who prophesies talks to men edification and
4 encouragement and consolation. One who talks with a
tongue edifies himself; whereas one who prophesies edifies
5 the Church. I wish you all talked with tongues, but most of
all that you should prophesy. Greater is one who prophesies
than one who talks with tongues, unless it be that he interprets,
that the Church may receive edification.

Futility of unintelligible speech. Edification is the supreme end of public worship, and its essential condition is intelligibility. The end was served by the presentation of a revelation and the knowledge which it supplied, or by prophecy, or by a Teacher's repetition of the Evangelic Tradition; but what profit could accrue from listening to 'inarticulate groanings'? These were indeed a language, but the meaning was hidden from the hearers. The ecstatic outpouring might be, as Edward Irving claimed,[2] no 'unmeaning gibberish, as the thoughtless and heedless sons of Belial have said,' but 'regularly formed, well-proportioned, deeply-felt discourse, which evidently wanteth *only the ear of him whose native tongue it is*, to make it a very masterpiece of powerful speech'; yet, so long as that ear was wanting, it was, for practical purposes, no better than a foreign language, and it remained unprofitable though it were 'the tongue of the angels.' xiii. 1.

6 This being so, brothers, what shall I profit you if I come to
you talking with tongues and do not talk to you in the way of
revelation or of knowledge[3] or of prophecy or of teaching?
7 In the case of mere lifeless instruments giving sound—say a

[1] ἀκούει, cf. Dt. xxviii. 49 LXX: ἔθνος ὃ οὐκ ἀκούσῃ τῆς φωνῆς αὐτοῦ.
[2] *Life*, p. 329.
[3] Cf. n. on xii. 8.

flute or a harp—if they give no distinction in their notes, how
will it be recognised what it is that is being played on either?
8 Ay, and if a trumpet give an uncertain sound, who will prepare
9 for war? So with you also in using the tongue, if you give
unintelligible speech, how will it be recognised what it is that
Cf. ix. 26. 10 you are talking? You will be talking 'into the air.' There
are, it may be, such and such a number of different languages
11 in the world, and nothing lacks a language. If, then, I do
not know the force of the language, I shall be to the man who
is talking it a foreigner, and the man who is talking it will be a
12 foreigner in my esteem. So with you also, since you are
striving so zealously for spirits, let it be for the Church's
edification that you seek to abound in them.

No 'speaking with tongues' without interpretation.

The remedy was that the gift of tongues should never be exercised in public assembly without interpretation. This was a distinct gift. Sometimes it accompanied the gift of tongues, and then, when his ecstasy passed, the enthusiast could explain the significance of his inspired utterances. But sometimes he lacked it, and then, unless one who possessed it were present to interpret them, they remained unintelligible to speaker and hearers alike. What was this gift of interpretation if the tongues were not, as they were popularly conceived, unknown languages? Articulate speech is not the sole language. It is man's peculiar gift, distinguishing him from the rest of the animals, which express their emotions by inarticulate cries. These cries, however, are also a language, and each has its proper significance. 'With the domesticated dog,' says Darwin,[1] 'we have the bark of eagerness, as in the chase; that of anger, as well as growling; the yelp or howl of despair, as when shut up; the baying at night; the bark of joy, as when starting on a walk with his master; and the very distinct one of demand or supplication, as when wishing for a door or window to be opened.' And, besides the inarticulate speech which is his normal mode of expression, man, in certain moods, 'uses, in common with the lower animals, inarticulate cries to express his meaning, aided by gestures and movements of the muscles of the face. This especially holds good with the more simple and vivid feelings, which are but little

[1] *The Descent of Man*, I. iii.

connected with our higher intelligence. Our cries of pain, fear, surprise, anger, together with their appropriate actions, and the murmur of a mother to her beloved child, are more expressive than any words.' Such cries were the 'inarticulate groanings' of the enthusiasts, and they were a language. They expressed distinct emotions—prayer, praise, adoration, thankfulness; and, meaningless as they were to others, they were intelligible to one who shared the emotions which prompted them. The spiritual expert understood the language of the spirit. He had 'the gift of interpretation.'

13 Wherefore let one who talks with a tongue pray that he
14 may interpret. For, if I pray with a tongue, my spirit
15 prays but my mind is barren. What follows, then? I
will pray with my spirit, but I will pray with my mind
also; I will praise with my spirit, but I will praise with my
16 mind also. Else, if you bless with spirit only, how shall
one who fills the place of the plain man[1] say the Amen at
your thanksgiving, since he does not know what you are
17 saying? Your thanksgiving indeed is beautiful, but your
18 neighbour is not edified. Thank God, I talk with tongues
19 more than any of you; yet in Church I had rather talk five
words with my mind, so as to lodge them in the memories
of others also, than ten thousand words in a tongue.

An appeal to good sense.

And now he appeals to the good sense of the Corinthians. Was there not something childish in those unintelligible raptures? What end did they serve? They availed neither for conversion nor for edification. There was a lesson for the Church in the ancient Scriptures. Long ago, when the scornful men of Jerusalem scoffed at the simplicity of his message, the Prophet had warned them that the Lord would address them after another fashion. The Assyrians would invade Jerusalem, and she would hear their foreign tongue. It was because they would not hearken to His gracious Word that the Lord had spoken to His people in a language which they could not understand; and so, argues the Apostle, was it still. There was no grace in those unintelligible tongues of which the Corinthians were so proud.

[1] ὁ ἰδιώτης, 'the plain man' as distinguished from 'the expert,' ὁ τέχνην ἔχων, whatever his τέχνη—the statesman, the physician, the poet, the soldier, the churchman. Precisely equivalent to 'layman' in its old use. Cf. Sir Philip Sidney, *Sonnet* 74.

They neither edified believers, as prophecy did ; nor did they, like prophecy, convert unbelievers, though they might make the latter wonder and scoff.

20 Brothers, do not prove children in your wits. No, in evil
21 be very babes, but in your wits prove full-grown men. It is
Is. xxviii. 11, 12. written in the Law : 'By men of strange tongues and by lips
of strangers will I talk to this people, and not even thus will
22 they hearken to Me, saith the Lord.'[1] And so tongues serve
as a sign not for those who hold the Faith but for strangers
to it ; whereas prophecy serves not for strangers to the Faith
23 but for those who hold it. If, then, the whole Church assemble
together and all talk with tongues, and there enter plain men
or strangers to the Faith, will they not say that you are mad ?
24 But if all prophesy and there enter a stranger to the Faith or
25 a plain man, he is convicted by all, he is examined by all, the
secrets of his heart become manifest ; and so he will fall on his
Is. xlv. 14. face and worship God, proclaiming that 'God is indeed among
you.'

A practical regulation.

And so the Apostle lays down a practical rule. The plague of the Corinthian Church was the profusion of its spiritual gifts. At each meeting so many were eager to bear a part. One would lead in a psalm of praise, another would recite a lesson from the Evangelic Tradition, another had a revelation to communicate, another would break out with a tongue, while another would furnish the interpretation. It was a scene of wild and unedifying confusion. The worst disorder was occasioned by talking with tongues, and when several enthusiasts talked simultaneously, it was a very babel. And so for the regulation of this exuberant gift the Apostle enjoins that it should never be exercised without interpretation : where there was no interpreter, there should be no talking with tongues. And in any case it should be exercised sparingly—twice or, at the utmost, thrice at a single meeting, and always one at a time.

26 What follows, then, brothers ? Whenever you assemble,
each has a psalm, has a lesson, has a revelation, has a tongue,
has an interpretation : let everything be done with a view to
27 edification. In the case of talking with a tongue : let two or,

[1] Not the LXX rendering, which is here very erroneous. Origen (*Philoc.* IX. 9) says he had found the equivalent of the Apostle's rendering in Aquila's Version.

at the most, three talk at one meeting, and each in turn ; and
28 let one interpret. But if there be no interpreter, let the man
keep silence in Church, and talk to himself and to God.

Regulation of prophecy.

The Apostle is here content with imposing these stringent limitations on the exercise of the gift of tongues, but it would seem that ere long, like Erskine of Linlathen, he adopted a less tolerant attitude and absolutely discountenanced it. At all events 'talking with tongues' has no place in his subsequent enumerations of spiritual gifts. (Cf. Rom. xii. 6-8; Eph. iv. 11, 12.) Meanwhile he allows that it is indeed a divine endowment, but he pronounces the gift of Prophecy better, inasmuch as it served the grand use of spiritual edification. Yet even the gift of Prophecy was liable to abuse, and apparently it was doubly abused at Corinth. It fostered spiritual pride and self-deception. The former displayed itself in the eagerness of the Prophets to thrust themselves forward and proclaim their revelations. Several would rise simultaneously and endeavour to speak each other down. Their inspiration was their pretext : they must utter the divine message. And the result was disorder and strife. Moreover, they were prone to self-deception. Erskine tells how on two occasions he heard James Macdonald prophesy with remarkable power, and afterwards 'discovered the seed of his utterances in the newspapers.'[1] It was not imposture ; it was self-deception. What he had read had lodged in his mind, and he had brooded over it until at length he mistook it for a revelation. 'I thus see,' remarks Erskine, 'how things may come into the mind and remain there, and then come forth as supernatural utterances, although their origin be quite natural.' It appears that similar deceptions had chanced at Corinth, demonstrating the necessity of 'discerning' the prophetic spirits.[2]

29 And as for Prophets : let two or three talk, and let the
30 others discern. And if a revelation be made to another sitting
31 by, let the first keep silence. For you can all prophesy one

[1] *Letters*, p. 209. Several of Irving's followers ultimately recognised and confessed that their inspiration had been a delusion. Cf. *Life*, pp. 323, 357 f., 364.

[2] Irving's test of the prophets was twofold : 'blameless walk and conversation' and 'nothing contrary to sound doctrine, but everything for edification, exhortation, and comfort' (*Life*, p. 319).

32 by one, that all may learn and all be encouraged. And Pro-
33 phets' spirits are subject to the Prophets; for God is not
a God of disorder but a God of peace, as He is in all the
churches of His saints.[1]

Women prophesying.

Here arose the question of the legitimacy of women prophesying. There had been prophetesses in ancient Israel, and there were prophetesses also in the Apostolic Church like the four daughters of Philip the Evangelist. The gift was a divine endowment, and its possession attested its legitimacy; and Paul, recognising as he did the oneness of male and female in Christ Jesus, would have been the last to 'make channels for God's Spirit, as men make channels for the water-courses, and say, "Flow here, but flow not there."' He acknowledged the legitimacy of women prophesying, but in view of the scandals which he has already censured in dealing with the question of the veil,[2] he prohibits them from public exercise of the gift.

Ac. xxi. 9.

Gal. iii. 28.

34 Let the women keep silence in the Churches; for it is not
permitted them to talk. No, let them be subject, as the Law
35 also says. And if they wish to learn anything, let them
question their own husbands at home. For it is disgraceful
for a woman to talk in Church.

Cf. Gen. iii. 16.

Catholic usage.

Cf. xi. 16.

The Apostle knew by experience how wilful the Corinthians were, and he reminds them once more of the deference due to catholic custom. The Corinthian Church was not Christendom but merely a Christian community, and they had no right to practise innovations at their own discretion. They must reverence the Lord's authority and the *consensus fidelium.*

36 Was it from you that the Word of God went forth, or did
37 it reach to you alone? If any one fancies he is a prophet or
a spiritual, let him fully recognise that what I am writing to
38 you is the Lord's commandment; and if any one ignores it,
he is to be ignored.[3]

[1] This last clause is otherwise construed (1) with ver. 31, vers. 32, 33*a* being parenthetical (W. H.); (2) with ver. 34 (Tisch.)—'as in all the churches of the saints, let the woman keep silence in your churches.'

[2] Cf. p. 282.

[3] ἀγνοεῖται, pres. (cf. Mt. xxiv. 40, xxvi. 2), 'this is his doom—to be ignored.' For the variant ἀγνοείτω, 'if any one ignores it, let him ignore it,' cf. vii. 15; Rev. xxii. 11.

39 And so, my brothers, be zealous for prophesying and do
40 not hinder talking with tongues; but let everything be done
in a seemly and orderly fashion.

5. The Resurrection of the Body.

The next question which the Corinthian rescript submitted concerned the resurrection of the body; and it is not surprising that this problem should have been debated in a Gentile community. The constant burden of the Apostle's preaching was twofold: the Lord's Death and His Resurrection with its corollary, the resurrection of believers; (Cf. Ac. xvii. 3.) and while the former presented a special difficulty to Jewish minds with their secular ideal of the Messiah as a victorious King, it was the latter that chiefly offended the philosophic Greeks. (Cf. 1 Cor. i. 23.) To the Apostle's audience in the Court of the Areiopagos it had seemed a grotesque impossibility, and it had been greeted with contemptuous ridicule; (Ac. xvii. 32.) and a like sentiment prevailed at Corinth. It was a postulate of ancient philosophy that matter is essentially and necessarily evil; and hence impurity is inseparable from our present condition. The mortal body is the prison-house of the immortal spirit, and only when it attains disembodiment will the latter escape corruption. Meanwhile impurity is inevitable, and it has no moral significance. The Apostle had dealt with this mischievous theory in his first letter.[1] He had insisted on the sanctification of soul and body alike, since the body is no perishing vesture one day to be cast aside. (1 Cor. vi. 12-20.) It was worn by the Lord in the days of His flesh, and even as His body was raised by the power of God, so will ours.

The Resurrection of the Lord.

His doctrine had excited a lively controversy in the Corinthian Church. The idea of the resurrection of the body presented insuperable difficulties to the Greek intellect, and these were submitted to the Apostle. It was indeed a profound problem, and his argument ranks as his noblest achievement. It is a truly prophetic vision, and the subsequent progress of human thought has only served to illumine it and discover more of its inexhaustible fulness. He begins with a reaffirmation of the historic fact of the Resurrection of the Lord and a repetition of the Evangelic Tradition which he had already delivered to the Corinthian Church—the eye-

[1] Cf. p. 236.

witnesses' testimonies to the manifestations of the Risen Lord during the forty days betwixt His Resurrection and His Ascension,[1] besides his personal testimony to the manifestation which had been vouchsafed to himself on the road to Damascus.

xv. 1 I recall to you, brothers, the Gospel which I preached
to you, which also you received, in which also you stand
2 firm, through which also you are being saved—the very
terms in which I preached it to you, presuming you hold it
3 fast—unless it be that your faith was all to no purpose. I
delivered to you primarily [2] the tradition which I had also
received: Christ died for our sins according to the Scrip-
4 tures, and He was buried, and He has been raised [3] on the
5 third day according to the Scriptures; and He appeared
6 to Cephas, then to the Twelve; next He appeared to
upwards of five hundred brothers all at once, of whom
the greater number remain to this day while some have
7 gone to their rest; next He appeared to James, then to all
8 the Apostles. Last of all, He appeared also to me, as it
9 were, the poor weakling.[4] For I am the least of the
Apostles; I am not fit to be called an Apostle, inasmuch
10 as I persecuted the Church of God. But by God's grace
I am what I am. And the grace which He showed me
proved no empty thing. No, I toiled more abundantly
than any of them; yet it was not I but the grace of God
11 aiding me. Whether, then, it be I or they, this is the
message we are proclaiming and this the faith you embraced.

No resurrection, no salvation.

It does not appear that the Corinthians questioned the Resurrection of the Lord. It was merely the resurrection of believers that they denied; but they could not stop there.

[1] Cf. *The Days of His Flesh*, p. 520.

[2] ἐν πρώτοις, not 'at the beginning of my teaching' (Chrys.: ἐξ ἀρχῆς, οὐ νῦν), but 'in the place of primary importance' (Grot.: 'inter præcipua quæ credere debetis').

[3] ἐγήγερται, perf., since His Resurrection is not merely an historic fact (ἠγέρθη) but a present and abiding force.

[4] ἔκτρωμα (cf. LXX Num. xii. 12; Job iii. 16; Eccl. vi. 3), 'an abortion' or 'premature birth,' and so a stunted weakling. The idea, as explained in next ver., is twofold: (1) the *irregularity*, not the *lateness*, of Paul's conversion; (2) the imperfection of his growth: he was, in his own estimation, the weakling of the apostolic brotherhood. He was always ready to confess this. It was not the quality but the reality of his apostleship that he asserted, and the necessity of asserting it was distasteful to him. His achievements were not his own but triumphs of God's grace through his poor instrumentality.

Their contention that 'there was no such thing as a resurrection of the dead' ruled out not merely the resurrection of believers but the Resurrection of Christ as well; and see what would then ensue. Not only would the testimony of the Apostles be discredited, but the faith of their converts would be betrayed. Salvation lay in union with Christ—identification with Him in His Death, His Burial, His Resurrection, and His Life; and if He had never been raised, their hope of salvation was belied, and their expectation of reunion with their beloved dead was an idle dream. They were the pitiable dupes of a fond delusion.

Cf. Rom. vi. 2-11.

12 Now if it is proclaimed that that Christ has been raised from
the dead, how is it that some among you are saying that
13 'there is no such thing as a resurrection of the dead'? If
'there is no such thing as a resurrection of the dead,' neither
14 has Christ been raised; and if Christ has not been raised,
it turns out that the message we proclaim is an empty thing,
15 your faith also is an empty thing. Yes, and we are being
found false witnesses of God, because we bore witness against
God that He raised Christ; and He did not raise Him, if
16 indeed it turns out that the dead are not raised. For, if the
17 dead are not raised, neither has Christ been raised; and if
Christ has not been raised, your faith is futile: you are still
18 in your sins. It turns out also that those who have gone
19 to their rest in Christ, have perished. If it be for this life
that we have set our hope in Christ, and that be all, we are
the most pitiable of mankind.

It was an appalling issue, and the Apostle dismisses it and turns with exultant relief to the glorious reality. Christ has been raised, and His Resurrection is the prophecy and pledge not only of the future resurrection of all who are united to Him but of the final triumph of God's redemptive purpose. He is the new head of humanity. Adam was the original head, and by the profound principle which links the generations and makes each the heir of the last, his sin became the heritage of the race. And, conversely, since Christ is the new head of humanity, His grace flows down the ages like a healing stream; nor will its beneficent operation cease until evil has been purged from the Universe and God the Father reigns in undisputed dominion.

The glorious reality.

20 But, as it is, Christ has been raised from the dead, the
21 first-fruits of those who have gone to rest. For, since it
is through a man that there is death, it is also through a
22 man that there is a resurrection of the dead. For, just as
in Adam all die, so also in Christ all shall be made live.
23 But each in the proper order: Christ the first-fruits; next
24 Christ's people at His Advent; then the end, when He
surrenders the Kingdom to the God and Father, when He
shall have crushed every principality and every authority
25 and power. For He must be King until 'He put all things
26 under His feet.' The last enemy to be crushed is death;
27 for 'He has subjected all things under His feet.' And
when He shall say: 'All things have been subjected'
(plainly with the exception of Him who subjected them
28 all to Him)—when they shall all be subjected to Him, then
the Son shall Himself also be subjected to Him who subjected them all to Him, that God may be all in all.

Pss. viii. 6, cx. 1.

The issues at stake.

Such was the Christian faith in the Resurrection; and the Apostle proceeds to remind his converts how precious it was to their own hearts, and what sacred issues depended on it. Their dearest affections were at stake. Those were sorrowful days at Corinth. A pestilence had visited the city,[1] and death was busy in her dwellings. It was the call of God, and many had hearkened to it. Unbelieving husbands or wives, bereaved of their beloved, turned in their desolation to the Saviour whom they had hitherto rejected and, moved by the hope of a blessed reunion, confessed their faith in the Gospel. They were 'baptised for the sake of their dead.' If there was 'no such thing as a resurrection,' that tender hope was a fond delusion.

And there was more at stake. The Corinthian Christians were bearing constant sacrifice and suffering for their Lord. The Apostle reminds them of the persecutions which he had endured in their midst and those which he had endured and was still enduring at Ephesus. He was facing death daily in the hope of winning the glory of the Resurrection. If that hope were a dream, then his sacrifices and theirs were unavailing, and it were better to embrace the Epicurean philosophy and snatch the fleeting pleasures of the passing hour.

[1] Cf. p. 288.

29 Else, what will they do who are baptised for the sake of
their dead? [1] If the dead are not raised at all, why are they
30 actually baptised for their sake? Why, too, are we running
31 risks every hour? Daily I am facing death—ay, by that Cf. 2 Cor.
boasting in you, brothers, which is mine in Christ Jesus our i. 8.
32 Lord. If it was from merely human motives that I fought
with wild beasts at Ephesus,[2] what am I the better for it?
If the dead are not raised, 'let us eat and drink, for on the Is. xxii. 13.
morrow we die.' [3]

A warning against libertinism.

The Apostle had a purpose in quoting that Epicurean maxim. Too many of the Corinthians were actually prac-

[1] A much vexed passage. A mere enumeration of all the various interpretations would require, says Bengel, a dissertation. Cf. collection in Poole's *Synops. Crit.* occupying four folio pages. The clue to the Apostle's meaning lies in ver. 18: the hope of reunion in Heaven with their beloved dead who had 'gone to their rest in Christ,' had induced some, hitherto unbelieving, to profess faith and be baptised. Of other interpretations suffice it to indicate three which have had a long and wide vogue: 1. *Vicarium baptisma*, 'Vicarious Baptism' (Ambrstr., Grot.). Believers submitted themselves to the Sacrament in name of their unbaptised dead, that these might rank as Christians and share in the felicity of the Resurrection. The practice certainly prevailed in the time of Tertullian (cf. *De Resurr. Carn.* 48; *Adv. Marc.* v. 10), but only, it would seem, among heretics—the Marcionites (cf. Chrys.) and the Cerinthians (cf. Epiphan. *Hær.* xxviii. 7). There is, however, no evidence that it was known at Corinth, and it probably originated in a misunderstanding of the text. 2. After pouring scorn on that heretical practice Chrys. propounds his own view. He explains the passage by the fashion obtaining in his time at the administration of Baptism: the catechumen repeated the article of the Creed 'I believe in the Resurrection of the Dead,' and on the strength of this confession of his faith he was then immersed in token of his burial and resurrection with Christ. Thus 'baptism for the dead' was supposed to mean 'baptism on the ground of faith in the resurrection of the dead.' 3. *Baptisma clinicorum*, 'Death-bed Baptism,' administered on the approach of death to those who had postponed the observance of the Sacrament for fear of mortal sin (Epiphan., Calv., Beng.). But (1) *ὑπὲρ τῶν νεκρῶν* cannot mean 'on the verge of death,' *jam morituri*; and (2) it was not until a later period that the custom of delaying Baptism arose (cf. Append. VI).

[2] The same metaphor occurs in iv. 9 (cf. p. 254). *θηριομαχεῖν* is certainly figurative. It is incredible that Paul, a Roman citizen, should actually have fought in the circus as a *bestiarius*. Cf. Ignat. *Rom.* v, where the saint, on his way to martyrdom at Rome, says he is 'fighting with wild beasts all the while,' *ἐνδεδεμένος δέκα λεοπάρδοις*, meaning his brutal guards. 'Wild beasts' was a common metaphor for savage men (cf. Pompey in Appian, II. ix. 61: *οἵοις θηρίοις μαχόμεθα*. Ps. xxii. 12, 13), especially the mob or tyrants (cf. Philostr. *Vit. Apoll.* IV. 38). For a graphic picture of *θηριομαχία* cf. *Act. Paul. et Thecl.* 33 ff.; *Martyr. Polyc.* ii-iv.

[3] 'Epicureorum vox' (Wetstein, who quotes classical parallels). Cf. Hor. *Od.* I. xi. 7, 8.

tising it. They reasoned from the philosophical principle of the essential evil of matter that, since the body was a perishing thing, they might indulge its appetites as they would. It was a mischievous delusion, and it came of their converse with pagan thought and pagan manners, exemplifying that saying of the Greek poet:[1] 'Ill company corrupts good characters.' In truth their doubt of the Resurrection was moral as well as intellectual.

33 Be not deceived. 'Ill company corrupts good characters.'
34 Awake from your debauch to righteousness, and give over
sinning; for there are some who have no recognition of God.
It is to move you to shame that I am talking.

Two objections:

And now the Apostle addresses himself to a consideration of the intellectual problem of the Resurrection of the Body. Two difficulties had presented themselves to the minds of the Corinthians.

35 But some one will say: 'How are the dead raised? And
with what sort of body do they come?'

(1) The dissolution of the body.

These are difficulties which have been felt all down the ages and are still as vital as ever. The first is presented by the experience of our mortal bodies after death. The early Christians abhorred the pagan fashion of burning their dead in funeral pyres and preserving the ashes in urns. The body was sacred in their eyes, and they committed it reverently to the earth.[2] Reverence was their sole motive, but the pagans imputed to them a fond solicitude to preserve the body intact until it should be reanimated at the Resurrection; and it is told that during the persecution in the reign of the Emperor Verus they outraged the bodies of the martyrs at Lyons and Vienne, and then burned them and cast the ashes into the river Rhone, that they might have no hope of resurrection. 'Now let us see,' they jeered, 'if they will rise again, and if their God can succour them and snatch them out of our hands.'[3] It would indeed have been a just taunt had the Christians entertained that notion. For when the

[1] Cf. p. 24.
[2] Cf. Minuc. Fel. *Oct.* 11, 34.
[3] Eus. *Hist. Eccl.* v. 1 (*ad fin.*).

body is committed to the earth, it does not lie there 'with meek hands folded on its breast,' awaiting the Resurrection-morning. It decays and turns to dust. The sum of matter is definite and constant, and our bodies are composed of the common stuff; and even as the leaves of autumn do not perish when they wither and fall, but are cast into Nature's alembic, and the mantle which arrays her each spring-time is no new garment but the old fabric refashioned, rewoven, and dyed with fresh colours, so our bodies when they die are resolved into their elements. They 'melt into the general mass of nature, to be recompounded in the other forms with which she daily supplies those which daily disappear, and return under different forms—the watery particles to streams and showers, the earthly parts to enrich their mother earth, the airy portions to wanton in the breeze, and those of fire to supply the blaze of Aldebaran and his brethren.' And how, then, are the dead raised? Can the dispersed elements ever be re-collected and redintegrated? These bodies which are ours now, have served other uses in the bygone ages, and they will serve yet others in the ages to come; and at the Resurrection where will they be and to whom will they belong?

(2) Unsuitability of a material body to a spiritual world.

Nor is this the only difficulty. If the dead are raised, 'with what sort of body do they come?' The Eternal World is a spiritual realm, and what place will there be there for material bodies? 'Flesh and blood,' said the Corinthians, 'cannot inherit the Kingdom of God, nor does corruption inherit incorruption.' The Anthropomorphites solved the problem by materialising the spiritual world. They read in the Scriptures of the image of God, His face, His eyes and ears and hands and feet; and taking this language literally they accounted the doctrine of His incorporeality a blasphemy and anathematised the books of Origen where it was taught.[1] It is told of Serapion, that venerable monk of the Nitrian Desert, that when the doctrine was presented to him, he wept and wailed and cast himself on the ground. 'Woe is me!' he cried. 'They have taken away from me my God; and I have none to hold now, nor know I any longer

[1] Cf. Socr. *Eccl. Hist.* VI. 7; Aug. *Contra Epist. Manich.* 25.

whom to adore or address.'[1] And so precisely reasoned the Corinthians from their diverse point of view. As Serapion saw no place in the Eternal World for an incorporeal God, so they saw none for a material body.

Analogy of seed and harvest.

These are no frivolous objections. The difficulties were very real, and they were propounded in all seriousness; yet how does the Apostle receive them? 'Senseless man!' he exclaims; and it seems a sorry beginning. But consider what the epithet means. It is well defined by the use which Socrates makes of it when, in the course of his theistic argument, he applies it to a statue.[2] A sculptor's noblest creation is but 'a senseless image,' seeing nothing, hearing nothing, understanding nothing. And this is the idea which leaped into the Apostle's mind when those doubting questions were presented to him. 'Senseless man!' he cries; 'unperceiving as an inanimate statue! open your eyes to the wonders which surround you. Look at the fields and see the seed cast into the ground and springing up in a rich and golden harvest: there is the miracle of the Resurrection enacted before your eyes.' The seed dies, but it dies that it may live again, and live more abundantly. For death is not merely, in St. Bernard's phrase, 'the gate of life'; it is the pathway to an ampler and nobler life.

> 36 Senseless man! what you yourself sow is not made live
> 37 unless it die. And what you sow—it is not the body which
> is to come into being that you sow, but a bare grain of
> 38 wheat, perchance, or some of the other sorts; and God
> gives it a body as He has chosen, and each of the seeds its
> proper body.

Varieties of body.

But will this suffice? The harvest is no less material than the seed, and will the nobler body which will spring from it be less material than the mortal body or better fitted to inherit the Kingdom of God? Consider, argues the Apostle, what 'body' is. It is a larger term than 'flesh.' There are indeed bodies of flesh, but even these are widely diverse. There is human flesh, and there is the flesh of beast and bird

[1] Cassian. *Collat. Patr. Scet.* x. 2.

[2] Xen. *Mem.* I. iv. 4: πότερά σοι δοκοῦσι οἱ ἀπεργαζόμενοι εἴδωλα ἄφρονά τε καὶ ἀκίνητα ἀξιοθαυμαστότεροι εἶναι ἢ οἱ ῷ ἔμφρονά τε καὶ ἐνεργά;

and fish; and these are all different, yet they are all flesh. And they are all bodies, but they are not the only sorts of body. There are heavenly bodies as well as earthly bodies, and the heavenly bodies are not bodies of flesh. And, moreover, like the earthly bodies, they are of different sorts. Sun, moon, and stars have each a peculiar glory.

39 Every flesh is not the same flesh, but men's is one kind,
cattle's flesh another, fowls' flesh another, and fishes' another.
40 And there are heavenly bodies and earthly bodies, but the
glory of the heavenly is of one sort, and that of the earthly
41 of another. There is one glory of sun, and another glory of
moon, and another glory of stars; for star differs from star in
glory.

The animal body and the spiritual body.

'Flesh,' then, and 'body' are not synonymous terms; and while flesh cannot inherit the Kingdom of God, it by no means follows that body cannot. And hence the Apostle carries forward the argument. He distinguishes between 'animal bodies' and 'spiritual bodies.' The former are bodies of flesh, and they are earthly and cannot inherit the Kingdom of God; but the latter are heavenly bodies, and they can. 'In the heavenly,' says St. Augustine,[1] 'there is no flesh, but bodies simple and lucid, which the Apostle styles "spiritual," while others call them "ethereal."' And, furthermore, there is a relation betwixt the two. The animal body is in truth the rough cast of the spiritual body. There is, 'as it were, a brain within the brain, a body within the body, something like that which the Orientals have for ages spoken of as the "Astral Body"';[2] and in due season the scaffolding will be taken down, 'this muddy vesture of decay' will fall off, and the spiritual body will emerge purged of its grossness and fit to inherit the Kingdom of God. Our bodies meanwhile are only in the making. Their evolution began when 'the Lord God formed man of the dust of the ground, (Gen. ii. 7.) and breathed into his nostrils the breath of life'; and the agelong process will be complete when the Lord Jesus Christ has 'refashioned the body of our humiliation into conformity (Phil. iii. 21.) with the body of his glory,' and we wear no longer 'the

[1] *De Fid. et Symb.* 24.
[2] McConnell, *Evol. of Immort.*, p. 166.

image of the earthly man' but 'the image of the Heavenly Man.'[1] And the Resurrection is the achievement of this consummation.

42 Thus also the resurrection of the dead. It is sown in cor-
43 ruption, it is raised in incorruption; it is sown in dishonour,
it is raised in glory; it is sown in weakness, it is raised in
44 power; it is sown an animal[2] body, it is raised a spiritual.
45 If there is an animal body, there is also a spiritual. Thus also
Gen. ii. 7. it is written: 'The first man Adam became a living soul':
46 the last Adam is become a life-giving spirit. But what comes
first is not the spiritual but the animal; then comes the
47 spiritual. The first was 'a man formed of the dust of the
48 ground'; the second is a Man from Heaven. What the man
formed of the dust was, that also are the men formed of the
dust; and what the Heavenly Man is, this also are the heavenly
Gen. v. 3. 49 men. And as we wore the image of the man formed of the
dust, we shall wear[3] also the image of the Heavenly Man.

Final glorification of living and dead.

Thus it was a just contention that 'flesh and blood cannot inherit the Kingdom of God,' but it was no disproof of the Resurrection of the Body. For when the body is raised, it will be no longer flesh and blood but a spiritual body. And this, adds the Apostle, is a sure prospect; for it is no mere speculation: it is 'a mystery.' And, as he employed the term, 'a mystery' signifies not a hidden truth but a truth once hidden and now revealed.[4] Such a truth was the Resurrection of the Body. In bygone ages it had been a vague dream, a yearning inspired by the heart's rebellion against dissolution and disembodiment; but the Resurrection of Christ had triumphantly confirmed it. He had been raised from the dead, 'the first-fruits of those who have gone to rest.' (Cf. vers. 20-23.) One with Him in His Death and Burial, they will at His Advent share also His Resurrection and Glorification. Some three and a half years previously the Thessalonians, uninstructed as yet in the hope of the Resurrection, had vexed themselves with the question whether their friends who had already gone to rest would be excluded from the (1 Th. iv. 13-18.)

[1] Cf. p. 52.
[2] Cf. p. 249.
[3] Though φορέσωμεν, 'let us wear,' is more strongly supported, φορέσομεν, 'we shall wear,' is certainly authentic. The exhortation is impossible, since the resurrection of the body is God's work. Such itacism is frequent. Cf. Rom. v. 1.
[4] Cf. p. 440.

triumph of the Second Advent, which they regarded as imminent; and the Apostle had reassured them by telling them that the appearance of the Lord would be the signal for the resurrection of all who had died in faith.[1] And now it seems that a converse misgiving had assailed the minds of the Corinthians. They too believed in the imminence of the Second Advent; and since it is through death and resurrection that the corruptible body attains incorruption, they wondered what would happen to those who survived until the Lord's Appearing and never died. Would their bodies remain mortal and corruptible, unfit to inherit the Kingdom of God? The Apostle answers by assuring them that all, whether asleep or awake, would share the glorious transformation.

50 And this I admit, brothers, that 'flesh and blood cannot
inherit the Kingdom of God, nor does corruption inherit
51 incorruption.' Look you, it is a mystery that I am telling you.
52 We shall not all be laid to rest, but we shall all be changed, in
a moment, in the twinkle of an eye, at the last trumpet. For Cf. 1 Th.
the trumpet will sound, and the dead will be raised incor- iv. 16.
53 ruptible, and we shall be changed. For this that is corruptible
must clothe itself with incorruption, and this that is mortal
54 clothe itself with immortality. And when this that is corruptible has clothed itself with incorruption and this that is
mortal has clothed itself with immortality, then will come
to pass the word that is written: 'Death is swallowed up in Is. xxv. 8;
55 victory.' 'Where, death, is thy victory? where, death, is Hos. xiii.
56 thy sting?' The sting of death is sin, and the power of sin 14.
57 is the Law; but thanks to God who gives us the victory
through our Lord Jesus Christ.
58 And so, my beloved brothers, prove steadfast, immovable,
abounding in the work of the Lord always, knowing that your
toil is no empty thing in the Lord.

3. Collection for the poor at Jerusalem.

The last question in the rescript concerned the Gentile collection on behalf of the poor Christians at Jerusalem.[2] The scheme had been submitted to the Corinthians by Titus and the colleague whom the Church of Antioch had associated with him in the management of the business,[3] and it had in the first instance been well received; but amid the subsequent dissension it had encountered opposition. Already,

[1] Cf. p. 163. [2] Cf. p. 223. [3] Cf. p. 234.

it would seem, there were mutterings of a calumny which was afterwards unblushingly alleged—that in his zeal for the poor Paul had a dishonest end in view, and under the pretext of charity was seeking his own enrichment; and apparently these had reached his ears. The rescript, however, made no mention of the odious insinuation, raising merely a question of procedure—whether the Church should proceed immediately with the collection or await his arrival. His answer is that the Corinthians should adopt the method which he had instituted in the Churches of Galatia, and lay by each Lord's Day as much as they could afford of their week's earnings. There was a double advantage in this method: not only would a gradual accumulation prove less burdensome but it would yield a better result.[1] The collection would, moreover, be ready when he arrived, and it could be at once forwarded to its destination. And, he adds significantly, he would not himself undertake its conveyance thither. They must appoint deputies, and these he would furnish with a letter of credit to the Church at Jerusalem; or else, he says, evidently to incite their liberality, if the contributions proved sufficiently generous, he would, instead of furnishing the deputies with a letter of credit, accompany them in person and introduce them to the Church.

xvi. 1 Regarding the collection for the saints: Follow the order
2 which I prescribed to the Churches of Galatia. Every
First Day of the Week let each of you lay by him in store
as he may be prospered, that, when I come, there may
3 then be no making of collections. And when I arrive, the
persons whom you approve I shall send with a letter of
4 credit [2] to convey your benefaction to Jerusalem. If,
however, it be worth my going too, they will go in my
company.

The Apostle's plans.

And now the letter closes with various personal concerns. First, the Apostle explains his plans for the future. He had intended leaving Ephesus at an early date and sailing

[1] Cf. Ambrstr.: 'quia quod paulatim colligitur, nec grave est, et invenitur multum.'

[2] Literally 'letters' (δι' ἐπιστολῶν); but it is unlikely that each of the deputies would be furnished with a letter, and ἐπιστολαί was used of a single letter. Cf. Lightfoot, *Phil.* pp. 140 ff.

direct to Corinth; but this purpose had been overruled by the emergence at once of large opportunities and of corresponding difficulties which required his presence yet a while in Asia. In truth there was another reason for delay. Had he proceeded forthwith to Corinth, he must have dealt sternly with the Church; and his hope was that, if he postponed his visit, wiser counsels would in the interval prevail, and he would then be absolved from that hateful necessity. This motive, however, he meanwhile conceals and simply intimates his intention of remaining at Ephesus until Pentecost of next year and then travelling overland through Macedonia. He would thus reach Corinth in the autumn of 56, and perhaps he might be able to spend the winter there.

Cf. 2 Cor. i. 23-ii. i.

5 I shall come to you after travelling through Macedonia;
6 for through Macedonia I am to travel. And with you, perhaps,
I shall make a stay or even spend the winter, that you may
7 send me on my way wherever I may be going. For I do
not wish to pay you just now merely a passing visit: I hope
8 to stay some time with you, if the Lord permit. I shall,
9 however, stay on at Ephesus until Pentecost; for a wide door
for active work has opened to me, and there are many opposing.

Recommendation of Timothy.

Another matter he mentions with peculiar solicitude. Timothy and his party were on their way to Corinth by the overland route through Macedonia, and Paul reckoned that their arrival would synchronise with the delivery of his letter.[1] He apprehended that the Corinthians might make it a grievance that he had sent them so youthful an ambassador on so delicate an errand, and he bespeaks for him a kindly reception. He was indeed young, but he was, as they knew by experience, a true comrade of the Apostle. It would have been well that a more experienced delegate should have been sent, and Paul had been anxious that Apollos should undertake the office; but he had declined it. The unpleasant experience which had driven him from Corinth was fresh in his remembrance, and he judged, perhaps wisely, that his presence there would meanwhile be inopportune. So Timothy was being sent, and they must receive him graciously.

[1] Cf. p. 260.

The Apostle was anxiously awaiting the report which he and his companions would bring back from Corinth.

10 If Timothy comes, see to it that there is nothing to affright
him in his intercourse with you; for he is doing the Lord's
11 work like myself. Therefore let no one set him at naught.
Send him on his way in peace, that he may come to me; for
12 I am expecting him and the brothers with him. Regarding
our brother Apollos, I repeatedly besought him to go to you
with the brothers, and he would on no account go at present.
He will go, however, whenever it is opportune.

Appreciation of the Corinthian deputies.

He pleads with them to rally their faith and love. Their letter and the personal statements of their three messengers had gladdened him; and he makes special mention of his friend Stephanas, who with his household had been steadfastly loyal during the trouble; and begs them to be guided by that example.

13 Be vigilant: stand firm in the Faith; play the man;
14, 15 be strong. Let all that you do be done in love. I beseech
you, brothers—you know the household of Stephanas, how
they are the first-fruits of Achaia, and they enlisted in the
16 service of the saints—that you on your part enlist under
men of this sort and under everyone who shares their
17 work and toils hard. It is a joy to me that Stephanas and
Fortunatus and Achaicus have come: the service which
18 you could not render me, they have made up. They have
refreshed my spirit and yours too. Recognise the full
worth of men of their sort.

Greetings.

This ends the letter, and here the customary greetings are entered. The first is a fraternal greeting to the church of Corinth from the churches of Asia, not merely the church of Ephesus but all the churches of the Province; and this indicates how protracted had been the stay of the Corinthian delegates and how widespread was the interest which their visit had created. The second is a greeting from Aquila and Prisca. Corinth was their former home, and they had many friends there; and so they send 'many greetings.' Their house was one of the meeting-places of the Ephesian Christians, and they associate their fellow-worshippers in their expression of good-will. And since the Corinthian trouble had excited general solicitude at Ephesus, a third greeting is added—from 'all the brothers.'

19 The churches of Asia greet you. Aquila and Prisca send
you many greetings in the Lord, and in these the church at
20 their house joins. All the brothers greet you. Greet one
another with a holy kiss.

And now the Apostle appends his sign-manual.

The Apostle's autograph.

21, 22 MY GREETING WITH MY OWN HAND—PAUL'S. IF ANY
ONE DOES NOT LOVE THE LORD, LET HIM BE ACCURSED.
23 'O OUR LORD, COME!'[1] THE GRACE OF THE LORD JESUS
24 BE WITH YOU. MY LOVE BE WITH YOU ALL IN CHRIST
JESUS.

Corinthian obduracy.

The letter was forthwith conveyed to Corinth by Stephanas, Fortunatus, and Achaicus. Stephanas had been steadfastly loyal to the Apostle; and if his companions had been disaffected in the recent controversies, their experience at Ephesus had disarmed their hostility, and on their return to Corinth they would co-operate with Timothy. There is no record of what transpired, but the issue is indubitable. The effort at conciliation proved futile, and Timothy and his companions returned to Ephesus with a disheartening report. The feud between the dissident parties of the Judaists and the Spirituals continued, and both alike were incensed against the Apostle and assailed him with cruel and insulting charges. The former persisted in their denial of his apostleship; and his explanation of the generous motives which had prompted him to waive his apostolic privileges, was contemptuously flouted. His forgoing of the right to maintenance they construed as a cunning device to ingratiate himself, and they insinuated that his collection for the poor at Jerusalem was a selfish imposition. And as for the Spirituals, they maintained their antinomian attitude, and accused him of carnality in insisting upon moral obligations; and, as though conscious of the untenability of their position, they resorted to personal abuse. They raised the old cry of the simplicity of his preaching. His letter indeed

Cf. 1 Cor. ix.

2 Cor. xii. 16-18.

x. 2.

[1] *μαραναθά*, an Aramaic prayer which passed into a Christian watchword. It is a question how the phrase should be divided. (1) *μαρὰν ἀθά*, 'our Lord has come,' or rather 'is coming' (patristic). Cf. Phil. iv. 5: ὁ Κύριος ἐγγύς. (2) *μαράνα θά* (מָרַנָא תָא), 'our Lord, come!' Cf. Dalman, *Words of Jesus*, p. 328. The latter is preferable. Cf. Rev. xxii. 20: ἀμήν, ἔρχου, Κύριε Ἰησοῦ. The phrase occurs at the close of the eucharistic prayer in the *Didache*, x: εἴ τις ἅγιός ἐστιν, ἐρχέσθω· εἴ τις οὐκ ἔστι, μετανοείτω. μαραναθά· ἀμήν.

was characterised by strength of argument and fulness of
knowledge; and, unable to dispute this, they sneered not
x. 10, xi. 6. only at the rudeness of his speech but at his physical weakness
xi. i, 16. and the ungainliness of his appearance; they called him
xv 23; cf. i. 13. 'senseless,' and they even went the length of suggesting that
his enthusiasm was stark madness.

Hasty and ineffectual visit to Corinth.

Such was the report which his deputies brought; and so
grievous was it to the Apostle that he interrupted his ministry
at Ephesus and paid a hasty visit to Corinth.[1] His faith in
the erring church had been sorely tried, but he still clung
to the hope that reason would prevail, and he went in a
gracious and conciliatory spirit. The issue was a bitter
disappointment. His forbearance was misconstrued. His
critics contrasted it with the 'courage,' the 'confidence,'
the 'boldness' which his letter had exhibited; and they
accused him of pusillanimity. His language, they sneered,
Cf. x. 1, 2, 9, 10. was very stout when he was writing to them at Ephesus
with the breadth of the Ægean betwixt him and them; but
when he met them face to face, he was all meekness—a
faltering and pitiful weakling. His loudest detractors were
Cf. x. 7, xi. 4, 5, xii. 11. the Judaist propagandists, especially their leader, who had
come from Jerusalem with a 'letter of commendation' and
boasted of his authority, his commission from 'the superlative Apostles.'

A stern letter.

It was an impracticable situation. Remonstrance was
useless; reason was unavailing: it would only have provoked recrimination and created fresh exasperation. And
Cf. xiii. 2. so the Apostle took his departure with an intimation that
he would ere long return and deal decisively with the prime
Cf. ii. 2-4, vii. 8. offenders. On reaching Ephesus he wrote a letter, defining
the situation and reiterating his warning.[2] It was a stern
message; and it seems that, like St. Ambrose in the brave
protest which he addressed to the Emperor Theodosius on
the Thessalonian massacre in the year 390,[3] he wrote it with
his own hand, dispensing with the service of an amanuensis.[4]

[1] Cf. Append. I. [2] Cf. Append. I. [3] *Epist.* li. 14.

[4] This seems the most reasonable interpretation of αὐτὸς δὲ ἐγὼ Παῦλος (x. 1), which is otherwise explained either (1) as contrasting Paul with Timothy and the others whom he had previously sent to Corinth, or (2) as contrasting his gentleness with the undutiful behaviour of the Corinthians, or (3) as contrasting his present forbearance with the apostolic severity which he would shortly display. Cf. Bengel.

Not only was his grief too poignant for deliberate expression but he would not put his erring Church to heedless shame. No unsympathetic ear must hear his reproaches. He wrote with strong emotion, with a trembling hand and dim eyes; and there are passages which, as even without his express testimony one might well imagine, were blotted with tears. Cf. ii. 4.

A last appeal.

It was indeed a stern letter, the sternest perhaps that he ever wrote. It flashes keen sarcasm and breathes indignation and scorn; nevertheless it is instinct with tenderness, 'the meekness and sweet reasonableness of Christ.' It is not a sentence of condemnation; it is rather a warning of the impending judgment and a final appeal to the Corinthians to repent and spare him the grief of dealing severely with them. He recognised that the blame rested on the ringleaders. They indeed were hopeless, and their doom was inevitable; but the mass of the Church were mere dupes, and he would fain believe that they were sound at heart and would bethink themselves betimes. Cf. x. 1-11; xiii. 1-3. Cf. xiii. 5-10.

Third Letter to Corinth

(2 Cor. x-xiii. 10)

Obscurity of the letter.

It is only the body of the letter that has been preserved, and the opening address and the final greetings are lacking. There is no writing of the Apostle which is so obscure; and the reason is that it abounds in personal references. It bristles with quotations—words and phrases which had been hurled at the Apostle during his unhappy visit to Corinth and which rankled in his memory. These the Corinthians would recognise, but they are frequently puzzling to ourselves.

The taunt of cowardice.

He begins with the charge of cowardice. His letters from his secure vantage-ground at Ephesus, it was alleged, were very 'courageous,' but when he came to Corinth and faced his critics, he was all meekness and humility, 'valiant as the wrathful dove or most magnanimous mouse.' This was the taunt especially of the party which posed as 'the Spirituals' and resisted his disciplinary mandate on the ground that flesh and spirit were distinct domains, charging him, when he insisted on moral purity, with 'comporting himself according to the flesh' and not 'according to the spirit.' His answer is that they misconstrued his attitude. His gentleness was not cowardice; it was forbearance. The Corinthian Church was like a revolted city, and he had laid siege to it. Meanwhile he would not assail it with the weight of his artillery and raze it to the ground, but after the Lord's example would summon it to surrender and recall it to its allegiance. Only in the event of persistent obduracy would he resort to severity. And this was no empty threat; for, let the Judaists deny it as they would, he was armed with apostolic authority: he too, 'held by Christ.'

Cf. 1 Cor. i. 12.

x. 1 I Paul myself exhort you by the meekness and sweet
reasonableness of Christ—I who 'to your face am humble
among you, but when far away am so courageous against
2 you'—I beg that I may not when with you show my
'courage' with the 'confidence' wherewith I reckon on
'dealing boldly' with some that reckon us as 'comporting
3 ourselves according to the flesh.' Though it is in the flesh
that we are comporting ourselves, it is not according to the
4 flesh that we are warring; for the weapons of our warfare
are not fleshly but divinely powerful[1] for the pulling down
5 of strongholds. We pull down 'reckonings' and everything
that lifts itself on high against the knowledge of God; and
we bring every thought captive into submission to Christ;
6 and we are in readiness to take vengeance on every rebellion
7 whenever your submission is complete. It is at the face-
value of things that you look. If any one has confidence
in himself that he 'holds by Christ,' let him bethink himself
and take this into his reckoning that, just as he 'holds by
8 Christ,' so also do we. For if I boast somewhat too abundantly of our authority which the Lord gave for your upbuilding and not for your downpulling, I shall not be put
9 to shame. That I may not seem as though I were merely
10 'terrifying you through my letters'—'his letters,' says my
critic, 'are indeed weighty and vigorous, but his bodily
11 presence is weak and his speech contemptible'—let such a
man take this into his reckoning,[2] that what we are in our

[1] *δυνατὰ τῷ Θεῷ*, a Hebraism, equivalent to a superlative. Cf. Jon. iii. 3: *πόλις μεγάλη τῷ Θεῷ*, 'an exceeding great city.' Ac. vii. 20: *ἀστεῖος τῷ Θεῷ*, 'exceeding fair.'

[2] So Chrys., beginning a new sentence with *ἵνα μή*, connecting ver. 9 with ver. 11, and regarding ver. 10 as parenthetical. Ver. 9 is commonly attached to *οὐκ αἰσχυνθήσομαι*, and *ἵνα μή* is then elliptical: '(and this I say) in order that I may not seem'; 'non addam plura ea de re, ne quis inania esse putet *terriculamenta*' (Grot.); 'hoc eo dico, *ne*, etc.' (Beng.).

speech by letter when far away, that shall we be also when we are among you and take action.

Sarcastic rejoinder to Judaist criticism.

And now he assails the Judaists with keen sarcasm. They arrogated to themselves a superiority which he would never have had the 'boldness' to claim; and their pretensions had no better foundation than their colossal self-complacency. They saw themselves fair

> 'none else being by,
> Themselves poised with themselves in either eye.'

They stigmatised him as a usurper of apostolic functions, but in truth they were the usurpers. His rule was to preach the Gospel only where it was still unknown, always respecting the boundary between his field of operations and another man's. Corinth was his domain, for he had been the first to preach there; and his hope—a hope which was actually realised ere long when he carried the Gospel thence to Epirus and Illyricum and Dalmatia [1]—was that he might advance beyond Achaia into regions yet untrodden. And this was his complaint against the Judaists, that with the world before them they had dogged his footsteps and sown dissension in the Churches which he had founded.

Rom. xv. 20.

Rom. xv. 19.

12 We have not indeed the 'boldness' to class or compare
ourselves with some of the self-commenders. No, in their
measurement of themselves by themselves and their comparison of themselves with themselves they have no under-
13 standing. As for us it is not outwith our measured domain
that we shall boast, but according to the measure of the
boundary-line which God apportioned to us for a measure to
14 reach as far as you. There is not, as there would be if we did
not reach to you, any overstretching on our part; for we
were the first to get as far as you in the preaching of the
15 Gospel of Christ. We do not boast ourselves outwith our
measured domain in other men's toils, but our hope is that,
as your faith grows, we may, still keeping to our boundary-line,
16 be so abundantly enlarged among you as to preach the Gospel
in the regions beyond you, without intruding on another's boun-
17 dary-line or boasting of work which we found already done. 'He Jer. ix. 23.
18 that boasts, let him boast in the Lord'; for it is not the 24; cf. 1
self-commender, it is not he, that stands the test; no, it is Cor. i. 31.
the man whom the Lord commends.

[1] Cf. p. 612.

Apology for his self-vindication.

It was distasteful to the Apostle to write thus. It looked like boasting, and it might seem to justify his enemies' designation of him as 'senseless.' But he had a good excuse. He was actuated by solicitude for his Corinthian converts, lest they should be seduced from the Gospel of salvation by faith in Christ. They showed a fine patience with that aggressive person, the ringleader of the Judaist propagandists who were subverting the true evangel; and surely they might bear with him. He had no less authority than 'the superlative Apostles' whom the Judaists exalted at his expense, denying the validity of his ordination and pronouncing him a mere 'layman'; and, say what his critics would about the rudeness of his speech, they could hardly disparage his knowledge, at all events at Corinth, where it had been so amply displayed.

xi. 1 Would that you could have patience with me in some
2 little senselessness! Nay, do have patience with me. I
am jealous for you as God is jealous; for I betrothed you
3 to one husband to present a pure virgin to Christ, and my
Gen. iii. 13. fear is that, as 'the Serpent beguiled' Eve in his craftiness,
your thoughts may be corrupted from their simplicity and
4 purity toward Christ. For if your visitor is proclaiming
another Jesus whom we did not proclaim, or you are
receiving a different Spirit which you did not then receive
or a different Gospel which you did not then accept, your
5 patience is beautiful![1] For I reckon that I am nothing
6 inferior to 'the superlative Apostles.' And though I be
a mere 'layman'[2] in speech, I am no layman in knowledge.
No, in every respect we made this manifest in every one's
judgment in our relations with you.

His preaching without salary.

Cf. 1 Cor. ix. 1-18.

Cf. 1 Cor. ix. 15.

The Judaists were making a vast ado about Paul's receiving no remuneration during his ministry at Corinth. Despite what he had said in his previous letter, they construed it as a confession that he lacked apostolic authority, and with stupid inconsistency they alleged further that it evinced an ungracious attitude toward his converts, adducing perhaps his proud protestation that he would rather starve than accept a grudging requital. It was a preposterous con-

[1] καλῶς, ironical; cf. Mk. vii. 9. Instead of bearing with him they should have counted him accursed (cf. Gal. i. 8).

[2] Cf. p. 307.

tention, and he makes merciless sport of it. At all events it could be no grievance to the Corinthians that he had refrained from making himself a burden to them. If there was any grievance in the matter, it belonged rather, he remarks with a touch of sarcasm, to his Macedonian converts whom they had allowed to come to his rescue. The truth was that the Judaists were feeling sore about it. They were greedy men and exacted their own salary, and the contrast between them and him was the talk of the whole Province of Achaia; and he certainly would not dam up the stream of boasting in regard to himself by altering his practice and demanding payment. That would be playing the game of the Judaists. It would put him and them on a level, and would afford an outlet for their boasting which his generosity had dammed up. Their complaint was their condemnation. It revealed what sort of men they were. They were false Apostles. They called him 'a trickster' and accused him Cf. xii. 16.
of 'craft'; but they were the tricksters, 'crafty workmen' masquerading as Apostles of Christ.

7 Or did I commit a sin in humbling myself that you might
be exalted, inasmuch as I preached the Gospel of God to you
8 gratuitously? Other churches I despoiled by taking a salary
9 from them in order to minister to you. And when I was
with you and had lack, I cramped no one;[1] for the brothers
came from Macedonia and supplied my lack, and in everything
10 I kept myself and will keep myself unburdensome to you. As
Christ's truth is in me, this boasting in regard to me will not
11 be dammed up[2] in the regions of Achaia. Wherefore? Be-
12 cause I do not love you? God knows. But what I am doing
I shall keep on doing, that I may cut off their outlet who are
desirous of an outlet[3] that, wherein they boast, they may be
13 found on a level with us. For men of this sort are false
Apostles, 'crafty workmen,' assuming the guise of Apostles
14 of Christ. And no wonder; for Satan himself assumes the

[1] *καταναρκᾶν*, 'benumb,' from *νάρκη*, *torpor* (whence 'narcotic'); cf. Aristoph. *Wasps*, 713 f.: *οἴμοι, τί ποθ' ὥσπερ νάρκη μου κατὰ τῆς χειρὸς καταχεῖται; /καὶ τὸ ξίφος οὐ δύναμαι κατέχειν ἀλλ' ἤδη μαλθακός εἰμι*, 'Why is a numbness poured upon my hand? I cannot grip my sword.' The verb occurs in N. T. only here and xii. 13, 14; and it is said to have been one of Paul's Cilician provincialisms (cf. Hieronym. *Algas.*, *Quæst.* x.).

[2] *φράγησεται*, cf. Rom. iii. 19; Heb. xi. 33. *φράσσειν*, 'block up,' *e.g.*, a stream (cf. Herod. II. 99), the entrance of a harbour (cf. Thuc. IV. 13).

[3] *ἀφορμήν* (cf. p. 215), continuing the metaphor of *οὐ φράγησεται*.

15 guise of an angel of light. It is therefore nothing great if his
ministers also assume a guise as ministers of righteousness.
Their end will be according to their works.

Apology for boasting.

Cf. ver. 1.

Cf. Ac. xv. 10; Gal. v. 1.

Cf. Mt. xxiii. 4.

Cf. Mk. xii. 40.

Cf. Mt. v. 39.

1 Tim. iii. 3; Tit. i. 7.

It was more particularly on the score of his preaching without remuneration that the Judaists had branded the Apostle with the insulting epithet of 'senseless.' He has already scornfully alluded to it; and now after his merciless castigation of his critics he reverts to it. They had his answer, and if they still called him 'senseless,' he would exercise his privilege and indulge in a little boasting—a senseless employment which they practised largely. And what boasting theirs was! what arrogance! what insolence! Not only had they enslaved the Corinthians by imposing on them the yoke of the Law and all its heavy burdens, but they emulated the methods of the Jewish Rabbis—their greedy exactions [1] and their tyrannous contumelies. They thought nothing, when one offended them, of smiting him on the face; and if this seem incredible, it should be remembered how by and by it was necessary for the Apostle to require of an aspirant to the office of Overseer that he should not be 'ready with his fists,' and how, moreover, in later days corporal chastisement was inflicted not merely by abbots on their monks but by bishops on their inferior clergy.[2] If the Corinthians endured the insolence of the Apostle's Judaist traducers, surely they might have patience with a little boasting on his part, a little vindication of his title to honour.

16 I repeat, let no one fancy me to be 'senseless'; or else
even as 'senseless' accept me, that I too may boast some
17 little. Here it is not according to the Lord that I am
talking, but as in 'senselessness,' in this well founded
18 boasting.[3] Since many are boasting according to the flesh,

[1] Cf. *The Days of His Flesh*, p. 414.

[2] Cf. Bingham, *Antiq.* VIII. iii. 12; XVII. iv. 12.

[3] ἐν ταύτῃ τῇ ὑποστάσει τῆς καυχήσεως, 'in this standing-ground of boasting.' His boasting might be called 'senseless,' but it was really well founded. ὑπόστασις, properly 'underlying basis'; cf. Ps. lxix. 2 LXX: ἐνεπάγην εἰς ἰλὺν βυθοῦ καὶ οὐκ ἔστιν ὑπόστασις. Hence, as a philosophical term, the 'underlying reality' of a thing, its 'substance,' *substantia* (cf. Heb. i. 3). So (1) 'assurance' objectively (cf. Heb. xi. 1) and (2) subjectively 'confidence,' the feeling of assurance (cf. Heb. iii. 14; 2 Cor. ix. 4).

19 I shall do it too. For you are sweetly patient with the
20 ‘senseless,’ having your own senses about you. You are
patient if one enslaves you, if one devours you, if one
‘catches’ you,[1] if one gives himself lofty airs, if one strikes
you on the face.

His heroic ministry.

And now he makes his boast. His enemies sneered at his forbearing gentleness, so conspicuous during his hasty visit to Corinth, and called it ‘weakness,’ construing it as a confession that he lacked apostolic authority; and he retorts that he had more reason for ‘boldness’ than any of them. Which of the Judaists could claim a purer lineage than his? They boasted themselves ‘Hebrews’—members of the chosen race; ‘Israelites’—members of the theocracy; ‘the seed of Abraham’—heirs of the Promise: all these dignities were his no less than theirs. And in the matter of service to the cause of Christ, which of them had a record like his? He recites his experiences as a missionary of the Cross—his ‘moving accidents by flood and field,’ his toils, his persecutions, his privations. It is a long catalogue that he gives, yet, as he remarks, it was incomplete. He could not tell the whole story, and even the history of the Book of Acts omits much. It says nothing, for example, of his five scourgings in Jewish synagogues, of two of his three floggings by Roman lictors, or of his three shipwrecks and his drifting on a broken spar. Only a meagre record of his ordeals has survived, and the heaviest of them all was one which could not be written—his ceaseless solicitude for the welfare of his churches. His letters are its best memorial, yet how inadequate it is! His extant letters are the merest fragments of his voluminous correspondence: had it all survived, it would fill a library.

21 I am speaking self-disparagingly, supposing that we have
been ‘weak’; but, whatever ground any one has for ‘boldness’—it is in ‘senselessness’ that I am speaking—I have it too.
22 Are they Hebrews? So am I. Are they Israelites? So am
23 I. Are they the seed of Abraham? So am I. Are they
ministers of Christ? (It is in very ‘madness’ that I am
talking.) So am I still more than they. My toils outnumber

[1] Referring to the charge that he had ‘caught them by craft’ (xii. 16). The Judaists caught them with violent hands.

theirs ; my imprisonments outnumber theirs ; my stripes have
been more severe ; I have been many a time at death's
Cf. Ac. xvi. 22, 23. Cf. Ac. xiv. 19.
24 door. At Jewish hands I five times got forty lashes save one ;[1]
25 thrice I was beaten by the lictors' rods ; once I was stoned ;
thrice I was shipwrecked ; a night and a day I have drifted on
26 the deep.[2] My journeyings have been many ; I have faced
dangers in fording rivers, dangers of brigands, dangers from
my own race, dangers from Gentiles, dangers in the city,
Cf. 1 Th. ii. 9 ; 2 Th. iii. 8.
dangers in the wild, dangers at sea, dangers among false
27 brothers. I have borne toil and moil ; I have kept vigil
many a time, have hungered and thirsted, have fasted many a
28 time, have suffered cold and nakedness. Besides all else that
I omit, there is my daily besetment—my anxiety for all the
29 churches. Who is weak, and I am not weak ? Who is made
to stumble, and my heart is not fired ?

His visions and revelations.

It was a moving story. ''Twas pitiful, 'twas wondrous pitiful.' It showed his 'weakness,' but not the sort of weakness which his enemies imputed to him. It was heroic weakness. Boasting was distasteful to him, but if he must boast, he would boast of that record of 'weakness' ; and God knew it was all true. At the same time he had another and higher ground for boasting in the marvellous revelations which the Lord had vouchsafed him.

30 If boast I must, it is of the things which show my 'weak-
31 ness' that I shall boast. The God and Father of the Lord
Jesus knows—He who is blessed evermore—that I am not
Cf. Ac. ix. 23-25.
32 lying. (At Damascus the governor under King Aretas was
33 guarding the city of the Damascenes to apprehend me, and
through a window I was lowered in a hamper through the
xii. 1 wall and escaped his hands.)[3] Boast I must--indeed it
is unprofitable, but I shall come to visions and revelations
of the Lord.

Two ineffable experiences.

He cites two transcendent and ever memorable experiences which had befallen him in the course of the nine years which

[1] Forty lashes and no more were the punishment prescribed by the Law (cf. Dt. xxv. 2, 3), and by a later ordinance the fortieth was omitted lest the limit should be exceeded through an error in enumeration. Cf. Wetstein.

[2] Cf. the experience of Josephus when in the course of his voyage to Rome his ship foundered in the Adriatic : περὶ ἑξακοσίους τὸν ἀριθμὸν ὄντες δι' ὅλης τῆς νυκτὸς ἐνηξάμεθα (*Vit.* 3).

[3] A manifest interpolation, interrupting the argument. Most probably another *marginale*—a note entered by the Apostle on the margin after the letter was written as an example of 'dangers from my own race, dangers from Gentiles, dangers in the city' (ver. 26).

he had spent in his native Province between his conversion and his commission as Apostle of the Gentiles.[1] That was a heart-stirring period, and his soul, employed in earnest meditation and heavenly communion, had been marvellously visited. What happened remained mysterious to him, and he describes it in the religious language of his day. The Jewish imagination pictured not one heaven but seven—'the heavenly regions' as they were designated. The lowest was denominated 'the Veil'; and it was gloomy, 'since it beholds all the unrighteous deeds of men.' In the second, 'the Firmament,' are 'fire, snow, and ice made ready for the Day of Judgment.' In the third, 'the Clouds,' are the angelic hosts ordained for the Day of Judgment. In the fourth, 'the Habitation,' are thrones and dominions, always praising God. In the fifth, 'the Dwelling,' are the angels who carry the prayers of men to 'the angels of the presence of the Lord,' who in turn present these before the Throne. In the sixth, 'the Place,' are 'the archangels, who minister and make propitiation to the Lord for all the sins of ignorance of the righteous.' The seventh was *Araboth*, 'the Broad Fields,' or Paradise, 'the Garden.' It was 'the Heaven of Heavens'; and there 'dwelleth the Great Glory, far above all holiness.'[2]

The Seven Heavens. Eph. i. 3, 20, ii. 6, iii. 10, vi. 12.

Cf. Col. i. 16; Eph. i. 21.

1 Ki. viii. 27.

A vision of the Third Heaven.

It was thus that the Jewish mind envisaged the Unseen Universe, and the Apostle employs the familiar imagery to express his ineffable visions. The first was an elevation to 'the Third Heaven'; and this, since the Third Heaven was the abode of 'the angelic hosts ordained for the Day of Judgment,' would be a terrible vision of the righteousness of God. What precisely it was that happened—whether

[1] Cf. p. 62.

[2] Cf. *Test. XII Patriarch.*, *Levi*, II, III. The Rabbinical designations of the Seven Heavens were (1) וִילוֹן, Latin *velum*, 'the Veil'; (2) רָקִיעַ, 'the Firmament' (cf. Gen. i. 6, 7, 8; Ps. xix. 1); (3) שְׁחָקִים, 'the Clouds' (cf. Job xxxvii. 18, xxxviii. 37); (4) זְבוּל, 'the Habitation' (cf. Ps. xlix. 14; Is. lxiii. 15; Hab. iii. 11); (5) מָעוֹן, 'the Dwelling' (cf. Pss. xxvi. 8, lxviii. 5; Dt. xxvi. 15); (6) מָכוֹן, 'the Place' (cf. Ps. xxxiii. 14; Ex. xv. 17); (7) עֲרָבוֹת, 'the Broad Fields' (cf. Ps. lxviii. 4) or פַּרְדֵּס (*παράδεισος*), 'Paradise,' 'the Garden' 'or 'Pleasance' (cf. Neh. ii. 8; Eccl. ii. 5; Song iv. 13).

he was rapt away bodily or his soul parted from his body and conversed in the Unseen while his body remained inanimate on earth—he confesses that he knew not, warning his readers, as St. Chrysostom remarks, against futile curiosity.

2 I know a man in Christ fourteen years ago—whether in the
body I know not, or out of the body I know not: God knows—
such a man rapt away as far as the Third Heaven.

A vision of Paradise.

This experience was followed by another more wonderful and more gracious. It was an elevation to Paradise; and, since Paradise is 'the dwelling-place of the Great Glory' or, in Christian language, the abode of God and the Glorified Lord and His redeemed, this was no mere ecstasy. It was a revelation of the Risen Christ. The Apostle saw Him and heard His voice.

Cf. Lk. xxiii. 43; Rev. ii. 7.

3 And I know such a man—whether in the body or parted
4 from the body I know not: God knows—that he was rapt
away into Paradise and heard ineffable words which a human
being may not talk.

Why he would not boast:

(1) His sense of unworthiness.

One so transcendently privileged might justly have boasted, but it was not his high privileges that were his boast; it was rather his weaknesses. And what was the reason why he was thus minded? It was, in the first instance, a sense of his unworthiness. It is told of St. Francis of Assisi that one day, as he was returning from the forest where he had been in prayer, Brother Masseo to try his humility exclaimed: 'Why after thee? Why after thee? . . . Thou art neither comely nor learned, nor art thou of noble birth. How is it, then, that men go after thee?' 'Wouldst thou,' was the answer, 'learn the reason? Know that it is because the Lord, who is in heaven, who sees the evil and the good in all places—because, I say, His holy eyes have not found among men a more wicked, a more imperfect, or a greater sinner than I am; and to accomplish the wonderful work which He intends doing, He has not found a creature more vile than I am on earth; for this reason He has chosen me, to confound force, beauty, greatness, birth, and all the science of the world, that man may learn that every virtue and every good gift comes from Him, and not from the creature; that none may glory before Him ; but if any one glory, let him glory in the Lord, to whom belongeth all glory in eternity.'[1] And even such was the thought of the Apostle, His high privileges were of the Lord's amazing and unmerited grace, and they belonged not to himself. It was not himself, so weak and worthless, that had been so highly honoured ; and therefore, when he tells the story, he tells it as of another : 'I know a man in Christ rapt away.'

5 On such a man's behalf I shall boast, but on my own behalf
6 I shall not boast except in my weaknesses. If I desire to
boast, I shall not be 'senseless,' for it is truth that I shall be
telling ; but I refrain, lest any one should reckon to my
account more than he sees in me or hears from me.

(2) His 'thorn.'

And, moreover, he had been taught a needful and salutary lesson. He had been in danger, after those transcendent experiences, of spiritual pride, and he had been delivered by the Lord's stern mercy. In the course of his first mission he had been stricken by that distressing malady which ever since had clung to him, humbling him in the sight of the world and thwarting his purposes ; and for a while it had seemed to him an emissary of Satan, the Enemy of the Gospel. He had carried it to the Throne of Grace and repeatedly prayed for its removal ; but his request had always been denied. At length he had bowed to the Lord's will ; and no sooner had he accepted his affliction in loving trust than it was transfigured. What had appeared a frustration of his purposes was recognised as a hedge of thorns enclosing the way which the Lord would have him take and deterring him from futile paths of his own choosing. His weakness had proved his strength and his painful experience a gracious discipline. And now it seemed to him a very Shekinah, the Cloud of the Lord's presence overshadowing his life.[2]

7 And lest by the transcendence of the revelations I should
be uplifted,[3] there was given me a thorn for my flesh, a mes-
8 senger of Satan to buffet me, lest I should be uplifted. On
this behalf I thrice besought the Lord that I might be rid of

[1] *Fioretti di S. Francesco*, x.

[2] Cf. Append. III.

[3] Reading with Tisch. ἐξ ἐμοῦ. καὶ τῇ ὑπερβολῇ τῶν ἀποκαλύψεων ἵνα μὴ ὑπεραίρωμαι, which is the Western emendation of an evidently corrupt passage.

9 it. And He has said to me : ‘ My grace suffices you ; for
power is perfected in weakness.’ Most gladly then will I rather
boast in my weaknesses, that the Cloud of Christ’s Power may
10 overshadow me.[1] Wherefore I am well pleased in weaknesses,
in contumelies, in necessities, in persecutions and straits on
Christ’s behalf ; for when I am weak, then it is that I am
powerful.

A pained remonstrance.

Here ends the Apostle’s self-vindication, and he turns from it with relief. It had indeed been a ‘ senseless ’ employment, and his excuse was that it had been forced upon him by the Judaist aspersions. He would have been spared the odious task had the Corinthians rated these at their proper worth. His apostolic ministry among them was a sufficient evidence of his apostleship ; and if it was a grievance with them that he had never exacted remuneration from them, he craved their pardon, but he would promise no amendment. He contemplated paying them a third visit, and he would then pursue his accustomed course. Not, he playfully repeats, that he did not love them ; on the contrary, they were his spiritual children, and he would perform a father’s part by them, grudging no sacrifice. And what of the base insinuation that he was making a good thing of the collection for the poor at Jerusalem, and his forgoing remuneration was a mere blind ? Its refutation was that in this business he had never had any personal dealings with them. It had been negotiated by Titus and his companion-delegate of the Church of Antioch.[2] They were his deputies, and their conduct had been irreproachable.

Cf. xi. 11.

11 I have proved ‘ senseless ’ : it was you that compelled me.
I ought to have been commended by you ; for nothing inferior

[1] *ἵνα ἐπισκηνώσῃ ἐπ’ ἐμὲ ἡ δύναμις τοῦ Χριστοῦ.* Later Jewish theology was dominated by the thought of Divine Transcendence, and the idea was jealously guarded by the Targumists. An example of their devices is their manipulation of those O. T. passages which speak of the Lord as ‘dwelling (שָׁכַן) with men.’ They coined the noun שְׁכִינָה, and employed a reverential periphrasis. Thus in Ex. xxv. 8 Onqelos has : ‘I will cause My Shekinah to rest among them.’ The Shekinah was the Cloud of the Lord’s Presence which had accompanied the Israelites in the Wilderness and overshadowed the Mercy-seat ; and it was represented in Greek, on the strength of the assonance, by *σκηνή, σκηνόω* (cf. Rev. xxi. 3, vii. 15 ; Jo. i. 14). Cf. *The Atonement in the Light of History and the Modern Spirit*, p. 162.

[2] Cf. p. 234.

was I to 'the superlative Apostles,' though I am nothing.
12 The signs of an Apostle were wrought among you in unflagging
13 endurance by signs and portents and powers. For what disadvantage is there that you were put to above the rest of the
churches, except that I personally never cramped you?
14 Forgive me this injustice! Look you, this is now the third
time that I am ready to visit you, and I will not cramp you;
for it is not your money that I am seeking but yourselves.
It is not the children that should store up for the parents;
15 it is the parents that should store up for the children. And
for my part most gladly will I spend and be spent to the uttermost on your souls' behalf. If I love you more abundantly,
16 am I to be the less beloved? So be it; I was never a burden
on you, but I was all the while 'a trickster' and 'caught you
17 by craft.' Is there any of the deputies I have sent to you
18 through whom I overreached you? I enlisted Titus and
deputed the brother to accompany him: did Titus in anything
overreach you? Did we not comport ourselves by the same
spirit? Did we not tread the same path?

An explanation.

And now the Apostle closes with some plain yet affectionate speaking. First he corrects a possible misapprehension in the minds of the Corinthians. His letter was not a personal apologia; else it would not have been addressed to them, since God alone was his Judge. It was a call to repentance, and his only personal concern was their welfare.

19 You have been fancying all this while that we are making
our defence to you. It is before God in Christ that we are
20 talking, and it is all, beloved, for your upbuilding. My fear
is that I may come and find you not what I desire, and that I
may be found for you what you do not desire; that there
may be strife, jealousy, frenzies, intrigues, slanders, whisper-
21 ings, windy braggings, disorders; that on my return my God
may humble me among you, and I may have to mourn many
of those who have sinned in the past and never repented for
the uncleanness and fornication and sensuality which they
practised.

A warning.

Continued obduracy would have serious and distressing consequences. He contemplated a third visit to Corinth, and he reiterates the intimation which he had left with them on the painful occasion of his last visit. On his return, unless the situation had been meanwhile amended, he would take severe measures. He would arraign the offenders and deal with them no longer in the way of remonstrance but by judicial process, leading evidence and pronouncing sentence. Thus he would furnish the proof which was desiderated that he was indeed an Apostle, and that, while one with Christ in the weakness of His incarnate Humiliation, he was one with Him also in the power of His glorious Exaltation.

Dt. xix. 15. xiii. 1 This is the third visit that I am paying you: 'at the
mouth of two witnesses and three shall every word be
2 established.' I have given warning, and that warning
which I gave when I was with you the second time, I repeat
now when I am far away, to those who have sinned in the
past and to all the rest, that if I come back, I shall not
3 spare, since you are seeking proof[1] that it is Christ who
talks in me. He is not 'weak' toward you; no, He is
4 powerful among you. For though it was weakness that
brought Him to the Cross, yet He lives by God's power;
and though we are weak in Him, yet by God's power we
5 shall share His life in dealing with you. Try yourselves
whether you are in the Faith; put yourselves to proof.
Or have you no clear recognition regarding yourselves that
Jesus Christ is in you? He is, unless indeed you be
6 counterfeits. I hope you will recognise that we are no
7 counterfeits; but our prayer to God is that you do nothing
evil, not that we may show good coin, but that you may
8 ring true though we should be as counterfeits. For it is
not against the Truth that we have any power but only on
9 the Truth's behalf. We are glad when we are weak and
you are powerful; this is also our prayer—your knitting
10 together.[2] Therefore it is that I am writing thus when
far away, that when with you I may not handle you
Cf. x. 8. severely in the exercise of the authority which the Lord
gave me for upbuilding and not for downpulling.

Titus the bearer of the letter.

Cf. 2 Cor. ii. 13; vii. 13-15.

The business of conveying the letter to Corinth and not merely presenting it to the Church but enforcing its appeal was a difficult office, demanding both courage and tact, qualities which are seldom combined. Happily a competent delegate was available in Titus, that young Antiochene who had been attached to the mission as superintendent of the Gentile collection for the poor at Jerusalem, and who had acquitted himself so successfully when with his colleague he visited Corinth in its interest some two years previously.[3] He was a young man, and on that occasion it was not without

[1] Cf. n. on 1 Th. v. 21, p. 165.
[2] Cf. n. on 1 Th. iii. 10, p. 161.
[3] Cf. p. 234.

reluctance that he had faced the ordeal, and it was only the Apostle's encouragement that had conquered his diffidence.[1] It was a still harder ordeal that he was now called to encounter, and he would doubtless dread it. Nevertheless he faced it stoutly. Its very difficulty was a challenge, and how nobly he met it the event proves.

IV

RETREAT TO MACEDONIA

Ac. xix. 23-41; 2 Cor. i. 8-10; Ac. xx. 1; 2 Cor. ii. 12, 13; vii. 5-7; 2 Cor. i-ix, xiii. 11-14.

Riot at Ephesus.

It was toward the close of the year 55 when the letter was despatched to Corinth; and thereafter the Apostle resumed his ministry at Ephesus. His design was to remain in the Asian Capital until the ensuing May, but it was presently overruled by a distressing *dénouement*. His situation had for some time been difficult, and six months previously in his second letter to Corinth he had referred to the dangers which beset him. It was the animosity of the heathen populace which then threatened him; and so far from abating it had increased, and now it culminates in an outbreak of violence.

Cf. 1 Cor. xvi. 9.

Grievance of the silversmiths.

The grievance was ostensibly religious, but in fact it was commercial. The worship of Artemis had created an extensive and lucrative industry, especially in the manufacture and sale of silver models of the celebrated Temple;[2] and this had been seriously curtailed by the progress of Christianity not alone in the city but throughout the Province.[3] It was natural that the craftsmen and merchants whose interests were involved should take alarm; and their resentment found vent when Demetrius, a silversmith who employed numerous workmen, convened the latter, probably

[1] Cf. 2 Cor. xii. 18: παρεκάλεσα Τίτον, 'I exhorted' or 'encouraged Titus.'

[2] Cf. p. 227.

[3] Here as at Philippi (cf. pp. 129 ff.) it was when their worldly interests were affected that the Gentiles opposed the Gospel. And similarly it was its interference with trade, especially the sale of sacrificial victims, that provoked the persecution in the Province of Bithynia during the reign of Trajan (cf. Plin. *Epist.* x. 101).

in their guildhall, and represented the seriousness of the issue were Paul suffered to pursue his propaganda and discredit the worship of the Great Goddess. It was an appeal to self-interest in the name of religion, and it fired the assemblage. They raised the cry 'Great Artemis of the Ephesians!'—the accustomed acclamation at sacred processions;[1] and it was taken up by the populace. An excited mob surged through the streets, headed by Demetrius and his craftsmen.

Cf. Ac. xx. 4. Cf. Col. iv. 10, 11.

They would have seized Paul but he happened to be out of the way, and they found two of his associates, Gaius of Derbe and Aristarchus, a Jewish Christian of Thessalonica who was then at Ephesus perhaps as a delegate from the troubled churches of Macedonia.[2] They laid hands on both and tumultuously dragged them to the theatre, the customary scene of popular gatherings.[3] Tidings of their predicament reached the Apostle, and he would have hastened to their support had he not been restrained at once by the remonstrance of his followers and by the authority of some of the Asiarchs[4] who, concerned both for his safety and for the preservation of order, sent him a message to keep away.

Scene in the theatre.

The theatre was meanwhile a scene of wild confusion. The rabble had merely caught up the cry of Demetrius and his company, and concluded that some affront had been offered to their goddess; but what it might be they did not know, and various theories were bandied about. The Jews in the assemblage took alarm lest the blame should be attached to them on the score of their general unpopularity and their notorious antipathy to image-worship; and so they prompted one of their number named Alexander to

[1] According to the reading of Cod. Bez. (D)* in vers. 28, 34, μεγάλη Ἄρτεμις Ἐφεσίων.

[2] The best attested reading in Ac. xix. 29 is Μακεδόνας, making Gaius and Aristarchus both Macedonians and differentiating the former from Gaius of Derbe (cf. xx. 4). Several MSS., however, have Ἀρίσταρχον Μακέδονα, 'Aristarchus a Macedonian'—a probable reading, Μακεδόνας being dittographic. συνέκδημος apparently denoted a deputy appointed by his church to travel with the Apostle to Jerusalem in connection with the collection for the poor (cf. 2 Cor. viii. 19); and Aristarchus is so designated here by anticipation, since the Macedonians had not yet made their collection (cf. 2 Cor. ix. 2, 3).

[3] Wetstein. Cf. the horrible story of a popular atrocity in the theatre of Ephesus in Philostr. *Apoll. Tyan.* IV. 10.

[4] Cf. p. 225.

protest their innocence.[1] He essayed to address the crowd, but when they recognised him for a Jew, they would not listen to him and shouted as with one voice : 'Great Artemis of the Ephesians !'

The town-clerk's intervention.

For two hours the uproar continued, until the town-clerk arrived on the scene. His appearance calmed the tumult, and he remonstrated with the rabble. It was quite unnecessary for them, he represented, to protest their devotion to the Great Goddess. Her honour was safe, and Gaius and Aristarchus had never impugned it. If Demetrius and his craftsmen had any grievance, they could obtain redress in the law-courts. And such tumultuary proceedings were dangerous : they were an affront to the majesty of Roman law, and they would be sternly handled. It was a salutary reminder, and the mob dispersed.

Paul's departure to Troas. Cf. 2 Cor. i. 8-10. Cf. Rom. xvi. 3, 4. Cf. 2 Cor. i. 1 ; Ac. xx. 4.

The riot was ended, but the hostility against the Apostle remained unabated. It was very bitter. He was menaced with actual violence. His lodging was attacked, and his host and hostess, Aquila and Prisca, shared his peril. It seemed to him a veritable miracle that he survived. By the mercy of God and the help of his friends he escaped from the city and got away by sea. He did not go alone. Timothy accompanied him, and so apparently did the Ephesians Tychicus and Trophimus as well as Aristarchus of Thessalonica and Gaius of Derbe. His intention had been that on leaving Ephesus he should proceed to Macedonia and thence betake himself to Corinth ; and now that his departure had been so rudely precipitated he adhered to his plan, all the more that he would thus meet Titus on his return journey and learn how his mission had prospered. It was the month of

[1] The best attested reading (ver. 33) is συνεβίβασαν, 'instructed' (cf. 1 Cor. ii. 16). The subject is ἐκ τοῦ ὄχλου, sc. τινες (cf. Jo. vii. 40, xvi. 17 ; Rev. xi. 9), 'some of the multitude,' and the parenthesis προβαλόντων αὐτὸν τῶν Ἰουδαίων explains who these were. T. R. προεβίβασαν (cf. Mt. xiv. 8), 'they advanced Alexander out of the multitude,' means that his co-religionists put him forward and the crowd hustled him to the front. Another variant is κατεβίβασαν, *detraxerunt* (Vulg.), evidently 'put him down out of the press into the arena.' If there were any reason for identifying him with 'Alexander the coppersmith' who was so active in procuring Paul's condemnation at Rome (cf. 2 Tim. iv. 14), it might be supposed that he was one of Demetrius' craftsmen, and therefore qualified to explain the situation.

January, and there was meanwhile no direct communication between Ephesus and Macedonia. Not until spring could ships venture out on the broad Ægean; but he found a coasting vessel bound for Troas, and he sailed thither. That seaport lay on the route which Titus must follow, and Paul awaited him there with the less impatience that an unexpected opportunity presented itself for preaching the Gospel.

Cf. 2 Cor. ii. 12.

Removal to Macedonia.

Cf. 2 Cor. ii. 13.

Time passed, and still Titus never appeared; and at length the Apostle could no longer repress his anxiety and determined to push forward to Macedonia. It would be early summer when he left Troas, and he would follow the familiar route of the autumn of the year 50,[1] sailing to Neapolis and settling at Philippi. There he would receive a gracious welcome from the friends who had cherished him in affectionate remembrance and repeatedly succoured him in his need; and he would meet Luke, 'the beloved physician,' whom he had left there at the close of the year 50 and who had ministered there ever since.[2] It was a glad reunion; nevertheless he was confronted by a situation which oppressed his already overburdened spirit. The controversy which the Judaist propagandists had excited in Macedonia in the course of their mischievous progress from Galatia to Achaia was still raging, and he had to address himself to its settlement with anxiety for Corinth gnawing at his heart all the while.

Cf. 2 Cor. vii. 5.

A healing ministry.

Cf. 2 Cor. viii. 18.

Cf. Ac. xx. 2.

Cf. 2 Cor. vii. 5.

It was a large and difficult task, but he was effectively reinforced by his followers from Ephesus and more especially by Luke who was known and beloved all over the Province. In their company he passed from town to town, visiting the distracted churches and allaying the strife. He encountered fierce opposition, since there was no abatement of the Jewish hostility which had threatened his life at Thessalonica and Berœa five years previously; nevertheless his efforts prevailed, and by the autumn he had not merely restored peace but engaged the churches in zealous support of the collection for the poor at Jerusalem. In Macedonia as in Galatia that generous enterprise served to heal the estrangement of the Jewish and Gentile Christians.[3]

Cf. viii. 1-4.

[1] Cf. p. 126. [2] Cf. p. 135. [3] Cf. p. 224.

It was now the month of September,[1] and the Apostle's cup of gladness was filled to overflowing by the arrival of Titus, bringing good news from Corinth. His mission had been crowned with complete and triumphant success. He had delivered the Apostle's letter, so stern yet so compassionate, and had reinforced it by his personal appeal. The Corinthians, already assailed with misgivings, had been overcome. They had recognised the unreasonableness of their lawless attitude and the gravity of the issues which it involved; and when he reminded them how much they owed to the Apostle and told them how sorely they had grieved him, they were overwhelmed with shame, and addressed themselves in good earnest to the business of reformation. The *fons et origo mali* was that flagrant scandal which had emerged a year previously, and which the Apostle had so sternly condemned, requiring that disciplinary proceedings should be instituted against the offender. It had, however, been thrust out of sight by the ensuing controversies, and the culprit had hitherto gone free. He was now arraigned, and he was unanimously condemned. Thus far there was no divergence of sentiment. All recognised his guilt, but a difference arose on the question of his punishment. Some advocated extreme severity; and these were doubtless the Apostle's party, who had throughout stood loyal to him and now desired to honour him by a complete and unqualified execution of his original mandate. But there were others who favoured a more lenient sentence. It appears that the offender shared the general repentance. He confessed and mourned his sin, and it seemed right that he should be pardoned and suffered to continue in the Church's fellowship. This counsel was approved by the majority, but a minority remained dissatisfied and protested against the decision. And not without reason, since there were certain of the majority who hardly realised the enormity of the offence. They condemned it indeed, but they were disposed to make light of it.

Success of Titus' mission. vii. 6-16.

Cf. 1 Cor. v. 3-5.

Cf. 2 Cor. ii. 6, 7.

[1] Cf. Append. I.

Fourth Letter to Corinth

(2 Cor. i-ix, xiii. 11-14)

The address. Cf. ix. 2.

It is uncertain where precisely Titus found the Apostle. It was in Macedonia, but whether at Philippi [1] or some other of the Macedonian cities does not appear. Wherever it may have been, his tidings were right welcome. Paul was already rejoicing in the happy termination of the Macedonian trouble; and when he learned of his deputy's success at Corinth, his heart overflowed and he poured forth his gladness in a gracious letter to the penitent Church. By a felicitous coincidence it was the season of the Feast of Tabernacles, the joyous harvest thanksgiving,[2] and his heart kept festival, 'rejoicing according to the joy in harvest.' His last letter to Corinth he had written with his own hand, hiding the shame of his erring converts; but concealment was now unnecessary, and he employed Timothy as his amanuensis. And, moreover, he addressed the letter not alone to the Church of Corinth but to 'all the saints in the whole of Achaia.' It was a chivalrous thought. The Corinthian scandal was notorious throughout the Province, and he would have the Church's repentance as widely published. And therefore he desired that his letter should be treated as an encyclical and circulated among the neighbouring Churches.[3]

i. 1 Paul, an Apostle of Christ Jesus through God's will, and
Timothy the brother, to the Church of God which is at
2 Corinth with all the saints in the whole of Achaia. Grace to
you and peace from God our Father and the Lord Jesus
Christ.

Distress and comfort.

He begins with a glad thanksgiving. The penitent Corinthians had apparently expressed through Titus their sorrow not only for the grief which they had occasioned him but for the tribulation which he had of late been experiencing at Ephesus. The latter was indeed, as he tells them, more

[1] According to the subscription: πρὸς Κορινθίους δευτέρα ἐγράφη ἀπὸ Φιλίππων τῆς Μακεδονίας διὰ Τίτου καὶ Λουκᾶ.

[2] Cf. *The Days of His Flesh*, pp. 300, 330 f.

[3] *E.g.*, Cenchreæ (Rom. xvi. 1). Cf. p. 189.

serious than they knew; for it was after the departure of Titus for Corinth that the malice of his enemies had reached its height and driven him from the city. But now he could bless God for it all. His distress had been a sacred fellowship in the sufferings of Christ; and if he had shared Christ's sufferings, so he had experienced also Christ's comfort, and had thus been better fitted for the task of comforting and confirming the Corinthians. Cf. Col. i. 24.

3 Blessed be the God and Father of our Lord Jesus Christ,
4 the Father of compassions and the God of all comfort, who
comforts us in all our distress in order that we may be able
to comfort the distressed of all sorts through the comfort
5 with which we are ourselves comforted by God. For, just as
the sufferings of Christ overflow on us, so through Christ our
6 comfort also overflows. And if we are distressed, it is for your
comfort and salvation; if we are comforted, it is for your
comfort, which is put in operation by endurance of the same
7 sufferings which we are experiencing. And our hope is firm
on your behalf, since we know that, as you are partakers of the
8 sufferings, you are partakers also of the comfort. For we do
not wish you to be ignorant, brothers, of our distress which befell
in Asia. Its weight was excessive, so overpowering that we
9 despaired even of life; nay, in our hearts we had come to the
decision [1] that we must die, that our confidence might not
10 rest upon ourselves but upon God who raises the dead. And
from so terrible a death He rescued us and is rescuing us; [2]
and we have set our hope in Him that He will rescue us in the
11 future also, while you also co-operate on our behalf by prayer,
so that for the blessing which they have played a part in
winning for us,[3] thanks may be rendered by many on our
behalf.

[1] ἀπόκριμα, an official decision (cf. Moulton and Milligan, *Vocab.*). ἐσχήκαμεν, aoristic perf. (cf. ii. 13, vii. 5). The perf. of ἔχω was thus used since the aor. ἔσχον had acquired the meaning 'got,' 'received' (cf. i. 15). Cf. Moulton, *Proleg.*, p. 145.

[2] ῥύεται $\mathrm{D^c}$EFGKLM, Vulg., Ambrstr. ῥύσεται, though strongly attested (ℵBCP), is hardly possible with the future following. It is the emendation of a copyist who failed to perceive that Paul is referring to his immediate dangers in Macedonia (cf. vii. 5).

[3] ἐκ πολλῶν προσώπων, 'from many actors,' connected with τὸ χάρισμα. πρόσωπον, (1) 'face,' (2) 'mask,' particularly an actor's mask (cf. *persona*), (3) an actor, *dramatis persona*, (4) an actor on the stage of life, *i.e.*, 'a person'—a late use. The word may here be taken in the sense of 'face,' ἐκ πολλῶν προσώπων being then connected with εὐχαριστηθῇ—'that thanksgiving may be made from many faces,' the glad faces bespeaking grateful hearts.

The Apostle's constant affection.

The Apostle had merited their affection. He could claim with a clear conscience that his devotion to them had never wavered. The tenderness which he was now expressing was no new thing. Even when he had dealt sternly with them, it had been ever present alike in his correspondence and in his personal intercourse, as some of them had always perceived and, as he hoped, they would all henceforth recognise.

12 For this is our boasting—the testimony of our conscience
that it was in God-given holiness and sincerity, not in carnal
wisdom but in God's grace, that we conducted ourselves in
13 the world and most of all in relation to you. For it is nothing
else that we are writing to you than what you know from our
letters or indeed from personal recognition—and I hope you
14 will recognise our disposition to the full,[1] as indeed you have
done in a measure—that we are your boast, even as you are
ours, on the Day of our Lord Jesus.

Complaint that he had broken his promise to visit Corinth. 1 Cor. xvi. 5-9.

What prompted this asseveration was the old grievance of his tardiness in visiting Corinth despite his promise.[2] He had already explained it in his second letter, but even yet, in their longing to see him and demonstrate their newborn affection, they were inclined to think hardly of him. They were suspecting him of levity and of a disposition, after the way of the world, to play fast and loose with his promises.

15 And it was with this confidence that I purposed formerly
16 to visit you, that you might receive a second grace, and to
pass by way of Corinth to Macedonia, and return from Macedonia to you and be sent by you on my journey to Judæa.
17 This, then, being my purpose, did I, as it has turned out,
show levity? Or are the plans I lay laid on the carnal principle that I may say with one breath 'Yes, yes' and with
the next 'No, no'?[3]

[1] ἕως τέλους, like εἰς τέλος (cf. *The Days of His Flesh*, p. 436, n. 2), not 'to the end' but 'to the full,' contrasted with ἀπὸ μέρους.

[2] Cf. p. 323.

[3] The word of one who is guided by mere worldly wisdom, ἐν σοφίᾳ σαρκικῇ (ver. 12), is unreliable; it is 'Yes' to-day and 'No' to-morrow. On the emphatic iteration cf. Mt. v. 37. Chrys. (followed by Beng.) takes the second ναί and the second οὔ as predicates (cf. Ja. v. 12): 'that my "Yes" should be "Yes" and my "No" "No"'—an unalterable decision, regardless of providential eventualities. This is 'planning according to the flesh,' and it is the way of 'the carnal man' (ὁ σαρκικὸς ἄνθρωπος, τουτέστιν, ὁ τοῖς παροῦσι προσηλώμενος καὶ ἐν τούτοις διαπαντὸς ὢν καὶ τῆς τοῦ Πνεύματος ἐνεργείας ἐκτὸς τυγχάνων); whereas

He meets the insinuation with a flat denial: 'our word to you is not "Yes" and "No"'; and then he delicately indicates that the blame lay not with him but with themselves. There are always two parties to a promise, and its fulfilment rests with both. Think, for example, of the promises of God. He says 'Yes' in Christ, but is this enough? Nay, it is faith that receives the promise; and it is only when His 'Yes' is answered by our 'Amen' that the promise is fulfilled. Perhaps indeed it is not fulfilled immediately, but in the grace of His Holy Spirit we have 'the earnest' of its ultimate fulfilment.

A promise conditional on the recipients' attitude.

Here is a thought which the Apostle loved. The Greek term is *arrhabon*,[1] and it signified the caution-money deposited on the conclusion of a bargain as a pledge of full payment in due course.[2] Originally a Phœnician word, it was naturally borrowed from that nation of merchants by the Hebrews, the Greeks, and the Romans. In the Apostle's day it was a common business-term,[3] precisely synonymous with the Scottish 'arles'[4] and the Old English 'wedde'[5]; and he enlisted it in the service of the Gospel. The idea is that the operation of the Holy Spirit in our souls constitutes a guar-

'The earnest of the Spirit.'

'the minister of the Spirit' (ὁ ὑπηρέτης τοῦ Πνεύματος) is like a good slave who makes a promise to his fellow-slaves and then, finding that his master disapproves, does not fulfil it. So the Apostle's promise was conditioned by the will of God. This makes excellent sense, but it appears from vers. 18-20 that Ναὶ ναί and Οὔ οὔ are merely reduplications.

[1] ἀρραβών, עֵרָבוֹן (cf. Gen. xxxviii. 17, 18), *arrhabo*, *arrha*.

[2] Suid.: ἡ ἐν ταῖς ὠναῖς περὶ τῶν ὠνουμένων διδομένη πρώτη καταβολὴ ὑπὲρ ἀσφαλείας.

[3] Cf. *Oxyrh. Pap.* 299 (a letter of late 1st c.): 'As regards Lampon the mouse-catcher, I gave him as earnest-money (ἀραβῶνα) on your account 8 drachmæ to catch the mice while they are still with young.' Also Milligan, *Select.* 45.

[4] Cf. Scott, *Redgauntlet*, Letter XI: 'he had refused the devil's arles.' *Abbot*, chap. XI: 'St. Catherine broke up house-keeping before you had taken arles in her service.'

[5] Wycl.: 'a wedde (or ernes) of the spirit.' Chaucer, *Knightes Tale*, 1218: 'Let him be war, his nekke lyth to wedde!' There was also a verb ἀρραβωνίζειν, 'hire' or 'take into one's service.' As an ecclesiastical term it signified 'espouse'; and in Mod. Gk. ἡ ἀρραβωνι(α)σμένη is 'the betrothed' and ἡ ἀρραβῶνα 'the engagement-ring'—an earnest of the full payment of the marriage-debt (cf. Moulton and Milligan, *Vocab.*). In the early Church *sponsalitiæ arrhæ* were presents which a man made to his betrothed as tokens and pledges of the espousal (cf. Bingham, *Ant.* XXII. iii. 3).

Cf. Eph. i. 13, 14. Cf. Phil. i. 6. Rom. viii. 23.

antee of God's propriety in us and the ultimate consummation of His gracious design. It is His 'seal' marking us His, a foretaste of our full heritage, a pledge that the good work which He has begun in us, He will perfect until the Day of Jesus Christ. It is 'the first-fruits of the Spirit,' the earliest sheaf of the rich harvest.

18 But, as God is faithful, our word to you is not 'Yes'
19 and 'No.' For the Son of God, Christ Jesus, who was
proclaimed among you through us—through me and
Silvanus and Timothy—did not prove 'Yes' and 'No';
20 nay, it has proved 'Yes' in Him. For to every promise
of God in Him is the 'Yes,' and therefore also through Him
21 is the 'Amen' that God may have glory through us. And
He who is confirming us and you together in Christ and put
22 His chrism on us, is God, who also sealed us and gave us
the earnest of the Spirit in our hearts.

Why he had stayed away.

And just as our response to God's promises is the condition of their fulfilment, so it was with the Apostle's promise to the Corinthians. It was their behaviour that had prevented its fulfilment. While the trouble was in progress, he had pleaded the emergence in Asia of unexpected claims; but there had been another and more potent reason, and now that the trouble was so happily ended, he was free to avow it. It was consideration for them that had kept him away. Had he visited them at that distressful crisis, he must have dealt sternly with them; and he had remained away in the hope that wiser counsels would prevail among them. He had indeed been compelled eventually to pay them a hasty visit, and it had confirmed his worst apprehensions. It was an experience which he would not willingly repeat, and so he had told them in the stern letter which he had written them on his return to Ephesus. That was indeed a stern letter, but it was love for them that had inspired it, and he had written it with a breaking heart.

Cf. 2 Cor. xii. 19-xiii. 10.

23 But I call God to witness, as my soul shall answer it, that
it was by way of sparing you that I came no more to Corinth.
24 Not that we have lordship over your faith; no, we are
helpers in working out your joy, for it is by faith that you
ii. 1 stand fast. And this was my determination in my own
interest, that I should not visit you again on a grievous

2 errand. For if I grieve you, then who is it that gladdens
3 me but the man who has grief from me? And I wrote
precisely this, that I might not, when I came, receive grief
from those who should have given me joy, confident as I
was regarding all of you that my joy is the joy of you all.
4 For out of great distress and anguish of heart I wrote to you
through blinding tears, not that you might be grieved, but
that you might perceive how my heart was full to overflowing with love for you.

Approval of the Church's judgment on the case of immorality.

This reference to his own sorrow was skilfully designed to introduce the vexed question of the Church's decision on the case of immorality. It had been a disputed judgment, and in approving it he at the same time deftly rebukes both the extreme parties. His sorrow had indeed been poignant, but it was rather a vicarious than a personal sorrow. It was not himself but the Church that had been injured, and it was the Church that had been grieved, at all events, he adds, 'in a measure,' ostensibly extenuating the culprit's offence yet withal suggesting that it were well had there been no extenuation, had the Church's grief been not merely partial but universal. Nevertheless the sentence was right. Censure was sufficient, and the dissentients must acquiesce in the decision and admit the penitent to loving fellowship. They were the Apostle's friends, and they would best evince their loyalty to him by following his example in this particular. Severity would only play into Satan's hands by driving the penitent to despair.

5 But if some one has caused grief, it is not to me that he
has caused it; no, in a measure—not to be too hard on him—
6 it is to you all.[1] Sufficient for such a man is this censure
7 pronounced by the majority; so that you should reverse
your attitude toward him and rather forgive and comfort
him, lest such a man should be swallowed up by his excessive
8 grief. And therefore I exhort you to assure him of your love;
9 for it is to this end indeed that I am writing,[2] that I may put
you to the proof and discover whether you are obedient in
10 every respect. One whom you forgive anything, I also
forgive. For indeed what I have forgiven, if I have forgiven

[1] ἀπὸ μέρους anticipates ὑπὸ τῶν πλειόνων (ver. 6). The qualification has a double purpose: (1) to alleviate the responsibility of the offender; (2) to rebuke the lax minority: the censure should have been unanimous.

[2] ἔγραψα, epistolary aorist. Cf. p. 219.

11 anything, is on your account in the presence of Christ, that we may not be overreached by Satan; for we do not ignore his devices.

Titus' report. Cf. i. 8-11.

And now the Apostle resumes his personal narrative. Driven from Ephesus he had betaken himself to Troas. His ministry there was successful, but all the while Corinth was in his thoughts, and he was wondering how Titus had fared and what report he would bring. Still Titus never appeared, and at length, that he might meet him the sooner, he had quitted Troas and passed over to Macedonia. There he had heard the joyful tidings; and now, as he looks back on those days, so dark and troubled yet so rich in blessing to Troas and Macedonia, he recognises how God had been leading him all the while, and he breaks into a pæan of thanksgiving. He likens his experience to the magnificent pageant of a Roman triumph.[1] The victorious general, followed by his troops and preceded by his fettered captives, entered the city and rode in his chariot along the Via Sacra and up the slope of the Capitol to the Temple of Jupiter amid the applause of the spectators and the fragrance of floral garlands and the odour of incense from the altars in the open temples.[2] And just as the Apostle elsewhere boasts himself 'the slave' and 'the prisoner' of Christ, so here he conceives of himself and his comrades as Christ's captives adorning His triumphal progress. He had been Christ's captive ever since the day when his rebellious will was broken on the road to Damascus; and it was a blessed condition. For the Victor was Sovereign Love, and His dominion was liberty and peace.

'I have no cares, O blessed Will!
For all my cares are Thine;
I live in triumph, Lord! for Thou
Hast made Thy triumph mine.'

The captives were the conqueror's trophies, publishing his renown; and even so the Apostle was a trophy of Christ,

[1] Cf. the descriptions of the triumphs of Pompey (Appian. *Bell. Mith.* 116, 117), Æmilius Paulus (Plut. *Æm. Paul.* 32-34), and Vespasian and Titus (Jos. *De Bell. Jud.* VII. v. 4-6).

[2] Cf. Plut. *Æm. Paul.* 32: πᾶς δὲ ναὸς ἀνέῳκτο καὶ στεφάνων καὶ θυμιαμάτων ἦν πλήρης. Hor. *Od.* IV. ii. 51, 52. Dion Cass. lxxiv. 1.

and Christ's glory was the end of his ministry. His sufferings for Christ's sake were the odours which breathed on the Conqueror's path. They were 'a fragrance of Christ,' though to the world they seemed mere ignominy, even as, says St. Chrysostom, the light is darkness to weak eyes and honey bitter to distempered palates.

12 And when I came to Troas to preach the Gospel of Christ,
13 though a door had been opened for me in the Lord, I had no
relief for my spirit through my not finding Titus my brother.
14 No, I bade them farewell and set out for Macedonia. But
thanks to God who always leads us in His triumphal train[1]
in Christ and wafts the odour of His knowledge abroad through
15 us in every place! For we are a fragrance of Christ for God's
honour among those who are on the way to salvation and
16 among those who are on the way to ruin: to the latter an
odour death-exhaled and death-exhaling, to the former an
odour life-exhaled and life-exhaling.

Efficacy of the Apostle's message.

It was a tremendous claim, nothing less than this—that the Apostle's ministry had an inherent and inevitable efficacy whether for weal or for woe; and now he proceeds to justify it. The efficacy lay in his message, inasmuch as it was the pure Word of God, unadulterated, like the teaching of the Corinthian intellectuals, with human wisdom or, like that of the Judaists, with dead tradition. Here he was not resuming the odious employment of self-commendation. There had been enough of that in his last letter, where he had perforce vindicated himself from the aspersions of the Judaists, and he would leave the graceless business to them. They had come to Corinth armed with letters of commendation from their superiors at Jerusalem, but he needed no such credentials. His converts were his letter of commendation, a letter written by Christ, not with ink but with the Holy Spirit's grace.

17 And for this who is qualified? Well, we are not, like so
many, adulterators of the wine of God's Word. No, it is in

[1] A.V. 'causeth us to triumph' represents the Apostle and his companions as occupying the place of the honoured friends who sat beside the victor in his triumphal chariot (cf. Dion Cass. li. 16, lxiii. 20). This, however, is an impossible rendering, since θριαμβεύειν is always 'lead in triumph.' Cf. Plut. *Rom.* 4: βασιλεῖς ἐθριάμβευσε. *Ant.* 84 (Cleopatra to dead Antony): μηδ' ἐν ἐμοὶ περιίδῃς θριαμβευόμενον σεαυτόν, 'suffer not thyself in my person to be led in triumph.'

its purity, it is just as God gave it, that we speak it before
iii. 1 God in Christ.[1] Are we beginning again to commend ourselves? Or do we need, like some, commendatory letters
2 to you or from you? You are our letter, inscribed on our
3 hearts, recognised and read by all men, since it is manifest
that you are a letter of Christ, ministered by us, inscribed
not with ink but with the Spirit of the living God, not on
'tablets of stone' but on 'the tablets of the heart,' tablets
of flesh.[2]

Ex. xxxiv. 1. Prov. iii. 3, vii. 3.

Its twofold excellence:

Here was the Apostle's answer to the question 'Who is qualified for this?' the justification of his claim that he was 'a fragrance of Christ,' an odour life-exhaled and life-exhaling or death-exhaled and death-exhaling according to the attitude which men assumed toward him. The efficacy lay not in himself but in his message. And what was the transcendent excellence of his message? It was twofold.

(1) A ministry of life. xxxi. 31-34.

In the first place, it was, in the language of the Prophet Jeremiah, the Gospel of 'a new covenant.' The Old Covenant was embodied in the Law, the written code of Mount Sinai. It was a series of stern and inexorable commandments, and since these were too hard for weak and sinful man, it issued in condemnation and death. But the New Covenant is a covenant of grace. It is not a written code; it is a ministry of the Spirit. It does not command; it succours and strengthens, and it issues in life.

4 And such is the confidence which we have through Christ
5 toward God. Not that by our own resources we are qualified
6 for any reasoning as proceeding from ourselves. No, our
qualification proceeds from God, who also qualified us for
the ministry of a New Covenant, not a written code but a
Spirit; for the written code kills, but the Spirit gives life.

[1] *οὐ γάρ*, ellipt.: '(we are qualified), for we are not.' *κάπηλος*, 'a trader,' especially 'an innkeeper' (*caupo*). Hence *καπηλεύειν* (1) 'trade,' especially as an innkeeper (*cauponari*); (2) 'trade dishonestly,' especially as an innkeeper who adulterates his wine. Cf. Is. i. 22 LXX: *τὸ ἀργύριον ὑμῶν ἀδόκιμον· οἱ κάπηλοί σου μίσγουσι τὸν οἶνον ὕδατι.* Ecclus. xxvi. 29. *ἐξ εἰλικρινίας* carries on the metaphor, according to the old and in nowise discredited etymology which explains *εἰλικρινής* as 'tested in the sunlight (*εἵλη*)'; the idea being that the glass of wine is held up against the light and no impurities are discovered by the searching rays.

[2] The chief MSS. read *πλαξὶν καρδίαις σαρκίναις*, 'hearts of flesh as tablets'; but T. R. *πλαξὶ καρδίας σαρκίναις* has the more ancient attestation of Iren. (v. xiii. 4), at all events according to the Latin translation.

And, in the second place, it was a ministry of transcendent and unfading glory. Here he bases his argument on that passage which relates how, when Moses descended from the Mount, bearing the two tablets of stone, 'the skin of his face shone' or, as the Septuagint Version has it, 'was glorified.' It was the lingering reflection of the glory which had shone upon him while he communed with the Lord; and when they saw it, the people were afraid. That was only a transient glory, and it quickly faded away; but the glory of the New Covenant is permanent. It is no mere reflection on the face of a human mediator; it is the divine glory which shines in the face of Jesus Christ—not a glorified but the glorifying face.

(2) A ministry of glory.

Ex. xxxiv. 29-35.

Cf. iv. 6.

7 And if the ministry of death, engraved on stones in written
characters, was invested with glory, so that the children of
Israel could not gaze on the face of Moses by reason of the glory
8 of his face—the transient glory, how shall not rather the
9 ministry of the Spirit be invested with glory? For if the
ministry of condemnation be glory, far rather does the ministry
10 of righteousness abound in glory. For the glorified has been
dimmed of its glory in this particular on account of the tran-
11 scendent glory.[1] For if the transient was attended with glory,
far rather is the permanent invested with glory.

Here lay the inspiration of the Apostle's preaching. He was proclaiming a full and abiding revelation, and it was fitting that he should use 'much boldness of speech.' The Gospel was the fulfilment of the Law, and the transience of the latter had appeared in the very hour of its promulgation. The glory which lit the face of Moses was a transient thing, a lingering reflection of the awful glory which had shone upon him while he communed with the Lord on the Mount. The people saw it while he talked with them, but he would not have them witness its disappearance lest they should think it meant that the Lord had forsaken him; and so, 'whenever he had done speaking with them, he put a veil on his face,' and took it off only 'when he went in before the Lord to speak with Him.' It was an attempt to conceal the transience of the Law, and the Jews had never to that day discovered it. The glory of the Old Covenant had faded before the

Transience of the Old Covenant.

Ex. xxxiv. 33 R.V.

[1] 'The glory of the New Covenant, overshadowing and hiding the glory of the Old, as the light of the sun that of the other stars' (Euth. Zig.).

glory of the New as the light of the stars is quenched by the sunrise, but this they had not perceived. For their thoughts were dull. It was as though a veil covered their heart, and just as they had not seen the glory fading from the face of Moses, so they had not seen it fading from the Law. They did not recognise that a new glory had dawned, nor would they recognise it till they turned from the written code to the life-giving Spirit. As it was only 'when Moses went in before the Lord to speak with Him' that the 'veil was taken from his face,' so only when their heart turned to the Lord, would its veil fall off. Then they would be emancipated from the bondage of the Law. They would see the glory of the Spirit, the tender grace of redeeming love, shining in the face of Jesus Christ, and it would irradiate and transfigure them.

12 Since, then, we have such a hope, we use much boldness
13 of speech, and are not like Moses who 'put a veil on his
face' in order that the children of Israel might not gaze
14 at the end of the transient thing. But their thoughts were
dulled;[1] for to this day the same veil remains upon the
reading of the Old Covenant, since the fact is not unveiled
15 to them that in Christ it is passing away.[2] No, down to
this day, whenever Moses is read, a veil lies on their heart;
16 but whenever it turns to the Lord, the veil is taken off.
17 'The Lord' is here the Spirit; and where the Spirit of
18 the Lord is, there is freedom. And we all, seeing with
unveiled face the reflection[3] of the Lord's glory, are trans-

[1] *πωρόω*, properly 'petrify,' *λιθοποιῶ* (Suid.). So 'make dull.' Of the heart, 'make hard' or 'callous' (cf. Mk. vi. 52, viii. 17); of the eyes, 'make dim' or 'blind' (cf. Job xvii. 7 LXX).

[2] *ἀνακαλυπτόμενον*, accus. absol., 'the fact not being unveiled that it (the Old Covenant) is being done away' (R.V. marg., Meyer). Otherwise (1) *μένει μὴ ἀνακαλυπτόμενον· ὅτι, κ.τ.λ.*, 'remains unlifted, because it (the veil) is being done away in Christ' (Vulg., Ambrstr.); (2) *ἀνακαλυπτόμενον· ὅ, τι, κ.τ.λ.*, 'remains unlifted; which (veil) is being taken away' (Bez., Luth., A.V., R.V.). It rules out both these constructions that the subject of *καταργεῖται* is not 'the veil' but 'the Old Covenant' (cf. vers. 7, 11, 13). The verb for 'removing the veil' is not *καταργεῖν* but *περιαιρεῖσθαι*.

[3] *κατοπτριζόμενοι*, not 'reflecting as a mirror' (R.V.), which would require the act. *κατοπτρίζοντες*. *κατοπτρίζεσθαι* (mid.) is 'to see the reflection' either (1) *of oneself* (cf. Diog. Laert. *Socr.* II. 33: *ἠξίου δὲ καὶ τοὺς νέους συνεχῶς κατοπτρίζεσθαι, ἵν', εἰ μὲν καλοὶ εἶεν, ἄξιοι γίγνοιντο.* *Plat.* III. 39: *τοῖς μεθύουσι συνεβούλευε κατοπτρίζεσθαι· ἀποστήσεσθαι γὰρ τῆς τοιαύτης ἀσχημοσύνης.*) or (2) *of another* (cf. Phil. *Leg. Alleg.* III. p. 107, Mangey: *μηδὲ κατοπτρισαίμην ἐν ἄλλῳ τινὶ τὴν σὴν ἰδέαν ἢ ἐν σοὶ τῷ Θεῷ*). The mirror which reflects the glory of the Lord the Spirit, is the face of Christ (cf. iv. 5, 6).

formed into the same image from glory to glory according to the wonted operation of the Lord the Spirit.[1]

In this glad letter to his penitent converts the Apostle is in no mood for controversy, yet he cannot forget the strife which had so lately raged among them and which might so easily be revived, all the more that the Judaists remained in their midst. And therefore all through his exultant congratulation there runs a note of anxious solicitude and covert admonition. That argument, so impassioned yet so restrained and elusive, on the transience of the Old Covenant and the transcendent and abiding glory of the New is a refutation of the Judaist insistence on the permanent obligation of the Law; and now he proceeds to deal with some of the personal allegations of his traducers. The first is that coarse calumny which branded him as 'a trickster,' seeking selfish ends and deceiving his dupes by flattering speech and professions of disinterestedness. His answer is that trickery was impossible for one who had been entrusted with so lofty a ministry. Its glory put cowardice and duplicity to shame. His constant appeal was to men's consciences; and if they failed to respond, the reason was that their moral sense was blinded; as he had already said, there was 'a veil on their heart' and the light of the Gospel could not penetrate it. The light which shone in the face of Christ had illumined his own heart, and his divine call was to illumine others. It was Christ, not himself, that he proclaimed; and if he proclaimed himself, it was as an example of the Gospel's illuminating efficacy.

The charge of 'trickery.'

Cf. xii. 16.

iv. 1 Therefore, having a ministry like this, in view of the
2 mercy we have experienced, we never lose heart. No, we
have renounced shame's concealments, never playing 'the
trickster' or sophisticating the Word of God,[2] but by the

[1] As in the renewal of the earth (cf. Mk. iv. 28), so in the renewal of the soul the operation of the Creator Spirit is gradual, from one degree of glory to another.

[2] *δολοῦν* is synonymous with *καπηλεύειν*, 'adulterate' (ii. 17). Cf. *ἄδολος*, 'pure,' 'unadulterated,' used of milk (1 Pet. ii. 2), grain (*Oxyrh. Pap.* 1124. 11: *πυρὸν νέον καθαρὸν ἄδολον ἄκρειθον*), wine (*ibid.* 729. 19: *τὸν μὲν οἶνον παρὰ ληνὸν νέον ἄδολον*). Cf. Moulton and Milligan, *Vocab.* Precisely equivalent is the old

manifestation of the truth commending ourselves to every
3 human conscience in the sight of God. If, however, our
Gospel is veiled, it is in the case of those who are on the
Cf. ii. 15. 4 way to ruin that it is veiled; and in their case the god of
this age has blinded the thoughts of the faithless to shut
out the illuminating beams of the Gospel of the glory of the
Gen. i. 27. 5 Christ who is 'the image of God.' For it is not ourselves
that we proclaim; it is Christ Jesus as Lord and ourselves
6 as your slaves for Jesus' sake, because it is the God that
said 'Light shall shine out of darkness,' who shone in our
hearts that we might illumine others with the knowledge
of the glory of God in the face of Christ.

The taunt of bodily weakness.

Cf. Lev. xxi. 16-24

Cf. x. 10.

Next he notices his adversaries' sneer at his physical infirmity. It was indeed a graceless taunt, yet on the lips of the Judaists it was not without excuse, since the ancient Law had required that not only the sacrificial victim but the priest who offered it should be 'without blemish,' and later legislation so far from relaxing the restriction had strengthened it, specifying no fewer than a hundred and forty-two physical defects as disqualifying for the sacred office.[1] It was thus natural that the weakness of Paul's bodily presence should figure in the Judaist indictment against his apostolic claim. And what is his reply? The fact was indisputable. He was little of stature; he was the victim of a chronic malady; and he was worn with toil and travel and bore the scars of stoning and scourging. But this was no disqualification. On the contrary, it redounded to the glory of God. As a jewel shows the more resplendent in a base setting, so the power which employed so feeble an instrument, was the more conspicuously divine. And, moreover, since his bodily infirmities were the scars of his apostolic service, they were invested with a double glory. They were his portion in the sufferings of Christ and the evidence of his devotion to the souls of men. 'It is all for your sakes.'

use of 'sophisticate' in the sense of 'corrupting by admixture.' Cf. Scott, *Woodstock*, chap. x: 'there was a vintner, his green apron stained with wine, and every drop of it sophisticated.' Similarly O. E. 'card.' Cf. Shak. 1 *King Hen. IV*. III. ii. 62 f.: 'carded his state, | Mingled his royalty with capering fools'; where Temple ed. quotes Green's *Quip for an Upstart Courtier*: 'You card your beer if you see your guests begin to get drunk, half small, half strong.'

[1] Cf. Schürer, II. i. p. 214.

7 But we have this treasure in earthen vessels[1] that the
transcendence of the power may be God's and no achieve-
8 ment of our own. At every turn we are distressed yet never
9 straitened; perplexed yet never at our wits' end; hard
pressed yet never left in the lurch; stricken down yet never
10 destroyed; always carrying about in our body the mortal
agony of Jesus, that the life of Jesus also may be manifested
11 in our body. Ever are we that are alive being delivered to
death for Jesus' sake, that the life of Jesus also may be mani-
12 fested in our mortal flesh. And so death is operative in us
13 but life in you. Having, however, the same spirit of faith
expressed in that scripture 'I had faith, and therefore I spoke,' Ps. cxvi 10.
14 we also have faith, and therefore also we speak; knowing as
we do that He who raised the Lord Jesus will raise us also with
15 Jesus and will present us with you. For it is all for your
sakes, that grace may spread from soul to soul and make
thanksgiving abound to the glory of God.

The comfort of the Resurrection.

The Apostle had a double purpose in introducing the thought of the Resurrection. He desired, in the first instance, to display the comfort which that glorious hope afforded and which sustained him amid his mortal sufferings.

16 And therefore we never lose heart. No, though our outward
man is wasting away, yet our inward man is being renewed
17 day by day. For the light distress of the moment is working
out for us, ever more and more transcendently, an eternal
18 weight of glory; while we look not at the things visible but
at the things invisible; for the things visible are temporary,
but the things invisible are eternal.

The horror of disembodiment.

The hope of the Resurrection was impressively presented at that juncture, at all events to the minds of Jewish Christians. For it was the season of the Feast of Tabernacles, which was at once a celebration of the ingathering of the harvest and a commemoration of the wilderness wanderings. For forty years the children of Israel had made their weary pilgrimage in quest of the Promised Land, pitching their tents at nightfall and striking them on the morrow to continue their march; and their experience served in after generations as a parable of this earthly life. (1 Chr. xxix. 15.) So the Apostle now employs it, and the image would appeal the more to the Corinthians when they recalled how he had earned his bread

[1] ἐν ὀστρακίνοις σκεύεσιν, 'in britel vessels' (Wycl.), worthless and fragile earthenware (cf. Ps. ii. 9). On σκεῦος cf. n. on 1 Th. iv. 4, p. 161.

among them by plying his craft of tent-making. He likens the mortal body to a tent, 'the soul's frail dwelling-house.' When it is dismantled by the rude hand of death, the soul is not left shelterless; for there awaits it a nobler habitation —that spiritual body whereof he had told them in his second letter. It was indeed a glorious prospect, yet it would seem that despite his masterly handling of the problem a perplexity still remained in their minds, and its solution is his second and main concern. Even where the hope of immortality is cherished, there is an instinctive horror in the thought of death. For how will the soul fare when it is stripped of its corporeal vesture and goes forth naked into the unknown,

> 'To bathe in fiery floods, or to reside
> In thrilling regions of thick-ribbed ice;
> To be imprison'd in the viewless winds,
> And blown with restless violence round about
> The pendent world'?

The blank misgiving which the thought inspires is poignantly expressed in that question of the dying Emperor Hadrian:[1]

> 'Soul of mine, thou fleeting, clinging thing,
> Long my body's mate and guest,
> Ah now, whither wilt thou wing,
> Pallid, naked, shivering,
> Never, never more to sport and jest?'

There was indeed reassurance in the Christian revelation of
Cf. 1 Th. iv. 16. the resurrection of the body, yet it was but partial. For it is at the Second Advent that the dead will be raised, and meanwhile their souls must remain naked, divested of their mortal bodies and yet unclothed with their 'heavenly habitation.' Here, in large measure, lies the *raison d'être* of the hope which animated the primitive Christians that the Coming of the Lord was at hand. Their longing was that they might live to witness it and thus escape death and never experience the
1 Cor. xv. 52. desolation of disembodiment. For them, 'in a moment, in

[1] 'Animula vagula, blandula,
Hospes comesque corporis,
Quæ nunc abibis in loca,
Pallidula, rigida, nudula,
Nec, ut soles, dabis jocos?'

the twinkle of an eye,' the transformation would be wrought and 'the mortal thing be swallowed up by life.' The Apostle shared this hope, this eager longing; yet even though it were denied him, he was undismayed. For in any case the resurrection of the body was a blessed certainty. It was the end which God had in view, and the present experience of the sanctifying operation of the Holy Spirit was 'the earnest' of its ultimate consummation. With this prospect in view he went his way with a stout heart; and while he would fain be home, his only ambition was that, whether here or there, he might please the Lord and be ready for the inquisition of His Judgment-seat.

v. 1 For we know that if our earthly tent-dwelling be dismantled, we have one of God's building, an house which no
2 hands have made, eternal, in the heavens. For in this we
groan, longing to put on over it our heavenly habitation,
3 if so be that by putting it on we shall not be found naked.
4 For indeed we who are in the tent groan under its weight,
on the understanding that it is not our desire to put off our
vesture, no, but to put on a vesture over it, that the mortal
5 thing may be swallowed up by life. But He who wrought
us for this very end is God, who gave us the earnest of the
6 Spirit. Therefore, being always courageous and knowing
that, while we are at home in the body, we are exiled from
7 the Lord; for it is by faith that our steps are guided, not
8 by sight—ay, we are courageous and are well content rather
9 to be exiled from the body and get home to the Lord. And
therefore also our ambition is that, whether at home or in
10 exile, we should be well pleasing to Him. For all of us must
appear in our true colours before the Judgment-seat of
Christ, that each may receive what his body has earned
according to his actions, whether a good award or an evil.

This was the Apostle's attitude. He left the unknown future in God's hands, confident that it would be wisely and mercifully ordered. He was animated by that spirit which the Old Testament Scriptures so largely inculcate—'the fear of the Lord,' that spirit of reverent and trustful submission to the Sovereign Will of Almighty God which is evermore 'the beginning of wisdom,' 'a strong confidence' and 'a fountain of life.' He left the future in God's hands, and his one concern was the discharge of the ministry which had

The ministry of reconciliation.

Ps. cxi. 10; Prov. i. 7. Prov. xiv. 26, 27.

been entrusted to him. His ambition was to 'persuade men'; and though his pleading was construed by his Judaist adversaries as unscrupulous plausibility,[1] God knew his motive, and he hoped he was justified by the consciences of the Corinthians. In saying that he was not 'commending himself' to them; he was rather seeking to show them the realities. His critics called him 'mad,' but what they deemed madness was a passion for God and for the souls of men. The love of Christ had possessed him, and it had revolutionised his estimate of life, of men, and of the world. Life for him was now life in Christ, since he had died with Christ and had been raised with Him. And his estimate of men was correspondingly altered. Earthly distinctions no longer counted. He 'knew no man according to the flesh.' He is thinking here of the Judaists and their insistence on the efficacy of external rites and more especially their denial of his apostleship because he had never known the Lord in the days of His flesh. That contention was valid only if the Lord were a mere historic personage, 'a Christ according to the flesh'; and though the Apostle had once shared that Jewish ideal of a secular Messiah, he had now attained to a loftier conception. Christ was for him the Risen and Glorified Saviour, truly known not according to the flesh but according to the Spirit, not by historic tradition but by immediate and vital fellowship. And thus, furthermore, the universe was transfigured in his eyes. The old order had passed away and a new order had arisen; and what made the difference was Christ's revelation of God's thoughts and purposes. The world was alienated from God. It had rebelled against Him; and it had seemed that there was no hope for guilty sinners save the averting of His wrath. It lay with them to approach Him with overtures of reconciliation. And, behold, He had visited the world in Christ, and had taken on Himself the burden of its guilt and demonstrated that the enmity is all on man's side. It is the world that needs to be reconciled to God, not God that must be reconciled to the world.[2] And this amazing revelation defined the Apostle's

Cf. Gal. ii. 19, 20.

[1] Cf. p. 197.

[2] On the Pauline doctrine of 'reconciliation' cf. *The Atonement in the Light of History and the Modern Spirit*, pp. 111 f.

ministry. He was Christ's ambassador, presenting God's overtures and offering a full atonement and a free forgiveness.

11 It is, then, because we know 'the fear of the Lord' that we Cf. Gal. i.
'persuade men'; and to God we have appeared in our true 10.
colours, and I hope that at the bar of your consciences also
12 we have so appeared. We are not again commending ourselves to you; no, we are giving you an outlet [1] for a boast
on our behalf, that you may counter those whose boasting is
13 all concerned with face-value and not with heart-reality. If
14 we are 'mad,' it is for God; if we are sane, it is for you. For
the love of Christ has us in its grasp, and this is our judgment:
15 One died on behalf of all, consequently all died; and He died
on behalf of all that those who live should no longer live for
themselves but for Him who on their behalf died and was
16 raised. And so we henceforth know no one according to the
flesh. Though we have conceived of a Christ according to
17 the flesh, yet now that is no longer our conception. And so,
if one be in Christ, there is a new creation: [2] the old order
18 has passed away; see, a new order has arisen. And it is all
from God, who reconciled us to Himself through Christ and
19 gave us the ministry of reconciliation, to this effect—that God
was in Christ, reconciling a world to Himself, not reckoning
their trespasses to them and having entrusted to us the message
20 of reconciliation. On Christ's behalf, then, we are ambas-
sadors, as though God were appealing to you through us. We
21 pray you on Christ's behalf, be reconciled to God. Him who
never knew sin, He made sin on our behalf, that we might
become God's righteousness in Him.[3]

This is the message of the Gospel, and the Apostle now enforces his argument with a personal appeal. The Corinthians had welcomed the message when they heard it from his lips during his ministry among them, and would they now disown it and embrace the teaching of his Judaist adversaries? It was a momentous issue; and it would commend his appeal and determine their decision if they remembered his credentials—his constant devotion and his many sufferings in the ministry of the Gospel. A personal appeal.

vi. 1 And in co-operation with Him we also appeal to you that
2 it be not in vain that you welcomed the grace of God. For
He says:

[1] Cf. p. 215. [2] Cf. p. 220.
[3] Cf. n. on Gal. iii. 13, p. 204.

Is. xlix. 8.

'At an acceptable moment I hearkened to thee,
And in a day of salvation I succoured thee.'

See, now is the right 'acceptable moment'; see, now is
3 'the day of salvation.' Never in anything do we put a
hindrance in the way, lest blame be cast upon the ministry.
4 No, in everything we commend ourselves as God's ministers
should—in much endurance, in distresses, in necessities, in
5 straits, in stripes, in imprisonments, in riots, in toils, in
6 vigils, in fastings, in purity, in knowledge, in long-suffering,
7 in kindness, in the Holy Spirit, in unaffected love, in the
preaching of the Truth, in the power of God; by the weapons
8 of righteousness in the right hand and in the left; by glory
and dishonour; by ill report and good report; as deceivers
9 and true men; as ignored and acknowledged; as 'dying'
and, see, we 'live'; as 'chastened and not put to death';
10 as grieved yet always rejoicing; as poor yet enriching
many; as having nothing yet possessing everything.

Ps. cxviii. 17, 18.

Apology for digression.

Here the Apostle bethinks himself. He has wandered far from the path of his argument, and he playfully apologises. His long digression was an outpouring of his overflowing tenderness, and it proved how large a space the Corinthians occupied in his affection. If there was any narrowness of heart, it was manifestly not on his side; and he begs them to open their hearts to him as he had opened his to them. He deserved it; for he had always treated them generously. No one had ever been the poorer for him during his ministry among them. Here, he need not reassure them, he was not reproaching them. He was talking frankly in the fulness of his pride and gladness.

Pss. li. 15, cxix. 32.

11 'Our lips have been opened' to you, Corinthians; 'our
12 heart has been enlarged.' It is not in us that you are
straitened for room; it is in your own affections that you
13 are straitened. And as a recompense in kind—I say it
vii. 2 as to my children—be you also enlarged.[1] Make room for us.
We wronged no one, we damaged no one, we overreached
3 no one. I am not saying it to condemn you; for I have
already said that you are in our hearts to die with us and to
4 live with us. I am very frank with you; I am always
boasting on your behalf. I am filled with comfort; my joy
is overflowing upon all our distress.

Cf. ix. 2.

[1] Vers. 14—vii. 1, a fragment of the first Corinthian letter. Cf. p. 236.

The good news from Corinth.

After his long digression he resumes his personal narrative. He has told how, in his anxiety to meet Titus and learn how he had fared at Corinth, he quitted Troas and crossed over to Macedonia; and now he tells what happened there. The Judaist controversy was raging, and it was a difficult and indeed a dangerous situation since he had not only to deal with internal dissension but to face the violence of his ancient and inveterate enemies, the Macedonian Jews. And thus it was an unspeakable comfort and gladness to him when Titus arrived and reported the successful issue of his mission.

Cf. ii. 13.

5 For after we had come to Macedonia our flesh had no relief.
At every turn we were distressed—fightings without, fears
6 within. But the Comforter of the humble, even God, com-
7 forted us by the arrival of Titus; and not only by his arrival
but by the comfort which the thought of you afforded him in
telling us the story of your longing, your lamentation, your
8 zeal on my own behalf to the enhancement of my joy, because,
though I grieved you in my letter, I do not regret it. Though
I did regret it, perceiving [1] that that letter grieved you, though
9 but for a brief hour, I now rejoice, not that you were grieved,
but that your grief issued in repentance; for you were grieved
as God would have you, that in nothing might you suffer loss
10 by us. For the grief which God would have works a repentance which issues in salvation—a repentance which is never
11 regretted; whereas the world's grief works out death. For
see, this very circumstance that you were grieved as God would
have you—what earnestness it wrought out in you, ay, what
self-defence, what vexation, what fear, what longing, what
zeal, what vindication! In everything you proved yourselves
12 to be pure in the affair.[2] The fact is that, though I wrote
you, it was not that the wrong-doer might be punished or his
victim righted but that your earnestness on our behalf might
13 be manifested among you in the sight of God. On this score
it is that we have been comforted.

An achievement of Titus.

It was the Apostle's stern letter that had achieved the happy result, yet it would have availed nothing without the personal address of Titus. By his courage, wisdom, tact, and kindliness he had succeeded where the gentle and timorous Timothy had failed. He had amply justified the Apostle's

[1] Reading βλέπων with Vulg. (*videns*), which satisfactorily rectifies a manifestly corrupt passage. The MSS. have βλέπω or βλέπω γάρ.

[2] τῷ πράγματι, a delicate reference to the unnamable scandal. Cf. 1 Th. iv. 6.

confidence, and he was well entitled to the satisfaction which so signal a triumph afforded him.

> And besides our comfort we were still more abundantly
> rejoiced at the joy of Titus because his spirit has received
> 14 refreshment from you all. However I may have boasted to
> him on your behalf, I was not put to shame; no, as it was all
> truth that we spoke to you, so our boasting to Titus also turned
> 15 out truth. And his affection is flowing out to you the more
> at the remembrance of your unanimous obedience—how with
> 16 fear and trembling you received him. I rejoice that in every-
> thing I have courage in you.

Neglect of the collection for the poor at Jerusalem.

There was one alloy in the Apostle's gladness: the Corinthians had neglected the collection for the poor at Jerusalem. Soon after his settlement at Ephesus he had sent Titus and his Antiochene colleague to Corinth to commend the beneficent enterprise, and it had been espoused with much good will.[1] Presently, however, a dispute had arisen regarding the method to be pursued in taking the collection, and the question had been referred to the Apostle in the consultative rescript which the Corinthians had addressed to him the previous summer. The dispute was concerned merely with the mode of procedure, and after his decision he had assumed that the business was in progress until, to his discomfiture, he learned from Titus that nothing had been done.

Cf. 1 Cor. xvi. 1-4.

Macedonian liberality.

And so he appeals to them to repair their neglect; and by way of incentive he begins by telling them of the splendid generosity of the Macedonian churches, which was the more remarkable since Macedonia was at that period groaning under an oppressive burden of imperial taxation.[2] The people were desperately poor, yet they had insisted on bearing their part in the charity. It was an act of self-consecration, signalising their happy deliverance from the Judaist controversy, and it had occurred to the Apostle that the Corinthians might well follow the example and attest their penitence by a like devotion. And so he had enlisted Titus to revisit them and complete his good work by engaging their liberality.

[1] Cf. p. 234.

[2] Cf. Arnold, *Later Roman Commonwealth*, II. pp. 381 ff.

viii. 1 But we acquaint you, brothers, with the grace of God
2 vouchsafed among the churches of Macedonia—that it is
in the thick of a distressing ordeal that their joy is so
abundant, and their deep poverty issued in the abundant
3 riches of their liberality. According to their ability, I
4 testify, and beyond their ability, of their own free will with
much appeal they begged of us the privilege of participating
5 in the ministry to the saints. And it was not merely as
we had hoped; no, they first gave themselves to the Lord
6 and to us through the will of God, insomuch that we
appealed to Titus that he should follow up the good beginning he had already made by accomplishing among you this
7 grace also. Ay, as you abound in everything—faith and
eloquence and knowledge and the love which we have
inspired in you—see that you abound in this grace also.

An appeal of honour.

It was not a command that he was addressing to them; it was an appeal to their honour. And their incentive was threefold: the example which their Macedonian neighbours had set; the gratitude which they owed to Christ for His infinite self-sacrifice; and, furthermore, the obligation which, in the Apostle's judgment, rested upon them, for their own credit, to make good the enthusiastic protestations of last year. The collection was no oppressive or inequitable imposition. They were asked to contribute according to their resources; and the appeal was addressed not to Corinth alone but to all Gentile Christendom, and they were required merely to play their proper part.

8 I am not saying it in the way of a commandment; no, I am
employing the earnestness of your neighbours to prove the
9 genuineness of your love. For you recognise the grace of our
Lord Jesus Christ—that for your sakes, when He was rich,
He became poor, that you by His poverty might become rich.
10 And I give you an opinion in this matter: this is to your
advantage, since you made a beginning a year ago not merely
11 in doing it but also in desiring it. And now accomplish the
doing also, that your eagerness in desiring it may be matched
by your accomplishment of it out of the resources you have.
12 For if the eagerness be there, it is acceptable according to the
13 means it may have, not according to what it has not. The
intention is not that others should be relieved and you dis-
14 tressed. No, it is that, on the principle of equality, at the
present crisis your abundance may meet their lack in order
that their abundance in turn may meet your lack, so that

Ex. xvi. 18. 15 equality may result, as it is written: 'He who gathered much had no more, and he who gathered little had no less.'

Delegates to Corinth.

It was not without reluctance that Titus had undertaken his first mission to Corinth some two years previously; but after his recent experience he was otherwise disposed. He welcomed the Apostle's proposal and was eager to set out. He was not going alone. Two others would bear him company. One was a preacher who had gained a distinguished reputation in Macedonia, and who had been elected by the churches of the province to accompany Paul when he returned to Jerusalem, and convey their contributions thither. This the Apostle is careful to mention, and it would bring the blush to the faces of the Corinthians. His enemies in their midst had charged him with malfeasance in the administration of the collection,[1] and it was that cruel calumny which had dictated this arrangement. He would not handle the fund: each church must appoint a delegate to convey its contribution to the Holy City. It would seem that this distinguished delegate was none other than Luke, who for the last five years had laboured in Macedonia [2] and henceforth bore the Apostle company. Philippi had been the headquarters of his Macedonian ministry, and the Philippian church would naturally entrust him with the conveyance of its contribution. The other companion of Titus was doubtless his Antiochene colleague who had attended him on his first eleemosynary mission to Corinth and who had abundantly proved his capacity. For all three the Apostle bespeaks a gracious reception. Titus needed no introduction, and it was a strong recommendation of his companions that they were 'commissioners of churches.' It became the Corinthians to show them honour not only in their personal but in their representative capacity. Their slighting would be an affront to the churches which had commissioned them.

16 And thanks be to God who is putting the same earnestness
17 on your behalf into the heart of Titus. He not merely accepts
our appeal but his reluctance is all gone and of his own free
18 will he is setting out to visit you.[3] And we are sending with

[1] Cf. pp. 321 f. [2] Cf. p. 135.

[3] ἐδέξατο, ἐξῆλθεν, συνεπέμψαμεν (vers. 18, 22), ἔπεμψα (ix. 3), epistolary aorists. Cf. p. 219.

him the brother whose praise in the Gospel is all over the
19 churches,[1] and who, moreover, has been elected by the churches
as our fellow-traveller in connection with this grace which is
being ministered by us. It is the Lord's own glory and our
20 eagerness that we have in view; this being our concern—
that no one should blame us in connection with this rich store
21 which is being ministered by us; for we are 'safeguarding our Prov. iii. 4
honour' not only 'in the Lord's sight' but 'in the sight of LXX.
22 men.' And we are sending with them our brother whose
earnestness we have proved many a time in many a matter
and now find largely increased by his large confidence in you.
23 As regards Titus, he is my comrade and fellow-worker for you;
and as for our brothers, they are commissioners of churches,
24 they are the glory of Christ. Therefore in demonstrating
toward them your love and our boasting on your behalf you
are doing it in the face of their churches.

Incentives to liberality. And now the Apostle commends the collection to the liberality of the Corinthians. First, he reminds them that their credit was at stake. On the strength of their protestations a year ago he had boasted to the Macedonians how much Corinth was doing, and now it turned out that Corinth had done nothing. Some of the Macedonians intended accompanying him to Achaia presently, and what would they think if they discovered on their arrival that his boasting had been groundless? It was to obviate this unpleasant *dénouement* that he was sending the three delegates in advance; and he bids the Corinthians retrieve their neglect and save his face, and their own faces too. Then he reminds them of the religious motive. It is the testimony of Scripture that 'God loves a blithe giver' and recompenses liberality. It is the sowing of a rich harvest. And there was a peculiar incentive in the present instance. The Gentile collection

[1] The general opinion of the Fathers that this distinguished brother was Luke (Orig. in Eus. *Hist. Eccl.* VI. 25; Hieronym.; 'certain' quoted by Chrys. Cf. Grot.) has been discredited by their fancy that ἐν τῷ εὐαγγελίῳ refers to his Gospel, which in fact was not yet written. Nevertheless the identification is highly probable. He had laboured for over five years in Macedonia, and of no other, so far as evidence goes, could it have been said that 'his praise was all over the churches.' And from his introduction of the first pers. pron. in Ac. xx. 4, 5 it appears that he had been with Paul at Corinth and accompanied him on his return journey through Macedonia. From ver. 2 it appears that he did not accompany him from Macedonia to Corinth, and it is a reasonable supposition that he was one of the delegates who had preceded him (cf. ix. 3-5).

for the Jewish poor was not merely a worthy charity; it was a statesmanlike enterprise. It was an effective irenicon, tending to the reconciliation of Christendom by demonstrating to the Jewish Christians that Gentile Christianity was a practical reality. 'Thanks to God,' cries the Apostle, 'for His unspeakable bounteousness'—the regal munificence of His grace![1] That was the supreme and overmastering incentive.

ix. 1 Regarding the ministry to the saints[2] it is indeed super-
2 fluous for me to write you. For I know your eagerness,
and I am boasting of it on your behalf to the Macedonians—
that Achaia has been prepared a year ago; and your zeal
3 stimulated most of them. And I am sending the brothers
that our boast on your behalf may not be an empty one in
this particular—that, as I was saying, you may be prepared,
4 lest it be that, if Macedonians come with me and find you
unprepared, we—to say nothing of you—may be put to
5 shame where we thought we had standing-ground.[3] Therefore I deemed it necessary to appeal to the brothers that
they should go beforehand to you and arrange beforehand
your promised blessing, that it may thus be ready as a bless-
6 ing and not as an exaction. And here is the rule: 'Niggardly
sowing, a niggardly harvest; bountiful sowing, a bountiful
7 harvest.'[4] Let each give as he has decided beforehand in
Prov. xxii. his heart, not as a grievous or necessary duty; for 'God
8 LXX. 8 loves a blithe giver.' And God has the power to bestow
abundance of every grace upon you, that you may in everything ever have every sufficiency[5] and abound in every good
Ps. cxii. 9. 9 work, as it is written: 'He scattered; he gave to the poor;
10 his righteousness abides for ever.' And He who furnishes
Is. lv. 10. 'seed to the sower and bread for eating' will furnish and
Hos. x. 12 multiply your seed, and make 'the fruits of your righteous-
LXX. 11 ness' grow; while at every turn you are enriched for every
sort of liberality which through us works out thanksgiving
12 to God, because the ministry of this sacred service does not
only supply the wants of the saints but also overflows in

[1] Cf. n. on Rom. v. 15, p. 407.

[2] περὶ μὲν γὰρ τῆς διακονίας, 'I have written of my delegates and not of the collection, *for* it is superfluous to write of the latter'—a courteous expression of confidence in their liberality.

[3] Cf. n. on xi. 17, p. 332.

[4] A proverb. Cf. n. on Gal. vi. 7, p. 218.

[5] αὐτάρκεια, properly a philosophical term, 'self-sufficingness,' 'independence,' but frequent in Common Greek in the sense of 'the necessary and fitting amount.' Cf. Moulton and Milligan, *Vocab.*

13 a stream of thanksgiving to God. The proof of you which
this ministry affords moves them to glorify God for your
confessed allegiance to the Gospel of Christ and the liberality
14 of your impartation to them and to all; while they also
in prayer on your behalf long for you by reason of God's
15 surpassing grace toward you. Thanks to God for His
unspeakable bounteousness!

Exhortations and sign-manual.

The letter closes with exhortations to reconciliation, unity, and peace, befitting the penitent Church;[1] and the Apostle appends his accustomed sign-manual.

xiii. 11 And now, brothers, farewell. Be knit together,[2] be comforted, be of the same mind, be at peace; and the God
12 of love and peace will be with you. Greet one another
13 with a saintly kiss. All the saints greet you.
14 THE GRACE OF THE LORD JESUS CHRIST AND THE LOVE
OF GOD AND THE FELLOWSHIP OF THE HOLY SPIRIT BE
WITH YOU ALL.

V

SOJOURN AT CORINTH

Ac. xx. *2b*, *3a*; Rom.

Paul's departure to Corinth.

It was in the month of September, 56 A.D., that the glad letter was despatched to Corinth. The Apostle remained yet a while in Macedonia not merely to complete his ministry there but to afford the Corinthians time to make their collection ere he should arrive among them; and it was probably about the beginning of December when he set out. He did not go alone. Several of the Macedonians accompanied him—a Berœan named Sopater, the son of Pyrrhus, and two Thessalonians, Aristarchus who had been at Ephesus when the riot took place and had been rudely handled by the mob, and his fellow-townsman Secundus. He was attended also by Gaius of Derbe[3] who had suffered with Aristarchus in the riot, and by Tychicus and Trophimus,

Cf. 2 Cor. ix. 1-5.

Cf. Ac. xix. 29.

[1] x-xiii. 10, the stern letter. Cf. pp. 327 ff.

[2] Cf. n. on 1 Th. iii. 10, p. 161.

[3] He is styled 'Gaius of Derbe' (Ac. xx. 4) to distinguish him from Gaius of Corinth, Paul's host. Valckenaer, followed by Blass, emends Γάϊος Δερβαῖος καὶ Τιμόθεος into Γάϊος, Δερβαῖος δὲ Τιμόθεος, 'Gaius, and Timothy of Derbe' in view of the reading Μακεδόνας in Ac. xix. 29 (cf. p. 342). Timothy, however, belonged not to Derbe but to the neighbouring Lystra. Cf. p. 100.

the two Ephesians who had shared his flight from the Asian Capital.[1] All these, at all events, were with him when he took his departure from Corinth three months later, and it is likely that they accompanied him thither. Corinth was merely a station in his journey to Jerusalem, and the three Macedonians had doubtless been delegated to convey their churches' contributions.

Cf. 2 Cor. viii. 19, 20; Rom. xv. 25, 26.

His employment there.

Cf. 1 Cor. i. 14; Rom. xvi. 23.

He had a gracious reception on his arrival. He no longer needed to earn his daily bread; for his convert and friend, the large-hearted Gaius, welcomed him into his home and hospitably entertained him. His visit lasted three months, and to outward appearance it was an uneventful time. He engaged in no missionary activities; indeed, in view of the perils and anxieties which he had recently sustained in Asia and Macedonia, it may well be supposed that he had need of repose and welcomed the breathing-space which his sojourn at Corinth afforded. Yet the days did not pass unprofitably. His mere presence was a benediction, and his gracious converse would comfort and confirm the penitent church. Above all, he employed himself in a task of measureless and enduring value; for it was then that he composed the grandest of his extant Epistles, a work which ranks as his chief literary monument and constitutes not the least precious of Christendom's sacred possessions.[2]

A treatise on the Judaist controversy.

From the outset of his career Jewish hostility had been the Apostle's chief obstacle; and more embarrassing than the enmity of the unbelieving Jews who accounted him a renegade, a traitor to his people and his God, was the opposition of those Jewish Christians who insisted on the permanent obligation of the ceremonial Law and reprobated his Gospel of salvation for Jews and Gentiles by faith in Christ. It had seemed as though the controversy were settled by the decree of the Council of Jerusalem at the beginning of the year 50, and he had gone on his second mission with a light heart;

[1] For Ἀσιανοί (Ac. xx. 4) Cod. Bez. (D) reads Ἐφέσιοι. Trophimus was certainly an Ephesian (cf. Ac. xxi. 29), and so, it would appear (cf. Eph. vi. 21; 2 Tim. iv. 12), was Tychicus also.

[2] Cf. Coleridge, *Table Talk*, June 15, 1833: 'St. Paul's Epistle to the Romans is the most profound work in existence; and I hardly believe that the writings of the old Stoics, now lost, could have been deeper.'

but on his return to Syrian Antioch in the spring of 53 he learned that Judaist propagandists had followed him through Galatia and sown dissension in his churches there. He had remedied the mischief first by a hasty letter and then by a personal visit; but as he proceeded on his third mission it appeared that they had tracked his footsteps westward and poisoned the minds of his converts in Macedonia and Achaia. It was a grave menace to the progress of the Gospel, demanding more serious and effective treatment than he had hitherto, amid his manifold distractions, been able to accord it. His sojourn at Corinth afforded him a fitting opportunity, and he availed himself of it. He resumed the argument which he had roughly sketched in his impassioned remonstrance with the churches of Galatia,[1] defining the relation between the Law and the Gospel, expounding and enforcing his doctrine of Justification by Faith, and examining the problems which it involved.

The problem of its destination.

This treatise is the letter which is commonly known as 'the Epistle to the Romans'; and though the title is merely traditional, yet it seems to carry the Apostle's express attestation. For he addresses 'all who are at Rome' and presently affirms his eagerness to 'preach the Gospel to you also who are at Rome'; and thus it would appear that the destination of the letter was the Christian community in the Imperial Capital. On closer scrutiny, however, a difficulty emerges. (i. 7, 15.)

The Apostle's intimacy with his readers.

Turn to the closing chapter. This is a personal appendix. It begins with a 'commendation' of Phœbe, the bearer of the letter, attesting her *bona fides* and bespeaking a welcome for her; and then follows a long series of greetings to friends of the Apostle in the church which he is addressing. It is here that the difficulty lies; and it is twofold. On the one hand, though this was an ambition which he had long cherished and hoped ere long to realise, he had never visited Rome; and how then is it possible that in a church which he had never seen he should have had so many acquaintances, nay intimate, personal friends—all that extensive catalogue of (Cf. xv. 22-29. Cf. i. 10-15.)

[1] Cf. Lightfoot, *Galatians*, p. 49: 'The Epistle to the Galatians stands in relation to the Roman letter, as the rough model to the finished statue.'

men and women whom he specifies by name and greets with such close knowledge and tender affection?

Ephesians among them.

Again, while the majority are strangers to us, there are three whom we recognise, and these belong not to Rome but to Ephesus. First of all, and with special honour and affection, he mentions Prisca and Aquila. It is true that they belonged originally to Rome; but they had been banished thence by the anti-Jewish edict of the Emperor Claudius and had migrated to Corinth, where Paul had made their acquaintance in the autumn of the year 51.[1] They had left Corinth with him in the spring of 53 and accompanied him to Ephesus.[2] There they settled, and they were still there when he returned in the ensuing October.[3] Their house was his abode during his Ephesian ministry, and they risked their lives on his behalf in the riot which so abruptly terminated it in January, 56.[4] They were still at Ephesus some ten years later; and hence it would appear that they were there at the time of the Apostle's sojourn at Corinth betwixt December, 56, and February, 57. Another to receive a greeting is Epænetus; and he is designated 'Asia's first-fruits for Christ.'[5] That is to say, he was the earliest convert in the Province, and it was doubtless during the Apostle's brief stay at Ephesus in the year 53, on his return journey to Syrian Antioch, that he was won.[6] In any case, he was an Ephesian, since it was at Ephesus that the Gospel was first preached in the Province of Asia.

Cf. 2 Tim. iv. 19.

The destination apparently not Rome but Ephesus.

The situation, then, is that this closing chapter of the letter is addressed, not to a community which, like the church at Rome, Paul had never visited, but to one where he was well known and had numerous intimates. Such a community was the church at Ephesus; and it is to it that the only familiar names in the catalogue of the Apostle's friends actually belonged. This circumstance, if it stood alone, would indicate that Ephesus was the destination of the

[1] Cf. p. 151.
[2] Cf. p. 189.
[3] Cf. p. 228.
[4] Cf. p. 343.
[5] Rom. xvi. 5: ἀπαρχὴ τῆς Ἀσίας ℵABCD*FG. T.R. Ἀχαΐας is disproved not only by documentary evidence but by the fact that 'the first-fruits of Achaia' were the household of Stephanas (cf. 1 Cor. xvi. 15).
[6] Cf. p. 191.

letter; but the fact remains that it is expressly addressed to the church at Rome.

The truth is that 'the Epistle to the Romans' is an encyclical or circular letter.[1] It deals, not with a local question, but with a matter of universal concern, a far-reaching controversy which had already disturbed the Churches of Galatia, Macedonia, and Achaia, and menaced the future progress of the Faith. The Apostle had dealt with it personally in those particular arenas; but his adversaries were prosecuting their malign activities, traducing him where he was yet unknown and creating a prejudice which would be hard for him to overcome when he should journey thither. To obviate this embarrassment he wrote an encyclical dealing exhaustively with the question, and despatched it to the communities which were exposed to the assaults of the Judaist propagandists. His solicitude turned mainly in two directions. In the Province of Asia there were numerous Churches which, though he had never seen them, had been created by his ministry at Ephesus, particularly in the valley of the Mæander and the Lycus, that populous district whence his physical malady had hitherto debarred him.[2] Among these were the Churches of Colossæ, Laodiceia, and Hierapolis, and others which had been established by the labours of his Ephesian colleagues and converts but which had never 'seen his face in the flesh.' Then there was Rome, the Imperial Capital. She was the goal of the Apostle's desire. The Gospel would never dominate the world until the mistress of the world was won; and as he travelled ever farther westward, he yearned more and more for the day when he would reach Rome.

An encyclical.

Cf. Col. ii. 1.

Cf. Ac. xix. 21, xxiii. 11; Rom. xv. 22-24.

[1] This was first perceived by Renan, who distinguished four copies. The encyclical is i-xi; and it was sent to (1) the Roman Church with xv added; (2) to the Ephesian Church with xii-xiv, xvi. 1-20 added; (3) the Thessalonian Church with xii-xiv, xvi. 21-24 added; and (4) an unknown Church with xii-xiv, xvi. 25-27 added. His view is criticised by Lightfoot (*Bibl. Ess.*, pp. 287 ff.), who supposes that the Epistle as it stands was addressed to the Roman Church, and the Apostle subsequently adapted it for use as an encyclical by cutting off chaps. xv, xvi and substituting the doxology (xvi. 25-27), and also omitting ἐν Ῥώμῃ (i. 7, 15). Cf. Hort's criticism in same volume (pp. 321 ff.); also Appendix to W. H., pp. 110-13). The question is luminously treated by Lake (*Earlier Epistles of St. Paul*, chap. VI).

[2] Cf. pp. 121 ff., 224.

Original address.

It was thus needful, in the interest of the cause which lay so near his heart, that the truth should be presented in Asia and, above all, in Rome; and it was for the Christians in the Imperial Capital especially that he composed this treatise, this exposition of the issues involved in the Judaistic controversy. As it stands, it is addressed 'to all who are at Rome, God's beloved,' 'to you also who are at Rome'; but this is not the original text. Our earliest manuscript dates from the fourth century,[1] and in the text which Origen employed a century earlier the words 'in Rome' are absent from the address.[2] This means that in the original draft of the encyclical the destination was left undefined. The address ran: 'to all who are at ——, God's beloved,' 'to you also who are at ——'; and when the letter was assigned to a particular locality, the destination was entered in the blank space. The copies for the Province of Asia would be addressed 'to all,' 'to you also, who are at *Colossæ*,' '*Laodiceia*,' and so forth; and the copy for Rome 'to all,' 'to you also, who are at *Rome*.'

Multiplicity of benedictions.

And now turn to the close of the letter. What here arrests attention is the multiplicity of benedictions. A benediction commonly marks the conclusion of a letter, yet there are here no fewer than three. The first closes the fifteenth chapter: 'Now the God of peace be with you all. Amen.' This should be the end; but the Apostle proceeds further,
xvi. 20. and then he pronounces a second benediction: 'The grace

[1] Codex Sinaiticus (א).

[2] Origen's commentary on Rom. exists only in a Latin version, and this reads 'omnibus qui sunt Romæ, dilectis Dei' (ver. 7), 'et vobis qui Romæ estis' (ver. 15); but that ἐν Ῥώμῃ was absent from his text is proved by a scholium in S (Codex Athous Lauræ, 8th or 9th c., based on the lost text of Origen's commentary): *τοῦ 'ἐν Ῥώμῃ' οὔτε ἐν τῇ ἐξηγήσει οὔτε ἐν τῷ ῥητῷ μνημονεύει*, 'he mentions "at Rome" neither in the exposition nor in the passage' (*i.e.*, the text prefixed to the exposition). This means that, while inserting ἐν Ῥώμῃ in his text in deference to the MSS. of his day, the scribe explains that the phrase was absent from the text of Origen which he is reproducing. It was necessary that the hiatus should be supplied in lectionary use, and ἐν Ῥώμῃ was naturally inserted, since the encyclical was destined *in primis* for the Roman Church. Another device, however, appears in G (Codex Bœrnerianus Dresdensis, 9th c.), which in ver. 15 omits τοῖς ἐν Ῥώμῃ and in ver. 7 reads τοῖς οὖσιν ἐν ἀγάπῃ Θεοῦ, 'to all who are in the love of God.' This was an early reading. Cf. Ambrstr. (4th c.): 'Quamvis Romanis scribat, illis tamen scribere se significat qui in charitate Dei sunt.'

of our Lord Jesus Christ be with you.' And neither is this the end. Fresh greetings follow, and then a third benediction: 'The grace of our Lord Jesus Christ be with you all. Amen.' And thereafter the letter at length closes with a doxology. Ver. 24. Vers. 25-27.

Appendix of local messages.

It seems a bewildering tangle; but a clue to its unravelment is furnished by the fact that the final doxology is placed by numerous authorities at the close of the fourteenth chapter.[1] And this, it appears, was its original position. The fourteenth chapter concluded the encyclical, which, being properly a treatise and not a letter, fitly closed with a doxology rather than a personal benediction. And conceive what happened when the encyclical was despatched to its various destinations. Not only was the address inserted at the beginning but a personal message was appended at the close. It was sent to Rome, and indeed it was Rome that lay chiefly on the Apostle's heart when he wrote it; and then the fifteenth chapter was added by way of a personal message. It was sent also to the Churches of Asia; and then it was addressed to the mother-church at Ephesus for circulation in the Province, and it was accompanied by a personal message to the Ephesian Christians—the first twenty verses of the sixteenth chapter. And what of the ensuing paragraph? It is a special greeting from the inner circle of the Apostle's friends and his amanuensis; and it would be inserted after his personal message in every copy of the encyclical. All that he had written was accounted precious in after days, and it was inevitable that his messages to the great Churches of Rome and Ephesus should be permanently incorporated. The doxology, properly the close of the encyclical, was generally transferred to the end as a fitting Vers. 21-24.

[1] L (Cod. Angel. Rom., 9th c.), Syr. and Arm. Verss., Chrys. Origen (*In Ep. ad Rom. Comm.* x. 43) observes that the heretic Marcion (2nd c.) had cut away not only the doxology but the whole of chaps. xv, xvi, making xiv. 23 the close of the Epistle; while in the other copies, uninfluenced by Marcion, he found the doxology diversely placed. In some codices it followed xiv. 23, whereas in others it stood at the end of the Epistle, *ut nunc est positum*. The fact is that Marcion's text was not, as Origen supposes, a deliberate mutilation of the Epistle; it was the original encyclical. And Tertullian also seems to have known the Epistle in that abbreviated form; at all events, he refers to xiv. 10 as occurring 'in the closing section' (*in clausula*). Cf. *Adv. Marc.* v. 14.

xvi. 24. conclusion of the whole ;[1] and then the preceding benediction appeared superfluous. It seemed to copyists an accidental repetition of the previous benediction ; and hence it is omitted in the principal manuscripts.[2]

Ver. 20.

The amanuensis. Cf. xvi. 21, 22.

Though Timothy was with the Apostle, he did not on this occasion serve as his amanuensis. The office was performed by one Tertius, who is otherwise unknown. An expert hand was required for the execution and reduplication of so important a document, and Tertius was doubtless a professional scribe ; possibly he may have been the private secretary of Gaius. In any case he was a Christian ; and it is evident that he was a personage of some consequence in the Corinthian Church, else he would hardly have presumed to send his greeting to the various Churches which received the encyclical.

ENCYCLICAL ON JUSTIFICATION

('Epistle to the Romans')

INTRODUCTION (i. 1-15)

The address.

The letter opens with the customary address ; and the Apostle with characteristic skill elaborates the stereotyped formula, and defines at the outset the main issues of the controversy. The Judaist attack was directed principally against his Apostleship and his Gospel ; and here he vindicates both. His Apostleship rested on a double basis. He was an Apostle by *redemption,* since he was 'a slave of Jesus Christ,' 'bought for freedom' ;[3] and by *divine appointment,* since he had been 'set apart,' first, in God's eternal purpose and, then, by his 'calling' in due season. And as for his Gospel, his message of salvation for Jew and Gentile, it was no innovation, as the Judaists alleged, but the fulfilment of an ancient promise enshrined in the prophetic Scriptures—the Saviour's Incarnation and His glorious Resurrection.

[1] The theory that the doxology is a liturgical addition (cf. Lake, *Earlier Epistles*, pp. 359 ff.) is so far supported by its omission from Marcion's text.

[2] ℵABC.

[3] Cf. p. 265.

i. 1 Paul, a slave of Jesus Christ,[1] by calling an Apostle, set Cf. Gal. i. 15; Ac. xiii. 2.
2 apart to preach God's Gospel which He promised in advance
3 through His Prophets in the Holy Scriptures, concerning
His Son, who was a descendant of David according to the
4 flesh and was defined 'Son of God' in power, according to
the Spirit of Holiness, by the resurrection of the dead[2]—
5 Jesus Christ our Lord. Through Him we received grace and
apostleship for the achievement of faith's surrender among
6 all the Gentiles on His Name's behalf, including you who by
7 calling are Jesus Christ's. To all who are at ——, God's
beloved, by calling saints. Grace to you and peace from God
our Father and the Lord Jesus Christ.

Personal explanations. The Apostle was addressing churches which he had never yet visited, and he apprehended that they might be aggrieved at his seeming neglect. Indeed it is likely that during his long ministry at Ephesus he had intended visiting the numerous churches in the Province and they had complained of his remaining all the while in the capital and denying them the privilege of seeing his face and hearing his voice. And so, ere entering upon his argument, he absolves himself from blame. He assures his readers of his affectionate and prayerful interest in them, his desire to see them, and his hope that he might ere long achieve it. It was notorious how his purpose had hitherto been overruled by the providence of God, and it could simply be 'wilful ignorance' on their part if they persisted in suspecting him of deliberate neglect.

8 First,[3] I thank my God through Jesus Christ for you all,

[1] The authorities vary between 'Ιησοῦ Χριστοῦ (ℵAEGKLP, Chrys.) and Χριστοῦ 'Ιησοῦ (B, Arm., Orig., Aug., Ambrstr.). The distinction is that 'I. X. starts from our Lord's humanity and rises to His deity (cf. Chrys.: καὶ τὰ τῆς οἰκονομίας ὀνόματα προβάλλεται, κάτωθεν ἀναβαίνων ἄνω)—the Synoptic order; whereas X. 'I. starts from His deity and descends to His humanity—the Johannine order.

[2] The Christ (Messiah) of Jewish expectation was 'the Son of God' merely as the King of Israel (cf. Pss. ii. 6, 7, lxxxix. 27) of David's lineage; but our Lord was defined 'Son of God' in a deeper sense by (1) His miraculous power, ἐν δυνάμει (cf. xv. 19), (2) His perfect holiness, κατὰ πνεῦμα ἁγιωσύνης, and (3) His Resurrection. ἐξ ἀναστάσεως νεκρῶν, not simply the resurrection of Christ (which would be ἐξ ἀναστάσεως αὐτοῦ ἐκ νεκρῶν), but that also of all who are united to Him. His resurrection was not solitary: it involved the resurrection of believers (cf. 1 Cor. xv. 20-23).

[3] πρῶτον μέν should be balanced by εἶτα δέ, but grammatical sequence is characteristically overborne by the rush of thought.

9 that your faith is being noised all over the world. God whom
I serve in my spirit in the Gospel of His Son, is my witness
10 how unceasingly I make mention of you, always in my prayers
asking that now at length the way may, in the will of God,
11 be cleared for me to visit you. For I am longing to see
you, to impart to you some spiritual gift that you may be
12 strengthened, or rather that we may both be comforted while
13 I am among you by our mutual trust, yours and mine. And
I do not wish you to ignore the fact,[1] brothers, that many a
time I have proposed to visit you—and I have been prevented
up to this point—that I might win some harvest among you
14 as I have done among the rest of the Gentiles. Both to
Greeks and to Barbarians, both to wise and witless,[2] I am
15 a debtor; so I am all eagerness[3] to preach the Gospel to you
also who are at ——.

I

DOCTRINAL (i. 16–v)

The Apostle's Conception of Christianity: Justification by Faith (i. 16–iv)

The thesis.

First he enunciates his thesis in a twofold proposition: *salvation is by faith* and *it is universal*—not for the Jews only but for 'every one who has faith, both the Jew, in the first instance, and the Greek.' It may seem as though he invalidated his argument by inserting the phrase 'in the first instance' and thus, apparently, according the Jews a position of preference.[4] This, however, were a misconstruction of his thought. He indeed ascribes a priority to the

[1] ἀγνοεῖν, cf. n. on 1 Th. iv. 13, p. 163.

[2] A comprehensive designation of the Gentile world. The Greeks were the cultured and enlightened Gentiles (σοφοί), and the Barbarians the rude races (ἀνόητοι). Cf. Hesych.: Ἕλληνες, φρόνιμοι εἴτε σοφοί· βάρβαροι, ἀπαίδευτοι. βάρβαρος is onomatopoetic, and denotes a foreigner who spoke an unintelligible language, mere 'babble' in Greek ears.

[3] Three possible constructions: (1) τὸ κατ' ἐμέ (cf. Eph. vi. 21; Col. iv. 7; Phil. i. 12) subj. and πρόθυμον pred.: 'my disposition is eager to preach the Gospel.' τὸ κατ' ἐμέ is then a periphrasis for ἐγώ. (2) τὸ κατ' ἐμὲ πρόθυμον subj. and εὐαγγελίσασθαι pred.: 'my eager desire (*propensio ad me attinens*) is to preach the Gospel.' (3) τὸ κατ' ἐμέ adverbial and parenthetic and πρόθυμον nominal: 'thus, so far as I am concerned, there is an eager desire to preach the Gospel.'

[4] Hence πρῶτον is omitted by several authorities (BG, Tert.).

Jews, but it is a priority in opportunity and responsibility and not in privilege. They were the elect nation, and their history had been a *præparatio Evangelii*. They were God's witnesses, the repositories and vehicles of His universal grace. The Synagogue was a divinely prepared nidus for the Gospel; and therefore it was that wherever the Apostle arrived in the prosecution of his world-wide mission, he first of all sought the Jewish community and presented his message to them; and it was only when they rejected it and refused their vocation, that he turned to the Gentiles. The Jews stood first in opportunity, and when they failed, they stood first in condemnation.

Cf. Ac. xiii. 14, 46; xxviii. 17-28.

16 I am not ashamed of the Gospel: it is God's power for
salvation to every one who has faith, both the Jew, in the
17 first instance, and the Greek. For God's righteousness is
evermore revealed in it as faith grows from more to more,[1] as
it is written: 'The righteous man on the score of faith will
live.'

Hab. ii. 4, cf. Gal. iii. 11.

Its demonstration.

And now he proceeds to demonstrate his thesis. His argument is that other methods have been tried and have conspicuously and lamentably failed. He adduces successively the experiences of the Gentile world and the Jewish, and shows how neither has attained righteousness; and then he introduces the divine remedy. What mankind has failed to achieve has been made possible in Christ.

1. *Failure of the Gentiles to attain Righteousness* (18-32)

Neglect of the revelation in Nature.

The law of the moral order is twofold: first, unrighteousness is ever pursued by the wrath of God, the indignation wherewith, inasmuch as He is holy, He must needs regard it and which, however its operation be delayed, issues in inevitable judgment; and, second, knowledge is the measure

Cf. Ps. xxxiv. 16.

[1] ἐκ πίστεως εἰς πίστιν, a Jewish phrase denoting gradual progress, advancement from stage to stage. Cf. the Rabbinical maxim (quoted by Wetstein): 'A man sitting and studying in the Law advances from law to law, from ordinance to ordinance, from verse to verse.' This is the principle of intellectual progress, and it is the principle also of spiritual progress. Cf. 2 Cor. iii. 18: ἀπὸ δόξης εἰς δόξαν.

Cf. iii. 20; Lk. xxiii. 34; 1 Tim. i. 13.

of guilt: there is no guilt where there is no knowledge, no transgression where there is no law. It may seem as though the latter clause cleared the Gentiles. They had no Law like the Jews, and their ignorance should have absolved them. In fact, however, they were not ignorant. They 'possessed the truth,' and their condemnation was that they 'possessed it in unrighteousness.' They had indeed neither the Jewish revelation in the Law nor the better revelation in Christ; but they had the revelation in Nature, 'that universal and public manuscript that lies expans'd unto the eyes of all,' proclaiming the existence, the power, and the beneficence [1] of God. It was indeed meagre in comparison with the revelation of grace; yet it was amply sufficient to render the unrighteousness of the Gentiles inexcusable.

Idolatry.

They had a revelation, and they perverted it. They closed their eyes to the light, and they were stricken with judicial blindness.[2] The tragedy began in pride, and it ended in folly—the folly of idolatry. There were two sorts of idolatry in the ancient world. One was the idolatry of the Greeks—the worship of the human. Their gods were 'magnified men,' more beautiful than mortals and also more passionate. They deified human attributes, and worshipped not only Apollo, the god of light and beauty, but Dionysus, the god of the wine-cup; not only Athene, the goddess of wisdom, but Aphrodite, the goddess of lust. Then there was animal-worship, which had its chief home in Egypt, that land of prehistoric civilisation. It was a gross superstition, and it was derided by the heathen of the West,[3] who were thus far at least superior, that in worshipping the human they worshipped a true 'image of God.' Nevertheless both kinds of idolatry degraded their votaries. The law is that men grow like the objects of their worship; and the heathen were like their idols—licentious and brutal.

18 For God's wrath is evermore revealed from heaven against
all impiety and unrighteousness of men who possess the truth

[1] Implied in ηὐχαρίστησαν (ver. 21). Cf. Ac. xiv. 17; xvii. 25.

[2] Cf. vers. 21, 22. Observe the transition from act. (ἐδόξασαν, ηὐχαρίστησαν) to pass. (ἐματαιώθησαν, ἐσκοτίσθη, ἐμωράνθησαν). The perversion of the revelation was their own act, and the consequence was God's judgment. They closed their eyes, and God blinded them.

[3] Cf. Juv. xv. 1-4.

19 in unrighteousness,[1] inasmuch as what may be perceived of
God is manifest among them; for God manifested it to them.
20 For ever since the creation of the world His invisible attributes
—His everlasting power and divinity—have been clearly seen,[2]
being conceived by His works, that they might be inexcusable,
21 inasmuch as, though they had recognised God, they did not
glorify Him as God or give Him thanks. No, they were
stricken with futility in their reasonings, and their stupid
22 heart was darkened. Professing to be wise, they were be-
23 fooled, and 'changed the glory' of the incorruptible God Ps. cvi. 20.
'for the similitude' of an image of corruptible man and fowls
and quadrupeds and reptiles.[3]

Moral degradation.

The evidence lay before all eyes in the actual condition of the heathen world in those days; and the Apostle points to the prevalence of that unnatural vice which disgraced pagan society and stains so many pages of classical literature. He sees in it a direct judgment of God. The heathen abandoned God, and God abandoned them to uncleanness. Nor did the tragedy end there. Lust is, in the first instance, self-degradation; but its malignant operation extends beyond the individual. 'It hardens all within, and petrifies the feeling,' and it makes the sinner a curse to his fellows. The prevailing licentiousness blasted the heathen world; and the Apostle depicts this final stage of the moral declension.

24 And therefore God abandoned them in the lusts of their
hearts to uncleanness, that their bodies might be degraded
25 among them;[4] since they exchanged the truth of God for the
lie,[5] and adored and served the creature rather than the
26 Creator,[6] who is blessed for ever. Amen. For this reason it
is that God abandoned them to degrading passions. Their
27 females exchanged the natural use for the unnatural; and

[1] κατέχειν, not 'hold down' (R.V.), but a strengthened ἔχειν, 'have in one's grasp,' 'have and hold,' 'possess.' Cf. 2 Cor. vi. 10.

[2] καθορᾶν (cf. κατέχειν), a strengthened ὁρᾶν. Cf. Job x. 4: ἢ ὥσπερ βροτὸς ὁρᾷ, καθορᾷς; 'Is Thy clear vision as a mortal's vision?'

[3] Cf. Strabo, 812.

[4] The MSS. vary between ἐν αὐτοῖς (the better attested) and ἐν ἑαυτοῖς. With the former ἀτιμάζεσθαι is pass.: 'that their bodies might be dishonoured among them'; with the latter, mid.: 'that they might dishonour their bodies with one another.'

[5] That is, 'the idol' (cf. Rev. xxi. 27, xxii. 15), since an idol (1) is itself false and (2) deceives its worshippers.

[6] Cf. p. 220.

the males likewise forsook the natural use of the female and
were inflamed in their desire for one another, males with males
working unseemliness and receiving in their own persons the
28 inevitable retribution of their error. And as they did not
think God worth keeping in recognition, God abandoned them
29 to a worthless mind to do unfitting things.[1] They were
replete with every sort of unrighteousness, rascality, greed,
malice; they were laden with 'murdering mischief,'[2] strife,
30 craft, spitefulness; whisperers, calumniators, haters of God,[3]
bullies, swaggerers, braggarts,[4] inventors of evils,[5] disobedient
31 to parents, stupid, faithless, destitute of natural affection,
32 pitiless. Fully cognisant of God's righteous ordinance, that
those who practise such things are worthy of death, they not
only do them but applaud those who practise them.

Justification of the Apostle's indictment of heathendom:

It is a ghastly picture of cruelty and terror and despair, yet it is a sober delineation. It is drawn from life, and perhaps the surest demonstration of its verisimilitude is a recital of certain large and definite enormities which cast a lurid light on the multitudinous details of the Apostle's indictment.

(1) The practice of delation.

(1) The practice of delation. A despot is never secure, and the Roman Emperors were haunted by continual

[1] A play upon *δοκιμάζειν* and *ἀδόκιμος* (cf. note on 1 Th. v. 21, p. 165). Literally, 'as they did not approve God to have Him in full recognition, God abandoned them to a reprobate mind.'

[2] *φθόνος φόνος*, a jingling byword (cf. Gal. v. 21 T. R.), not to be pressed literally. Cf. Iamblichus (in Suidas): *τὸ δεύτερον τοῦ φθόνου γράμμα ξέσας εὕροις ἐν αὐτῷ τὸν φόνον γεγραμμένον.*

[3] Either *θεοστύγεις* (act.), 'hating God,' *Dei osores* (Cypr., Euth. Zig.) or *θεοστυγεῖς* (pass.), 'hated by God,' 'hateful to God,' *Deo odibiles* (Vulg.). The former is the more suitable to the context, all the other epithets being active. 'Agitur enim de vitiis, non de pœnis' (Grot.). It is true that, wherever else it occurs in extant literature, the word is passive; but the active use is equally possible, and Suidas assigns both uses to it and takes it as act. here: *οἱ ὑπὸ θεοῦ μισούμενοι, καὶ οἱ Θεὸν μισοῦντες. παρὰ δὲ τῷ Ἀποστόλῳ 'θεοστυγεις' οὐχι οἱ ὑπὸ Θεοῦ μισούμενοι ἀλλ' οἱ μισοῦντες τὸν Θεόν.*

[4] *ὑβριστάς, ὑπερηφάνους, ἀλαζόνας.* *ὕβρις*, coarse insolence, exhibited in physical violence (cf. Mt. xxii. 6; Lk. xviii. 32). *ὑπερηφανία*, insolent, overweening pride, the spirit of a haughty and scornful aristocrat (cf. Lk. i. 51). *ἀλαζονία*, 'braggadocio,' vain and unwarranted pretension. *Def. Plat.*: *ἕξις προσποιητικὴ ἀγαθοῦ ἢ ἀγαθῶν τῶν μὴ ὑπαρχόντων.* Cf. 1 Jo. ii. 16: *ἡ ἀλαζονία τοῦ βίου*, 'the braggart boast of life.' This article of the Apostle's indictment is illustrated by Juvenal's picture of the dangers of the city streets after nightfall (III. 268 ff.).

[5] Existing vices lost their piquancy, and men taxed their ingenuity to invent new ones. Cf. Tac. *Ann.* VI. 1: 'tuncque primum ignota antea vocabula reperta sunt.'

apprehension of conspiracy. What reason they had appears from the startling fact that of the twelve who reigned during the first century, only three were suffered to die natural deaths; and it is little wonder that, breathing an atmosphere of suspicion, they pursued a policy of jealous surveillance and ruthless intimidation. It was a reign of terror. The merest trifle—a word, a jest, a look, a gesture—was liable to a sinister construction, and was visited with condign vengeance. The only safety lay in fulsome adulation and denunciation of offences against the imperial majesty; and a law of Tiberius, assigning to the informer a share in his victim's property,[1] encouraged the iniquity which darkened the life of Rome until it was abolished during the brief reign of Pertinax (A.D. 192-193). A mere accusation sufficed. Condemnation was certain, and the victim generally anticipated his doom by self-destruction.[2] It is told that during the dark days of Nero's reign a drunken fellow used to go about the city singing the Emperor's songs and denouncing all who did not listen admiringly and contribute liberally.[3] The Roman satirist speaks of an informer 'slitting throats with a fine-edged whisper'; [4] and it is the informers that the Apostle has in view when he speaks of 'whisperers, calumniators.'

(2) The prevalence of suicide.

(2) The prevalence of suicide. Here is the conclusion of an epistle where the philosopher Seneca discourses on the uncertainty of the world: [5] 'You know this—to how many death is useful, how many it frees from tortures, poverty, complaints, punishments, disgust. We are not in the power of any so long as death is in our own power.'

'Nor stony tower, nor walls of beaten brass,
Nor airless dungeon, nor strong links of iron,
Can be retentive to the strength of spirit;
But life, being weary of these worldly bars,
Never lacks power to dismiss itself.
If I know this, know all the world besides,

[1] Tac. *Ann.* II. 32.
[2] Cf. Sen. *De Benef.* III. 26.
[3] Philostr. *Vit. Apoll. Tyan.* V. 39.
[4] Juv. IV. 110: 'tenui jugulos aperire susurru.'
[5] *Epist.* xci.

That part of tyranny that I do bear
I can shake off at pleasure.'[1]

Suicide was appallingly frequent in that age and, it is significant, less among the lower orders than among the wealthy and distinguished members of society. Sometimes it was resorted to as an escape from tyranny, but in most cases the motive was sheer weariness of life, the disgust of hearts sated with pleasure and sick of disillusionment. Amid the wealth and luxury and pride of her high civilisation Rome was stricken with the curse of her own iniquity.

'On that hard Pagan world disgust
And secret loathing fell.
Deep weariness and sated lust
Made human life a hell.'

(3) The cruelty of heathen society.

(3) The sadness of heathen society was matched by its cruelty. It was, as the Apostle observes, not merely 'pitiless' but 'destitute of natural affection,' that tenderness which the very brutes have for their kind and especially for their offspring.[2] If evidence be required, there is no lack. There is, for example, the horrible custom of destroying weakly children. Realise what it means that Seneca, a Roman scholar and gentleman, could write thus with never a qualm:[3] 'We strike down mad dogs; we butcher a fierce and wild ox, and knife sickly cattle lest they infect the herd; we destroy monstrous offspring; children too, if they are born weakly and deformed, we drown. It is not anger but reason to separate the useless from the healthy.' And there is the barbarity of exposing infants. As soon as a child was born, it was brought and laid at its father's feet. If he 'took it up,'[4] it was reared in his family; but he need not take it up unless he chose. If he shrank from the trouble and expense of rearing it or had already as many children as he desired and objected to further subdivision of the inheritance, he would let it lie; and then it was 'exposed'—thrown out to die on a mountain-side or other desolate place, like the

[1] Shak. *Jul. Cæs.* I. iii. 93 ff.

[2] *στοργή*. Chrys. compares Ecclus. xiii. 15: *πᾶν τὸ ζῶον ἀγαπᾷ τὸ ὅμοιον αὐτοῦ, καὶ ἄνθρωπος τὸν πλησίον αὐτοῦ.*

[3] *De Ira*, I. 15.

[4] *Sustulit*, *suscepit*.

infant Œdipus on Mount Cithæron. It is an eloquent fact that, though the Greek and Latin languages have each several words for 'house,' neither has a word for 'home.' And the reason is that it is 'natural affection' that makes a home, and lust had banished natural affection from the heathen world. Natural affection, and pity too. What pity was there in a society which tolerated the institution of slavery [1] and was entertained with gladiatorial combats and fights between criminals and wild beasts in the circus ? [2]

And these enormities provoked no protest. The heathen 'not only did such things but applauded those who practised them.' That was the climax of their guilt, their utter condemnation. The mere doing of evil need not argue depravity, since one may be hurried by passion into conduct which he disapproves in calmer mood, and one never realises the enormity of a sin until it has been committed and stands before him in hideous actuality. But it condemns a man if he contemplates wickedness and accords it his sympathy and approval.

2. *Failure of the Jews to attain Righteousness* (ii, iii)

The Apostle's indictment of heathendom would command the approval of his Jewish readers. They despised the Gentile world, and the exhibition of its depravity would gratify their national prejudice. But now he turns to the other side of his argument and shows that, if the Gentiles have failed to attain righteousness, the Jews have failed no less signally and with far less excuse. The very iniquities which they condemned in the Gentiles, they practised themselves. **Indictment of the Jews.**

ii. 1 And therefore you are inexcusable, you man whoever you are that judge. In passing judgment on your neighbour you pronounce judgment against yourself; for you practise the self-same things, you that judge.

It vitiated the moral judgment of the Jews that they conceived themselves as occupying a privileged position. They were Abraham's descendants, and they reasoned that, **Refutation of their false confidence:**

[1] Cf. pp. 569 ff. [2] Cf. p. 254.

Cf. Mt. iii. 8-10; Jo. viii. 33, 39.

since God had made a covenant with Abraham and his seed after him to all generations, they were permanently secure: whatever they might do, the engagement stood. Against this fatal confidence the Apostle arrays two stern truths.

(1) Impartiality of God's judgment.

One is the impartiality of God's judgment. His sentence is 'according to truth': it is not arbitrary; it is determined by realities. The sole test recognised by Scripture is conduct: 'He will render to each according to his works'; and the mistake of the Jews lay in their failure to perceive that their peculiar privileges were gracious appeals, and if they disregarded these, they would then receive the heavier doom. First in opportunity, they would be first in condemnation.

2 We know that the doom of God lights according to truth on
3 those who practise such things. But is this your reckoning,
you man that pass judgment on those who practise such things
and do them the while—that *you* will escape the doom of
4 God? Or is it that you despise the riches of His kindness
and forbearance and long-suffering, ignoring the fact that the
5 kindness of God is drawing you to repentance? But, obdurate
as you are and impenitent in heart, you are storing up for
yourself wrath on the Day of Wrath—the Day when the
6 righteousness of God's judgment will be revealed. He 'will
7 render to each according to his works': to those who by the
path of persistence in good work are seeking glory and honour
8 and incorruption, life eternal; while to those who are factious
and disobedient to the truth but obedient to unrighteousness,
9 the award will be wrath and fury. Distress and anguish will
light upon every human being who works out evil, both the
10 Jew, in the first instance, and the Greek. But glory and
honour and peace are the portion of every one who works
11 good, both the Jew, in the first instance, and the Greek. For
there is no respect of persons with God.[1]

Ps. lxii. 12; Prov. xxiv. 12.

(2) Universality of moral obligation.

The other truth is the universality of moral obligation. Neither Jews nor Gentiles were exempt. For both alike sin involved condemnation—for the Gentiles who have no Law, since they have the revelation in Nature and Conscience; and for the Jews who have the Law, since it is not the knowledge of the Law that avails but its observance.

12 All who have sinned without the Law, without the Law will
also perish; and all who have sinned within the Law, in terms

[1] An epigram disposing of the Jewish claim to special privilege. On προσωποληψία cf. p. 199.

13 of the Law will be judged. For it is not the hearers of the Law
that are righteous with God; no, it is the doers of the Law
14 that will be accounted righteous (For, when Gentiles who have
no Law, do by natural instinct the Law's requirements, these
men, though they have no Law, are a Law to themselves,
15 since they display the Law's work written on their hearts,
their conscience bearing witness with it and their reasonings
16 debating in condemnation or defence.)[1] on the Day when
God judges the secrets of men according to my Gospel through
Christ Jesus.

Here is the principle which condemned the Jews and justified the Apostle's indictment of them as no less guilty than the Gentiles. The vain boast of the Law.
Their very name was a proud distinction, since in the Hebrew Jew means 'praised'; and they boasted of their high privileges, oblivious that these were their heavy condemnation. Cf. Gen. xxix. 35; xlix. 8.
Here he has the Rabbis particularly in view—those Scribes and Pharisees whom the Lord had so terribly impeached. Mt. xxiii.
They were the custodians and interpreters of the Sacred Law, 'the Teachers of Israel'; Jo. iii. 10.
and the Apostle's allegation, like the Lord's, is that their conduct was a flagrant violation of their teaching and a stark invalidation of their pretensions. The Law forbade theft, and the Rabbis practised it in the most heartless fashion by their cruel impositions and greedy exactions in the name of religion. Cf. Mt. xxiii. 14, 25.
The Law forbade adultery, and they were grossly incontinent.[2] They abhorred idols, yet, says the Apostle, they had no scruple in enriching themselves by the plunder of heathen temples. And the charge is amply authenticated. It is recorded[3] that in the year 19 A.D. a Jew, who had committed

[1] Another *marginale* (cf. p. 245). The Apostle is here enforcing the universality of moral obligation, and in order to beat down the Jewish pretension to special privilege he has affirmed that the obligation rests no less on the ἔννομοι than on the ἄνομοι. On reading over the manuscript he perceives the probability of the objection being raised that, while it is just that the Jews who sinned in spite of the restraint of the Law should be punished, it were unjust that the Gentiles, lacking that advantage, should be held guilty. And so he adds this marginal comment, recalling his previous statement (cf. i. 19, 20) that, though they have no special revelation, the Gentiles have the revelation in Nature and Conscience and are therefore inexcusable. Observe the graphic metaphor: a law-court with legal code, witness, prosecutor, advocate, judge. The Unwritten Law (γραπτὸν ἐν ταῖς καρδίαις αὐτῶν) is the statute, Conscience the witness, their reasonings prosecutor and advocate, God the Judge.

[2] Cf. *The Days of His Flesh*, p. 414.

[3] Jos. *Ant*. XVIII. iii. 5.

some illegality in his own country and escaped to Rome, set up there as a Rabbi, and gained such influence over a wealthy proselyte, a Roman lady named Fulvia, that she entrusted him and three accomplices with the conveyance of a costly offering of purple and gold to the Temple at Jerusalem, and they appropriated it to their own use. The rascality which plundered the Lord's treasury, would not spare heathen shrines; and the Jews of the Dispersion were notoriously addicted to temple-robbery, insomuch that a notion prevailed in the Gentile world that the name of their capital was originally *Hierosyla*, 'the Temple-robber,' and they had subsequently altered it to *Hierosolyma*.[1] Such was the odium which they thus incurred that a Jewish Law was enacted for the repression of the scandal. 'Let no one,' it ran,[2] 'blaspheme the gods which other cities recognise. No one must plunder alien temples or reset a treasure dedicated to any god.'

Cf. Ac. xix. 37.

17 But if you bear the grand name of 'Jew,' and pillow your
18 head on the Law,[3] and boast in God, and read His will, and
19 are an adept in casuistry,[4] having the Law by heart,[5] and are
confident that you are yourself 'a guide of the blind,' 'a light
20 to those in darkness,' 'an instructor of the senseless,' 'a
teacher of babes,' possessing the embodiment of knowledge
21 and truth in the Law;[6]—you, then, that teach your neighbour,
do you not teach yourself? You that preach against stealing,
22 do you steal? You that talk about not committing adultery,
do you commit it? You that abhor idols, do you pillage

[1] Jos. *Contra Apion.* I. 34.

[2] Jos. *Ant.* IV. viii. 10.

[3] Alexander the Great so admired Homer that he slept with the volume under his pillow. Cf. Plut. *Alex.* 8. Eustath. *Præfat. Iliad.* i. 20: τὴν Ὁμηρικὴν βίβλον ἀπαγόμενος καὶ τὴν κεφαλὴν, ὅτε ὑπνοῦν δέοι, ἐπαναπαύων αὐτῇ.

[4] δοκιμάζεις τὰ διαφέροντα. δοκιμάζειν, either 'test' or 'approve' after testing (cf. note on I Th. v. 21, p. 165). διαφέρειν, either 'differ' or 'be better than.' Hence δοκιμάζειν τὰ διαφέροντα, either 'test the things that differ' or 'approve the things that are excellent.' The former is preferable, the reference being to the Rabbical *penchant* for casuistical refinements, nice distinctions. Cf. *The Days of His Flesh*, pp. 132, 299, 413.

[5] κατηχούμενος ἐκ τοῦ νόμου, 'being catechised out of the Law.' Oral instruction was the method in the Jewish schools, and a Jew had the Law committed to memory in childhood. Cf. p. 23. *The Days of His Flesh*, p. xvii.

[6] μόρφωσις, either 'shaping,' or 'the thing shaped,' 'embodiment.' Suid.: μόρφωσιν· σχηματισμόν, εἰκόνα. Here 'embodiment.' What a statue is to the sculptor's conception, that the Law is to knowledge and truth.

23 temples? You who boast in the Law, do you by the trans- Is. lii. 5;
24 gression of the Law dishonour God? For 'the name of God Ez. xxxvi.
is on your account being calumniated among the Gentiles,' as 20; 2 Sam.
it is written. xii. 14; Neh. v. 9.

The vain boast of Circumcision. Cf. Gen. xvii. 7-13.

And no less futile was the Jewish confidence in the rite of Circumcision. It was the seal of the Covenant between God and Abraham and his seed after him throughout their generations, the symbol of Israel's separation from defilement, her consecration, her fellowship with God.[1] In course of time, however, the Jews had fallen into the crass error of confounding the symbol and the reality. They ascribed a magical efficacy to the mere rite and conceived it as constituting them heirs of the Promise and differentiating them from the Gentiles whom they stigmatised as 'uncircumcised dogs.' And thus, instead of keeping ever before them the necessity of purity of heart and life, it rendered them heedless of ethical distinctions and inspired them with a spirit of national pride and religious bigotry. To this fatal misconception the Apostle opposes a twofold principle: since the value of Circumcision lies not in the mere rite but in its spiritual significance, it follows that, though the rite be observed, there is no true Circumcision where the spiritual reality is lacking, and, conversely, wherever there is the spiritual reality, there also is Circumcision, though the rite be lacking. A circumcised transgressor of the Law has no title to 'the grand name of Jew'; and an uncircumcised Gentile who keeps the Law is a son of Abraham and an heir of the Promise.

25 For circumcision profits if you practise the Law; but if you
be a transgressor of the Law, your circumcision has turned
26 out uncircumcision. If, then, one who is circumcised keep
the righteous requirements of the Law, will not his uncircum-
27 cision be reckoned as circumcision? And the man who from
natural circumstances is uncircumcised, will in performing the
Law judge you who, in possession of a written code and of
28 circumcision, are a transgressor of the Law. For it is not the
visible Jew that is really a Jew, nor is it the visible circum-

[1] Circumcision was older than the time of Abraham, and it was practised in after days not by the Jews alone but by the Edomites, the Ammonites, the Moabites, the Phœnicians, and the Egyptians (cf. Jer. ix. 25, 26). It was a Semitic usage, and its distinction in Israel was the significance attached to it. Cf. Hardwick, *Christ and Other Masters*, pp. 490 ff.

29 cision in the flesh that is really circumcision. No, it is the
secret Jew that is really a Jew; and his circumcision is circumcision of heart, in spirit, not in a written code. And his
'praise' is not from men but from God.

Jewish objections:

The Apostle has now established his thesis. He has demonstrated the failure of mankind, the Jews no less than the Gentiles, to attain righteousness; and it remains that he should press home the inevitable conclusion and exhibit God's remedy for the universal malady—Justification by Faith. But here he pauses and, to 'make assurance double sure' and close every loophole of escape, he reviews a series of objections which a Jew might urge. They are the difficulties which had engaged his own mind at the crisis of his religious experience; and he presents them in a sort of musing soliloquy. Meanwhile he merely states them summarily and dismisses them abruptly, reserving their discussion. And he resumes them in the subsequent course of his argument.

1. What of Israel's pre-eminence?

First, on the principle of Justification by Faith in Christ apart from the Works of the Law, what becomes of Israel's historic pre-eminence? If her distinctive rite of Circumcision was worthless, she was reduced to the common level of the nations of mankind. The answer is that Israel's supreme distinction was that she had been the repository of revelation; and that was an imperishable glory.

iii. 1 'What becomes, then, of the pre-eminence of the Jew, or
2 of the profit of the Circumcision?' It is a great thing
from every point of view. Primarily because they were
entrusted with the Oracles of God.[1]

2. What of God's faithfulness?

Again, what of the faithfulness of God? He was pledged to Israel by an inviolable covenant; and whatever her unfaithfulness, He would stand true. Of course a covenant is a mutual agreement and it is cancelled by the disloyalty of either party; but the Apostle does not stay to expose the fallacy. He simply repudiates the vain argument.

3 'Very well; if some proved unfaithful, will their unfaithful-
4 ness invalidate the faithfulness of God?' Away with the

[1] λόγιον in classical literature 'an oracle'; so generally 'a divine utterance.' Cf. Philo's περὶ τῶν δέκα λογίων, the Ten Commandments (cf. Ac. vii. 38). Here, the O. T. Scriptures.

idea! No, let God prove true and 'every man a liar'; as it is written, 'that Thou mightest be found righteous in Thy causes and prevail when Thou pleadest.'[1]

Ps. cxvi. 11. Ps. li. 4.

Further, according to the teaching of the Gospel, our unrighteousness serves to illustrate God's righteousness, which shows all the clearer against the dark background; and this suggests the question whether He can fairly visit us with His displeasure. The Apostle dismisses the suggestion as preposterous. It is a denial of the moral government of the world.

3. What of His title to condemn?

5 'But if our unrighteousness commends God's righteousness,
what are we to say? Is God unrighteous who inflicts wrath?
6 It is mere human language that I am using.' Away with the
idea! In that case how will God judge the world?

And here emerges also a moral problem: If sin redounds to the glory of God, there is no harm in sinning. Rather should we sin the more that God may be the more glorified. This is the odious charge of antinomianism which the Judaists urged against the Gospel and which the Apostle presently handles at length. Meanwhile he dismisses his traducers with indignant contempt: 'Their doom is righteous.'

4. What of moral obligation?

Cf. vi, vii.

7 'But if my lie advanced God's glory by magnifying His
8 truth, why am *I* still judged as a sinner? And why not'—as
we are calumniously represented and some allege that we say—
'"let us do evil that good may come"?' Their doom is
righteous.

He has thus swept away every subterfuge. His opponents have shot their last bolt but, reluctant to acknowledge defeat, they petulantly exclaim: 'So it comes to this, that we Jews are actually worse than the Gentiles!' 'Not at all,' he answers. 'That is not my contention. My charge is not that the Jews are worse than the Gentiles, but that

Jews and Gentiles alike condemned by Scripture.

[1] ἐν τοῖς λόγοις σου, 'in Thy causes' (cf. Ac. xix. 38). κρίνεσθαι, mid., 'plead,' 'go to law' (cf. 1 Cor. vi. 6), not pass., 'be judged.' The LXX rendering, which the Apostle follows, is a mistranslation. The Hebr. means: 'that Thou mightest be justified when Thou speakest, and be clear when Thou judgest,' where the Psalmist (not God) is on trial and confesses the justice of God's sentence. The Apostle's use of the O. T. is literary rather than dogmatic, and the LXX rendering here illustrates his argument.

they are both in the same case: both alike have failed to attain righteousness and stand condemned before God.' And he appeals to the Scripture, that tribunal which was authoritative and final in Jewish eyes. It pronounced a verdict of universal guilt, bringing not the Gentiles alone but the whole world under condemnation.

9 'What, then? Are we worse than they?'[1] Not at all;
we have already laid it to the charge of both Jews and Greeks
10 that they are all under sin. And so it is written:

Ps. xiv. 1-3. 'There is none righteous, not even one;
11 There is none that understands, there is none that seeks after God;
12 They have all turned aside, they have all with one accord become unprofitable;
There is none that does kindness, there is not so much as one.
Ps. v. 9. 13 A sepulchre wide open is their throat;
With their tongues they have spoken guile.
Ps. cxl. 3. The poison of adders is under their lips.
Ps. x. 17. 14 Whose mouth of cursing and bitterness is full.
Is. lix. 7, 8. 15 Swift are their feet to shed blood;
16 Destruction and wretchedness are in their ways,
17 And the way of peace have they not recognised.
Ps. xxxvi. 1. 18 There is no fear of God before their eyes.'[2]
19 Now we know that every word of the Law is spoken[3] to
those who are within the Law, that every mouth may be
stopped and all the world be brought under the condemnation
Ps. cxliii. 2. 20 of God; because on the score of works of law 'shall no flesh

[1] So R.V. ('are we in worse case than they?'), taking προεχόμεθα as pass.: 'are we excelled' or 'surpassed' (by the Gentiles)? A petulant question of the baffled Jews. Otherwise: (1) προεχόμεθα in act. sense: 'are we better than they?' So A.V. after Vulg. *præcellimus eos?* That is, 'have we Jews any superiority over the Gentiles?' And then the Apostle's answer is: 'None whatsoever; for we have just found Jews and Gentiles equally guilty.' It is a fatal objection to this construction that it would require προέχομεν. The mid. προέχεσθαι never occurs in the sense of 'excel.' (2) προέχεσθαι in mid. sense: 'do we excuse ourselves?' (R.V. marg.), 'have we any plea to urge, any excuse to offer, any defence to make?' προέχεσθαι is frequent in the sense of 'hold out a πρόσχημα,' *i.e.*, a defence or excuse; but this is here inadmissible, since the verb in this sense is always followed by an accus. denoting the pretext offered.

[2] This array of O. T. proof-texts was probably derived from a primitive collection of 'testimonies' (cf. p. 229). The entire passage (vers. 10-18) stands in LXX Version of Ps. xiv, having doubtless been interpolated from the Epistle by a Christian copyist.

[3] λέγειν refers to the *meaning*, λαλεῖν to the *language*. Cf. Mt. xxvi. 73; Jo. iv. 41, 42, viii. 43.

be accounted righteous in His sight.' For through law is full recognition of sin.[1]

3. *God's Way to attain Righteousness* (iii. 21-31)

Justification by Faith.

The Apostle's argument has now reached its goal. He has demonstrated the failure of the Gentiles to attain righteousness and the no less disastrous failure of the Jews despite their privileges ; and so he proceeds to the inevitable conclusion. Other methods have failed, and we are shut up to God's method—Faith in the Lord Jesus Christ. This he has already defined in stating the thesis of his argument ; (Cf. i. 16, 17.) and here he presents a more precise definition as a basis for subsequent discussion. First, it is no novel device. It is attested by the Old Testament Scriptures ; and even as the Incarnation was a 'manifestation' of the Eternal Saviour, so the Gospel is the 'manifestation' of an eternal grace. (Cf. Col. i. 26; 1 Jo. i. 2.) Further, it is the satisfaction of a universal need. Jews and Gentiles alike are under condemnation, and justification is a free gift of God. It is offered in Christ, and it is appropriated by faith. And, finally, it offers a righteous remission, at once meeting the requirements of the moral order and satisfying the moral instincts of the soul. And the reason is that it rests on 'redemption.' Sin has been expiated by the vicarious love of God in Christ. Christ is the Mercy-seat, the meeting-place between God and sinners ; and the Mercy-seat is sprinkled with sacrificial blood.

21 But, as the case stands, apart from the Law a righteousness
of God has been manifested, being attested by the Law and
22 the Prophets ; a righteousness of God, however,[2] through
faith in Jesus Christ reaching all who have faith. There is
23 no distinction ; for all have sinned and lack the glory of God.[3]
24 They are freely accounted righteous by His grace through the
25 redemption which is in Christ Jesus, whom God has set forth

[1] This principle is elaborated in vii. 7-25.

[2] Not righteousness simply, but a righteousness of a particular sort. Cf. ix. 30.

[3] ἥμαρτον, aor. defining the past as one great aggregate of transgressions. ὑστεροῦνται, mid., 'feel their want of' (cf. Lk. xv. 14). Sin is not merely a past fact but a present and conscious misery. 'The glory of God' is His irradiating and gladdening presence, and sinners feel sorrowfully their lack of it.

as a Mercy-seat[1] through faith, besprinkled with His blood,
for a demonstration of His righteousness on the score of the
prætermission of sins previously committed during the for-
26 bearance of God[2]—to demonstrate, I repeat, His righteousness
at the present hour, that He may be Himself righteous while
accounting the man righteous who holds by faith in Jesus.

Cf. ii. 17, 23.

27 Where, then, is the boasting? It is excluded. Through
what manner of law? That of works? No, but through
28 faith's law. For we reckon that a man is accounted righteous
29 by faith apart from works of law. Or is God the God of Jews
only? Is He not the God of Gentiles also? Yes, of Gentiles
30 also, seeing that God is one, and He will account the circumcised righteous on the score of faith and the uncircumcised
through their faith.[3]
31 Are we, then, invalidating the Law through faith? Away
with the idea! No, we are establishing the Law.

4. *Consonance of Justification by Faith with Scripture* (iv)

Scriptural evidence of the Apostle's doctrine.

The Apostle has concluded his definition of the doctrine of Justification by Faith in Christ with an emphatic contradiction of the Jewish objection that it invalidated the Law. This was *prima facie* a reasonable objection; and he proceeds to consider it and prove that his doctrine was consonant with the Law. 'The Law' had a double signification. In its narrower use it denoted the Mosaic code of ceremonial prescriptions, and this had indeed been abrogated by the Gospel. It was merely a preparatory discipline, and it had served its function. In its larger use, however, the term signified the Scriptures of the Old Testament—the Prophets and the

[1] ἱλαστήριον. Cf. *The Atonement in the Light of History and the Modern Spirit*, pp. 160 ff.

[2] Until Christ came and made atonement for the sin of the world, there was no ἄφεσις, 'remission,' 'letting go'; only πάρεσις, 'prætermission,' *i.e.*, 'letting go in the meantime' in view of a future settlement. The disposition which prompted the πάρεσις was ἀνοχή, 'forbearance.' Cf. Ac. xvii. 30.

[3] ἐκ and διά are here practically interchangeable, yet there is a subtle distinction. ἐκ denotes the *source*, διά the *instrument*. The Jews derived justification from works, and the Apostle derived it from faith. The Law, again, is the instrument of salvation; and since the Gentiles had no Law, it might seem that they had no instrument. But, says the Apostle, the true instrument of salvation is faith. The Jews regarded the Law as the source of salvation, and he tells them that faith is the source; the Gentiles might regard the Law as the means of salvation, and he tells them that faith is the means and they do not need the Law.

Hagiographa as well as the Law of Moses;[1] and with these, the Apostle will now demonstrate, the doctrine of Justification by Faith is in profound agreement.

The case of Abraham:

He appeals to the history of Abraham, the father of Israel; and there are three links in the chain of his argument.

(1) Justified not by works but by faith.

Abraham was justified not by works but by faith. He did not earn righteousness; he received it. It was a free gift of grace. Nor was his experience singular. It was the experience of the Psalmist long afterwards. Justification by Faith is thus the doctrine of the Scriptures. They recognise no other way.

iv. 1 What, then, shall we say of Abraham, the forefather of
2 our race?[2] If Abraham was accounted righteous on the
score of works, he has something to boast of. But he has
3 nothing to boast of in relation to God. For what says the
Scripture? 'And Abraham had faith in God, and it was Gen. xv. 6.
4 reckoned to him as righteousness.' Now to one who works
the wage is not reckoned in terms of grace but in terms
5 of debt; whereas to one who does not work but reposes
faith on Him who accounts the impious righteous, his faith
6 is reckoned as righteousness. Thus David also speaks of
the blessedness of the man to whom God reckons righteousness apart from works:
7 'Blessed are they whose lawlessnesses have been remitted Ps. xxxii. 1, 2.
and whose sins have been covered;
8 Blessed is the man whose sin the Lord will never reckon.'

(2) Circumcision only the seal of his justification. Cf. Ac. xv. 1.

Circumcision was not the ground but the seal of Abraham's justification. The Jewish doctrine was that, unless a man was circumcised, he could not be saved. He was outside the Covenant. Look, says the Apostle, at Abraham. He was accounted righteous on the ground of his faith, and then he received the rite of Circumcision. It was not the ground of his justification but merely its seal. The order was Faith, Justification, Circumcision; and the Jewish error lay in omitting Faith and putting Circumcision before Justification as its antecedent and necessary condition.

[1] Cf. iii. 19 (referring to the foregoing quotations from Psalter and Isaiah); 1 Cor. xiv. 21; Jo. x. 34.

[2] Most authorities insert εὑρηκέναι either (ℵACDEFG) after ἐροῦμεν ('what shall we say that Abraham, our forefather after the flesh, has found?'), or (KLP) after τὸν προπάτορα ἡμῶν ('that Abraham, our forefather, has found after the flesh?'). It is omitted by B 27 Chrys., and is probably a grammatical gloss.

9 Is this blessedness, then, the portion of the circumcised or
of the uncircumcised also? We say: 'His faith was reckoned
10 to Abraham as righteousness.' How, then, was it reckoned?
When he was circumcised or while he was still uncircumcised?
Not when he was circumcised but while he was still uncircum-
Gen. xvii. 11. 11 cised. And he received 'the sign' of Circumcision, a seal of
the righteousness which his faith, while he was still uncircumcised, won him; that he might be the father of all who
have faith though in a state of uncircumcision, that righteous-
12 ness might be reckoned to them, and a circumcised father for
those who do not hold by Circumcision only but also tread[1]
in the steps of the faith which our father Abraham displayed
while still uncircumcised.

(3) The basis of the Promise not the Law but Faith.

Gal. iii. 17.

The Promise did not rest on the Law but on Faith. The Apostle has already demonstrated this proposition in his letter to the Galatians by appealing to the historical fact that the promise to Abraham preceded the delivery of the Law to Moses at Mount Sinai by fully four centuries. Here, however, his argument is theological. He shows that the idea of Promise is alien from the domain of Law. It belongs to the domain of Grace, and the domains of Law and Grace are incompatible, mutually exclusive. In the former it is merit that counts; and if the inheritance is to be won by merit, then the Promise and the faith which grasps it are eliminated: faith has been made an empty thing and the Promise invalidated. Experience attests this. For there is no merit in sinful man; the Law merely discovers his sinfulness and establishes his liability to the wrath of God. It brings not promise but condemnation. Where there is no Law, there is sin indeed, but no transgression, no guilt, and hence no wrath. And the Promise belongs not to the domain of Law but to the domain of Grace. It is received by faith. It was indeed on the ground of his righteousness that Abraham received it; but then it was on the ground of his faith that he was accounted righteous, and it was his faith that held fast the Promise in face of all that seemed to belie it.

[1] The art. (τοῖς) before στοιχοῦσιν is superfluous, making it appear as though two distinct classes were intended—'those who hold by faith' and 'those who tread in the steps of Abraham's faith'; whereas there is only one class—believing Jews who are circumcised and at the same time share the faith which justified Abraham while still uncircumcised.

13 It was not the Law that brought the Promise to Abraham
or his seed, that he should be heir of the world; no, it was the
14 righteousness which faith won him. If it be those who hold
by Law that are the heirs, faith has been made an empty
15 thing and the Promise invalidated. For the Law works out
wrath; but where there is no Law, neither is there trans-
16 gression. Therefore it is on the score of faith, that it may
be in terms of grace, in order that the Promise may be firm
for all the seed—not those who hold by the Law only but
also those who hold by the faith of Abraham, who is the father
17 of us all, as it is written: 'The father of many nations have Gen. xvii. 5.
I made you.' And they hold by Abraham's faith in the sight
of Him in whom he reposed it, even God who makes the dead
live and calls things which have no being as though they Cf. 1 Cor. i.
18 had. On hope where hope there was none, he built his faith, 28.
that he might become 'the father of many nations,' according
19 to the saying: 'So shall your seed be.' And without weaken- Gen. xv. 5.
ing in his faith he contemplated his own body with its vitality
gone, since he was some hundred years old, and the devitalisa-
20 tion of Sarah's womb; yet in view of the promise of God he
never wavered for lack of faith. No, his faith put power into
21 him, and he gave glory to God, satisfied [1] that what He has
22 promised He has power also to do. And therefore also 'it
was reckoned to him as righteousness.'
23 Now it was not written for his sake only that 'it was reckoned
24 to him,' but also for the sake of us to whom it shall be reckoned
—us who repose faith on Him that raised Jesus our Lord from
25 the dead, who 'was delivered up for our trespasses' and raised Is. liii. 12
that we might be accounted righteous. LXX.

5. *A Devotional Interlude* (v)

A pause in the argument.

The Apostle has now accomplished his main task: he has established his thesis that Justification is by Faith in Christ and not by the Works of the Law. Serious problems still remain, but ere addressing himself to these he pauses to commend his doctrine and enforce its blessed consequences.

The privileges of the justified:

He begins with an exhortation. Our faith in Christ has won us a new standing in God's sight: let us realise it and appropriate its privileges.

[1] πληροφορηθείς. The verb was used in the Common Greek of satisfying a person by paying him his due. Cf. *Oxyrh. Pap.* 509, 10 f.: τυγχάνω δὲ πεπληροφορημένος τοῖς ὀφειλομένοις μοι, 'it happens that I have been satisfied in respect of the sums due to me.' So here the idea is that Abraham regarded God's promise as equal to the fulfilment.

(1) Peace with God.

The first of these is peace with God—the peace of reconciliation. We are done with our guilty past. Christ has dealt with it. His infinite Sacrifice has expiated the sin of the whole world, and forgiveness is ours. The invitation of the Gospel is not 'Have faith in Christ, and you will be forgiven,' but 'You are forgiven: have faith and be at peace.'

(2) A glorious hope.

Nor is it the past alone that Christ has transfigured. He has transfigured the future also; and the second privilege of the justified is a glorious hope. Our destiny is Heaven, our heritage the Glory of God; and though we may not boast in the Law, we may well boast in this.

Cf. iii. 27, iv. 2.

(3) A present comfort.

And our third privilege is a present comfort. It is ours not merely to boast in the glory which awaits us but to boast in the distresses which now encompass us. And the secret lies in recognising the precious use which life's sorrow and suffering are designed to serve, the blessing which, when they are employed aright, they surely bring. Distress is a sacred discipline. It is like the testing of a bar of metal. First, it 'works out endurance,' discovering our weakness and our strength. If we be weak, it breaks us; if we be strong, we stand the strain. And then we are 'approved.' And, finally, 'approbation works out hope.' It confirms our 'hope in the glory of God'; for it is only a present experience of the operation of grace that assures us of its future consummation. What God has already done for us is an earnest of the greater things which He will yet do.

v. 1 Being, then, accounted righteous on the score of faith, let
us have [1] peace with God through our Lord Jesus Christ,
2 through whom also we have gained the *entrée* [2] by faith into
this grace in which we stand; and let us make the hope
3 of the glory of God the ground of our boasting.[3] And, more
than that, let us boast in our distresses; knowing that

[1] The overwhelming weight of documentary evidence supports ἔχωμεν. The variant ἔχομεν is a mere itacism, and even if it were more strongly supported, it should be rejected on internal evidence. Cf. 1 Cor. xv. 49, where the weakly attested φορέσομεν is certainly authentic.

[2] προσαγωγή (cf. Eph. ii. 18, iii. 12; 1 Pet. iii. 18), 'introduction,' admission to the king's audience, presentation at court (cf. Xen. *Cyrop.* I. iii. 8; VII. v. 45). Christ is our προσαγωγεύς. Cf. Heb. vi. 20.

[3] καυχώμεθα may be either indic. or conj. Both here and in next ver. it is best regarded as conj., continuing the exhortation of ἔχωμεν.

4 distress works out endurance, and endurance approbation,[1]
5 and approbation hope. And the 'hope does not put to shame,' because the love of God has been poured forth in our hearts through the Holy Spirit who was given us.

Ps. xxii. 5; cf. Ps. xxxiv. 5; Ecclus. ii. 10, 11.

Their objective guarantee.

Perhaps, it may be objected, our hope of the glory of God is no better than a mere dream, a fond illusion; and when the cold reality is discovered it will put us to shame. No, the Apostle answers, it is no empty dream, and its guarantee is not simply the subjective testimony of the Holy Spirit's revelation of God's love but the objective testimony of our Lord's Death. Here is the supreme demonstration of the love of God; and it is an amazing love, transcending the utmost range of human devotion. 'Greater love,' says our Lord, 'has no man than this, that a man lay down his life *for his friends.*' He would never die for an enemy; he would hardly die for 'a righteous man'—one like the Roman Cato, upright and just yet stern and pitiless; he might die for 'a good man,' kindly and generous. This is the farthest reach of human love; but here is the wonder of the love of God—that, when we were not 'good,' when we were not even 'righteous,' when we were 'sinners,' nay, 'enemies,' Christ died for us. And this is the guarantee that our hope of the glory of God is no fond illusion. A love like that will never fail us. It will carry our salvation to its eternal consummation.

Jo. xv. 13.

6 For if Christ, while we were still weak,[2] in due season died
7 for the impious (Hardly for a righteous man will one die;
it is for the good man that perhaps one even has the hardihood

[1] Cf. n. on I Th. v. 21, p. 165.

[2] The text is very uncertain. (1) The best supported reading is ἔτι γὰρ Χριστὸς ὄντων ἡμῶν ἀσθενῶν ἔτι. This simplifies the construction of the passage, but the double ἔτι is intolerable. (2) εἴ γε (B, Aug.), 'seeing that,' *quandoquidem* (a questionable rendering), making ver. 6 a continuation of ver. 5. (3) εἰς τί γάρ (D^bFG, Iren., Vulg. *ut quid enim*), 'for wherefore?' (4) εἰ γάρ (Isid. Pel. *Ep.* II. 117, and a few Latin authorities, *si enim*), making ver. 6 the protasis, vers. 7, 8 a parenthesis, and ver. 9 the apodosis. This is probably the original reading. Vers. 7, 8 are, as the omission of οὖν in ver. 9 by numerous authorities indicates, a *marginale* (cf. p. 245 and n. on ii. 14, 15); and the various readings are copyists' devices to smooth the construction after the comment had been introduced into the text. Vers. 6, 9 and ver. 10 are thus similarly constructed sentences.

8 to die ; [1] but God commends His own love toward us inasmuch
9 as, while we were still sinners, Christ died for us.), much
more, being accounted righteous now that we are sprinkled
with His blood,[2] we shall be saved through Him from the
10 Wrath. If, being enemies, we were reconciled to God through
the death of His Son, much more, being reconciled, we shall
11 be saved in His life—being reconciled and, more than that,
boasting in God through our Lord Jesus Christ, through whom
we have now obtained the reconciliation.

The principle of Reconciliation—Imputation.

Reconciliation was a master-thought in the Apostle's theology,[3] and his contemplation of the privileges which it brings has kindled his heart ; and now, ere resuming his argument, he lingers over it and unfolds its significance. First he exhibits the principle which underlies it. It is the principle which theologians have denominated Imputation and which modern science has illumined by its doctrines of Heredity and the Solidarity of the Race.[4] Humanity is not a congeries of isolated individuals but a vital organism ; and generations and individuals are all interrelated. The principle has a twofold operation. On the one hand, the sin of the fathers is their children's heritage and the curse of wrong rests upon the innocent. And, on the other hand, the righteousness of the fathers is likewise their children's heritage, and each noble life blesses the race. Hence not only is the sin of Adam, its first head, imputed to mankind, but so also is the righteousness of Christ, its Second
2 Cor. v. 19. Head ; and thus God is 'in Christ reconciling the world to Himself.'

[1] δίκαιος, 'righteous,' observing the letter of the law, doing strict justice—a character of rigid rectitude not without severity. ἀγαθός, 'good,' 'kindly,' an epithet of Barnabas (Ac. xi. 24). The idea appears in Marcion's distinction between the *justus Deus* of the Old Testament and the *bonus Deus* of the New. Cf. *Sayings of the Fathers*, v. 16 (Taylor, p. 89) : 'There are four characters in men. He that saith "Mine is mine, and thine is thine" is an indifferent character : he that saith "Mine is thine, and thine is mine" is a worldling [practising 'give and take'] : "Mine and thine are thine," pious : "Thine and mine are mine," wicked.' Cf. Plut. *Cat. Maj.* v : καίτοι τὴν χρηστότητα τῆς δικαιοσύνης πλατύτερον τόπον ὁρῶμεν ἐπιλαμβάνουσαν, 'goodness moves in a larger sphere than justice.'

[2] Cf. iii. 25. The worshippers as well as the Mercy-seat were sprinkled with sacrificial blood (cf. Ex. xxiv. 8 ; Heb. ix. 19).

[3] Cf. *The Atonement in the Light of History and the Modern Spirit*, pp. 111 f.

[4] *Ibid.*, pp. 182 ff.

The imputation of Adam's sin proved by the universality of death.

Cf. iv. 15.

The Apostle does not merely affirm the principle of Imputation: he demonstrates it. And his argument is that death is the penalty of sin, and since death is universal, it follows that sin is universal also. But 'where there is no Law, neither is there transgression.' There may indeed be sin where there is no Law, but there is no guilt, since 'sin is not taken into the reckoning when there is no Law.' Now it was ages after the Fall that the Law was delivered at Sinai. Throughout the long interval between Adam and Moses there was no Law and therefore there should have been no death. But in fact death reigned even then. Sin was taken into the reckoning, and was visited with the penalty of death; and what was the reason? It might be alleged that mankind had never lacked the knowledge of God. Ere the Law was given at Sinai, it was written on their hearts; and thus they 'sinned after the similitude of the transgression of Adam.' They sinned with open eyes, and merited the penalty of death. This, however, will not suffice, since death was absolutely universal. It was the portion of unconscious infants and those who lacked the light of reason. And thus no other reason remains save that Adam's sin was imputed to his posterity. *Omnes peccarunt, Adamo peccante.* His sin was theirs; and, sharing his sin, they shared also its penalty.

Cf. i. 19-21, ii. 14, 15.

12 Therefore, as through one man sin entered into the world,
and through sin death, and thus death spread to all mankind
13 inasmuch as all sinned;[1]—for prior to the Law sin was in the
world, but sin is not taken into the reckoning when there is
14 no Law; yet death reigned from Adam on to Moses even over
those who did not sin after the similitude of the transgression of Adam, who is the type of the future Saviour.

Is death the penalty of sin?

The apparent flaw in this chain of reasoning is the assumption, which the Apostle treats as a self-evident axiom, that death is the penalty of sin. That was indeed the Jewish

[1] ἐφ' ᾧ, (1) 'because,' 'inasmuch as,' *propterea quod*; (2) 'on condition that,' *eâ lege ut*. Cf. Moulton and Milligan, *Vocab.* Vulg., with Fathers, *in quo*, 'in whom (*i.e.*, Adam) all sinned.' This construction is impossible, since (1) the anteced. ἑνὸς ἀνθρώπου is too remote, and (2) it would require ἐν ᾧ. Nevertheless it truly defines the Apostle's thought: 'all sinned,' not actually but in Adam, as he proceeds to explain.

Cf. Gen. ii. 17. doctrine. 'There is no death,' taught the Rabbis, 'without sin, and no chastisement without iniquity';[1] and the idea established itself in Christian theology. It was accounted a heresy by St. Augustine and St. Jerome when Pelagius denied it and maintained that Adam was created mortal and would have died though he had never sinned. Nevertheless it is an untenable notion. Death is no curse entailed by sin. It is, as the Stoic philosophers recognised,[2] an ordinance of Nature; and, says our English essayist,[3] 'all that Nature has prescribed must be good; and as Death is natural to us, it is absurdity to fear it.' It is a natural law, and its operation is universal. The leaves and flowers, the birds and beasts, no less than sinful man, obey it. And it is a beneficent ordinance. 'Death,' says St. Bernard, 'is the door of life.' It is not destruction but transition into a larger, richer, and nobler condition.

> 'All that lives must die,
> Passing through nature to eternity'—

Jo. xii. 24. a truth which our Lord proclaimed when He said: 'Unless the grain of wheat fall into the earth and die, it remains itself alone.' Yet the Apostle affirms that death is the consequence and penalty of sin: 'through one man sin entered into the world, and through sin death.' It may seem at the first glance as though, like St. Augustine and St. Jerome, he were here following in the footsteps of the Rabbis and repeating the doctrine which he had learned in the school of Gamaliel; but this were a hasty conclusion, and on closer scrutiny the profound truth of his argument is recognised.

The Apostle's use of the term 'death.'

1 Cor. xv. 22. His affirmation is that 'through one man sin entered into the world, and through sin death,' and 'just as in Adam all die, so also in Christ all shall be made live'; and the essential question is what the term 'death' here signifies. If it be merely the dissolution of the body, then the Apostle's argument breaks down. For Christ does not exempt His people from death in that sense of the term. All still die, believers

[1] Cf. Wetstein on Rom. v. 12.

[2] Cf. Sen. *Nat. Quæst.* VI. 32: 'Mors naturæ lex est, mors tributum officiumque mortalium, malorum omnium remedium est.'

[3] Addison, *Spect.* 152.

and unbelievers alike. It is incredible that this flaw in his reasoning, at once so fatal and so obvious, should have eluded his acute observation. He must have attached another significance to the term; and that he actually did appears from the fact that in the course of his magnificent argument on the Resurrection of the Body he expressly affirms the necessity of the dissolution of the physical organism in order to the fuller life which is the goal of redemption. 'What you sow,' he says, 'is not made live unless it die.' The 'animal body' must die that it may be raised 'a spiritual body.'

Cf. 1 Cor. xv. 36-44.

Not physical dissolution but its distressing concomitants.

Hence it is evident that, when he affirms that 'through sin death entered into the world,' it is not the mere dissolution of the physical organism that he has in view. This is a necessary, and not merely a necessary but a beneficent process; and by 'death' he means not the process but its distressing concomitants. And these have resulted from sin; they are the curse which it has entailed. 'This death,' says William Ames, that profound and saintly theologian of Puritan England,[1] 'the punishment inflicted on man for sin, is the miserable privation of life. It is not privation of life simple and bare but conjoined with subjection to misery; and therefore it is not the annihilation of the sinner, because, were the subject of the misery done away, the misery itself would be done away.' Hence the Apostle's affirmation that 'through sin death entered into the world' does not mean that, if man had never sinned, he would have continued for ever on the earth—an event neither possible nor desirable, since space would quickly have failed on this little planet for the accumulating generations, nor is this man's perfect condition but merely a stage in the progress toward his goal. It means rather that, had man never sinned, his dissolution would have been, according to the Creator's design, a natural and easy transition, without grief or apprehension, from the lower condition to the higher, like the passage from childhood to manhood or the bursting of the bud into the flower.

Gen. ii. 17; Rom. v. 12.

Death 'a sleep' according

That this is indeed the Christian conception is attested by the teaching of our Lord. He never spoke of His people's

[1] *Theol. Med.* I. xii. 28, 29, 32.

to our Lord. Cf. 2 Tim. i. 10. 'death.' For them there is no 'miserable privation of life.' He has 'undone' this: yet the natural process of dissolution remains, and they must sustain it in order that they may attain the full and perfect life. And this transition He always designated 'falling asleep.'[1] Cf. Jo. xi. 11-13.

The Christian conception. Thus, in Christian phraseology, 'death' never signifies the mere dissolution of the physical organism, but the gloom and terror wherewith sin has invested that natural, necessary, and truly beneficent process. It is in this sense that the Apostle employs the term when he affirms that 'through sin death entered into the world'; and when he says that 'our Saviour Christ Jesus has undone death,' he means that the natural process has, in the believer's thought, been divested of its alien associations and reconstituted what it was in the Creator's purpose—the perfecting and consummation of life. The process remains, but the terror is gone.

The redemption of death. In truth our Lord's dealing with death is but an instance of His redemptive ministry, His undoing of the work of sin. Sin creates nothing; it only mars God's creation. Thus, the Scriptures represent work no less than death as a curse which sin has entailed on the race. Cf. Gen. iii. 19. And Christ removes the curse, not by absolving us from work, but by restoring its primal and proper idea.

'After Adam work was curse:
The natural creature labours, sweats, and frets.
But, after Christ, work turns to privilege;
And henceforth one with our humanity,
The Six-day Worker, working still in us,
Has called us freely to work on with Him
In high companionship.'[2]

And it is precisely thus that He has removed the curse of dissolution also—not by cancelling the necessity but by revealing its true significance, its proper glory. He has given believers a new idea of it, and thus He has robbed it of its sting. Cf. 1 Cor. xv. 56, 57; Heb. ii. 14, 15.

The imputation of Christ's righteousness. Here, then, is the principle of redemption: 'as through one man sin entered into the world, and through sin death, so through one man righteousness entered into the world,

[1] Cf. p. 163.

[2] E. B. Browning, *Aurora Leigh*, viii.

and through righteousness life.' The work of Christ is an undoing of the work of Adam; but, the Apostle proceeds, it is incomparably grander. Grace is matched against the Curse, but it is no equal conflict. Look at the quality of the antagonists: on the one side, the trespass of Adam and, on the other, the grace of God in Christ, so bountiful and overflowing. And look again at the issues: on the one side, humanity doomed for a single trespass and, on the other, humanity acquitted of a multitude of trespasses for the righteousness of one man. And here is the attestation of the doctrine of Justification by Faith. Salvation is a gracious gift, a magnificent bounty oi God. It is not earned by the works of the Law; it is received by faith in Christ. The Law cannot save. Its function is not justification but condemnation. 'Where there is no Law, neither is there transgression'; and the Law's office was not to heal the malady but to reveal it, to show men their sinfulness and lead them to the Saviour.

15 Yet the trespass and the gift of grace did not correspond. For
if by the trespass of the one the race[1] died, much more the grace
of God and the bounteousness[2] in grace—the grace of the one
16 man, Jesus Christ—overflowed to the race. Neither did the
result of the one's sinning and the bounty correspond. For
the doom on the score of one trespass issued in a verdict of
guilt; while the gift of grace on the score of many trespasses
17 issued in a verdict of righteousness.[3] For if by the trespass of

[1] οἱ πολλοί, not 'many' (A.V.), but 'the many,' *i.e.*, not merely the majority, but the mass of mankind, the race as distinguished from ὁ εἷς. 'By this accurate version some hurtful mistakes about partial redemption and absolute reprobation had been happily prevented. Our English readers had then seen what several of the Fathers saw and testified, that οἱ πολλοί *the many*, in an antithesis to *the one*, are equivalent to πάντες *all* in ver. 12 and comprehend the whole multitude, the entire species of mankind, exclusive only of *the one*' (Bentley, *Works*, III. p. 244).

[2] δωρεά, in the Papyri the Emperor's *largesse* to his soldiers (cf. Moulton and Milligan, *Vocab.*); in N. T. God's *regal munificence*, the bounteousness of His grace (cf. Ac. ii. 38; Heb. vi. 4). δώρημα (ver. 16) is His *bounty*, His χάρισμα.

[3] δικαίωμα, (1) 'a righteous ordinance' (cf. i. 32, ii. 26, viii. 4; Lk. i. 6); (2) 'a righteous act,' 'an achievement of righteousness' (cf. Rev. xv. 4, xix. 8); (3) 'a verdict of acquittal,' δικαίωσις (ver. 18; cf. iv. 25) being the pronouncing of the verdict. Here 'a verdict of acquittal,' since εἰς δικαίωμα stands in antithesis to εἰς κατάκριμα ('a verdict of guilt'). In ver. 18, where the antithesis is δι' ἑνος παραπτώματος, δι' ἑνὸς δικαιώματος, the meaning is 'an achievement of righteousness.'

the one death reigned through the one, much more will those who receive the flood of grace and of the bounteousness of righteousness, reign in life through the one, Jesus Christ.
18 So then,[1] as one trespass resulted for mankind in a verdict
of guilt, so also one achievement of righteousness resulted for
mankind in a life-giving pronouncement of them righteous.
19 For, as through the disobedience of the one man the race was
constituted sinful, so also through the obedience of the one
20 the race will be constituted righteous. And as for the Law, it
stole in that trespass might multiply; but where sin multi-
21 plied, grace overflowed the more, that, as sin reigned in death,
so also grace might reign through righteousness to life eternal
through Jesus Christ our Lord.

II

APOLOGETIC (vi-xi)

Problems presented by the doctrine of Justification by Faith:

The Apostle has demonstrated his doctrine of Justification by Faith, but his task is still incomplete. For the doctrine was open to grave perversion and presented a serious stumbling-block, especially to Jewish minds; and he now proceeds to vindicate it from misconstruction and solve the problems which it involved.

1. *The Ethical Problem* (vi)

(1) Emboldenment to persist in sin.

First there was an ethical problem, and this was defined by two Jewish objections to the doctrine of Justification by Faith. One was a specious sophistry which would doubtless commend itself all too readily to the laxer sort of believers —that, since salvation is a gift of grace, not won by works but bestowed on faith, it was actually a pious duty to 'persist in sin' that the grace of God might be the more displayed. 'Are we,' asks the Apostle, 'to "persist in sin that grace may multiply"?' and he first answers with his indignant repudiation 'Away with the idea!' and then meets the suggestion with a profound argument.

[1] Resuming the interrupted protasis of ver. 12. The sentence should have run: 'As through one man sin entered into the world, and through sin death, so through one man righteousness entered into the world, and through righteousness life.' Ver. 18 is elliptical. Supply from ver. 16 τὸ κρίμα (ἐγένετο), τὸ χάρισμα (ἐγένετο).

vi. 1 What, then, shall we say? Are we to 'persist in sin
2 that grace may multiply'? Away with the idea! We
who died to sin—how shall we any more live in it?

The Apostle's answer: Mystic Union with Christ.

The argument rests upon the mystic union between Christ and believers. Faith unites us with Him. We are one with Him in His Death, His Burial, His Resurrection, and His Life; and this mystic experience is symbolised by the Sacrament of Baptism according to the mode of Immersion.[1] Consider, says the Apostle, what your Baptism into Christ signified. Your plunging in His name beneath the water symbolised your burial with Him, and your re-emergence your resurrection with Him. You died with Him, you were buried with Him, you were raised with Him, and henceforth you live with Him. His death was crucifixion, and crucifixion was a *servile supplicium.* When you died with Him, you died a slave's death. You were sin's slave; and now you are acquitted from its thraldom, since 'the end of life cancels all bands.'

A Christian experience.

This is the mystic union between Christ and the believer; and, as it is stated here in theological terms, it wears an artificial look. What is the vital nexus which unites the believer to Christ and welds him to Christ as the graft is welded to the tree? The answer transcends theology. It is furnished by Christian experience, and the Apostle stated it when he wrote to the Corinthians: 'The love of Christ has us in its grasp, and this is our judgment: One died on behalf of all, consequently all died; and He died on behalf of all that those who live should no longer live for themselves, but for Him who on their behalf died and was raised.' This is not theology: it is experience; and it is a blessed reality for every true believer whom the love of Christ has mastered and inspired with a responsive devotion. The Apostle's readers knew the glorious mystery. They confessed it in their hymns of praise; and it has been the experience of myriads of souls in succeeding generations.

2 Cor. v. 14, 15.

'For ah! the Master is so fair,
His smile so sweet to banished men,
That they who meet it unaware
Can never rest on Earth again.

[1] Cf. Append. VI.

'And they who see Him risen afar
At God's right hand to welcome them,
Forgetful stand of home and land,
Desiring fair Jerusalem.' [1]

A Stoic thought.

The true life, taught the Stoic philosophy, was 'life according to Nature,' and the secret of attaining it lay in accounting oneself dead to the past. 'Consider that you have died,' says Marcus Aurelius,[2] 'and at this point ended your existence; and henceforth live according to Nature.' The true life, teaches the Apostle, is 'life in Christ'; and his precept is: 'Reckon yourselves to be dead to sin, but alive to God in Christ Jesus.' You are absolved, he argues, from the bondage of sin: be its slaves no longer. God is now your King, and it is His battles that you must henceforth fight. It is a debt of honour. You owe it to grace. It were a shame to be irresponsive to the Love of Christ. Sin must not, it will not, be your lord.

3 Are you ignoring the fact that all of us who were baptised
4 into Christ Jesus, were baptised into His death? With
Him, then, we were buried through our baptism into His
death, that, as Christ was raised from the dead through
the glory of the Father, so we also may comport our-
5 selves in a new order of life. For if we have been vitally
welded with Him [3] by the similitude of His death, then so
6 shall we be by that also of His resurrection; recognising
this—that our old self was crucified with Him, that sin's
thrall [4] might be invalidated, so that we should no more be
7 slaves to sin. For one who has died is acquitted from sin.[5]
8 And 'if we died with Christ,' our faith is that 'we shall also
9 live with Him'; since we know that Christ

'Once raised from the dead, dies no more;
Death is His lord no more.

[1] *The Desire to Depart* in *Ezekiel and Other Poems* by B. M.

[2] VII. 56.

[3] σύμφυτοι, 'grown together with Him,' like a graft with the tree. Cf. Shak. 2 *King Henry IV*, II. ii. 67: 'so much engraffed to Falstaff.'

[4] τὸ σῶμα τῆς ἁμαρτίας, not 'the body of sin,' 'the sinful body,' but 'the slave of sin.' σῶμα in the sense of 'slave' is frequent in Biblical and Common Greek. Cf. Gen. xxxiv. 29; Rev. xviii. 13.

[5] δεδικαίωται ἀπὸ τῆς ἁμαρτίας, a legal maxim. In old Scottish phrase a criminal was 'justified' when he was hanged: he had 'tholed assize,' paid the penalty and satisfied justice; and the law no longer had a hold on him. Cf. Shak. *Temp.* III. ii. 140: 'He that dies pays all debts.'

10 For the death He died,
He died to sin once for all;
And the life He lives,
He lives to God.'[1]

11 So with you also: reckon yourselves to be dead to sin, but
alive to God in Christ Jesus.
12 Let not sin, then, reign in your mortal body, that you
13 should obey its lusts. And never present your members to
sin as weapons of unrighteousness. No, present yourselves
to God as men once dead and now alive, and your members
14 as weapons of righteousness to God. Sin must not be your
lord;[2] for you are not under Law but under Grace.

(2) The charge of antinomianism.

This leads the Apostle to the second perversion of his doctrine. It was the charge of antinomianism which the Judaists had so often urged, and which derived a show of reason from the frequent laxity of his Gentile converts.[3] Since, it was alleged, we are justified by Faith, we are done with Law and absolved from moral restraint. Solicitude for good works is mere legalism. The believer is above Law. The spirit is his domain, and the passions of the flesh belong for him to the category of 'things indifferent.' He is at liberty to sin as he pleases.

15 'What then? Are we to sin because we are not under
Law but under Grace?'

Lawlessness not liberty but a worse bondage.

The Apostle's answer is that lawlessness is not liberty; and the libertines, who fancied that their emancipation from the Law absolved them from moral obligation, simply exchanged their old bondage for another and a still worse bondage. Some master we must always have. Whatever we obey is our master, and the choice lies between three masters—the Law, Sin, and Righteousness. The service of the Law was indeed, as it had proved in the experience of the Jews, an intolerable bondage; but the service of Sin is far more grievous, and so the Gentiles had found it. It brings shame and issues in death. The service of Righteousness is the true emancipation. God's slaves are the only free

[1] Snatches of Christian hymns. Cf. 2 Tim. ii. 11.

[2] ἁμαρτία γὰρ ὑμῶν οὐ κυριεύσει, not a promise but an expectation, a confident challenge. *Noblesse oblige*. Cf. Mt. v. 48: ἔσεσθε οὖν ὑμεῖς τέλειοι.

[3] Cf. p. 161.

men. Take Him, says the Apostle, for your Master, and serve Him henceforth as devotedly as you have served Sin. It is told of an Egyptian monk, named Pambos, that he once visited Alexandria on the invitation of the Bishop Athanasius and, encountering an actress in the city, he burst into tears. His companions inquired what ailed him. 'Two things,' he answered: 'the creature's perdition, and the thought that my zeal to please God is less than hers to please base men.'[1] And this is the Apostle's argument: 'As you presented your members as slaves to uncleanness and to lawlessness waxing ever worse, so now present your members as slaves to Righteousness issuing in increase of holiness.' God's is the best, the most profitable service. Sin is a cruel tyrant, and its soldiers' pay is death—the inglorious death of ignominious defeat; but God's kingly largesse, His precious donative, is life eternal—the victor's unfading crown.

16 Away with the idea! Do you not know that whatever
you present yourselves to as slaves to obey it, you are slaves
of what you obey, whether sin issuing in death or obedience
17 issuing in righteousness? And thanks to God that, though
you were once slaves of sin, you have heartily obeyed the
18 standard of teaching to which you were given over.[2] Set
19 free from Sin, you were enslaved to Righteousness. (I am
speaking after the fashion men use in consideration of your
human weakness.[3]) As you presented your members as
slaves to uncleanness and to lawlessness waxing ever worse,
so now present your members as slaves to Righteousness

[1] Socr. *Eccl. Hist.* IV. 23.

[2] τύπος, either (1) a type or image of something yet future (cf. v. 14) or, more commonly, (2) a pattern or exemplar for imitation or avoidance (cf. 1 Cor. x. 6; Phil. iii. 17; 1 Th. i. 7; 2 Th. iii. 9; Tit. ii. 7; Heb. viii. 5; 1 Pet. v. 3). Here the latter. τύπος διδαχῆς does not mean the distinctively Paul doctrine. It is an anachronism to conceive of distinct types of Christian teaching at that period. In those days when the N. T. was only in the making, there was no *regula fidei morumque*, no authoritative rule of Christian faith and conduct; and it appears that, to supply the lack, concise statements, like Luke's manual (cf. pp. 594 f.), were formulated (cf. 2 Tim. i. 13; 2 Jo. 9; Jud. 3; Polycrates in Eus. *Hist. Eccl.* v. 24: ὁ κανὼν τῆς πίστεως), less theological than religious and ethical. Eph. iv. 20-24 is evidently a reference to such a 'rule of faith.' Cf. Hatch, *Influence of Gk. Ideas*, p. 314; Hort, *Rom. and Eph.*, p. 32. The rule of faith was not 'delivered to the believers'; they were 'delivered to it,' to be shaped by it like metal in a mould.

[3] An apology for the expression 'enslavement to righteousness.'

20 issuing in increase of holiness. For while you were slaves of
21 Sin, you were free as regards Righteousness. What, then,
was the fruit that you had in those days? Things of which
you are now ashamed;[1] for the end of those things is death.
22 But now that you are set free from Sin and enslaved to God,
the fruit you have makes for increase of holiness, and the end
23 is life eternal. For Sin's pay is death, but God's donative is
life eternal in Christ Jesus our Lord.[2]

2. *The Position of the Law* (vii, viii)

Abrogation of the Law.

And now the Apostle addresses himself to a problem of poignant interest to every Jewish heart—the question of the position of the ancient Law in the new order of Grace. According to the doctrine of Justification by Faith the Law was abrogated. The very idea was sacrilege in the eyes of devout Jews, and he seeks to demonstrate its reasonableness and reconcile them to the inevitable *dénouement*. Following up occasional suggestions which he has already dropped, he defines the proper office of the Law and displays its essential and necessary insufficiency as an instrument of salvation.

Analogy of a second marriage.

Its abrogation was inevitable. A law by its very nature is necessarily temporary, since it is designed for the regulation of a particular situation and its obligation ceases when the situation changes. This was plain to the Apostle's readers, living as they did under the rule of Imperial Rome and enjoying her just and wise administration; and he quotes an apposite instance. The law of marriage imposes on a wife the obligation of fidelity; but the obligation is not interminable. She is bound to her husband as long as he lives; but with his death her obligation ceases and she is at liberty to contract another marriage. And here is a parable. The believer was formerly wedded to Sin or the Old Self; and it was a grievous union. It was the Law that made it hard by its stern prohibition of sinful passions. But now

[1] Punctuating εἴχετε τότε; Otherwise τότε ἐφ' οἷς νῦν ἐπαισχύνεσθε; The sentence is then elliptical: 'What fruit had you then of those things whereof (ἐκείνων ἐφ' οἷς) you are now ashamed? [None]; for the end, etc.'

[2] A military metaphor (cf. vers. 13, 14). ὀψώνια, the soldier's 'pay' (*stipendia*), properly the small sum which he received to purchase relish (ὄψον) for eating with his rations (σιτομέτρημα). χάρισμα, the *donativum* in recognition of good service. 'Solent Reges egregiis militibus præter stipendium dare coronas, laureas, honores' (Grot.).

Cf. vi. 6. the Old Self has been 'crucified with Christ'; it is dead, and the believer is absolved from the galling obligation and has entered into a new and blessed union. The analogy seems somewhat fanciful, and indeed it is playfully propounded; yet the principle which it illustrates is real and conclusive. Law is provisional and temporary; and when a new order emerges, the obligations of the old order cease. And so it happened with the Jewish Law. Christ has instituted a new order, and in Him we are no longer under Law but under Grace.

vii. 1 Are you ignoring the fact, brothers—I am talking to men
who know what law is—that the law lords it over the person
2 during his life-time? The woman who is under a husband
is bound by the law to the living husband; but if the
husband die, the law which held her to him is invalidated.
3 So then, during the husband's life, she will be termed an
adulteress if she pass to a second husband; but if the
husband die, she is free from the law, so that she is not
4 an adulteress by passing to a second husband. And so,
my brothers, you also were put to death as regards the
Law through the body of Christ, that you might pass to a
second—Him who was raised from the dead in order that
5 we may bear fruit for God. For, while we were in the flesh,
the sinful passions provoked by the Law were ever being
set in operation in our members to bear fruit for death;
6 but, as the case stands, the law which bound us was
invalidated by our dying to what held us fast, so that we
are slaves in the new order of the Spirit and not the old
order of a written code.

Evidence of the Apostle's personal experience.

Here arises an objection—the petulant objection of a Jew who perceives the principle yet is loath to acknowledge it: Is the Law synonymous with Sin? The Apostle repudiates the suggestion, and proceeds to define the difference between the Law and Sin and their mutual relation. His argument is a personal testimony. He narrates his spiritual autobiography, and shows how, beginning as a Pharisee, he had sought righteousness by the Works of the Law and had been driven by painful experience to the blessed refuge of Faith in Christ.[1]

[1] Cf. pp. 32 f. The passage is plainly autobiographical. The Apostle speaks in his own name and not merely as a representative either of the Jews (Euth. Zig.) or of the human race (Theophyl.). It is a personal confession exemplifying the universal experience.

(1) His awakening.

His youth had been serene, unvexed by the consciousness of alienation from God; but one unforgotten day his peace had been broken. Lust had mastered him, and immediately the flood-gates were opened. Conscience gripped him. The Law intervened, and its commandment 'Thou shalt not lust' rang in his ears, and he recognised himself a sinner. It was the Law that brought him the discovery; and this indeed is the Law's proper function. 'Through law is full recognition of sin,' and 'where there is no law, neither is there transgression'; for 'sin is not taken into the reckoning when there is no law.' Had there been no law, the Apostle's sin would have been dead; but conscience quickened it, and he found himself in the Law's deadly grasp. The Law was not Sin; it was the discoverer of Sin. It was holy, and its prohibition of lust was holy and righteous and good. It had been instituted as a deterrent for the gracious purpose of preventing sin, and had he obeyed it, it would have been his friend; but when it was violated, it became his remorseless enemy.

iii. 20; iv. 15; v. 13.

7 What, then, shall we say? Is the Law sin? Away with
the idea! No, I had never recognised sin save through law.
For I had never known lust had not the Law kept saying
8 'Thou shalt not lust.' And sin got an outlet[1] through the
commandment to work out in me every sort of lust; for
9 apart from law sin is dead. I was alive apart from law once;
but when the commandment came, sin sprang into life, while
10 as for me, I died; and the commandment which aimed at
11 life—I found it resulted in death. For sin got an outlet
through the commandment to 'deceive' me and through it Cf. Gen.
12 to slay me. And so the Law is holy, and the commandment iii. 18.
13 is holy and righteous and good. Did what is good, then,
prove death to me? Away with the idea! No, but sin did,
that it might be shown as sin, by working out death for me
through what is good, that sin might come out in its transcendent sinfulness through the commandment.

(2) His conflict.

From that day his career of Pharisaic zeal was a struggle against sin, a feverish effort to rehabilitate himself with the Law and avert its condemnation by obedience to its commandments. But the struggle always issued in defeat; his efforts proved always unavailing. Sin was too strong for

[1] ἀφορμήν, cf. p. 215.

him. It held him in thraldom, thwarting each resolution and compelling him to do the evil which he hated. In the language of the Latin poet,[1] 'if he could, he would have been saner; but a strange force dragged him unwillingly. Lust prompted one thing, reason another. He saw the better things, and approved them; he followed the worse.' And here he made a second discovery. There was within him a dual personality—a higher self and a lower, his reason and his flesh, and these were in conflict. His reason would fain obey the Law of God, but his flesh obeyed the law of Sin. Here he found a measure of comfort, since his reason was his true self; yet his plight remained pitiful. The struggle seemed hopeless, and he saw no prospect of emancipation. 'Wretched man that I am!' was his lament, 'who will rescue me from the body laden with this death?'

14 For we know that the Law is spiritual, but I am a creature
15 of flesh,[2] sold into sin's thraldom. What I am working out I
do not recognise; for it is not what I will that I practise; no,
16 what I hate, it is this that I do. But, if it be what I will not
17 that I do, I admit the beauty of the Law; and, as the case
stands, it is no longer I that am working out the thing but the
18 sin which has its dwelling in me. For I know that there
dwells in me, that is, in my flesh, no good. It lies within my
reach to will what is beautiful, but to work it out does not;
19 for it is not the good which I will that I do, but the evil which
20 I will not, it is this that I practise. But if it be what I will
not that I do, it is no longer I that am working out the thing;
21 no, it is the sin which dwells in me. I find therefore the
law: when I will to do what is beautiful, it is what is evil
22 that lies within my reach. For my delight is with the Law of
23 God, so far as my inmost self is concerned; but I perceive a
different law in my members warring against the law of my
reason and taking me captive under the law of sin, the law
24 which is in my members. Wretched man that I am! who will
rescue me from the body laden with this death?[3]

[1] Ovid, *Met.* VII. 18-21.

[2] σάρκινος, 'carneous,' 'made of flesh' (cf. p. 249). He was not σαρκικός, 'carnal,' else there would have been no spiritual conflict. He was a spiritual being inhabiting flesh.

[3] ἐκ τοῦ σώματος τοῦ θανάτου τούτου, the body which is the seat of sin (cf. vi. 6), which in turn works out death (cf. ver. 13). If it were permissible to construe τούτου with σώματος, 'this body of death,' *i.e.*, 'this dead body' (Erasm., Calv.), the idea would be that the Apostle regarded himself as a living man bound to a corpse, like the victims of the tyrant Mezentius (cf. Verg. *Æn.* VIII. 485-8).

Brought thus low he made a final discovery. He found in Christ the rescue of which he had despaired. The conflict continued, but victory was assured. Deliverance was in sight.

(3) Peace in Christ.

25 Thanks to God through Jesus Christ our Lord! So, then,
I my own self with the reason am a slave to the Law of God
but with the flesh a slave to the law of Sin.

Controversy between the sinner and sin before the Law.

And now he proceeds to unfold the happy situation. He pictures a controversy before the Law between himself and Sin. The Law was his friend, and it would fain have pronounced a verdict in his favour; but its benevolent intent was frustrated: 'it was weak through the flesh.' There was a moral antinomy in his nature. His reason approved the Law of God, but his flesh was enslaved to the law of Sin, and the flesh had proved too strong for the reason. He had obeyed its unholy dictates, and thus there was nothing for it but that the holy Law should pronounce a verdict against him. It would fain have acquitted him, but it could not: 'it was weak through the flesh,' and it had to condemn him. Here redemption interposed. Christ had assumed frail, sin-laden humanity, and He had conquered the allurements of the flesh. He had resisted the law of Sin and obeyed the Law of God. And thus what the Law could not do in our case it was able to do in His: it found Him righteous, and 'condemned Sin in the flesh'—the Sin which had invaded humanity and which the Incarnate Saviour had resisted.

viii. 1 So, as the case stands, there is no condemnation for those
2 who are in Christ Jesus; for the law of the Spirit of life
freed you in Christ Jesus from the law of sin and death.
3 For what the Law could not do inasmuch as it was weak
through the flesh, God by sending His own Son in the
similitude of sinful flesh [1] and to deal with sin condemned
4 sin in the flesh, that the righteous requirement of the Law
might be fulfilled in us who follow not the ways of the flesh
but those of the spirit.

[1] Cf. Phil. ii. 7; Heb. ii. 17. Our Lord assumed not 'sinful flesh' but a human body like Adam's at his creation—'a true body' yet different from the bodies of the children of men inasmuch as it was untainted by Original Sin. Cf. *The Days of His Flesh*, Append. I.

Abiding antinomy between flesh and spirit.

It was thus that the Apostle found by faith in Christ the peace which he had vainly sought by the works of the Law. The antinomy remained, but the condemnation was gone. And this happy issue resulted from his mystic union with Christ. The Son of God had by His Incarnation been identified with humanity, and by conquering its solicitations had mastered the sin inherent in our flesh. He had died and had been raised and glorified; and the Apostle, united with Him by faith, had died with Him, had been raised with Him, and lived with Him. It was indeed true that his old self, though crucified, still lived, and the conflict between the Law of God and the law of sin still persisted and would persist while he tenanted the sin-laden body; but his union with Christ had effected a momentous and blessed difference. His life in Christ was his true life, and his peace lay in resolutely maintaining it.

5 For those who take the ways of the flesh espouse the cause
of the flesh; while those who take the spirit's ways espouse
6 the spirit's cause.[1] The espousal of the cause of the flesh is
death; while the espousal of the spirit's cause is life and
7 peace because the espousal of the cause of the flesh is enmity
against God, for it is not subjected to the Law of God, indeed
8 it cannot be; and those who are in the flesh cannot please God.

Life in the spirit by union with Christ and surrender to His Spirit.

The Apostle's argument here is illumined by recollection of his conception of the two hostile domains, the two antagonistic forces in human nature—the flesh and the spirit.[2] The flesh is not simply the body—man's physical nature, that side of his complex being which relates him to the animal creation. It is the body enslaved and corrupted by sin. It is the domain where the law of sin prevails. The spirit, on the other hand, is that side of our nature which is akin to God. It is the domain dominated by the Spirit of God. And thus our destiny depends on our relation to these two domains. The flesh is mortal, and if we live in it and obey

[1] *φρονεῖν τὰ τῆς σάρκος*, 'take the side of the flesh,' 'support its cause.' Cf. *The Days of His Flesh*, p. 268. Socr. *Eccl. Hist.* I. 24, where *ἁ Σαβελλίου φρονεῖν* is synonymous with *Σαβελλίζειν*. It is a political phrase, and the idea is continued by *ἔχθρα εἰς Θεὸν* and *Θεῷ ἀρέσαι* (vers. 7, 8). *ἀρέσκειν* occurs in inscriptions commemorating services to the state (cf. Moulton and Milligan, *Vocab.*).

[2] Cf. p. 214.

the law of sin, our destiny is death. If, on the contrary, we live in the spirit and surrender ourselves to the Holy Spirit's dominion, then our destiny is life. And in this destiny our mortal bodies will participate; for they will be delivered from the debasing tyranny of sin and share the Resurrection of Christ. The flesh will be redeemed from corruption and raised incorruptible, a body of glory.

> But you are not in the flesh; no, you are in the spirit, if
> indeed God's Spirit is dwelling in you. If one has not Christ's
> 10 Spirit, this man is not His. And if Christ be in you, then,
> while the body is dead by reason of sin, the spirit is life by
> 11 reason of righteousness. And if the Spirit of Him who raised
> Jesus from the dead is dwelling in you, He who raised Christ
> Jesus from the dead will make even your mortal bodies live
> through His Spirit who has His dwelling in you.

Hence the secret lies in eschewing the domain of the flesh and resolutely living in the domain of the spirit; and this the Apostle designates 'a debt'—a debt of honour, a sacred obligation. He is thinking here of the mystic union between the believer and Christ and is recalling his previous argument: 'We who died to sin—how shall we any more live in it? Reckon yourselves to be dead to sin, but alive to God in Christ Jesus.' *A debt of honour.* *vi. 2, 11.*

> 12 So then, brothers, we are debtors, not to the flesh that we
> 13 should live in accordance with the flesh. For if you are living
> in accordance with the flesh, you will soon die; but if by the
> spirit you are putting the body's practices to death, you will
> live.

The antinomy indeed persists and the conflict continues; but it is no longer a hopeless conflict, for our union with Christ and our surrender to the dominion of His Spirit have brought us magnificent reinforcements. And these the Apostle proceeds to display. *A threefold reinforcement:*

The first is the restoration of our divine sonship. Sonship is our primal birthright, and even while we are following the ways of the flesh, we are still God's sons, though, as our Lord has it, lost sons, sons who have wandered from the Father's House, forgotten Him, and forfeited their heritage.[1] *(1) The restoration of our divine sonship.*

[1] Cf. *The Atonement in the Light of History and the Modern Spirit*, pp. 143 ff.

When we forsake the ways of the flesh and follow the Spirit's ways, then our faces are turned homeward and we cry '*Abba*, our Father!' Perhaps there is a reference here to that prophetic word of the Lord: 'How shall I put thee among the children, and give thee a pleasant land, the goodliest heritage of the nations? And I said, Ye shall call Me, My Father; and shall not turn away from following Me.' When our hearts turn homeward and we yearn for our Father, that is the awakening within us of the spirit of sonship, but we are not yet reinstated in our heritage,

Jer. iii. 19.

> 'not inheritors as yet
> Of all our own right royal things.'

Sonship is ours in possession, but the heritage is ours only in prospect. It will be ours in possession when we get home, and meanwhile we must travel the painful road in eager expectation. Christ won His glory by suffering, and we must share His suffering if we would share His glory.

14 For they who are led by God's Spirit, these are all God's
15 sons. For you did not receive a spirit of slavery to be again
in fear; no, you received a spirit of restored sonship in which
16 we cry '*Abba*, our Father!'[1] The Spirit Himself testifies
17 with our spirit that we are God's children. And if we are
children, we are also heirs—God's heirs and Christ's fellow-
heirs, if indeed we are His fellows in suffering that we may be
made also His fellows in glory.

(2) The glory which awaits us.

And this golden hope is the second reinforcement which surrender to the Spirit's dominion brings. Our present sufferings dwindle into insignificance in view of the glory which awaits us. They are our portion in the universal curse, that tide of woe which streamed from Adam's sin and has flooded all nature, animate and inanimate, 'turning to dross the gold of nature's dower.' Our Lord endured it in His vicarious anguish when He 'submitted Himself to cursing on our behalf,' and He is calling us to take up the cross and follow Him, His fellow-workers in the universal redemption.

Gal. iii. 13.

18 I reckon that the sufferings of the present crisis are not
worth mentioning in view of the glory which will soon be

[1] Cf. p. 209.

19 revealed as our portion. For the creation, eagerly intent, is
20 awaiting the revelation of the sons of God. The creation was
subjected to futility,[1] not of its own choice but because of
21 him who subjected it; [2] yet was there a hope to sustain it,
forasmuch as the creation itself also will be freed from enslavement to corruption and attain the freedom belonging to
22 the glory of the children of God.[3] For we know that all
the creation has been groaning and travailing with mankind [4]
23 to this day. And, more than that, ourselves also, though we
have the first-fruits of the Spirit [5]—we ourselves also are inly
groaning while we await our restoration to sonship—the
24 redemption of our body. It is by the hope that we were
saved; but when a hope is seen, it is not a hope; for a thing
25 which one sees, why is he hoping for it? But if it be for a
thing which we do not see that we are hoping, we enduringly
await it.

And a third reinforcement is the Spirit's help. We are not alone on the painful road: 'the Spirit lends a helping hand to our weakness.' It is a homely and kindly word that the Apostle employs here. It occurs in only one other passage in the New Testament—the Evangelist Luke's story of the supper at Bethany, where it is told how Martha, 'distracted about much service,' appealed to the Master to bid Mary 'lend her a helping hand.' It is a long compound—the simple verb, meaning 'to lay hold of,' and two prepositions, one signifying 'along with' and the other 'over against,' 'at the opposite side.' And thus the idea is that you are

(3) The Spirit's help.

Lk. x. 40.

[1] Cf. Ps. xxxix. 5: *τὰ σύμπαντα ματαιότης, πᾶς ἄνθρωπος ζῶν.*

[2] That is, Adam, whose sin cursed not only his posterity but the whole creation, even inanimate nature (cf. Gen. iii. 17), which consequently 'groans and travails with sinful man' (cf. ver. 22). So Chrys. Not God (Orig., Ambrstr., and most moderns). It was sin, not God, that inflicted the curse. Adam by his sin subjected the creation to futility; God redeems it by subjecting it to Christ (cf. 1 Cor. xv. 27, 28).

[3] *ἐπ' ἐλπίδι*, 'in reliance on hope,' with *ὑπετάγη*. On the view that *διὰ τὸν ὑποτάξαντα* refers to God, *ἐπ' ἐλπίδι* may be construed either with *ὑπετάγη* or with *ὑποτάξαντα*. In the latter case it is necessary to read, not *διότι*, 'because' (ℵD*FG), but *ὅτι*, 'that' (ABCD^c EKLP)—'with hope that.'

[4] The present sufferings are 'the birth-pangs' of a new creation, a better world (cf. Mt. xxiv. 8=Mk. xiii. 8: *ἀρχὴ ὠδίνων*); and all nature, cursed by man's sin, shares his anguish. On the view that *διὰ τὸν ὑποτάξαντα* (ver. 20) refers to God, *συν* in *συνστενάζει* and *συνωδίνει* must be regarded as a mere strengthening of the simple verbs or as introducing the idea of a chorus of groaning in Nature. On this use of the pres. cf. Jo. xiv. 9: *τοσοῦτον χρόνον μεθ' ὑμῶν εἰμι;*

[5] Cf. p. 350.

struggling to lift a burden beyond your strength, and a friend comes to your aid. He lays hold of it, and then betwixt you—you on this side and he on that—it is lifted easily.

This is the office of the Holy Spirit. He does not relieve us of our burdens: He 'lends us a helping hand.' And the Apostle adduces a particular case—the task of prayer. We are ignorant and bewildered. Our prayers are only confused cries, 'inarticulate groanings'; but the Spirit pours meaning into them; He pleads for us; and, interpreted by Him, our 'inarticulate groanings' are prevailing supplications in God's ear. This is the Spirit's 'intercession.' It is the complement of the intercession of Christ. The Holy Spirit is our Lord's Successor. In the days of His flesh our Lord was the mind of God and the love of God in contact with human need. When He took His departure, that point of contact was removed; but another was established by the Holy Spirit's advent. He is now what our Lord was in the days of His flesh—God's earthly representative, on the one hand advocating God's cause with men, and on the other conveying their responses to God. His intercession is the pledge of our acceptance. It is the taking up of our prayers by God, their entrance into His very heart. It is God's espousal of our cause.

Cf. ver. 34.

Cf. Jo. xiv. 16-18, 25, 26.

26 Likewise the Spirit also lends a helping hand to our weakness. For what to pray for as we should we do not know, but
the Spirit Himself pleads for us with inarticulate groanings;[1]
27 and the Searcher of hearts knows what cause the Spirit espouses,
because it is as God would have it[2] that He pleads the cause
28 of the saints. And we know that with those who love God
He co-operates in everything for good[3]—with those who are
29 called in accordance with His purpose. For those whom He

[1] The groanings are ours, not the Spirit's. Cf. Aug. *In Joan. Ev. Tract.* VI. 2: 'In nobis gemit, quia gemere nos facit. Nec parva res est, quod nos docet Spiritus sanctus gemere: insinuat enim nobis quia peregrinamur, et docet nos in patriam suspirare, et ipso desiderio gemimus.'

[2] *κατὰ Θεόν*, cf. 2 Cor. vii. 9-11.

[3] This construction makes the sentence an amplification of *κατὰ Θεόν*, and it is attested by (1) the addition of ὁ Θεός after *συνεργεῖ* in AB, and (2) the absence of ὁ Θεός in ver. 29, implying that *συνεργεῖ* and *προέγνω* have the same subj. The rendering 'for those who love God all things co-operate for good' is, however, grammatically no less possible.

foreknew, He also foreordained for conformation to the
image of His Son, that He might be the first-born among
30 many brothers; and whom He foreordained these He also
called; and whom He called, these He also accounted righteous; and whom He accounted righteous, these He also Cf. ver. 17.
glorified.

The eternal security of the believer.

And now the Apostle draws to a conclusion. He surveys his argument, and exults in the believer's eternal security confirmed by a double guarantee. God is on our side, and the evidence is the Cross of Christ: 'He did not spare His own Son but surrendered Him for us all.' The love which faced that supreme Sacrifice will withhold nothing. And our acquittal is absolute. It is God's verdict, and God's verdict is final. We are one with Christ, not only in His Death but in His Resurrection; and the presence of our Representative at God's right hand is the pledge of our future glory. His love is our security, and it is an unfailing love. It holds us in its grasp, and it will never let us go.

That was the Apostle's persuasion, and it was born of experience. The love of Christ had succoured him in all the manifold distresses of the bygone years, and brought him (Cf. 2 Cor. xi. 23-27.) through every conflict a conqueror and more than a conqueror; and he recognised in the experience of the past a prophecy of the future. The love which had blessed him hitherto, would never fail him. It would attend him to the end of his days, nor would it cease there. It would reach out into the unknown Eternity. He conjures up the mysterious terrors of the Unseen, marshals them in grim array, and sets them at defiance. 'Neither death'—that black shadow which is ever travelling toward us across the waste and will presently engulf us. 'Nor life'—a worse terror still, more mysterious, more perilous.

> 'Many there be that seek Thy face
> To meet the hour of parting breath;
> But 'tis for life I need Thy grace:
> Life is more solemn still than death.'

What dread chances it holds! what appalling possibilities of disaster, suffering, and shame! 'Nor angels nor principalities nor powers'—the innumerable hosts which encompass us, those mysterious forces which play upon our lives, incalculable, uncontrollable. 'Nor things present nor things future, nor height nor depth'—all dimensions of time and space; this world, the next; Heaven, Hell. And what more remains? The Apostle sums up every possibility under one final and comprehensive category—'nor any different creation.' 'I know not,' he means, 'what new environment may yet confront me, what strange world, what unimagined order, what play of forces more dread and solemn than I have hitherto experienced; but I fear not even that. For there is nothing here, nothing there, nothing anywhere which I need dread, since, wherever I may be and whatever may emerge, the Love of Christ will be with me, my comrade and my portion.'

It is told of Robert Bruce, the Scottish saint in the generation succeeding the Reformation, that, as he lay a-dying, attended by his daughter, he suddenly exclaimed: 'Hold, daughter, my Master calls me.' And then he bade her fetch the Bible. 'Cast me up,' he said, 'the eighth chapter of Romans, and place my finger on these words, "I am persuaded."' And thus he died, with his finger and his heart resting there.

31 What, then, shall we say in view of all this? If God is
32 for us, who is against us? Seeing that He did not spare
His own Son but surrendered Him for us all, how will He
not also with Him graciously bestow everything upon us?
33 Who will bring a charge against God's elect? It is God
Is. l. 8. 34 'that accounts righteous: who is it that condemns?' It
is Christ Jesus that died, or rather, was raised, He who is
35 at the right hand of God, who is also pleading for us. Who
will separate us from the love of Christ? Will distress or
anguish or persecution or famine or nakedness or danger or
36 sword? As it is written:

Ps. xliv. 22. 'For Thy sake we are being put to death all the day long;
We were reckoned as sheep for slaughter.'

37 But amid all this we more than conquer through Him who
38 loved us. For I am persuaded that neither death nor
life, nor angels nor principalities nor powers,[1] nor things

[1] The words οὔτε δυνάμεις in the vast majority of MSS. stand after μέλλοντα, but they should certainly stand after ἀρχαί, forming a triple category οὔτε ἄγγελοι οὔτε ἀρχαὶ οὔτε δυνάμεις. Unless indeed they are a mere interpolation (cf. 1 Cor. xv. 24; Eph. i. 21; 1 Pet. iii. 22), their transposition is probably due to their

39 present nor things future, no height nor depth, nor any
different creation [1] will have the power to separate us from
the love of God, the love which is in Christ Jesus our Lord.

3. *The Problem of the Election of Israel* (ix-xi)

The tragedy of Israel's rejection.

The Apostle's task is accomplished. He has defined and demonstrated his doctrine of Justification by Faith, and answered the objections which were urged against it. But he does not conclude here. A problem still remained which was very grievous to his own heart and well-nigh disposed him to wish that a doctrine involving so terrible a consequence might be false. Its offence in the eyes of the Judaists lay in its obliteration of the distinction between Jews and Gentiles; but the Apostle recognised that a heavier disaster had befallen Israel than the loss of her ancient prestige, her exclusive privilege. It was the tragedy of her utter rejection. She had refused her Saviour, the promised Messiah, and her heritage had passed to the believing Gentiles. They were now the people of God, and she was an outcast from His grace. It was a dire catastrophe, and well-nigh broke the Apostle's heart. For he loved his people. Their sacred tradition was precious and glorious in his eyes; and when he contemplated the tragic *dénouement*, the prayer of Moses rose to his lips: 'Oh, this people have sinned a great sin. Yet now, if Thou wilt forgive their sin . . . ; and if not, blot me, I pray Thee, out of Thy book which Thou hast written.' (Ex. xxxii. 31, 32.)

ix. 1 It is truth that I am telling in Christ, it is no lie, my
conscience supporting me with its testimony in the Holy
2 Spirit—that I have great grief and my heart has ceaseless [2]
3 pain. I caught myself praying that I should be myself
an accursed outcast from the Christ for the sake of my
4 brothers, my kinsfolk according to the flesh. For they are

accidental omission from the text of an early MS. They would then be noted on the margin and might easily be misplaced in the text by a subsequent copyist. The Apostle is here alluding to the elaborate Jewish angelology which, especially in Gnostic circles, tended to develop into angelolatry. Cf. p. 550.

[1] Cf. Chrys.: *ὃ δὲ λέγει τοιοῦτόν ἐστιν· εἰ καὶ ἄλλη τοσαύτη κτίσις ἦν ὅση ἡ ὁρωμένη, ὅση ἡ νοητὴ, οὐδέν με τῆς ἀγάπης ἐκείνης ἀπέστησε.*

[2] *ἀδιάλειπτος*, 'incessant,' 'unremitting'; used of a racking cough—*ἀδιαλίπτως δὲ ἐπαγωνιζόμενος* (Moulton and Milligan, *Vocab.*).

Cf. Heb. ix. 1, 6.

Israelites; theirs are the restoration to sonship, and the
Glory,[1] and the Covenants, and the Lawgiving, and the
5 Temple-service, and the Promises; theirs are the Fathers,
and of them sprang the Christ according to the flesh—He
who is over all, God blessed for ever. Amen.[2]

Its threefold justification:

To the discussion of this bitter problem he now addresses himself, and he grapples with it in anguish of soul: now vindicating God's righteousness and laying the responsibility on Israel; then gladly recognising that her rejection is only partial, and there is still 'a remnant according to the election of grace'; and finally emerging into the triumphant assurance of her ultimate restoration and humanity's universal salvation.

His argument turns on three ideas which figured largely in Jewish theology—Election, the Sovereignty of God, and His Irresponsibility.

(1) Election.

Israel was the elect nation, and the Jews derived thence a fatal assurance of unassailable security. God had promised

[1] The Shekinah (cf. Jo. i. 14; Heb. ix. 5). Cf. n. on 2 Cor. xii. 9, p. 338.

[2] The great Fathers and the ancient versions agree in attaching ὁ ὢν ἐπὶ πάντων Θεὸς εὐλογητὸς εἰς τοὺς αἰῶνας to ὁ Χριστός, but this construction was early challenged in the interests both of orthodoxy and of heresy. On the one hand, the text was quoted, as identifying Christ with God, by the Patripassians (cf. Hippolyt. *Contra Noet.* vi; Epiphan. lvii. 2, 9); while, on the other hand, it offended the Arians (cf. Epist. of Co. of Antioch to Paul of Samosata, A.D. 269, Routh, *Reliq. Sacr.*, III. pp. 291 f.). And so the construction was altered by manipulation of the punctuation—a legitimate procedure, since punctuation was lacking in the earliest MSS. 1. A period was placed after σάρκα, and the ensuing words were rendered either (1) 'He who is over all, even God, be (or 'is') blessed for ever,' or (2) 'He who is over all is God blessed for ever.' 2. The period was placed after πάντων: 'the Christ according to the flesh, who is over all (cf. x. 12; Ac. x. 36). God be (or 'is') blessed for ever.' The objection to these latter constructions is that an ascription of glory to God is here abrupt and purposeless; and, moreover, in a doxology εὐλογητός always stands at the beginning (cf. Lk. i. 68; 2 Cor. i. 3; Eph. i. 3; 1 Pet. i. 3). It is a decisive confirmation of the former construction that it provides a natural and necessary antithesis to τὸ κατὰ σάρκα: the Christ who was an Israelite 'according to the flesh' was in truth the blessed and eternal God. It is no valid objection that nowhere else does Paul expressly designate Christ 'God,' but always 'the Lord' as distinguished from 'God the Father' (cf. 1 Cor. viii. 6); for the designation is in no wise alien from his thought. Cf. the interchange of Πνεῦμα Θεοῦ and Πνεῦμα Χριστοῦ in viii. 9-11. The Apostolic Father St. Ignatius could not have used phrases like Ἰησοῦς Χριστὸς ὁ Θεὸς ἡμῶν so freely as he does (cf. *Eph.* inscr., i, xviii; *Rom.* inscr., iii, vi; *Polyc.* viii; *Smyrn.* i) unless the idea had been apostolic.

to be the God of Abraham and his seed after him ; and thus, they argued, He was bound by an inviolable pledge, and could never disown them. The Apostle meets this contention by demonstrating from the Scriptures that Election had a narrower compass than they supposed. Not all Abraham's descendants are his children and heirs of the Promise. There is an election within the election. The Scriptures recognise this, and he adduces an historic instance. Ishmael was a son of Abraham no less than Isaac, yet Ishmael was not 'a child of the Promise.' He was indeed Abraham's son by a heathen concubine, and it might be urged that this invalidated his title to rank with Isaac, the child of Sarah ; but then Jacob and Esau were sons of Isaac by the same mother, Rebecca, yet God, in the prophet's grim phrase, 'loved Jacob and hated Esau.'

6 Not that the word of God has lapsed. For not all who are
7 of Israel's race are Israel ; nor because they are Abraham's
seed are they all his children. No, 'in Isaac shall thy seed
8 be called.' That is, it is not the children of the flesh that are Gen. xxi.
children of God ; no, it is the children of the Promise that 12.
9 are reckoned as seed. For the word is a word of promise, and
it is this : 'At this season next year I will come, and Sarah
10 shall have a son.' And, more than that, there is also the case xviii. 10.
of Rebecca when she conceived by one man, our father Isaac.
11 Ere the children were born or had done aught good or ill, that
God's elective purpose might abide on the score not of works
12 but of His call, it was told her : 'The elder shall be slave to xxv. 23.
13 the younger' ; and accordingly it is written : 'Jacob I loved, Mal. i. 2, 3.
but Esau I hated.'

Here the question emerges whether this was fair : and the Apostle answers it by asserting the Sovereignty of God—that stern truth which finds exemplification in the story of Pharaoh. God shows mercy where He will, and where He will He hardens men's hearts ; and there is here no unfairness, since none has a claim upon Him. None is entitled to mercy or compassion, and where He displays either, it is pure unmerited grace.

(2) The sovereignty of God.

14 What, then, shall we say ? Is there unrighteousness with
15 God ? Away with the idea ! He says to Moses : 'It will be Ex. xxxiii.
mercy wherever I have mercy, and compassion wherever I 19.
16 have compassion.' So then it depends not on man's will or

ix. 16. Cf. Ex. iv. 21, vii. 3, ix. 12, xiv. 4, 17.

17 effort but on God's mercy. For the Scripture says to Pharaoh :
'For this very end I raised thee up, that I might demonstrate
in thee My power, and that My name might be proclaimed
18 abroad in all the earth.' So then on whom He will He has
mercy, and whom He will He 'hardens.'

(3) His irresponsibility. Cf. Is. xxix. 16, xlv. 9; Jer. xviii; Wisd. xv. 7-17; Ecclus. xxxiii. 13.

But then, it may be urged, if it be God that has hardened our hearts, why should He blame us for our unbelief? This objection the Apostle meets by affirming the Irresponsibility of God, borrowing an image which figures largely in Jewish literature and likening God to a potter and man to the clay which the potter fashions as he will.

'For the potter, pressing soft earth toilsomely,
fashioneth each vessel for our service;
Nay, of the same clay he is wont to fashion both the vessels
which minister pure offices
and those of a contrary sort, all alike;
And what is the use of each vessel of either sort
the workman is judge.'

Here, suggests the Apostle, may lie the answer to that Jewish question why God first hardened Israel's heart, and then condemned her for her unbelief. Perhaps her privilege had an ulterior purpose. Perhaps the Jews were all the while 'vessels of wrath' doomed to destruction, and His long forbearance with them was nothing else than the working out of His gracious purpose toward His 'vessels of mercy'—His believing people whether Jews or Gentiles. The idea found support in Scripture. Was it not the Gentiles that Hosea meant when he prophesied of the calling of those who were no people to be the people of God? And did not Isaiah declare that, however numerous the nation of Israel might be, only 'the remnant' would be saved?

Is. xxix. 16, xlv. 9. Jer. xviii. 6. Jer. l. 25; Is. liv. 16.

19 You will say to me, then : 'Why does He still find fault?
20 For who is withstanding His will?' Nay, rather, man, who
are you that are bandying words with God? 'Shall the thing
moulded say to him who moulded it : "Why didst thou make
21 me thus?"' Has not 'the potter' authority over 'the clay,'
of the same lump to make one vessel for honour and another
22 for dishonour? Suppose that, while it was God's will to
demonstrate His wrath and publish His power, He bore in
much long-suffering with 'vessels of wrath' fitted 'for destruc-

23 tion,' that He might publish [1] the riches of His glory toward
vessels of mercy which He prepared beforehand for glory—
24 even us whom He also called, not only from among the Jews
25 but from among the Gentiles also? As He says also in Hosea:

'I will call them that are no people to be My people ii. 23.
and her that is not beloved to be beloved.
26 And it shall be that in the place where it was said to them, i. 10.
"No people of Mine are ye,"
There shall they be called to be sons of the Living God.'

27 And Isaiah cries concerning Israel: 'Though the number of x. 22, 23.
the sons of Israel be as the sand of the sea, it is but the remnant
28 that shall be saved. For a reckoning complete and concise
29 will the Lord make upon the earth.' And, as Isaiah has previously said, i. 9.

'Unless the Lord of Hosts had left us a seed,
as Sodom we would have become, and like Gomorrah
would we have been made.'

Thus the long history of humanity had issued in a surprising *dénouement*. The Gentiles had won the prize which they had never sought; and the Jews, though they had pursued it, had never reached the goal. The prize was righteousness, and the Jews had missed it because they had pursued it along a false track. They had sought to win it by the works of the Law; and the Gentiles, in their need and helplessness, had found it by faith in Christ. **An amazing issue.**

30 What, then, shall we say? That Gentiles, who were not
pursuing righteousness, won righteousness, a righteousness,
31 however, which comes of faith; whereas Israel, though pur-
32 suing a law of righteousness, never reached one. Wherefore?
Because their starting-point was not faith but what they
deemed works. They stumbled over 'the stone of stumbling,' [2]
33 as it is written:

'Behold, I place in Sion a stone of stumbling and a rock of Is. viii. 14,
tripping, xxviii. 16.
and he who rests his faith on Him shall not be put to
shame.' [3]

[1] Omitting καί before ἵνα γνωρίσῃ with W. H.

[2] A continuation of the metaphor of the race in ver. 16 (τοῦ τρέχοντος) and vers. 30, 31. Cf. the description of a disaster at the Pythian Games through a chariot striking the turning-post in Soph. *Elect.* 743-48.

[3] These two passages are similarly conjoined in 1 Pet. ii. 6. The quotation is evidently taken from a collection of 'testimonies.' Cf. 229.

Purpose of the preceding argument.

To appreciate this passage it should be observed that the Apostle is grappling in anguish of soul with a grim and baffling problem; and he thus far presents no adequate and final solution. He merely throws out a series of suggestions based on theological postulates which were indubitable to the Jewish mind but which appear less cogent from the Christian point of view. It was enough at the moment that he should silence the objections of his Jewish readers and lead them to recognition of the dire fact of Israel's rejection, and he presently emerges into a larger conception of God's providential dealings.

Its limitations.

Stern as it is, his idea of Election hardly admits of criticism, since it is nothing else than a reading of history. Ishmael and Esau stood in his thought for their descendants; and the descendants of the former were the fierce tribe of the Ishmaelites, whose hand was against every man and every man's hand against them, and the accursed Edomites, the enemies of Israel and Israel's God. He reasons back from the actual issue to the eternal purpose. But the Christian spirit refuses to acquiesce in the Jewish dogmas of the Sovereignty and Irresponsibility of God. It repudiates the idea that God owes nothing to man. The creature has a claim on his Creator; the child has a claim on his Father. It is indeed true that 'wherever He has mercy, it is mercy, and wherever He has compassion, it is compassion'; but He owes both, since He is 'a faithful Creator' and, still more, since He is a Father. He would not be a Father if He did not love His children, especially His lost children, and do the utmost which love can devise to bring them home.[1] And as for the assertion of the Irresponsibility of God, it is open to obvious and fatal objections. Grant that we are but as clay in the hands of the potter, and He may make of us what He will—a vile utensil or a festal cup; yet it were a shame

Gen. xvi. 12. Ps. cxxxvii. 7. I Pet. iv. 19.

[1] Cf. George Eliot, *Life*, Append. to Chap. x by Mrs. John Cash: 'To something that followed from her intimating the claim of creatures upon their Creator, my father objected, "But we have no claim upon God." "No claim upon God!" she reiterated indignantly; "we have the strongest possible claim upon Him."' . . . '"There may be," she would say, "conduct on the part of a parent which should exonerate his child from further obligation to him; but there cannot be action conceivable which should absolve the parent from obligation to serve his child, seeing that for that child's existence he is himself responsible."'

to Him if He deliberately fashioned vessels for destruction and not for use. His character as a good craftsman is at stake, and He owes it to Himself to make the best of His material and compel it to His purpose.

> ' So, take and use Thy work :
> Amend what flaws may lurk,
> What strain o' the stuff, what warpings past the aim !
> My times be in Thy hand !
> Perfect the cup as planned !
> Let age approve of youth, and death complete the same ! '

This is indeed God's way. ' The Lord will perfect that which concerneth me : Thy mercy, O Lord, endureth for ever ; forsake not the works of Thine own hands.' Nor is this the final definition of the relation between God and man. We are more, much more, than senseless clay in the Potter's hands. We are God's reasonable creatures ; we are His children created after the image of His Eternal Son, and He owes us a Father's love and sympathy and care.

Ps. cxxxviii. 8.

All this the Apostle duly recognises in the sequel ; and the fact is that he is not here expounding his own doctrine. His purpose is to beat down Jewish arrogance, and he confronts its pretensions with its own theological postulates.

Israel's inexcusability:

He has been writing hard things of his people ; and since he has harder things still to write, he reasseverates the undying affection which he bore them, and his grief at the disaster which had overtaken them. He was not exulting in their humiliation. On the contrary, their salvation was his constant and eager desire ; yet he could not close his eyes to their unhappy plight, and he proceeds to show that it was their own doing. They had indeed sought righteousness, but they had sought it in their own laborious and futile way by the works of the Law, and had refused God's way—the easy and sure way of faith in Christ.

x. 1 Brothers, my heart's craving [1] and my prayer to God on
2 their behalf are for their salvation. I bear them testimony
that they have a zeal for God, but it is an uninstructed zeal.
3 For, ignoring God's righteousness and seeking to set up one

[1] ἡ εὐδοκια τῆς ἐμῆς καρδίας, 'the good pleasure of my heart,' what would content it. Chrys. : εὐδοκιαν ἐνταῦθα τὴν σφοδρὰν ἐπιθυμιαν φησί.

of their own, they were not subjected to the righteousness of God.

(1) The accessibility of the Word.

Dt. xxx. 11-14.

And they were inexcusable, since the very Law which required Works revealed the better way of Faith. He adduces a passage in Moses' address to the Israelites when he was giving them the Law: 'This commandment which I command thee this day, it is not too hard for thee, neither is it far off. It is not in heaven, that thou shouldest say, "Who shall go up for us to heaven, and bring it unto us, and make us to hear it, that we may do it?" Neither is it beyond the sea, that thou shouldest say, "Who will go over the sea for us, and bring it unto us, and make us to hear it, that we may do it?" But the word is very nigh unto thee, on thy lips, and in thy heart, that thou mayest do it.' The Lawgiver is here warning the Israelites of their responsibility. They knew God's requirement, since it was plainly written in the Law which he had delivered to them. It was no unrevealed mystery, no inaccessible lore. The passage is an assertion of the simplicity and sufficiency of the Law, but the Apostle, handling the ancient Scriptures with his accustomed freedom, invests it with a significance which Moses never intended. In fact his reference is not a quotation but an adaptation, a mere literary allusion. He recalls the familiar words and fits them to his purpose. Here, he says, is the difference between the Law and the Gospel. The Law says: 'Do, and thou shalt live'; but the Gospel inculcates no laborious observances. Its command is: 'Have faith in Christ.' He has wrought out salvation by His Incarnation and Resurrection, and these are accomplished facts. You need not ask: 'Who will go up to heaven and bring Him down?' for He came down and lived and died. Nor need you ask: 'Who will go down to the deep and raise Him from the dead?' for He is risen and ascended. He is the Living and Glorified Saviour, and nothing is required but a glad, brave faith in Him. 'We need not,' St. Chrysostom puts it, 'go a far road or sail the ocean or cross mountains in order to be saved. No, though you will not so much as step over your threshold, you may be saved sitting at home.'

Faith is all; for is it not written that 'no one who sets his faith on Him shall be put to shame'? This is the charter of universal salvation. Salvation is by faith in Christ, and it is offered to Jew and Gentile indiscriminately. His mercy is for all who 'call upon His name'; and here lay the Apostle's justification in preaching to all, Jews and Gentiles alike.

4 For the Law's goal is Christ,[1] that righteousness may accrue
5 to every one who has faith. For Moses writes that 'the man Lev. xviii.
who doeth' the righteousness which comes of the Law 'shall 5.
6 live in it.' But the righteousness which comes of Faith speaks
thus: 'Say not in thy heart: "Who will go up to heaven?"
7 that is, to bring Christ down; or, "Who will go down to the
deep?"[2] that is, to bring Christ up from the dead.' No,
8 what is it that it says? 'The Word is nigh thee on thy
lips and in thy heart,' that is, the Word of Faith which we are
9 proclaiming—that, if you take the confession 'on thy lips'
JESUS IS LORD, and have the faith 'in thy heart' that God Cf. 1 Cor.
10 raised Him from the dead, you will be saved. It is with the xii. 3.
heart that one has faith and attains righteousness, and it is
with the lips that one makes confession and attains salvation.
11 For the Scripture says: 'No one who rests his faith on Him Is. xxviii.
12 shall be put to shame.' There is no distinction between Jew 16.
and Greek; for the same Lord is Lord of all, rich toward all
13 who call upon Him. For 'whosoever calls upon the name of Joel ii. 32.
14 the Lord shall be saved.' How, then, are they to call upon
One in whom they never had faith? And how are they to
have faith in One whose message they never heard? And
15 how are they to hear it without one to proclaim it? And how
are they to proclaim it unless they be commissioned? As it
is written, 'How beautiful are the feet of those who preach Is. lii. 7.
the Gospel of good things!'

[1] So Chrys., taking τέλος as 'the aim,' 'the end sought' (cf. 1 Tim. i. 5). The end of the Law is Christ and the righteousness He bestows (cf. Gal. iii. 24), just as the end of the physician's art is health. Most of the Fathers understand by τέλος 'fulfilment' (cf. Lk. xxii. 37). Clem. Alex. *De Div. Serv.* 9, where πλήρωμα (cf. Rom. xiii. 10) is read for τέλος. Aug. *Contra Adversar. Leg. et Proph.* II. 26: 'Finis perficiens, non interficiens.' *Ad Oros. contra Priscill. et Orig.* 8: 'finem non consumentem sed perficientem significat . . . quo lex perficiatur, non quo aboleatur. Quod et illic significat, ubi ait: *Non veni legem solvere sed adimplere* (Mt. v. 17).' Similarly Orig., Ambrstr. Most moderns take τέλος in the sense of 'termination': 'Christ has put an end to the Law' (cf. Mt. xi. 13; Lk. xvi. 16).

[2] ἄβυσσος, 'the depth of the sea' (cf. Ps. cvii. 26). Quoting freely, the Apostle writes τίς καταβήσεται εἰς τὴν ἄβυσσον; for τίς διαπεράσει ἡμῖν εἰς τὸ πέραν τῆς θαλάσσης; making the two questions correspond.

(2) Her disregard of it.

And this was the condemnation of the Jews: they had not hearkened to the Gospel. And what was the reason? It was not that they had never heard it; for it had been published near and far. There was no corner of the wide-spread Empire whither it had not penetrated.[1] In truth it was like 'the music of the spheres,' filling the broad firmament and unheard only by inattentive ears, unperceived only by dull hearts. And this was the reason of Israel's faithlessness. The music of the Gospel was in her ears, but she had never perceived it. And the Gentiles had perceived it and hearkened to it—the stupid, despised Gentiles.

Cf. xv. 19.

Cf. Ps. xix. 1-6.

16 But they did not all hearken to the Gospel. No, for Isaiah
says: 'Lord, who had faith in the message he heard from
17 us?' So faith springs from the message one hears, and the
18 message one hears is conveyed by the word of Christ. But,
I say, did they never hear it? Yes, indeed:

liii. 1.

'To all the earth went forth their speech,
and to the limits of the world their words.'

Ps. xix. 4.

19 But, I say, did Israel never perceive it? First there is Moses,
and he says:

'I will stir you to jealousy against a nation which is no nation,
against a nation without understanding will I stir you to wrath.'

Dt. xxxii. 21.

20 But Isaiah speaks out boldly:

'I was found by those who were not seeking Me;
I was made manifest to those who were not inquiring Me';

lxv. 1, 2.

21 while with reference to Israel he says: 'All the day long I
stretched forth My hands to a people disobedient and rebellious.'

Assurance of Israel's restoration:

There was no evasion of the tragic fact. Israel by her faithlessness had forfeited her ancient glory. She was no longer the holy nation, the people of God. But was her rejection complete and irrevocable? The very suggestion was intolerable to the Apostle. It was ruled out, in his judgment, alike by personal and providential considerations. He was himself an Israelite, and not only did the destiny of his people engage his sympathy but it involved his own. He knew that he was saved by faith, and this sufficed to

[1] Cf. Chrys.: *οὐδὲ γὰρ ἐν γωνίᾳ μικρᾷ τὸ γενόμενον ἦν, ἀλλ' ἐν γῇ καὶ θαλάττῃ καὶ πανταχοῦ τῆς οἰκουμένης.*

assure him that the Israelites were not outcasts from grace. And, moreover, God's purpose was invincible and His love inexhaustible. He 'never regrets His gifts of grace and His calling.' Where He once loves, He loves for ever. This is the assurance on which the Jews built their false security; and the assurance was just: it was their inference that was delusive. God's faithfulness did not bind Him to them despite their disloyalty; it was rather a pledge that He would yet conquer their disloyalty and make them true to their vocation. Cf. xi. 29.

And so the Apostle sets himself *con amore* to the task of vindicating the faithfulness of God and disclosing the golden hope which shone for Israel behind the dark cloud of her present shame. God had not, and He never would, cast her off.

xi. 1 I say, then, 'did God cast off His people?' Away with Pss. xciv.
the idea! I am an Israelite, sprung of Abraham's seed, a 14, xcv.
2 member of the tribe of Benjamin. God never cast off His 3 LXX: 1 Sam. xii.
people whom He foreknew. 22.

(1) The faithful remnant. Cf. ix. 27. Cf. ix. 7-13.

The argument is twofold. First, the Apostle resumes and elaborates the idea which he has already introduced of a faithful remnant in Israel. In all ages there had been an election within the election, and this was the true Israel. In Elijah's day Israel was not the idolatrous nation but the seven thousand who had stood faithful and had never bowed a knee to Baal; and now in like manner she was represented by those Jews who had welcomed the Gospel and inherited by faith the ancient promises.

Do you not know what the Scripture says in the story of 1 Ki. xix.
3 Elijah—how he pleads with God against Israel? 'Lord, 10, 18.
they have killed Thy prophets, they have dug down Thine
altars; and I am left alone, and they are seeking my life.'
4 But what says the divine response to him? 'I have left
for Myself seven thousand men, who never bowed a knee to
5 Baal.'[1] Thus, then, at the present crisis also there has

[1] τῇ Βάαλ (LXX τῷ Βάαλ). The fem. was formerly explained either by an ellipse of εἰκόνι, 'the image of Baal' (Euth. Zig., A.V., Grot.) or by the supposition that Queen Jezebel worshipped a feminine idol (Wetstein). The fact is that ἡ Βάαλ, which occurs frequently in LXX (cf. 1 Sam. vii. 4; Jer. ii. 28, xi. 13, xix. 5, xxxii. 35; Hos. ii. 8; Zeph. i. 4), is Q'ri: in reading the Scriptures αἰσχύνῃ, 'shame,' was substituted for the unholy name 'Baal,' and the fem. art. indicated this.

turned out to be a remnant according to the election of grace.
6 And if it be by grace, it is no longer on the score of works;
else the grace turns out to be no longer grace.
7 What, then? The thing which Israel is seeking after, she
never obtained; but her elect obtained it. And all the rest
8 grew callous, as it is written: 'God gave them a spirit of
stupefaction—eyes to see nothing and ears to hear nothing—
9 until this very day.' And David says:

Is. xxix. 10; Dt. xxix. 4.

'Let their table be made a snare and a prey
and a trap[1] and a retribution to them;
10 Let their eyes be darkened, that they may see nothing,
and bow down their back continually.'

Ps. lxix. 22, 23; cf. xxxv. 8.

(2) Provocation of the faithless multitude to repentance.

But what of the multitude of faithless Jews? Was their rejection final, their ruin irretrievable? It were indeed a sorry issue of those long centuries of abundant grace that only a meagre remnant should be saved from the nation's wreck. Here the Apostle reverts to the thought which he has already quoted from the Scriptures—that the ulterior purpose of God's mercy to the Gentiles was to stir the faithless Jews to jealousy and move them, in very chagrin, to repent and seek penitently the grace which they had forfeited.

Cf. x. 19.

11 I say, then, did they stumble to their fall? Away with the
idea! No, by their lapse salvation has accrued to the Gentiles,
12 to 'stir them to jealousy.' And if their lapse be the enrichment of the world and their loss the enrichment of the Gentiles,
how much more their full restoration!

Dt. xxxii. 21.

Warning to believing Gentiles.

He addresses particularly his Gentile readers. He was their Apostle; he had, in the providence of God, been commissioned to preach the Gospel to them, and he 'glorified his ministry.' They knew how devotedly he discharged it; but in truth their salvation was not his sole concern. He had his Jewish countrymen constantly in view, and his hope was that by the success of his Gentile ministry he might 'stir them to jealousy' and turn their hearts. Nor was it an unreasonable expectation. The profound principle of Imputation[2] operated here. The blood of Abraham and Isaac and Jacob and all the saints of old flowed in the veins of the faithless Jews, and even in their faithlessness they were 'beloved for their fathers' sake.' As in the ancient heave-

[1] σκάνδαλον, cf. n. on 1 Cor. viii. 13, p. 272.

[2] Cf. pp. 402 f.

offering the consecration of the first of the dough sanctified the whole mass, so its fathers' faith was evermore the nation's heritage, its inspiration and rebuke.

This is a Jewish illustration, and the Apostle immediately passes to another which his Gentile readers could better appreciate. 'If the root be holy, so also are the branches.' Israel was the tree—a good olive-tree; and the Jews were the native branches. Some of them had proved barren. These were the unbelieving Jews; and they had been broken off, and in their stead shoots of a wild olive-tree had been ingrafted on the stock. These latter were the believing Gentiles, and the purpose of the parable was to warn them against exulting in their preferment. That were a repetition of the offence which had cost the Jews so dear. They were alien branches; and if they departed from the faith which had ingrafted them, the doom which had befallen the native branches would surely befall them. And if the Jews repented, they would be restored. They were the native branches, and if it were possible to ingraft alien shoots, it was more possible to reingraft them. **The olive and the ingrafted branches.**

13 It is to you Gentiles that I am speaking. Inasmuch as[1] I
14 am an Apostle to Gentiles, I glorify my ministry in the hope of
stirring my countrymen to jealousy and saving some of them.
15 For if their rejection be the reconciliation of the world, what
16 will their reception be but life from the dead? If 'the first- **Num. xv.**
fruits' be holy, so also is 'the dough'; and if the root be **17-21 LXX.**
17 holy, so also are the branches. And if some of the branches
were broken off and you, though but a wild olive, were ingrafted among them, and were given a share in the root which
18 holds the sap of the olive-tree, boast not against the branches.
If you do, it is not you that are carrying the root; it is the
root that is carrying you.
19 You will say, then: 'Branches were broken off that I might
20 be ingrafted.' Very good: it was for their faithlessness that
they were broken off, while, as for you, it is by your faith that
you stand fast. Be not uplifted with conceit; no, be afraid.
21 For if God did not spare the native branches, neither will He
22 spare you. See, then, God's kindness and His severity. On
the fallen rests God's severity, and on you His kindness, if
you persist in His kindness; otherwise you also will be cut off.

[1] Omitting μὲν οὖν (ℵABCP) with DEFG. There is no reasonable interpretation of μὲν οὖν, *imo vero*; and the simple μέν (L, Vulg., Chrys., Orig., Ambrstr.) implies an unexpressed antithesis (δέ).

23 And as for the others, if they do not persist in their faithlessness, they will be ingrafted; for God has the power to ingraft
24 them again. If you were cut off from your native wild olive
and, contrary to nature, were ingrafted into a good olive, how
much more will these, the native branches, be ingrafted on
their proper olive-tree!

A technical inexactitude.

It is indeed a telling parable; yet 'it is not,' observes an ancient commentator,[1] 'in accordance with the law of husbandry,' and it is well for the success of the Apostle's argument that it was addressed to readers who dwelt in cities and had no skill in arboriculture. The use of grafting is to provide the shoots with a vigorous root that they may be nourished by its sap and bear abundance of their proper fruit. Cuttings of an oleaster ingrafted on an olive would still bear their wild fruit, 'since,' says St. Jerome, 'the manner is rather for the branch to assimilate the strength of the root than for the root to change the branch into its own quality.' And no less impracticable is the idea of the reingrafting of the severed branches. Their fate, as our Lord remarks in His parable of the True Vine, is to be 'cast out and withered, and gathered and cast into the fire and burned.' (Jo. xv. 6.)

The Apostle's inexperience of Nature.

It is vain to allege, in needless solicitude for his technical exactitude, that the Apostle, dealing with a miracle of grace, intentionally describes an unnatural process. (Cf. ver. 24.) His purpose was to demonstrate by a familiar analogy the reasonableness of God's providential dispensation, and it was essential that the analogy should be true to nature. The truth is that the passage is characteristic. The life of cities was the only life which Paul knew. Tarsus was his birthplace and the home of his childhood; he had been educated at Jerusalem; and the cities of Asia Minor, Macedonia, and Achaia had been the exclusive scenes of his apostolic ministry. It was the teeming centres of population that he always sought in the course of his missionary journeys. He hastened from city to city; and it is significant that he has mentioned nothing which he encountered by the way save the obstacles which inter- (Cf. 2 Cor. xi. 25, 26.)

[1] Ambrstr. Cf. Orig.: 'Sed ne hoc quidem lateat nos in hoc loco, quod non eo ordine Apostolus olivæ et oleastri similitudinem posuit quo apud agricolas habetur. Illi enim magis olivam oleastro inserere et non olivæ oleastrum solent: Paulus vero apostolica auctoritate ordine commutato res magis causis quam causas rebus aptavit.'

rupted his progress—shipwrecks, floods, and brigands. He had no eye for scenery, no interest in historic monuments; and he never stayed to preach in the villages along his route. It was not that he despised those humble peasants, but that they were inaccessible to his message. They knew only their local dialects, and could not have understood his preaching in the Common Greek.

Contrast with our Lord.

And thus it came to pass that the city was his world, and his letters abound in allusions to its institutions and manners —its craftsmen and traders; its martial glitter and pomp; its law-courts;[1] its theatres and games; its architecture.[2] It is another atmosphere that one breathes in reading the Gospels. The Lord in the days of His flesh had His home in Galilee, and He loved its people and looked with kindly and sympathetic eyes on their employments and on all the wild and beautiful things of field and woodland.

Cf. Rom. ix. 21; 2 Cor. ii. 17; Eph. i. 14; 2 Cor. i. 22, v. 5; 1 Cor. ix. 7, xiv. 8; Eph. vi. 10-17; 2 Cor. ii. 14; Rom. xiv. 10; 2 Cor. v. 10; 1 Cor. iv. 9, ix. 24-27; 1 Cor. iii. 10-15.

'The Lake,
The lonely peaks, the valleys, lily-lit,
Were synagogues. The simplest sights we met—
The Sower flinging seed on loam and rock;
The darnel in the wheat; the mustard-tree
That hath its seed so little, and its boughs
Widespreading; and the wandering sheep; and nets
Shot in the wimpled waters—drawing forth
Great fish and small:—these, and a hundred such,
Were pictures for Him from the page of life,
Teaching by parable.'

But that page of life was hidden from the Apostle, and his rare allusions to it betray his inexperience. When he quotes that humane ordinance of the ancient Law: 'Thou shalt not muzzle the ox while it is treading out the grain,' it seems to him, oblivious of the Master's word that 'not a sparrow falls on the ground without our Father,' incredible that God should be concerned for oxen; and so he spiritualises the precept and interprets it of the preacher's right to maintenance.

1 Cor. ix. 9, 10; 1 Tim. v. 18.

Mt. x. 29.

Spiritual truth his sole interest.

And here again, when he essays an illustration from husbandry, he betrays his inexperience. His blunder would

[1] Cf. the terms δικαιόω, δικαίωμα, δικαίωσις: κρίσις, κρίμα, κρίνειν, ἀνακρίνειν, κατακρίνειν.

[2] Cf. the term οἰκοδομή.

hardly be observed by his city-bred readers, nor would it have discomposed him greatly had he been informed that he had misconceived the method of grafting. His concern was not with husbandmen and their management of trees but with God and His ways with men; and his illustration, such as it was, sufficed to enforce his argument, checking the confidence of his Gentile readers and opening an avenue of hope for the faithless Jews.

The 'mystery' of Israel's restoration and the redemption of humanity.

And now he proceeds to a second argument. He recognises in the dark tragedy of Israel's rejection a 'mystery'; and a mystery, be it remembered,[1] signified a providential secret, a gracious purpose of God once hidden but now revealed. The supreme mystery in the Apostle's thought was God's long neglect of the Gentile world; and it had been revealed by the discovery in Christ of a limitless grace. Humanity had been dear to God all down the ages, and His election of Israel had been the working out of His purpose of universal redemption. And here the Apostle makes a bold venture of faith. The past was in his sight a prophecy of the future, and he recognised in every dark dispensation a mystery of God, a providential secret still hidden but one day to be gloriously revealed. Such a mystery was Israel's rejection. It was not, it could not be, final. 'God never regrets His gifts of grace and His calling.'

> 'My own hope is a sun will pierce
> The thickest cloud earth ever stretched;
> That, after Last, returns the First,
> Though a wide compass round be fetched;
> That what began best, can't end worst,
> Nor what God blessed once, prove accurst.'

The enrichment of the Gentiles would discover to Israel her own loss; and her desolate heart would turn to God, and she too would be saved—not a poor remnant but the whole nation. And thus, in God's unsearchable providence, the ultimate issue would be the redemption of universal humanity.

25 I do not wish you, brothers, to ignore this mystery, lest
you harbour conceit—that callousness has partially befallen
Israel until the complement of the Gentiles have come in;
26 and thus all Israel will be saved, as it is written:

[1] Cf. p. 320.

'There will come out of Sion the Deliverer; Is. lix. 20,
He will turn away impieties from Jacob. 21; xxvii.
27 And this will be for them My fulfilment of the Covenant— 9.
when I have taken away their sins.'

28 As regards the Gospel they are enemies for your sake, but
as regards the Election they are beloved for their fathers'
29 sake; for God never regrets His gifts of grace and His calling.
30 As you once disobeyed God but have now experienced mercy
31 by their disobedience, so they also have now disobeyed Him
that, by the mercy you enjoy, they also on their part may
32 now experience mercy. For God locked all up in the prison
of disobedience that He might have mercy on all.
33 Ah, the depth of God's riches and wisdom and knowledge! [1] Cf. Job v.
How unsearchable are His judgments and untrackable His 9; ix. 10;
ways! xxxiv. 24.

34 'Who ever took knowledge of the Lord's mind? or who Is. xl. 13;
ever shared His counsels? Job xli. 11.
35 Or who first gave to Him that it should be repayed him?'
36 For from Him and through Him and to Him are all things.
To Him be the glory for ever. Amen.[2]

III

PRACTICAL (xii-xiv)

The Apostle's theological argument is now complete, but his last word has yet to be spoken. Doctrine is valueless unless it issue in holiness; and the doctrine of Justification by Faith is peculiarly liable to ethical perversion. And so

A call to consecration.

[1] So Orig., Chrys., taking πλούτου, σοφίας, and γνώσεως as co-ordinate genitives after βάθος. πλοῦτος, 'riches in grace' (cf. ii. 4, ix. 23, x. 12). σοφία is ratiocinative and γνῶσις intuitive. Ambrstr. takes σοφίας and γνώσεως as dependent on πλούτου: 'the depth of the riches of both the wisdom and the knowledge of God.' This is grammatically legitimate, but the former construction is established by vers. 34, 35, where the Apostle repeats the three attributes of God in reverse order: His γνῶσις—τίς ἔγνω νοῦν Κυρίου; His σοφία—τίς σύμβουλος αὐτοῦ ἐγένετο; His πλοῦτος—τίς προέδωκεν αὐτῷ, κ.τ.λ.

[2] Orig. sees here 'the mystery of the Trinity'—God the Father from whom are all things, our Lord Jesus Christ through whom are all things, and the Spirit in whom all are revealed; and also in ver. 33, where 'depth of riches' signifies the Father from whom are all things, 'depth of wisdom' Christ who is His wisdom (cf. 1 Cor. i. 24), and 'depth of knowledge' the Holy Spirit who knows the deep things of God (cf. 1 Cor. ii. 10, 11). Similarly Ambrstr. This is a mere fancy. It would require (1) ἐν αὐτῷ for εἰς αὐτόν and (2), as Aug. (*Enarr. in Psalm. V*, 4) observes, αὐτοῖς for αὐτῷ of the Three Persons.

he concludes his encyclical with a series of practical counsels and exhortations.

He begins with a call to consecration.

xii. 1 I exhort you, then, brothers, by the compassions of God,
to present your bodies as a living sacrifice to God. This
2 is your spiritual worship.[1] And do not follow the fashion of
this age, but be transformed by the renewal of the mind,[2] so
that you may prove what is the will of God, His good and
well-pleasing and perfect will.

Occasions of dissension:

And now he proceeds to deal with three questions which confronted all the communities of Gentile Christendom and disturbed their peace.

(1) Diversity of spiritual endowments.

The first was presented by the diversity of spiritual endowments and the heart-burning, the pride and jealousy which it engendered. This unhappy dissension had been rampant at Corinth a year previously. It was one of the questions which had been submitted to the Apostle's consideration by that contentious community, and he had discussed it exhaustively in his reply;[3] and here he merely reiterates his conception of the Church as an organic unity. It is a living body, and each believer is a member with his peculiar function essential to the corporate welfare. Our spiritual endowments, whatever they may be, are God's appointments; and our duty is to employ them faithfully. And he enforces this duty by a succession of practical precepts, pithy and memorable maxims relating to personal character and conduct, behaviour to fellow-Christians, and the proper attitude toward outsiders, especially persecutors.

1 Cor. xii-xiv.

3 By the grace which was given me I bid every one among you
not to harbour a higher estimate of himself than he should,
but to aim at a sober estimate in accordance with the measure
4 of faith which God has apportioned to each. For just as in
one body we have many members, and the members have not

[1] λογικός, (1) 'spiritual' as opposed to *σωματικός* or *σαρκικός* (cf. 1 Pet. ii. 2, 5). Cf. Chrys.: *λογικὴν λατρείαν· τουτέστιν, οὐδὲν ἔχουσαν σωματικὸν, οὐδὲν παχὺ, οὐδὲν αἰσθητόν*, in contrast with Jewish sacrifice, *ἐκείνη γὰρ σωματική*. (2) 'Reasonable,' 'rational,' in contrast with the sacrifice of *ἄλογα ζῶα* (cf. 2 Pet. ii. 12; Jude 10).

[2] Cf. n. on Phil. ii, 6, p. 514.

[3] Cf. pp. 289 ff.

5 all the same function, so we, many as we are, are one body
in Christ and are individually related to one another as
6 members. Since we have gifts of grace differing according
to the grace which was given us, if it be prophecy, let us
7 prophesy in proportion to our faith;[1] if it be deaconship,[2]
let us devote ourselves to our deaconship; if one be a teacher,
8 let him devote himself to his teaching;[3] if one's office be
exhortation, let him devote himself to his exhortation; if it
be charity, let him do it with a spirit of liberality;[4] if it be
ruling, let him do it with earnestness; if it be showing compassion, let him do it cheerily.
9 Let your love be unaffected.[5] Abhor what is evil; cleave
10 to what is good. In the matter of brotherly friendship have 1 Th. iv. 9.
a friendly affection for each other; in the matter of honour
11 give each other precedence; in earnestness be unslacking, in
12 spirit fervent, the Lord's slaves; in your hope rejoice, in your
13 distress endure, in your prayer persevere; have fellowship
14 with the necessities of the saints; prosecute hospitality. Bless
15 your persecutors; bless, and never curse. Rejoice with
16 them that rejoice, weep with them that weep. Share one
another's interests; harbour no lofty ambitions but embark
on the stream of lowly duties. 'Have a sober estimate of Prov. iii. 7.
17 yourselves.' Never repay evil with evil. 'Safeguard your Prov. iii.
18 honour in the sight of all men.' If possible, on your part, be 4 LXX; cf.
19 at peace with all men. Never avenge yourselves, beloved, 2 Cor. viii. 21.
but give room to the Wrath.[6] For it is written: 'It is for Me Dt. xxxii.
20 to avenge: I will repay,' says the Lord. No, 'if your enemy 35. Prov. xxv.
is hungry, feed him; if he is thirsty, give him a drink; for 21, 22.

[1] Preaching is real only as it is the testimony of faith, the declaration of an actual experience (cf. Jer. xxiii. 28; 2 Cor. iv. 13). Or τῆς πίστεως may be understood as 'the Faith,' the objective standard of truth to which preaching must conform.

[2] διακονίαν, not 'ministry' generally (Chrys.) but the office of the deaconship. Cf. Pelag.: 'ministerii sacerdotalis vel diaconatus officii.'

[3] Cf. p. 80.

[4] Cf. Sen. *De Benef.* II. vii.: 'Fabius Verrucosus beneficium ab homine duro aspere datum "panem lapidosum" vocabat.'

[5] Cf. 2 Cor. vi. 6. Anne Brontë, *Agnes Grey*, chap. xv: '"Stupid things!" muttered she. . . . She greeted them, however, with a cheerful smile, and protestations of pleasure at the happy meeting equal to their own.'

[6] Chrys.: 'What "wrath"? That of God. For since this is the chief desire of one who has been wronged—to see himself in the enjoyment of redress, He gives this very thing in large abundance. For if he does not himself retaliate, God will be his Avenger. Permit Him therefore, he says, to prosecute.' Jer. Taylor, *The Great Exemplar*, II. xii, Disc. XI, Part i. 1: 'To that "wrath we must give place," saith St. Paul; that is "in well-doing" and evil-suffering "commit ourselves to His righteous judgment," leaving room for His execution, who will certainly do it if we snatch not the sword from His arm.'

21 by doing this you will heap coals of fire upon his head.' [1] Be not conquered by evil, but conquer evil with good.

(2) Obedience to civil rulers.

The Apostle now turns to a second practical question—the Christian duty of obedience to civil rulers. There is no evidence that the primitive Christians were ever turbulently disposed; and they ere long proved themselves loyal and serviceable citizens of the Roman Empire.[2] Nevertheless in those early days they were generally regarded as a mere Jewish sect, and the Jews were the most troublesome of all Rome's subject races. The Messianic Hope was a powerful incentive to sedition, since the Saviour of Israel was conceived as a mighty king of David's lineage who should arise and crush the oppressor and establish the ancient throne in more than its ancient splendour; and the fanatical Zealots were continually fanning the smouldering indignation and kindling the flame of insurrection.[3] Their identification with the Jews exposed the Christians to the suspicion of the imperial government; and the Apostle had learned by experience how his preaching of Christ, the King of Israel, might be misconstrued into a treasonable propaganda. It was thus a counsel of prudence that the Christians should disarm suspicion by loyal submission to the constituted authorities.

Cf. Ac. xvii. 6-8.

A divine ordinance.

But it was more. It was an absolute duty inasmuch as civil government is a divine ordinance. 'The existing authorities are ordered by God; and so one who opposes the authoritative order is in resistance to God's ordinance.' It was to this passage that the Royalist divines of the seventeenth and eighteenth centuries appealed in vindication of their doctrines of the divine right of kings and the duty of passive obedience;[4] but they overlooked the essential consideration that, as St. Chrysostom remarks, the Apostle inculcates here submission not to governors but to government. 'He did not

[1] Cf. Ps. cxx. 4. The burning shame which your kindness will enkindle in your enemy's heart is the sorest punishment you can inflict upon him. Cf. Aug. *De Doct. Chr.* III. 24: 'ad beneficentiam te potius charitas revocet, ut intelligas carbones ignis esse urentes pœnitentiæ gemitus, quibus superbia sanatur ejus qui dolet se inimicum fuisse hominis a quo ejus miseriæ subvenitur.'

[2] Cf. *Epist. ad Diogn.* V; Tert. *Apol.* 37, 42.

[3] Cf. *The Days of His Flesh*, pp. 35 f.

[4] Cf. Jer. Taylor, *Duct. Dub.* III. iii. 3.

say, " No *ruler* exists but by God's appointment." No, it is of the thing that he is discoursing. " No *authority*," he says, " exists but by God's appointment; and the existing authorities are ordered by God." Thus also, when a wise man says: " A wife is fitted to a man by the Lord," his meaning is that God made marriage, not that it is He who unites every man in his association with a woman. For we see many associating with each other for evil and not by the law of marriage.' The question of the legitimacy of resistance to tyranny does not here arise. The Apostle has in view a righteous and beneficent government; and such a government he and his readers enjoyed in those days. Roman law was just and impartial; and repeatedly in the course of his travels—at Thessalonica, at Corinth, and at Ephesus—its strong arm had succoured him and shielded him alike from Jewish and from heathen violence. 'The authority' had indeed proved 'God's minister for his good'; and he recognised what disasters would ensue from its dethronement. 'Everything,' says St. Chrysostom, 'would go to wrack; neither city nor farm, neither house nor market nor aught else would stand, but everything would be overturned.' Government was a beneficent institution. It was the bulwark of society, and anarchy was a crime against God and humanity.

Prov. xix. 14 LXX.

Cf. Ac. xvii. 8, 9; xviii. 12-17; xix. 35-41.

xiii. 1 Let every person be in subjection to the supreme authorities. For no authority exists but by God's appointment; and the existing authorities are ordered by God.
2 And so one who opposes the authoritative order is in resistance to God's ordinance; and the resisters will bring doom upon
3 themselves. For it is not good conduct but evil that need be afraid of rulers. Would you have no fear of the authority?
4 Do good, and you will win its praise; for it is God's minister for your good. But if you do evil, be afraid; for it is not to no purpose that it wears the sword: it is God's minister taking wrathful vengeance on evil be-
5 haviour. And therefore you must needs be in subjection not only on account of the wrath but also on account of conscience.

It was thus incumbent upon Christians, wherever they might be, to revere the civil authority and loyally obey its requirements, paying their taxes cheerfully, remarks the Apostle with a smile, though the taxgatherers might play the

Taxes a debt.

bully. For governmental imposts are not an exaction; they are a debt,[1] and they must be paid; for it is a religious duty to 'owe nothing to any,' except, adds the Apostle, that debt which can never be discharged—the debt of love, 'so burdensome; still paying, still to owe.'[2] And this, as our Lord has taught us, is the only and all-sufficient fulfilment of the Law. Love your neighbour, and you will do him no manner of wrong; all particular precepts will be superfluous.

Cf. Mt. xxii. 34-40.

6 It is for this reason also that you pay taxes. For the tax-
7 gatherers are God's officers devoted to this very task. Pay
in every instance what you owe: gear where you owe gear,
tribute where you owe tribute, fear where you owe fear, honour
8 where you owe honour.[3] Owe nothing to any except mutual
9 love. One who loves his fellow has fulfilled the Law. For
the commandments 'Thou shalt not kill,' 'Thou shalt not
steal,' 'Thou shalt not covet,' and every other, are summed
up in this word: 'Thou shalt love thy neighbour as thyself.'
10 Love works no evil to one's neighbour; therefore love is the
fulfilment of the Law.

An exhortation.

In kindly and dutiful love lies the golden secret of good citizenship; and the obligation was strengthened by the prevailing expectation of the Lord's immediate Return. It was natural that the Jews with their secular ideal of the Messianic Salvation should entertain seditious dreams of the overthrow of the Roman dominion and the restoration of the kingdom to Israel; but it was a nobler consummation that the Christians had in view—the passing of the long night and the breaking of the Eternal Day. And that hope incited them not to political but to spiritual emancipation.

11 And this, knowing the crisis, that it is high time for you to
be roused from sleep; for now is the Salvation nearer to us
12 than when we embraced the Faith. The night is far advanced,
and the day is near. Therefore let us lay aside the works of
13 darkness and clothe us with the armour of light. Let us
comport ourselves becomingly as in the day-time, not in
revelry and drunkenness, not in chambering and wantonness,

[1] Cf. Mt. xxii. 21. Chrys.: οὐ χαριζόμεθα αὐτοῖς τὴν ὑπακοὴν ἀλλ' ὀφείλομεν.

[2] Milton, *Par. Lost*, IV. 52-57.

[3] Observe the paronomasia φόρον ('custom'), φόβον ('fear'). On the oppression of the *publicani* and the resentment which it provoked, cf. *The Days of His Flesh*, pp. 123 ff.

14 not in strife and jealousy. No, clothe you with the Lord Jesus Christ,[1] and make no provision for the gratification of your carnal lusts.[2]

And now the Apostle turns to a third practical question. A tendency to asceticism had invaded the Church and had of late extended widely; especially, as will appear in due course, in the Province of Asia, where it manifested itself in dietary restrictions, in fasting and in celibacy. It had indeed an affinity with the Jewish prohibition of unclean food and with that antipathy to meat offered in heathen sacrifice which had recently excited such keen contention in the Church at Corinth; but it was a much larger question than either. It was a creation of the spirit of the age, and it had both its Jewish and its pagan phase. (3) The question of asceticism. Cf. Col. ii. 16-23; 1 Tim. iv. 1-5. Cf. 1 Cor. viii-x.

Its Jewish phase was Essenism.[3] The Essenes make their first appearance in Jewish history about the middle of the second century B.C.; and though never numerous—only some four thousand in the days of Philo and Josephus—they figured conspicuously in the national life and are ranked by the Jewish historian with the Pharisees and Sadducees as the third Jewish sect.[4] They were a monastic order, and their principal settlement was in the Wilderness of En-Gedi on the western shore of the Dead Sea. They maintained themselves by industry, chiefly agriculture; and they eschewed sexual intercourse, abstained from flesh and wine, and practised fasting.[5] Essenism.

Just as Sadduceeism was likened by the Rabbis and the

[1] Cf. n. on Gal. iii. 27, p. 207.

[2] This (vers. 13, 14) is the passage on which St. Augustine's eyes lighted when, amid his spiritual distress, he opened his copy of St. Paul's Epistles in obedience to a voice—a child's at play in the neighbouring garden—chanting 'Take. read: take, read.' Cf. *Confess.* VIII. 12.

[3] On the Essenes cf. Jos. *De Bell. Jud.* II. viii. 2-13; *Ant.* XIII. v. 9, XVIII. i. 5; Philo, *Quod Omnis Probus Liber*, 12 f.; Plin. *Nat. Hist.* v. 15. Also Lightfoot, *Colossians*, pp. 347 ff.; Schürer, *Jewish People*, II. ii. pp. 188 ff.; Keim, *Jesus of Nazareth*, I. pp. 365 ff.; Hausrath, *N. T. Times*, I. pp. 153 ff.

[4] Jos. *Ant.* XIII. v. 9; *De Bell. Jud.* II. viii. 2; *Vit.* 2.

[5] Their abstinence from flesh and wine is expressly affirmed by St. Jerome on the alleged authority of Josephus (*Adv. Jovinian.* II.), and it is implied by the historian in *De Bell. Jud.* II. viii. 5. Cf. the Essenic characterisation of James the Lord's brother by Hegesippus (Eus. *Hist. Eccl.* II. 23): οἶνον καὶ σίκερα οὐκ ἔπιεν οὐδὲ ἔμψυχον ἔφαγε. Lightfoot, *Col.* p. 84.

Neopythagoreanism. Christian Fathers to Epicureanism [1] and Pharisaism, with more justice, to Stoicism,[2] so Essenism had its pagan counterpart in Neopythagoreanism. It was, according to Josephus, merely Neopythagoreanism ingrafted on the stem of Judaism; [3] but the truth is rather that they are kindred manifestations of the spirit which in those days was everywhere stirring in the souls of men. The Pythagoreans were vegetarians, and their abstinence from flesh was a corollary of their doctrine of the Transmigration of Souls, since it might happen that in slaying and eating an animal one was guilty of a criminal impiety, 'unwittingly assailing a parent's soul and violating by blade or tooth the lodging of some kindred spirit.' But they recommended it also for humanitarian and valetudinary reasons, and it gained numerous adherents. Seneca tells us [4] that in his youth he was won to the practice of vegetarianism by his Pythagorean tutor Sotion, and abandoned it only at the instance of his unphilosophical father to escape the odium which was excited in the reign of Tiberius against alien superstitions.[5]

Asceticism in the Church. It is thus no marvel that asceticism should have invaded the Christian Church. It is recorded of St. Matthew the Apostle and Evangelist that he was a vegetarian, living on 'seeds and nuts and herbs without flesh'; [6] and of James the Lord's brother that he 'neither drank wine and strong drink nor ate flesh.' [7] Such examples would be potent with the Jewish Christians, and would facilitate the spread of Neopythagoreanism in Gentile communities. Nevertheless it was an unfortunate development. Asceticism is essentially antagonistic to the spirit of Christianity. Its offence
Cf. ver. 14. is twofold—on the one hand, its underlying assumption of
Cf. ver. 17. the inherent evil of matter, and, on the other, its despiritualisation of religion. And apart from its theoretical implicates it was inevitable that its invasion of the Church should occasion grave dissension and hot recrimination, since the ascetics, probably a minority in each community, would fain

[1] Cf. Keim, *Jes. of Naz.*, I. p. 354.
[2] Cf. Jos. *Vit.* 2.
[3] *Ant.* XV. x. 4.
[4] *Epist.* CVIII.
[5] Cf. Tac. *Ann.* II. 85.
[6] Clem. Alex. *Pædag.* II. i. 16.
[7] Hegesippus in Eus. *Hist. Eccl.* II. 23.

have made their practices universally obligatory. They 'passed judgment' on the laxity of their liberal-minded neighbours, and the latter retaliated by 'setting them at naught' as worthless bigots.

An open question. The Apostle's sympathies were with the liberal party, and he expressly ranges himself on their side by ascribing the scrupulosity of the ascetics to the weakness of their faith. Yet he recognises that they too were in fault. They had failed, not without provocation, in the paramount duty of Christian charity. He will not enter upon a controversy: that were unprofitable work, issuing only in embitterment, and there was already too much of it. And so he adopts the wiser course of defining the attitude which the two parties should maintain toward each other.

xiv. 1 One who is weak in faith receive—not for discussion of
2 disputed opinions. One man's faith lets him eat every
sort of food, while one who is weak eats only vegetables.
3 The man who eats must not set at naught the man who
abstains; and the man who abstains must not pass judgment on the man who eats; for God received him.

The right of personal judgment. First he asserts the right of personal liberty. Every man is entitled to think and act according to his own judgment. He may indeed be mistaken, but he is responsible to the Lord alone.

4 Who are you that pass judgment on another's servant?
It is for his own lord that he stands or falls. And stand he
5 will; for the Lord has power to make him stand. One man
judges this day different from that; another judges every
6 day alike: let each be satisfied[1] in his own mind. The
man who observes the day observes it for the Lord. And
the man who eats eats for the Lord, for he gives thanks to
God; and the man who abstains abstains for the Lord, and
gives thanks to God.
7 None of us lives for himself, and none dies for himself;
8 for if we live, it is for the Lord that we live, and if we die, it
is for the Lord that we die. Therefore, whether we live or
9 die, we are the Lord's. For it was for this purpose that the
Lord died and came to life again—that He might be Lord of
both dead and living.
10 But you—why are you passing judgment on your brother?
Or you, again—why are you setting your brother at naught?

[1] Cf. n. on iv. 21, p. 399.

11 We shall all stand side by side at the Bar of God. For it
is written:

Is. xlv. 23.

> 'As I live, saith the Lord, to Me shall every knee bow,
> And every tongue shall make confession to God.'

12 So then each of us will give account of himself to God.

The duty of charity.

In this thought of direct and personal responsibility to God lay the sovereign corrective alike of ascetic censoriousness and of the impatience which it provoked; and the Apostle proceeds to reprobate the latter disposition, reaffirming the principle which he has already enunciated in dealing with the kindred controversy at Corinth regarding the eating of meat sacrificed to idols, and speaking the more freely inasmuch as he shared the liberal sentiment. He recognised the evil of asceticism, but he recognised also the duty of charity and respect even for an unreasonable scrupulosity. No food indeed is unclean *per se*; yet if a man deems it unclean, it is unclean for him, and it were an injury to his soul to insist upon his partaking of it against the dictates, the mistaken dictates, of his conscience.

Cf. 1 Cor. viii.

13 Let us therefore no longer pass judgment on one another. No,
let this rather be your judgment—never to place a stumbling-
14 block in your brother's way or a snare. I know and am
persuaded in the Lord Jesus that there is nothing defiling in
itself; but if one reckons a thing defiling, it is defiling for
15 him. If by reason of the food you eat your brother is being
grieved, you are no longer walking in the path of love. Do not
16 destroy him by your food—one for whom Christ died. There-
17 fore let not your common good be calumniated. For the
Kingdom of God is not eating and drinking but righteous-
18 ness and peace and joy in the Holy Spirit. One who is herein
a slave to Christ is well pleasing to God and approved by men.
19 So then let us pursue the interests of peace and of mutual
20 upbuilding. Do not for food's sake demolish the work of
God. All food is clean, but it is bad for one to eat if he has
21 scruples about it. The noble course is to refrain from eating
flesh and drinking wine and everything which is a stumbling-
22 block to your brother. As for you, the faith which you hold,
hold it for yourself in the sight of God. Blessed is the man
who does not pass judgment on himself in what he approves.
23 But one who has misgivings stands condemned if he eats,
inasmuch as it is not the outcome of faith; and everything
which is not the outcome of faith is sin.

Doxology concluding the encyclical.

The encyclical concludes with a noble doxology :[1]

xvi. 25 Now to Him who has power to strengthen you according
to my Gospel and the message of Jesus Christ, according to
the revelation of the mystery kept silent throughout the
26 course of times eternal, but manifested now, and through
the prophetic scriptures according to the commandment of
the Eternal God made known for the achievement of faith's
27 surrender among all the Gentiles, to the only, the wise
God through Jesus Christ—to whom be the glory for ever
and ever. Amen.

A retrospect of the argument.

It is an effective conclusion skilfully summarising the argument of the Epistle ; and its significance appears when we observe how the Apostle here reverts to his introduction. There he defines his Gospel. Its theme was ' the Son of God, Jesus Christ,' and here he terms it ' the message of Jesus Christ.'[2] And it was no innovation, as the Judaists alleged. It was the fulfilment of the prophetic promise of a world-wide salvation ; and here he reiterates this and introduces his grand conception of the ' mystery,' God's eternal purpose so long hidden from the blind eyes of men but intimated in the prophetic scriptures and illumined by the Christian revelation. In his introduction, again, he had spoken of his longing to visit his readers and ' impart to them some spiritual gift, that they might be strengthened ' ; and here he expresses a better wish—that they may be strengthened by God Himself.

A confession of the Lord's deity.

The most significant feature of the doxology, however, is its syntactical confusion. The Apostle's purpose at the outset is to ascribe glory to God, and he shapes the sentence with this end in view. ' To Him,' he says, ' who has power to strengthen you—the only, the wise God.' Here he adds ' through Jesus Christ,' since it is through Him that God is known and worshipped ; and he would naturally have continued ' be the glory.' But that Blessed Name captivates his thoughts ; and, throwing syntax to the winds, he writes ' through Jesus Christ, to whom be the glory.' Copyists have rectified the construction by omitting the relative and reading ' to the only, the wise God through Jesus Christ be

[1] On the position of the Doxology (xvi. 25-27) cf. p. 377.

[2] That is, 'the message which has Christ for its theme' (cf. 1 Cor. i. 23, xv. 12 ; 2 Cor. i. 19, iv. 5, xi. 4), not 'the message which Christ preached' (Chrys. : τὸ κήρυγμα Ἰησοῦ Χριστοῦ· τουτέστιν, ὃ αὐτὸς ἐκήρυξεν).

the glory,' or by substituting the demonstrative pronoun: 'to the only, the wise God through Jesus Christ, to Him be the glory.' But in thus amending the Apostle's grammar they have eliminated his thought. It was no mere inadvertence when he turned aside and ascribed to Christ the glory which belongs to God. It was a confession of his faith in the oneness of the Eternal Son with the Eternal Father.

PERSONAL MESSAGES TO THE VARIOUS CHURCHES

(1) *To Rome* (xv)

Exhortation to mutual sympathy between Jewish and Gentile Christians.

The primary *motif* of the encyclical, be it remembered, was to forestall the machinations of the Apostle's Judaist adversaries; and, since the Roman Church was a mixed community, he appropriately begins his personal message with an exhortation to mutual forbearance and sympathy. The more liberal party of the Gentile converts must have patience with the scrupulosity of their Jewish fellows. Christ was the sovereign Exemplar for both. His grace had comprehended Jews and Gentiles, and they should have room in their hearts for one another. There was here an especial lesson for the Jewish party. The Lord had indeed been 'a minister to the circumcised.' (Cf. ix. 5.) He had been a Jew according to the flesh, and the land of Israel had been the scene of His earthly ministry; but the reason was purely dispensational—not that He was the Redeemer of the Jews alone but that He might link His universal grace with the historic preparation and 'confirm the promises given to the fathers.' And these promises, as the Apostle shows by a series of scriptural testimonies, culled from the three divisions of the sacred literature—the Law, the Prophets, and the Hagiographa, were not limited to the Jews but embraced the Gentiles too.

1 Now we who have strength ought to bear their weaknesses
2 who have none, and not to please ourselves. Let each of us
please his neighbour for his good with a view to his upbuilding.
3 For even the Christ did not please Himself. No, as it is
Ps. lxix. 9. written, 'the reproaches of them that reproach Thee fell upon
4 Me.' All that was written of old was written for our instruction, that through endurance and the comfort of the Scrip-
5 tures we may have hope. And may God, the giver of this

endurance and comfort, grant you mutual sympathy according
6 to Christ Jesus, that with one mind and voice you may glorify
the God and Father of our Lord Jesus Christ.

7 Therefore receive one another, as the Christ also received
8 us [1] for the glory of God. I mean that Christ has been made a
minister to the circumcised in vindication of God's truthfulness, that He might confirm the promises given to the fathers
9 and that the Gentiles might glorify God for His mercy, as it
is written :

'Therefore I will give thanks unto Thee among the Gentiles, Ps. xviii.
and unto Thy name will I sing praise.' 49.

10 And again says the Scripture : 'Rejoice, ye Gentiles, with His Dt. xxxii.
11 people.' And again : 43.

'Laud the Lord, all ye Gentiles, Ps. cxvii. 1.
and let all the people belaud Him.'

12 And again Isaiah says :

'There will be the Root of Jesse, xi. 10.
And One that ariseth to rule the Gentiles ;
on Him the Gentiles will set their hope.'

13 Now may God, the giver of this hope, fill you with all joy and
peace in the exercise of faith, that you may have the hope
abundantly in the power of the Holy Spirit.

Personal explanation.

And now, with that tactful courtesy which always characterised him, he proceeds to obviate a possible misconception. He had written his encyclical with unrestrained freedom, and he recognised that certain of the sterner passages in the course of his impassioned argument might be personally construed and resented as unjust aspersions on a community which he had never visited. And so he assures his readers that he had harboured no such intention. On the contrary, all that he had heard of them had persuaded him of the excellence of their Christian character and their doctrinal attainments. His argument was merely an affirmation of truths which they knew and believed but which they might easily forget ; and his emphasis was inspired by his apostolic authority and the momentousness of the issue. It was a vital cause that he was advocating—the universality of redemption ; and his achievements entitled him to vindicate it boldly. He had carried the Gospel for Jew and

[1] ὑμᾶς, though more strongly supported (ℵACD^{b}) than ἡμᾶς (BD*P), is plainly a copyist's emendation, suggested by προσλαμβάνεσθε.

Gentile to every land in the long circuit from Jerusalem to Illyricum, and his labours had been crowned with signal success.

14 I am persuaded, my brothers—yes, I am myself persuaded—
regarding you, that you are yourselves laden with goodness,
replete with all knowledge, well able also to admonish one
15 another. Yet I am writing to you somewhat boldly here and
there, with the idea of putting you in remembrance, on the
16 strength of the grace given me from God, that I may perform
the office of Christ Jesus to the Gentiles in the priestly work
of the Gospel of God, in order that the offering up of the
Gentiles may prove acceptable, having been sanctified in the
17 Holy Spirit. It is, then, in Christ Jesus that I have the right
18 to boast in my service of God. For I will not make bold to
talk of anything save what Christ has wrought through me
19 to win the Gentiles to obedience by word and work in the
power of signs and portents, in the power of the Holy Spirit,
insomuch that from Jerusalem and all round as far as
20 Illyricum I have fulfilled the Gospel of the Christ; yet
always with the ambition of thus preaching it—not where
Christ's name was known, lest I should be building on another
21 man's foundation, but as it is written:

Is. lii. 15.

'They will see to whom no announcement of Him was ever made;
and they who have not heard will understand.'

His purpose to visit Rome.

Cf. Ac. xix. 21.

It was indeed a magnificent triumph, but it had been hardly won. It had cost him ten weary years of toil and suffering. All the while the Imperial Capital in the West had been the goal of his ambition, and he had hasted to accomplish his eastern ministry that he might betake himself thither. With that end in view he had steadfastly adhered to the rule of never preaching where the Gospel was already known; but this had afforded him little absolution, since he was the only 'Apostle to the Gentiles,' and it had lain with him to evangelise all the wide circuit of Asia Minor, Macedonia, and Achaia. But for him those lands would never have heard Christ's name, and others had visited them only to undo his work and excite dissension in his Churches. Thus his cherished design of preaching at Rome had remained hitherto unfulfilled. Now, however, his eastern ministry had at length been accomplished, and the realisation of his dream was in sight. He was on the eve of quitting Corinth

Cf. 2 Cor. x. 15, 16.

and returning to Jerusalem with the contributions which the Churches of Macedonia and Achaia had entrusted to him for the relief of the poor in the Sacred Capital ; and his purpose was, as soon as he had discharged that errand, to inaugurate a far-reaching campaign in the West. His ultimate destination was Spain, and in the course of his progress thither he would visit Rome. Such was his design, but in the inveterate hostility of the Judaist party he recognised a menace to its fulfilment. He anticipated trouble during his visit to Jerusalem, and he begs the Christians of Rome to intercede with God on his behalf.

22 And this is the reason why I was so often hindered from
23 visiting you ; but now, since I have no more ground to occupy
in these regions and have been longing to visit you for many
24 years past, whenever I journey to Spain—for I am hoping in
the course of my journey to get a sight of you and be forwarded
to my destination by you, in the event of my first enjoying in
25 a measure the satisfaction of your company. Just now, however, I am journeying to Jerusalem on an errand of ministra-
26 tion to the saints. For it was the good pleasure of Macedonia
and Achaia to impart something to the poor among the saints
27 at Jerusalem. Yes, it was their good pleasure, and they owe
it to them ; for if the Gentiles have participated in their
spiritual blessings, they ought in turn to perform their office
28 by them in their material goods. So, after accomplishing this
errand and putting them in possession of this harvest, I shall
29 set out for Spain and take you by the way. And I know that,
when I visit you, it will be in the plentitude of Christ's blessing.
30 But I beseech you, brothers, by our Lord Jesus Christ and
by the love of the Spirit to join me in wrestling in prayers to
31 God on my behalf, that I may be rescued from the enemies
of the Faith in Judæa and that the ministration I am conveying
32 to Jerusalem may prove acceptable to the saints, so that I
may, if God will, visit you in joy and find refreshment in your
company.
33 Now may God, the giver of peace, be with you all.
Amen.

(2) *To Ephesus and the other Cities of Asia* (xvi. 1-20)

The office of conveying the encyclical to Ephesus was entrusted to an old and valued friend of the Apostle—Phœbe, that deaconess of the Church of Cenchreæ who had tended him in his sickness four years previously on the eve of his

Commendation of Phœbe.

departure from Achaia ;[1] and he begins his personal message to the Churches of Asia with a note of introduction, at once attesting her *bona fides* and bespeaking for her the consideration which she so well deserved. Apparently she had an errand of her own to Ephesus, and she undertook to carry the letter thither.

> 1 Now I commend to you Phœbe our sister, who is a deaconess
> 2 of the Church at Cenchreæ, that you give her a welcome in
> the Lord worthy of the saints, and befriend her in any matter
> where she may need you ; for she on her part has proved a
> friend in need to many and to myself.

Greetings.

Then, as was natural in a communication to a city where he had ministered so long, he addresses affectionate greetings to an extensive list of personal friends. First come his ancient and tried comrades, Prisca and Aquila, who had shared his toils and perils ever since he had encountered them at Corinth, and who were now playing a foremost part in the Christian community at Ephesus. Their house was one of the meeting-places of the Church, and he includes in his greeting the company which assembled there for fellowship and worship.

Cf. Ac. xviii. 1-3.

These two are the only familiar names in the catalogue. The others are mentioned nowhere else, and not a few are names which were common among slaves—Andronicus, Ampliatus, Urbanus, Persis, Rufus, Asyncritus, Philologus, and Nereus. The households of Aristobulus and Narcissus were also slaves—the *familiæ* of citizens who do not appear to have been themselves Christians.[2] There is not one

[1] Cf. p. 189.

[2] On the hypothesis that the epistle is a simple letter to the Church at Rome and the persons mentioned in xvi. 1-20 Roman Christians, an interesting explanation of οἱ ἐκ τῶν Ἀριστοβούλου and οἱ ἐκ τῶν Ναρκίσσου has been suggested (cf. Lightfoot, *Phil.*, pp. 171 ff.). Aristobulus, the grandson of Herod the Great, resided at Rome during the reign of Claudius (cf. Jos. *De Bell. Jud.* II. xi. 6 ; *Ant.* XX. i. 2), and it is supposed that he may have bequeathed to the Emperor his retinue of slaves, who would thenceforth belong to the imperial household and be distinguished by the title of *Aristobuliani.* It countenances the idea that (1) there were, subsequently at all events, members of the imperial household in the Church at Rome (cf. Phil. iv. 22), and (2) the Jew Herodion (ver. 11) was evident'v from his name a freedman of some prince of the Herodian family, and might be one of the *Aristobuliani.* Similarly a wealthy freedman in the reign of Claudius was named Narcissus (cf. Juv. XIV. 329 ; Tac. *Ann.* XIII. 1), and he

personage in the list who was distinguished in the eyes of the world. They were all obscure folk, and their names have been rescued from oblivion by their association with the Apostle and their devotion to the Lord.

At least six were Jews—Prisca, Aquila, and, as her name demonstrates, Mary;[1] Andronicus, Junias, and Herodion. The Apostle designates the three last his 'fellow-countrymen'; and the reason is that he would fain disarm the natural hostility of their Jewish hearts to his argument against Jewish privilege, his impassioned vindication of the equality of Jew and Gentile in the sight of God. And therefore he accords them that tender appellation which he had employed in his poignant protestation of undying affection for the
people of Israel, 'my brothers, my kinsmen according to the ix. 3.
flesh.' He evinces no such solicitude regarding Prisca, Aquila, and Mary. Prisca and Aquila were his tried fellow-workers, and Mary had proved her devotion during his ministry at Ephesus: 'she laboured so much for us.' If, like those other 'labourers,' Tryphæna and Tryphosa, who were probably sisters, she was a deaconess, it may be that she had nursed him in sickness.[2]

After all those personal greetings the Apostle adds yet another of a larger sort: 'all the Churches of the Christ are greeting you.' It were an attenuation of his purpose to conceive that he meant merely 'all the Churches in Achaia,' and that these had formally commissioned him to convey on their behalf an affectionate greeting to their fellow-Christians in Asia. The fact is that the fame of the Churches of Ephesus and the adjacent cities was noised abroad. Wherever the

also may be supposed to have bequeathed his *familia* to the Emperor. If it were possible to regard xvi. 1-20 as addressed to the Church at Rome, these identifications would be attractive; yet even then they would be precarious, since (1) the names Aristobulus and Narcissus were both common, especially in the East, and (2) the slaves, on the purely conjectural supposition of their bequeathal to the Emperor, would have been styled Ἀριστοβουλιανοί and Ναρκισσιανοί, and Paul would have employed these designations. It may be added that, while epigraphic evidence shows that most of the other names in the passage were in use at Rome, it shows also that they were no less common in the East. Cf. *Corp. Inscript. Græc.*, where Epænetus, Hermas, and Hermes appear in Ephesian and Tryphosa in Carian inscriptions.

[1] Most MSS. have the Hebr. form Μαριάμ (ℵDEFGL).

[2] Cf. p. 189.

Cf. ver. 19. Apostle had travelled, he had heard their praises. It was a universal chorus, and here he conveys it to their ears: 'all the Churches of the Christ are greeting you.'

3 Greet Prisca and Aquila, my fellow-workers in Christ
4 Jesus: they risked their own lives for mine; and it is not
I alone that am thankful to them, but all the Churches of
5 the Gentiles. And greet the Church at their house. Greet
my beloved Epænetus, who is Asia's first-fruits for Christ.
6, 7 Greet Mary, who laboured so much for us.[1] Greet Andronicus and Junias,[2] my fellow-countrymen and once my
fellow-captives:[3] they are men of note among the Apostles,[4]
8 and they have been in Christ longer than I. Greet
9 Ampliatus, my beloved in the Lord. Greet Urbanus, my
10 fellow-worker in Christ, and my beloved Stachys. Greet
Apelles, that approved Christian. Greet the household of
11 Aristobulus. Greet Herodion, my fellow-countryman.
Greet those of the household of Narcissus who are in the
12 Lord. Greet Tryphæna and Tryphosa, who labour in the
Lord. Greet the beloved Persis: she laboured so much
13 in the Lord. Greet Rufus, that choice disciple, and his
14 mother and mine. Greet Asyncritus, Phlegon, Hermes,
Patrobas, Hermas, and the brothers of their company.
15 Greet Philologus and Julia, Nereus and his sister, and
16 Olympas, and all the saints of their company. Greet one
another with a saintly kiss. All the Churches of Christ
are greeting you.

Heresy at Ephesus. Nevertheless even in Asia mischief was at work. The Churches were indeed untouched by the Judaist controversy,

[1] The bulk of the MSS. vary between *εἰς ὑμᾶς*, 'for you' (ℵ*ABC*P), and *ἐν ὑμῖν*, 'among you' (DEF^{gr}G), but *εἰς ἡμᾶς*, 'for us' (C^{2}L), seems preferable. If Mary's labour had been for the Church merely, no addition would have been necessary (cf. ver. 12). Paul is recalling her services to himself and his companions during their sojourn at Ephesus. Cf. Chrys.: *ἀποστόλων καὶ εὐαγγελιστῶν ἀναδεξαμένη δρόμους.* The phrase occurs in a wife's epitaph on her husband in the cemetery of Pontianus at Rome: *τεὶς* (*i.e.*, *ὅστις*) *μοι πολλὰ ἐκοπίασεν* (*Corp. Inscript. Græc.* 9552).

[2] Or 'Junia,' when Andronicus and Junia, like Aquila and Prisca, Philologus and Julia, would doubtless be husband and wife.

[3] *συγγενεῖς* (cf. ix. 3), not 'kinsmen' but 'fellow-Jews.' Cf. ver. 21, where the designation distinguishes Lucius, Jason, and Sosipater from the half-Gentile Timothy (cf. Ac. xvi. 1). *συναιχμαλώτους μου*, on some unrecorded occasion during his troubled ministry at Ephesus (cf. 2 Cor. i. 8) or elsewhere ere they had settled there.

[4] Not, as the Fathers generally, that they were themselves Apostles in the wide use of the term (cf. p. 60), but that they were esteemed by the original Apostles. They were old Christians, converted ere the rise of the Judaist controversy.

but a subtle and pestilent heresy had emerged in their midst. It was, as will appear in due course, a shameless antinomianism in the guise of heathen philosophy; and the Apostle entreats his friends to beware of it.

17 Now I beseech you, brothers, to observe those who are
creating divisions and snares contrary to the teaching which
18 you learned. And shun their company; for it is not to our
Lord Christ that men of this sort are slaves, but to their own
appetites, and by their affability and plausibility they deceive
19 the hearts of the innocent. The fame of your loyalty has
travelled all abroad; over you, therefore, I rejoice, but I
wish you to be wise in what is good and simple in what is bad.
20 And God, the giver of peace, will crush Satan under your feet
ere long.

THE GRACE OF OUR LORD JESUS BE WITH YOU.

Greeting from the Apostle's Friends and his Amanuensis at Corinth, appended to the Personal Message in each copy of the Encyclical (xvi. 21-24).

21 Timothy, my fellow-worker, greets you; and Lucius and
22 Jason and Sosipater, my fellow-countrymen. I Tertius, who
23 am writing the letter, greet you in the Lord. Gaius, my host
and the host of the whole Church, greets you. Erastus, the
City Treasurer, greets you; and brother Quartus.
24 THE GRACE OF OUR LORD JESUS CHRIST BE WITH YOU ALL.
AMEN.

VI

THE JOURNEY TO JERUSALEM

Ac. xx. 3-xxi. 16.

The start. After the encyclical had been despatched to its various destinations there was no more to be done at Corinth. It was now the beginning of February, A.D. 57; and since the Apostle was desirous, according to his wont, of reaching Jerusalem in time for the celebration of the Passover, which fell that year on April 7, it was necessary that he should address himself to the journey thither. A ship was about to sail from the port of Cenchreæ with a complement of Jewish pilgrims, and he and his company arranged to travel by her; but on the very eve of their departure it came to their knowledge that a Jewish plot was a-foot against his life. Evidently **A Jewish plot.** the intention was murder on the high seas, and amid that crowd of devotees it would have been easy for a fanatic to stab him in his sleep and cast his body overboard.[1] Fortunately he received timely warning and checkmated the murderous design. The rest of his companions—the three Macedonians, Sopater, Aristarchus, and Secundus, the two Galatians, Gaius and Timothy, and the two Asians, Tychicus and Trophimus—quietly embarked; but he and Luke remained behind, and then unobserved, since it was supposed that they had gone with the others, they quitted Corinth and pursued the overland route by way of Thessaly and Macedonia. It was a toilsome journey, and the Apostle could no longer hope to reach Jerusalem in time for the Passover. This, however, was a lesser concern. His chief errand was the presentation of the bounty which the Churches of Macedonia and Achaia had charged him and his colleagues to convey to the Sacred Capital; and it was arranged that the seven should rejoin him in the course of the journey. The ship would put in at Ephesus, and they were to leave her there and betake themselves northward to Troas and await his arrival.[2]

The overland route.

At Troas.

It was a long journey that Paul and Luke had to make, and their progress was so delayed by the necessity of visiting the Churches *en route* at Berœa, Thessalonica, Apollonia, Amphipolis, and Philippi that it was the middle of April [3] ere they set sail from the port of Neapolis. The passage to

[1] Cf. the plot of the crew against the poet Arion on the voyage from Tarentum to Corinth: τοὺς δὲ ἐν τῷ πελάγει ἐπιβουλεύειν τὸν Ἀρίονα ἐκβαλόντας ἔχειν τὰ χρήματα (Herod. I. 24).

[2] Luke's narrative here (Ac. xx. 3-6) is very concise, and the situation has been obscured by two scribal attempts at elucidation: (1) the insertion of ἄχρι τῆς Ἀσίας after συνείπετο αὐτῷ and (2) the alteration of προελθόντες into προσελθόντες. The idea then is that none of the seven were with Paul when he started from Corinth, and Sopater, Aristarchus, and Secundus attached themselves to him during his progress through Macedonia and accompanied him to Asia, where he was joined by Gaius and Timothy from Galatia and by Tychicus and Trophimus from Ephesus. The fact is that ver. 4 is a catalogue of the companions who set out with him from Corinth, and ver. 5*a* indicates their procedure on the discovery of the plot: 'they went on (by the ship) and waited for us (Paul and Luke) at Troas.' After his wont Luke makes no express mention of himself, but his use of the first pers. pron. indicates his presence and the part he played. Titus also was at Corinth (cf. p. 368), and as there is here no mention of him, it may be inferred that he remained with the Church which he had already served so well.

[3] Cf. Append. I.

Troas occupied four full days, and there they found their seven friends.

Resuscitation of Eutychus.

Paul was no stranger at Troas. Twice already he had visited it,[1] and there was a considerable community of Christians in the city. He remained with them for a week. The last day of his sojourn was a Sunday, and in the evening the Church assembled for worship, concluding with the customary celebration of the Lord's Supper. The Apostle preached, and in the fulness of his heart he protracted his discourse until midnight.[2] The scene was an apartment in a poor house on the topmost storey of a tenement ;[3] and since it was not only crowded but lit with numerous lamps the atmosphere was stifling. One of the congregation, a lad named Eutychus, was seated on the ledge of an open window, and, falling a-drowse, he toppled over and was precipitated to the ground. The company hastened down ; and to their consternation found him dead ;[4] but Paul embraced the inanimate form and presently assured them that his life was in him. The lad was removed, and they returned to the upper room and partook of the Holy Supper, and thereafter the Apostle conversed with them until daybreak. It was then time for him to take his leave, and it was no small alleviation of their grief in parting with him that Eutychus was recovered. His friends brought him, and he joined in the farewell.

Cf. 2 Ki. iv. 34.

Progress to Miletus.

Troas lay remote from the route of commerce, and it appears that the Apostle and his companions hired a ship to convey them on their journey.[5] She would be a small craft, and she sailed early in the morning to profit by the northerly breeze which on that coast blows all day and falls in the evening. It was thus only by day that she could prosecute her voyage, and her first station for the night would

[1] Cf. pp. 124, 344.

[2] 'Spiritual teachers,' observes Bengel, 'ought not to be too strictly bound by the clock, especially on a solemn and rare occasion.'

[3] The third storey of an *insula*, immediately under the tiling, was occupied by the humbler sort of tenants. Cf. Juv. III. 199.

[4] On the verdict of Luke the physician (*ἤρθη νεκρός*). Had the lad been merely stunned, he would have written *ἤρθη ὡς νεκρός*. Paul's words *ἡ γὰρ ψυχὴ αὐτοῦ ἐν αὐτῷ ἐστιν* do not mean that his life had been in him all the time but that it had just returned. Cf. Grot. : 'jam nunc cum loquor vita ei rediit.'

[5] A regular trader would have followed her own course, and it would have been impossible for Paul to determine what ports she should visit (cf. ver. 16).

be Assos. All the others embarked at Troas and sailed round Cape Lectum, but Paul chose to go a-foot across the promontory, a distance of fully twenty miles. It would be no hardship for one so accustomed to travel, and he desired a season of solitude that he might ponder what lay before him; and therefore he went all alone, unaccompanied even by Luke. He joined the ship at Assos, and the next day's run brought her to Mitylene on the east of the island of Lesbos; the third day (Wednesday) she reached an anchorage on the mainland abreast of the island of Chios, perhaps at Cape Argennum; and, sailing thence next morning, she emerged on the Caÿstrian Gulf and, striking across and rounding the western extremity of the island of Samos, put in for the night at Cape Trogyllium,[1] and on the fifth day (Friday) proceeded to Miletus.

Citation of the Ephesian Elders.

There she made a stay, since the Apostle had an office to discharge. The murderous plot of the Jews on the eve of his departure from Corinth had revealed to him the inveteracy of their hostility, and he had encountered fresh evidences of it in every town he had visited in the course of his journey through Macedonia. It had inspired him with gloomy forebodings of the fate in store for him at Jerusalem. He anticipated the worst; he was sure that he was going to his death. He would never pass that way again, and therefore he would fain deliver a last message to his friends at Ephesus, all the more that they were threatened with the invasion of a malignant heresy. His obvious course would have been to steer from Cape Argennum up the Caÿstrian Gulf and land at Ephesus; but he was in haste to reach Jerusalem in time for the Feast of Pentecost, which fell that year on May 28, and a visit to a city where he had so many friends would have detained him too long. And so he had held on to Miletus, and thence he summoned the Ephesian Elders to wait upon him and receive his counsels.

Cf. vers. 22-25.

Conference with them.

It was a short run from Trogyllium to Miletus, and the ship would reach the latter by noon. The route to Ephesus lay

[1] According to the interpolation in DHLP *καὶ μείναντες ἐν Τρωγυλίᾳ* (Τρωγυλλίᾳ, al. Τρωγυλίῳ, Τρωγυλλίῳ). Cape Trogyllium (Τρωγύλλιον ἄκρον) was the western extremity of Mount Mycale, and in front of it lay an islet or rather three islets of the same name. Cf. Strabo, 636; Plin. *Nat. Hist.* v. 37.

across the gulf of the Mæander, now silted up by the river's deposit, to the town of Priene, a distance of some ten miles, and thence some twenty miles by land; and a courier would accomplish the journey in about eight hours. If the Elders set out betimes next morning (Saturday), they would, at their slower rate of travel, reach Miletus in the evening. It was thus in the night-time, after a brief repose, that the
Apostle held his conference with them; nor was it, as he Cf. ver. 31.
reminded them, the first occasion in their experience when he had turned night into day. Luke would be present at the interview, and he has preserved a report of the Apostle's moving farewell.[1]

xx. 18 You know, from the first day when I set foot in Asia,
19 how I conducted myself among you all the time, as the
Lord's slave with all humility and tears and trials which
20 fell to my lot amid the plots of the Jews. I never shrank
from declaring to you anything that was profitable and
21 teaching you in public and in your homes, always testifying
both to Jews and to Greeks repentance toward God and
faith in our Lord Jesus.

22 And now, look you, bound in spirit, I am on the way to
Jerusalem, not knowing what will happen to me there,
23 except that the Holy Spirit is testifying in city after city
24 and telling me that bonds and distresses await me. But
I set everything at naught, nor do I count my life precious
to me, if only I may accomplish my course and the ministry Cf. 2 Tim.
which I received from the Lord Jesus—to testify the Gospel iv. 7.
of the grace of God.

25 And now, look you, I know that you will never see my face
again—all you amongst whom I went about, proclaiming
26 the Kingdom. Therefore I testify to you this day that I Cf. xviii. 6.
27 am clean of the blood of all; for I never shrank from
declaring all the will of God to you.

28 Take heed to yourselves and all the flock among which
the Holy Spirit appointed you overseers,[2] that you shepherd

[1] The accuracy of the report is attested by its Pauline diction. Cf. *δουλεύειν τῷ Κυρίῳ*, *ταπεινοφροσύνῃ* (ver. 19), *συμφέροντα* (ver. 20), *διακονία* (ver. 24), *φείδομαι* (ver. 29), *νουθετεῖν* (ver. 31), *οἰκοδομεῖν* (ver. 32), *κοπιᾶν* (ver. 35).

[2] *ἐπισκόπους*, 'bishops.' Here (cf. 1 Pet. v. 2-4) it is the Elders (*πρεσβύτεροι*) of the Church that are addressed, and they are designated *ἐπίσκοποι*. 'Bishop' is simply a corruption of the Greek term, and it should be expunged from the N. T. in view of the ecclesiastical significance which it subsequently acquired. There were not three orders in the Apostolic Church—*ἐπίσκοποι*, *πρεσβύτεροι*, and *διάκονοι*, but only two—*πρεσβύτεροι* or *ἐπίσκοποι* and *διάκονοι* (cf. Phil. i. 1;

the Church of the Lord which He won with His own
29 blood.[1] I know that after my departure grievous wolves
30 will come in among you and will not spare the flock; and
from your own midst men will arise and talk perverted
31 things to draw the disciples away after them. Therefore
be watchful, and remember that for three years night and
day I never ceased with tears to admonish every one.

Cf. Mt. vii. 15.

32 And now I commend you to God and to the Word of His
grace which has power to upbuild you and give you the
33 'heritage' among 'all His sanctified.' No man's gold or
34 silver or clothing did I ever covet: you are yourselves
aware that these hands[2] served my needs and my com-
35 panions. I gave you every example that you ought to
toil thus and help the weak, and remember the words of
the Lord Jesus how He said Himself: 'It is more blessed
to give than to receive.'[3]

Dt. xxxiii. 3, 4.

The farewell.

Thereafter the Apostle kneeled down and prayed with them. They were deeply moved, especially by his announcement that they would never see his face again; and, as they gave him the parting kiss,[4] they clung about his neck with loud lamentation. It was now morning, and the breeze was rising and the ship was unfurling her sails. It was Sunday, but the Apostle had cast off the bondage of Jewish Sabbatarianism and had no scruple in pursuing his journey on the

Cf. Rom. xiv. 5.

1 Tim. iii. 1-13). ἐπίσκοπος, 'overseer,' was a common appellation of a shepherd (cf. 1 Pet. ii. 25), since a shepherd's business was to 'oversee' (ἐπισκοπεῖν) his flock (cf. 1 Pet. v. 2); and the N. T. conception is that Christ is the supreme Shepherd or Overseer of the Church, and its ministers or presbyters His under-shepherds. Hence He is styled ὁ Ἀρχιποίμην (1 Pet. v. 4). Cf. p. 590.

[1] The chief MSS. are divided between τὴν ἐκκλησίαν τοῦ Κυρίου (AC*DE) and τὴν ἐκκλ. τοῦ Θεοῦ (ℵB), but the oldest authorities (*e.g.*, Iren. III. xiv. 2) attest the former. The interchange of Θεός and Κύριος is frequent (cf. ver. 32: τῷ Θεῷ ℵACDEHLP; τῷ Κυρίῳ B), their abbreviation (Θ̅Σ̅, Κ̅Σ̅) facilitating their confusion. It is decisive in favour of τοῦ Κυρίου that, while the phrases Ἰησοῦς Χριστὸς ὁ Θεὸς ἡμῶν and αἷμα Θεοῦ are frequent in sub-apostolic literature (cf. Ign. *Eph.* inscr., i), they are alien from N. T., which always maintains the distinction between 'God,' the Unseen Father, and 'the Lord,' His visible manifestation, *Dei inaspecti aspectabilis imago* (cf. n. on Rom. ix. 5, p. 426). It would support τοῦ Θεοῦ if the Apostle's words were regarded as a reference to Ps. lxxiv. 2; but it would then be necessary to construe τοῦ ἰδίου as a gen. dependent on τοῦ αἵματος, 'the blood of His own [Son].' Cf. Rom. viii. 32. See Wetstein's extensive and erudite critical note.

[2] Displaying his toil-worn hands: 'callosæ, ut videtis' (Beng.).

[3] A *logion* from the oral tradition, not preserved by our Evangelists. Cf. *The Days of His Flesh*, p. xix; *Unwritten Sayings of Our Lord*, pp. 4 f.

[4] Cf. p. 166.

Christian Day of Rest. The Ephesian Elders escorted him from the scene of the interview, probably a house of entertainment in the city, to the harbour, and would hardly let him go. The travellers had to 'tear themselves away.'

Their course lay direct south, and with the wind astern they reached the island of Cos that evening. Next morning they steered south-east, and still the breeze was fair, since they were entering the Levant, and there the prevailing winds are westerly. That evening they made the port of Rhodes at the northern extremity of the island of the same name; and next day they reached Patara on the coast of Lycia, 'a great city with a harbour and many temples.'[1] There they found a large ship bound for Phœnicia, and, dismissing their little hired craft, they embarked in the more commodious and expeditious vessel. It seems that she coasted along to Myra;[2] and thence, putting out to sea, she steered past the west of Cyprus and made for the port of Tyre.

Voyage to Tyre.

Her cargo was consigned to Tyre, but her destination was Ptolemais some five and twenty miles southward, and after unlading she would proceed thither. It was a long way from Tyre to Jerusalem, and since he was evidently desirous of husbanding his strength in view of the ordeal which awaited him, the Apostle decided to remain by the ship to the end of her voyage. The unlading occupied a week, but the time was well employed in fellowship with the Christians of Tyre. They were a small community; and, since they were unapprised of his advent, he had to search them out, and it was not without difficulty that he discovered them in that great city.[3] When, however, he succeeded, they showed him lavish kindness. They were acquainted with the Jewish sentiment toward him, and they confirmed his apprehensions and solemnly warned him to keep away from Jerusalem. Their entreaties were unavailing, and when he took his departure, all the little community, even the women and children, escorted him and his companions to the harbour. They kneeled down on the beach and prayed, and then bade each other an affectionate farewell; nor was it until the

Sojourn there.

[1] Strabo, 666.

[2] Cod. Bez. (D) *εἰς Πάταρα καὶ Μύρα.*

[3] Cf. Ac. xxi. 4: *ἀνευρόντες δὲ τοὺς μαθητάς.* Blass: '*ἀνευρεῖν* est *quærendo* reperire; erat enim urbs magna, Christiani pauci.'

travellers were on board that their friends returned sorrowfully home.

At Cæsarea.

Steering southward along the coast, the ship reached Ptolemais. This was her destination,[1] and the travellers quitted her. They spent a day with the Christians of the city, waiting for a coasting vessel to convey them to Cæsarea,[2] fully thirty miles farther on their way. At Cæsarea they found a hospitable welcome in the house of Philip the Evangelist, one of the Seven Deacons; [3] and there they remained 'a good many days,' evidently, in view of what transpired, a full week at the least. Philip had four maiden daughters endowed with the spirit of prophecy,[4] and the danger which menaced the Apostle would not be hidden from them. Their sex precluded them from free remonstrance, but they would not suffer him to go unwarned to his doom. In the Church at Jerusalem there was a venerable prophet—that Agabus who had predicted the great famine some fourteen years previously; [5] and it would seem that they appealed to him. At all events he appeared on the scene and delivered an impressive warning after the histrionic manner of his order.[6] He entered the assembly of the brethren and, taking Paul's girdle, bound with it his own feet and hands and intimated that the Jews would so bind its owner at Jerusalem and deliver him into the hands of the Gentiles.

Cf. 1 Cor. xiv. 34.

Warning of Agabus.

The Apostle's solution.

The announcement, chiming with the Apostle's own foreboding at Miletus and the warning of the Christians at Tyre and deriving from the character of the speaker the authority of a divine oracle, profoundly moved his companions; and the whole assemblage besought him to abandon his purpose of going up to Jerusalem. Their entreaties grieved him. He was going on the Lord's errand, and he was affected by

[1] *τὸν πλοῦν διανύσαντες* (ver. 7) can only mean 'having finished the voyage'; and *ἀπὸ* Τύρου must be construed, not with *πλοῦν* (as though *τὸν ἀπὸ* Τύρου *πλοῦν*, 'the voyage from Tyre'), but with *κατηντήσαμεν*, 'we arrived from Tyrc at Ptolemais.'

[2] If they had travelled by land from Ptolemais, they would never have gone near Cæsarea; they would have struck inland and followed the direct route to Jerusalem.

[3] Cf. pp. 39 f.

[4] Cf. p. 310.

[5] Cf. p. 72.

[6] Cf. *The Days of His Flesh*, p. 345.

their affectionate importunity as the Lord had been by Peter's protest at Cæsarea Philippi when He intimated His approaching Passion. (Cf. Mt. xvi. 21-23.) It was cruel kindness to dissuade him thus from the ordeal, and he told them that he was ready not merely to be bound but to die at Jerusalem for the name of the Lord Jesus. This put them to silence, and they mournfully acquiesced.

Progress to Jerusalem.

They did not, however, desist from their solicitude on his behalf; they rather redoubled it. With the fear of a recurrence of his chronic malady before his eyes he had latterly, doubtless on the advice of Luke the physician, spared himself unnecessary fatigue; and now in prospect of the journey they made all provision for his easy transit. Jerusalem was some sixty miles distant from Cæsarea, and they procured beasts of burden for his conveyance.[1] Nor would they permit him to make a single day's march of the journey. At a village on the route, perhaps Lydda, there dwelt a venerable Christian named Mnason. He was a native of Cyprus, (Cf. xi. 20.) and had perhaps been won to the Faith by Peter in the course of the latter's mission in that district quarter of a century previously. (Cf. ix. 32-35.) Lydda, situated thirty-seven miles from Cæsarea and twenty-three from Jerusalem, would be a convenient station, and it was arranged that the Apostle should break his journey there and pass the night at Mnason's house. Accordingly, when he set out, a deputation of the Cæsarean Christians escorted him so far on his way and committed him to the care of his gracious host.[2] Next day he continued his journey, and on his arrival at the Sacred Capital on the eve of the Day of Pentecost he was joyfully welcomed. (Cf. xxiv. 11.)

[1] *ἐπισκευάσασθαι* (Ac. xxi. 15) denoted especially 'putting a load on beasts.'

[2] The narrative is here (xxi. 16, 17) very obscure, and it is thus happily elucidated by Cod. Bez. (D): *συνῆλθον δὲ καὶ τῶν μαθητῶν ἀπὸ Καισαρείας σὺν ἡμῖν· οὗτοι δὲ ἤγαγον ἡμᾶς πρὸς οὓς ξενισθῶμεν, καὶ παραγενόμενοι εἴς τινα κώμην ἐγενόμεθα παρὰ Μνάσωνί τινι Κυπρίῳ, μαθητῇ ἀρχαίῳ. κἀκεῖθεν ἐξιόντες ἤλθομεν εἰς Ἱεροσόλυμα, ὑπέδεξάν τε ἡμᾶς ἀσμένως οἱ ἀδελφοί*, 'and there went with us also some of the disciples from Cæsarea; and these conducted us to our entertainers, and on arriving at a certain village we were lodged with a certain Mnason, a Cyprian, an early disciple. And setting out thence we came to Jerusalem, and the brothers welcomed us gladly.'

BOOK III

PAUL THE PRISONER OF JESUS CHRIST

'O comrade bold, of toil and pain!
  Thy trial how severe,
When sever'd first by prisoner's chain
  From thy loved labour-sphere!

'Say, did impatience first impel
  The heaven-sent bond to break?
Or, could'st thou bear its hindrance well,
  Loitering for JESU'S sake?'

JOHN HENRY NEWMAN.

ARREST AT JERUSALEM

Ac. xxi. 17-xxiii.

Reception by the Presbytery.

On the following day the Presbytery of the Church convened under the presidency of James, the Lord's brother;[1] and Paul and his companions appeared beforc it. They would present the contributions which they had brought from the Churches of Macedonia and Achaia, and the Apostle told the story of his ministry among the Gentiles during these last four years. It was a thrilling narrative, and it was received with devout gratitude.

Judaist animosity.

It would have been well had this sentiment been universal in the Church of Jerusalem, but the Presbytery was aware of the prevalence of a bitter animosity against the Apostle. Most of the Judæan Christians belonged to the Judaist party, and they regarded him as a renegade who went about seeking to pervert the Hellenistic Jews and persuading them to discontinue the observance of the Mosaic Law, particularly the rite of Circumcision. It was of course a mischievous misrepresentation. His actual contention was that Circumcision mattered nothing. Salvation was by faith in Christ and not by the rites of the Law, and he refused to impose Circumcision on his Gentile converts; but he never forbade it to the Jews. They were free to practise it and other Mosaic rites if they would, so long as they rested on Christ for salvation. His Judaist adversaries, however, ignored this essential distinction, and they had dinned their grievance into the ears of the Judæan Christians.[2]

Cf. 1 Cor. vii. 18-20.

Association of the Apostle with Nazirite votaries.

The consequence was that he was regarded in Jerusalem with inveterate hostility. The situation was perilous, and the Presbytery had planned a remedy, a politic device for openly defining his attitude toward the Law and clearing

[1] Again (cf. pp. 60, 111) apparently the original Apostles were absent.

[2] κατηχήθησαν, cf. *The Days of His Flesh*, p. xvii.

himself of those malicious aspersions. It happened that there were four members of the Church who, on account of ceremonial defilement, had five days previously [1] assumed the Nazirite vow. It was accounted meritorious in those days that a Jew should associate himself with a poor votary and defray the Temple-charges for his purification; [2] and the Presbytery's proposal was that Paul should undertake this charitable office on behalf of the four, and thus publish his reverence for the Law. It would involve no compromise of his principles, since he had himself assumed the Nazirite vow on the occasion of his last visit to Jerusalem.[3] He agreed, and repaired with the votaries to the Temple and intimated to the priest his association with them and his responsibility for their charges.

Riot in the Temple. Cf. Num. vi. 9.

Since the vow ran for a week, it was accomplished on the following day, and Paul then returned with them to the Temple to discharge his liability. So far he had been unmolested, and it had seemed as though the Presbytery's stratagem would succeed; but it was frustrated by an unfortunate circumstance. Among the pilgrims who had resorted to Jerusalem to celebrate the Feast of Pentecost were some Jews from the Province of Asia, and it chanced that they encountered the Apostle in the city in company with Trophimus. The latter was an Ephesian, and they recognised him; and presently they espied Paul within the Temple-precincts on his errand to the priest, and leaped to the conclusion that he had brought his Greek follower with him. It was an intolerable desecration that the feet of an 'uncircumcised dog' should tread the sacred court, and they seized the Apostle and shouted 'Israelites, to the rescue!' A wild tumult ensued. The whole city was roused, and Paul was beset by a mob of fanatics, who dragged him outwith the Temple and, lest he should elude their grasp and find sanctuary by the altar, shut the gates. Once in the street they showered blows upon him, and would have done him to death had not the uproar reached the adjacent barracks of Fort Antonia, and the commander, Claudius Lysias, promptly appeared on the scene with a detachment of soldiers.

[1] Cf. Append. I, p. 657.
[2] Cf. Jos. *Ant.* XIX. vi. 1.
[3] Cf. p. 190.

He rescued the Apostle from his murderous assailants, and put him in charge of two soldiers who coupled him to themselves by a chain on either wrist; and then he inquired who he was and what he had done. The only answer was a confused and unintelligible clamour, and he ordered that the stunned prisoner should be conveyed within the Castle for examination. A suspicion had crossed his mind. Those were troublous days in Judæa. The Assassins, that extreme party of the Zealots sworn to undying enmity against the Roman tyranny, were active; and recently there had been a wild outbreak under an Egyptian Jew who professed himself a prophet and played upon the fanaticism of the populace. It had been suppressed by the Procurator Felix, and the leader had escaped and disappeared.[1] And now the idea had occurred to Lysias that the Apostle might be that desperado and the deluded mob was taking its revenge.

The Apostle's rescue by Claudius Lysias.

The Castle adjoined the Temple to the north, and it was entered by a double stairway in the north-east angle of the outer court.[2] On the way thither the crowd hustled the prisoner and his guards, shouting 'Away with him!' until on reaching the stair the soldiers had to carry him up the steps. Just at the doorway he accosted the commander for the first time and craved a word with him. 'Do you understand Greek?' was the surprised answer. 'Are you not the Egyptian?' 'No,' said the prisoner, 'I am a Jew of Tarsus in Cilicia, a citizen of no undistinguished city. Pray, permit me to talk to the people.' Lysias consented, and, taking his stand on the broad landing, Paul faced the tumultuous assemblage in the court beneath, and, with that characteristic gesture which Luke had remarked the first time he ever heard him in the Synagogue of Pisidian Antioch,[3] raised his hand to bespeak attention. The tumult subsided, and he addressed the crowd in their Aramaic vernacular. It would be unintelligible to the Roman Lysias, and probably also to the Greek Luke who witnessed the scene from his place in the court; but it was kindly in the ears of the Jewish fanatics and won their attention.

His speech to the mob.

The speech was a biographical narrative, designed to

His personal apologia.

[1] Cf. Jos. *Ant.* xx. viii. 6; *De Bell. Jud.* II. xiii. 5.

[2] Cf. *De Bell. Jud.* v. v. 8.

[3] Cf. p. 92.

justify the Apostle's attitude toward the Jewish Faith. He styled his hearers, with all honour, after the Jewish fashion, 'brothers and fathers,' thus claiming kinship with them; and he told them of his Jewish birth at Tarsus, his education in their own College under the celebrated Rabbi Gamaliel, and how he had once been as zealous for the Law as any of them and a ruthless persecutor of the followers of Jesus. And then he told them how he had been converted on the road to Damascus by a vision of Jesus, Risen and Glorified; and how, thirteen years later,[1] there in the court of the Temple the Lord had again appeared to him and, sorely against his will, had imposed on him the office of preaching salvation to the Gentiles.

Renewed uproar. Hitherto they had listened eagerly, but this mention of the Gentiles infuriated them. 'Away with such a fellow from the earth!' they shouted, and struggled and gesticulated till the very air was thick with the dust they raised.

Sentence of scourging. The uproar discomposed Lysias. He was responsible for the maintenance of order in the city, and in the hope of pacifying the mob he adopted an illegal course: he ordered that the prisoner should be scourged until he confessed his crime. The illegality was twofold. It was only when a prisoner had refused, in the course of examination, to state the truth that resort was had to torture; and Paul had not refused; he had not even been put upon his trial. Moreover, he was, though Lysias was unaware of this, a Roman citizen, and to inflict the ignominy of the scourge on the sacred person of a Roman was sacrilege.[2]

His protest. The soldiers were binding him to the whipping-post when he said to the centurion in charge: 'Have you the right to scourge a man who is a Roman and has had not trial?' The protest was effective. The centurion turned to Lysias. 'What are you going to do?' he asked. 'This man is a Roman.' Lysias was aghast. He stepped over to the prisoner. 'Tell me,' he said, 'are you a Roman?' 'Yes' was the answer. It seemed incredible. It was indeed common for a rich provincial to purchase that precious privilege,[3] and it was thus that Lysias had obtained it; but Paul was only a poor Jew. 'For a large sum,' exclaimed

[1] Cf. p. 76. [2] Cf. p. 20. [3] *Ibid.*

the officer, 'I gained this citizenship.' 'But I,' was the proud rejoinder, 'am a Roman born.'

Arraignment before the Sanhedrin. Cf. Ac. xvi. 35-39.

Lysias would have been glad if, like the magistrates of Philippi in a similar embarrassment, he could have dismissed the prisoner with an apology; but Jerusalem was not Philippi, and he durst not provoke the resentment of the turbulent Jews. The best he could do was to secure him a fair trial. Since Paul was a Jew, he was under the jurisdiction of the Jewish tribunal, and so the commander required the Sanhedrin to meet on the following day. The august court assembled in due course in the Hall of Hewn Stone under the presidency of the High Priest Ananias; and Lysias, evidently apprehending violence, conducted the prisoner thither from the Castle under a military escort. On his own account he hoped for an amicable issue in view of the illegality which he had perpetrated; and it appears, moreover, that he was well disposed to the Apostle and desired his acquittal.

His stout bearing.

Paul's attitude too is remarkable. He had plainly abandoned all expectation of justice at the hands of the Jews; and it seems as though he had regretted his attempt to conciliate their prejudices by assuming the Nazirite vow and had determined to have done with compromises. Probably also, as St. Chrysostom suggests, he reckoned that a resolute bearing would impress the commander and stiffen his resolution to see justice done.

Rencontre with the High Priest. Cf. Ac. iv. 8. Cf. Eph. ii. 12; Phil. i. 27, iii. 20. Cf. 2 Cor. xi. 20; Mt. v. 39.

At all events he faced the Sanhedrin fearlessly and indeed cavalierly. Instead of meekly awaiting examination he immediately entered a protest. 'Brothers,' he said abruptly —not 'Rulers of the people and Elders of Israel,' which was the customary formula in addressing the supreme court— 'I have with a perfectly good conscience been a citizen of the Commonwealth of God to this day.' It was an assertion of his loyalty to the Jewish Faith, and it so angered the High Priest that he ordered his attendants to silence the audacious prisoner by smiting him on the mouth. It was the grossest of insults, a piece of sheer ruffianism perpetrated by a minister of justice; and the Apostle's indignation blazed up. 'God will smite you,' he cried, 'you whited wall![1]

[1] A proverbial phrase. Cf. Mt. xxiii. 27.

And sit you there as my legal judge, and illegally bid me be smitten?' The tyrant's minions were horrified, and exclaimed against such language to 'God's High Priest'; but their reproof merely exposed Ananias to a sharper thrust. Paul looked round the court. 'I knew not, brothers,' he said, 'that he was High Priest, for it is written: "Thou shalt not speak ill of a ruler of thy people."' It was no apology but a biting sarcasm: 'Certainly the High Priest should be reverenced, but who could have supposed that this ruffian was a High Priest?'[1]

Ex. xxii. 28.

It was indeed a dramatic episode, and the natural heart applauds the Apostle's brave defiance; yet perhaps he would bethink himself by and by in calmer mood that there was a nobler way. His Lord had once stood like him before the High Priest and been subjected to the self-same contumely; and His only answer had been a gentle remonstrance. 'Where,' asks St. Jerome,[2] 'is that patience of the Saviour, who, "led as a lamb to the slaughter, opened not His mouth," but spoke gently to the smiter: "If I have spoken ill, testify of the ill; but if well, why do you strike Me?" We do not detract from the Apostle but we proclaim the glory of the Lord who, when He suffered in the flesh, rose superior to the injury and weakness of the flesh.'

Cf. Jo. xviii. 22, 23.

Embroilment of Sadducees and Pharisees.

It was clear to Paul that he would receive no justice in the Sanhedrin, and he resorted to an adroit stratagem. The court was composed of representatives of the rival parties of the Sadducees and the Pharisees, who were sharply divided on the question of Immortality.[3] Here lay his opportunity. He was himself a Pharisee by birth and education, and amid the excitement which ensued upon his defiance of the Sadducean President, he appealed to the partisan sympathies of the Pharisaic members. 'Brothers,'

Cf. xxvi. 5; Phil. iii. 5.

[1] This interpretation was common in Chrysostom's day (τινὲς μὲν οὖν φασὶν ὅτι εἰδὼς εἰρωνεύεται); but his own view is that Paul spoke seriously: he really did not know that it was the High Priest, since he had been long absent from Jerusalem and was unacquainted with Ananias, and, moreover, in the thronged court he would not distinguish the speaker. But the High Priest was unmistakable. He occupied the presidential seat in the middle of the semicircle of Sanhedrists, and the prisoner stood before him during the trial.

[2] *Dial. adv. Pelag.* III.

[3] *The Days of His Flesh*, p. 42.

he cried, 'I am a Pharisee, the son of a Pharisee: it is on the question of hope for the dead and their resurrection that I am being judged.' The ruse succeeded. The Scribes, the leaders of the Pharisaic party, immediately espoused his cause and asserted his innocence. And so fierce grew the quarrel that he was in danger of being torn limb from limb, until Lysias interfered and had him conveyed to the Castle.

The Apostle's misgivings.

There he passed a troubled night. He could have little satisfaction in reviewing the day's proceedings or indeed the part which he had played ever since his arrival in Jerusalem. His initial blunder had been his acquiescence in the politic proposal of the Presbytery. This involved indeed no compromise of principle, but it was alien from the spirit of 'simplicity toward Christ.' Once before, when he had circumcised Timothy in deference to Jewish prejudice, he had resorted to diplomacy, only to discover its unprofitableness; and now again he had essayed it, and it had failed him disastrously. It was perhaps his chagrin that prompted him to assume so defiant an attitude before the Sanhedrin, forgetful of 'the meekness and sweet reasonableness of Christ.' This also had proved futile; and then in his desperation he had resorted to an ignoble trick, enkindling the mutual animosity of his enemies, and it was only the intervention of Lysias that had extricated him from his embarrassment.

2 Cor. xi. 3.

2 Cor. x. 1.

His reassurance.

His situation was indeed disquieting, and it was largely his own creation. It seemed as though there were no escape, but in that dark hour he was visited by a thought which he hailed as a divine assurance. His long-cherished dream that he would crown his ministry by testifying for Christ in the Imperial Capital had become a settled conviction. That was, to his mind, God's indubitable purpose; and, dark as was his immediate prospect, the cloud would lift. He would not perish in Jerusalem but would live to preach at Rome.

A plot for his assassination.

His faith was justified by the event, and already God was working out His providential design. The Apostle's escape from the Sanhedrin had been an exasperating disappointment to the Jewish rabble; and next morning a company of over forty desperadoes mustered and swore that they would have his life. They waited upon the rulers of both parties, and unfolded their plot. It was that a requisition be addressed to Lysias in name of the Sanhedrin, desiring him to bring the prisoner once more before the court, on the pretext of instituting a stricter examination; and they undertook to assassinate him on the way from the Castle, though it should cost them their own lives.[1] The Sadducees and the Pharisees had so far composed their dissension of the previous day that they were now agreed in desiring the Apostle's life; and the plot was sanctioned.

Its frustration.

Happily, however, it was frustrated. A nephew of Paul, his sister's son, was resident in Jerusalem, and he discovered what was a-foot. Evidently he was not a Christian but a Jew; and it may be that, like his uncle once, he was a student in the Rabbinical College. At all events, he had access to the inner circle of the Jews and got wind of the plot. Like the rest of Paul's relatives,[2] he regarded him as a traitor to the ancestral Faith, but natural affection triumphed over religious animosity, and, repairing to the Castle, he obtained an interview with the prisoner and told him the tidings. Paul desired one of his guards to conduct the lad to the commander; and it is an evidence of the latter's goodwill toward his prisoner that, when he learned that the business concerned Paul, his interest was at once engaged, and he grasped the lad's hand and drew him aside and heard his story.

Reference to the Procurator.

He took prompt and effective measures not merely to circumvent the conspiracy, but to remove the prisoner from his perilous situation. Since the case had assumed so serious an aspect, he would refer it to the Roman Procurator and have Paul conveyed to Cæsarea, where the Procurator had his seat. He enjoined the lad to keep silence and, summoning two trustworthy centurions, instructed them to provide a strong escort of seventy horsemen and two hundred guardsmen, with asses for the prisoner and his attendant Luke.[3] And he wrote a letter to the Procurator, informing

[1] In xxiii. 15 several authorities have *ἀνελεῖν αὐτόν, ἐὰν δέῃ καὶ ἀποθανεῖν*, 'to kill him even if we must die for it.'

[2] Cf. p. 61.

[3] The text in vers. 23, 24 is uncertain and confused, and it is simplified by (1) omitting *διακοσίους* after *στρατιώτας* with several minuscs., and (2) either omitting *καὶ* before *ἱππεῖς* (Fl.) or taking it as epexeg., 'even' (cf. Gal. vi. 16). *στρατιώτας* is then the entire force, and *ἱππεῖς* and *δεξιολάβους* its constituents.

him of the circumstances. He suppressed his own initial error in sentencing a Roman citizen to the scourge, and merely told how Paul had been mishandled by the mob, and in the course of his examination before the Sanhedrin all that had been laid to his charge was some offence against the Jewish religion. He had committed no crime, but it had transpired that a plot was on foot against his life; and so Lysias was sending him to the Procurator and bidding his accusers prosecute their grievance at Cæsarea.

The danger was that, if the conspirators discovered that the Apostle was being conveyed from Jerusalem, they might attempt a surprise *en route*; and so the departure was delayed until nightfall. At nine o'clock the troop set forth and marched under cover of the darkness as far as Antipatris, a distance of over thirty miles. Once beyond Judæa there was no need of apprehension; and from Antipatris the guardsmen marched back to Jerusalem, while the horsemen rode forward apace to Cæsarea and delivered the letter and handed over the prisoner to the Procurator at the Prætorium, his official residence, formerly the palace of King Herod the Great. And thus, after an absence of only nine days, the Apostle found himself back in Cæsarea.

Conveyance of the Apostle to Cæsarea.

IMPRISONMENT AT CÆSAREA

Ac. xxiv-xxvi.

The Procurator Felix.

THE Procurator at that time was Antonius Felix.[1] He had held office since the year 52,[2] and these had been sorrowful days in Judæa. He was a freedman of Antonia, mother of Claudius, and a brother of Pallas, the Emperor's notorious favourite. He was the first freedman who had ever held a procuratorship, and he owed his appointment to his brother's influence. The taint of his base origin clung to him throughout his career ; and, as the historian Tacitus expresses it in his epigrammatic fashion, he 'exercised the prerogative of a king, with all cruelty and lust, in the spirit of a slave.'

His evil administration.

Cruelty and lust—these were indeed the vices which darkened his Judæan administration. He exhibited the latter in his matrimonial relations. He was thrice married, and each of his wives, it is said,[3] was a princess. The first is unknown, but the second was a grand-daughter of Mark Antony and Cleopatra, and the third the Jewish princess Drusilla, daughter of Agrippa I and sister of Agrippa II. Shortly after his accession to office, though she was already married to Azizus, King of Emesa, he was captivated by her beauty and persuaded her to forsake her husband and ally herself with him. Of his cruelty that insurrection under the Egyptian Jew constitutes one of many instances. It was provoked by his tyranny, and he repressed it with sanguinary ferocity. Such tragedies were frequent during his malign administration. It was a veritable reign of terror, and it ended in his recall by Nero in the year 59.

His reception of the prisoner.

Such was the man who now controlled the Apostle's destiny. And indeed it was better in his hands ; for, with

[1] Cf. Tac. *Ann.* XII. 54 ; *Hist.* v. 9. Jos. *Ant.* XX. viii. 5, 6 ; *De Bell. Jud.* II. xiii. 2-6.

[2] Cf. Schürer, I. ii. p. 174.

[3] Suet. *Claud.* 28 : 'trium reginarum maritum.'

all his faults, Felix was a Roman magistrate, and under his administration Paul was sheltered by the strong bulwark of Roman law. On reading the letter of Lysias he merely inquired of the prisoner what province he belonged to, and then informed him that he would be brought to trial as soon as his accusers presented themselves, and therewith dismissed him to a cell.

Representatives of the Sanhedrin.

Meanwhile the implacable Jews were not idle. The Sanhedrin appointed a deputation consisting of the High Priest Ananias to represent the Sadducees and several Elders to represent the Pharisees, and associated with them a Jewish lawyer named Tertullus to submit the case before the Roman tribunal. These preparations and especially the instruction of Tertullus required time, and Paul had lain five days in prison ere the prosecutors appeared at Cæsarea.

The indictment.

The trial opened with a speech by Tertullus. Though a Jew and the spokesman of the Sanhedrin, he began with fulsome and servile adulation of the tyrant. Then he proceeded to the indictment, and laid three distinct charges: treason, heresy, and sacrilege. Paul, it was averred, went about exciting insurrection among the Jews throughout the Empire; he was a ringleader of 'the sect of the Nazarenes,' as the Jews contemptuously designated the Christians; and he had attempted to desecrate the Temple at Jerusalem. The deputies corroborated the indictment; and then the Procurator nodded to the Apostle, and the latter replied.

The Apostle's defence.

His defence was prefaced by no flattering exordium, nor would the omission impair its effectiveness, since Felix would duly appreciate the hollow sycophancy of the Jewish delegates. He simply expressed the satisfaction which he sincerely felt in pleading his cause before one who after five years' experience was accurately acquainted with Jewish questions; and then he proceeded to deal with the indictment. As for the charge of sedition-mongering, it was palpably absurd. It was only twelve days since he had entered Jerusalem;[1] and what was the record of the six days which he had spent there? He had never harangued the people either in the Temple-court or in the Synagogue or in the street. It was indeed true that he was a Christian,

[1] Append. I, p. 657.

but that involved no disloyalty to his ancestral Faith. On the contrary, he held by the Scriptures and cherished the hope of the Resurrection, which his accusers, at all events the Pharisees, themselves avowed. His loyalty to the Faith was as unimpeachable as theirs, and it was attested by the errand which, after years of absence, had brought him to Jerusalem. He had come on a mission of charity, conveying alms for the poor Jews; and when the cry of desecration was raised against him by some Asian Jews in the Temple-court, he was actually engaged in the discharge of a legal vow. And in his trial before the Sanhedrin he had been convicted of no wrong. His solitary offence, as he now frankly confessed, was his impulsive provocation of the mutual antagonism of his judges.

Adjournment of the case.

Felix knew enough of the sentiment of his province to recognise that the Jews were actuated merely by their notorious hostility to the harmless sect of the Christians. He should have dismissed the Apostle forthwith; but experience had rendered him suspicious of seditious designs, and he determined to adjourn the case and detain the prisoner in custody until he had an opportunity of conferring with Lysias. Evidently, like all the Roman officials who had to do with Paul, he was attracted to him; and he directed that, instead of being remanded to his cell, he should be granted the indulgence of *libera custodia*, enjoying superior fare and the society and ministration of such friends as might choose to visit him.

Paul's interview with Felix and Drusilla.

The case had naturally a peculiar interest for the lady Drusilla.[1] She was herself a Jewess, and she was curious to see this Jew who had created so much stir and hear something of his novel doctrine from his own lips. To gratify her the Apostle was summoned into the presence of the sinful pair, and he faced them undismayed. He first proclaimed his Gospel of Faith in Christ Jesus, and then, after the fashion of a Hebrew prophet, he spoke home to their consciences, discoursing of 'righteousness, self-control, and the future judgment.' The Procurator's guilty soul quailed and shuddered. It was the first time, perhaps, that he had ever

[1] xxiv. 24 Syr$^{p\ mg}$: 'she asked to see Paul and to hear his word. Therefore, wishing to content her, he sent for Paul.'

been so confronted by his sin, and it might have proved the turning-point in his career; but he stifled the divine impulse. 'For the present,' he said, 'go, and when I get an opportunity, I shall summon you.'

His prolonged detention.

And he did summon the Apostle again, but in the meantime he had hardened his heart. He shared that lust for gold which so often disgraced the imperial administration of the provinces; and he had conceived the idea of extorting a bribe from the prisoner as the price of his release. It was indeed no unreasonable expectation; for not only was Paul liberally befriended in his captivity by the Christians of Cæsarea but it would seem that he had brought with him some little store of money. It is likely that he had been well provided by the penitent Corinthians on his departure from their midst. At all events he had the means of hiring the vessel which conveyed him and his company from Troas to Patara and also for defraying the Temple-charges of the four Nazirites on his arrival at Jerusalem. It was indeed no large store, and it soon dwindled away; but it was sufficient to excite the Procurator's cupidity, and he detained the prisoner and frequently summoned him into his presence and conferred with him.

Cf. Phil. iv. 10-20.

His employments.

Thus vexatiously the days passed and lengthened into months until two years had elapsed. It was a weary time, and the heart of the Apostle, daily expectant of release and daily disappointed, must have sickened with hope deferred. And his ardent spirit must have fretted at his enforced inactivity. That long space is a blank in the narrative of his ministry. There is no extant letter which he wrote from Cæsarea; nor is it recorded that he won a single convert in the garrison of the Prætorium. Yet it is incredible that the two years should have passed idly. He would fain indeed have been prosecuting his mission and achieving his cherished dream of visiting Rome and carrying the Gospel to the western limit of Europe; but he would not neglect the lesser employments which lay to his hand. He would be mindful of his Churches; and, though none have survived, he would write many a letter of counsel and encouragement. Luke was with him to serve as his amanuensis; nor would there be lacking among the friends who visited him at the Prætorium,

Cf. Rom. xv. 23, 24.

Cf. 2 Cor. xi. 28.

willing hands to perform this and kindred offices on his behalf. And he would be very busy with the Holy Scriptures, searching them and meditating on them and finding in them ever fresh testimonies to the Gospel of salvation in Christ Jesus. In truth his chamber would be no prison but a study, a school of Christ, an house of prayer.

Cf. xxvi. 24.

Accession of Festus.

It was in the year 59 that his captivity ended.[1] Felix was recalled from the Procuratorship of Judæa, and Porcius Festus was appointed in his room.[2] It would have been well for the departing tyrant to dismiss the prisoner and thus cover up the wrong he had done by detaining him in the hope of gaining a bribe; but that might have involved him in a worse embarrassment. The Jews were bitter against him for his many cruelties, and it would have intensified their exasperation had he released their victim. And so of the two risks he preferred the lesser, and in the hope of conciliating the Jews he left the Apostle still a prisoner.

Resumption of the case.

It appears from the little that is recorded of him that Festus was a prudent and honourable man, and in happier circumstances he might have proved a successful ruler. But he was charged with an impossible task. His province, always a seething hotbed of bigotry, faction, and intrigue, had been inflamed by his predecessor's maladministration, and within two years he died of despair. On his accession, however, he faced the ordeal hopefully, in the fond belief that justice and generosity would prevail. Cæsarea was his seat of government, but Jerusalem was the Sacred Capital; and, anxious to demonstrate his friendliness toward his tumultuous subjects, he betook himself thither three days after his accession. Immediately he found himself involved in a characteristic web of intrigue. The Jewish authorities were as bitter as ever against Paul, and they begged that the Procurator would have the prisoner conveyed to Jerusalem and forthwith pass sentence on him. Their design was to execute the plot which had been baulked two years previously and have him assassinated in the course of the journey; and perhaps they had their gang still in readiness despite the oath of the ruffians that they would neither eat

[1] Cf. Append. I.

[2] Cf. Jos. *Ant.* XX. viii. 9-11; *De Bell. Jud.* II. xiv. 1.

nor drink until they had killed Paul, for absolution from such a vow was easily obtained.[1] Festus was shrewd enough to suspect a sinister purpose, and he courteously refused their request on the ground that there was no time. He must return to Cæsarea in little over a week ; but they might send thither with him a deputation to prosecute the case, and he would dispose of it without delay.

Appeal to Cæsar.

They agreed, and a deputation accompanied him to Cæsarea. The day after their arrival the trial was instituted. The Apostle was arraigned on the old charges of heresy, sacrilege, and treason, and he repudiated them. The question could be decided only by taking evidence ; and Festus, a stranger to Jewish institutions and customs, recognised his incompetence to deal with it. It was a question for a Jewish court ; and, anxious to win the confidence of the Jewish rulers and at the same time do justice to the prisoner, he suggested that the case should be referred to the Sanhedrin, with himself as assessor. It seemed to him a reasonable proposal ; and indeed it would have been the best possible procedure had the Sanhedrin been an impartial tribunal. He did not know its actual disposition, but Paul knew it. He remembered how he had fared in the Hall of Hewn Stone in the time of Felix, and he would not consent to a repetition of the outrage. He was entitled to a fair trial ; and since he had no chance of obtaining it under a Procurator ignorant of the Jewish machinations, he claimed a privilege which was his hereditary prerogative. He was a Roman citizen ; and it was the right of a Roman citizen, if he were dissatisfied with the procedure of a subordinate tribunal, to enter his protest and appeal to the Emperor's judgment. Paul availed himself of his privilege : 'I appeal to Cæsar.'

Cf. xxv. 8.

Sanctioned by the Procurator.

It was an unexpected *dénouement*, and it unpleasantly surprised the Procurator. The challenging of his first administrative act would prejudice him in the eyes of the

[1] Cf. *Hieros. Abod. Zar.* xl. 1 : 'For one who has vowed that he will abstain from food, woe if he eat, woe if he do not eat. If he eat, he sins against his vow ; if he do not eat, he sins against his life. What must he do here? Let him go to the wise, and they will absolve him from his vow, as it is written : "The tongue of the wise is health" (Prov. xii. 18).'

imperial government; and in the hope of averting this embarrassment he turned to his assessors [1] and held a hasty consultation with them. It did not lie with a magistrate to refuse an appeal to the Emperor; and the only question was whether the appeal was valid. Apparently it was the first intimation Festus had received that Paul was a Roman citizen; and once he was assured of it, he could do nothing but allow the appeal: 'You have appealed to Cæsar; to Cæsar you will go.'

State-visit of Agrippa and Bernice. Cf. xxv. 26.

It only remained for Festus to despatch the prisoner to the Imperial Capital; but certain preliminaries were necessary, particularly the preparation of an official report for submission to the Emperor. And this was a difficult task for the Procurator, ignorant as he was alike of previous proceedings and of the true issues. His perplexity, however, was presently resolved. His main reason for abridging his sojourn at Jerusalem had been that he expected a state-visit from his neighbour, King Herod Agrippa II.[2] This potentate was the son of Herod Agrippa I who figures at an earlier stage in the history of the Book of Acts. He was a great-grandson of King Herod the Great, the tyrant of Judæa in the days when our Lord was born at Bethlehem, and a brother of Drusilla, the sinful spouse of Felix. On the death of Herod the Great his kingdom had been apportioned between his three sons, who ruled under the title of tetrarchs; but in the year 37 A.D. the Emperor Caligula restored the regal title to his grandson, who thenceforth ruled as King Herod Agrippa I over the tetrarchies of Philip and Lysanias, comprising Batanæa, Trachonitis, Gaulanitis, and Abilene. His son, Herod Agrippa II, inherited his dominion, and Nero added to it a large part of Galilee and Peræa. He was a mere puppet, reigning by grace of the Emperor and deferring to his master with servile submissiveness. His character was weak and indolent, and he was freely charged with the vilest of moral infamy. His widowed sister Bernice resided with him in his palace at Cæsarea Philippi, and they were credited with the maintenance of incestuous intercourse.[3]

Cf. xii. 1-3, 19-23.

Cf. Lk. iii. 1.

[1] Cf. Schürer, *Jewish People*, I. ii. p. 60.

[2] Cf. Jos. *Ant.* XIX. ix-XX. ix.

[3] Cf. Jos. *Ant.* XX. vii. 3; Juv. VI. 156-60.

Nevertheless—such moral mixtures will the human heart contain—he was an ardent devotee of the Jewish religion. And Bernice shared his devotion; at all events, it is recorded of her that she once assumed the Nazirite vow.[1]

Agrippa's interest in Paul. In due course Agrippa and Bernice arrived with their retinue. Their errand was to greet the new Procurator. It was a state function, and the city was *en fête*. It was an opportunity for Festus to ingratiate himself with his subjects; and he made the most of it, receiving the native prince with courteous observance and inviting representatives from all parts of the province.[2] The visit extended over a good many days, and in the course of it he took occasion to confer with Agrippa on the perplexing case which his predecessor had bequeathed to him. He narrated the circumstances, and Agrippa's interest was aroused. He had heard of Paul, and had been wishing to hear him. Festus grasped at the hint. 'To-morrow,' he said, 'you will hear him.' Agrippa was a Jew, and it would clarify the situation if he conducted an examination of the prisoner in the Procurator's presence.

Paul's appearance before him. Next day the royal party, with all the glitter of military and civic pomp, was ushered into the audience-hall of the Prætorium. The prisoner was introduced, and after a statement of the case by Festus the King granted him permission to speak. He began with his characteristic gesture and, addressing Agrippa, avowed his satisfaction in laying his defence before one so intimately versed in Jewish affairs.

His statement. His defence was a personal narrative. His antecedents, he claimed, were notorious, especially the fact that at the outset of his career he had been a Pharisee of the strictest order. Nor had he since proved recreant. The historic faith of Israel was the hope of the Messiah's Advent and the Resurrection of the Dead; and it was for his advocacy of this hope that he was arraigned. One difference indeed there was. He had seen that hope's fulfilment; he had recognised in Jesus of Nazareth the Promised Saviour. And he proceeded to show how he had attained that momentous assurance. It had been forced upon him. The name of Jesus

[1] Cf. Jos. *De Bell. Jud.* II. xv. I.

[2] In xxv. 23 Syr$^{p\ mg}$ mentions, with the military officers and magnates of Cæsarea, 'those who had come down from the province.'

had at first been abhorrent to him; and by authority of the Sanhedrin he had instituted a ruthless persecution of His followers. He had harried them in Jerusalem and pursued them to the neighbouring cities; and it was at the very height of his fury that he had been arrested. He was on the way to Damascus, urging the pursuit, when he had an awful vision of Jesus, risen and glorified, and received from His lips the commission to proclaim His salvation to Jews and Gentiles. From that hour he had obeyed the heavenly vision; and that was the reason why the Jews had arrested him. He was no heretic. His Gospel of a Suffering Messiah, whose Resurrection had illumined the darkness for Jew and Gentile, was no novel invention; it had been foreshadowed by the Prophets and Moses.

The Procurator's astonishment.

It is merely a summary that the historian has furnished of the Apostle's defence; but even so it is a moving argument, and what would be its effect upon the audience beholding his rapt look and thrilled by his impassioned tones as the torrent of eloquence poured from his lips? It was the first that Festus had ever heard of the miracle of Christian faith, and it amazed him. He was a shrewd, practical, unimaginative Roman, and the idea crossed his mind that the nervous, studious prisoner, whose cell was littered with volumes, was a crazed idealist. As he listened, he forgot his surroundings; and when the flood of eloquence ceased, he cried out: 'You are mad, Paul! Your great learning is turning you mad.'[1] 'No,' answered the Apostle, 'I am not mad, Festus your Excellency. They are words of truth and sanity that I am uttering.'

Appeal to Agrippa.

And then he appealed to Agrippa. The facts which he had stated were notorious. They were familiar to every Jew, and Agrippa, being a Jew, was aware of them. 'King Agrippa,' he said, 'do you believe the Prophets? I know that you do.' Agrippa perceived his intention. He was about to clinch the argument and drive it home: 'You admit that my Gospel is approved by the Scriptures? Then, as a faithful Jew, you must accept it.' It was an embarrassing predicament for the King. He was indeed impressed, but he must at all hazards maintain his submission to the

[1] Like the minister of St. Ronan's, 'just dung donnart wi' learning.'

imperial government, and he durst not commit himself in presence of the Procurator after the latter's unflattering pronouncement. He writhed and feebly protested against thus being driven into a corner : 'You are for persuading me by a short argument to become a Christian.'[1] 'Would to God,' was the reply, 'that, by a short argument or a long one, not only you but all my hearers to-day became such as I am, apart from these bonds !'

This ended the proceedings. The great personages and their train withdrew and discussed the case. They agreed that the prisoner was guilty of no crime ; and Agrippa's verdict was that he might have been released if he had not appealed to the Emperor.

The Apostle pronounced innocent.

[1] ἐν ὀλίγῳ με πείθεις (ℵBEHLP) Χριστιανὸν γενέσθαι (EHLP, Vulg.). The only question here regards the meaning of ἐν ὀλίγῳ. A.V. renders 'almost,' making Agrippa confess himself on the verge of conversion. But 'almost' (*propemodum*) would be ὀλίγου or παρ' ὀλίγον. ἐν ὀλίγῳ can only mean either (1) 'in brief,' 'by a short argument,' sc. λόγῳ (cf. Eph. iii. 3), or (2) 'in a short time,' sc. χρόνῳ (cf. Plat. *Apol.* 22 B). In the latter sense it would be a sneer : 'It will take you longer than you imagine to persuade me to turn Christian.' For γενέσθαι ℵAB read ποιῆσαι. This could only mean 'in a little' (whether 'in a short time' or 'by a short argument') 'you are persuading me, so as to make me a Christian,' which R.V., with questionable legitimacy, paraphrases 'with but little persuasion thou wouldest fain make me a Christian.' If ποιῆσαι be accepted, it is then necessary to read πείθῃ (A) for πείθεις, 'you are confident of making me a Christian' ; but γενέσθαι is attested by its occurrence in Paul's echo of Agrippa's words (ver. 29).

THE VOYAGE TO ROME

Ac. xxvii-xxviii. 15.

The prisoner despatched to Rome. It was now the close of July 59,[1] and nothing remained but to despatch the Apostle to Rome. Several other prisoners were to be transported with him, probably condemned criminals destined to play their part as *bestiarii*, fighting with wild beasts in the circus for the entertainment of the populace;[2] and they were consigned to a military guard, a detachment of the Augustan or Imperial Cohort. This was a corps attached to each provincial legion and charged, like the *Frumentarii* at a later date, with the duty of communicating between the Emperor and his forces abroad, especially in the way of conveying despatches and escorting prisoners. They were known at Rome as the *Peregrini* or 'soldiers from abroad,' and during their visits to the Capital they were quartered in the *Castra Peregrinorum* on the Cælian Hill adjacent to the imperial residence on the Palatine.[3] A ship belonging to the Mysian port of Adramyttium was in the harbour of Cæsarea, preparing to set sail on a trading voyage along the coast of the Province of Asia; and the intention apparently was that she should convey the prisoners and their escort to the busy port of Ephesus, where they would be likely to find a ship bound for Rome; or, failing this, they might proceed with her to Adramyttium, whence they would sail to Neapolis and march by the Egnatian Road to Dyrrachium.

Attended by Luke and Aristarchus. It would have been a distressing experience for the Apostle had he been obliged, during the long voyage, to herd

[1] Cf. Append. I.

[2] Cf. note on 1 Cor. iv. 9, p. 254.

[3] Cf. Ramsay, *St. Paul the Traveller*, pp. 315, 348. The σπεῖρα Σεβαστή is otherwise explained as a cohort of Sebastenes, originally levied under Herod the Great at Sebaste or Samaria and now incorporated with the imperial army (cf. Schürer, *Jewish People*, I. ii. pp. 51 ff.). But the designation would then be σπεῖρα Σεβαστηνῶν.

with that gang of desperadoes; but he was spared this ignominy. He would hardly have been subjected to it in any case, since he was no condemned criminal, but a Roman citizen going to plead his cause before the Emperor; and it appears, moreover, that he enjoyed a certain distinction. He was accompanied by Luke and Aristarchus.[1] It seems strange that their presence should have been permitted, and the explanation is suggested by a story which Pliny tells [2] of Arria, the heroic wife of the Stoic Thrasea Pætus. Her husband was being conveyed a prisoner from Illyricum to Rome, and at the embarkation she vainly entreated that she might accompany him. 'You will give a man of consular rank,' she pleaded, 'some attendants to serve his food, to attire him, to put on his sandals: I will singly perform every office.' Thus it appears that, though he might not take friends with him, a prisoner might have attendants; and it was doubtless in this capacity that those two devoted followers accompanied the Apostle. His health was broken by all that he had recently undergone, and Luke would go with him as his physician and Aristarchus as his servant. Their attendance would lend him dignity and procure him exceptional consideration; and from the outset he was courteously treated by Julius, the centurion in command of the convoy.

Course to Myra.

It would be August ere the ship set sail. She had to call at Sidon, some seventy miles north of Cæsarea, to complete her lading, and during her stay there Julius allowed Paul the privilege of going ashore and enjoying among the Christians of that great Phœnician city the attention which his infirmity required.[3] From Sidon their direct course lay west-north-west to the island of Rhodes, but at that season the wind in the Levant blows steadily from the west, and working to windward was impossible for an ancient ship with her single mast amidships and one huge square sail. And so she steered northward with the wind a-beam under the lee of Cyprus, until she fetched Cilicia; and then, availing

[1] The historian's presence is indicated by the use of the first pers. pronoun 'we' throughout the narrative.

[2] *Epist.* III. 16.

[3] ἐπιμέλεια (xxvii. 3) is one of Luke's medical terms. Cf. Hobart, *Med. Lang. of St. Luke*, pp. 269 f.

herself of the land-breezes and the current which there sets steadily westward,[1] crept along the southern coast of Asia Minor for fifteen days [2] until she gained the port of Myra in Cilicia.

Transhipment.

There Julius had the good fortune, as he deemed it, to find a large ship hailing from Alexandria and bound for
Cf. xxvii. 38. Italy with a cargo of corn, and he put his convoy on board
of her. Egypt was the chief granary of the Empire, and the ships which conveyed to the Capital the immense supplies which its teeming populace required, were numerous and large. Lucian [3] has furnished a minute description of one named 'The Isis' which was driven into the Piræus by stress of weather, and which amazed the Athenians by her enormous dimensions. Her length was a hundred and eighty feet, her breadth forty-five, and the depth of her hold forty-three and a half. Her crew was like a camp, and her cargo, it was said, would have fed all Attica for a year. 'The Isis' indeed was a marvel for size, and this ship would be smaller; still she was a large vessel, and it is some indication of her dimensions that, when they were all on
Cf. xxvii. 37. board, she carried, besides her cargo, a complement of
two hundred and seventy-six.

Wind-bound at Fair Havens.

From Myra the ship crept a hundred and forty miles along the coast until she cleared it abreast of Cnidus and lost the aid of the land-breeze and the current. Unable to cross the Ægean in face of the westerly wind she held southward to Crete, and, rounding Cape Salmone, the eastern extremity of the island, crept along the southern coast to Fair Havens, a bay still bearing the same name five or six miles to the east of Cape Matala and close to the town of Lasæa.[4] It was impossible meanwhile to proceed farther, since on passing Cape Matala the ship would be exposed to the westerly wind. She fretted at her moorings 'for a considerable time'; and at length, when the first week of October had passed,[5] the situation grew serious, since navigation was dangerous after the autumnal equinox and

[1] Cf. Smith, *Voyage and Shipwreck of St. Paul*, pp. 68 f.

[2] After διαπλεύσαντες (xxvii. 5) 112, 137, Syr^{p} add δι' ἡμερῶν δεκάπεντε.

[3] *Navig. seu Vot.*

[4] Cf. Smith, *Voyage and Shipwreck*, Append. I.

[5] Cf. Append. I.

would be entirely suspended by the winter storms from November 11 to February 8.[1]

Departure for winterage at Phœnix. Cf. 2 Cor. xi. 25.

Accordingly a council was held, and Paul, as an experienced traveller who had thrice been shipwrecked, was admitted to it. The owner of the ship and the sailing master were of course present, but Julius, though a military officer, presided over the deliberations, since the ship was in the service of the imperial government. The Apostle perceived the danger of putting to sea, and strongly advised that they should remain at Fair Havens; but the owner and the sailing master opposed him. Fair Havens was a poor harbour for wintering in, and they recommended shifting some fifty miles westward to Phœnix, the modern Lutro, a land-locked bay facing east and confronted by an island which formed a natural breakwater.[2] There the ship would have lain secure whatever wind might blow.

A N.E. gale.

It was a seamanlike course, and Julius naturally approved of it. And it seemed to justify his decision that the wind opportunely veered round and blew gently from the south. If it held, the ship on rounding Cape Matala would have the breeze over her port quarter, and would make Phœnix easily and swiftly. It occasioned, however, a preliminary difficulty that the Cape jutted southward, and it seemed doubtful whether the cumbrous craft could lie sufficiently close to the wind to weather it. She came perilously near the rocks,[3] and the life-boat had been lowered and was towing astern in case of need; but she contrived to scrape past, and then eased off and steered W.N.W. across the Gulf of Messara. She had not proceeded far when a terrific tempest burst upon her. It was the Euraquilo,[4] a tearing nor'-easter,

[1] Cf. Append. I, p. 648.

[2] *βλέποντα κατὰ λίβα καὶ κατὰ χῶρον* (xxvii. 12), 'looking down the south-west wind and down the north-west wind,' in the directions towards which these winds blew, *i.e.* north-eastward and south-eastward. The island lay across the mouth of the bay, and thus there were—from the view-point of a ship at anchor within—two exits, one to the north-east and the other to the south-east. On weighing anchor and setting sail, she would run either 'down the south-west wind' or 'down the north-west wind.' [3] xxvii. 13: *ἆσσον παρελέγοντο τὴν Κρήτην*.

[4] *εὐρακύλων* ℵAB*, 'north-east wind,' compounded of *εὖρος*, 'east wind,' and Lat. *aquilo*, 'north wind.' The variants *εὐροκλύδων*, 'east wind wave,' and *εὐρυκλύδων*, 'broad wave,' are meaningless corruptions. Cf. *εὐρόνοτος*, 'south-east wind.'

the dread of seamen in those parts; and it smote the ship on the starboard side, and she had to pay off and drive before it. The strain of the huge sail was severe, and there was danger of the timbers starting and the ship foundering; but fortunately there lay some thirty miles to leeward the islet of Clauda, and, running under its shelter, the crew were able to make her snug. They brought her head to wind, and got the swamped small-boat on board; then they 'frapped' the ship, passing cables under her keel and binding them round her hull to hold her together; and finally they lowered the great sail with its heavy yard, and 'hove her to' under a storm-sail. Their only other resource would have been to let her scud before the tempest under short canvas; but this would have been rushing to destruction, since right to leeward, at a distance of between three and four hundred miles, lay the dreaded quicksands of the Syrtis off the African coast. The sole remedy therefore was to 'heave her to' and ride out the gale.

Ship 'hove to' under the lee of Clauda.

Driving westward.

It had caught her on the starboard side as she was crossing the Gulf of Messara, and it was on the starboard tack that she now lay heading it under Clauda. So situated, she kept drifting astern but always forging northward, and thus she was carried almost due westward. The sea grew ever wilder, and the leaky ship laboured heavily. There was imminent danger of her sinking under them; and so next day the crew lightened her of all superfluous lumber, and the following day, by the united effort of all hands, 'flung the gear' overboard, probably the huge sail-yard with its cumbrous tackle. Thus relieved, she rode more easily, but her condition remained parlous. Her strained timbers were leaking badly, and at any moment she might settle down. The only hope lay in running her ashore somewhere; but ever since the storm broke, the sky had been obscured by dense, black clouds and no reckoning could be taken. All hands were continually toiling at the pumps, and they had hardly tasted food; for cooking was impossible, and their provisions were soaked.

The Apostle's good cheer.

In their extremity Paul came to the rescue one morning, and heartened his despairing comrades with a brave reassurance. He reminded them that it was against his judgment that they had quitted Fair Havens, and the event had justified his counsel. Nevertheless there was no reason for despair. During the past night his God had vouchsafed him a revelation. An angel had assured him that his life would be preserved and he would undergo his trial before the Emperor; and they would all share his deliverance. The ship alone would perish: she would be cast on some island. In view of the Jewish manner of recognising the voice of God in His providential orderings [1] it is hardly reasonable to postulate here an actual angelophany. On board the storm-tossed ship as in his cell in the Castle at Jerusalem on the (Cf. xxiii. 11.) night after the scene in the Sanhedrin, his visiting Rome was an indubitable certainty in the Apostle's mind. It was ordained of God, and it must come to pass. Thus on that fearful night, as he considered his position, he was assured that he would not perish in the tempest. The ship was plainly doomed, but he would escape; and if he escaped, his fellow-voyagers would escape too.

Land discovered.

Whether they believed his assurance or not, it would appear that his prediction of the ship being cast on some island was not lost on the crew. They kept a vigilant outlook, and on the fourteenth night of the frail vessel's desperate battle with wind and wave they detected land under their lee. They could not see it, for it was midnight; but they heard the sullen boom of breakers, and perhaps, as they peered into the black darkness, they might descry the white spray dashing high. They took soundings, and found twenty fathoms; and presently, sounding again, they found only fifteen. Plainly they were driving down on a rock-bound coast, and their only hope was that there might be some creek into which they could steer the ship and beach her. The dawn would disclose their situation, and meanwhile they must stay the vessel's drift, lest she should strike in the darkness. They accordingly lowered four anchors.

Preparation for beaching.

They lowered them from the stern, thus letting her swing round head to land in readiness for running ashore. The ancient steering-gear consisted of two large paddles projecting from either quarter; and now that the ship was

[1] Cf. p. 122.

riding by the stern, they raised these and secured them with lashings. They would also lower the storm-sail which had hitherto kept her 'hove to'; and it seems that they also cut away the heavy mast. And thus they held on, eagerly expecting what the dawn would reveal.

Crew's attempt to abandon the ship.

It was a distressful situation, since the wallowing ship might founder at her anchors. At any moment a heavy sea might break over her poop and engulf her. The seamen were alive to the danger, and, evidently with the connivance of their officers, they resolved to desert the ship and take to the life-boat on the chance of getting ashore. They lowered the boat on the pretext of putting out an anchor at the bow. It was a transparent trick, since an anchor at the bow would have been useless; and Paul detected their base intention. He turned to Julius and told him that there was no chance of escape unless the sailors stood by the ship to execute the difficult manœuvre of beaching her; and the soldiers promptly cut the boat's hawser and let her go adrift.

Cf. xxvii. 40.

Paul rallies his comrades.

At that anxious crisis Paul was the one 'still, strong man,' and he realised the expediency of rallying his panic-stricken comrades and bracing them for the final ordeal. All those terrible days they had eaten little, and, as they crouched on the wave-swept deck, he counselled them to take some food. It would be their last meal on board the doomed ship, and there was no longer any necessity for sparing their scanty provision. And he set the example. He took a piece of bread, and after the Christian fashion which turned every common meal into a sacramental feast, 'gave thanks and broke it and ate.' The whole company joined with him, and their spirits rose. The sullen mariners resumed their duties. The less the ship's draught the higher would she drive on the beach and the better the chance of escape; and so they set to work and lightened her by throwing her cargo of grain overboard.

Cf. 1 Cor. xi. 24.

The island of Melita.

Presently the dawn broke, and the prospect opened to their wistful gaze. They saw an island under their lee. It was Melita, the modern Malta; [1] but none of them, not even

[1] There was another Melita, the modern Meleda, in the Adriatic Gulf off the coast of Dalmatia; and it has been maintained (cf. Coleridge, *Table Talk*, August 18, 1832) that this was the scene of the shipwreck. The reasons alleged

the sailors, recognised it, since it was off the course which they were accustomed to steer in making the voyage to Rome. To the left lay a rocky headland, the Point of Koura, where the sea was breaking with that thunderous roar which had been booming in their ears all night. But right ahead was a deep bay with a fringe of smooth sand excellently adapted for beaching the ship. It was a welcome sight, and they hastened to avail themselves of the opportunity. They unlashed the rudders, and, since the mast was gone, set the little foresail which, in its normal use, served to facilitate the operation of putting the ship about by making her 'pay off' on the other tack after she had been brought head to wind.[1] Then they slipped the anchors, and the ship bore down toward the beach.

All safely landed.

Ere she reached it, she ran on a sunken reef.[2] The stern was battered to pieces by the terrific impact of the pursuing billows, but the bow stuck fast in the soft clay. There was still a chance of escape, since the reef acted as a breakwater, and the sea betwixt it and the beach, though deep, was smooth, and it would be easy to swim or paddle ashore. It might have been expected that the common danger would

are: (1) The island was in the Adria (cf. ver. 27), and Malta lies close to Sicily in the open Mediterranean. But ὁ Ἀδρίας was not merely the gulf on the east of Italy; it included also the whole middle basin of the Mediterranean. The geographer Ptolemy distinguishes 'the Adrian Gulf' (Ἀδρίας κόλπος), which bounds Italy on the east, and 'the Adriatic Sea' (Ἀδριατικὸν πέλαγος), which bounds it on the south, and also bounds Sicily on the east, the Peloponnesus on the west and south, and Crete on the west. (2) The inhabitants are termed 'barbarians' (xxviii. 2), whereas the Maltese were highly civilised. But βάρβαρος means simply 'a foreigner.' Cf. n. on Rom. i. 14, p. 380. (3) There are no vipers (xxviii. 3) in Malta. But the extinction of noxious creatures is nothing uncommon. Cf. Smith, *Voyage and Shipwreck*, pp. 150 ff.

[1] ὁ ἀρτέμων (xxvii. 40), not 'the mainsail' (A.V.), but 'the foresail' (R.V.), set on a little mast over the prow. In his description of the shipwreck of his friend Catullus, Juvenal (XII. 69) tells how the mast was cut away during the storm, and then, when it abated, 'the wretched prow ran before the wind with a poor device of clothes outspread and its own sail, the only one remaining' (*et, quod superaverat unum, velo prora suo*); where the scholiast annotates: *artemone solo velificarunt*, 'they sailed with the *artemon* only.'

[2] τόπος διαθάλασσος (ver. 41), 'a place dividing the sea.' '*Tæniam* intelligit, quales multæ solent esse non procul a littore, ita tamen ut inter eas et littus mare interluat' (Grot.). Thus Dion Chrysostom (V. 9) speaks of the shoals of the Syrtis as βραχέα καὶ διαθάλαττα καὶ ταινίαι μακραὶ making the sea impassable (ἄπορον).

have established a bond of brotherhood between the hapless castaways; but self-preservation is a strong and pitiless instinct, and just as the sailors had attempted to take to the boat and desert their comrades, so now the soldiers planned a still worse brutality. The Roman law held them answerable with their lives for the safe delivery of their prisoners,[1] and they proposed to butcher the wretched gang lest they should swim ashore and make off. Julius would have agreed but that Paul would have been included in the massacre. His respect and affection had been enlisted by the Apostle's bearing throughout that terrible fortnight; and for his sake he prohibited the atrocity, and directed that such as could swim should plunge in and strike out for the shore, and that the others should construct rafts of the wreckage. And presently all the two hundred and seventy-six were safe on the beach.

Kindly islanders.

Luke in his Greek manner calls the islanders 'barbarians,' meaning not that they were savages but merely that they were not Greeks.[2] Melita was originally a Phœnician settlement; subsequently it passed under Greek dominion; but since 218 B.C. it had belonged to Rome and was included in the Province of Sicily. The inhabitants were thus highly civilised. Their language would be the Common Greek, the *lingua franca* of the Empire.[3] And, albeit heathen and superstitious, they were a kindly folk. All in the vicinity had trooped down to the beach on espying a ship in peril; and they helped the castaways ashore and entreated them humanely. 'They afforded us,' says Luke, 'uncommon philanthropy'; and it is remarkable that the word occurs
xxvii. 3. but thrice in the New Testament—once of the kindness which Julius, a Roman soldier, showed his prisoner; here of the kindness of those heathen to the shipwrecked voyagers;
Tit. iii. 4. and again of the kindness which God has manifested in Christ to sinful man. It would be the beginning of November,[4] and the castaways were shivering in the biting north-east blast and the driving rain. There was no immediate refuge for so many, since the town of Melita stood inland, remote from the scene of the shipwreck; but the

[1] Cf. p. 133.
[2] Cf. n. on Rom. i. 14, p. 380.
[3] Cf. pp. 7 f.
[4] Cf. Append. I.

islanders kindled a bonfire [1] in some sheltered nook, and warmed and fed the forlorn strangers.

Here an incident occurred which afforded Paul a golden opportunity. In that spirit of self-forgetfulness which he had displayed on board the doomed ship, he employed himself in gathering a faggot of brushwood, and he was putting it on the fire when a viper which had lodged in it fastened on his hand. The islanders expected to see him drop dead, and in their superstitious fashion concluded that he was a criminal overtaken by vengeance. But ere the half-numbed reptile had struck its fangs into his flesh, he calmly shook it off into the fire, and was none the worse. It was an entirely natural occurrence ; but it seemed a miracle to the islanders and, like the folk of Lystra, they now concluded that he was a god. Forthwith he was invested with sanctity in their eyes, and hence a substantial benefit presently accrued. Hard by lay the estate of Publius, the chief magistrate or, as the native title was, 'the Primate' of the island,[2] and he invited the Apostle and his attendants, Luke and Aristarchus, to his residence until they should procure a lodging of their own.

The chief magistrate's entertainment of Paul and his companions.

Ac. xiv. 11.

His gracious hospitality was richly rewarded. His father was prostrate with a malady which Luke, with professional accuracy, defines as dysentery with intermittent fever ; [3] and the Apostle was introduced into his chamber, and after praying by his couch laid his hands on him, as the Master had been wont, and healed him. The miracle was a proclamation of the Gospel. Paul indeed wrought it, but he wrought it in the name of Christ and ere working it he openly invoked Christ's aid. The wonderful story spread over the island, and from near and far the sick repaired to the house of Publius and were healed. Their gratitude was boundless.

Healing of his father.

Cf. Lk. iv. 40, xiii. 13.

[1] πυρά, in 1 Macc. xii. 28 'a camp-fire.'

[2] ὁ πρῶτος τῆς νήσου. The plur. (οἱ πρῶτοι) is frequent in the sense of 'the principal men' of a place or community (cf. xiii. 50, xxv. 2, xxviii. 17), but the sing. is never so used. Nor could Publius have been called 'the principal man of the island' while his father was still alive unless in a public or official capacity; and it appears from two inscriptions found at Citta Vecchia, the ancient Melita, that ὁ πρῶτος was an official appellation. Cf. Lewin, *Fast. Sacr.*, 1901.

[3] The plur. πυρετοί is a technical medical term. Cf. Hobart, *Med. Lang. of St. Luke*, p. 52.

They compassed Paul and his companions with observances and loaded them with benefactions. Their generosity was opportune. It would enlarge the Apostle's scanty store and furnish him and his companions for the months which they must pass on the island. It enabled him to procure a lodging and remove thither after a sojourn of only three days under Publius' hospitable roof.

Voyage to Italy.

It happened that another Alexandrian corn-ship, named 'The Twin Brothers' after Castor and Pollux, the patrons of seamen, had been stayed in her passage and had found in the island a safe winter-harbour; and it was arranged that she should carry Julius and his convoy to Italy. On February 8 navigation was resumed, and Paul embarked with his companions laden with parting gifts from the grateful people. The ship set sail, and a favouring breeze sped her on her course as far as Syracuse. There the wind headed her, and she was forced to put into the anchorage. After she had lain for three days it veered to the north-west, and she managed by dint of tacking to fetch Rhegium; but, unable for lack of sea-room to beat through the Strait of Messina, she lay there for twenty-four hours. Then the wind set in from the south, and she ran directly and swiftly on her course. Within twenty-four hours she reached her destination, the port of Puteoli on the Bay of Naples.

Sojourn at Puteoli and progress to Rome.

Puteoli was the principal harbour in the south of Italy; and, though over a hundred miles distant from Rome, it was the regular port of the Egyptian corn-ships.[1] There they unladed, and there the passengers disembarked and proceeded to the Capital by the Appian Road.[2] The Apostle and his company did not set out immediately. Julius had to communicate his arrival to his superior officer and await instructions regarding the disposal of his prisoners; and meanwhile they were detained at Puteoli.[3] The detention

[1] Cf. Sen. *Epist.* lxxvii.

[2] On his journey from Alexandria the Emperor Titus followed the Apostle's route. Cf. Suet. *Tit.* 5: 'Festinans in Italiam, cum Rhegium, deinde Puteolos oneraria nave appulisset, Romam inde contendit expeditissimus.'

[3] In xxviii. 14 the chief authorities have ἐπιμεῖναι, 'we were besought (by the brothers) to remain among them.' But it was Julius and not Paul who had the ordering of the march, and thus the variant ἐπιμείναντες is inevitable: 'having found brothers, we remained among them for seven days and were comforted.'

was grateful to Paul; for he was unnerved by his rough experience, and his heart was troubled as the supreme ordeal approached. In a city so important as Puteoli and so intimately connected with the Capital there was naturally a community of Christians. They were unapprised of the advent of the famous Apostle; but he searched them out,[1] and was received with warm kindness. It comforted him and his companions; and after a week's sojourn among those sympathetic friends they started on their march. Tidings of his approach had reached Rome, and the Christians hastened out to meet him. They had never seen his face, but they had heard his fame and they had read the great encyclical which he had sent them from Corinth three years previously. One contingent encountered him at Appii Forum and a second at Tres Tabernæ, and their welcome was like a royal ovation.[2] It dispelled his misgivings. It showed him that the appeal of his encyclical had not fallen on deaf ears and that the hearts of the Roman Christians were open to him. 'He thanked God and took courage.'

[1] *εὑρόντες*, cf. xxi. 4.
[2] *εἰς ἀπάντησιν*, cf. p. 130.

THE FIRST IMPRISONMENT AT ROME

Arrival at at Rome.

ON reaching Rome Julius marched his gang of prisoners to the *Castra Peregrinorum* on the Cælian Hill, and handed them over to the commander, the *Princeps Peregrinorum*.[1] Paul, however, doubtless on the ground of the report of Festus and the testimony which Julius would bear to his behaviour during the terrible voyage, was accorded a welcome privilege. He was allowed to reside outside the barracks, apparently in the house of some hospitable Christian,[2] in the enjoyment of comparative freedom. He was not indeed suffered to stir abroad, and he was linked by the wrist day and night to a military guard; but his attendants, Luke and Aristarchus, might go where they would, and visitors had unrestrained access to him.

Cf. xxviii. 20.

Hostile reception by the Jewish leaders.

Throughout his ministry his constant rule had been 'to the Jew, in the first instance, and to the Greek,'[3] and he pursued it on his arrival at Rome. He allowed himself only three days of much needed repose; and then, precluded from visiting the Synagogue, he invited the representatives of the Jewish community, probably the Rulers of the Synagogue, to wait upon him, and told them the story of his arrest, his imprisonment, and his appeal to the Emperor, affirming at the same time his loyalty to his people and the ancient Faith. They accorded his statement but a chill reception. No letter regarding him, they said, had been

[1] The Old Latin (Gig.) rendering of the term *στρατοπεδάρχης* in the sentence which HLP insert in ver. 16: *ὁ ἑκατόνταρχος παρέδωκε τοὺς δεσμίους τῷ στρατοπεδάρχῃ, τῷ δὲ Παύλῳ ἐπετράπη, κ.τ.λ.* Cf. p. 490.

[2] His abode is called a *ξενία* (ver. 23), which may signify either an inn (Suid.: *καταγώγιον, κατάλυμα*) or a hospitable lodging with a *ξένος* (cf. Rom. xvi. 23; Ac. xxi. 16). The latter seems most suitable in Phm. 22, the only instance of the term in N. T. In any case it was only a temporary accommodation, for he presently removed to a rented lodging.

[3] Cf. p. 83.

sent them from the Sanhedrin, nor had any evil report of him reached their ears; but they knew the hostility with which his sect was universally regarded, and therefore they must hear what his opinions were ere they could pronounce upon them. A day was fixed, and at an early hour they came to his abode in large numbers; and he expounded his Gospel to them, and right on to the evening adduced from the Scriptures testimonies to the Messiahship of Jesus. Some of his hearers were convinced, but others rejected his arguments; and when they fell a-wrangling, he announced that he must leave them alone and devote himself to the Gentiles.

The Emperor Nero:

It was thus that the Apostle's ambition to see Rome was realised; and if his fortunes were dark, those of the Imperial City were still darker. It was the sixth year of Nero's reign. Born on December 15, A.D. 37,[1] he had at the death of Claudius on October 13, 54, been acclaimed Emperor at the early age of seventeen.[2] Though the child of a wicked father, Cnæus Domitius Ahenobarbus, and a still more wicked mother, the younger Agrippina, who had plotted for his elevation to the throne and hesitated at no crime to attain her end,[3] his youth was rich in fair promise.

His early promise.

It won him the regard of the populace not only that his maternal grandparents were the good Germanicus and the elder Agrippina but that he had inherited from his infamous father the charm of physical beauty.[4] He was, moreover, singularly fortunate in possessing two wise counsellors.[5] One was his tutor, the Stoic philosopher, L. Annæus Seneca, brother of Gallio, that Proconsul of Achaia who had befriended Paul at Corinth in the year 52. And the other was Afranius Burrus, the Prefect of the Prætorian Guard, a distinguished soldier who exhibited in a degenerate age the ancient Roman austerity and rectitude.

[1] Suet. *Ner.* 6.

[2] Tac. *Ann.* XII. 69; Suet. *Ner.* 8. Lewin, *Fast. Sacr.*, 2066.

[3] When Domitius was congratulated on the birth of his son, he is said to have remarked that a child of himself and Agrippina could be nought but a thing of detestation and a public ill (Suet. *Ner.* 6). And it is told of Agrippina that she consulted the astrologers about Nero, and when they told her that he would be Emperor and kill his mother, she replied: 'Let him kill me, provided he is Emperor' (Tac. *Ann.* XIV. 9).

[4] Tac. *Ann.* XI. 11, 12.

[5] *Ibid.* XIII. 2.

Quinquennium Neronis.

Seneca and Burrus dominated the youthful Emperor, and his reign opened auspiciously. On his accession he declared his intention of reverting to the precedent of Augustus; and he made good his profession, on the testimony of his merciless biographer,[1] by 'omitting no opportunity of liberality, clemency, or courtesy.' He abolished or diminished the more oppressive taxes, repressed the malign activities of the informers,[2] and treated the Senate with respect while refusing the servile honours which it would have heaped upon him. He also ameliorated the administration of justice. Extreme penalties were rarely inflicted; and it is told how on one occasion when he was asked to sign a death-warrant, the young Emperor sighed: 'How I wish that I could not write!'

Subsequent reign of terror.

Such was the manner of Nero during the first five years of his reign; and it is no wonder that after forty years of atrocity under Tiberius, Caligula, and Claudius this benignant regime, the *quinquennium Neronis*, should have seemed a very age of gold and been wistfully remembered in the dark days which ensued.[3] It was, however, short-lived. It is said that Seneca was early aware of his pupil's latent ferocity, and would remark to his intimates that 'once the lion tasted blood, his native cruelty would return.' And the prediction was terribly fulfilled in the month of April, 59, when Nero, now in the twenty-second year of his age, impatient of the domination of his mother Agrippina, procured her assassination.[4]

Paul's discouragement.

This was the end of the happy *quinquennium* and the beginning of that reign of terror which has invested the name of Nero with lurid horror and unrivalled infamy. It had happened less than a year ere the Apostle's arrival. Perhaps it was at Puteoli that he had his first intelligence of the ominous crime, and this would account for the gloom which there enshrouded his soul. He had been trusting that he would find justice in the court of the Emperor and soon be set free to prosecute his ministry in the Capital; but now

[1] Suet. *Ner.* 10-15.

[2] Cf. pp. 384 f.

[3] Cf. Aurel. Vict. *Cæs.* 5: 'uti merito Trajanus sæpius testaretur procul differre cunctos principes Neronis quinquennio.'

[4] Tac. *Ann.* XIV. 1-9. Cf. Lewin, *Fast. Sacr.*, 1874.

that dream was rudely dispelled. And, as the days passed and he learned in his seclusion how events were shaping, his hope would wax ever fainter.

It is an evidence of his anticipation of a speedy trial that he had accepted the hospitality of some Christian in the city. It was a temporary accommodation, and he availed himself of it only for the brief space which, he expected, would elapse ere the hearing of his appeal. But the days passed, and still he was never summoned before the imperial tribunal. Nor is the reason obscure. There was open enmity between him and the Jews of Rome, and it lay with the latter to sustain his prosecution in name of the Sanhedrin. They could hardly hope for the condemnation of a prisoner whom the Procurator Festus had pronounced innocent, but they might delay his trial and thus prevent him from propagating his heresy in their midst; and this end they would easily compass by requesting time for the accumulation of evidence and the production of witnesses.[1] It would be at the best a tedious process, since the sphere of the Apostle's activities was so remote and so extensive; and they would be at no pains to expedite it. Moreover, they had a friend at court in the person of the infamous Poppæa Sabina, subsequently Nero's Empress and now his mistress.[2] Despite her flagrant immorality she was, like not a few ladies of rank at that period,[3] a votaress of the Jewish religion, and at least two instances are recorded where she successfully supported Jewish interests.[4]

Deferment of his trial.

Cf. Ac. xxiv. 5.

It is thus in no wise inexplicable that Paul's case should have been deferred. No less than two years elapsed ere he was brought to trial, and it was a repetition of his experience at Cæsarea. Every day he hoped that the summons would come, and every day he was disappointed. Yet he did not let the time pass unimproved. He removed from his friend's hospitable abode to a lodging which he rented in the city, and there in the freedom of his own dwelling he received numerous visitors and instructed them in the faith of the Gospel. Notwithstanding its limitations his ministry achieved signal success; and indeed those very limitations

A rich ministry. Ac. xxviii. 30.

Cf. Phil. ii. 23, 24; Phm. 22.

[1] Cf. Tac. *Ann.* XIII. 43, 52.
[2] *Ibid.* XIII. 45, 46; XIV. 1, 60, 61.
[3] Cf. pp. 6 f.
[4] Jos. *Vit.* 3; *Ant.* XX. viii. 11.

procured him a rare and unexpected opportunity. He was constantly under the surveillance of a Prætorian guardsman; and it proved no irksome duty for the soldiers who were told off to discharge it. The gracious prisoner won their hearts. They heard his discourses to the visitors who at stated hours thronged his chamber, and the letters which he dictated to his amanuensis for the comfort and instruction of his Churches; and in his leisure hours he would converse with them and tell them of the Saviour for whose sake he wore the chain. When they returned to the barracks, they carried
Cf. Phil. i. 12, 13. a report to their comrades, and it quickly spread abroad. The Apostle and his Gospel became the talk of the city. The
Cf. Phil. iv. 22. slaves of the imperial palace heard it, and some of them repaired to his lodging and were won to the Christian Faith.

Judaist enmity. There was thus much to gladden the captive, yet there was not a little also to grieve him. The hostility of the Jews was inevitable, and it would sit lightly upon him; but it vexed him that he encountered enmity in the Church. The Christian community at Rome was mixed, partly Jewish and partly Gentile. Its origin is obscure, but it is certain that the Gospel had early obtained a footing in the Metropolis, and it was probably introduced by those Jews from
Cf. Ac. ii. 10. Rome who witnessed the outpouring of the Holy Spirit on the great Day of Pentecost. Hence it would appear that the first Roman Christians were Jewish converts, but they were ere long reinforced by Gentile believers. The Roman satirist lamented some fifty years later that Syrian Orontes had long poured its stream into the Tiber—a turbid flood of oriental jargon, mountebankery, and immorality.[1] But these were in no wise the sole contributions which Syria made to the Imperial City. Antioch on the Orontes was the metropolis of Gentile Christendom, and she would send many a Christian to Rome. Thus the Roman Church was a mixed community, and it was rent by the troublous controversy which Paul had encountered in Galatia, Macedonia, and Achaia. The Judaists raised the old outcry against his Gospel of universal grace, and insisted on the permanent obligation of the Mosaic Law and the necessity of imposing its ceremonies on Gentile converts. It grieved the Apostle,

[1] Juv. III. 62 ff.

yet he recognised that even this vexatious controversy was serving the supreme end. The Judaists, notwithstanding their narrow prejudice, were Christians, and even a Judaist Gospel was better than paganism. Moreover, he had confidence in his message of salvation by faith, and he was sure that discussion would inevitably issue in its triumph. Cf. Phil. i. 15-18.

Epaphroditus of Philippi.

Such was the course of events at Rome while Paul awaited his citation to the Emperor's tribunal. It appears that Luke and Aristarchus had left him soon after his arrival.[1] He would doubtless despatch them on errands to some of the Churches whose welfare was his constant care; and it seems that Luke went to Philippi where he had ministered so long and where his appearance would be warmly welcomed.[2] The Apostle, however, had not been left alone; for Timothy had joined him, and not only acted as his amanuensis but ministered to him with that beautiful tenderness which had always characterised his attitude toward his father in Christ and which was specially conspicuous amid the distresses of those later years. And by and by he was gladdened by the advent of another true-hearted comrade. This was Epaphroditus of Philippi, and he came as the deputy of his Church. The Philippians had been apprised of the Apostle's fortunes. Secundus of Thessalonica on returning from Jerusalem to Macedonia three years previously would report his arraignment before the Sanhedrin and his imprisonment at Cæsarea, and occasional intelligence of his situation would subsequently be conveyed to Philippi. Indeed it is likely that he would write to so important a Church during his two years' seclusion.[3] Communication

Cf. 2 Cor. xi. 28.

[1] The evidence is twofold. (1) They are not expressly included in the greeting at the close of Phil. (iv. 21, 22) as, in view of their intimacy with the Philippians, they must have been had they been present. They had rejoined the Apostle when he wrote Col. and Phm., and they are mentioned in these letters (cf. Col. iv. 10, 14; Phm. 24). (2) Had they, especially Luke, been present, Paul could not have written Phil. ii. 19-21.

[2] Luke's visit to Philippi is proved by Phil. iv. 3, if he was indeed the γνήσιος σύνζυγος.

[3] The canonical epistle is the only extant letter of the Apostle to the Philippians; but Polycarp (*Phil.* iii) speaks of 'letters' (ἐπιστολάς) which Paul had written to them and which they then possessed. This indeed is not conclusive, since the plur. ἐπιστολαί might denote a single letter (cf. Lightfoot, *Phil.*, pp. 138 ff.); but the probability remains.

would cease on his departure for Rome; but now, if Luke had indeed gone to Philippi, he would tell the story of the eventful voyage and inform the brethren of their revered teacher's plight in the Imperial Capital.

Letter and gift from the Philippian Church.

Their sympathy was awakened, and they promptly displayed it in their own practical and generous fashion. The Apostle was in sore need. He was not indeed actually destitute, for he had been well furnished by the liberality of the people of Melita; but he had to meet the expense of his rental and maintenance at Rome, nor was he permitted to go abroad and earn a wage by plying his craft of tent-making. And he was a stranger in the vast Metropolis. The Church there was not his foundation. Its members were bound to him by no ties of gratitude and affection, and the converts whom he had won since his arrival belonged to the poorer order—soldiers of the Prætorian Guard and slaves of the imperial household. They could afford him nothing. His little store was fast dwindling, and unless he were brought speedily to trial he must be destitute. His plight was grievous, and it appealed to the Philippians. Their generous souls were conscience-stricken. Nine years previously, when his need was sore, they had repeatedly relieved it;[1] but when the need passed, their liberality had ceased. It was not that their hearts had been estranged. Their love was as true and fond as ever, and had they known of his distress, they would gladly have succoured him. And now that they were apprised of it, they hastened to make amends. They levied contributions, and they wrote a letter of gracious sympathy. They deplored the long winter of their apparent neglect, and assured him that it had been occasioned not by any defect of love but solely by their ignorance of his need; and they begged him to cheer them with tidings of his condition. And they deputed Epaphroditus to convey their letter and their gift to Rome.

Cf. ii. 19; iv. 10.

Devoted service of Epaphroditus at Rome.

It was probably midsummer when Epaphroditus presented himself. Paul and his two companions had arrived there about the beginning of March, and Luke would hardly leave him immediately. The journey to Philippi *via* Dyrrachium and the Egnatian Road occupied little less than a

[1] Cf. pp. 137, 152.

month;[1] and if he set out in April, he would arrive in May. A considerable time would be consumed by the telling of his story and the raising of the contribution, and thus July would be well advanced ere Epaphroditus joined the Apostle. He proved himself a true friend and a staunch ally. He made no haste to return home, but stayed on with the Apostle and aided him in his ministry, particularly, it would seem, in his controversy with the Judaists. And for this 'warfare' he was well qualified, since the question had so recently been debated in Macedonia and he was familiar with the issues. His zeal, however, cost him dear. The autumn was an insalubrious season at Rome,[2] and Epaphroditus sickened amid his labours, and for a while his life was in danger. During his tedious convalescence his heart turned homeward, and his longing became insupportable when he received an anxious message from his friends. They had heard of his sickness and would fain know how he was faring; and he decided to set out immediately and relieve their apprehension.

Cf. ii. 25.

A letter to Philippi.

He would convey to Philippi an answer to the letter which he had brought, and the Apostle addressed himself to its composition. It had been long delayed. In view of his activities at Rome it can hardly have been earlier than September when Epaphroditus fell sick; and it would take the better part of two months for the report of his illness to find its way to his friends and their anxious inquiry to travel back to Rome. And thus it would be the month of November when Paul wrote. His letter is an outpouring of his heart's gratitude and affection. It is the sweetest and tenderest of all his surviving letters, and its tone evinces how much he owed to the sympathy of his Philippian friends and the kindness of their deputy. His situation was indeed distressful. He was a prisoner; and not only was he vexed by the hostility of a powerful party in the Roman Church but

[1] The distance between Rome and Brundisium was about 360 miles, and it occupied some ten days (cf. Ovid, *Epist.* IV. v. 7 f.: 'Luce minus decima dominam venietis in Urbem, | Ut festinatum non faciatis iter.'). The passage from Brundisium to Dyrrachium depended on weather conditions, but a single day commonly sufficed. From Dyrrachium to Philippi the distance was about 370 miles, and this would consume about a fortnight, since travel was less expeditious there than in Italy.

[2] Cf. Hor. *Epist.* I. vii. 1-9.

his prospect was dark and ominous. The long deferment of his appeal was disquieting, and the rumours which reached him of Jewish machinations and imperial tyranny justified gloomy forebodings of the final issue. His spirit might well have been oppressed, yet it was light and glad. 'Joy' is the letter's refrain, occurring oftener within its brief compass than in any other.[1]

LETTER TO PHILIPPI

Address and commendation.

After the formal address, making special mention of the Elders, 'the Overseers' or Shepherds of the Flock,[2] and the Deacons, since it was they who had directed the Church's contribution on his behalf, the letter opens with an assurance of the Apostle's continual and affectionate regard.

i. 1 Paul and Timothy, slaves of Christ Jesus, to all the saints
in Christ Jesus who are at Philippi, with the Overseers and
2 Deacons. Grace to you and peace from God our Father and
the Lord Jesus Christ.
3, 4 I thank my God whenever I think of you, ever in my every
supplication for every one of you making my supplication
5 with joy for the part you have taken in spreading the Gospel
6 from the first day until the present hour. Just this is my
confidence, that He who inaugurated a good work in you
7 will carry it to perfection until the Day of Christ Jesus. And
indeed it is right for me to be thus disposed on behalf of you
all, since I hold you in my heart, being as you all are, alike in
my imprisonment and in my defence and confirmation of the
8 Gospel, my partners in grace. For God is my witness how I
9 am longing for you all in the tenderness of Christ Jesus. And
this is my prayer—that your love may still more and more
10 overflow in full knowledge and all perception, that you may
11 have moral discernment[3] so as to be sincere and offenceless
against the Day of Christ, replete with that harvest of righteousness which is wrought by Jesus Christ to the glory and
praise of God.

The Apostle's situation at Rome.

In their letter the Philippians had commiserated the Apostle on his unhappy situation; and now he hastens to

[1] χάρα, 'joy,' five times (i. 4, 25; ii. 2, 29; iv. 1); χαίρειν, 'rejoice,' eleven times (i. 18 *bis*; ii. 17 *bis*, 18 *bis*, 28; iii. 1; iv. 4 *bis*, 10).

[2] Cf. n. on Ac. xx. 28, p. 463.

[3] εἰς τὸ ιμάζειν ὑμᾶς τὰ διαφέροντα, cf. n. on Rom. ii. 18, p. 390.

show them how wonderfully it had eventuated. It had procured the Gospel an entrance into the barracks of the Prætorian Guards and had stirred most of the Roman Christians to courage and zeal, while even the opposition of the Judaists was serving a gracious end by compelling reflection. And so they must not grieve. It was true that his personal prospect was dark. His fate was hanging in the balance, and there seemed little likelihood of his escaping condemnation and a martyr's death. But his resolution was so to bear himself that, whatever the issue, Christ might be magnified. Indeed he had no fear of death. It would be a blessed release, and he would almost choose it. Yet when he considered how eagerly the Philippians desired him, he could not but believe that he would be spared and have the joy of seeing them again.

12 Now I desire you to recognise, brothers, that my fortunes
have actually issued in the advancement of the Gospel.
13 It has become notorious among the whole of the Prætorian
Guard and all the rest of the citizens that it is for my
14 relation with Christ that I am a prisoner; and the majority
of the brothers have gained confidence in the Lord by my
imprisonment and with more overflowing boldness are
15 fearlessly talking of the Word of God. There are some
indeed who are preaching the Christ for envy and strife,
but there are some also who are doing it for good will.
16 The latter are prompted by love, knowing that I am
17 appointed for the defence of the Gospel, while it is by
partisanship that the former are prompted to proclaim the
Christ, in no pure spirit, thinking to aggravate the distress
18 of my imprisonment. And what then? Only that in every
way, whether in pretence or in truth, Christ is being proclaimed; and in this I rejoice. Yes, and I will rejoice;
19 for I know that 'this will result for me in salvation' Job xiii.
through your supplication and a rich supply of the Spirit 16 LXX.
20 of Jesus Christ, according to my eager expectation and
hope that in nothing shall I be put to shame, but with all
boldness of speech now as always Christ will be magnified
in my body whether through life or through death.
21, 22 For to me living is Christ and dying is gain. But if living
in the flesh be my portion, this means for me a harvest of
23 work; and which I shall choose I cannot tell. I am in a
dilemma: I have the longing to strike my tent and be Cf. 2 Cor.
24 with Christ, for this were far, far better; yet my staying v. 1.
25 still in the flesh is more necessary for your sakes. And of this

> I am confident, and I know that I shall stay, I shall stay on
> among you, for your advancement and joy in the Faith,
> 26 so that in me you may have in Christ Jesus abundant
> reason for boasting through my advent again among you.

Twofold incentive to Christian unity:

Unhappily the music of the sweet letter is broken by a jarring note. The peace of the Philippian Church had been disturbed by a petty dissension. It was indeed no very serious matter, but it grieved the Apostle that even so slight a blot should sully the fair fame of this the noblest of his Churches. But for that his pride in the Philippians would have been without alloy, and he lovingly yet passionately pleads with them to banish it and 'complete his joy.'

(1) The Heavenly Citizenship.

i. 27; cf. iii. 20.

He sets before them two inspiring ideals. First he appeals to them to be worthy of their Christian 'citizenship,' here introducing a new conception which had of late captivated his imagination and thenceforth moulded his thought of the Church. It grew out of his Roman citizenship, and it had taken definite shape in his mind when he found himself within the gates of the Imperial Capital, the Queen of the Nations, the Mistress of the World, and surveyed from that proud centre 'the wide arch of the ranged empire.' It seemed to him, as to St. Augustine three and a half centuries later, an earthly adumbration of the *Civitas Dei*, the Heavenly Commonwealth. The imperial spirit was strong in the Roman colony of Philippi, and he appeals to his friends to recognise their nobler citizenship and prove worthy of it, all the more that they were surrounded by jealous and malignant enemies.

> 27 Only be worthy in your Citizenship of the Gospel of Christ,
> that, whether I come and see you or be far away, the account I
> have of you may be that you are standing fast in one spirit,
> with one soul supporting the Faith of the Gospel in its struggle,
> 28 and never for a moment intimidated by your opponents. This
> is for them an evidence of ruin, but it is an evidence of your
> 29 salvation—an evidence from God; because the privilege has
> been granted you on Christ's behalf, not only to have faith in
> 30 Him but to suffer on His behalf, engaged as you are in the same
> sort of contest which you saw me maintaining and now hear
> of my maintaining.

But there was another and far more moving ideal. It was

(2) The Lord's self-humiliation.

always the Apostle's wont to invest the commonest of duties with the loftiest of sanctions; and just as he had incited the Corinthians to Christian liberality by setting before them the example of the Lord's sacrificial self-impoverishment (2 Cor. viii. 9), so now he presents to the Philippians a like incentive to self-effacement. He reminds them of Christ's self-humiliation. He was the Eternal Son of God, yet He freely surrendered that dignity. He became man; the Lord of Glory made Himself a slave. It was a reversal of creation. At his creation man was 'made in the image of God, after His likeness' (Gen. i. 26); and that Divine Image, the Archetype of Humanity, was the Eternal Son (Cf. 2 Cor. iv. 4; Col. i. 15, iii. 10). God's purpose was 'the conformation of humanity to the image of His Son' (Cf. Rom. viii. 29); but this was frustrated by sin. The Divine Image in humanity was defaced, and to remedy the disaster the Eternal Son was 'made in the likeness of men.' It was a temporary humiliation. Observe how the Apostle distinguishes between the 'form' and the 'fashion.' Form is permanent, fashion transient. Man's form is the eternal image of God, and his fashion the frail and perishing estate into which sin has brought him (Cf. 1 Cor. vii. 31); and the Archetype of Humanity, that He might 'conform humanity to His own image,' shared its fashion and endured to the uttermost its suffering and shame. And this infinite self-renunciation is His glory. It has exalted the name of Jesus and won Him universal adoration.

ii. 1 If, then, the appeal of union with Christ counts for anything, if love's persuasion counts for anything, if the Spirit's
fellowship counts for anything, if tenderness and com-
2 passion count for anything,[1] complete my joy by espousing
the same cause. Cherish the same love; be united in
3 soul; espouse the one cause. Never be actuated by
partisanship or vaingloriousness, but with humility deem

[1] The difficulty here lies in εἴ τις σπλάγχνα. The obvious emendation εἴ τινα (Chrys., Ambrstr., Vulg., T. R.) has no MS. authority. εἴ τις σπλάγχνα is generally regarded as a mere grammatical slip on the part of the Apostle; but since Cod. Bez. (D) and several minuscs. have also εἴ τις παραμύθιον, some ancient interpreters take the nouns as predicates: 'if any one would be a comfort to me, if any one would be a consolation to my love, if any one would be a fellowship of spirit to me, if any one would be tenderness and compassion.' Cf. Euth. Zig. One authority (Euthal [cod]) has εἴ τι οὖν παράκλησις, and the probability is that εἴ τι, *si quid valet*, should be read throughout. Cf. Moulton, *Proleg.*, p. 59.

4 one another more important than yourselves, with an eye
not to your own several interests but also to those of your
5 neighbours. Harbour this sentiment which dwelt even in
6 Christ Jesus. Though He existed primally in God's form,[1]
He did not deem His equality with God a treasure to be
7 clutched.[2] No, He emptied Himself by taking a slave's
8 form, being made in the likeness of men. And, being found
in fashion as a man, He humbled Himself by carrying His
9 obedience as far as death, yes, death on a cross. And
therefore God also highly exalted Him and bestowed on
10 Him the Name which is higher than every name, that at
Is. xlv. 23. the name of Jesus 'every knee might bend,' among 'the
11 denizens of heaven and earth and the nether world,'[3] 'and
every tongue confess' that JESUS CHRIST IS LORD to the
glory of God the Father.

12 And so, my beloved, as you have always been obedient,
now—not merely as you would if I were with you but all the

[1] *ὑπάρχων*, cf. note on Gal. ii. 14, p. 200. *μορφή* is *forma*, the distinctive and unchangeable form. Cf. Chrys.: *τὸ ἀπαράλλακτον ἡ μορφὴ δείκνυσι καθώς ἐστι μορφή.* It is impossible to be of one essence and have the 'form' of another essence. *E.g.*, no man has the form of an angel, nor has an irrational beast the form of a man. *σχῆμα* is *habitus*, *figura*, the 'fashion' or 'shape,' which may change while the 'form' remains. Thus, the *σχῆμα* of the world passes away (1 Cor. vii. 31), but not its *μορφή*: the world itself remains though its 'fashion' changes. Satan may *transfigure* himself (*μετασχηματίζεσθαι*) but he could not *transform* himself (*μεταμορφοῦσθαι*) into an angel of light (cf. 2 Cor. xi. 14). Hence *ἐν μορφῇ Θεοῦ ὑπάρχων* affirms our Lord's essential and eternal deity (as against Arianism); *μορφὴν δούλου λαβών* His true humanity (as against Doketism). The reality of His incarnate humanity is further affirmed by *σχήματι εὑρεθεὶς ὡς ἄνθρωπος*: in the days of His flesh He exhibited the 'fashion' of a man—'*habitus*, cultus, vestitus, gestus, sermones victus, et actiones' (Beng.). It may seem impossible that one who was 'in the form of God' should take 'the form of a slave'; and thus Spinoza (*Epist.* xxi) pronounces it no less absurd to say that God assumed human nature than to say that a circle has assumed the nature of a square. This, however, ignores the basal postulate of the Incarnation, viz., man's kinship with God, his creation 'in God's image.' Hence Christ, 'existing primally in God's form,' could nevertheless 'take a slave's form'; He could become man without ceasing to be God. And conversely, just as He, being in a slave's form, could be 'transformed' (*μεταμορφοῦσθαι*) into His primal glory (cf. Mt. xvii. 2; Mk. ix. 2), so we, without ceasing to be men, can be 'transformed' into His image (cf. Rom. viii. 29, xii. 2; 2 Cor. iii. 18)—the *εἰκών* in which we were created (cf. 1 Cor. xi. 7; Col. iii. 10)—and be 'made partakers of the divine nature' (2 Pet. i. 4).

[2] *ἁρπαγμός*, a 'catch,' a prize to be greedily clutched as a lion seizes his prey (cf. Moulton and Milligan, *Vocab.*). Here not, as the Arians understood it, a *ἕρμαιον*, a privilege which Christ might have grasped and made His own, but, as the argument requires, a dignity which He actually possessed and would not retain like a miser clutching his gold. Cf. Isid. Pel. *Epist.* IV. 22.

[3] A phrase of contemporary Gnosticism. Cf. Hippolytus, *Refut.* v. 8.

more since I am far away—with fear and trembling work
13 out your own salvation; for it is God that operates in you
both the willing and the operating in pursuance of His
14 good pleasure. Do everything without murmurings and
15 disputations, that you may prove blameless and pure,
'God's spotless children' in the midst of 'a crooked and Dt. xxxii.
perverse generation,' among whom you are seen shining like 5.
16 stars in the world, holding forth a message of life, that I Cf. Gen. i.
may have reason for boasting on the Day of Christ that I 14.
did not run my race in vain or 'spend my labour in vain.' Is. xlix. 4;
17 Nay, though my life-blood be poured out over the sacrifice lxv. 23.
and priestly ministration of your faith, I rejoice and I
18 share the joy of you all. And in the same manner I would
have you also rejoice and share my joy.

The Apostle's present arrangements.

And now the Apostle passes to a personal explanation. In their letter the Philippians had begged him to 'cheer them with information of his concerns,' and he tells them that he hopes ere long to send Timothy to them and be cheered with information of their concerns. He was only waiting until he should be able to tell them how his case was likely to go; and his expectation was that he would soon be set at liberty, and then he would visit them himself. Meantime he was sending Epaphroditus back to Philippi to relieve the anxiety which the tidings of that good friend's sickness had occasioned them; and they must honour him all the more for the service which he had rendered in their name during his stay at Rome.

19 Now I am hoping, if the Lord Jesus will, to send Timothy to
you ere long, that I too may be 'cheered by information of
20 your concerns.'[1] I have no one with a soul like his—no one
21 who will have a kindly regard for your concerns; for they are
22 all seeking their own ends, not those of Christ Jesus. But you
are aware what he has proved himself: like father and child he
23 and I slaved together in the service of the Gospel. Him, then,
I am hoping to send as soon as ever I make out my prospects;
24 but I am confident in the Lord that I shall myself also come
25 ere long. I deemed it necessary, however, to send to you
Epaphroditus, my brother and fellow-worker and fellow-
soldier, whom you sent on an errand of priestly ministration
26 to my need, since he was longing after you all and was home-
27 sick[2] because you had heard that he was ill. Indeed he was

[1] κἀγώ, 'I also,' a reference to the Philippians' letter. They had hoped to be cheered with tidings of his welfare, and he reciprocates their courtesy.

[2] ἀδημονεῖν, cf. *The Days of His Flesh*, p. 457.

ill, almost at death's door ; but God had mercy on him, and
not on him only but on me too, lest I should have grief upon
28 grief. I am sending[1] him, then, the more eagerly, that you
may be rejoiced by the sight of him and my grief may be
29 lessened. Welcome him, then, in the Lord with all joy, and
30 hold men like him in honour ; for it was his devotion to the
work of Christ that brought him nigh to death. He hazarded
his life to make up to me the ministry which you could not
render.

Cf. 1 Cor. xvi. 17.

Final charge.

And now he draws to a conclusion. Ere he closes he reverts to the dissension which was disturbing the Philippian Church, and would reiterate his counsel.

iii. 1 For the rest, my brothers, rejoice in the Lord. To repeat
what I have already written to you is not irksome for me, and
it is safe for you——

An interruption.

Here he breaks off. Something has occurred which interrupts the stream of his dictation and arrests Timothy's pen ; and when he resumes, it is to pour forth a torrent of burning indignation. The occasion was plainly a peculiarly offensive exhibition of Judaist animosity ; but he does not stay to define it, and hence it may be inferred that Epaphroditus had been the victim. It was unnecessary to recount the incident, since he would explain the circumstances when he delivered the letter. It was probably a rencontre at a meeting of the Church. Epaphroditus had been discoursing and had been assailed by the Judaist faction ; and now he has returned vexed and pained, and tells the story.

A Judaist attack.

Apparently the attack was threefold. First, the Judaists had indulged in coarse vituperation. They had stigmatised the Gentile converts as 'uncircumcised dogs'—that foul epithet which the Jews were so fond of hurling at the Gentiles,[2] likening them to the pariahs which prowled in quest of garbage among the refuse-heaps outside an oriental town ; and this enkindled a flame of chivalrous resentment in the Apostle's breast. He retorted the epithet. The Judaists were the real pariahs, and their legal rites were the garbage. Their boasted circumcision was only a symbol of spiritual grace, and the symbol without the grace was valueless. It

Cf. Rev. xxii. 15.

Cf. Rom. ii. 29; Col. ii. 11.

[1] ἔπεμψα, epistolary aor. Cf. n. on Gal. vi. 11, p. 219.

[2] Cf. *The Days of His Flesh*, p. 250.

was no true *circumcision* but mere *concision*, mere mutilation, mere 'cutting in the flesh.' Again they had assailed the Apostle; and he replies that he was a better Jew than any of them, and his present attitude was no jealous depreciation of a privilege which he did not possess. He had been 'born in the purple.' He was an heir of the sacred traditions, and had once been devoted to the Law; but he had found in Christ a nobler righteousness, and recognised that legal rites were in comparison naught but 'refuse.' Then they had preferred their old charge that the Gospel of salvation by faith relaxed moral obligation; and this touched him in the quick. His Gentile converts, even the Philippians, too often lent colour to the calumny by their retention of the pagan taint; and he implores them to realise the ethical requirements of the Gospel. The Christian life was a continual conflict, a strenuous struggle toward the goal of a Christlike character, and he was himself striving to attain it. Cf. Lev. xxi. 5.

2 Beware of the 'dogs'; beware of the 'evil workers'; be- Cf. 2 Cor.
3 ware of the concision.[1] For we are 'the circumcision'—we xi. 13.
who serve God's Spirit and boast in Christ Jesus and have no
confidence in the flesh.
4 And yet I have reason for confidence even in the flesh. If
any one else fancies he may have confidence in the flesh, still
5 more may I: circumcised as I was when eight days old; born
of Israel's race and of Benjamin's tribe, a Hebrew of Hebrew
6 parentage; as regards the Law a Pharisee; as regards zeal a
persecutor of the Church; as regards righteousness—legal
7 righteousness—past blame. But all these which were once
8 gains to me, I have for Christ's sake deemed loss. Yes, and
more than that: I deem everything to be loss for the sake of
the transcendent advantage of knowing Christ Jesus my Lord.[2]

[1] A contemptuous parody—not περιτομή but κατατομή, not 'circumcision' but 'amputation' (cf. Gal. v. 12). Such paronomasia was congenial to the ancient mind. Diogenes the Cynic was addicted to it. Cf. Diog. Laert. VI. 24: 'He called the σχολή (school) of Euclid χολή (bile) and the διατριβή (discourse) of Plato κατατριβή (waste of time).' It is frequent in N. T. generally as a play upon words like the jingling proverb μαθήματα παθήματα, 'experience teaches' (cf. Herod. I. 207; Æsch. *Agam.* 170), and in this kindly fashion our Lord employed it (cf. Mt. xvi. 18). Cf. Moulton's Winer, p. 794-6.

[2] Deissmann (*Light from Anc. East*, p. 383, n. 8) quotes a 1st c. Byzantine inscription which records of a citizen of Olbia that he had 'advanced to knowledge of the Augusti' (*i.e.*, the Emperors Augustus and Tiberius), μέχρι τᾶς τῶν Σεβαστῶν γνώσεως προκόψαντος. On this analogy it is *personal* not *speculative* knowledge of Christ that the Apostle means. Cf. Jo. x. 15, xiv. 7, xvii. 3, 25.

For His sake I suffered the loss of everything and deem it but
9 refuse,[1] that I may gain Christ and be found in Him, not having
a righteousness of my own—the legal righteousness—but that
which comes by faith in Christ, the righteousness which God
10 gives on the ground of faith, that I may know Him and the
power of His Resurrection and the fellowship of His sufferings,
11 being conformed to His death in the hope of attaining to the
resurrection from the dead.[2]

Cf. Ac. xx. 24.

12 Not that I have already laid hold or have already accomplished the course; but I am pressing on in the hope of laying
fast hold on that for which Christ Jesus laid fast hold on me.
13 Brothers, I do not yet reckon myself to have laid fast hold on it,
but one thing I do: forgetting what lies behind and straining
14 out toward what lies ahead, I am pressing on to the goal for
the prize of God's upward call in Christ Jesus.

15 Let all of us, then, who are mature,[3] be thus minded; and if
in aught you are differently minded, this also will God reveal to
16 you. Only, so far as we have reached, let us march in unbroken
rank.

17 Unite in imitating me, brothers, and keep an eye on those
who comport themselves after the pattern which we have set
18 you. For there are many who comport themselves—I used
often to speak of them to you, and now I speak of them even
19 with tears, as the enemies of the Cross of Christ. Their end
is ruin, their god is their appetite, and their glory is in their
20 shame—men who mind earthly things. Our Eternal Commonwealth is in Heaven;[4] and thence we are expecting a Saviour,
21 the Lord Jesus Christ, who will refashion the body of our
humiliation into conformity with the body of His glory after
the operation of the power He has even to subject the universe
to Himself.

Resumption of final charge.

And now the Apostle resumes the exhortation which had been so rudely interrupted. He names the two ladies—Euodia and Syntyche—who had occasioned the dissension. Nothing is known of them beyond this unhappy reference. Their record had hitherto been honourable. They had been won to the Faith during his ministry at Philippi and had lent him valiant assistance in the founding of the Church, and throughout the ten years which had since elapsed they had served it well, perhaps in the capacity of deaconesses.

[1] A reversion to 'the dogs' (ver. 2), *σκύβαλα* being refuse thrown to dogs. Cf. Suid.: *σκύβαλον, κυσίβαλόν τι ὄν, τὸ τοῖς κυσὶ βαλλόμενον.*

[2] *ἡ ἀνάστασις τῶν νεκρῶν*, the general resurrection; *ἡ ἀνάστασις ἡ ἐκ νεκρῶν*, the resurrection of believers (cf. Ac. iv. 2 with Ac. xvii. 32; 1 Cor. xv. 12).

[3] *τέλειοι*, cf. n. on 1 Cor. ii. 6, p. 248.

[4] *ὑπάρχει*, cf. n. on Gal. ii. 14, p. 200.

Hence he was the more grieved by their present behaviour; and he appeals to Luke, who had proved his skill in spiritual no less than physical healing, to help them to a better frame. The ranks of his old comrades had been thinned in the process of the years, and he bespeaks kindly consideration of the survivors, particularly one named Clement. Undistinguished as they might be in the world's esteem, their names were in the Book of Life.

iv. 1 And so, my brothers beloved and longed after, my joy and
2 crown, thus stand fast in the Lord, beloved. I exhort
Euodia[1] and I exhort Syntyche to espouse the same cause
3 in the Lord. Yes, and I ask you, true yoke-fellow,[2] help them
—those women who shared my struggle in the cause of the
Gospel, they and Clement[3] also and the rest of my fellow-
workers whose names are in 'the Book of Life.' Cf. Ps. lxix. 28.

[1] Not Euodias (masc.). The fem. pronouns *αὐταῖς, αἵτινες* (ver. 3) show that both persons were women. And the reiterated *παρακαλῶ* makes the admonition impartial: both needed it.

[2] *γνήσιε σύνζυγε.* Whom the Apostle thus designates is problematic, but four suggestions may perhaps be confidently dismissed. 1. The quaint notion that, despite the masc. terminations, *γνήσιος σύνζυγος* denotes a woman and that she was Paul's wife (Clem. Alex. *Strom.* III. vi. 53; Orig. *ad Rom. Comm.* I. 1), whom Renan (*St. Paul*, VI) identifies with Lydia of Philippi. 2. The idea that *Σύνζυγος* is a proper name, and the Apostle plays upon the common meaning of the word (cf. Phm. 10, 11)—'Synzygus (yoke-fellow), truly so named.' This notion, like the former, was prevalent in Chrys.'s day (*τινὲς δέ φασιν ὄνομα ἐκεῖνο κύριον εἶναι*). 3. Chrys., while rejecting the idea that the reference is to Paul's wife, thinks it may have been to some other woman but more probably to the brother or the husband of Euodia or Syntyche; cautiously adding, however, *πλὴν εἴτε τοῦτο εἴτε ἐκεῖνο οὐ σφόδρα ἀκριβολογεῖσθαι δεῖ.* 4. Paul here apostrophises either Epaphroditus (Grotius, Lightfoot), the bearer of the letter, or Timothy (Estius), whom he intended sending to Philippi (cf. ii. 19-23). But, though he might have given such an injunction to either, he could hardly have introduced a personal 'aside' into the letter. It remains that he is addressing some prominent personage at Philippi, to whom the letter was consigned and who would read it to the Church; and Luther hits the mark when he understands 'the chief Bishop' or Presbyter. That had been Luke's position during his ministry at Philippi, and on revisiting the Church he would resume the dignity if not the office. There was no one whom Paul could more fittingly have designated his 'true yoke-fellow,' a phrase which recalls Agamemnon's designation of Odysseus (Æsch. *Agam.* 815): *ζευχθεὶς ἕτοιμος ἦν ἐμοὶ σειραφόρος*, 'when yoked he was ever to me a ready trace-horse.'

[3] Connecting *μετὰ καὶ Κλήμεντος* with *συνήθλησάν μοι.* It may also be connected with the remote *συνλαμβάνου αὐταῖς*: 'help them, you and Clement also.' On the former construction Clement and the rest of Paul's converts were partisans of Euodia and Syntyche, and hence it would appear that the dissension arose from a feeling on the part of the original members of the Church that they received less deference than they deserved from the later adherents.

The secret of peace.

The mischief of dissension was that it broke the Church's peace, and banished joy, and dishonoured the Gospel. The remedy lay in the cultivation of a spirit of 'sweet reasonableness'; and this was attained by the unburdening of the soul at the Throne of Grace and the resolute pursuit of lofty ideals.

4, 5 Rejoice in the Lord always; again will I say it, rejoice. Let
your sweet reasonableness[1] be known to all men. The Lord
6 is nigh. Be anxious about nothing, but in everything by
prayer and supplication with thanksgiving let your requests
7 be made known in God's presence. And the peace of God,
which transcends all understanding, will be the warden of
your hearts and thoughts in Christ Jesus.

Cf. Jo. i. 1, 2 (Gk.).

8 For the rest, brothers, all that is true, all that is dignified,
all that is righteous, all that is pure, all that is lovely, all that
is winsome, whatever virtue there may be and whatever
9 praise, take these things into your reckoning. All that you
learned and received and heard and saw in me, put in practice;
and God, the Giver of Peace, will be with you.

Acknowledgment of the Philippian bounty.

One matter remains—the monetary relief which the Philippians had sent the Apostle, and he acknowledges it in a few sentences which only a gentleman could have written—a rare blending of gratitude, dignity, and humour. They had explained, somewhat grandiloquently, their apparent neglect—the tardy 'revival of their drooping mindfulness' of him; and he accepts their apology. He was glad of their gift; not for the relief which it afforded, since he had learned to endure privation, but for the assurance which it conveyed of their constant kindness. And he thanks them for it. It was like them to send it. Some ten years previously, when he was driven out of Macedonia,[2] they alone had considered his need and 'settled accounts' with him. He uses this phrase significantly, indicating that their contribution was no charity. It was a debt which they owed him for his precious service of them, and had they disowned it, they would have been the losers. And now that they have sent him another payment, he playfully writes

[1] τὸ ἐπιεικές (ἡ ἐπιεικία), the quality which, according to Matthew Arnold, distinguished Jesus, the temper which maintained His 'sure balance.' Cf. 2 Cor. x. 1.

[2] Cf. p. 152.

a formal receipt: 'Paid in full; received from Epaphroditus.' At the same time their gift was hallowed by their love. It was more than a payment; it was a fragrant offering, and it would win them God's rich blessing.

10 Now it rejoiced me greatly in the Lord that 'at long last' you
had 'revived your drooping mindfulness of me.' And in this
connection you were indeed mindful of me all the while, but
11 you never had an opportunity. Not that I am speaking under
pressure of want; for I have learned, whatever my circum-
12 stances, to be content. I know how to be brought low; I know
how to be affluent. Into each and every experience I have
been initiated—fulness and hunger, affluence and want.
13 I have strength for everything in Him who puts power into
14, 15 me. Yet thank you for participating in my distress.[1] And
you Philippians know as well as I do that in the early
days of the Gospel, when I quitted Macedonia, no Church
16 settled accounts with me[2] but you alone. For not
only at Thessalonica but again and yet again you sent me
17 help in need. Not that I am seeking after your gift; no,
it is the interest which accumulates to your account that
18 I am seeking after. I am paid in full,[3] and I am affluent.
My wants are all supplied now that I have received from
Epaphroditus what you sent me, 'an odour of a sweet Ex. xxix.
fragrance,' a sacrifice acceptable, well pleasing to God. 18; Ez.
19 And my God will supply all your need according to His xx. 41.
20 riches in glory in Christ Jesus. And to our God and
Father be the glory for ever and ever. Amen.
21 Greet every saint in Christ Jesus. The brothers who are
22 with me greet you. All the saints greet you, especially
those belonging to Cæsar's household.
23 THE GRACE OF THE LORD JESUS CHRIST BE WITH YOUR
SPIRIT.

It was toward the close of the year 60 when Epaphroditus took his departure for Philippi, carrying the letter with him. The Apostle would miss his gracious and helpful presence, The prisoner's companions.

[1] *καλῶς ποιεῖν*, a Common Greek colloquialism, frequent in papyri. (1) The aor. 'thank you.' Cf. Ac. x. 33. *Oxyrh. Pap.* 1066, 3: *καλῶς μὲν ἐποίησας ἀποστίλας μοι τὴν ῥίνην*, 'thank you for sending me the file.' The fut. 'please.' Cf. 3 Jo. 6. *Oxyrh. Pap.* 300, 5: *καλῶς ποιήσεις ἀντιφωνήσασά μοι ὅτι ἐκομίσου*, 'please send me a reply that you received it.'

[2] *εἰς λόγον δόσεως καὶ λήμψεως*, 'on the score of payment and receipt.' Cf. Moulton and Milligan, *Vocab.*

[3] In Common Greek *ἀπέχω* (cf. Mt. vi. 2), 'I have received it,' was the technical acknowledgment of payment. *ἀποχή*, 'a receipt.' Cf. *Oxyrh. Pap.* 91, 25: *κυρία ἡ ἀποχή*, 'the receipt is valid.'

but he was not left alone. Timothy was with him, and by and by others joined him. Luke and Aristarchus returned from their expeditions with the old kindness in their hearts. It seems that his health had been impaired by his long confinement, his ceaseless employment, and his wearing anxiety; and thus the advent of 'the beloved physician' was doubly welcome. Aristarchus too did his part. So assiduous was he in his tendance, never quitting the Apostle's chamber, that the latter playfully styled him 'my fellow-captive.' Another arrival was Demas. He seems to have belonged to Thessalonica; and since his name is coupled with Luke's, it may be presumed that he had accompanied the latter from Macedonia, conveying doubtless his Church's sympathy. He is merely mentioned without commendation, and this evident coldness is justified by the part which he subsequently played.

Cf. Col. iv. 10, 14; Phm. 24.

Cf. Col. iv. 10.

Cf. 2 Tim. iv. 10.

Arrival of John Mark and Tychicus.

Time wore away, and the year 61 would be nearing its close when the Apostle was gladdened by a welcome surprise. It was the arrival of John Mark who ten years previously had occasioned the tragic rupture between him and his noble-hearted comrade Barnabas.[1] Of Mark's doings during the interval there is no record, but it is plain that he had redeemed his character. Though a Jew, he was loyal to Paul's Gentile Gospel; and since in the immediate sequel he is found ministering in the Province of Asia, the likelihood is that it was thence that he had come to Rome. Nor is it without suggestion that another who appears on the scene at this juncture is Tychicus the Ephesian. He was one of the deputies who accompanied the Apostle to Jerusalem in the spring of 57 to present the Gentile contributions for the poor Christians in the Sacred Capital; and when his errand was accomplished he had returned to Ephesus. There, probably, he had encountered Mark; and when the latter was apprised of his intention to visit Rome, he would propose to accompany him that he might make his peace with the Apostle. The reconciliation was complete; and Paul not merely renewed the old fellowship with him but publicly absolved him by writing to the Churches of Asia and commending him to their confidence.

Cf. Col. iv. 10; 2 Tim. iv. 11.

Cf. Eph. vi. 21; Col. iv. 7, 8.

Cf. 2 Tim. iv. 11.

Cf. Col. iv. 10.

[1] Cf. p. 117.

Jesus Justus.

Nor should it go unnoticed that there was yet another who cheered the Apostle during his weary captivity—Jesus, a Jewish Christian, who, after the fashion of that period,[1] bore also the Gentile name of Justus. Since he is an unknown personage, and thus can hardly have been a provincial deputy, he was probably a member of the Roman Church; and this invested him with an honourable distinction. He was the only Jewish Christian in the city who befriended the Apostle: all the rest were Judaists.

Cf. Col. iv. 11.

Heresy in the Province of Asia.

It was a serious errand that had brought Tychicus to Rome. A heresy had arisen in the Province of Asia and was working deadly mischief in the Church; and he had been deputed to convey the tidings to the Apostle and obtain his counsel. The intelligence was no surprise to Paul; for he had long foreseen the evil. Already during his ministry at Ephesus he had perceived the trend of thought; and four years previously, in the message to the Churches of Asia annexed to his encyclical on Justification by Faith, he had sounded a note of warning, and he had repeated it with stronger urgency in his moving address to the Ephesian Elders at Miletus. And now he learns that his forebodings have been realised.

Cf. Rom. xvi. 17-20.

Cf. Ac. xx. 29, 30.

Incipient Gnosticism.

What was the heresy? It was the initial phase of that subtle philosophy which was known in after days as Gnosticism. Gnosticism was, at all events in the domain of Gentile Christianity, a fusion of Oriental theosophy and Greek philosophy; and it was natural that it should have its home in the Province of Asia, that borderland betwixt East and West. It were indeed illegitimate to anticipate later developments and identify the heresy which confronted the Apostle with the elaborate, complex, and fantastic system which flourished in the second century; at the same time it were no less illegitimate to ignore their affinity. Systems are never born in a day, and the full-blown Gnosticism which appears on the pages of St. Irenæus was no sudden growth but the development of ideas which had been operative for generations. It were reasonable to assume *a priori* that they had already emerged in the Apostle's day, and the assumption is historically attested. Thus, according to St. Irenæus,[2] the

[1] Cf. p. 21.

[2] IV. li. 3; cf. III, *præfat.*

Gnostics were disciples of Simon Magus, 'the father of all heretics'; and Hippolytus early in the third century designates the Gnostic sect of the Ophites or Naasenes 'the progenitors of subsequent heresies' and places them in the order of his discussion before Simon Magus and before Cerinthus, the Apostle John's adversary during his ministry at Ephesus.[1] Hence it is no mere surmise but an historical fact that Gnosticism had already appeared in the days of the Apostles. It was indeed still undeveloped, but its characteristic ideas were thus early in vogue; and it was these that were disturbing the Churches of Asia and engaged Paul's attention.

The problem of God's relation to the world.

Its basal principle was that persistent postulate of ancient thought—the inherent and essential evil of matter; and this presented the twofold problem of the mode of creation and the relation of God to the world. If the world were God's direct creation out of nothing or an immediate emanation from His own essence, then He would be the author of evil. And if He be perfect goodness and purity, then it is impossible for Him to have contact with evil and impure matter. There is thus a wide gulf between God and the world; and the question was how that gulf should be bridged.

Gnostic theory of emanations.

Cf. Rom. viii. 38; Col. i. 16.

The answer was furnished by a theory of successive emanations, a series of intermediaries between God and the world. These were the *æons*, a hierarchy of angels designated 'thrones,' 'lordships,' 'principalities,' 'authorities,' and 'powers,' and inhabiting, in order of dignity, 'the heavenly regions' which rose, tier above tier, to the Throne of God.[2] The *pleroma* or 'fulness' dwelt in God, and it was weaker in each successive emanation until the lowest rank was

Eph. vi. 12.

reached—'the world-making angels,'[3] 'the rulers of this

[1] *Refut.* v. 6; vi. 1.

[2] According to *Test. of Levi* (cf. p. 335) in the Sixth Heaven are the Archangels, the Angels of the Presence; in the Fifth the Messengers of God, who bear the prayers of men to the Angels of the Presence; in the Fourth Thrones and Authorities, the Holy Ones; in the Third the hosts of avenging angels. Orig. *De Princip.* I. v. 3 (Latin translation) specifies, in ascending order, (1) the Holy Angels (*sancti angeli*), (2) Principalities (*principatûs*, ἀρχαί), (3) Powers (*potestates*, δυνάμεις), (4) Thrones (*throni*), (5) Lordships (*dominationes*, κυριότητες).

[3] κοσμοποιοὶ ἄγγελοι (cf. Iren. I. xix; xx. 1).

dark world, the spiritual hosts of wickedness,' under Satan, 'the *æon* of this world, the Prince of the authority of the air.' Eph. ii. 2.

A ruinous heresy:

Fantastic as the theory appears, it was no frivolous speculation. It was, on the contrary, a serious attempt to solve an ancient and abiding problem—the problem of the origin of evil;[1] and it stimulated much profitable inquiry in the course of the early Christian centuries. Nevertheless it was a pernicious heresy, and, had it prevailed, the Faith must have perished. How widely it diverged from Christianity appears by its very name. It was the doctrine of *gnosis* or 'knowledge,' and its advocates distinguished themselves from the simple multitude who had only 'faith' by assuming the designation of 'Gnostics.'[2] They were 'the spiritual' or 'the perfect,'[3] while mere believers, uninitiated into the mysteries of the *gnosis*, were 'the animal.'[4] It was just the old distinction between the *esoterics* and the *exoterics* in the philosophic schools, a revival of the spirit of caste which the Gospel had exorcised.

(1) Its denial of the Incarnation.

The poison of the heresy lay in its dualism, and its mischief was both theological and ethical. In the former connection it struck at the very foundation of the Faith. Since matter was essentially evil, there could be no true Incarnation. Christ was not God manifest in the flesh, 'the fulness of deity embodied,' but merely an *æon*, an angelic intermediary. This pernicious doctrine had already emerged in Paul's day; and it was subsequently developed by Cerinthus. 'He alleged,' says St. Irenæus,[5] 'that the world had not been made by the First God, but by a power separate and remote from the Authority which is over the Universe, and ignorant of the God who is over all. And Jesus, he supposed, had not been begotten of a virgin, but He had been born of Joseph and Mary, a son, in like manner to all the rest of men, and had become more righteous and wise. And after His Baptism the Christ descended into Him from the Sovereignty which is over the Universe, in the form of a

Cf. Eph. iv. 9, 10; Col. i. 15-19, ii. 8-10.

Cerinthus.

[1] Cf. Tert. *De Præscript.* 7; *Adv. Marc.* I. 2; Eus. *Hist. Eccl.* V. 27.

[2] Cf. Iren. I. i. 11; Clem. Alex. *Strom.* II. iii. 10.

[3] οἱ πνευματικοί, οἱ τέλειοι (cf. n. on 1 Cor. ii. 6, p. 248).

[4] οἱ ψυχικοί (cf. n. on 1 Cor. ii. 14, p. 249).

[5] I. xxi.

dove; and then He proclaimed the unknown Father and accomplished miracles; and at the end the Christ withdrew from the Jesus; and the Jesus had suffered and been raised, but the Christ had remained throughout impassible, being spiritual.'

(2) Its unethical implicate.

This distinction between the Divine Christ and the human Jesus, who were never truly one but were merely associated during the three years of our Lord's ministry, is the inevitable issue of the theory. In Paul's day, however, the heresy was as yet primarily ethical, and this mischief also flowed from its dualistic presupposition. The argument with Gentile converts was that, since matter and spirit are distinct domains, the things of sense are, for the spiritual man, 'indifferent,' and he is free to indulge his carnal appetities as he pleases.[1] This doctrine had already been urged in the Corinthian Church,[2] and it was professed and practised in
Cf. Rev. ii. 6, 14, 15.
the Churches of Asia by a school of sectaries who were still active in the days of the Apostle John. They were known
The Nicolaitans. Ac. vi. 5.
as the Nicolaitans, and they derived their name from Nicolaus, one of the Seven Deacons. He was a Gentile, belonging to Syrian Antioch; and since he had been a proselyte to Judaism ere his conversion to Christianity, it may be inferred that he was a restless spirit. At all events he soon went far astray. His position was defined by his maxim that 'we should disregard the flesh';[3] and a story is told which illustrates his meaning. He was taunted by his fellow-apostles with jealousy regarding his beautiful wife, and he brought her forward and intimated that any one who would might marry her.[4] So entirely did he 'disregard the flesh.' His attitude, however, was liable to misconstruction. It is Clement of Alexandria who tells the story, and, while expressly absolving Nicolaus of personal incontinence, he affirms that 'the adherents of his sect followed up the incident and the maxim simply and inconsiderately and committed fornication without restraint.' They were, he alleges elsewhere,[5] 'dissolute as he-goats.'

[1] Cf. Iren. I. xx. 2, 3; II. xlix. 1.
[2] Cf. p. 238.
[3] ὅτι παραχρᾶσθαι τῇ σαρκὶ δεῖ.
[4] Clem. Alex. *Strom.* III. iv. 25; cf. Eus. *Hist. Eccl.* III. 29.
[5] *Ibid.* II. xx. 118. Cf. Tert. *Adv. Marc.* I. 29; Hippol. *Phil.* VII. 36.

Gentile ignorance of Jewish ethic.

Such scandal would have been impossible among Jewish Christians, disciplined by the stern ethic of the Mosaic Law; but this restraint was lacking in the Churches of Asia. Their members were Gentiles, and it appears that they had travelled beyond that repudiation of moral obligation which the Apostle had so frequently to deplore in his converts from heathenism and which furnished the Judaists with so effective an indictment of his Gospel of Salvation by Faith. Judaism was nothing to them. They despised the Jews and ignored the historic basis of Christianity. And hence arose a striking reversal of the accustomed conditions. Hitherto it had been necessary for the Apostle to plead with the Jews for the recognition of the Gentiles, but now he has to exhibit the glory of the ancient Covenant to his Gentile converts and warn them against despising that precious heritage.

The Asian Presbyters appeal to the Apostle.

Such was the situation which had emerged in the Province of Asia, and it occasioned the leaders of the Churches no small disquietude. It would appear that they held a representative conference, and resolved to communicate with the Apostle. They wrote a letter in name of all the Churches, acquainting him with their perplexity and soliciting his counsel; and they deputed Tychicus to convey it to Rome.[1]

An encyclical letter.

The report was no surprise to Paul. He had detected symptoms of the heresy during his ministry at Ephesus, and after his departure he had kept himself informed of its progress. It had engaged his anxious consideration, and thus he was able to deal effectively with it; and he forthwith addressed himself to the task and composed an encyclical letter.[2] This is the letter which stands in the New Testament

[1] καὶ ὑμεῖς, 'you also' (vi. 21), proves that Paul had received a letter from his readers: they had told him of their concerns, and Tychicus would tell them of his. Cf. κἀγώ, 'I also' (i. 15).

[2] Beza was apparently the first to perceive that the letter is an encyclical. 'Suspicor,' he says in his note on the subscription, 'non tam ad Ephesios ipsos proprie missam epistolam quam Ephesum ut ad ceteras Asiaticas ecclesias transmitteretur.' The evidence is twofold. 1. The address ἐν Ἐφέσῳ (i. 1) is omitted by the two earliest and most authoritative MSS. (א*B), and it was absent from the still earlier text of Origen. Reading τοῖς ἁγίοις τοῖς οὖσιν καὶ πιστοῖς, he attached a metaphysical significance to τοῖς οὖσιν, connecting it with the Ineffable Name (cf. Ex. iii. 14): 'the saints who share the essence of the Eternal.' The fact is that here, as in 'the Epistle to the Romans' (cf. p. 376), the address was left

Canon as 'the Epistle to the Ephesians.' It was not written for the Ephesians alone. It is an encyclical, and it was designed not exclusively for the metropolitan Church, but for all the others in the Province—the Churches at Smyrna, Pergamos, Thyatira, Sardes, Philadelphia, Magnesia, Tralles, Hierapolis, Laodiceia, and Colossæ. Tychicus was charged with its conveyance to Asia and its presentation at its several destinations; and this was a large commission, involving extensive travel and much negotiation. His itinerary was arranged. He would return to Ephesus and deliver the letter there; and thence he would set forth on his tour of the Province. Probably he would betake himself northward to Smyrna and Pergamos, and then strike inland to Thyatira, and thence by Sardes and Philadelphia to Magnesia. From Magnesia he would ascend the valley of the Mæander to Tralles and pursue his journey eastward to Hierapolis, Laodiceia, and Colossæ in the valley of the Lycus. The letter, being an encyclical, lacked the element of *personalia*, and he was charged not merely to deliver it

Cf. vi. 21, 22.

but to convey to each Church the affectionate greetings and particular counsels of the Apostle. It is unlikely that he was furnished with a special copy for each Church. The same manuscript would serve for all. A blank had been left in the address, and in reading it to each community he would supply the name; and doubtless ere his departure a copy would be made and preserved for future reference among the Church's records.

ENCYCLICAL TO THE CHURCHES OF ASIA

'The Epistle to the Ephesians is evidently a catholic epistle, addressed to the whole of what might be called St. Paul's diocese. It is the divinest composition of man. It embraces every doctrine of Christianity;—first, those doctrines peculiar to Christianity, and then those precepts common to it with natural religion.'

S. T. COLERIDGE.

blank in the original draft and the destination was entered in each copy. 2. The absence of *personalia* and, more particularly, sentences like i. 15 and iii. 2 prove that Paul is addressing strangers and not the Church of Ephesus which he knew so intimately. Theod. Mops. recognised this difficulty, and evaded it by supposing that the letter had been written to the Ephesians before the Apostle visited them.

Introduction of the argument.

After the customary address and greeting, the letter begins with an elaborate thanksgiving for the rich heritage of Christian blessings. Here the Apostle skilfully introduces his argument. He tacitly assails the Asian heresy by employing several of its distinctive terms—' spiritual,' ' the heavenly regions,' ' wisdom,' ' fulness '—and exhibiting the true satisfaction of their claims in the Gospel. The heresy contrasted ' spiritual ' and ' material,' ' the heavenly regions ' and ' the world '; the Gospel unites them: ' God has blessed us with every spiritual blessing in the heavenly regions in Christ.' It is not by escaping from ' the prison of the body ' and material environment that we attain spiritual perfection; already this is ours by union with the Cf. ii. 6.
Risen Lord.

The Christian heritage.

Then he enumerates the Christian blessings. The first is our eternal election in Christ; next, its realisation in time —our redemption in Christ; and, finally, the discovery in Christ of God's providential purpose, ' the mystery of His will.' In the heretical philosophy ' mystery ' signified the secret lore which only the ' spiritual ' knew; but on the Apostle's lips it had a grander meaning. It was God's purpose of grace so long hidden but now gloriously manifested in Christ.[1] And its discovery brings ' wisdom '—a truer and nobler wisdom than the heretics imagined. The wisdom which they flaunted was intellectual, and it went hand in hand with moral foulness; but the Christian wisdom was a holy thing: ' He poured the riches of His grace on us to overflowing in wisdom *and moral discernment.*'

The discovery of ' the mystery of His will ' brought wisdom inasmuch as it revealed the oneness of the Universe, ' gathering it under one Head in the Christ '; but in revealing the oneness of the Universe it revealed also the oneness of humanity. The Jews indeed possessed a peculiar prestige in their long history of faith in God and hope in the Promised Saviour; but, though this was lacking to the Gentiles, they had heard the glad tidings of salvation; faith had made it theirs; and the Holy Spirit had sealed their title to the future heritage.

i. 1 Paul, an Apostle of Christ Jesus by God's will, to the saints
2 who are —— and hold the Faith in Christ Jesus. Grace to

[1] Cf. p. 320.

you and peace from God our Father and the Lord Jesus Christ.
3 Blessed be the God and Father of our Lord Jesus Christ,
who has blessed us with every 'spiritual' blessing in 'the
4 heavenly regions' in Christ, in pursuance of His election of us
in Him ere the world's foundation, that we might be holy and
5 blameless in His sight. In love [1] He foreordained us to be
restored to the status of sonship [2] through Jesus Christ,
6 according to the good pleasure of His will, to the praise of the
glory of His grace which He lavished on us in His Beloved.
7 And in Him we have our redemption through His blood, the
remission of our trespasses, according to the riches of His
8 grace, which He poured on us to overflowing in all wisdom
9 and moral discernment [3] when He discovered to us the
mystery of His will according to His good pleasure which He
10 purposed in Him for the establishment of a new order when the
seasons had run their course, to gather the Universe under one
Head in the Christ, the heavens and their belongings and the
11 earth and all that is on it; even in Him in whom we were made
God's heritage, having been foreordained according to the
purpose of Him who operates the Universe according to the
12 counsel of His will, that we might be for the praise of His
13 glory—we who had beforehand hoped in the Christ. And in
Him you also, on hearing the Word of Truth, the Gospel of
your salvation—in Him you also had faith and were sealed
14 with the Spirit of promise, the Holy Spirit, who is the earnest
of our inheritance,[4] that God might redeem His ownership
for the praise of His glory.

Cf. Dt. xxxii. 9.

I. The Theological Question (i. 15-iii)

Commendation of two truths:

And now the Apostle embarks on his argument. He courteously reciprocates the kindness which the letter from Asia had expressed, and assures his readers of his warm regard. With most of them indeed he had no personal acquaintance; but he had heard of their faith and love during his sojourn at Ephesus, and since his departure his

[1] So Chrys., Theod. Mops., Theodrt., construing *ἐν ἀγάπῃ* with *προορίσας*. Otherwise either (1) with *ἐξελέξατο*, 'elected us . . . in love' (Oecum.), or (2) with *ἁγίους καὶ ἀμώμους*, 'holy and blameless in love' (Ambrstr., Vulg.).

[2] Cf. n. on Gal. iv. 5, p. 209.

[3] *σοφία* is theoretical, *φρόνησις* practical. Cf. *Plat. Def.*: *σοφία ἐπιστήμη ἀνυπόθετος· ἐπιστήμη τῶν ἀεὶ ὄντων· ἐπιστήμη θεωρητικὴ τῆς τῶν ὄντων αἰτίας. φρόνησις δύναμις ποιητικὴ καθ' αὑτὴν τῆς ἀνθρώπου εὐδαιμονίας· ἐπιστήμη ἀγαθῶν καὶ κακῶν· διάθεσις καθ' ἣν κρίνομεν τί πρακτέον καὶ τί οὐ πρακτέον.* Arist. *Eth. Nic.* VI. 7.

[4] Cf. p. 349.

interest in them had never flagged. It was his constant prayer that they might miss nothing of their rich heritage in Christ.

(1) The Universal Sovereignty of the Risen Christ.

Here, with the heresy in view, he introduces two profound truths. The first is the Universal Sovereignty of the Risen Christ. Observe how here and throughout his argument he speaks not of 'Christ' but of 'the Christ,' and, in view of the doctrine which Cerinthus ere long advocated and which was already in vogue, identifies Him with the human Jesus, who died and was raised from the dead. The Christ was truly incarnate. He was no mere *æon*, no mere link in a chain of angelic intermediaries between God and the world. He is the Supreme Lord enthroned evermore at God's right hand 'above every "principality" and "authority" and "power" and "lordship" and every name in vogue.'

(2) His Headship over the Church.

Cf. 1 Cor. vi. 15, 16, xii. 12-31; Rom. xii. 4, 5.

And with this truth he links another—Christ's Headship over the Church. The idea is not an absolute novelty. Already he has spoken of the corporate unity of Christians, likening them, in their mutual relationships, to members of one body;[1] but here he enlarges the conception. Christ is the Living Head, and the Church is His Body, 'the fulness of Him who fills the Universe in every part.' It is the perpetuation of the Incarnation. What the flesh was to the Lord in His humiliation, that the Church is in His exaltation. And thus there is no impassable gulf between God and the world.

15 Therefore I too, since I heard of the faith in the Lord Jesus
which prevails among you and the love which you have for all
16 the saints, never cease to give thanks on your behalf, making
17 mention of you in my prayers, that the God of our Lord Jesus
Christ, the Father of Glory, may give you a spirit of wisdom
18 and revelation in full knowledge of Him; the eyes of your
heart being so enlightened that you may know what is the hope
of His calling, what is the riches of the glory of His 'inheritance Dt. xxxiii.
19 in the saints,' and what is the surpassing greatness of His 3, 4.
power for us who have faith according to the operation of His
20 strength's might which He has exhibited in the Christ by
raising Him from the dead and 'seating Him at His right Ps. cx. 1.
21 hand' in 'the heavenly regions' far above every 'principality'
and 'authority' and 'power' and 'lordship' and every name
22 in vogue, not only in this but in the future age. And He 'put Ps. viii. 6.

[1] Cf. p. 291.

everything in subjection under His feet,' and gave Him to the
23 Church as her Supreme Head—the Church which is His Body,
the 'fulness' of Him who fills the Universe in every part.

Life by union with Christ.

This thought completes the argument. Christ is the Church's Head, and she is His Body in vital union with Him. His people, Gentiles and Jews alike, once 'dead through their trespasses and sins,' now share His life, His resurrection, His enthronement 'in the heavenly regions.' 'Because,' says St. Augustine,[1] 'your Head has risen, hope, you other members, for this which you see in your Head. It is an ancient and true proverb: "Where the head is, the other members are too." Christ has ascended into Heaven, and thither we shall follow.'

ii. 1 And you, when you were dead through your trespasses
2 and sins, in which you once comported yourselves according
to 'the *æon* of this world,' according to 'the Prince of the
authority of the air,' the spirit who is now operating in the
3 sons of disobedience—and in them we too were all once
occupied in the lusts of our flesh, doing all that our flesh
and our thoughts would; and we were by nature children
4 of wrath like the rest. But God, rich as He is in mercy,
5 because of the great love with which He loved us, dead
though we were through our trespasses, made us alive with
6 the Christ—it is by grace that you have been saved—and
raised us with Him and seated us with Him in 'the
7 heavenly regions' in Christ Jesus, that He might demonstrate in the ages to come the surpassing riches of His
8 grace by His kindness toward us in Christ Jesus. For it is
by grace that you have been saved through faith; and that
9 not of yourselves: it is God's gift; not of works, that no
10 one may boast. For we are His making, created in Christ
Jesus for good works, which God had arranged beforehand
that we might comport ourselves in them.

Reconciliaion of Jews and Gentiles:

It is not without design that the Apostle here introduces his doctrine of Salvation by Faith. He is about to deal with another aspect of the situation—the cavalier attitude which the Churches of Asia had adopted toward Judaism; and lest his remonstrance should be misconstrued, it was well that he should preface it with a reaffirmation of his Gospel of free grace. The Asian Christians were predominantly,

[1] *In Psalm. XXIX Enarr.* ii. 14.

if not exclusively, converts from heathenism; and they knew the Jews only as their Apostle's adversaries and bitter assailants of their own title to salvation. It was natural that they should retaliate and disdain the Jews and the Jewish religion. And the mischief was twofold. The Church was rent in twain, and the agelong estrangement which Christ had come to heal was perpetuated. And the Gentiles were themselves the chief sufferers. For the Jewish Faith was a precious heritage. It was the historic basis of the Gospel; and when they ignored it and construed Christianity in terms of human speculation, they were forsaking the fountains of heavenly wisdom and turning the Gospel into a barren philosophy.

(1) The Commonwealth of God.

The Apostle confronts this twofold danger with a magnificent conception—the Commonwealth of God. It was originally an Old Testament ideal. Israel was a theocracy, and the holy nation was the Commonwealth of God. Its citizens were the Chosen People, and the rest of the nations were aliens. But the Gospel had enlarged the ideal. The boundaries of the Commonwealth of God had been extended, and they included not Israel alone but humanity. Christ had revealed 'the mystery of God's will,' His eternal purpose of universal grace. He had healed the enmity between Jews and Gentiles and 'reconciled them both in one Body to God.'

Imperial conception of the Church.

And, as has already appeared, this larger and nobler ideal had been revealed to the Apostle by his imperial environment. Rome was the capital of the world, the fountain of law and civilisation, the centre whence so many highways radiated, like rich arteries, carrying their vitalising streams to the remotest province. All the nations, in themselves strangers and foreigners, were united in her, and each shared her glory, her strength, her peace. And here he recognised an emblem of the Commonwealth of God and rose to a loftier conception of the Church. It is significant that in his earlier letters the term 'church' denotes a particular community. Thus, in the year 51 he addressed 'the Church of the Thessalonians'; in the year 53 'the Churches of Galatia,' meaning the Christian communities of Pisidian Antioch, Iconium, Lystra, and Derbe; and in the years 55 and 56 'the Church of God which is at Corinth.' But now

1 Th. i. 1; 2 Th. i. 1. Gal. i. 2.

1 Cor. i. 2; 2 Cor. i. 1.

he employs a new style. The Church is in his thought no longer a particular community of Christians, nor even the sum of all the communities. She is the Body of Christ, her Sovereign Head; she is the Commonwealth of God, embracing in her universal citizenship all the faithful on earth and in Heaven. And thus he addresses, not 'the Church of the Philippians' or 'the Church of the Colossians,' but 'all the saints in Christ Jesus who are at Philippi' and 'the saints and faithful brothers at Colossæ.'

Phil. i. 1. Col. i. 2.

(2) The Living Temple.

It is a noble conception, yet it failed to satisfy the Apostle. It seemed too secular; it needed consecration. And so he glides into another ideal. The Church is more than a Commonwealth; she is a Living Temple. Christ is the foundation or, in the prophetic phrase, 'the chief corner-stone,' which signifies 'the primary foundation-stone at the angle of the structure by which the architect fixes a standard for the bearings of the walls and cross-walls throughout.'[1] On that foundation the spiritual fabric is reared. Stone is added to stone, not only the Apostles and Prophets—the men who had companied with the Saviour and their fellows who were inspired by the Holy Spirit—but all faithful souls. And thus the Living Temple grows from age to age toward its glorious completion.

Cf. 1 Cor. iii. 11. Is. xxviii. 16; cf. 1 Pet. ii. 6.

11 And therefore remember that once you, the Gentiles in the
flesh, 'the Uncircumcision' as you are called by what is called
Cf. Rom. ii. 28, 29. 'the Circumcision,' a circumcision made with the hand in the
12 flesh—that you were at that season apart from Christ, alienated
from the Commonwealth of Israel and strangers to the
Covenants of the Promise; no hope had you and no God in
Is. lvii. 19. 13 the world. But now in Christ Jesus you who once were 'far
off' have been brought 'nigh' in the blood of the Christ.
14 For He it is that is our peace, He who made both one and
pulled down the wall which fenced off one from the other,[2]

[1] ἀκρογωνιαῖος, cf. Moulton and Milligan, *Vocab.*

[2] The area of the Temple at Jerusalem was divided into two courts, the outer and the inner, separated by a balustrade three cubits in height, with pillars at regular intervals on which was inscribed in Latin and Greek an intimation that no alien (ἀλλόφυλον) might pass into the inner court but on pain of death (cf. Jos. *De Bell. Jud.* V. v. 2; *Ant.* XV. xi. 5). One of these pillars with its Greek inscription was discovered by M. Clermont-Ganneau in 1871 (cf. Schürer, *Jewish People*, II. i. p. 266). This is doubtless the reference of τὸ μεσότοιχον τοῦ φραγμοῦ, and it would appeal all the more to the Gentile Christians of Asia,

15 even the enmity between them, by invalidating in His flesh
the Law of commandments expressed in ordinances, that He
might in Himself create the two into one new man, thus making
16 peace, and might reconcile them both in one Body to God
17 through the Cross, slaying the enmity by it. And He came Is. lii. 7,
and 'preached the Gospel of peace to you who were far off and lvii. 19.
18 peace to those who were nigh.' For through Him we have
both of us the *entrée* [1] in one Spirit to the Father.
19 So, then, you are no longer strangers and sojourners. No,
you are the saints' fellow-citizens and members of God's house-
20 hold. You have been built upon the foundation of the Apostles
and Prophets,[2] the 'chief corner-stone' being Christ Jesus
21 Himself. And in Him all the building,[3] being welded together,
22 grows into a holy temple in the Lord. And in Him you also
are being built together into a habitation of God in the Spirit.

The Apostle has now completed his discussion of the speculative aspect of the heresy; and his heart prompts him to a devotional conclusion, a prayer for the establishment of the Churches in the truth. He introduces it by reminding his readers of the proof which he had given them of his devotion to their eternal welfare, and the title which this conferred upon him to their grateful and affectionate regard. He was 'the prisoner of Christ Jesus on their behalf—if indeed,' he adds, 'you have heard of the stewardship of that grace of God which was given me for you.' He is not here suggesting a doubt. Of course they had heard of it, and knew what his devotion in the cause of the Gentiles had cost him. And this constitutes his plea: 'If you know, you must hearken to my appeal.' The thought of the trust

A personal appeal and a prayer.

since it was Paul's supposed violation of the prohibition by introducing their countryman Trophimus into the inner court that had occasioned the riot at Jerusalem and his subsequent imprisonment (cf. Ac. xxi. 28).

[1] Cf. n. on Rom. v. 2, p. 400.

[2] Not (1) 'the foundation which consists of the Apostles and Prophets' (Chrys.: τουτέστι, θεμέλιος οἱ ἀπόστολοι καὶ οἱ προφῆται), since Christ is the foundation (1 Cor. iii. 11), nor (2) 'the foundation which they have laid' (Ambrstr.), since it is God that lays the foundation (cf. Is. xxviii. 16), but 'the foundation on which they are built and on which you also are built in their goodly company.' 'The Prophets' are here, as the order proves, not the ancient (cf. Ambrstr.: 'hoc est, supra novum et vetus Testamentum collocati') but the Christian Prophets (cf. p. 72), who were reckoned next in dignity to the Apostles (cf. iv. 11; 1 Cor. xii. 28).

[3] πᾶσα ἡ οἰκοδομή ℵ[a]ACP. The more strongly attested πᾶσα οἰκοδομή, 'every building,' 'each part of the building' (cf. Mt. xxiv. 1), would denote each separate Christian community.

which had been committed to him diverts him for a brief space from his purpose, and he lingers over it and reiterates that grand conception of 'the mystery of the Christ,' His discovery, to 'His holy Apostles and Prophets,' of God's universal grace. Here Paul not merely includes himself in that august fellowship but arrogates to himself a unique position, inasmuch as he had been specially charged with the proclamation of the mystery. And, lest his claim should seem to savour of boastfulness, he hastens to avow his sense of personal unworthiness: 'To me, the very least of all saints, was this grace given.' Nor, when he spoke of his sufferings on their behalf, would he have the Churches fancy that he grudged these. His Apostleship was a supreme honour, and it was worth all and more than all that it had cost him.

iii. 1 For this reason I Paul, the prisoner of Christ Jesus on
2 behalf of you Gentiles [1]—if indeed you have heard of the
stewardship of that grace of God which was given me
3 for you, how that by revelation was the mystery dis-
Cf. i. 9. covered to me, as I have already written in a brief
4 sentence, in view of which you can, in reading the
Scriptures,[2] perceive what I understand by 'the mystery
5 of Christ,' which in former generations was not discovered to the sons of men as it is now revealed to His
6 holy Apostles and Prophets in the Spirit, that the
Gentiles share with us in the Inheritance and belong
to the same Body and participate with us in the Promise
7 in Christ Jesus through the Gospel, of which I was made
a minister according to the bounteousness [3] of the grace of
God which was given me according to the operation of His
8 power. To me, the very least of all saints, was given this
grace—to preach to the Gentiles the untrackable riches
9 of the Christ, and to show in clear light what my stewardship is—the stewardship of the mystery which from age
to age has been hidden in God, the Creator of the Universe,
10 that now may be discovered to 'the principalities' and
'the authorities' in 'the heavenly regions,' through the

[1] The sentence is resumed at ver. 14 after the digression (vers. 2-13).

[2] ἀνάγνωσις (cf. 1 Tim. iv. 13; Mt. xxiv. 15) was the public reading of the Law and the Prophets in the Christian assemblies according to the synagogal practice (cf. Lk. iv. 16-20; Ac. xiii. 15; 2 Cor. iii. 14). Paul means that, if they kept his doctrine of 'the mystery of Christ' in view during the reading of the O. T., they would find it corroborated διὰ γραφῶν προφητικῶν (cf. Rom. xvi. 25, 26).

[3] τὴν δωρεάν, cf. n. on Rom. v. 15, p. 407.

11 Church, the richly woven 'wisdom' of God, according
to the agelong purpose which He has achieved in Christ
12 Jesus our Lord, in whom we have such boldness and such
13 a confident *entrée* through our faith in Him. And therefore I ask you never to lose heart amid my distresses on
your behalf; for these are your glory.

14 For this reason I bend my knees in the presence of God Cf. Phil. iv. 6.
15 the Father, from whom all 'fatherhood' in heaven and
16 on earth derives its name,[1] that He may grant you,
according to the riches of His glory, to be mightily endued
with power through His Spirit to the inmost core of your
17 being, that the Christ may dwell through faith in your
18 hearts, so that, rooted and founded in love, you may
have the strength to grasp, with all the saints, in its
19 breadth and length and height and depth, and to know,
though it surpasses knowledge, the Christ's love, that you
may be filled up to all 'the fulness' of God.

20 And to Him who has all-transcendent power to do far,
far beyond our requests or thoughts, according to the
21 'power' which is operative in us, to Him be the glory in
the Church and in Christ Jesus to all generations age after
age. Amen.

2. The Ethical Question (iv-vi. 20)

1. Dissension.

And now the Apostle turns to the ethical aspect of the heresy. The trouble which it had created in this connection was twofold. It had, in the first place, excited a bitter controversy, and the Churches were rent by fierce animosities. This temper the Apostle rebukes by reiterating and elaborating his conception of the corporate unity of the Church. Christ was her Living Head, and she was His Body. There was one Body and there was one Spirit, and it behoved the members to 'maintain the unity of the Spirit in the bond of peace.'

There was room indeed for infinite diversity, since to each member a peculiar function was assigned, and the Risen Lord had bestowed on the Church all the rich and various

[1] The Heavenly Fatherhood is the archetype of all earthly fatherhood. Cf. Theodrt.: ὃς ἀληθῶς ὑπάρχει πατὴρ ὃς οὐ παρ' ἄλλου τοῦτο λαβὼν ἔχει ἀλλ' αὐτὸς τοῖς ἄλλοις μεταδέδωκε τοῦτο. πατριά is here *paternitas* (Vulg.), not *gens*, 'family,' 'tribe' (cf. Lk. ii. 4; Ac. iii. 25). In the latter sense πᾶσα πατριά would signify 'every family' (R.V.), not 'the whole family' (A.V.), which would be πᾶσα ἡ πατριά (cf. ii. 21).

gifts which He had won by His redemptive conflict, according to the Psalmist's word :

> ' He ascended on high and led captive a train of captives ;
> He gave gifts to men.'

The quotation diverts the Apostle for a moment from his argument, and he pauses to indicate its Christological significance, employing that Rabbinical manner of exegesis which he had learned in the school of Gamaliel. He saw in the passage an affirmation of the reality of the Incarnation and a refutation of the dualistic heresy. The Lord's 'ascension' implied His previous 'descent.' 'He descended,' says he, quoting from another psalm, '"into the lower parts of the earth,"' that is, into the darkness of the womb. There He was clothed in mortal flesh ; and when He re-ascended to His seat at God's right hand, He carried with Him His glorified humanity. And thus had the gulf between God and man been bridged, not by a hierarchy of angelic intermediaries but by the Incarnate Lord.

Cf. i. 20.

From this digression he returns to his argument. The gifts of the Exalted Redeemer were manifold. There were various offices in the Church of larger or lesser dignity, but these all served the self-same end—'the knitting of the saints together, the upbuilding of the Body of the Christ' ; and there was no occasion for rivalry or jealousy. It was only as each member discharged his proper office that he shared the corporate life and attained his full Christian manhood.

iv. 1 I beseech you, then—I, the prisoner in the Lord—that
you comport yourselves worthily of the call which you have
2 received, with all humility and meekness, with long-suffering,
3 forbearing one another in love, earnest to maintain the
4 unity of the Spirit in the bond of peace. There is one Body,
and there is one Spirit, just as there was one hope which
5 your call inspired when you received it ; there is one Lord,
6 one Faith, one Baptism, one God and Father of all, who
rules all, wields all, and pervades all.

7 Yet to every one of us was grace given as it was measured
8 out by the bounteousness of the Christ. And therefore the
Spirit says :

Ps. lxviii. 18.

> ' He ascended on high and led captive a train of captives;
> He gave gifts to men.'

9 Now what does 'He ascended' mean but that He also
10 'descended' into 'the lowest parts of the earth'?[1] The Ps. cxxxix.
very One who 'descended' is also the One who 'ascended' 15.
far above all the heavens, that He might 'fill' the Universe.
11 And He it is that 'gave' here Apostles, there Prophets,
12 there Evangelists, there Pastors and Teachers,[2] to knit the
saints together[3] for the work of ministration, for the up-
13 building of the Body of the Christ, until we all of us attain
to the unity of the Faith and of the full knowledge of the

[1] εἰς τὰ κατώτατα τῆς γῆς, cf. Ps. cxxxix. 15: ἐν τοῖς κατωτάτω (v. l. κατωτάτοις) τῆς γῆς. If the phrase be a quotation from the psalm, then κατώτατα should be preferred to the more strongly attested κατώτερα. In any case μέρη is a manifest gloss. The interpretation of the passage is much disputed. 1. The Fathers generally (Iren., Tert., Hieron., Ambrstr.) find here a reference to the *Descensus ad Inferos*, the belief, so picturesquely presented in the apocryphal *Evang. Nicod.* and incorporated in the Apostles' Creed (c. A.D. 500), that during the three days between His Death and His Resurrection, while His body lay in the sepulchre, our Lord descended to Hades, where the souls of the saints of old were kept imprisoned until their redemption was accomplished, and brought them forth in triumph. This was known in mediæval English as 'the Harrowing' or 'Harrying of Hell' (cf. Chaucer, *Milleres Tale*, 3512). In its earliest form the idea was that His errand was exclusively to the saints of Israel, the righteous who had believed the promise of His coming, from Adam to John the Baptist (cf. Just. M. *Dial. cum Tryph. Jud.*, Sylb. ed., p. 298; Iren. III. xxii, xxxii. 1; IV. xlii. 4; V. xxxi; Tert. *De Anim.* 55); but by and by a larger hope was cherished. (1) It had been a fancy of Hermas, early in 2nd c., that the Apostles also had descended and preached to the departed and given them the seal of Baptism (*Sim.* IX. xvi), and Clem. Alex.. with characteristic large-heartedness, seized upon it and supposed that, whereas the Lord had preached in Hades to righteous Jews, the Apostles had preached to virtuous heathen (*Strom.* VI. vi. 45; cf. II. ix. 44). (2) Still later it was held, with a yet wider charity, that the Lord's preaching in Hades was addressed to all its captives; and Augustine, while refraining from dogmatism, expresses his sympathy with the idea (cf. *Epist.* clxiv). If the Apostle were indeed referring here to the *Descensus ad Inferos*, his argument would be that Christ had established a universal dominion—from the depth of Hell to the height of Heaven. But the reference is more than dubious. The idea of the *Descensus* is a later growth, alien from N. T., even, on a just interpretation, from 1 Pet. iii. 19, iv. 6. It first appears, though vaguely, in Ign. *ad Magn.* ix. 2. Chrys. and Theod. Mops. understand by the Lord's descent 'into the lowest parts of the earth' His death and burial; and this is the view of most modern interpreters. 3. Though it has found little acceptance, there is good reason for the view of Witsius, Beza, and others, who recognise here a quotation of the Psalmist's phrase (cxxxix. 15), which signifies 'in the darkness of the womb' (cf. Æsch. *Eum.* 635: ἐν σκότοισι νηδύος τεθραμμένη). The passage is thus an affirmation of the Incarnation (cf. Gal. iv. 4; Jo. i. 14), most relevant to the Apostle's argument in view of the heretical denial of its possibility.

[2] ποιμένες, 'shepherds,' were the Overseers (ἐπίσκοποι) or Presbyters (cf. n. on Ac. xx. 28, p. 463); διδάσκαλοι, the Catechists (cf. pp. 80, 218).

[3] πρὸς τὸν καταρτισμὸν τῶν ἁγίων, cf. n. on 1 Th. iii. 10, p. 161.

Son of God, to mature manhood, to the measure of the
14 stature of the Christ's 'fulness,'[1] that we may be no longer
babes, wave-tossed mariners, carried hither and thither
by every wind of the discipline[2] which originates in men's
sleight of hand, in trickery for the furtherance of error's
15 wiles; but, holding the truth in love, may in every respect
16 grow into Him who is the Head, even Christ. From Him
all the Body, linked and welded together by every joint
supplying vital energy as each single part requires, derives
its growth for its own upbuilding in love.

2. Licentiousness.

Dissension, however, was by no means the worst scandal. The heresy relegated the sins of the flesh to the category of 'things indifferent'; and the gross licence which had disgraced the Corinthian Church was rampant in the Churches of Asia. Christian and heathen morals were indistinguishable.

17 This, then, I say and testify in the Lord, that you no
longer comport yourselves as the Gentiles do, in the
18 futility of their mind, being darkened in their thought,
alienated from the life of God by reason of the wilful
ignorance which is in them and the callousness of their
19 heart. Sunk in insensibility, they have abandoned themselves to wantonness to work all uncleanness greedily.
20, 21 But it is not thus that you have learned the Christ, if indeed
you have heard Him and been taught in Him—and this is
22 the truth in Jesus—that you should lay off, as regards your
former behaviour, your old self which is doomed to the
23 corruption that the lusts of error ever bring, and be
24 renovated by the spirit of your mind, and clothe you with
the new self which was created after God's likeness in the
righteousness and piety of the truth.

The prevailing vices.

The Apostle now proceeds to deal with this aspect of the situation; and how appalling it was appears from his

[1] ἡλικία, either 'stature' (cf. Lk. xix. 3) or 'age' (cf. Jo. ix. 21; Heb. xi. 11). It was taken here in the latter sense by the Latin versions (cf. Vulg.: 'in mensuram ætatis plenitudinis Christi'); and Augustine found in the passage an intimation of the condition of the redeemed in the hereafter (cf. *De Civ. Dei*, XXII. xv). They will 'attain to the measure of the age of His fulness'; and since He died and was raised and ascended at the age of thirty-three, in the very prime of manhood when He had passed the immaturity of youth and was still untouched by the decay of age, this will be the condition of all who are raised in Him and share His glory. They will 'flourish in immortal youth.' There will be neither immaturity nor infirmity in our glorified humanity. Cf. Thom. Aquin. *Summ. Theol.* III, Q. xlvi, Art. ix.

[2] Cf. p. 593.

catalogue of the prevailing iniquities—lying, quarrelsomeness, dishonesty, uncleanness, and drunkenness.

25 And therefore lay off falsehood and 'speak truth every Zech. viii.
one with his neighbour,' inasmuch as we are one another's 16.
26 members. 'Be angry and sin not' Let not the sun set Ps. iv. 4.
27 upon your angerment;[1] and never give room to the Devil.
28 Let the thief be a thief no longer, but rather let him toil
with his own hands at honest work, that he may have
29 something to share with one in need. Never let unwholesome speech pass your lips, but only such as is good for
improvement of the occasion, that it may give grace to the
30 hearers.[2] And do not grieve God's Holy Spirit in whom
31 you were sealed for the day of redemption. Let all
bitterness and passion and anger and clamour and reviling
be banished from your midst, and withal every sort of
32 malice. Treat one another kindly and tenderly, forgiving
v. 1 each other just as God in Christ forgave you. Follow
2 God's example, then, as His beloved children, and comport
yourselves lovingly, just as the Christ loved you and gave Ps. xl. 6.
Himself up on your behalf, 'an offering and a sacrifice' Ex. xxix.
to God 'for an odour of a sweet fragrance.' 18; Ez. xx. 41.
3 And as for fornication and every sort of uncleanness or
greed, let them never be even named among you, as befits
4 saints; obscenity, too, and foolish talking or levity,[3]
which are all misbecoming. Your business is rather
5 thanksgiving. For keep this fact in recognition—that
every one addicted to fornication or uncleanness or greed
—and greed is idolatry—has no inheritance in the Kingdom
of the Christ and God.
6 Let no one deceive you with empty words. These are
the things which bring down the anger of God upon the
7 sons of disobedience. Take, then, no part with them.
8 For you were once darkness, but now you are light in the

[1] The Pythagorean rule (Plut. *De Frat. Am.* 488 c). Cf. Jer. Taylor, *Great Exemplar*, II. xii. 30.

[2] Cf. Plut. *Pericl.* viii. 4: 'He was so scrupulous in regard to his speech that always, when he was going to the platform, he would pray to the gods that not a word might fall from him unwittingly unfitted to the occasion in question (πρὸς τὴν προκειμένην χρείαν ἀνάρμαστον).'

[3] εὐτραπελία, 'versatility.' In a good sense in classics. Cf. Arist. *Rhet.* II. xii. 16: ἡ γὰρ εὐτραπελία πεπαιδευμένη ὕβρις ἐστίν. Plato (*Rep.* VIII. 563 A) couples εὐτραπελία and χαριεντισμός, 'pleasantry.' The εὐτράπελος was distinguished, on the one hand, from the γελωτοποιός, 'buffoon,' and, on the other, from the σκληρός, 'churl.' The word, however, degenerated, and Suidas defines it as μωρολογία, κουφότης, ἀπαιδευσία. The Antiochenes termed their boasted scurrility (cf. p. 67) εὐτραπελία (Julian, *Misop.* 344 B). Cf. Trench, *N. T. Syn.*; Jer. Taylor, Serm. XXIII, 'The Good and Evil Tongue.'

9 Lord. As children of light comport yourselves—for the
fruit of light grows in the soil of every sort of goodness
10 and righteousness and truth,—always proving what is
11 well-pleasing to the Lord; and have no dealings with
the unfruitful works of the darkness; rather expose them.
12, 13 For it is disgraceful even to speak of their secret doings. But
being exposed, they all are manifested by the light; for
14 all that is manifested is light. And therefore it is said:[1]

'Awake, O sleeper,
And arise from the dead,
And the Christ will give thee light.'

15 Take careful heed, then, how you comport yourselves.
16 Let it not be as unwise men but as wise, buying up the
17 opportunity, because these are evil days. Therefore do
not lose your moral sense, but understand what is the will
of the Lord.

18 And never get drunk with wine—that way lies profligacy
19 —but be filled with the Spirit. Talk to each other in
psalms and hymns and spiritual songs; sing and make
20 music in your heart to the Lord. Give thanks always
for all things in the name of our Lord Jesus Christ to the
21 God and Father. Be subject to one another in Christ's
fear.

Social relationships.

Here is the sovereign antidote to the moral plague—the grace of the Holy Spirit. It satisfies the soul; it quenches unholy desires; it makes the heart grateful and glad and gentle; it banishes selfishness and establishes the law of love. Every domain of society had been infected with the foul contagion, and the Apostle proceeds to commend the blessed remedy to every class—husbands and wives, parents and children, masters and slaves.

Cf. 1 Cor. xi. 3.

22 Wives, be subject to your own husbands as to the
23 Lord, because a husband is his wife's head as the Christ
also is the Church's Head, Himself His Body's Saviour.
24 But, as the Church is subject to the Christ, so let the wives
be to the husbands in everything.

25 Husbands, love your wives just as the Christ also loved
26 the Church and gave Himself up for her, that He might
make her holy, after cleansing her with the laver of water,
27 by the Word,[2] that He might present the Church to Himself

[1] A verse of a Christian hymn.

[2] ἐν ῥήματι belongs to ἁγιάσῃ. The Word of God (cf. vi. 17), His truth, is the means of sanctification (cf. Jo. xvii. 17). Chrys., construing ἐν ῥήματι with καθαρίσας τῷ λουτρῷ τοῦ ὕδατος, understands by 'the word' the baptismal formula 'in the name of the Father and the Son and the Holy Spirit.'

all-glorious with never a spot or a wrinkle or aught of the
28 sort, but that she might be holy and blameless. Thus
also ought husbands to love their own wives—just as they
love their own bodies. One who loves his wife loves him-
29 self. For no one ever hated his own flesh ; no, he nurtures
30 and cherishes it just as the Christ does the Church, because
31 we are members of His Body. 'For this reason shall a
man forsake his father and mother, and shall be joined to Gen. ii. 24.
32 his wife ; and the two shall become one flesh.' This
mystery is great : my reference is to Christ and to the
33 Church. However, as regards you individually, let each
love his own wife just as he loves himself ; and as for the
wife, let her see to it that she fear her husband.[1]

vi. 1 Children, obey your parents in the Lord ; for this is a
2 duty. 'Honour thy father and mother'—this is the Ex. xx. 12;
3 first commandment with a promise attached to it—'that Dt. v. 16.
it may prove well with thee, and thy days be long upon the
earth.'

4 And, fathers, never anger your children, but nurture
them in the Lord's instruction and admonition.[2]

5 Slaves, obey your human lords with fear and trembling
in the simplicity of your heart as you obey the Christ,
6 not in the way of eye-services as though you had only men
to please, but as Christ's slaves, doing God's will with the
7 soul's devotion. Serve with good-will as the Lord's slaves
8 and not men's, knowing that whatever good each does, he
will get it back from the Lord, whether he be a slave or a
free man.

9 And, lords, act on the same principles toward them. For-
bear your threating, knowing that both theirs and yours
is the Lord in Heaven, and there is no respect of persons
with Him.

The panoply of God.

Human effort is impotent without heavenly reinforcement. It was a hard warfare that his readers must wage—a warfare against strong and subtle spiritual forces ; and the Apostle not only summons them to the conflict but shows them 'the panoply of God.' Already in writing to the Thessalonians and the Corinthians he had employed the metaphor of the soldier and his armour ; but now he elaborates it and portrays in minute detail a mail-clad warrior. Here is another evidence of his Roman environment ; and it was doubtless the prætorian guardsmen who took their turns in

Cf. 1 Th. v. 8; 2 Cor. x. 4.

[1] As the Christian fears Christ (cf. ver. 21).
[2] Cf. p. 61.

the wardenship of the prisoner, that furnished him with the material of the picture. His nimble imagination caught the spiritual analogy, and he turned it into an effective parable.

10 Henceforth find your power in the Lord and in the might of
11 His strength. Clothe yourselves with the panoply of God,
that you may have power to stand against the stratagems of the
12 Devil. For it is not with flesh and blood that we have to
wrestle, but with 'the principalities,' with 'the authorities,'
with 'the rulers of this dark world,' with 'the spiritual hosts
13 of evil'[1] in 'the heavenly regions.' Therefore take up the
panoply of God, that you may have power to stand your ground
in the evil day, and after every achievement still stand firm.
14 Stand, then, with 'the girdle of truth about your waist' and
15 'the cuirass of righteousness on your breast' and the equip-
16 ment of 'the Gospel of peace on your feet.' In every encounter take up the shield of faith, on which you will have
17 power to quench the flaming missiles[2] of the Evil One. And
receive 'the helmet of salvation' and 'the sword of the Spirit,'
18 that is, 'the Word of God.' With all prayer and supplication
pray at all seasons in the Spirit, and for that be vigilant in all
19 perseverance and supplication for all the saints, and on my
behalf that speech may be given me, whenever I open my
20 mouth, to publish boldly the mystery of the Gospel on behalf
of which I am an ambassador—in a chain![3]—that in telling it
I may speak as boldly as I ought to do.

Is. xi. 5; lix. 7; lii. 7.

Is. lix. 17; xlix. 2, xi. 4; Hos. vi. 5.

Cf. 2 Cor. v. 20.

Conclusion.

An encyclical, being intended for various communities, was necessarily couched in general terms and lacked the greetings wherewith the Apostle was wont to conclude his letters. When he despatched his great encyclical on Justification by Faith he annexed a personal message to each copy, and he would probably have done the like in this instance had there been no better way. But Tychicus had undertaken the toilsome office of conveying the letter to

[1] Both οἱ κοσμοκράτορες and τὰ πνευματικὰ τῆς πονηρίας are Gnostic phrases. Cf. Iren. I. i. 10. The term ὁ κοσμοκράτωρ was derived originally from the Talmud, where it denotes the Angel of Death. Cf. *Vayik. Rab.* 18: 'At that time the Lord called the Angel of Death and said to him: "Although I have made thee Kosmocrator (קוזמוקרטור) over the creatures, yet hast thou no power over this nation, because they are My sons."'

[2] The *falaricæ* or *malleoli*, fitted with pitch and tow and launched ablaze to fire houses and other buildings.

[3] 'Paradoxon,' says Bengel. 'Mundus habet legatos splendidos.' An ambassador's person was sacrosanct.

Asia and delivering it to the various churches, and he would, more effectively than any written message, express to each all that was in the Apostle's heart.

21 That you also may know my situation and my employment,
Tychicus, the beloved brother and faithful minister in the Lord,
22 will acquaint you with everything. I am sending him to you
for this very purpose, that you may be acquainted with our
concerns, and that he may encourage your hearts.
23 Peace to the brothers and love and faith withal from God
the Father and the Lord Jesus Christ.
24 GRACE BE WITH ALL WHO LOVE OUR LORD JESUS CHRIST IN
'INCORRUPTION.'[1]

It was not without occasion that the Apostle introduced in his practical exhortation a counsel to slaves and masters. An addition had been made to his little company in the person of Onesimus, a fugitive slave. His master was Philemon, a prominent member of the Christian community at Colossæ and one of Paul's Asian converts. Though he belonged to a Christian master, Onesimus was not himself a Christian. He was a slave of the lowest order—a Phrygian slave, and a Phrygian slave was a byword for rascality. It was a common proverb that 'a Phrygian was the better of a flogging';[2] and Onesimus had acted up to the reputation of his class. He had stolen from his master and decamped. And he had naturally betaken himself to Rome. The vast metropolis was, in the phrase of a Latin historian,[3] 'the cesspool into which the refuse of the world streamed'; and nowhere could the fugitive find a safer refuge than in its

Conversion of a fugitive slave.

Cf. Phm. 19.

Cf. Phm. 18.

[1] *ἀφθαρσία*, one of the heretical terms. Cf. fragment of Gnostic Gospel (*Oxyrh. Pap.* 1081, 10-19): *εἶπεν· πᾶν τὸ γεινόμενον ἀπὸ τῆς φθορᾶς ἀπογείνεται ὡς ἀπὸ φθορᾶς γεγονὸς, τὸ δὲ γεινόμενον ἀπὸ ἀφθαρσίας οὐκ ἀπογείνεται ἀλλὰ μένει ἄφθαρτον ὡς ἀπὸ ἀφθαρσίας γεγονός*, 'He said: Everything that is born of corruption perishes as having been born of corruption; and what is born of incorruption does not perish but remains incorrupt as having been born of incorruption' (cf. Jo. iii. 6). One of the Gnostic 'syzygies' was *Ἀφθαρσία καὶ Χριστός* (cf. Iren. I. xxvii. 1). Paul here (1) affirms the reality of the Incarnation, the oneness of the Divine Christ and the human Jesus (*τὸν Κύριον ἡμῶν Ἰησοῦν Χριστόν*), and (2) places 'incorruption' in loving Him—not in the negation but in the consecration of matter.

[2] Cf. Suid.: *Φρὺξ ἀνὴρ πληγεὶς ἀμείνων καὶ διακονέστερος.* Cic. *Pro Flacc.* 27: 'Utrum igitur nostrum est an vestrum hoc proverbium *Phrygem plagis fieri solere meliorem?*'

[3] Sallust, *Catil.* xxxvii; cf. Tac. *Ann.* XV. 44.

teeming purlieus. He was soon in distress and needed a friend. Paul, confined to his lodgings, would never have encountered him; but his comrades were free, and they did the work of evangelists in the city; and it is an indication of the nature of their ministry that in the course of it one of them came across the wretched fugitive. Perhaps it was Tychicus. Since he was an Asian, he may have visited Colossæ and stayed at the house of Philemon; and he would recognise Onesimus. He brought the forlorn creature home, and the gracious Apostle won his poor soul for Christ. Kindness begat kindness, and Onesimus was like a son to his benefactor, tending him with affectionate devotion.

Advent of Epaphras of Colossæ.

By a curious coincidence hardly had Paul finished his encyclical to the Churches of Asia when another Colossian presented himself. This was Epaphras, and not only was he a native of Colossæ but it was he who had introduced Christianity into the city. He was one of the numerous provincials who had visited Ephesus during the Apostle's ministry there and been won to the Faith; and he had carried home the glad tidings and had ever since been the leader of the Church. Colossæ had not escaped the poison which had infected the Province, and Epaphras had come to acquaint the Apostle with the situation and obtain his counsel.

Cf. Col. i. 6, 7; iv. 12.

The cities on the Lycus:

He must of course have been aware of the appeal which the Churches of Asia had addressed to the Apostle, and it might be supposed that this should have sufficed him. But it appears that he was confronted by a peculiar difficulty and had need of special counsel. Colossæ, once a great city,[1] had in those days sunk into comparative insignificance.[2] It had been eclipsed by the rise of two prosperous neighbours. One was Laodiceia, which competed with Apamea Kibotos for the position of chief city in Phrygia. It lay on the left bank of the Lycus, fully five miles to the west of Colossæ, backed to the south by the snow-capped range of the Cadmus; and it had risen to importance under the imperial rule.[3]

Colossæ.

Laodiceia.

[1] Cf. Herod. VII. 30; Xen. *Anab.* I. ii. 6.

[2] Cf. Strabo, 576, 578.

[3] Strabo: *ἡ δὲ Λαοδίκεια μικρὰ πρότερον οὖσα αὔξησιν ἔλαβεν ἐφ' ἡμῶν καὶ τῶν ἡμετέρων πατέρων.*

Its situation favoured its advancement, since it was not only a station on the great trade route between Ephesus and the East but the junction of three busy highways—from Sardes in the north-west, from Dorylæum in the north, and from the southern port of Attaleia. The Province of Asia, under Roman administration, was divided into 'jurisdictions,' and the most important of these was the *jurisdictio Cibyratica*; and Laodiceia was its capital, where the taxes of the twenty-five subordinate towns were collected and the proconsular courts held their sessions.[1] It was a financial centre, and Cicero resorted thither during his Cilician proconsulship to cash his treasury bills.[2] Nor was its prosperity due merely to political circumstances. It derived a splendid revenue[3] from a breed of sheep peculiar to the neighbourhood with fleeces of raven gloss and fine texture; it excelled also in sandal-making;[4] and its fame and wealth were further augmented by the manufacture of a reputed eye-salve, the 'Phrygian powder,'[5] employed in a celebrated school of medicine between Laodiceia and Carura.[6] Laodiceia was thus a prosperous city, and it is a striking evidence not only of her wealth but of the spirit which animated her, that when, some three years later, she and the neighbouring cities of Hierapolis and Colossæ were laid in ruins by one of the earthquakes so frequent in that volcanic district, she repaired the destruction by her own resources without the usual subsidy from the imperial exchequer.[7] This magnanimous spirit had its perils, and it is no surprise that in the pride of their achievement the Laodiceans should have boasted of their material riches, oblivious of their spiritual destitution, and
needed the apocalyptic counsel to purchase 'gold tried with Rev. iii. 17, 18.
fire' and the 'white raiment' which was better than their

[1] Plin. *Nat. Hist.* V. 29.

[2] Cf. *ad Fam.* III. 5; *ad Attic.* V. 15.

[3] Strabo: προσοδεύονται λαμπρῶς ἀπ' αὐτῶν.

[4] Cf. Schürer, *Jewish People*, II. i. p. 44.

[5] Cf. Ramsay, *Cit. and Bish. of Phryg.*, I. p. 52.

[6] Strabo, 580.

[7] Tac. *Ann.* XV. 27. Tacitus assigns the earthquake to the year 60; and it would then be strange that the Apostle in writing to Colossæ early in 61 should have made no reference to the recent disaster. But Eusebius (*Chron.* Ol. 210), who has here a better title to credence (cf. Lightfoot, *Col.*, pp. 38 ff.), puts it after the burning of Rome in 64.

fine stuff of raven black, and anoint their blind eyes with a salve more efficacious than their ' Phrygian powder.'

Hierapolis. Across the Lycus, some four miles distant from Laodiceia, stood the city of Hierapolis, backed by the Mesogis range.[1] Its enduring fame is that there, about the year A.D. 50, was born that noblest of the Stoic teachers, Epictetus, ' a slave, and maimed in body, and a beggar for poverty, and dear to the immortals.' Its chief industry was the dyeing of woollen fabrics in scarlet and purple, but this was not the main source of its abundant prosperity. The physical peculiarities which distinguish the valley of the Lycus attain at Hierapolis their highest development. The neighbourhood teems with hot springs ; and so strongly are these impregnated with calcareous deposit that the courses of the cascades which leap down the mountain-side are marked by a snow-white incrustation, and it is told how the husbandmen used to embank trenches round their gardens and vineyards and flood these from the streams, and in a year's time the channels had hardened into fences of solid stone.[2] Some of the springs were poisonous,[3] especially one deep well known as the Plutonium which, like the Grotta del Cane near Naples, exhaled mephitic vapour fatal to any living creature that breathed it except, according to local fable, the priests of Cybele. Most of them, however, were merely medicinal ; and thus the city acquired fame as a health resort, and the numerous baths which still survive among its extensive ruins, show how largely it was frequented.

Jewish population. There was naturally an intimate fellowship between the Christian Churches in those adjacent cities. Probably all Cf. Col. iv. 13. three had been founded by Epaphras, and he maintained a constant and solicitous surveillance over them. The immediately significant fact, however, is that there was in that

[1] Cf. Strabo, 629 f. It is an evidence of the connection between the Asian heresy in the Apostle's day and the later Gnosticism that Hierapolis was subsequently designated Ophiorymè, 'the Serpent's stronghold' (cf. *Acta Philippi*, 107), as the home of the Jewish-Gnostic sect of the Ophites or Naasenes, so named because the serpent (ὄφις, נָחָשׁ) was the symbol of their worship (cf. Hippol. *Refut.* v. 4).

[2] Strabo : *τὸ μὲν γὰρ ὕδωρ εἰς πῶρον οὕτω ῥᾳδίως μεταβάλλει πηττόμενον ὥστ' ὀχέτους ἐπάγοντες φραγμοὺς ἀπεργάζονται μονολίθους.* Cf. Vitruv. VIII. 3.

[3] Hence the epigram (*Anthol.* I. 65) : *εἴ τις ἀπάγξασθαι μὲν ὀκνεῖ θανάτου δ' ἐπιθυμεῖ, | ἐξ Ἱερᾶς Πόλεως ψυχρὸν ὕδωρ πιέτω.*

locality a large and influential Jewish colony. It originated in the reign of Antiochus the Great (223-187 B.C.) who, in view of civil commotion in Lydia and Phrygia, deported thither from Mesopotamia two thousand Jewish households, that their proved loyalty might leaven the prevailing disaffection.[1] Some of these would certainly be settled in the valley of the Lycus, and they would share in the increasing prosperity of its cities and be continually reinforced by fresh accessions of their enterprising race. How numerous and important the Jewish population became is evinced by the circumstance that their annual tribute of a half-shekel apiece to the Temple at Jerusalem amounted to so large a sum that in 62 B.C. Flaccus, the Proprætor of the Province of Asia, took alarm. He prohibited the exportation of so much treasure and arrested in Laodiceia no less than twenty pounds weight;[2] representing, it has been calculated, over eleven thousand male adults irrespective of women, children, and slaves.

A Jewish phase of the Asian heresy. Cf. Col. i. 21, 27; ii. 11-13.

The Jewish population in the valley of the Lycus was thus very large; and, though the Churches were predominantly Gentile, they would include a proportion of Jewish converts.[3] These may have been few, but they were influential, and they had succeeded in turning the heresy into a Jewish channel and casting it in a Jewish mould. Intellectual movements are commonly epidemic. They are inspired by the spirit of the age, and their influence is all-pervasive. Thus, those Gnostic tendencies which in Gentile communities expressed themselves in terms of Greek philosophy, especially Neopythagoreanism, found a home also in Judaism.

Essene principles: (1) Essential evil of matter.

That home was Essenism,[4] and its affinity with the incipient Gnosticism which had invaded the Churches of Asia is distinctly apparent. Its fundamental principle was the essential evil of matter. The body was corruptible and evanescent. It was the prison-house of the immortal soul, and only on its severance from the body would the soul be

[1] Jos. *Ant.* XII. iii. 4.

[2] Cic. *Pro Flacc.* xxviii.

[3] It is not without significance in this connection that there were Phrygian Jews in the multitude of converts on the great Day of Pentecost (cf. Ac. ii. 10).

[4] Cf. p. 447.

released from its bondage and joyfully soar on high.[1] It does not appear, nor indeed is it likely, that the Essenes engaged in characteristically Greek speculation regarding the mode of creation, yet they had metaphysical theories of their own. No one was admitted to the order until he had served faithfully a noviciate of three years; and then he must pledge himself by 'awful oaths,' chiefly 'that he would neither hide anything from the members of the sect nor disclose anything regarding them to others, no, not under violence even unto death; that he should communicate none of their ordinances to any one otherwise than he had himself received them; but that he would refrain from robbery, and likewise closely guard the books of their sect and the names of the angels.'[2] Hence it appears that the Essenes had a hidden lore, enshrined in 'sacred books,'[3] and a doctrine of angels. The latter is especially significant. It is essentially Jewish, and it is illustrated by two specific ideas. One is the Rabbinical notion that the Law had been delivered to Moses by angelic mediators;[4] and the other the Philonic doctrine of the creation of man. It is written in the Book of Genesis, first, that God said, 'Let us make man in our image,' and, then, that 'God created man'; and Philo explains this as meaning that in the creation of man God co-operated with the angels. 'All else was made by God, but man alone was fashioned with the aid of other fellow-workers. The Father of the Universe converses with His own powers, to which He gave the fashioning of the mortal part of our soul, in imitation of His own art when He formed the rational in us; deeming it right that what rules in the soul should be wrought by the Ruler and what is subordinate by subordinates.'[5] Thus the Jewish doctrine conceived the angels as bearing a part in revelation and creation; and the Essenes elaborated it, especially by assigning names to the angels and defining their functions after the manner of the Book of Enoch.[6] Hence it appears that their doctrine exhibits a close analogy to the Gnostic theory of a hierarchy

Cf. Col. ii. 3.

(2) Angelic intermediaries.

i. 26, 27.

[1] Cf. Jos. *De Bell. Jud.* II. viii. 11.
[2] *Ibid.* 7.
[3] *Ibid.* 12.
[4] Cf. n. on Gal. iii. 20, p. 206.
[5] Phil. *De Profug.* 556 (Mangey).
[6] *Enoch*, xx, xl.

of angelic intermediaries between God and the world; and furthermore its elevation of the angels to the rank of God's fellow-workers issued in angel-worship.[1] Cf. Col. ii. 18.

(3) Asceticism.

Moreover, the Essenes were visionaries. They pored over the prophetic Scriptures and undertook to foretell the future.[2] Indeed, according to one widely approved though doubtful etymology, their name signified 'the Seers.'[3] Josephus affirms that their predictions rarely missed the mark, and he has furnished several striking instances.[4] Visionaries are commonly ascetics, 'lean-look'd prophets whispering fearful change'; and here is a clue to the Apostle's reference when he describes the ascetic teacher who was unsettling the Churches by the Lycus, as 'poring over his visions, idly puffed up by his carnal mind.' Col. ii. 18. For the Essenes were ascetics. Indeed this was their primary and fundamental characteristic; and if Philo's explanation of their name as signifying 'the Holy Ones' be etymologically untenable, it is at all events historically accurate. They shared with

[1] *Preaching of Peter*, quoted in Clem. Alex. *Strom.* VI. v. 41: *μηδὲ κατὰ Ἰουδαίους σέβεσθε, καὶ γὰρ ἐκεῖνοι μόνοι οἰόμενοι τὸν Θεὸν γινώσκειν οὐκ ἐπίστανται, λατρεύοντες ἀγγέλοις καὶ ἀρχαγγέλοις, μηνὶ καὶ σελήνῃ.* Orig. *Contra Cels.* V. 6: *πρῶτον οὖν τῶν Ἰουδαίων θαυμάζειν ἄξιον, εἰ τὸν μὲν οὐρανὸν καὶ τοὺς ἐν τῷδε ἀγγέλους σέβουσι· τὰ σεμνότατα δὲ αὐτοῦ καὶ δυνατώτατα.* Cf. the apocalyptic protest against the angelolatry which had invaded the Churches of Asia (Rev. xix. 10; xxii. 9). Theodrt. (on Col. ii. 18) says that angelolatry continued long in Phrygia and Pisidia, and even in his own time (5th c.) was still uneradicated.

[2] Cf. Jos. *De Bell. Jud.* II. viii. 12.

[3] Ἐσσαῖοι from חָזָה, 'see,' a derivation which seems to be countenanced by Suidas: *οἱ ἐπιμελοῦνται τῆς ἠθικῆς λέξεως θεωρίᾳ δὲ τὰ πολλὰ παραμένουσιν. ἔνθεν καὶ Ἐσσαῖοι καλοῦνται, τοῦτο δηλοῦντος τοῦ ὀνόματος, τουτέστι, θεωρητικοί.* The origin of the name is uncertain. Besides the above many explanations have been suggested (cf. Lightfoot, *Col.*, pp. 347 ff.), and of those three may be adduced. (1) 'The Holy Ones,' from *ὅσιος*. This Philo's derivation. Cf. *Quod Omnis Probus Liber*, 457 (Mangey): *διαλέκτου Ἑλληνικῆς παρώνυμοι ὁσιότητος.* Hence probably the form Ὀσσαῖοι. (2) 'The Healers' or 'Physicians,' from Aram. אֲסָא, 'heal.' Cf. the kindred Egyptian sect of the Θεραπευταί, 'Healers.' This is countenanced by the statement of Josephus (*De Bell. Jud.* II. viii. 6) that the Essenes 'with a view to the healing of ailments sought out remedial roots and the properties of stones.' (3) 'The Silent Ones,' from חָשָׁה, 'keep silence,' in reference to their secrecy regarding their hidden lore. Josephus (*ibid.* 5) says that 'to those without the silence of those within appeared as some awful mystery.'

[4] Cf. the predictions of Judas (*Ant.* XIII. xi. 2; *De Bell. Jud.* I. iii. 5), Menahem (*Ant.* XV. x. 5), and Simon (*De Bell. Jud.* II. vii. 3).

the Greek philosophers the initial postulate of the inherent and necessary evil of matter; but there the agreement ended. The common principle yielded two diametrically opposite inferences. It was argued, on the one hand, that material things are, for the spiritual man, 'indifferent'; and, on the other, that the flesh must be mortified that the spirit may be unfettered.[1] Thus the principle issued now in libertinism and now in asceticism, and it is remarkable that the Gnostic schools of the second century were divided between these two attitudes. The Gentile schools, like the Carpocratians, were libertine, while the Judaistic Encratites were ascetic. And already in the Apostle's day the distinction had asserted itself in the Province of Asia. The general attitude, defined in his encyclical, was libertine, but the attitude in the Churches by the Lycus was ascetic. And the reason is that in the latter the heresy was cast in the Essene mould, and the Essenes were ascetics.

Excessive veneration of the Mosaic Law.

They shared the Pharisaic reverence for the Mosaic Law, but they carried it beyond the utmost reach of Pharisaic scrupulosity. 'The chief object of veneration among them next to God was the name of the Lawgiver; and if any one blasphemed against him, he was punished with death.' They observed the Sabbath with extreme rigour. 'They not only prepared their food the day before, that they might not so much as kindle a fire on that day, but they durst not so much as remove a vessel nor do their natural office.'[2] Their ablutions were frequent. They bathed in cold water before each meal and whenever they incurred defilement. In the sultry East the practice of anointing the body after bathing was almost a necessity, but they would have none of it, regarding oil as a pollution; and they always wore white raiment.[3]

Sun-worship.

So resolute were the Essenes in eschewing the contamination of impure matter, and thus far they remained true to the spirit of Jewish ceremonialism. But their ascetic solicitude carried them further and betrayed them into a usage which

[1] Cf. Clem. Alex. *Strom.* III. v. 40: *φέρε δὲ εἰς δύο διελόντες πράγματα ἁπάσας τὰς αἱρέσεις ἀποκρινώμεθα αὐτοῖς. ἢ γάρ τοι ἀδιαφόρως ζῆν διδάσκουσιν, ἢ τὸ ὑπέρτονον ἄγουσαι ἐγκράτειαν διὰ δυσσεβείας καὶ φιλαπεχθημοσύνης καταγγέλλουσι.*

[2] Jos. *De Bell. Jud.* II. viii. 9.

[3] *Ibid.* 3, 5, 9.

approached perilously near idolatry and suggests Zoroastrian influence. Light is purity, and they worshipped the sun, oblivious of the Scriptures' denunciations. 'Before the appearance of the sun,' says Josephus,[1] 'they utter nothing of profane matters but only certain ancestral prayers to him, as though supplicating him to rise.' The Jewish Law had ordained that ordure should be buried in the earth, and the Essenes observed this precept; only, their anxiety was not lest the unclean thing should offend the eyes of the Lord but 'lest it should outrage the beams of the god'; and 'the god' is here the Sun. It is such idolatry that the Apostle has in view when he warns the Christians in the valley of the Lycus against the empty deception of the heretical teacher who was making them his booty 'according to the world's dim lights,' and reminds them that 'when they died with Christ, they left the world's dim lights.'

Cf. Dt. iv. 19; 2 Ki. xxiii. 5; Job xxxi. 26, 27; Jer. xliv. 17; Ez. viii. 16.

Cf. Dt. xxiii. 12-14.

Col. ii. 8, 20.

Essenism the mould of the Colossian heresy.

The Gnostic ideas were *en l'air* in those days, and they expressed themselves everywhere in terms of the prevailing thought. Just as in the Greek world their vehicle was the Neopythagorean philosophy, so in the Jewish world it was Essenism. It may indeed seem incredible that the doctrine of an isolated sect of anchorites in the Wilderness of Engedi should have been diffused abroad and travelled as far as the Province of Asia; but the truth is that the Essenes were not all recluses. Many of them remained in the world. There was a Gate of the Essenes in Jerusalem;[2] and Josephus says that 'they were numerous in every city.'[3] Thus their opinions and practices were notorious, and they would influence many who did not profess themselves Essenes. Indeed their principal use was that they served as a congenial nidus for the larger ideas which were everywhere stirring in the minds of men and which but for them would hardly have found a lodgment in Judaism.

An influential teacher.

The Churches in the valley of the Lycus, being predominantly Gentile, would naturally have fallen into line with their neighbours throughout the Province, but it appears that a persuasive teacher had arisen in their midst. He was a Jewish Christian; and while he taught the common heresy,

Cf. Col. ii. 8.

Cf. i. 16.

[1] Jos. *De Bell. Jud.* II. viii. 5. [2] *Ibid.* V. iv. 2. [3] *Ibid.* II. viii. 4.

Cf. Eph. iv. 17-v. 21; Col. ii. 16-23.

he gave it the distinctive Essene cast. The distinction was mainly ethical: elsewhere in the Province the heresy was libertine; in the valley of the Lycus it was ascetic.

Letter to the churches by the Lycus.

Such was the situation which had confronted Epaphras and which he reported to the Apostle; and the latter proceeded to deal with it in a letter addressed to the Church at Colossæ. To a large extent it traversed the same ground as his encyclical, since the intellectual problem was identical: the Gnostic ideas which had invaded the other churches of the Province prevailed also in those by the Lycus. Hence he thus far simply reiterates his argument and reproduces much of his phraseology. This was inevitable in writing immediately on the same theme.[1] Had the intellectual problem been all, the encyclical would have sufficed; but there was also the ethical question. He had dealt elaborately in the encyclical with the prevailing libertinism; but his argument there was irrelevant to the situation in the valley of the Lycus, and therefore he omits it and substitutes a disquisition on asceticism. Nevertheless there was much in the encyclical which was profitable for the Colossians and their neighbours, especially its full discussion of the Gnostic tendencies; and he would have them read and ponder it also.

Cf. Col. iv. 16.

So he adheres to the original plan. Tychicus would convey both letters. He would make his tour of the Province and deliver the encyclical to each of the churches by the way. Colossæ was his ultimate destination; and on reaching it he would deliver to the Christians there both their own letter and the encyclical which he had brought from Laodiceia, his previous station. And since their letter was designed for their neighbours as well, it must be transmitted first to Laodiceia and thence to Hierapolis.

[1] George Eliot's correspondence furnishes an apposite parallel. Writing to Madame Bodichon on 4th Dec. 1863 she says: 'You perceive that instead of being miserable, I am rather following a wicked example, and saying to my soul, "Soul, take thine ease."' Then on 28th Dec. she writes to Mrs. Peter Taylor: 'I am wonderfully well in body, but rather in a self-indulgent state mentally, saying, "Soul, take thine ease," after a dangerous example.' Cf. Sir Walter Scott's letter to Rev. Mr. Gordon, 12th Apr. 1825 (Lockhart's *Life of Scott*, chap. lxxv), repeating phrases which occur in his portraiture of Rev. Josiah Cargill in *St. Ronan's Well*, chap. xvi (published Dec. 1823)—'diminished the respectability,' '*concio ad clerum*,' 'walk through the parts.'

LETTER TO COLOSSÆ

Address and commendation. Cf. ii 1.

After the customary salutation and address the Apostle expresses his appreciation of the past record of the Colossians. He had never indeed visited them, but he had heard of their faith and love, and what Epaphras had told him had confirmed those pleasing reports—a needful assurance lest they should suspect their 'faithful minister' of an ungracious representation.

i. 1 Paul, an Apostle of Christ Jesus through the will of God,
2 and Timothy the brother, to the saints and faithful brothers
in Christ at Colossæ. Grace to you and peace from God our
Father.
3 We thank God, the Father of our Lord Jesus Christ, always
4 for you in our prayers, since we have heard of your faith in
5 Christ Jesus and the love which you bear to all the saints in
view of the hope laid up for you in the heavens, which you
heard of long ago in the word of the truth of the Gospel.
6 That Gospel has come to you in the fruitfulness and growth
which it displays throughout the world; and these it has
displayed among you also, ever since the day when you heard
7 and gained full knowledge of the grace of God in truth, as you
learned it from Epaphras, our beloved fellow-slave, who is a
8 faithful minister of the Christ on your behalf,[1] and who has
informed me of your love in the Spirit.

Assurance of continued regard.

And lest they should fancy that recent developments had alienated his own regard, he assures them also of his constant affection and his earnest solicitude for their spiritual advancement.

9 Therefore we also, ever since the day when we heard of it,
have never ceased praying on your behalf and asking that you
may be filled with the full 'knowledge' of His will in all
10 'wisdom' and 'spiritual' understanding, so that you may
comport yourselves worthily of the Lord and please Him in
everything by bearing fruit and growing in every good work
11 through the full 'knowledge' of God, by enduement with every
kind of power, according to the might of His glory, to be ever
12 enduring and long-suffering, with joyous thankfulness to the

[1] The authorities are fairly divided between ὑπὲρ ὑμῶν and ὑπὲρ ἡμῶν. The former ('on your behalf') reminds the Colossians of Epaphras' devotion to them. The latter ('on our behalf') would mean that he had preached to them as the Apostle's deputy; but in this case it should rather have been ὑπέρ μου.

Father who has qualified you to share in the lot of the saints in
13 light. He rescued us from 'the authority of the darkness' and
transported us into the Kingdom of the Son who is His love's
14 embodiment,[1] in whom we have our redemption, the remission
of our sins.

I. The Theological Question (i. 15-ii. 6)

The universal supremacy of Christ.

Here by interweaving several of its characteristic phrases —'knowledge,' 'wisdom,' 'spiritual,' 'the authority of the darkness'—the Apostle has introduced the heresy; and now he proceeds to its refutation. He affirms the pre-eminence of that 'Son who is the embodiment of the Father's love,' and defines His relation to God, to the Universe, and to the Church. He was no mere *æon*, no mere angelic intermediary, but the Eternal Son of God incarnate, in the fine phrase of Hugo Grotius, *Dei inaspecti aspectabilis imago*, 'the Visible Image of the Invisible God.' That is His relation to God, and His relation to the Universe is its corollary. The Father's heart is wide, and He created the Universe and peopled it that He might lavish upon it His overflowing affection. His Eternal Son was not enough, and He created a multitude of sons in His image 'that,' as the Apostle says elsewhere, 'He might be the first-born among many brothers.' (Rom. viii. 29.) But the Eternal Son, by right of primogeniture, remains evermore the Lord of all creation, the Father's universal household. That is His relation to the Universe: it is 'in Him' and 'through Him' and 'for Him.' But sin has destroyed the primal order and necessitated reconciliation; and what Christ was to the former order, He is also to the latter. He is the Head of the Church. He was the beginning of the former creation, and He is the beginning of the latter; as the First-born, the Eternal Son, He was Lord of the human family, and as the First-born from the dead He is Lord of the redeemed who share His Death and His Resurrection.

[1] τοῦ Υἱοῦ τῆς ἀγάπης αὐτοῦ. Cf. Aug. *De Trin.* xv. 37: 'The love of the Father, which is in His ineffably simple nature, is nothing else than His very nature and substance, as often already we have said and dislike not often to repeat. And therefore "the Son of His love" is none else than One who has been begotten of His substance.'

15 And He is the image of the invisible God, the First-born
16 Lord of all creation, because in Him was created the universe of
things in the heavens [1] and on the earth, the visible and the
invisible, whether 'thrones' or 'lordships' or 'principalities'
or 'authorities': the universe has been created through Him
17 and for Him; and He is before all things, and in Him they are
18 an ordered universe. And He is the Head of the Body, the
Church. He is the Beginning, the First-born from the dead,
19 that He may everywhere occupy the first place, because it was
God's good pleasure that all 'the fulness' should dwell in Him
20 and that He should through Him reconcile the universe to
Himself by making peace through the blood of His Cross—yes,
reconcile all through Him whether on the earth or in the
heavens.

This was no mere theory for the Colossians; they had experienced it. Once alienated from God, they had been reconciled through Christ's infinite Sacrifice—His true Incarnation and His Death 'in the body of His flesh'; and nothing could prevent their attainment of the final glory of His redemption but their own unfaithfulness, their abandonment of the Gospel which had already done so much for them. That was the peril which threatened them, and the Apostle addresses to them a double appeal, a double argument for resisting the heretical allurement and standing true to the Gospel. First, it was 'the Gospel which had been preached in all the creation under heaven.' Its efficacy had been proved in every land, and should they forsake it for an evanescent speculation? And, again, it was 'the Gospel of which he had been made a minister.' He was the Apostle of the Gentiles, and it was for the sake of the Colossians and their fellow-Gentiles that he had toiled and suffered and was at that hour in bonds. It was a delicate appeal to their chivalry, a suggestive challenge to their loyalty. He was their champion, and he was enduring the malice of that party which would have excluded them from the Church. There were, as he significantly observes later, only three Jewish Christians befriending him in his sore need. Would

Incentives to steadfastness.

Cf. iv. 10, 11.

[1] ἐν τοῖς οὐρανοῖς in the Colossian letter corresponds to ἐν τοῖς ἐπουρανίοις in the encyclical (cf. Eph. i. 3, 20, ii. 6, iii. 10, vi. 12). The phrases are distinctive of the Jewish and Gentile phases of the heresy respectively. The 'heavens' here are the Seven Heavens of Rabbinical Theology, and the conception was employed by the Judaist Gnostic Valentinus in the 2nd c. (cf. Iren. I. i. 9).

the Colossians forget this and espouse a Judaist propaganda ?

Not that he grudged his sacrifices for their sake. It was in a glorious cause that he was suffering ; and its glory lay in this—that he was not merely suffering on their behalf ; he was sharing the Redeemer's vicarious Sacrifice. His Death on Calvary was not the whole of Christ's Passion. He is the Head of the Church, and He shares the anguish of His meanest member. His Sacrifice is an agelong Passion, and it is continued by every believer who, according to His word, 'takes up his cross and follows Him.' That was the Apostle's inspiration. His sufferings were a sacred privilege ; they were his fellowship with the Glorified Lord, his contribution to the achievement of God's 'mystery,' the eternal purpose of universal redemption.

And that was the reason of his insistent solicitude. The heresy was, at the best, a message for the few, for the esoteric circle of 'the spiritual,' 'the perfect,' who were initiated into its 'secret wisdom.' But the Gospel was for 'every man' ; and therefore it was that he was so anxious for his friends in the valley of the Lycus who had never seen his face or heard the truth from his own lips, and strove so hard to confirm their faith and arm them against the plausible sophistries which were invading their minds.

21 And you, alienated as you once were, and enemies in your
22 thought amid your evil works, He has now reconciled in the
body of His flesh through His Death, to present you holy and
23 blameless and unchargeable in His sight, if indeed you abide
by the Faith, founded and steadfast and never moved away
from the hope of the Gospel which you heard—that Gospel
which has been preached in all the creation under heaven, and
of which I Paul was made a minister.

24 I am now rejoicing in my sufferings on your behalf, and I
am doing my part to complete in my person what is lacking
in the Christ's distresses on behalf of His Body, that is, the
25 Church, of which I was made a minister according to the
stewardship which God gave me for you to fulfil the Word
26 of God, the mystery which has been hidden from the ages and
the generations. But now it has been manifested to His
27 saints, to whom it was God's will to discover what is the
riches of the glory of this mystery among the Gentiles, which
28 is 'Christ in you, the hope of glory.' And Him we proclaim,
admonishing every man and teaching every man in every sort

Cf. Rom. viii. 10; 2 Cor. xiii. 5; Gal. iv. 19.

of 'wisdom,' that we may present every man 'perfect' in
29 Christ. And to this end I toil and contend with all the energy
wherewith His power endues me.
ii. 1 For I wish you to know what a hard contest it is that I am
waging on behalf of you and the people at Laodiceia and all
2 who have never seen my face in bodily presence, that their
hearts may be encouraged and that they may be welded
together in love and gain all the riches of intelligent satisfaction, till they attain a full 'knowledge' of the mystery of God,
3 even Christ, in whom all 'the treasures of wisdom' and
4 'knowledge' are 'hidden.' I say this that no one may befool
5 you with plausible sophistry. For, though I am far away in
bodily presence, yet I am with you in spirit and rejoice to see
your discipline and the solid front which your faith in Christ
presents.

Is. xlv. 3; Prov. ii. 3, 4.

2. The Ethical Question (ii. 6-iv. 6)

Christian purity.

And now the Apostle turns to the ethical aspect of the question. It was indeed well that the Christians in the valley of the Lycus had recognised their moral obligation and repudiated the libertinism which disgraced the other Churches of the Province. So far they were truly Christian; for Christ is His people's pattern, and they are His only as they are like Him. The Apostle has just spoken of the 'discipline' of the Colossians and 'the solid front which their faith in Christ presented'; and now he applies this military metaphor. A gallant leader is the inspiration of his troops. He is their exemplar, like Shakespeare's hero by whose light

'Did all the chivalry of England move
To do brave acts: he was indeed the glass
Wherein the noble youth did dress themselves:
He had no legs that practised not his gait;
. . . so that in speech, in gait,
In diet, in affections of delight,
In military rules, humours of blood,
He was the mark and glass, copy and book,
That fashion'd others.'

'As, then,' says the Apostle, 'you have received the Christ, Jesus the Lord, comport yourselves in Him.'

They were indeed right in seeking purity, but they sought it by a wrong method—not by glad fellowship with the Living

Lord but by the morose practice of Judaistic asceticism. Despite the Apostle's protest the error persisted and spread down the valley of the Mæander. Some fifty years later it prevailed in the Church at Magnesia,[1] and St. Ignatius laid his finger on the mischief when he exhorted the Magnesians to 'put away the evil leaven which had grown stale and sour, and betake themselves to the new leaven, which is Jesus Christ.' The stale leaven is the spirit of asceticism, and it embitters the soul. The new leaven is the love of Christ, and it floods the heart with health and gladness and makes it, in the Apostle's phrase, 'overflow in thanksgiving.'

6 As, then, you have received the Christ, Jesus the Lord, com-
7 port yourselves in Him. Be rooted, be built up in Him; be
confirmed by the Faith as you were taught it; and overflow in
thanksgiving.

Condemnation of asceticism.

And so he warns the Colossians against the 'philosophy and empty deception' of the ascetic heresy. It was an attempt to recall them from the free, glad life of the Gospel to the futile bondage of Judaistic ceremonialism. All that it offered, Christ had given them. They had in Him the true circumcision—the purity which the old rite merely symbolised. For what did their Baptism signify? It signified their union with Christ. They had died with Him; they had been buried with Him; they had been raised with Him; and now they shared His triumphant life. His victory over the powers of evil was their redemption. Here the Apostle flashes out a magnificent picture. The ceremonial Law had been the debtor's bond, and God had reckoned with it in Christ. He had met its claims, and He had nailed the cancelled bond to His Cross, advertising to the Universe that it was no longer valid. And in cancelling the bond He had disarmed the powers of evil. His Sacrifice was their defeat. The Cross was the Victor's chariot, and He had led the vanquished 'principalities and authorities' in His triumphal train.

8 See to it! Perhaps there will be [2] some one who is making
you his booty through his philosophy and empty deception,
according to the tradition of men, according to the world's

[1] Ignat. *Ad Magn.* viii-x.

[2] Cf. n. on Gal. ii. 2, p. 199.

9 dim lights,[1] and not according to Christ. For in Him dwells
10 all 'the fulness of deity' embodied; and you are 'filled' in
Him. He is the Head of every 'principality' and 'authority.'
11 And in Him you were circumcised with a circumcision not
made by hand when you put off the body of the flesh and
12 received the circumcision of the Christ by your burial with
Him in Baptism, in which you were also raised with Him
through your faith in the operation of God who raised Him
13 from the dead. And you, when you were dead by reason of
your trespasses and the uncircumcision of your flesh—He made
14 you alive with Him; He forgave us all our trespasses; He
obliterated the condemnatory bond[2]—the bond of legal
ordinances—which bore so hard against us; and He has taken
15 it out of court and nailed it to the Cross.[3] He despoiled 'the
principalities' and 'the authorities,' and paraded them openly[4]

[1] στοιχεῖα, cf. n. on Gal. iv. 3, p. 208. Here (cf. ver. 20) the term has perhaps a double reference—(1) to the 'rudimentary ideas' of Judaism and (2) to the Essenic sun-worship.

[2] The ancient writing material was papyrus, and since the ink did not permeate the fibre, it could be washed off, leaving the sheet clean.

[3] Grotius sees here a reference to the custom, which prevailed in some places in his day and which he supposes to have prevailed in Asia, of driving a nail through a cancelled bond. The suggestion has been rejected on the ground that there is no evidence of the custom in the Apostle's day, but Gal. iii. 1 (cf. n., p. 203) is sufficient. It was customary to post up magisterial announcements in public, but here, in contempt, it is not an edict cancelling the bond that is posted up, but the cancelled bond itself.

[4] The double compound ἀπεκδύεσθαι is apparently a Pauline coinage, occurring only here and iii. 9 (cf. the noun ἀπέκδυσις, ii. 11). The interpretation is much disputed. 1. It was taken generally by the Fathers as a proper reflex. mid., 'having stripped Himself'; and then the passage was construed in two ways: (1) The Greek Fathers took τὰς ἀρχὰς καὶ τὰς ἐξουσίας as the obj. of ἀπεκδυσάμενος, 'having stripped Himself of the principalities and the authorities, He paraded them openly' (Chrys., Theod. Mops., Theodrt.). So Lightfoot: 'The powers of evil, which had clung like a Nessus robe about His humanity, were torn off and cast aside for ever.' (2) The Latin Fathers supplied τὴν σάρκα as obj. of ἀπεκδυσάμενος and construed τὰς ἀρχ. καὶ τὰς ἐξ. with ἐδειγμάτισεν, 'having stripped Himself of the flesh, He paraded the principalities and the authorities' (Ambros. *Expos. Ev. sec. Luc.* v. 107; Aug. *Epist.* cxlix. 26). The objection to both is that they involve an abrupt change of subj., making Christ the subj. in ver. 15. God (cf. vers. 12, 13) is the subj. throughout the passage. 2. The mid. is not necessarily reflex. but may denote what one does in one's own interest (cf. Moulton's Winer, pp. 322 ff.); and so it was taken here by Hieron. ('exspolians principatus et potestates, traduxit confidenter') and Ambrstr. ('exuens principatus et potestates, ostentavit in auctoritate'), 'having stripped' or 'despoiled the principalities and the authorities, He paraded them,' in His triumphal procession (cf. p. 352). ἐδειγμάτισεν, cf. Hor. *Epist.* I. xvii. 33: 'captos ostendere civibus hostes.'

by leading them in triumphal procession in the chariot of the Cross.[1]

Its futility and harmfulness.

Here lay the condemnation of the heresy alike in its ascetic and in its speculative aspect. The reimposition of ceremonial ordinances was a reaffirmation of the cancelled bond, and the worship of angels a re-enthronement of the vanquished powers and a dethronement of the Victor. There is no need of angelic intermediaries; for Christ is our Head, and in union with Him we are in vital contact with God in all His fulness. And this is the one secret of purity. Asceticism is unavailing; for it deals with externals and never touches the inner springs. Nor is it merely unavailing; it is positively mischievous. It is an affectation of 'humility'; and, as the philosophic Emperor has shrewdly observed, 'the pride which is proud of the lack of pride, is most offensive of all.'[2]

16 Let no one, then, judge you in eating and in drinking or in
17 the matter of a feast or a new moon or a Sabbath.[3] These are
only the shadow of things to come, but the substance is the
18 Christ's. Let no one rule you out of the prize,[4] delighting in
'humility' and worship of angels, poring over his visions,[5]
19 idly puffed up by his carnal mind, and not holding fast the
Head, from whom all the Body, supplied and welded together
by means of its joints and ligatures, grows with a God-given
20 growth. If, when you died with Christ, you left the world's
dim lights, why, as though still alive in the world, are you
21 overridden by ordinances: 'Do not handle this'; 'Do not
22 taste that'; 'Do not touch the other thing'—things which
all waste away when they have served their use—according to
23 the 'commandments and teachings of men'? These restrictions
have all a show of 'wisdom' in self-imposed worship and

Is. xxix. 13; cf. Mt. xv. 9.

[1] *ἐν αὐτῷ, i.e., ἐν τῷ σταυρῷ* (cf. ver. 14). The Cross is here God's triumphal chariot, just as it is His throne according to the Christian variant in Ps. xcvi. 10 LXX (insisted on by Just. M., Tert., Aug.): *ὁ Κύριος ἐβασίλευσεν ἀπὸ τοῦ ξύλου.* Cf. Lat. hymn: 'Impleta sunt quæ cecinit | David fideli carmine, | Dicens in nationibus, | Regnavit a ligno Deus.'

[2] M. Aurelius, XII. 27: *ὁ γὰρ ὑπὸ ἀτυφίᾳ τῦφος τυφόμενος πάντων χαλεπώτατος.*

[3] The stereotyped catalogue of Jewish observances. Cf. 1 Chr. xxiii. 31; 2 Chr. ii. 4, xxxi. 3; Ez. xlv. 17; Hos. ii. 11; Is. i. 13.

[4] *καταβραβεύειν*, of an umpire (*βραβεύς*) who decides against the rightful winner. Cf. Suid.: *καταβραβευέτω· καταλογιζέσθω, κατακρινέτω, καταγωνιζέσθω. τὸ ἄλλου ἀγωνιζομένου ἄλλον στεφανοῦσθαι λέγει ὁ Ἀπόστολος καταβραβεύεσθαι.*

[5] *ἐμβατεύειν*, in the classics of a god 'haunting' sacred ground (cf. Soph. *O. C.* 679; Æsch. *Pers.* 449); in the ritual of the Greek Mysteries of the initiate 'setting foot on' the divine life (cf. Moulton and Milligan, *Vocab.*).

'humility' and ascetic rigour, but they possess no value for combating carnal indulgence.

After thus demonstrating the futility of asceticism the Apostle exhibits the Christian method of attaining purity. The believer is united with Christ at every stage of His redemptive progress—His Death, His Burial, His Resurrection, His Exaltation. He not only died with Christ to this world, but he was raised with Him and lives with Him. 'Your life,' says the Apostle, 'is hidden with the Christ in God. Recognise this; seek the things which are above, and set your minds on them.' It is precisely the counsel which he had administered to his Galatian converts eight years previously: 'Comport yourselves by the Spirit, and no desire of the flesh will you ever perform.' This is the golden secret. Experience has ever proved the futility of asceticism, and foul things were rife at Colossæ. The remedy lay in forsaking the dead past and breathing the atmosphere of the new creation, that high domain where the old distinctions are obliterated and the divine ideal which slumbers in every child of the human race, be he a wise Greek or a religious Jew or a degraded savage or an oppressed slave, is quickened and released.

Purity by union with Christ.

Cf. Rom. vi. 1-9.

Gal. v. 16.

iii. 1 If, then, you were raised with the Christ, seek the things
which are above, where the Christ is, 'seated at God's right Ps. cx. 1.
2 hand.' Set your minds on the things which are above, not
3 on those which are upon the earth. For you died, and your
4 life is hidden with the Christ in God. When the Christ is
manifested—He who is our life—then you also will be
5 manifested with Him in glory. Mortify, then, your members
which are upon the earth—fornication, uncleanness, sensual-
6 ity, evil desire, and the greed which is idolatry. These are the
7 things that bring down the anger of God; and that was the
arena where you also comported yourselves in the days when
8 your life was there. But now you also must lay them all off—
anger, passion, malice, reviling, obscene talk: let it never pass
9 your lips. Speak no falsehood against one another, since
you have divested yourselves of the old self with its practices,
10 and have clothed yourselves with the new self which is being
renovated to ever fuller knowledge 'after the image of its Gen. i. 27.
11 Creator.' And there is here no distinction between Greek
and Jew, circumcision and uncircumcision, barbarian,
Scythian, slave, free man; but Christ is everything and in
everything.

How to attain it.

But how is it possible always to inhabit this serene domain? The way is simple and practical. The fountain of all evil is selfishness and the pride and enmity which it breeds; and the remedy lies in the cultivation of a kindly, meek, patient, and forgiving spirit. And how may this be achieved? First, says the Apostle, remember how the Lord has forgiven you, and you will forgive others. Nay, you will not only forgive; you will love. Second, in every question which may arise, recognise that the supreme interest is the preservation of brotherly fellowship. Never seek a controversial triumph. Make the Peace of Christ the arbiter; let it decide your differences. Again, store your mind with Gospel teaching and sing the songs of redemption. There is a blessed efficacy in a holy text or a glad hymn. And, finally, in everything you say or do, have Christ's approval.

12 Clothe yourselves, then, as God's chosen, holy and beloved,
with tender compassion, kindness, humility, meekness, long-
13 suffering, forbearing one another and forgiving each other, if
one has a grievance against another. Just as the Lord forgave
14 you, so must you also. And over all these graces put on love:
15 this is the bond of 'perfection.' And let the Christ's peace be
umpire in your hearts; for it is indeed to peace that you were
16 called in one Body. And show yourselves thankful. Let the
Christ's Word dwell within you richly. In all 'wisdom'
teach and admonish each other with psalms and hymns and
17 spiritual songs in grace, singing in your hearts to God. And
everything that you do in word or in work, do it ever in the
name of the Lord Jesus, giving thanks to God the Father
through Him.

Consecration of the home.

The home is the sanctuary of life, and there especially should the Christian graces be displayed. And so the Apostle reiterates the precepts which he had addressed in the encyclical to husbands and wives, parents and children, masters and slaves.

18 Wives, be subject to your husbands, as is becoming in
19 the Lord. Husbands, love your wives, and never be bitter
20 against them. Children, obey your parents in everything;
21 for this is well-pleasing in the Lord. Fathers, never irritate
22 your children, lest they be discouraged.[1] Slaves, obey in
everything your human lords, not in eye-service, as though

[1] Cf. p. 61.

you had only men to please, but in simplicity of heart,
23 fearing the Lord. Whatever you are doing, work with the
24 soul's devotion, as for the Lord and not for men, knowing
that from the Lord you will receive the recompense of the
inheritance. It is to the Lord Christ that you are slaves.
25 For one who does wrong will get back the wrong which he
iv. 1 has done; and there is no respect of persons. Lords,
accord what is right and equitable to your slaves, knowing
that you also have a Lord in Heaven.

The proper conduct of the controversy.

It was a difficult situation that the faithful Christians in the valley of the Lycus occupied, confronted as they were with a subtle heresy and encompassed by keen and aggressive controversialists. They were guardians of the Faith, and it became them to bear themselves well and commend the truth to the unbelieving world. And so the Apostle counsels them to abound in prayer; and lest he should seem dictatorial and didactic, he begs them to remember him in their intercessions, since he too occupied a difficult situation and needed the aids of heavenly grace. 'Wisdom' was a catchword of the heresy, and they must exhibit a nobler wisdom. They must be ever watchful and miss no opportunity. Zeal, however, is insufficient. Controversy may confute, but it never convinces; it merely exasperates. It is only a gracious word that prevails; and 'grace,' says Samuel Rutherfurd, 'is a witty and understanding spirit, ripe and sharp.'

2 Persevere in prayer; be vigilant in it with a spirit of
3 thankfulness; and pray withal for us that God may open to
us a door for the Word, so that we may tell the mystery of the
4 Christ for the sake of which I am even in bonds, that I may
5 make it as manifest as I should tell it. Comport yourselves in
'wisdom' toward those without, buying up the opportunity.
6 Let your argument be always gracious, seasoned with salt,[1]
that you may know how you should answer every one.

Closing messages.

Here ends the argument. There was no need to encumber the letter with personal matters, since not only was Tychicus to convey it to Colossæ but Onesimus, the fugitive slave, was

[1] The use of salt is twofold—(1) to preserve from corruption and to flavour (cf. Job vi. 6); and thus λόγος ἅλατι ἠρτυμένος is opposed to λόγος σαπρός, 'rotten talk' (Eph. iv. 29), and (2) μωρολογία, 'foolish' or 'insipid talking' (Eph. v. 4). μῶρος (cf. *insipidus*), 'foolish,' had also the physical signification of 'insipid,' 'tasteless.' Cf. Mt. v. 13; Lk. xiv. 34.

returning thither in his company; nevertheless the Apostle thought fit to enter the greetings of his companions at Rome. And the reason was that there were two of these who required his special commendation. One was John Mark. The old quarrel was notorious, and now that it was healed, the Apostle would have the happy issue known, all the more that Mark purposed visiting Colossæ. Already, it seems, the Apostle had intimated this and bespoken a welcome for him, and now he reiterates the injunction. Then there was Epaphras, the Colossian Presbyter. By carrying to Rome a report of the controversy in the valley of the Lycus he had incurred not a little odium, and the Apostle takes occasion to certify his loyalty to the Colossians and their neighbours at Laodiceia and Hierapolis. The letter was addressed to Colossæ, but it was designed equally for the neighbouring churches. The Apostle had never visited them, yet there was at least one Laodicean whom he knew. This was a lady named Nympha, whose house was the meeting-place of the Christians in the city. Doubtless, like Epaphras, she had visited Ephesus during his ministry there, and had been won by his preaching; and so he sends his greeting to her and the congregation at her house.

7 With my situation Tychicus, the beloved brother and faithful
8 minister and fellow-slave in the Lord, will acquaint you. I
am sending him to you for this very purpose, that you may be
acquainted with our concerns, and that he may encourage your
9 hearts; and with him Onesimus, the faithful and beloved
brother who is one of yourselves. They will acquaint you with
all that is doing here.
10 Aristarchus, my fellow-captive, greets you; and Mark,
Barnabas' cousin—regarding him you have received my
11 injunction: 'if he comes to you, welcome him,'—and Jesus
called Justus. These are the only Jewish converts who are
my fellow-workers for the Kingdom of God, and they have
12 proved an encouragement to me. Epaphras, one of yourselves,
greets you. He is a slave of Christ Jesus, and he is ever wrestling on your behalf in his prayers, that you may stand 'perfect'
13 and satisfied in everything that is the will of God. For I bear
him testimony that he is deeply concerned for you and the
14 people at Laodiceia and those at Hierapolis. Luke, the beloved
physician, greets you, and Demas.
15 Greet the brothers at Laodiceia, and Nympha and the Church

16 at her house.[1] And when this letter has been read among you,
take care that it be read also in the Church of the Laodiceans,
17 and that you also read the one from Laodiceia.[2] And say to
Archippus: 'Look to the ministry which you received in the
Lord, that you fulfil it.'

The sign-manual. Cf. i. 1.

And now, according to his custom,[3] he takes the pen from his amanuensis Timothy and adds his sign-manual. His writing was ungainly at the best, and it was none improved by the fetter dangling from his wrist; and he surveyed the sprawling characters with a smile and inserted a pathetic apology: 'Remember my bonds.'

18 THE GREETING OF ME PAUL WITH MY OWN HAND. REMEMBER
MY BONDS. GRACE BE WITH YOU.

[1] The text here is uncertain. (1) *Νύμφαν καὶ τὴν κατ' οἶκον αὐτῆς ἐκκλησίαν*, 'Nympha and the Church at her house' (B 67** Syr$^{p\ txt}$). (2) *Νυμφᾶν καὶ τὴν κατ' οἶκον αὐτῶν ἐκκλησίαν*, 'Nymphas and the Church at their house' (ℵACP), *i.e.*, perhaps, 'the house of him and his friends.' Probably, however, *αὐτῶν* is due to the preceding *ἀδελφούς*. (3) *Νυμφᾶν καὶ τὴν κατ' οἶκον αὐτοῦ ἐκκλησίαν*, 'Nymphas and the Church at his house' (DEFGKL), obviously a copyist's correction.

[2] That is, the encyclical which Tychicus had presented at Laodiceia and brought on to Colossæ. Each church in the Province received it from the previous town in the circuit: for the Colossians it was 'the letter from Laodiceia,' and for the Laodiceans it would be 'the letter from Hierapolis,' and so forth. It is significant that 'the Epistle to the Ephesians' was entitled by Marcion 'to the Laodiceans' (cf. Tert. *Adv. Marc.* v. 17). Until it was recognised as an encyclical, the reference here was a puzzle. 1. It was supposed that 'the letter from Laodiceia' was one, no longer extant, which Paul had written to the Laodiceans and which he desired the Colossians also to read; and at an early date a forgery appeared, professing to be the lost letter. The text is given by Westcott (*Canon*, Append. E) and Lightfoot (*Col.*, pp. 285 ff.). It is fatal to this theory that Paul bids the Colossians convey his greeting to 'the brothers at Laodiceia' (cf. ver. 15). That was necessary when all that the latter had from him was an impersonal encyclical, but it would have been unnecessary had he just written them a personal letter. 2. Dislike of the idea that an apostolic writing had perished, accentuated by antipathy to the forgery, suggested another theory. It was pointed out that Paul speaks of a letter *from*, not *to*, Laodiceia, and hence it was argued that it was not a letter which he had written to the Laodiceans but one which they had written to him, consulting him about certain difficulties. Chrys. mentions this opinion as current in his day (*τινὲς λέγουσιν*) without indicating his own; but the theory was warmly espoused by Theod. Mops. and Theodrt. Such a letter, however, would have been in Paul's own hands, and he would not have directed the Colossians to procure it from Laodiceia but would have sent it to them. 3. The letter was one which Paul had written from Laodiceia, variously identified with 1 Tim. (Joan. Damasc., Theophyl.), 1 or 2 Th., Gal. It is a sufficient answer that the Apostle had never visited Laodiceia (cf. ii. 1); and, moreover, all those canonical epistles were certainly written elsewhere.

[3] Cf. p. 155.

Philemon and his household.

The Apostle's task was not complete when he had finished his letter to the Colossian Church. He had still another to write on behalf of Onesimus. The fugitive's master was [Cf. Phm. 11, 12; Col. iv. 9.] Philemon, who is known only from this correspondence. He was a citizen of Colossæ; and he was not only a Christian [Cf. Phm. 19.] but a convert of the Apostle, one of the fruits of his ministry at Ephesus. Since he owned at least one slave and probably [Cf. vers. 5, 6.] more, he was a man of means, and he was distinguished no less for his generosity than for his piety. His house was [Cf. ver. 2.] the Church's meeting-place, and he deserved the encomium [Rom. xvi. 23.] which the Apostle had bestowed on Gaius of Corinth, 'my host and the host of the whole Church.' He kept an open house, and Paul compliments him by intimating his intention [Cf. Phm. 22.] to avail himself of its lavish hospitality should he, as he hoped, visit Colossæ in the event of his speedy release. His wife Apphia[1] was like-minded, and their son Archippus[2] followed in their steps. He held some office in the Church, and the Apostle, who never dealt in cheap praise, styles him 'my fellow-soldier,' a title which he has bestowed only on [Cf. Phil. ii. 25.] one other, Epaphroditus of Philippi, and which speaks of strenuous devotion. It might indeed be construed as rather a challenge than a commendation; and in his letter to the [Cf. iv. 17.] Colossian Church the Apostle sends Archippus an express and emphatic injunction to diligence in his ministry, as though he had been exhibiting remissness.[3] But this is probably an unfair judgment. It is said that 'the ministry which he had received' was the charge of the Colossian Church during the absence of Epaphras;[4] and in view of the

[1] Not the Latin *Appia* but a Phrygian name (Ἀπφία) frequent in inscriptions (cf. Lightfoot, *Col.*, pp. 304 ff.; *Fresh Revision*, p. 186). The masc. is Ἀπφίανος, and they are derived from ἀπφά, a term of endearment for a brother or sister, ἀπφύς being the corresponding term for a father (Suidas).

[2] Cf. Phm. 2, where the addition καὶ τῇ κατ' οἶκόν σου ἐκκλησίᾳ indicates that Philemon, Apphia, and Archippus belonged to one household, the natural inference being that Philemon and Apphia were husband and wife and Archippus their son. It is curious that Theod. Mops. alone of the Greek Fathers draws this inference. Chrys. recognises Philemon and Apphia as husband and wife but dismisses Archippus as ἕτερόν τινα ἴσως φίλον.

[3] Cf. Chrys.: τίνος ἕνεκεν οὐ γράφει πρὸς αὐτόν; ἴσως οὐκ ἐδεῖτο, ἀλλὰ ψιλῆς μόνης ὑπομνήσεως ὥστε σπουδαιότερος εἶναι.

[4] Cf. Ambrstr.: 'Post enim Epaphram, qui illos imbuit, hic accepit regendam eorum Ecclesiam.' Since the warning to Archippus follows greetings to the

anxiety of the latter for his people's welfare, all the more since he contemplated remaining a while at Rome, it was natural that the Apostle should, without reproach, exhort the young teacher to gird himself to his heavy task. Cf. Col. iv. 12, 13.

Roman slaves.

Whether there were other members of Philemon's family or no, these were not his entire household. Slavery was a universal institution in the ancient world, and it was a poor house which had not its retinue of slaves. Ten were accounted a beggarly array, too few for dignity and barely enough for respectability.[1] Incessant conquest flooded Rome's slave-market with prisoners of war, and the abundant wealth of her citizens enabled them to maintain large households. Some were enormous. Just as ten were the fewest that decency permitted, so two hundred constituted an adequate equipment;[2] but this number was frequently far exceeded, and it is recorded that in the time of Augustus a wealthy freedman, C. Cæcilius Claudius Isidorus, notwithstanding considerable losses during the Civil War, left in his will 4116 slaves.[3] Of course wealthy Romans had their country estates as well as their town-houses, and such vast numbers included both the *urbana* and the *rustica familia*. The latter, being employed in tillage, would be the more numerous; nevertheless the domestic entourage was very large, and Horace speaks of the ridicule which the Prætor Tillius incurred because, on the journey of sixteen miles between Rome and Tivoli, he was attended by only five slaves.[4]

Their hard condition.

The lot of the ancient slave was pitiful.[5] He was defined by Aristotle as 'a live chattel,' and again as 'a live implement,' whereas an implement was 'a lifeless slave.'[6] And if this was his condition in Greece, it was worse at Rome, where luxury had hardened men's hearts. In the eye of the law slaves were not persons (*personæ*) but things (*res*). They

Laodiceans (cf. Col. iv. 15-17), Theod. Mops. infers that Laodiceia, not Colossæ, was the scene of his ministry; and Lightfoot approves the suggestion, illustrating the alleged remissness of Archippus by the prevalent lukewarmness of the Laodiceans (cf. Rev. iii. 15, 16).

[1] Hor. *Sat.* I. iii. 11 f.; Val. Max. IV. iv. 11.

[2] Hor. *ibid.*

[3] Plin. *Nat. Hist.* XXXIII. 47.

[4] *Sat.* I. vi. 107-9.

[5] Cf. Becker, *Charicles*, Excurs. to Sc. VII; *Gallus*, Excurs. to Sc. I.

[6] *De Rep.* I. 4: καὶ ὁ δοῦλος κτῆμά τι ἔμψυχον. *Eth. Nic.* VIII. 13: ὁ γὰρ δοῦλος ἔμψυχον ὄργανον, τὸ δέ ὄργανον ἄψυχος δοῦλος.

were their master's property, and he accounted them as cattle.[1] Like cattle they were bought and sold. They were stripped, and exposed, with a placard on their necks stating their qualities and blemishes, on a pedestal in the market, that intending purchasers might inspect and handle them, and they were trotted round like horses to prove their agility.[2] And they got names like those bestowed on horses and dogs—Onesimus, 'Profitable,' Chresimus, 'Useful,' Symphorus, 'Suitable,' Epictetus, 'Acquired,' and so forth. They were mated, too, like cattle. Their union was not marriage (*matrimonium*); it was mere cohabitation (*contubernium*), and their offspring were their master's property, an increase of his herd. They were absolutely at his mercy; and though a humane master would treat his slaves kindly, humanity was rare in 'that hard Pagan world.' It is told of Epictetus, the Stoic philosopher, that he was taken in childhood to Rome from his native Hierapolis, just about the time when the Apostle was there, and sold to Epaphroditus, the profligate freedman of Nero; [3] and one day his brutal master was amusing himself by to turing him. He twisted his leg. 'You are breaking it,' the child remonstrated. The ruffian persisted, and broke it; and all that the little Stoic said was: 'Didn't I tell you that you were breaking it?' [4] Such barbarities were painfully frequent. Offences were mercilessly punished.[5] Runaways (*fugitivi*) and pilferers (*fures*) were branded on the forehead with the letter F.[6] Scourging was common; [7] and so was crucifixion, the *servile supplicium*,[8] and it was often accompanied with brutal outrages—the hacking off of a limb or the cutting out of the tongue.[9] Slaves were cast to the wild beasts in the circus;

Cruelty.

[1] Cf. Sen. *Epist.* xlvii: 'nec tanquam hominibus quidem sed tanquam jumentis abutimur.'

[2] Cf. Plaut. *Bacch.* IV. vii. 17; Cic. *In Pis.* 15, *De Offic.* III. 17; Hor. *Epist.* II. ii. 1-19; Prop. IV. v. 51 f.; Sen. *Epist.* lxxx.

[3] Cf. Epict. I. i. 20.

[4] Orig. *Contra Cels.* VII. 53. The story is perhaps attested by the philosopher's own words (I. xii. 24): σκέλος οὖν μοι γενέσθαι πεπηρωμένον; ἀνδράποδον, εἶτα δι' ἓν σκελύδριον τῷ κόσμῳ ἐγκαλεῖς;

[5] Sen. *De Ira*, III. 3.

[6] Plaut. *Cas.* II. vi. 49, *Aul.* II. iv. 46; Mart. *Epigr.* III. xxi; Diog. Laert. *Bion.* IV. 46.

[7] Cf. Juv. XIV. 18 f.

[8] Hor. *Epist.* I. xvi. 47.

[9] Cf. Sen. *De Ira*, III. 3: 'lacerationes membrorum.' Cic. *Pro Cluent.* 66: 'Stratonem quidem in crucem actum esse exsecta scitote lingua.'

and it is said that a Roman knight, Vedius Pollio, practised a savage refinement on this atrocity. He had at his *villa*, after the luxurious fashion of the age,[1] a fishpond for the supply of his table, and offending slaves were thrown into it that he might enjoy the spectacle of the lampreys tearing their bodies.[2] Once, when Augustus was dining with him, a slave chanced to break a crystal cup, and Vedius ordered him to be thrown to the lampreys. The wretch escaped from the grasp of his executioners and cast himself at the Emperor's feet, asking only that he might be put to some less horrible death. Shocked by the cruelty, Augustus ordered that all the crystal cups should be broken in his presence and that the pond should be filled up.[3]

So trivial were the offences which were held to justify retribution so severe. And even when they gave no provocation, the slaves were treated with stern insolence. As they waited at table, they durst not speak or so much as move their lips. A whisper was checked with the rod; a cough, a sneeze, or a sigh was punished with scourging, and a word breaking the silence incurred a heavy penalty.[4] There were indeed masters, especially humanitarians of the Stoic school, who practised benevolence. 'I am glad,' writes Seneca to his friend Lucilius,[5] 'to be informed that you live familiarly with your slaves. This becomes your prudence and your erudition. Are they slaves? Nay, they are men. Are they slaves? Nay, sharers of our dwellings. Are they slaves? Nay, humble friends. Are they slaves? Nay, fellow-slaves. This is the gist of my injunction: so live with an inferior as you would wish a superior to live with you. Live kindly with your slave; courteously admit him to your conversation, to your counsel, and to your board. Let some dine with you because they are worthy, and some that they may be so.' This seemed, however, in those days grotesque eccentricity, and the prevalent sentiment was represented by Nero's freedman Pallas, the brother of the Procurator Felix, of whom it is recorded [6] that he would not degrade his voice by addressing

Contempt.

[1] Cf. Mart. *Epigr.* X. xxx. 21-4.
[2] Plin. *Nat. Hist.* IX. 39.
[3] Sen. *De Ira*, III. 40.
[4] Cf. Sen. *Epist.* xlvii.
[5] *Ibid.*
[6] Tac. *Ann.* XIII. 23.

his slaves, and intimated his wishes by a nod or a gesture or, where necessary, by writing. This may have been extreme insolence, yet it was characteristic of Roman society; and the general attitude is amusingly exemplified by an anecdote of Piso the orator.[1] His rule was that his slaves should never presume to address him save in answer to questions; and once he invited Clodius to a banquet. At the stated hour all the guests arrived except Clodius, and Piso repeatedly sent the slave who had conveyed the invitations, to see if he were coming. 'Did you invite him?' he at length inquired. 'I did,' was the reply. 'Then why has he not come?' 'He declined.' 'Then how did you not tell me at once?' 'Because you did not ask me this.' Even in the kindlier Greek world a like restraint was imposed, and the prohibition of 'freedom of speech' was accounted the worst hardship of a slave's lot[2]—a circumstance which illumines the thought in the minds of the Apostles when they reckon 'freedom of speech toward God' as the supreme privilege of reconciliation. It is the privilege of sonship: we are no longer slaves but sons.

Cf. Eph. iii. 12; 1 Jo. iii. 21, v. 14.

Cf. Gal. iv. 7; Jo. xv. 15.

Danger of insurrection.

There was indeed a measure of excuse for such severity in the overwhelming numbers of the slaves. The population of Rome under Augustus and Tiberius was about two million souls; and of these, it is reckoned,[3] between eight and nine hundred thousand were slaves, while the proportion was much larger in rural Italy. The presence of so vast a multitude of indignant serfs was a constant menace, and the peril was illustrated not merely by the memory of the Servile Wars in Sicily in the later years of the second century B.C. but by more recent insurrections nearer home.[4] It was a common proverb: *totidem esse hostes quot servos*, 'so many slaves, just so many enemies';[5] and though the philosopher counselled that they should be won by kindness,[6] it seemed a surer policy to hold them down with a strong hand and intimidate them by terrible examples. There was an old law that, if a slave murdered his master, not he alone but all

[1] Plut. *De Garrul.* 18.

[2] Eur. *Phœn.* 390-92.

[3] Furneaux, *Annals of Tacitus*, I. p. 90.

[4] Tac. *Ann.* IV. 27.

[5] Sen. *Epist.* xlvii.

[6] *Ibid.*: 'colant potius te quam timeant.'

his fellow-slaves should be put to death; and in A.D. 61, the very year when the Apostle wrote to Philemon on behalf of his fugitive, a case occurred which startled Rome. The Prefect of the city, Pedanius Secundus, was murdered by an aggrieved slave; and after an impassioned discussion in the Senate, the law was enforced, and the entire *familia*, four hundred unoffending creatures of both sexes and every age, shared the criminal's doom.[1]

A recognised institution.

Slavery was thus a monstrous institution, an outrage on humanity and religion; nevertheless it is no marvel that Philemon, that distinguished Christian, should have owned slaves, nor yet that Paul should have entered no protest. The institution was universally recognised, and it had been approved by the wisest teachers of antiquity. Thus, in depicting his ideal state, it never occurred to Plato that there should be no slaves in it. His only requirement was that the Greeks should spare their own race and not make slaves of fellow-Greeks.[2] And Aristotle defended the institution on the principle that there are differences between men: some are naturally slaves, since it is right that the better should rule the worse, as the soul rules the body and the husband the wife.[3] Even the Stoics never challenged its legitimacy. Freedom, they held, lies in the soul, not in the body. The body is external to the man and, like any other of his possessions, belongs to the category of 'things indifferent,' things which are not in his power and therefore should cost him no concern. 'He is free,' says Epictetus,[4] 'who lives as he wills.' 'No one is a slave while he is free in his choice.' 'Fortune is a sore bond of the body, but the soul's only bond is vice. For one whose body is at large while his soul is in bonds is a slave; and, contrariwise, one whose body is in bonds while his soul is at large, is free.'[5] '"I will put you in bonds." Man, what are you saying? Me? My leg you will put in bonds, but my choice not even Zeus can conquer. "I will throw you into prison." My poor body. "I will behead you." Well, when did I tell you that my neck, unlike all others, could not be severed?'[6]

Approved by Plato and Aristotle.

The Stoic attitude.

[1] Tac. *Ann.* XIV. 42-5.
[2] Plat. *Rep.* V. 469.
[3] Arist. *Rep.* I. 13.
[4] IV. i. 1.
[5] *Fragm.* 31, 32 (Schenkl).
[6] I. i. 23, 24.

The Apostle's attitude. Rom. vi. 12-23. 1 Cor. vii. 20-24. Cf. 1 Cor. xii. 13; Gal. iii. 28; Col. iii. 11.

Such was the Stoic attitude, and the Apostle's was much similar. The enslavement of the body was nothing to him. In his eyes sin was the only slavery, and Christ's slave was the only free man. Hence it never occurred to him to condemn the institution of slavery. It belonged to the old order which Christ had for ever abolished. It was doomed by the Christian revelation of the universal Fatherhood of God with its corollary, the universal brotherhood of man. And thus, when he wrote to Philemon on behalf of his fugitive slave, he did not require him to emancipate Onesimus; he imposed a larger injunction: 'Welcome him back no longer as a slave but something more than a slave—a brother beloved.'

His letter to Philemon.

This letter has a peculiar interest as the only surviving specimen of the Apostle's private correspondence; and it well deserves a place in the sacred canon. It contains indeed no doctrine, and for this reason, St. Jerome tells us, it was rejected by not a few in early days: 'it is not Paul's,' they alleged, 'or, even if it be Paul's, it contains nothing to edify us.' But the purpose of doctrine, as the Apostle says, is 'that the man of God may be perfect, equipped for every good work'; and the letter shows how well the Apostle's doctrine had served its use in his own person. It is the letter of a Christian gentleman, kindly, courteous, tactful, unselfish, and chivalrous, not too proud to solicit a favour yet incapable of servility, and withal possessing that quality of humour which is the salt of social intercourse. It is the sort of appeal which is irresistible. Philemon would recognise, when he read it, that the debt lay with him—a debt which he could never discharge.

2 Tim. iii. 17.

Cf. Col. iv. 6.

LETTER TO PHILEMON

1 Paul, a prisoner of Christ Jesus, and Timothy the brother,
2 to Philemon, our dear friend and fellow-worker, and
Apphia the sister, and Archippus our fellow-soldier, and
3 the Church at your house. Grace to you all and peace from
God our Father and the Lord Jesus Christ.
4 I thank my God always and make mention of you in my
5 prayers, when I hear of your love and faith—the faith which
you have toward the Lord Jesus and your love for all the

6 saints—that the generosity which your faith inspires may,
in a full discovery of all the good that is among us, effect
7 a closer union with Christ. For I have found much joy
and encouragement in your love, because the hearts of the
saints have been refreshed through you, brother.
8 And therefore, while I have in Christ no hesitation in
9 enjoining upon you what is becoming, for love's sake
I rather beseech, though I be the man I am — Paul,
an ambassador[1] but now also a prisoner of Christ Jesus.
10 I beseech you for my child whom I have begotten in my
11 prison—Onesimus, once so useless to you, but now right
12 useful both to you and to me.[2] I am sending him back to
13 you, though it is like tearing out my very heart. I would
fain have retained him by my side to minister on your
14 behalf to me while I am in prison for the Gospel; but I
decided to do nothing without your approval, that your
goodness may not be a matter of necessity but your own
15 free act. For perhaps it was for this reason that he was
severed from you for a brief hour—that you might have him
16 back for ever, no longer as a slave but something more than
a slave, a brother beloved, most of all to me, but how much
more than 'most of all' to you, both as a fellow-creature
and as a fellow-Christian!
17 If, then, you hold me your fellow, receive him as you
18 would myself. And if he has done you any wrong or is in
19 your debt, put this to my account—I PAUL WRITE IT WITH
MY OWN HAND: I WILL REPAY IT[3]—not to mention to you

[1] *πρεσβύτης* in classical Greek is 'an aged man' and *πρεσβευτής* 'an ambassador'; but it seems certain that *πρεσβύτης* means 'an ambassador' here. (1) Since the Apostle was about sixty, he might fairly have designated himself 'an aged man,' but he could hardly have urged his age as a plea for deference on the part of Philemon, who, if Archippus was his son, could be little younger. (2) *νυνὶ δέ*, 'but now,' makes *πρεσβύτης* and *δέσμιος* antitheses, contrasting the dignity of the ambassador and the ignominy of the prisoner. (3) The Apostle's language here is an expansion of his phrase *πρεσβεύω ἐν ἁλύσει* (Eph. vi. 20). Though *πρεσβύτης* is given by all MSS., Bentley conjectured *πρεσβευτής* as the true reading, and the frequent confusion of the two forms elsewhere would warrant the emendation. It is, however, unnecessary, since it appears that in later Greek they were interchangeable in the sense of 'an ambassador.' Cf. Lightfoot.

[2] A play on the name Onesimus, 'Profitable.'

[3] Here Paul takes the pen from his amanuensis Timothy and playfully writes and signs a debtor's bond, his 'note of hand' (*χειρόγραφον*), just as he had given the Philippians 'a receipt of payment' (cf. n. on Phil. iv. 18, p. 521). The debtor's formula was *ἀποδώσω*, 'I will repay,' or as here the stronger *ἀποτίσω*, implying liability to punishment or fine; and the formula of acquittance was *ἀπέχω*, 'I have received.' The formula had to be written with the party's own hand, or, if he could not write, a proxy wrote it for him with the note *ἔγραψα ὑπὲρ αὐτοῦ*. Cf. Deissmann, *Light from the Ancient East*, pp. 334 f.

20 that you owe me more than this—your very self. Yes,
brother, let me have 'profit'[1] of you in the Lord; refresh
my heart in Christ.
21 I am writing to you with full confidence in your compli-
ance, knowing that you will do far more than I mention.
22 And at the same time prepare hospitality for me;[2] for I
am hoping that through your prayers I shall be granted to
you.
23 Epaphras, my fellow-captive[3] in Christ Jesus, greets
24 you; also Mark, Aristarchus, Demas, Luke, my fellow-
workers.
25 THE GRACE OF THE LORD JESUS CHRIST BE WITH THE
SPIRIT OF YOU AND YOURS.

[1] Another play on 'Onesimus.' [2] ξενίαν, cf. p. 502.

[3] Epaphras, like Aristarchus (Col. iv. 10), is thus styled on account of his assiduous attendance on the captive Apostle (cf. p. 522).

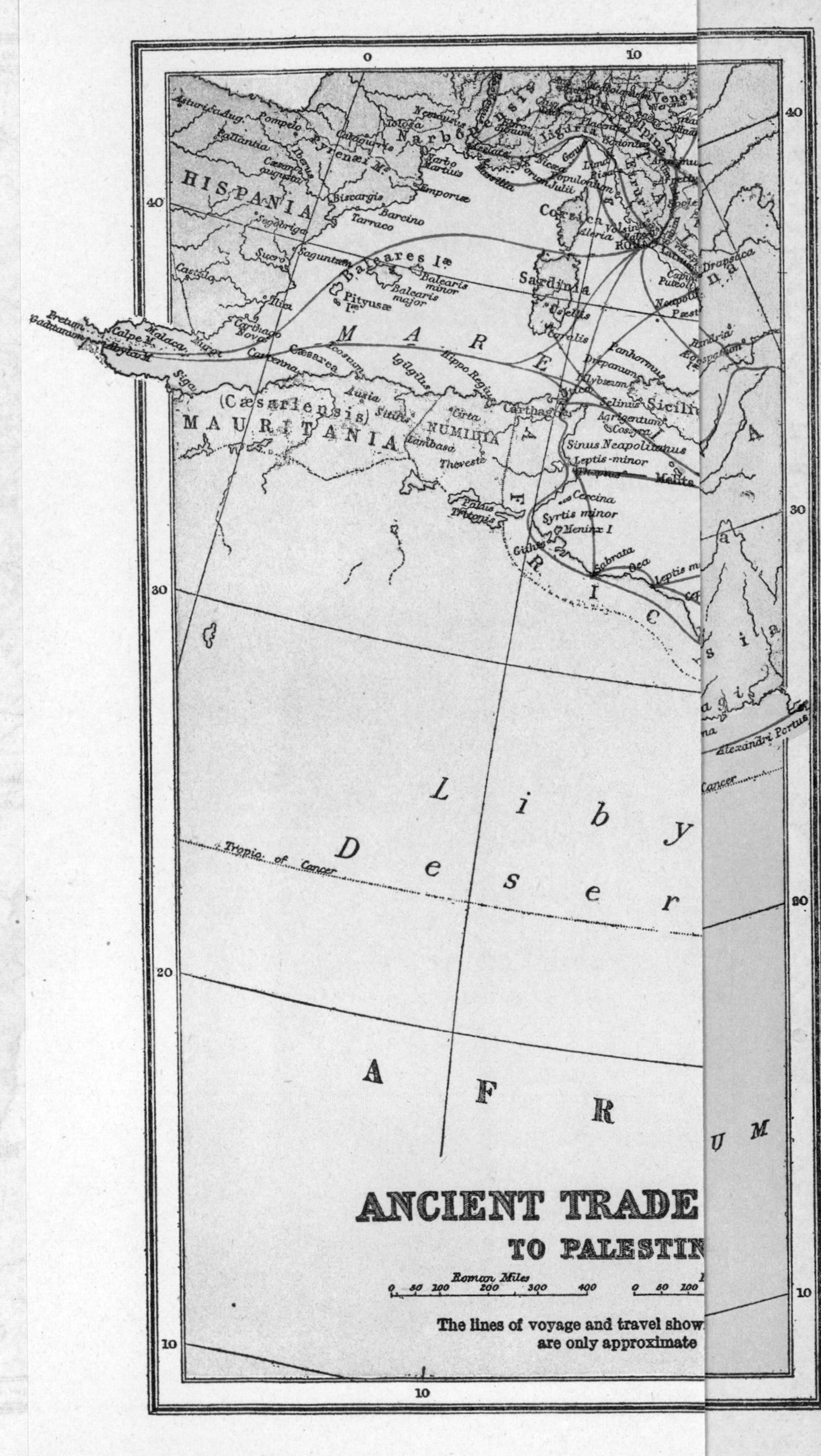

HISPANIA
Pyrenæi M.
Tarraco
Barcino
Emporiæ
Balcares Iæ
Balearis minor
Balearis major
Pityusæ Iæ
Carthago Nova
Malaca
Calpe M.
Corsica
Aleria
Sardinia
Caralis
ROMA
Puteoli
Neapolis
Panhormus
Drepanum
Lilybæum
Selinus
Agrigentum
Cossyra
Melite
MARE
Carthago
Utica
Hippo Regius
Cirta
NUMIDIA
Lambæsa
Theveste
(Cæsariensis)
MAURITANIA
Cæsarea
Auzia
Sitifis
Sinus Neapolitanus
Leptis-minor
Thapsus
Cercina
Syrtis minor
Meninx I
Sabrata
Oea
Alexandri Portus
Libyan Desert
Tropic of Cancer
AFRICUM
ANCIENT TRADE
TO PALESTIN
Roman Miles
0 50 100 200 300 400
The lines of voyage and travel show
are only approximate

BOOK IV

THE CLOSING YEARS

'O, but they say the tongues of dying men
Enforce attention like deep harmony:
Where words are scarce, they are seldom spent in vain,
For they breathe truth that breathe their words in pain.
He that no more must say is listen'd more
  Than they whom youth and ease have taught to glose;
More are men's ends mark'd than their lives before:
  The setting sun, and music at the close,
As the last taste of sweets is sweetest last,
Writ in remembrance more than things long past.'

SHAKESPEARE.

THE HISTORICAL PROBLEM

THE narrative of the Book of Acts recounts the Apostle's career from his conversion in the summer of 33 until his arrival at Rome in the spring of 60. He was brought thither as a prisoner in consequence of his appeal to the Emperor's judgment, and his trial was unexpectedly deferred. He was detained in *libera custodia*, occupying a private lodging and, though fettered and guarded, enjoying the society of his friends and freely conversing with all who chose to visit him. There the narrative leaves him, merely intimating that his captivity was protracted for two full years. Evidently he was then brought to trial; and, since there is no further record, the inference would seem to be that he was condemned and executed. History of the Book of Acts.

Against this conclusion, however, there are weighty considerations; and the chief is presented by that group of three letters, commonly known as 'the Pastoral Epistles,' which claim the Apostle as their author. It is not the least service which Luke has rendered to the Church, that he has illumined the correspondence of his beloved master. The latter teems with personal, local, and controversial references; and these, were they undefined, would be frequently puzzling and sometimes quite unintelligible. The Book of Acts, however, furnishes the contemporary background, and against this the Apostle's correspondence lives and moves and exhibits a varied and thrilling drama. Ten of his letters have hitherto fallen naturally and fittingly into position; but here is the difficulty which the Pastorals present and which constitutes the main reason why their authenticity has been so largely disputed—that they find no place in the historical framework. No place in it for the Pastoral Epistles:

Consider the First Letter to Timothy. It appears that, (1) First Timothy.

Cf. i. 3. 4. when the Apostle wrote it, he was at liberty. He had been at Ephesus and had found false teachers at work there; and on his departure for Macedonia he had left Timothy behind him to counteract their mischievous activities. It was a difficult ministry, and the purpose of the letter was to encourage Timothy in its prosecution. Where in the historical narrative can this incident be assigned a place? Twice, and only twice, is it recorded that the Apostle visited Ephesus. He called there in the course of his homeward voyage from Corinth at the close of his second mission in spring 53; but this cannot have been the occasion in question, for on taking his departure then he did not travel to Macedonia but continued his voyage eastward to Cæsarea. Nor had Christianity then been established in Ephesus; whereas, when the letter was written, there was a church in the city completely organised. His other appearance at Ephesus was in the ensuing autumn, and on this occasion he continued there for two years and a quarter. Thereafter, it is true, he proceeded to Macedonia; but he did not leave Timothy behind: he had despatched him in advance to Corinth by way of Macedonia. So neither is there a foothold for the letter here. It has been suggested [1] that he may have paid a hasty visit to Macedonia in the course of his protracted ministry in the Asian capital, leaving Timothy in charge of the Church during his absence, and it lends colour to the hypothesis that he actually paid such a visit to Corinth, though it is unrecorded in the Book of Acts.[2] The hypothesis, however, is ruled out not merely by the improbability that the Asian heresy should in so brief a space have attained such dimensions as the letter represents, but by the fact that in his interview with the Ephesian Elders in spring 57 upwards of a year after his departure from the city he warned them of the impending danger. The heresy which was rampant when he wrote the letter, was then still undeveloped.

Cf. Ac. xviii. 19-21.

Cf. iii. 14.

Cf. Ac. xx. 29, 30.

(2) Letter to Titus.

And what of the Letter to Titus? The situation here is that Paul had visited Crete in company with Titus, and had left him there to complete the organisation of the churches in the island. It was after his departure from Crete that he

Cf. i. 5.

[1] Cf. Wieseler, *Chronolog. des apostol. Zeitalters*, p. 286.

[2] Cf. p. 326.

wrote the letter; and when he wrote it, he contemplated Cf. iii. 12.
spending the winter at Nicopolis. On the assumption that it belongs to his recorded ministry, what place can be found for this episode? His sole connection with Crete was the Cf. Ac.
view he had of it from the bay of Fair Havens while the ship xxvii 7-13.
which was carrying him to Rome lay there wind-bound. The centurion Julius had indeed allowed him to land at Cf ver. 3.
Sidon and enjoy the society of his friends at the Phœnician port; but there is no evidence that he went ashore at Fair Havens, and even if he did, he had no time for winning converts and founding churches, since it seems that the ship stayed in the anchorage little over a week. Nor was Titus with him. His companions in the voyage were Luke and Aristarchus. It is indeed conceivable that somewhere in the course of his travels he may have paid a visit to Crete and engaged in a mission which the Book of Acts has left unnoticed; but this is improbable, and the improbability becomes extreme when it is remembered that his visit to Crete was followed by a winter's sojourn at Nicopolis, which also is unrecorded in the Book of Acts. It is inconceivable that so important and protracted an episode should have been ignored by the historian, nor is there room for it in the crowded narrative.

And what of the Second Letter to Timothy? It was (3) Second Timothy.
plainly written on the very eve of the Apostle's martyrdom; Cf. iv. 6-8.
and, on the assumption that it belongs to his recorded history, then it has its place at the close of the Book of Acts. It is there stated that he was detained a prisoner at Rome for two full years, and it is assumed that, when at length he was brought to trial, he was condemned and executed. Timothy was apparently at Ephesus, and the Apostle, fore- Cf. iv. 9-13.
seeing the fatal issue, wrote and summoned him to Rome.

This construction of the situation, however, involves insuperable difficulties. Timothy was not at Ephesus at the close of the two years' imprisonment. He was at Rome, and he had acted as the Apostle's amanuensis when, near the close, he wrote his letters to Colossæ and Philemon. Moreover, Paul had then been a captive for upwards of four consecutive years. He had passed two years in prison at Cæsarea, and had been conducted thence to Rome and there had passed two more weary years in bonds. Yet in this letter to Timothy he refers to incidents which had lately happened in the course of his travels in the East—how he had left his mantle and some precious literature at Troas, had parted from Erastus at Corinth, and had left Trophimus at Miletus sick.

Cf. iv. 13-20.

Peculiarities of the Pastorals:

It thus appears that there is no place for the Pastorals in the recorded history of the Apostle's ministry; and this further must be considered—that they are differentiated from the rest of his letters by peculiarities of style, language, and ideas. One misses in them his rugged and nervous eloquence, his glowing passion, his massive argumentation, the rush of his eager dialectic, his crowding thoughts, and his frequent digressions. The difference is indeed unmistakable, yet it in nowise precludes identity of authorship. It is a difference, not of personality, but merely of mood and circumstances; and it is a sufficient explanation, were there no other, that the Pastorals are private letters dealing mainly with practical affairs.

Style.

Language.

Less impalpable and elusive than the quality of style is the distinction of language; and the fact confronts us that the Pastorals abound in novel terms, alien from the Apostle's recognised vocabulary. Thus in the first letter to Timothy, which occupies six and a half pages in Westcott and Hort's edition, there are 123 peculiarities—over 18 to the page; in the second letter to Timothy, with four and three-quarter pages, there are 80—about 17 to the page; and in the letter to Titus, with two and three-quarter pages, there are 43—about 16 to the page. There are, moreover, 49 terms peculiar to the Pastorals, occurring in two or all of them and nowhere else in the Pauline writings. Thus the group exhibits in all 295 peculiarities—about 21 to the page.

Comparison with other groups:

(1) The Thessalonian letters.

And what does this mean? It has been construed as a conclusive evidence against the Pauline authorship of the Pastorals: their speech bewrays them. But consider the other letters. These fall into chronological groups, plainly distinguished by their linguistic peculiarities. The first group is the two letters to the Thessalonians, written in the autumn of 51 and dealing with the eschatological problem. That was the Apostle's earliest controversy, and his language is simple and untechnical. The first letter, with five and a half pages, exhibits 35 peculiarities; and the second, with three pages, 19—in both instances fully 6 to the page. There is, besides, one term which occurs in both and nowhere else in the Pauline writings; and thus there are in all 55 peculiarities in the group or between 6 and 7 to the page. The second group comprises the letter to the Galatians (June 53), the first to the Corinthians (early summer 55), the second to the Corinthians (close of 55—autumn 56), and the encyclical 'to the Romans' (beginning of 57). It belongs to the period of the Judaist controversy; and this is the *motif* of Galatians and Romans, while the Corinthian letters deal also with the special problems which had emerged in the Achaian capital. It was inevitable that the necessities of this complex argumentation should develop and enlarge the Apostle's vocabulary; and so we find in the Galatian letter, with eight pages, 70 peculiarities—almost 9 to the page; in First Corinthians, with twenty-four pages, 233—almost 10 to the page; in Second Corinthians, with sixteen and a half pages, 166—fully 10 to the page; and in Romans, with twenty-six pages, 180—about 7 to the page. There are also 174 words occurring in two or more of the group and nowhere else in the Pauline writings. And thus the sum of peculiarities is 823—fully 11 to the page. The third group is composed of the Prison Epistles: Philippians (toward the close of 60), a letter of grateful acknowledgment; Ephesians and Colossians (early in 62), dealing with the incipient Gnosticism of the Province of Asia; and their companion, the little letter to Philemon. Philippians, with six pages, has 65 peculiarities—almost 11 to the page; Ephesians, with eight and three-quarter pages, 74—between 8 and 9 to the page; Colossians, with six pages, 55—fully 9 to the page; and Philemon, with a page and a quarter, 8—between 6 and 7 to the page. There are also 20 words which are common to Ephesians and Colossians and occur nowhere else in the Pauline writings; and in the entire group there are 229 occurring nowhere else in the Pauline writings—between 10 and 11 to the page.[1]

(2) Those belonging to the Judaist controversy.

(3) The Prison Epistles.

Thus it emerges that the letters which relate to each of

Later date

[1] Cf. Append. VII.

of the Pastorals.

the historic controversies are plainly distinguished and the members of each group linked together by linguistic peculiarities. And when it is found that the Pastorals are similarly distinguished, being marked off from the other letters and interrelated by a still larger array of linguistic peculiarities, it follows not only that they constitute a separate group but that they belong, not to the Apostle's recorded ministry, but to a later period when novel conditions had arisen, new ideas, new problems, new institutions.

Evidence for the Apostle's later ministry: 1. Incompleteness of Luke's narrative.

Hence it would appear that, if it was indeed Paul who wrote the Pastorals, his career did not end where the history closes; and the inference is strongly attested. In his preface to the Book of Acts Luke refers to his Gospel, and it is significant that he styles it not 'the former' but 'the first narrative.'[1] He has left only two narratives; and had these been all that he had in view, then, when he referred in the second to its predecessor, he would have designated it 'the former,' and his phrase 'the first narrative' suggests that he had an ampler plan. He purposed writing a history of the origin and progress of the Christian Faith, and his Gospel was the first of a series of 'narratives.' It was followed by a second, our Book of Acts; but this did not complete his design. He had yet another 'narrative' in contemplation, and it would have carried the history down to his own day—a period of some twelve years, if there be truth in the tradition that he died in the year 74. His death arrested his literary labours, and his monumental work remains incomplete. The third 'narrative' was never written, and the Book of Acts evinces this by the abruptness of its conclusion. It leaves the Apostle a prisoner at Rome with the intimation that his captivity lasted 'two whole years,' thus plainly suggesting that thereafter something happened and the historian intended relating the issue in the ensuing narrative. What the issue may have been—whether the condemnation and execution of the Apostle or his acquittal

[1] Ac. i. 1: τὸν πρῶτον λόγον. The mere linguistic argument is not indeed conclusive, since in Hellenistic Greek the distinction between compar. and superl. was largely ignored (cf. Moulton, *Proleg.*, pp. 77 ff.) and πρῶτος was freely used for πρότερος (cf. Mt. xxi. 36; 1 Cor. xiv. 30; Heb. x. 9; Rev. xxi. 1). But the distinction was in nowise obliterated, and it would hardly be neglected by Luke, a literary Greek. Cf. Ramsay, *St. Paul the Traveller*, pp. 27 f.

and release—is left uncertain; but had it been the former, it would have been easily told, and the reservation suggests that much still remained. The prisoner was released and resumed his ministry, and the next narrative would have recounted his further travels and achievements.

Nor does this inference lack express corroboration. It appears, on the Apostle's own testimony, that, as his captivity dragged on its weary course, his prospects steadily brightened. Already toward the close of the year 60, though the issue remained uncertain, he had good hope of release; and thereafter his confidence so increased that about the beginning of 62 he could bid Philemon expect his speedy arrival at Colossæ and prepare for his entertainment. And according to primitive and trustworthy testimony his expectation was realised. In the last decade of the first century St. Clement of Rome, remonstrating with the contentious Christians at Corinth, appealed to historic examples. 'To leave,' he says, 'the ancient examples, let us pass to the champions who lived nearest to our day. By reason of jealousy and strife Paul pointed the way to the prize of endurance. After he had seven times worn bonds, had been exiled, had been stoned, had played the herald in the East and in the West, he won the noble renown of his faith, having taught the whole world righteousness and passed to the boundary of the West. And after testifying before the rulers so was he rid of the world and went to the Holy Place, having proved a very great exemplar of endurance.'[1] If, as seems indubitable,[2] by 'the boundary of the West' be meant the Pillars of Hercules, there is here a plain testimony by a contemporary of the Apostles that Paul not only was released and resumed his ministry but fulfilled his long cherished purpose of visiting Spain. And this is explicitly affirmed by that valuable document, the Muratorian Fragment, a mutilated and corrupt manuscript discovered in 1740 in the Ambrosian Library at Milan by an Italian scholar, Ludovico Antonio Muratori. Its author is unknown, but he mentions that he was a contemporary of Pius, Bishop of Rome (143-157). It was written at Rome after the death of Pius, probably about the year 170; and it says: 'The

[Margin notes: 2. The Apostle's testimony. — Phil. ii. 24. — Phm. 22. — 3. Primitive tradition. — Clemens Romanus. — Cf. Rom. xv. 28. — Muratorian Canon.]

[1] Clem. Rom. *Ad Cor.* v.

[2] Cf. Lightfoot *ad loc.*

Acts of all the Apostles are written in one book. Luke puts it shortly to the most excellent Theophilus that the several events were enacted in his presence, as he also evidently indicates by omitting the passion of Peter as well as Paul's departure from the city on his journey to Spain.' Here the Apostle's release and his journey to Spain are assumed as notorious facts.

Statement of Theodore of Mopsuestia.

It is needless to adduce the testimonies of later writers—Eusebius, St. Athanasius, St. Cyril of Jerusalem, Epiphanius, and St. Jerome; but it is worth while to quote the explicit statement of Theodore of Mopsuestia. 'St. Paul,' he says, 'twice visited Rome during the reign of Nero. First on his appeal to Festus in Judæa, when the latter to please the Jews would have sent him to Jerusalem. So he was conducted a prisoner to Rome; and thence, on his release by Nero's judgment, he was ordered to depart in safety. After his two years' stay at Rome he departed, and is seen to have preached to many the doctrine of piety. On a second occasion, however, he visited Rome, and while he stayed there it happened that by the sentence of Nero he suffered capital punishment for the preaching of piety.'[1] The passage survives only in a rude Latin version, but its meaning is indubitable. The Apostle suffered two imprisonments at Rome in the reign of Nero. The former followed on his appeal at Cæsarea to the Emperor's judgment, and it lasted for two years. Then he was brought to trial and acquitted and ordered to quit the capital. He resumed his apostolic labours and preached extensively; and by and by he paid a second visit to Rome and was again arrested. On this occasion apparently he suffered no long imprisonment. He was promptly tried and sentenced to death.

Are the Pastorals second century imitations?

Hence, though it is impossible to find a place for the Pastorals in the framework of his recorded ministry, it in nowise follows that they are not writings of the Apostle. The narrative of the Book of Acts is incomplete, and it is reasonable to seek a resting-place for the letters in the ensuing period. The question, however, arises whether the peculiarities of language and thought which exclude them from his recorded ministry, be consistent even with this

[1] Theod. Mops. *Ad Ephesios Argumentum*.

later date. The fact presents itself that, while each of the previous groups is distinguished by its linguistic peculiarities, the peculiarities of the Pastorals are much more numerous—thrice as many as those of the first group and twice as many as those of the second and third. And it has been alleged, moreover, that the letters breathe the atmosphere of a far later period. They exhibit theological ideas which are alien from the Apostle's recognised thought, giving, for example, the epithet of 'Saviour' not only, in his accustomed manner, to Christ but to God; they ascribe to him a novel interest in ecclesiastical organisation; and the heresy which they combat is the Gnosticism of the second century, Marcion's famous work *The Antitheses* being actually, it is alleged, mentioned by name. Hence it has been concluded that they are not the work of Paul but merely, as Coleridge puts it,[1] ἐπιστολαὶ Παυλοειδεῖς, controversial writings ascribed, after the ancient fashion,[2] to the great master.

Cf. 2 Tim. i. 10; Tit. i. 4, ii. 13, iii. 6.

Cf. 1 Tim. i. 1, ii. 3, iv. 10; Tit. i. 3, ii. 10, iii. 4.

Cf. 1 Tim. vi. 20.

Testimony of the Apostolic Fathers.

This judgment, however, ignores much important evidence. Not the least weighty is the testimony of the Apostolic Fathers. St. Clement of Rome had seen and conversed with the Apostles Paul and Peter,[3] and in his Epistle to the Corinthians, written during the last decade of the first century, not only are there several passages which seem clear echoes of the Pastorals[4] but there is one indubitable quotation from the letter to Titus.[5] There are numerous echoes also in the Epistles of St. Ignatius.[6] And in the Epistle of St. Polycarp, a disciple of the Apostles and especially the Apostle John,[7] there are, besides echoes, four distinct

[1] *Table Talk*, June 15, 1833.

[2] The Pythagorean philosophers ascribed their writings to the master, recognising him as the source of all their wisdom and claiming no glory for themselves. Cf. Iamblich. *De Vit. Pyth.* 198.

[3] Iren. III. iii. 2.

[4] Cf. vii with 1 Tim. ii. 3, v. 4; xxix with 1 Tim. ii. 8; lxi with 1 Tim. i. 17.

[5] ii: ἕτοιμοι εἰς πᾶν ἔργον ἀγαθόν. Cf. Tit. iii. 1.

[6] Cf. *Ad Magn.* xi with 1 Tim. i. 1; *Ad Polyc.* iii with 1 Tim. i. 3, vi. 3; *Ad Eph.* xx with 1 Tim. i. 4; *Ad Eph.* xiv with 1 Tim. i. 5; *Ad Rom.* ix with 1 Tim. i. 13; *Ad Trall.* vii with 1 Tim. iii. 9, 2 Tim. i. 3; *Ad Magn.* viii with 1 Tim. iv. 7, Tit. i. 14, iii. 9; *Ad Trall.* viii with 1 Tim. v. 14; *Ad Eph.* ii and *Ad Smyrn.* x with 2 Tim. i. 10; *Ad Polyc.* vi with 2 Tim. ii. 3, 4; *Ad Smyrn.* iv with 2 Tim. ii. 10.

[7] Cf. Iren. III. iii. 4.

quotations.[1] It is indeed conceivable that the debt might be on the other side, and that the Pastorals are Pauline imitations and their author quoted from the Apostolic Fathers; but it is unlikely that he should have so flagrantly convicted himself in view of the skill wherewith he has elsewhere executed his imitation. Thus, in the second letter to Timothy Paul is represented as sending a greeting from Linus. And who was Linus? He was the Overseer of the Roman Church after the martyrdom of the Apostles Paul and Peter.[2] Thenceforth he was a distinguished personage in the Church's annals, and his name would hardly have been introduced so slightly by a second century imitator who was capable of betraying himself by putting on the lips of Paul the language of the Apostolic Fathers.

iv. 21.

The peculiarities of the Pastorals congruous with their Pauline authorship:

The decisive question is whether the peculiarities which the Pastorals exhibit be inconsistent with their Pauline authorship and necessitate their relegation to a later period; and a little investigation of the historical data will disclose their entire congruity with the Apostle's circumstances. It may indeed be affirmed without temerity that, had Luke been permitted to continue his narrative and exhibit the historical background of the Pastorals, their authenticity would hardly have been challenged. As it is, the situation is indicated merely by suggestions and inferences; yet even so it is sufficiently illuminating.

1. Incidental usages. 1 Tim. vi. 1, Tit. ii. 9; cf. 2 Tim. ii. 21. Rom. xiv. 4, Eph. vi. 5, 9, Col. iii. 22, iv. 1. Cf. 1 Pet. ii. 18.

Not a few of the peculiarities are merely incidental. Thus, it has been remarked that in the Pastorals, when the Apostle speaks of slaves and slave-owners, he designates the latter 'masters,' whereas he elsewhere styles them 'lords.' But what does this mean? 'Master' was the regular term; and wherever in his earlier letters he speaks of slaves and their 'lords,' it is always with a didactic purpose. He is inculcating the reciprocal duty of kindness and faithfulness, and after the most sacred of examples he enforces it by a word-play and affirms that bond and free alike are all slaves—

[1] Cf. iv: *ἀρχὴ δὲ πάντων χαλεπῶν φιλαργυρία* with 1 Tim. vi. 10. iv: *οὐδὲν εἰσηνέγκαμεν εἰς τὸν κόσμον ἀλλ' οὐδὲ ἐξενεγκεῖν τι ἔχομεν* with 1 Tim. vi. 7. xii: *ὑπὲρ πάντων τῶν ἁγίων προσεύχεσθε . . . ὑπὲρ βασιλέων* with 1 Tim. ii. 1. ix: *τὸν νῦν ἠγάπησαν αἰῶνα* with 2 Tim. iv. 10. v: *καὶ συμβασιλεύσομεν* and 2 Tim. ii. 12 are probably independent quotations from a primitive hymn.

[2] Cf. Iren. III. iii. 2; Eus. *Hist. Eccl.* III. 2.

'slaves of Christ the Lord.' 'Slaves,' he says, 'obey in everything your human lords, fearing the Lord. Lords, accord what is right and equitable to your slaves, knowing that you also have a Lord in Heaven.'

Cf. Mt. vi. 24; Jo. xiii. 16, xv. 15, 20.

2. Medical terms.

Again, the peculiarities of the Pastorals include a little group of medical terms: 'gangrene' or 'cancer,' 'cautery,' 'distempered,' 'patient of ill,' 'healthful,' 'healthy,' 'bring to life'; and it seems reasonable to attribute these to the Apostle's constant intercourse with his 'beloved physician,' who bore him company throughout those closing years and tended him in his frequent ailings. Nor will this be deemed far-fetched if it be observed how many—no fewer than twenty-eight[1]—of the lexical peculiarities which distinguish the Pastorals from the other Pauline letters, occur elsewhere in the New Testament only in Luke's writings, his Gospel and the Book of Acts—an evidence of the influence which his converse had on the Apostle's language.

2 Tim. ii. 17; 1 Tim. iv. 2; vi. 4; 2 Tim. ii. 24; 1 Tim. i. 10, vi. 3, 2 Tim. i. 13, iv. 3, Tit. i. 9, 13, ii. 1, 2; 8; 1 Tim. vi. 13.

3. Interest in ecclesiastical organisation.

And what of the novel interest which the Pastorals evince in ecclesiastical organisation? There were two orders in the ministry of the primitive Church—the Elders or Overseers, who cared for its spiritual welfare, and the Deacons, who administered its temporal affairs; and, so far as the earlier letters indicate, it would appear that they bulked little in the Apostle's esteem. It is the congregations that engage his concern. Once and only once does he mention the two orders—when he addresses his Philippian letter 'to the saints in Christ Jesus, with the Overseers and Deacons.' This is his solitary mention of the first order; and as for the second, it appears again incidentally in his commendation of Phœbe, 'a deaconess of the Church at Cenchreæ,' who conveyed his great encyclical to Ephesus; and also in his inculcation of uncomplaining and faithful employment of the various 'gifts of grace': 'if it be deaconship, let us devote ourselves to our deaconship.' It is remarkable that he never in the earlier letters uses the term 'Elder' or 'Presbyter,' preferring in his solitary mention of the office the synonym 'Overseer.' And the reason seems to have been that Presbyter was a Jewish title. The Christian congregations were organised after the model of

Lacking in the earlier letters.

Rom. xvi. 1.

xii. 7.

[1] 15 in 1 Tim.; 9 in 2 Tim.; 4 in Tit. Cf. Append. VII.

the Synagogue; and as the latter had its Presbyters, so they had theirs. It was a venerable and appropriate title; yet by reason of its Jewish associations it lent itself to a mischievous perversion, encouraging the Judaist contention of the permanence of the ancient order and the abiding obligation of the Law. Hence in the stress of the Judaist controversy the Apostle naturally mistrusted it, and, though it was the official designation, rather employed the alternative 'Overseer.'

The term *episcopos.*

And this latter, in its primitive use, was a beautiful name. It was a pastoral term, and its proper idea appears in Paul's address at Miletus to the Ephesian Elders. 'Take heed,'
Ac. xx. 28. he says, 'to yourselves and all the flock among which the Holy Spirit appointed you overseers, that you shepherd the Church of the Lord which He won with His own blood.' And so the Apostle Peter counsels his fellow Elders:
1 Pet. v. 2, 4. 'Shepherd the flock of God which is among you, taking the oversight of it, not constrainedly but willingly after God's way; and when the Chief Shepherd is manifested, you will receive the unfading crown of glory.' This designation of our Lord, 'the Chief Shepherd,' occurs only here, and it used to be regarded as a Christian coinage after the pattern of 'Chief Priest'; but it is proved by a recent discovery to have been no high title but a homely and familiar designation in the Common Greek. Egyptian exploration chanced upon a wooden tablet which had hung about the neck of a mummy and bore a rude inscription commemorating the dead man's name and calling and age: 'Plenis the younger, chief shepherd, lived —— years.'[1] The pastures of the wilderness were widely scattered, and the sheep were led in several flocks where they could find sustenance. Each flock was tended by its own shepherd, and there was a chief shepherd who had the oversight of them all. Here is the apostolic conception of a Presbyter or Elder. He was a shepherd, and his congregation was the flock committed to his charge. But the Church was composed of many congregations. There were many flocks, and many shepherds

[1] Πλῆνις νεώ- | τερος ἀρχιποί- | μενος ἐβιώ- | σεν ἐτῶν - - -. ἀρχιποίμενος is a slip for ἀρχιποίμην, proving the illiteracy of the writer. Cf. Deissmann, *Light from the Ancient East*, pp. 97 ff.; Moulton and Milligan, *Vocab.*

each taking the oversight of his own flock; and over them all there was the Chief Shepherd, the Lord Jesus Christ, 'the Great Shepherd of the Sheep,' the supreme Shepherd and Overseer, 'the True Shepherd,' the Shepherd in whom the idea of shepherdhood is realised. Heb. xiii. 20; 1 Pet. ii. 25; Jo. x. 11, 14.

Ecclesiastical organisation an urgent concern in the Pastorals.

It was a beautiful conception, and it is no wonder that Paul should have loved it, and preferred it to the cold official designation when he was pouring out his heart to his converts and thinking not of ecclesiastical organisation but only of their doctrinal instruction and evangelical profit. It was otherwise, however, when he was addressing not a congregation but a Presbyter charged with the oversight of a congregation and embarrassed by administrative difficulties. And such was the occasion of the Pastorals. Timothy and Titus were charged, in peculiarly trying circumstances, with the business of government and organisation, and he deals with their actual and pressing needs. As it happened, both had need of counsel in the matter of the appointment of office-bearers, and in addressing himself to this practical concern he naturally uses the official terminology. In writing to Timothy he indeed retains the more congenial term 'Overseer,' but he presently drops it and employs the official designation 'Elder' or 'Presbyter'; and in his letter to Titus he reiterates his counsels and employs both terms interchangeably. 1 Tim. iii. 1, 2. v 17, 19. Tit. i. 5, 7.

Its importance always recognised by the Apostle.

It is true that the Apostle's interest in ecclesiastical organisation is peculiar to the Pastorals and has no parallel in his earlier letters; but the explanation lies in the novelty of the situation. If he has never heretofore written thus, the reason is simply that occasion has never heretofore arisen. And though questions of order and discipline were indeed secondary in his esteem, he had never slighted them or depreciated their importance. It appears from the Book of Acts that, wherever he preached in the course of his travels, he never reckoned his work complete until he had organised his converts into a congregation and ordained Presbyters over them; and thus it was no innovation when he enjoined Titus to organise the converts in the island of Crete and appoint Presbyters in every city. Cf. Ac. xiv. 23, xx. 17. Tit. i. 5.

The discussion of those questions of ecclesiastical organi-

4. The Asian heresy. sation and administration has furnished no inconsiderable proportion of the novel terms which distinguish the Pastorals; but there was a far graver problem which claimed the Apostle's attention, especially in his letters to Timothy; and this has put its impress on both his language and his thought. It was the Gnostic heresy which he had already foreseen during his ministry at Ephesus, and which had so quickly developed and overspread the Province of Asia. He had dealt with it during his Roman imprisonment in his encyclical 'to the Ephesians' and his letter to Colossæ; but his arguments had proved unavailing to arrest its malignant growth, and the situation in the Province and particularly in the capital was now more serious than ever.

Cf. Ac. xx. 29.

'Genealogies' of Gnostic *æons*.

He summarily and accurately defines the heresy and its implicates when he bids Timothy 'charge some not to teach strange doctrines or give heed to fables and interminable genealogies.' The phrase 'interminable genealogies' has been much disputed, but it can hardly be anything else than a contemptuous designation of the Gnostic theory of a succession of emanations from the Divine *Pleroma*, a hierarchy of *æons* mediating between God and the world.[1] Nor is this the sole reference in the Pastorals to that fantastic speculation, which rested on the philosophic postulate of the inherent evil of matter and the impossibility of direct contact between it and a holy God. It was only through angelic mediators that He could have to do with the world whether in creation or providence or redemption; and thus the Saviour was reduced to the rank of an *æon*. It is this theory that the Apostle has in view when he affirms that God created all kinds of food, and 'everything which God created is good,' thus denying the inherent evil of matter; and again when he affirms that there is 'one Mediator between God and man, Himself man, Christ Jesus,' thus at once asserting the divine dignity of our Lord and sweeping away the imagination of a hierarchy of angelic mediators.

I Tim. i. 3, 4.

I Tim. iv. 3, 4.

ii. 5.

Apocryphal 'fables.'

And what were the 'fables'? The Gnostics followed the allegorical method of interpretation, and just as the Neoplatonists had applied it to the Homeric Poems and Philo

[1] Cf. p. 524. Gnostic 'genealogising' is exemplified in the Naasene hymn which Hippolytus quotes (v. 5) as summarising all the mysteries of the heresy.

to the Jewish Scriptures, so they applied it to the narrative of our Lord's earthly life.[1] They saw in the evangelic history an allegory of the relation between God and the world, portraying the union of spiritual and holy powers with evil matter and their final triumph. It was all myth. And, not content with allegorising the history, they were ever weaving new fables until it was lost in a mass of wild and fantastic inventions. This is the origin of the apocryphal Gospels which appeared in such rank profusion during the early centuries. Such as have survived are indeed later than the Apostle's day, but Hippolytus mentions one which was current among the Naasenes and set forth their doctrine of the soul's rebirth from the earthly to the spiritual [2]—' the Gospel according to the Egyptians,' which survives only in a few patristic quotations.[3]

The peril was extreme. It menaced the very life of the Church. There was as yet no written Gospel; and the story of the Lord's earthly life was an oral tradition. The catechists who were charged with the business of its conservation and communication, were called *didaskaloi* or ' Teachers,' [4] and the cognate term *didaskalia* or ' discipline ' denoted both their office and its material. The Oral Tradition was the Church's most precious possession, and the task of its conservation was always supremely important, demanding scrupulous fidelity; but the appearance of those legend-mongers constituted an unprecedented menace and demanded tenfold vigilance, lest corruptions should steal in. And hence the Pastorals abound in importunate warnings and novel definitions. They speak of ' the heathful Discipline ' in contrast with ' the disciplines of demons,' ' the genuine Discipline ' in contrast with ' the profane and old-wifish fables ' of the heretical teachers, ' the Discipline which is the norm of religion.' And they call the sacred treasure by a significant name—' the deposit,' ' the genuine deposit.' This is a banker's term; [5] and the idea is that the Evangelic

The Evangelic Tradition.

Cf. 1 Tim. iv. 13, 16, v. 17; 2 Tim. iii. 16; Tit. ii. 7.

Cf. 1 Tim. i. 10, iv. 6, vi. 1; 2 Tim. iii. 10, iv. 3; Tit. i. 9, ii. 1, 10.

1 Tim. i. 10; Tit. i. 9, ii. 1.

1 Tim. iv. 1.

iv. 6, 7.

vi. 3.

1 Tim. vi. 20; 2 Tim. i. 14.

[1] Cf. Hippol. v. 3, 4. [2] *Ibid.* 5.

[3] Cf. Hilgenfeld, *Libr. Deperd. Fragm.*, pp. 42 ff.

[4] Cf. p. 80. Papias (Eus. *Hist. Eccl.* III. 39) says that Mark's Gospel was his report of the διδασκαλίαι of his master Peter.

[5] Cf. *The Days of His Flesh*, p. xv.

Tradition was a precious trust which amid the corrupting influences of the time must be sedulously guarded, preserved inviolate, and transmitted unimpaired. 'O Timothy,' pleads the Apostle, 'guard the Deposit, shunning the profane babblings and incongruities of the "Knowledge" (*gnosis*) so falsely named'; and again: 'The genuine Deposit guard through the Holy Spirit who dwells within us.' The Oral Tradition was 'the genuine Deposit,' and its commixture with those base counterfeits, the Gnostic fables, was the danger of the hour. And here lies the crowning evidence of the apostolic date of the Pastorals. Once the Tradition had been committed to writing, the Church possessed an authoritative record of the sayings and doings of her Lord in the days of His flesh; and their solicitude for the inviolate conservation of the Tradition demonstrates that the Pastorals were written ere the appearance of our Gospels. The earliest of these is the Gospel according to St. Mark; and if, as seems certain, it was composed shortly before the fall of Jerusalem in the year 70, then the Pastorals were written just before it in the extremity of the Church's need.

A Teacher's Manual. The Teachers were not left without aid in the discharge
Cf. 2 Tim. i. 13. of their difficult and responsible office. It appears that a
Manual had been prepared for their guidance.[1] It furnished
1 Tim. iii. 1-13. an 'outline' of the Evangelic Tradition; and besides this
2 Tim. iii. 16, 17. it seems to have contained rules regarding the offices of the
Eldership and the Deaconship; directions for the Christian
1 Tim. i. 15, iv. 9, 10; Tit. ii. 11-14, iii. 4-7. use of the Old Testament Scriptures; a variety of evangelical
truths and practical maxims; and a collection of Christian
1 Tim. iii. 16; 2 Tim. ii. 11-13. hymns. This is the source of those 'faithful words' which
the Apostle quotes, and of other passages which, though
1 Tim. i. 15, iii. 1, iv. 9, 10; 2 Tim. ii. 11-14; Tit. iii. 4-8. lacking express reference, are plainly quotations. And it is
significant that these exhibit striking affinities with the
language and thought of Luke. Thus, of the word 'equip'
which occurs in the Pastoral definition of the use of the Old
2 Tim. iii. 17. Testament Scriptures—'that the man of God may be perfect,
equipped for every good work,' there is only one other
Ac. xxi. 5. instance in the New Testament, and this is found in the Book
Tit. ii. 11, iii. 4. of Acts. Again, the word 'appear' which occurs twice in a
lengthy quotation in the letter to Titus, occurs elsewhere in

[1] Cf. p. 412.

the New Testament only twice—in Luke's Gospel, of the Lk. i. 79.
appearing of 'the dayspring from on high,' and in his Book Ac. xxvii.
of Acts, of the appearing of sun or stars to storm-tossed 20.
mariners. And no less striking is the word 'philanthropy' Tit. iii. 4.
or 'love of man' in the same passage. It is a Lucan word,
and occurs elsewhere only in the Book of Acts.[1] It is, xxviii. 2;
moreover, remarkable how characteristic of the quotations is cf. xxvii. 3.
the phrase 'God our Saviour.' It is a phrase of the Teacher's 1 Tim. iv.
Manual, and though the Apostle has adopted it in several 10; Tit. iii.
instances, he never disregards his accustomed differentiation 4. 1 Tim. i. 1,
between God and Christ the Lord.[2] It seems, however, ii. 3; Tit.
that the Manual ignored this distinction, and not only spoke i. 3.
of God and Christ equally as 'our Saviour' but styled Christ Cf. Tit. iii.
'our Saviour God.' Thus, according to the true rendering, 6.
it speaks of 'our great God and Saviour Christ Jesus'; and Tit. ii. 13.
it would appear that its outline of the Evangelic Tradition,
'the healthful words of our Lord Jesus Christ,' was entitled 1 Tim. vi. 3.
'The Discipline of Our Saviour God.' The significant fact Tit. ii. 10.
here is that the phrase 'God our Saviour' is found also in
Luke's hymn, the *Magnificat*, and nowhere else in the New Lk. i. 47.
Testament outside of the Pastorals save in the noble benediction at the close of the Epistle of St. Jude.

It seems a reasonable inference from all those linguistic Probably
coincidences between the writings of Luke and the Teacher's composed
Manual that the latter may have been his work. by Luke. And the inference is corroborated by the circumstance that the Manual contained Christian hymns; for 'the beloved physician' had the quality of a poet, and it is to him that the
Church owes three of her finest canticles—the *Magnificat*, Lk. i. 46;
the *Benedictus*, and the *Nunc Dimittis*. If the Teacher's 55; 68-79;
Manual was his work, then it was the forerunner of his ii. 29-32.
gracious Gospel; and, like his Gospel, 'the Gospel of the sinful,' it was, as the quotations in the Pastorals show, pervaded by the spirit of his revered master and beloved friend.

[1] Of the 295 linguistic peculiarities in the Pastorals no fewer than 28 are found in quotations from the Teacher's Manual. Cf. Append. VII.

[2] Cf. pp. 426, 464.

THE APOSTLE'S LATER MINISTRY

Its record. THE Apostle's later ministry extended from the close of his first Roman imprisonment in the spring of 62 until his re-arrest—a period, as will appear in the sequel, of some five and a half years. It is unrecorded by the sacred historian; but it was during its course that the Pastorals were written, and from their numerous and significant allusions it is possible, with the aid of tradition, to reconstruct its general outline with a measure of probability.

Expulsion from Rome. When at length after two weary years of captivity he was arraigned before the Emperor, he was acquitted; but since his continued presence in Rome would have provoked his Jewish enemies to fresh hostility, he was ordered, in the interest of the public peace, to quit the city. And whither did he betake himself? In his letter to his friends at Philippi
Phil. ii. 24. toward the close of the year 60 he had promised that in the event of his release he would pay them a visit; and quite recently, when the issue of his trial was assured, he had
Phm. 22. apprised Philemon of his intention to visit Colossæ and bidden him prepare for his entertainment. It is reasonable to assume that he was not unmindful of these engagements. He left Rome, accompanied by his beloved physician Luke and Timothy his son in the Faith who had both done so much to alleviate the hardship of his long imprisonment, and set out for the East.

Voyage to Ephesus. The sea was now open for navigation, and he took ship for Ephesus. This was not his destination, yet it was inevitable that he should make a considerable stay in the Asian capital, where he had so many associations and interests. Not only had he laboured there for two years and a quarter—the longest sojourn which he had made in a single city and the most eventful period in the whole course of his apostolic career, but there that subtle heresy which had since invaded the Province had its chief centre. Its mischievous operations had been reported to him during the second year of his imprisonment, and he had dealt with it by letter; and now he would be eager to ascertain what effect his arguments had produced.

Timothy stationed there. He quickly perceived that the mischief, so far from abating, had gathered strength. His worst forebodings had been realised. Alike in its doctrinal and in its ethical aspect the heresy had attained a larger development, and was poisoning the very fountain of the Faith. He would labour to counteract the mischief, and he doubtless protracted his sojourn to the utmost. But at the longest it was all too short; and when at length he took his departure in pursuance of his engagements elsewhere, he left Timothy behind to superintend the distracted Church and continue the work which he had begun. (1 Tim. i. 3, 4.)

Visit to Macedonia. His promise to the Philippians had been the first made, and it must be first fulfilled; and accordingly, when he left Ephesus, he betook himself to Macedonia. His chief interest lay at Philippi, and on their arrival he and Luke, who was held in affectionate remembrance for his long and gracious ministry there,[1] would receive a warm welcome. But their activities would extend much farther. Some six years previously the Province had been disturbed by Judaist machination,[2] and they would make a tour of the churches and confirm them in the Faith.

Overland journey to Colossæ. From Macedonia in pursuance of the promise to Philemon they travelled to Colossæ. They might have taken ship from Neapolis to Ephesus and journeyed up the valley of the Mæander; but since it appears that, when the Apostle by and by wrote to Timothy from the valley of the Lycus, he had never seen the latter since his settlement in the Asian capital, it may be inferred that they crossed to Troas and, disembarking there, travelled overland by Pergamos, Thyatira, Sardes, and Philadelphia. If, as is probable, it was now winter-time, early in 63, the difficulty of navigation would determine their choice of this route; and Paul would be glad of the opportunity of visiting those cities by the way (Cf. 1 Tim. i. 3.)

[1] Cf. p. 135. [2] Cf. pp. 260, 344.

and ascertaining how they were affected by the Gnostic heresy.

Sojourn in the valley of the Lycus.

On their arrival at Colossæ they would be hospitably welcomed by Philemon and his family, and they would meet at least two old friends, Epaphras, the leader of the Colossian Church, and Onesimus, Philemon's slave who had absconded to Rome and had heard from the captive Apostle of the freedom of the children of God and had returned to his master 'no longer as a slave, but something more than a slave—a brother beloved.' It was Paul's first and long desired visit to the valley of the Lycus, and his interest would extend to all its churches. It was natural that he should pass from Colossæ to its more important neighbour, the large and prosperous city of Laodiceia; and it was there, according to tradition,[1] that he wrote the first of the Pastorals.

Cf. Col. ii. 1.

Timothy's discouragement at Ephesus.

And what was the occasion? It is clearly indicated in the course of the letter. Of all the Apostle's friends perhaps the sweetest and gentlest was Timothy. There is none whom he more frequently and warmly commends, and none, save perhaps Luke, who had deserved better of him by personal devotion. Yet his very excellences involved limitations, and these seriously incapacitated him for the office which he held. He was charged with the oversight of the Ephesian Church and the eradication of the heresy which had taken root in its midst. It was a difficult task, demanding experience, discretion, and courage; and these qualities Timothy lacked. As the very name Presbyter or Elder implies, mature age, with the wisdom which it brings, was accounted essential in one who was entrusted with the oversight of a Christian community; and Timothy was still a young man. Since he was a mere lad living with his pious mother and grandmother in their home at Lystra when Paul enlisted him as his attendant in the summer of 50, he was now under thirty years of age; and it would be difficult for him to exercise the needful authority among the fathers of the Church. A strong and self-reliant personality might have succeeded, but Timothy was constitutionally timid.

Cf. 1 Cor. iv. 17, xvi. 10; Phil. ii. 19-22.

Cf. Ac. xvi. 1-3.

Cf. 1 Tim. iv. 12.

Cf. 1 Cor. xvi. 10.

[1] Subscript. A: ἐγράφη ἀπὸ Λαοδικείας, K: ἐγράφη ἀπὸ Λαοδικείας ἥτις ἐστι μητρόπολις Φρυγίας τῆς Πακατιανῆς, L.

He had a gentle and affectionate nature with a woman's tenderness and devotion, and in the Apostle's company he shrank from no hardship and feared no ordeal; but he could not stand alone, and years afterwards Paul still remembered how he had wept when they parted at Ephesus. That was an ill augury for the successful conduct of so difficult a charge; and whatever forebodings it may have awakened in Paul's breast were fully realised. It appears that Timothy's timidity so mastered him that he was disposed to shrink into retirement and shirk the public duties of his ministry. Lacking initiative and resolution, he was accessible to personal influence and lent a credulous ear to slanderous and plausible tongues. It seems that he was thus betrayed into painful and disastrous blunders through acting precipitately on groundless charges against Presbyters and, at the same time, ordaining unworthy men to the sacred office without sufficient investigation of their credentials. It is in keeping with his character that he was disposed to asceticism; and he suffered the inevitable penalty not only in physical weakness but also, as he had confided to his revered master, in morbid and impure imagination.

Cf Phil. ii. 19-23. Cf. 2 Tim. i. 4. Cf. 1 Tim. iv. 11-16. Cf. 1 Tim. v. 19-22. Cf. 1 Tim. v. 23. Cf. 2 Tim. ii. 22.

Letter to Timothy.

The Apostle was doubtless kept informed of the progress of events at Ephesus. Timothy would write him as opportunity offered; and it appears that after his arrival in the valley of the Lycus he received a communication which necessitated his energetic intervention. Timothy's embarrassments had multiplied until his position seemed intolerable, and he was disposed to resign his charge and quit the city. And the Apostle immediately wrote him and peremptorily vetoed the proposal, bidding him persevere in his ministry and discussing for his guidance the problems which confronted him.

Cf. 1 Tim. i. 3.

THE FIRST LETTER TO TIMOTHY

The address.

The letter opens with the customary address. It is natural that the Apostle's greeting to one so intimately and tenderly associated with him should be peculiarly affectionate, all the more that he has stern rebukes to administer; but it seems strange that he should have thought fit to affirm his apostleship. Did not Timothy know and acknowledge his divine calling? The reason is that the letter was no mere private communication. It deals with questions of general import; and, as appears from the final benediction, 'Grace be with you all,' it was designed for the instruction and correction of the whole Church. Paul had weighty judgments to pronounce, and therefore he affirms at the outset his apostolic authority.

i. 1 Paul, an Apostle of Christ Jesus according to the command
2 of God our Saviour and Christ Jesus our Hope, to Timothy,
a true child in faith. Grace, mercy, and peace from God the
Father and Christ Jesus our Lord.

Injunction to persevere.

He addresses himself at once to the immediate occasion—Timothy's discouragement and his proposal to demit his office; and this pusillanimous step he sternly vetoes and reiterates his original mandate. And what was that? The troublers of the Ephesian Church were Gnostic Judaists, and their doctrine was a blend of contentious philosophy and ascetic legalism; and Timothy's commission was to counter both by keeping the Church true to the Christian message of a love which cleanses the heart and renders legal restraint unnecessary.

3 As I exhorted you when I was going to Macedonia, stay on
at Ephesus,[1] that you may charge some not to teach strange
4 doctrines or give heed to fables and interminable genealogies,
since these occasion questionings rather than faithful discharge
5 of the stewardship which God has entrusted to us. And the
end which the charge should aim at is love springing from a
6 clean heart and a good conscience and unaffected faith; and
it is by missing these that some have swerved into futile
7 talking. They would be teachers of the Law, though they
do not understand either their own statements or the subjects
on which they dogmatise.

Cf. 1 Cor. ix. 17.

8 Now we know that the Law is beautiful if one use it law-
9 fully, recognising that law is not enacted for a righteous man
but for lawless and disorderly persons, impious and sinful,
unholy and profane, assaulters of their fathers or mothers,
10 murderers, fornicators, sodomites, kidnappers, liars, perjurers,

[1] The sentence is elliptic: 'as I exhorted you stay on, [so do].' Grotius avoids the anacolouthon by taking ἵνα παραγγείλῃς as imperat.: 'see that you charge' (cf. Eph. v. 33).

and whatever else is opposed to the healthful Discipline,
11 according to the Gospel of the glory of the Blessed God with
which I was entrusted.

The Apostle's own example.

It was a hard task, but by the Lord's grace it could be achieved. Was not Paul himself a conspicuous example of the efficacy of grace? He had been a blasphemer and a persecutor; and if he, 'the foremost of sinners,' had found mercy and been so signally used in the Lord's service, what was not possible to one whose early years had been so rich in promise? Here was an incentive to Timothy; and it was reinforced by the disastrous issue of the heresy, particularly in the case of two of its ringleaders whom for their blasphemous aberration the Apostle had recently excommunicated.

12 I am thankful to Him who put power into me, Christ Jesus
our Lord, because He deemed me faithful and appointed me
13 to His service, though I was formerly a blasphemer and a
persecutor and a bully. But mercy was vouchsafed me
because it was in ignorance that I did it while still a stranger
14 to the Faith; and the grace of our Lord multiplied exceedingly,
bringing that faith and love which come of union with Christ
15 Jesus. Faithful is the word and worthy of all acceptance
that 'Christ Jesus came into the world to save sinners'; and
16 of these I am foremost. But it was for this reason that mercy
was vouchsafed me, that in me as the foremost Jesus Christ
might demonstrate all His long-suffering as a pattern for those
who would afterwards rest their faith on Him for life eternal.
17 Now to the King of the Ages, incorruptible, invisible, only
God, be honour and glory for ever and ever. Amen.
18 This is the charge which I deposit in your keeping, my child
Timothy, according to the expectations which your early
promise inspired, that, begirt with them, you wage the
19 honourable warfare, keeping hold of faith and a good conscience. It is because they have thrust away the latter that
20 some have suffered shipwreck in relation to the Faith. Among
these are Hymenæus and Alexander, whom I 'delivered to
Satan'[1] that they might be instructed not to blaspheme.

Christian conduct.

And now he turns to practical instructions regarding the life of a Christian community. One inevitable corollary of the Gnostic heresy with its postulate of the evil of matter and its distinction between 'the spiritual' and 'the carnal'

[1] Cf. p. 256.

was a relaxation of civic and social obligation; and so he inculcates the primal duties of public loyalty and domestic piety.

ii. 1 I exhort, then, first of all that petitions, prayers, interces-
2 sions, thanksgivings, be made on behalf of all men, especially
on behalf of kings and all in high station, that we may lead a
3 tranquil and peaceful life in all religion and dignity. This is
honourable and acceptable in the sight of our Saviour God,
4 who wishes all men to be saved and reach a full knowledge of
5 the Truth. For there is one God, one Mediator also between
6 God and men, Himself man, Christ Jesus, who gave Himself
as a ransom on behalf of all—the testimony which God has
7 borne at proper seasons; and it was for this that I was
appointed a herald and an Apostle—it is truth that I am
telling, it is no lie—a teacher of Gentiles in faith and truth.

Cf. 1 Jo. v. 9-11. Cf. vi. 15; Tit i. 3. Cf. Rom. ix. 1.

8 It is my desire, then, that the men should pray in every
place, uplifting holy hands, without anger and disputation.
9 And it is my desire also that women should array themselves
in orderly attire modestly and discreetly, not with plaits and
10 gold or pearls or costly clothing,[1] but, as becomes women
11 professing godliness, by the practice of good works. Let
12 a woman be a peaceable and submissive learner. I do not
permit a woman to teach or to domineer over a man; no,
13 she must be peaceable. For Adam was fashioned first,
14 then Eve. And it was not Adam that was deceived; it was
woman that was out and out deceived and is involved in
15 transgression.[2] But she will find salvation in her office of
motherhood—if they continue in faith and love and
sanctification and discretion withal.[3]

Church offices.

Then he turns to the Church and its administration.

[1] Cf. a wife's epitaph at Heraclia on the Black Sea: ἡ φίλανδρος καὶ σώφρων ἡ φιλόσοφος ζήσασα κοσμίως.

[2] ἡ γυνή, not 'his wife,' but 'the woman,' involving womankind. Cf. Chrys.: πᾶσα ἡ φύσις ἐν παραβάσει γέγονε δι' ἐκείνης.

[3] The meaning of this difficult passage is clear in the light of the Rabbinical doctrine of the status of woman (cf. Taylor, *Sayings of the Fathers*, p. 15). She was forbidden to learn, much more to teach, the Law. But she was not therefore denied salvation. She found it in the performance of her proper offices; and these were to send her children to be taught in the synagogue; to attend to domestic concerns and leave her husband free to study in the schools; to keep the house for him till he returned. In the discharge of these womanly tasks women will find salvation, always, adds the Apostle, on the supposition that 'they continue in faith and love.' μείνωσιν plur., since ἡ γυνή (ver. 14) signifies 'womankind.' This interpretation rules out various notions which have been imported into the passage, as that τεκνογονία means (1) Baptism, 'quod est filiorum generatio' (Pelag.), (2) the Virgin Birth (anonym. in Theophyl.).

iii. 1 Faithful is the word; [1] 'If one aspires to Overseership, it is Cf. Mt.
"a beautiful work" that he is desiring.' xxvi. 10.
2 The Overseer, then, must be irreproachable, a faithful
husband,[2] sober, discreet, orderly, hospitable, apt at teach-
3 ing, not quarrelsome in his cups or ready with his fists, but
4 sweetly reasonable, no fighter, nor fond of money, ruling his
own house honourably, keeping his children in subjection
5 with all dignity—if one knows not how to rule his own house,
6 how will he manage God's Church?—no novice, lest he be
swollen with windy pride and incur the same condemnation
7 as the Devil.[3] And he must also have an honourable
reputation with outsiders, lest he incur reproach and fall
into the Devil's snare.
8 Similarly, Deacons must be dignified, not double-tongued,
9 nor hard drinkers or dirty money-makers; they must be
men who hold the mystery of the Faith in a clean conscience.
10 And let these also first be proved, and then let them take
11 office if nothing can be laid to their charge. Deaconesses [4]
similarly must be dignified, no slanderers, sober, trust-
12 worthy in everything. Let Deacons be faithful husbands,
13 ruling honourably their children and their own houses. For
those who have served honourably in the deaconship are
winning themselves an honourable station and much boldness
in preaching the Faith which is in Christ Jesus.

All these instructions have a personal bearing. It was for Timothy that the Apostle was concerned. His sojourn in the valley of the Lycus was drawing to a close, and he hoped that he might ere long revisit Ephesus, and then he would deal effectively with the situation. It was impossible, however, to forecast the future, and in the meanwhile he would have Timothy worthily administer his august office. He was charged with the oversight of the Church; and what was the Church? She was, according to one of the hymns in the Teacher's Manual, the repository and guardian of the truth, the witness to the high mystery of the Incarnation.

Timothy's high and difficult duty.

[1] Chrys., followed by W. H., attaches the formula to the preceding sentence (ii. 15). For πιστός here D* reads ἀνθρώπινος, 'human'—'a proverbial expression of general application and profane origin' (Zahn).

[2] Literally 'one woman's man.' There is no reference either to polygamy or to remarriage. The Apostle did not prohibit the latter (cf. v. 11, 14).

[3] It was through pride that Satan and the rest of the rebel angels fell. Cf. Ecclus. x. 13; 2 Pet. ii. 4; Jud. 6.

[4] γυναῖκας, not wives of deacons or women generally but women holding the office of deaconship, deaconesses. This is the patristic view. Cf. Theophyl.: οὐ περὶ τῶν τυχουσῶν γυναικῶν λέγει ἀλλὰ περὶ τῶν διακονισσῶν.

And the situation which had arisen at Ephesus was no surprise. It had been long impending; and the Apostle had foreseen it, and had strenuously protested against those ascetic tendencies and insisted on the truth that material things are God's creatures and nothing which God created is evil but, according to the Scriptures, 'all very good.' And Timothy's business now was the inculcation of that principle and the commendation, by precept and example, of the Christian ideal of holiness—not the mortification of the body but its consecration.

14 I am writing you all this though I hope to come to you
15 ere long. I am writing it in case I should be detained,
that you may know how you must conduct yourself in the
House of God, that is, the Church of the Living God, the
16 pillar and basement of the Truth. And confessedly great
is the mystery of our religion: He who[1]

'Was manifested in the flesh,
Was pronounced righteous by the Spirit, (Cf. Lk. iii. 22.)
Was seen by angels, (Cf. Mk. i. 13.)
Was heralded among the Gentiles,
Was trusted in the world,
Was received up in glory.'

iv. 1 But the Spirit expressly says that in later seasons some
will fall off from the Faith, giving heed to deceiving spirits
2 and disciplines of demons, through the masquerading[2] of
3 false talkers seared in their own conscience, prohibiting
marriage and enjoining abstinence from foods which God
created to be partaken of with thanksgiving by those who
hold the Faith and have attained full knowledge of the
4 Truth; because everything which God created is 'good,' (Gen. i. 4, 10, 12, 18, 21, 25, 31.)
and there is nothing that should be rejected if it be received
5 with thanksgiving; for it is hallowed through the Word of
God and intercession.

6 This principle inculcate on the brothers, and you will be
a genuine minister of Christ Jesus, feeding on the words of
the Faith and of the genuine Discipline which you have
7 followed. But their profane and old-wifish fables have
8 nothing to do with. Train yourself to religion; for
physical training is profitable for a little while, but religion
is profitable for everything, carrying as it does a promise
9 of life present and future. Faithful is the word and worthy

[1] Reading ὅς. The variant Θεός, 'God,' originated in a copyist's mistaking ΟΣ for Θ̄Σ, the uncial contraction of ΘΕΟΣ.

[2] ὑπόκρισις, properly 'play-acting.' Cf. *The Days of His Flesh*, p. 102.

10 of all acceptance : 'For this is the end of our toiling and
wrestling, that we have set our hope on a Living God who
is the Saviour of all men, especially of such as hold the
Faith.'

Call to devotion.

Cf. iv. 7b-10.

Timothy was a young man, and it would seem that his natural timidity had betrayed him into two fatal blunders. He had allowed himself to be overawed by the sanctimonious pretensions of the ascetics and had acquiesced in their practices instead of taking a resolute stand and boldly exhibiting the true ideal. And, further, he tended to seclude himself and neglect the public offices of his ministry, particularly the public 'reading' of the Old Testament Scriptures and the ensuing 'exhortation,' after the manner of the Jewish Synagogue, and the even more important institution of 'discipline'—the schooling of the Church in the Evangelic Tradition. This weak dereliction was a grievous disappointment to the Apostle, belying as it did the bright promise of Timothy's early years and the high hopes entertained of him at his ordination.

Cf. Ac. xiii. 15.

11, 12 Charge and teach all this. Let no man despise you for
your youth, but prove a pattern to those who hold the
13 Faith in word, in conduct, in love, in faith, in purity. Until
I come give heed to public reading, to exhortation, to
14 discipline. Be not neglectful of the gift of grace within
you, which was conferred upon you in the hope which you Cf. i. 18.
had inspired when the Presbytery laid their hands upon
15 you.[1] Practise these things, employ yourself in them, that
16 your progress may be manifest to every one. Take heed to
yourself and to the Discipline ; persist in your offices, for in
doing this you will save both yourself and your hearers.

The office of personal admonition.

Timidity was Timothy's snare, and it had involved him in many embarrassments. Not the least serious was the

[1] Ordination by 'the laying on of hands' was a primitive practice. Cf. Ac. vi. 6, viii. 17. The Presbytery was the college of Presbyters in each community; and its primitive constitution and procedure are illustrated by Clem. Rom. *Ad Cor.* xlii-xliv. (1) πρεσβύτεροι and ἐπίσκοποι were synonymous. Cf. Lightfoot, n. 9 on xlii. (2) The Christian office of Presbyter was Jewish in origin. It was not founded by Christ : the Apostles instituted it after the example of Moses. (3) That it might be permanent, they ordained that successors should be appointed as vacancies occurred through death. (4) These appointments were made by the ἐπίσκοποι or πρεσβύτεροι with the consent of the whole Church (συνευδοκησάσης τῆς ἐκκλησίας πάσης). Cf. the narrative of Polycarp's ordination in Pion. *Vit. Polyc.* xxiii.

difficulty which he experienced in the administration of personal admonition. It was a delicate duty, and when he braced himself to its performance, he was betrayed by sheer nervousness into excessive severity. The Apostle's counsel is: 'Never reprimand; remonstrate lovingly. Be like a son to older men and women and a brother to the younger.'

v. 1 Never reprimand an older man, but exhort him as a father;
2 and younger men as brothers; older women as mothers, and
younger as sisters in all purity.

The order of widows.

Cf. Ac. vi. 1, ix. 39, 41; Ja. i. 27.

A gracious characteristic of the Apostolic Church was its kindly solicitude for the poor. Almost from the outset of its career provision had been made for the maintenance of forlorn widows; and ere long, with a wise appreciation at once of the humiliation which charity inflicts and of the abuses which it inevitably occasions, those unfortunates were organised into an order resembling yet distinct from that of the Deaconesses. Capable widows were charged with a variety of gracious offices, especially the care of orphans and the nursing of the sick;[1] and thus they were serviceable to the Church, and their maintenance was no charity but a well earned remuneration. It was a beneficent institution, but it required vigilant surveillance. It was designed for the relief of the really necessitous, not for aged widows who had children or grandchildren well able to support them, nor for young widows who could earn their own livelihood and who, if they were supported in idleness, would turn mischievous and wanton. Thus a strict censorship was needed; and here apparently Timothy had proved remiss. Scandals had ensued, and to prevent their recurrence the Apostle lays down two rules; first, that no widow should be admitted to the order unless she were absolutely desolate; and, second, that none be admitted unless she had attained the age of sixty and bore a creditable character.

3, 4 Honour widows who are really widows; but if any widow
has children or grandchildren, let them learn first to act
religiously by their own house and recompense their fore-
5 bears; for this is acceptable in the sight of God. One who
is really a widow and left desolate has set her hope on God

[1] Cf. Lightfoot on Ignat. *Ad Smyrn.* xiii.

and continues at her supplications and her prayers night Cf. Lk. ii.
6, 7 and day; but gaiety in a widow is a living death. And 37.
8 press these charges, that they may be irreproachable. But
if any one does not provide for his own, especially his household, he has denied the Faith and is worse than one who is a stranger to it.
9 Let no widow be put on the list unless she be sixty years
10 of age, a faithful wife, with a reputation for 'beautiful works' Cf. Mt.
—the nurture of children, the entertainment of strangers, xxvi. 10.
the washing of the saints' feet,[1] the relief of distress, the
11 pursuit of every good work. But younger widows have
nothing to do with; for when they grow wanton against the
12 Christ, they want to marry, and incur condemnation for
13 cancelling their initial pledge. And at the same time they
learn to be idle, gadding from house to house; and not only
idle but tattlers and busybodies, talking about things which
14 should not be talked about. My wish then is that younger
widows[2] marry, bear children, be mistresses of houses, and
15 give the adversary no outlet for reviling; for some have
16 already swerved after Satan. If any woman who holds
the Faith is connected with widows, let her relieve them,
and let the Church not be burdened, so that it may relieve
the real widows.

Another difficulty which Timothy had experienced arose from his dealings with the Presbyters. His commission was the suppression of the disorders which the heresy had occasioned; and his jurisdiction was extensive, since in so large a city there would be several congregations,[3] and besides these he had the oversight of all the churches in the Province.[4] Each had its Presbyters, charged with the offices of administration and instruction; and it appears that they had in many cases been demoralised by the example of the heretical teachers. The latter were generally

Management of Presbyter

[1] Two true womanly qualities: (1) Motherliness, in the widest sense. 'One who is a mother only to her own children is not a mother; she is only a woman who has borne children' (George MacDonald). (2) Hospitality, so needful in those days when travellers went afoot. When Paul speaks of 'the washing of the saints' feet' (cf. *The Days of His Flesh*, p. 203), he is recalling his own experience in the course of his missionary journeyings, when he had found a kindly welcome in many a humble home.

[2] Curss., Chrys., Hier. add χήρας—a correct gloss.

[3] Cf. the multiplicity of synagogues in Damascus (Ac. ix. 2, 20) and Salamis (xiii. 5).

[4] Cf. ii. 8: ἐν παντὶ τόπῳ. Theod. Mops. *Argumentum*: 'ut omnem peragrans Asiam universam quæ illo sunt ecclesias gubernaret.'

Cf. vi. 5. mercenary adventurers, trading on their propaganda and reaping a rich harvest from the credulity of their dupes; and their abundant emoluments had excited envy and discontent in the breasts of the Presbyters. This unpleasant development had embarrassed Timothy, and the Apostle counsels him regarding it. He recognises that, in so far as the exactions of their sacred functions had impaired their livelihood, the Presbyters were entitled to remuneration, and there was a double claim on the Church's generosity in the case of those who had devoted themselves absolutely to her service, especially in the way of preaching and the laborious office of 'discipline,' the oral transmission of the Evangelic Tradition. That was fair, and it was sanctioned by the Scriptures; yet it was far from justifying the Presbyters in emulating the mercenary heretics and making a trade of religion. A decent livelihood was all that they should desire.

It is plain that this delicate question had occasioned much heart-burning. Hard things had been said of the Presbyters, and Timothy's handling of the situation had been injudicious. He had listened to evil reports, and had pronounced censure without strict investigation; and sometimes, when scandal had arisen, he was himself to blame. The simplicity which was credulous of malicious gossip, was credulous also of hypocritical pretension; and he had ordained unworthy men to office. A little prudence would have averted these disasters; for though a man's true character may not always be apparent at the first glance, it cannot remain hidden. A discerning eye soon penetrates the hollow mask, and detects also the modest worth which 'loves to be unknown and to be made of no reputation.'

17 Let the Elders who discharge their office honourably be
counted worthy of double remuneration, especially those who
Dt. xxv. 4; cf. 1 Cor. ix. 9. 18 toil in word and discipline. For the Scripture says: 'Thou
shalt not muzzle the ox while it is treading out the grain';
19 and 'worthy is the workman of his wage.'[1] Against an
Cf. Dt. xix. 15. Elder never admit an accusation unless it be supported by two
20 or three witnesses. As for those who sin, reprove them in the
sight of all, that the rest may be deterred.

[1] Not a quotation from Scripture but a proverbial maxim, quoted also by our Lord (cf. Lk. x. 7).

21 I solemnly charge you in the sight of God and Christ Jesus
and the elect angels, that you observe these instructions with-
22 out prejudice, doing nothing from partiality. Lay ordaining
hands on no one hastily, and be not a party to other men's
23 sins. Keep yourself pure. (Be no longer 'a water-drinker,'
but use a little wine for the sake of your stomach and your
24 frequent indispositions.[1]) There are some men whose sins are
patent and lead the way to a judgment of them; but there
25 are some also whose sins dog their steps. Similarly, 'beautiful
works' are patent, and such as are otherwise cannot be concealed.

Relations between masters and slaves.

At Ephesus, as in every great city of early days, the institution of slavery constituted a problem for the Church. Christianity recognised the brotherhood of the children of men and their equal worth in the sight of the Universal Father, and in a community where the distinction of bond and free was cancelled, it was inevitable that the relation of masters and slaves should be increasingly complicated. The abolition of slavery was indeed the necessary issue of the Gospel; but at that early date it was still unperceived, and the only practical remedy for the unrest was the inculcation of that love which would reconcile masters and slaves and banish both cruelty and resentment.

vi. 1 All who bear the yoke of slavery, let them deem their own
masters worthy of every honour, that the Name of God and
2 the Discipline may not be calumniated. And those who have
faithful masters, let them not despise them because they are
brothers, but be the more devoted because the recipients of
their good service are faithful and beloved.

Denunciation of the heretics.

All these were problems incidental to the normal administration of the Church, and besides them there were troubles from without. Timothy was confronted with that vexatious heresy, and the Apostle concludes his counsels with a denunciation of its emissaries and their evil ways—their departure from the Evangelic Tradition, their conceit, their ignorance, their contentiousness, and, above all, their mercenary greed. It proves how scandalous this last was

[1] A *marginale* (cf. p. 245), inserted in the margin after the letter was written as a needful corrective of Timothy's disposition to asceticism. ὑδροποτεῖν was a good Greek word, but it carried a suggestion of contempt. In the Comic Poets ὑδροπότης was 'a thin-blooded fellow.'

and how perilous its contagion that, when he read over the letter, he was moved to enforce his warnings by entering on the margin an additional exhortation.

3 All this teach and exhort. If any one teach otherwise and
do not accede to healthful words—those of our Lord Jesus
4 Christ—and the Discipline which is the norm of religion, he is
swollen with windy pride, knowing nothing but distempered
about questionings and verbal disputations which originate
5 envy, strife, calumnies, evil suspicions, persistent wranglings
on the part of men corrupted in their mind and bereft of the
6 Truth. They think that religion is a source of profit. And
religion *is* a great source of profit when contentment goes with
7 it. For we carried nothing into the world, nor [1] can we carry
8 anything out of it; but if we have food and covering, these will
9 suffice us. Those who would fain be rich fall into temptation
and a snare and many desires which are witless and mischievous,
10 since they sink men in wreck and ruin. For the love of money
is the root of all evils, and some in their ambition for it have
been led astray from the Faith and pierced themselves with
many a pang.

11 But you, man of God, flee from all this, and pursue righteous-
12 ness, religion, faith, love, endurance, meekness. Face the
Faith's honourable contest; win the Eternal Life for which you
were called and made the honourable confession in the sight of
13 many witnesses. My charge in the sight of God who brings
all things to life,[2] and Christ Jesus who at the bar of Pontius
14 Pilate witnessed the honourable confession, is that you keep
the commandment without spot or reproach until the Appearing
15 of our Lord Jesus Christ; and this will He display at His own
seasons who is the blessed and only Potentate, the King of the
16 kingly and the Lord of the lordly, who alone possesses immortality, inhabiting light unapproachable, and whom no man
ever saw or can see; to whom be honour and might eternal.
Amen.

17 (Those who are rich in the present age charge not to be
uplifted with conceit nor have their hope based on the visionari-
ness of riches, but to repose it on God who affords us everything
18 richly for our enjoyment, to be beneficent, to be rich in
19 'beautiful works,' to be open-handed and liberal, storing up
for themselves a sound foundation against the future, that
they may win the real life.) [3]

[1] Omitting ὅτι, which is probably 'an accidental repetition of the last two letters of κόσμον, ON being read as OTI' (W. H. Append.).

[2] ζωογονεῖν, 'bring to birth alive' (cf. Ex. i. 17, 18, 22), a medical term (cf. Hobart, *Med. Lang. of St. Luke*, p. 155); elsewhere in N. T. only in Lk. xvii. 33, Ac. vii. 19. Cf. p. 589.

[3] Another *marginale*, enforcing vers. 9, 10.

And now after his wont he takes the pen from his amanuensis and writes the closing sentence with his own hand. The Evangelic Tradition was the Church's most precious possession, and his last word is an earnest appeal to Timothy to preserve it inviolate and guard it from heretical corruption.

The Apostle's sign-manual.

20 O TIMOTHY, GUARD THE DEPOSIT, SHUNNING THE PROFANE
BABBLINGS AND INCONGRUITIES [1] OF THE 'KNOWLEDGE' SO
21 FALSELY NAMED. IT IS BY PROFESSING THIS THAT SOME HAVE
MISSED THE MARK IN RELATION TO THE FAITH. GRACE BE WITH
YOU ALL.

Progress to Syrian Antioch.

It was probably early in the year 63 that the Apostle had arrived at Colossæ, and his sojourn in the valley of the Lycus would continue for several months. Since it would have been perilous for him to linger in that malarial region during the heat of midsummer, it may be inferred that he took his departure by June at the latest; and it is hardly doubtful that he would travel eastward into the adjacent Province of Galatia and visit his Churches at Pisidian Antioch, Iconium, Lystra, and Derbe. Thence he would proceed to Syrian Antioch, the metropolis of Gentile Christendom and the constant base of his missionary operations; and he would arrive there in autumn, crossing the Taurus ere the passage was closed by the winter snows. This is indeed mere probability, but it finds a measure of confirmation in the circumstance that in the sequel he appears in the company of Titus, that young Greek who had attended him and Barnabas from Antioch on their eleemosynary mission to Jerusalem in the summer of 45,[2] and who had subsequently acquitted himself so creditably in the difficult negotiations with the recalcitrant Church of Corinth.[3] Antioch was the home of Titus, and it is likely that he would return thither when his work in the West was done, and labour there during the Apostle's long captivity. It is remarkable that his name is never mentioned in the Book

[1] ἀντιθέσεις, supposed by critics who regard the Pastorals as Pauline fictions of 2nd c., to be an express reference to Marcion's work 'The Antithesis.' But ἀντίθεσις was a familiar term both in Classical and in Common Greek (cf. Moulton and Milligan, *Vocab.*). Perhaps the Apostle was thinking of the Gnostic 'antitheses'—God and the world, spirit and matter, light and darkness, etc.

[2] Cf. pp. 73 f.

[3] Cf. pp. 340 f., 345.

of Acts, since, as it happened, he and Luke had hardly ever come into contact. He is known only from incidental allusions in Paul's letters; but these sufficiently testify to his rare qualities, and doubtless had the historian been permitted to complete his work, his later narrative would have rescued Titus from the obscurity which unfortunately invests him.

Mission to the extreme West.

The way was now open for the fulfilment of the Apostle's long cherished design of continuing the westward progress of the Gospel and carrying it as far as Spain; and he would set out on this momentous mission in the spring of 64, as soon as navigation was resumed on Feb. 8. He did not go alone. Luke and Titus accompanied him, and probably others. The ship would naturally call at the port of Ephesus, and he would land there and, in fulfilment of his promise, interview Timothy. With so large an enterprise in view he would make no long stay. The next station on the route was Corinth, and there in ordinary circumstances he would have continued his voyage to Italy, but that country was now closed against him. He had been banished from Rome on his acquittal in the spring of 62; and, moreover, it was probably at this very juncture that the world was startled by that appalling calamity, the conflagration of the Imperial capital. It broke out on July 19, 64, and raged for six days;[1] and since the blame of it was fastened on the Christians, it would have been certain death had the Apostle and his company appeared in the vicinity while the popular fury was at its height. And so it appears that he avoided Italy and travelled overland through Epirus and Dalmatia. These were new countries to him, but he had long cherished the hope of visiting them. And already he was no stranger to their people; for some seven years previously the Gospel had been diffused from Macedonia and Achaia to Illyricum, and along the route he would encounter Christian communities where his name was revered. On reaching the head of the Adriatic he would enter Venetia at Aquileia; and, journeying westward, he would traverse Gallia Cisalpina until he reached the port of Massilia (Marseilles), and thence he would take ship to Spain.

Cf. Rom. xv. 24, 28. — Cf. 1 Tim. iii. 14, iv. 13. — Cf. 2 Cor. x. 15, 16. — Cf. Rom. xv. 19.

[1] Cf. Lewin, *Fast. Sac.*, 1955 f.

All this is merely inferential, but it appears less precarious when it is remembered that Christianity was planted not only in Spain but in Gaul at a very early date, and St. Irenæus appeals to the churches in these countries as witnesses to the Apostolic Tradition.[1] The story of the Apostle's fortunes on those fresh fields would have made a stirring chapter in his biography ; and here one poignantly realises how grievous is the loss entailed by the cutting short of Luke's narrative. Regarding his ministry in Gaul there is indeed one uncertain suggestion. It seems that 'Galatia' was an alternative form of 'Gallia' ;[2] and if there be truth in the ancient opinion that, when the Apostle in the course of his last journey to Rome 'sent Crescens to Galatia,' it was not to the Asiatic Province that he sent him but to Gallia Cisalpina, then it appears that his ministry there had borne abiding fruit. As for his work in Spain, however, it is unillumined even by so doubtful a ray. The one certainty is that he would have no difficulty in obtaining a hearing for his message, since there were considerable Jewish colonies in Spain, especially along the eastern sea-board ;[3] and in each city he would, according to his wont, visit the synagogue and discourse to the congregation.

Ministry in Gaul and Spain.

2 Tim. iv 10.

It was probably in the spring of 66 that he once more turned his face eastward. Whatever his success in Spain, he had at least accomplished his purpose of carrying the Gospel to 'the Boundary of the West' ; and he now heard the call of other lands where he had never yet preached. One was the island of Crete, which had doubtless lain on his heart ever since in the autumn of 59 he had surveyed it from the deck of the ship which was conveying him to Rome. It was a large island, measuring, according to Pliny,[4] 270 Roman miles in length, 50 at the broadest, and 589 in circumference. It was an irregular ridge of mountains, forming three groups—Mount Leuke to the west, Mount Ida in the middle, and Mount Dicte to the east. The coastline was broken by sharp promontories and deep bays, and the

The island of Crete.

[1] Iren. I. iii.

[2] Cf. Lightfoot, *Gal.* pp. 3, 31 ; Moulton and Milligan, *Voc.* In 2 Tim. iv. 10 Tisch., following ℵC and other authorities, reads Γαλλίαν.

[3] Cf. Schürer, II. ii. p. 242.

[4] *Nat. Hist.* IV. 20.

surface was a tumble of hills and woodlands and fertile valleys.[1] It was closely populated, and contained, according to Pliny, a hundred famous cities. The chief of these were Gortyna, betwixt Mount Ida and the southern coast, and Cnossus toward the north. Crete figures largely in ancient mythology. There was the storied Labyrinth, the creation of Dædalus and the prison of the Minotaur; and at Mount Ida the infant Zeus had been nurtured, and his fabled tomb was the chief of the island's sacred shrines.

Character of the people.

The people bore an evil reputation. Their falsehood was proverbial. 'Cretising' was synonymous with 'lying,' and 'playing the Cretan with a Cretan' meant 'out-tricking a trickster.'[2] They were avaricious and unscrupulous; these vices, it was said, were indigenous, and the Cretans were the only people who counted them no disgrace.[3] The wine of Crete was famous,[4] and drunkenness prevailed. Even the women were addicted to it. It appears, moreover, from the record of history that the Cretans were a turbulent and lawless race. It was their complicity with the pirates, those pests of the Mediterranean, that provoked the war which issued in their subjugation to Rome by Metellus in the year 67 B.C.; and in later days they were still prone to sedition and rebellion.

Cretan Jews.

There were many Jews in Crete, especially in the cities;[5] and though not a few of them, like the family of the Cretan wife of the Jewish historian Josephus,[6] occupied the first rank in wealth and influence, they were frequently ringleaders of disorder. They remained true to their ancestral faith, winning proselytes and making pilgrimages to the Holy City at the seasons of the great Feasts; nor did their insularity exclude them from contemporary movements in the intellectual and religious domain. It is an evidence of this that the Gnostic ideas of the Province of Asia had been wafted across the Ægean and taken root in the island.

Cf. Ac. ii. 11.

Cf. Tit. i. 13-16; iii. 9-11.

Paul's ministry in Crete.

Crete had thus sore need of the Gospel. And it was

[1] Cf. Strabo, 475: *ἔστι δ' ὀρεινὴ καὶ δασεῖα ἡ νῆσος, ἔχει δ' αὐλῶνας εὐκάρπους.*

[2] Cf. Plut. *Æm. Paul.* 25. [3] Polyb. VI. 46.

[4] Juv. XIV. 270 f.

[5] 1 Macc. xv. 23; Phil. *Leg. ad Caium*, 36; Jos. *Ant.* XVII. xii. 1; *De Bell. Jud.* II. vii. 1. Cf. p. 4. [6] Jos. *Vit.* 76.

natural that the Apostle should turn thither. He had already planted the Faith in the countries on the northern shores of the Mediterranean basin and in the islands of Cyprus and Melita; and now, when he was warned by the decay of his physical powers and the increasing menace of his adversaries that the end was approaching, it would seem that the evangelisation of Crete, the one spot in the long circuit from Syria to Spain still untouched, would be the fitting crown of his life's labour. Of his mission in the island there is no record; but he would certainly follow his wonted procedure. He would visit the various cities, beginning perhaps with the capital Gortyna, and pass from place to place until he had traversed the whole island. It is plain from his references that he experienced to the full the obnoxious idiosyncrasies of the Cretan character, since after his departure from their midst he attested the justice of the people's odious reputation. Nevertheless his work was in nowise unsuccessful. He won many converts and founded numerous churches.

Cf. Tit. i. 12, 13.

Cf. ver. 5.

His departure. Cf. Tit. iii. 12.

He took his departure in the autumn, leaving Titus to continue and consolidate the work, particularly by the ordination of Presbyters in every city where a church had been formed. Much indeed had still to be done, and it would have been well for Crete could he have remained; but it seems that he was exhausted by the protracted strain and designed to spend the approaching winter in some peaceful retreat. There was constant and easy communication between Crete and Cenchreæ, the port of Corinth, and he would naturally voyage thither. He would find a cordial welcome among his numerous friends in the Achaian capital; and one of these was Apollos, who had doubtless fulfilled his intention of returning thither and resuming the powerful ministry which had been interrupted by the unhappy controversy in the Corinthian Church.[1]

Cf. 1 Cor. xvi. 12.

Winter residence at Nicopolis.

The Apostle's ultimate destination was uncertain when he left Crete, but he presently reached a decision and fixed upon Nicopolis for his winter residence. It happens that there were no fewer than eight places which bore this name, and it must remain questionable which of these is here

[1] Cf. pp. 240 f., 323.

intended. The most famous is the city of Epirus which Augustus had founded and named Nicopolis, 'the City of Victory,' in commemoration of his triumph over Antony and Cleopatra in the year 31 B.C. Two others were in Thrace—one in the west on the river Nessus, and the second on the Hæmus in the east. A fourth was in Armenia. A fifth was in Bithynia on the Bosporus.[1] A sixth was in Cilicia near the ridge of Amanus on the border of Cilicia and Syria.[2] A seventh was in Judæa—the town whose Jewish name was Emmaus. And there was still another in Egypt near Alexandria.[3] St. Chrysostom took the Apostle to mean Nicopolis in Thrace, presumably the town on the Nessus; but St. Jerome naturally thought of the famous city in Epirus, and this is the prevailing opinion. The probabilities, however, point rather to the Cilician Nicopolis. It was situated about equidistant from Tarsus, the Apostle's birthplace, whither his heart would instinctively turn in his old age, and Syrian Antioch, the headquarters of his ministry. It would recommend the Cilician town for his winter's residence that it was within easy reach of both. And the very indefiniteness of his reference is perhaps determinant. Titus belonged to Syrian Antioch, and when the Apostle intimated to him his intention of 'wintering at Nicopolis,' he would immediately think of the familiar town in his own Province of Syria-Cilicia. Any other Nicopolis would have required definition.

Letter to Titus at Crete.

On deciding where he would spend the winter Paul wrote to Titus; and the purpose of the communication was not merely to acquaint the latter with his movements but to counsel him on the fitting discharge of his heavy responsibilities. His position was difficult, and the Apostle, besides writing much helpful advice, entrusted the conveyance of the letter to two eminent Corinthians who would administer encouragement and inspiration. These were the brilliant Apollos and a converted Rabbi named Zenas.[4]

Cf. Tit. iii. 13.

[1] Plin. *Nat. Hist.* v. 43. [2] Strabo, 676. [3] Strabo, 795, 800.

[4] According to subscript. in Syr^{sch}, Theod. Mops. According to Cop. Vers. the bearer of the letter was Artemas (ver. 12).

THE LETTER TO TITUS

The address has a double purpose. It affirms Paul's apostleship, his title to speak with authority; and it defines the Gospel message in view of the Cretan situation. The Christians there would be largely Jewish converts, and the adversaries of the Faith were chiefly Jews more or less imbued with the Asian Gnosticism. Accordingly the Apostle emphasises the historic antecedents of Christianity. It was no novel institution. It was based on the ancient Promise which Israel had trusted from generation to generation and which, he observes with a reference to the Cretan character, was worthy of trust since it had been given by 'the God who never lies.' That Promise had been defined ever more clearly by successive revelations, and the Gospel was its final fulfilment.

The address.

Cf. i. 12.

i. 1 Paul, a slave of God and an Apostle of Jesus Christ for the
establishment of the faith of God's chosen and the advancement of the knowledge of the truth which is the norm of
2 religion and rests on the hope of life eternal which the God
3 who never lies promised ere the ages began, while at fitting
seasons He manifested His Word in the message which was
entrusted to me according to the commandment of our
4 Saviour God: to Titus, a true child after a common faith.
Grace and peace from God the Father and Christ Jesus our
Saviour.

The business of Titus was the consolidation of the Apostle's work in Crete. Converts had been won, but they would inevitably relapse unless provision were made for the confirmation of their Christian profession and their instruction in the Faith. And therefore it was necessary that the several congregations should be effectively organised. This was the business which had been entrusted to Titus; and his principal task was the ordination of Presbyters in each community. The Apostle reiterates the qualifications for the sacred office. The work of a Presbyter was mainly twofold: on the one hand, the communication and commendation of the Evangelic Discipline to the congregation; and, on the other, the refutation of the objections of unbelievers. And his qualifications were an irreproachable character and

Appointment of Presbyters and their qualifications.

scrupulous adherence to the Tradition as **he had himself** been instructed in it.

5 It was for this reason that I left you in Crete—that you might
put to rights what had still to be done, and appoint as Presbyters in every city, according to the direction I gave you,
6 men who have nothing laid to their charge, faithful husbands,
with believing children not accused of profligacy or unruly in
7 their behaviour. For an Overseer must, as a steward of God,
be one who has nothing laid to his charge, not churlish,[1] or
wrathful, or quarrelsome in his cups, or ready with his fists,
8 or a dirty money-maker, but hospitable, a lover of the good,
9 discreet, righteous, pious, self-controlled, maintaining the faithful Word as it was taught him, that he may be powerful
both at exhorting on the healthful Discipline and at refuting
our opponents.

Local difficulties.

It was specially needful that Titus should insist on these qualifications in view of local circumstances—the moral laxity of the Cretan character and the activity of the Gnostic Judaists, especially their ascetic propaganda which, by its false ideal of holiness, issued in moral disaster.

Cf. Gal. ii. 12.

10 For there are many disorderly persons, futile talkers and
11 deceivers, especially the champions of circumcision; and their
mouths you must shut, since they upset whole households by
teaching what they should not for the sake of dirty money-
12 making. Said one of them, a prophet of their own: [2]
'Cretans are ever liars, ill animals, indolent gluttons.'
13 This testimony is true. Wherefore refute them with sharp
14 severity, that they may be healthful in the Faith and give no
heed to Jewish fables and precepts of men who turn their backs
15 upon the Truth. Everything is clean to the clean; but to the
defiled and faithless nothing is clean; no, their very mind and
16 conscience are defiled. They profess to know God, but by
their works they deny Him, being abominable and disobedient
and for every good work worthless.

Advice in dealing with these.

The remedy lay in loyalty to the Evangelic Tradition, 'the healthful Discipline'; and the Apostle indicates what manner of exhortations Titus must address to the various classes of his hearers—the older men and women and the younger men. It is significant that, evidently for prudential

[1] αὐθάδης. Cf. Theophr. *Char.* III (Jebb): 'The churlish person is the sort who, when asked "Where is so-and-so?" says "Don't bother me," and when addressed does not answer.'

[2] Epimenides. Cf. pp. 11, 24.

reasons, he does not require Titus to address the younger women directly but relegates the task of schooling them to the older women. Titus was still comparatively young, and while it was expedient that he should refrain from personal dealing with the younger women, he was thus fitted for instructing the younger men; and the Apostle reminds him that his most potent influence resided in the example of his personal character. In Crete as elsewhere Christianity was confronted by the institution of slavery and the peculiar difficulties which it involved. Apparently the Cretan slaves were infected by the prevailing spirit, and the Apostle bids Titus exhort those converts who belonged to this unhappy order to eschew turbulence, insolence, and dishonesty, and by a display of kindly fidelity 'adorn the Discipline of their Saviour God,' exhibiting the grace of Christianity by reproducing in their own persons the life of the Incarnate Lord.

ii. 1 But as for you, speak things which befit the healthful
2 Discipline: that old men be sober, dignified, discreet,
3 healthful by their faith, their love, their endurance; old
women likewise reverend in demeanour, no slanderers or
4 slaves to wine, exemplars of honour, schooling the young
5 women to love their husbands and their children, to be
discreet, pure, good housewives, kindly, submissive to their
own husbands, that the Word of God may not be calumni-
6, 7 ated. The younger men likewise exhort to be discreet in
every respect, presenting in your own person a pattern of
'beautiful works'—exactitude[1] in the Discipline, dignity,
8 healthy speech which no one can condemn, that the opponent
may be discomfited through having nothing bad to say
9 about us. Bid slaves be submissive to their own masters
in all circumstances and give satisfaction, never speaking
10 back, never pilfering but displaying all kindly fidelity, that
they may adorn the Discipline of our Saviour God in all
circumstances.

All this he enforces by an apt and beautiful quotation from the Teacher's Manual, and charges Titus, as his message is so august, to proclaim it with due authority. 'Let no one despise you.' If he remembered the injunction to preserve

Quotation from the Teacher's Manual.

[1] ἀφθορία, 'incorruption,' scrupulous repetition of the Tradition in its proper purity. The adject. occurs in a papyrus contract with a wet-nurse binding her to feed the child 'with her own milk, pure and uncorrupt' (καθαρῷ καὶ ἀφθόρῳ). Cf. Moulton and Milligan, *Vocab.*

the Tradition inviolate and bear himself with becoming dignity, no one would despise either his message or himself.

11 For 'the grace of God appeared fraught with salvation
12 for all men, instructing us to deny irreligion and worldly
desires and live discreetly and righteously and religiously
13 in the present age, awaiting the Blessed Hope, even the
appearing of the glory of our great God and Saviour Christ
14 Jesus,[1] who gave Himself for us that He might "ransom
us from all lawlessness" and "purify for Himself a people
peculiarly His own," eager for "beautiful works."'
15 Speak all this, and exhort and rebuke with all imperative-
ness. Let no one despise you.

Ps. cxxx. 8. Ez. xxxvii. 23; Dt. xiv. 2.

Contentiousness and its remedy.

Turbulence was not peculiar to the slaves. It was a Cretan characteristic, and the Apostle enjoins Titus to inculcate respect for law and government and a neighbourly and peaceable disposition. Nor must he judge the Cretans too severely. The unlovely qualities so conspicuous in them were, in greater or less degree, universal in unregenerate humanity. It is, he says, quoting once more from the Teacher's Manual, the mercy of God that has saved us; and what the rich grace of His Holy Spirit has done for us it will do for them. That was the message which Titus must proclaim. And he must hold aloof from the foolish speculations and legalistic contentions of the adversaries of the Faith. Disputation is an unprofitable employment, availing nothing and issuing in worse hostility; and where an encounter was inevitable, he should simply state the truth and, if it were rejected, decline further controversy.

iii. 1 Remind them to be submissive to principalities and
authorities, to obey magistrates, to be ready for every good
2 work, to calumniate no one, to be peaceable, sweetly reason-
3 able, displaying all meekness toward all men. For we too
were once witless, disobedient, deceived, slaves of various
desires and indulgences, leading our lives in malice and envy,
4 detestable and hating each other. But 'when the kindness
5 and philanthropy of our Saviour God appeared, not on the

[1] It appears from numerous instances in the papyri that this was a regular formula among Greek Christians. It was indeed alien from the Pauline manner thus *θεολογεῖν τὸν Χριστόν* (cf. p. 426); but linguistic evidence proves this passage a quotation from the Lucan Manual (cf. pp. 594 f.), and it is therefore unnecessary to Paulinise the formula by rendering it ungrammatically 'the great God and our Saviour Christ Jesus.' Cf. Moulton, *Prol.* p. 84.

score of works—works in the way of righteousness—which we
did, but according to His mercy He saved us through the
6 laver of regeneration and renewal of the Holy Spirit whom
He poured forth upon us richly through Jesus Christ our
7 Saviour, that, being accounted righteous by His grace, we
might enter on our heritage according to the hope of life
eternal.'

8 Faithful is the word, and on all this I would have you
insist, that those who have put their faith in God may be
careful to practise 'beautiful works.' These are beautiful Cf. Mt.
9 and profitable for men. But foolish questions and genea- xxvi. 10.
logies and strife and legalistic quarrels avoid, for they are
10 profitless and futile. With a factious person after admon-
11 ishing him once or twice have nothing to do, knowing that
a man of this sort is perverted; he is a sinner and is self-
condemned.

Personal matters.

And now the letter concludes with some personal matters. The Apostle was retiring to Nicopolis, but he would only pass the winter there. Then he would set forth on a fresh mission and would require the assistance of Titus. In due time he would send a messenger to summon him, and this would be either Artemas or Tychicus. The latter was an old friend. He was an Ephesian,[1] and when he last appeared, it was as the bearer of the encyclical to the Churches of Asia and the letter to Colossæ. (Eph. vi. 21; Col. iv. 7.) As for Artemas, this is his first and only mention; and it may be that he was a young Corinthian or perhaps a Cretan convert who was accompanying the Apostle in the capacity of his attendant.[2] Zenas and Apollos were the bearers of the letter to Crete. They would make no long stay in the island, and Paul pointedly enjoins Titus to see to it that, when they took their departure, they were adequately provided for the homeward journey. It lay with the Cretan Church to furnish them; and the Apostle, aware of the Cretan avarice, apprehended neglect. And, in case the plea of poverty might be offered, he takes occasion to bid Titus inculcate on the Cretan Christians the duty of industry, that they might earn an honest livelihood and discharge their just liabilities.

12 When I send Artemas to you or Tychicus, do your best to
join me at Nicopolis; for there I have decided to winter,

[1] Cf. p. 371. Cf. p. 79.

13 And equip Zenas, the Teacher of the Law,[1] and Apollos for their
14 journey as best you may, that they may lack nothing. And let
our people also learn to practise honourable crafts for their
necessary needs, that they may not live barren lives.

The sign-manual. 15 ALL MY COMPANIONS GREET YOU. GREET OUR FRIENDS IN
FAITH. GRACE BE WITH YOU ALL.

Wintering at Nicopolis. Tit. iii. 12. It was the winter of 66-67 that Paul spent at Nicopolis; and while it was a season of much needed repose, it would be no season of inactivity. 'Wintering' was a military phrase; and, like a wise general, he would 'prepare in winter-quarters for the summer campaign.'[2] His residence was in the very centre of the Province of Syria-Cilicia where, betwixt his conversion and his call to the Apostleship of the Gentiles, he had laboured for some nine years. He was thus in the midst of friends; and while he refrained from travel, he would receive numerous visitors and hold frequent communication, especially with Tarsus and Syrian Antioch. Cf. 2 Tim. iv. 13. He would, moreover, be daily engaged in the study of the ancient Scriptures, his constant companions.

[1] *νομικός*, a Scribe, a teacher of the Jewish Law. Cf. Mt. xxii. 35: *εἷς ἐξ αὐτῶν νομικός* = Mk. xii. 28: *εἷς τῶν γραμματέων*.

[2] Cf. Epict. I. ii. 32.

THE SECOND IMPRISONMENT AT ROME

THE advent of spring summoned him to resume his labour, and he would doubtless repair to Syrian Antioch and thence set forth, with the Church's benediction, on a fresh mission. He did not go alone. The faithful Luke, his 'beloved physician,' had never left his side; Tychicus the Ephesian too had accompanied him to Nicopolis, and Titus had been summoned thither from Crete. These three, at all events, bore him company.

A mission westward.

Tit. iii. 12.

Cf. 2 Tim. iv. 10.

It appears that they betook themselves to the Province of Asia, where the Gnostic heresy was still distracting the churches. Paul would surely visit Ephesus, probably taking ship thither from Seleuceia; and it seems that his retinue was augmented at Ephesus by the accession of at least two old friends—Erastus, who during his ministry in the Asian capital had shared with Timothy the office of his attendant, and his fellow-townsman Trophimus. On his departure he visited other cities in the Province, among them Miletus, where Trophimus fell sick and had to be left behind.

The Province of Asia.

Ac. xix. 22.

Cf. 2 Tim. iv. 20.

The dream of his heart during the years of his missionary labours had been to visit the Imperial capital and win it for Christ; and it had been realised after a fashion when he was taken thither in bonds and pined in captivity for two long years. On his release he was banished from Rome; but he had clung to the hope of returning thither, and it seems that now, after the lapse of five years, he had resolved to venture back. It was a momentous enterprise, and so powerfully did it appeal to his friends in Asia that some of them were ambitious to share it and joined his train. Foremost among these enthusiasts were Phygelus and Hermogenes.

Resolution to venture back to Rome.

Cf. 2 Tim. i. 15.

Conscious of the risk he was running, he would fain visit by the way as many of his churches as he might; and so, it

Progress through

Macedonia to Corinth. appears, he determined not to take ship from Ephesus to Italy, but to travel overland through Macedonia to Achaia and thence proceed to Rome. Accordingly he turned his steps to Troas. During his stay there he was entertained by a Christian named Carpus; and it perhaps betokens the burden of anxiety which pressed upon his heart in those days, that on his departure he forgot his mantle and his books, including his precious rolls of the Old Testament Scriptures. From Troas he would make the familiar passage to Neapolis, the port of Philippi; and thence he travelled by Amphipolis and Apollonia to Thessalonica, where Demas joined his company.[1] From Thessalonica he journeyed on to Corinth, and there, for some unspecified reason, Erastus remained. It may have been that his services were needed in Achaia, and with so large a retinue the Apostle could easily spare him. There also, perhaps, he parted with two others of his followers. Tidings of his progress toward Rome had, it would seem, reached the Churches of Dalmatia and Gallia Cisalpina, and they desired that he should travel thither overland and visit them *en route*. This was impracticable, since his mission brooked no delay; but he responded to the appeal by despatching two delegates. To Dalmatia he sent Titus, and to Gaul Crescens who is otherwise unknown and who may perhaps have been one of his Asian followers.

(Margin: Cf. 2 Tim. iv. 13. — Cf. ver. 10. — Cf. 2 Tim. iv. 10.)

Arrival at Rome. With his retinue thus diminished he took ship for Rome. It would be late in the summer of 67 when he arrived, and he found himself confronted by active hostility. His acquittal in the spring of 62 had been a grievous disappointment to the Roman Jews; and when they heard of his return, they would bestir themselves to frustrate his design of propagating the Christian heresy in the capital. Nor was this a difficult task. His banishment from Rome had never been repealed, and his reappearance was a defiance of the judicial sentence. It might indeed, after so long an interval, have been condoned by the authorities, who were concerned solely with the maintenance of public order; but if the question were raised and the old quarrel rekindled, they would in all likelihood enforce the decree. Here the Jews recognised their opportunity. They had an energetic leader in one Alexander,

Arrest.

[1] Cf. p. 522.

a Jew who plied the trade of coppersmith in the city.[1] He delated the Apostle, and the latter was arrested.

The Emperor was not then at Rome. In the autumn of 66 he had betaken himself to Greece, where he played the mountebank after his manner by competing at the public games and winning a succession of easy victories.[2] In the summer of 67 he had been present at the Isthmian Games, and in the autumn he was still at Corinth, busied with the ambitious project of cutting a canal across the Isthmus.[3] Of course his absence did arrest the course of justice in the capital, and the Apostle would be arraigned before his representatives, perhaps the freedman Helius, who had been left in command of the city, or Nymphidius Sabinus, the second Prætorian Prefect,[4] who had remained when his colleague Sofonius Tigellinus accompanied their imperial master to the East.[5] Absence of Nero.

The initial stage in the proceedings was the *prima actio* or precognition ; [6] and here he experienced a painful disappointment. None of the Roman Christians had the courage to appear on his behalf. And indeed this is hardly surprising. The blame of the firing of Rome in midsummer 64 had been laid upon the Christians, and they had been subjected to savage reprisals,[7] and public odium still rested upon them. This aggravated the Apostle's danger, and it would deter the Roman Christians from taking his part and refuting the charges which Alexander urged against him. Less excusable were the friends who had accompanied him to the capital. So alarmed was Demas for his personal safety that he incontinently decamped and returned home to Thessalonica ; and the Asian contingent also took themselves off. Precognition. Cf. 2 Tim. iv. 16. Cf. iv. 10. Cf. i. 15.

The preliminary investigation might have concluded the case. Had the prisoner offered no defence, he would forthwith have been condemned ; while, had he succeeded in establishing his innocence, he would have been acquitted. But neither happened. He had no advocate, and pleaded Remanded for trial.

[1] A different person from Alexander of Ephesus (cf. 1 Tim. i. 20).
[2] Cf. Lewin, *Fest. Sac.*, 1995 f.
[3] *Ibid.*, 2053-55. [4] *Ibid.*, 1919, 1968. [5] *Ibid.*, 1994.
[6] Cf. pp. 252 f.
[7] Cf. Tac. *Ann.* xv. 44 ; Suet. *Ner.* 16 ; Juv. I. 155 ff.

Cf. Ac. xxiv. 10-21, xxvi. 1-23.

his own cause; and, as in the court of Felix and at his examination before Agrippa, his defence was a statement of the Gospel which he preached, defining its true nature and showing that it was no seditious propaganda. His very forlornness threw him back upon God, and his impassioned pleading made a powerful appeal. It is an evidence of the profound impression which it produced that, unsupported as it was by witnesses, it convinced the court of the necessity of fuller investigation, and he was remanded to prison for further trial.

Cf. 2 Tim. iv. 16, 17.

Faithful friends.

It was no small success, and it justified him in hoping that his trial might issue in his acquittal. His case was indeed perilous, but it was in nowise desperate; and as he lay in his cell, he would employ his mind in ordering the arguments which he would urge in his defence, taking counsel with God and staying his heart upon His sovereign will. Nor did he lack at that anxious crisis the support of human affection. Luke and Tychicus had both stood faithful; and another friend presently appeared on the scene. This was Onesiphorus. If there be any credibility in a romance of later days,[1] he was an old acquaintance. He had belonged originally to the town of Iconium in Southern Galatia, and when the Apostle arrived there in the autumn of 48 after his expulsion from Pisidian Antioch, he was welcomed and entertained by him and his wife Lectra and their two sons, Simmias and Zeno.[2] Be this as it may, Onesiphorus and his household were now resident at Ephesus, and he was a devoted member of the Church there. It seems that he was a deacon,[3] and he was zealous in the discharge of the charitable functions belonging to his office. It happened that he had occasion to visit Rome in those days, probably on some business errand; and on learning the Apostle's plight he fearlessly sought him out and gained admission to his cell. Since his visits were frequent, it would appear that he made a considerable stay in the capital, perhaps protracting his sojourn that he might cheer the venerable prisoner.

Onesiphorus.

Letter to Timothy.

In their converse they would talk much of Ephesus, and

[1] *Act. Paul. et Thecl.* 2.

[2] Several MSS. introduce their names in 2 Tim. iv. 19.

[3] Cf. i. 18, where the best authorities omit μοι.

the Apostle would inquire how the Church had been faring of late in the troubled city. He learned that the situation had in nowise eased. The Gnostic heresy was still active, and Timothy was still disheartened. A fresh apprehension invaded the Apostle's mind. His Asian followers had returned home, and they would publish the story of his arrest and his perilous situation. He knew Timothy's timidity, and he feared lest the heavy tidings should overwhelm him. And so he set about the writing of a letter which would rally his courage and keep him faithful to his charge.

THE SECOND LETTER TO TIMOTHY

At the outset he strikes the keynote of his message by the use of a novel formula. In his first letter to Timothy, writing amid his missionary activities, he styled himself 'an Apostle of Christ Jesus according to the command of God our Saviour'; now, writing under the shadow of death, he styles himself 'an Apostle of Christ Jesus according to the promise of life in Christ Jesus.' The address.

i. 1 Paul, an Apostle of Christ Jesus through the will of God
2 according to the promise of life in Christ Jesus, to Timothy,
a beloved child. Grace, mercy, peace from God the Father
and Christ Jesus our Lord.

He begins with an exquisitely tender expression of his personal regard and affection for Timothy. Their long intimacy was a gracious memory which filled his heart with gratitude to God. It grieved him that so gentle a spirit should be so hardly bested, and he would fain be with him; yet it reassured him when he thought of the beautiful faith which had sanctified his early home and which, he was confident, dwelt in his own heart. Expression of personal affection.

3 I am thankful to God, whom I serve as my ancestors did
before me with a clean conscience, that I have such unceasing
4 remembrance of you in my prayers night and day. Mindful
of your tears, I am longing to see you, that I may be filled
5 with joy; and I recall the unaffected faith which is in you—a
faith which dwelt first in your grandmother Lois and your
mother Eunice, and I am persuaded that it dwells in you too.

Challenge to Timothy's manhood. It was this persuasion that had moved him to ordain Timothy to his hard ministry at Ephesus, and he bids him justify it. His position was indeed difficult, and this constituted a challenge to his manhood; and recent events had only accentuated it. The Apostle's peril was an appeal to Timothy's chivalry and devotion, his faith in the Gospel which had divested death of its terror and irradiated the hereafter with the assurance of immortality. This glorious prospect was the Apostle's inspiration in that black strait. His destiny was in safe keeping: Christ would 'guard the deposit.'

6 This is the reason why I remind you to fan into a flame God's
gift of grace which is in you through the laying on of my hands.
7 For the spirit which God gave us is not a spirit of cowardice;
8 no, it is a spirit of power and love and mastery. Do not, then,
be ashamed of the testimony which our Lord claims, nor of
me His prisoner; no, share my hardships for the Gospel, as
9 God gives you power, He who saved us and called us with a
holy calling, not according to our works but according to His
own purpose and the grace which was given us in Christ Jesus
10 ere the ages began, and has now been manifested through the
appearing of our Saviour Christ Jesus. He has undone death
11 and illumined life and incorruption through the Gospel, for
12 which I was set as a herald and apostle and teacher. And
that is the reason why I am suffering all this. Yet I am not
ashamed; for I know Him in whom I have reposed faith, and
I am persuaded that He has the power to guard what I have
deposited with Him against that Day.

Conservation of the Evangelic Tradition. This suggests a practical exhortation. His soul was the 'deposit' which the Apostle had committed to Christ's keeping; but there was another deposit which Christ had committed to His faithful ministers—the record of His revelation, that oral tradition which was so gravely imperilled in those days by the legend-mongering of the Gnostic heretics. Its inviolate preservation and its transmission, unimpaired and uncorrupted, constituted the supreme duty of every Christian teacher. There was as yet no written Gospel, but already Luke had anticipated his work as an Evangelist by drawing up an outline of 'the healthful words of our Lord Jesus Christ'; and Paul bids Timothy make faithful and loving use of it. (1 Tim. vi. 3.)

13 Provide yourself, in the faith and love which are in Christ
Jesus, with an outline of the healthful words which you heard
14 from me. The genuine Deposit guard through the Holy Spirit
who dwells in us.

The Asians who had deserted the Apostle in his need had returned home, and Timothy had heard the story of his arrest, particularly from the lips of the two Ephesians, Phygelus and Hermogenes. It was likely that their alarm would create a panic in the Church, and by way of antidote he mentions the courage which Onesiphorus had displayed. It had greatly cheered him, and he invokes a blessing not only on Onesiphorus at Rome but on his household at Ephesus.

Exemplary devotion of Onesiphorus.

15 You know this, that all your Asians turned their backs
16 on me, and among them Phygelus and Hermogenes. The
Lord grant mercy to the house of Onesiphorus; for he
many a time refreshed me, and he was not ashamed of my
17 chain, but on his arrival in Rome he eagerly sought for me
18 and found me. The Lord grant that he may find mercy
from the Lord on that Day! And of all his service in the
deaconship at Ephesus you are very well aware.

It was not merely for personal reasons that he mentioned the incident. His hope was that so fine an example would shame the pusillanimity of Phygelus and Hermogenes and rally the Church, especially Timothy. And so he exhorts the latter to prosecute his ministry in the strength of Christ's grace, particularly that transcendently important office—the guardianship of the Evangelic Tradition and the discipline of competent catechists, and to face the stern conflict manfully. Hardship was inevitable, but this is a condition of every gallant achievement. Think of the soldier and the athlete. And without it there is no reward. The husbandman is entitled to his harvest, but he must win it by hard toil. All this is a parable; and the truth finds its supreme exemplification in 'Jesus Christ, raised from the dead, a descendant of David.' Observe the significance of this appellation 'Jesus Christ' occurring side by side with 'Christ Jesus'—'the grace which Christ Jesus supplies,' 'an honourable soldier of Christ Jesus,' 'the salvation which is in Christ Jesus.' The former—first Jesus, then Christ—is

Exhortation to a like devotion.

the order which the Synoptic Gospels follow, beginning with our Lord's humanity and rising to His deity; the latter—first Christ, then Jesus—is the order of the Fourth Gospel, which begins in Eternity and tells how the Word became
1 Tim. i. 1. flesh.[1] 'Christ Jesus,' descending from Heaven and discovering the heart of the Unseen Father, is our Hope; 'Jesus Christ,' sharing our mortal weakness and attaining, through suffering and death, to the glory at God's right hand, is our Example, inspiring us to endurance and assuring us of ultimate triumph.

ii. 1 You then, my child, find your power in the grace which
2 Christ Jesus supplies; and what you heard from me with the
corroboration of many witnesses, deposit in the keeping of
faithful men, such as will be qualified in turn to teach
3 others. Take your share of hardship as an honourable
4 soldier of Christ Jesus. No one, when he goes a-soldiering,
entangles himself with the business of his livelihood: his
aim is to win the approval of the officer who enlisted him.
5 And if one engages in an athletic contest, he is not crowned
6 unless he have observed the rules of the contest. The
husbandman who does the toil must be the first to participate
7 in the fruits. Perceive my meaning: the Lord will give you
understanding in every case.
8 Keep in memory Jesus Christ, raised from the dead, a
9 descendant of David, according to my Gospel. It is in this
Gospel's service that I am suffering hardship and have been
put in bonds like a criminal. But the Word of God has not
10 been bound. Therefore I endure everything for the sake
of His chosen, that they too may obtain salvation—the
salvation which is in Christ Jesus, and with it glory eternal.
11 Faithful is the word:

'If we died with Him,
we shall also live with Him;
12 If we endure,
we shall also reign with Him;
If we shall deny,
He also will deny us;
13 If we are faithless,
He remains faithful:
Deny Himself He cannot.'

The surest refutation of the heresy.

Such was the message with which Timothy was charged, and it was by proclaiming and commending it that he would most effectively counteract the heretical teachers. Con-

[1] Cf. p. 379.

spicuous among the latter were two, Hymenæus and Philetus, who allegorised the Christian promise of the Resurrection as signifying not a future consummation but a present experience, the rising of the regenerate from the grave of their earthly bodies and their realisation of the spiritual life.[1] Such subtleties were indeed pernicious, poisoning men's minds and operating like a stealthy cancer. But controversy was useless and harmful, issuing only in strife and embitterment. The surest refutation of error is the exhibition of the truth. And the truth was secure. It was an ancient fashion with the Israelites to publish their faith by inscribing holy texts above their doorways; and the Church bore her seal. It was a double seal, one side visible to the eye of God alone and the other discernible by human judgment. What though there were impostors in the Christian community? The Lord recognised His own, and profession was tested by character. The commingling of true and false is meanwhile inevitable; and just as the Lord had likened the Church to a field where wheat and tares grow side by side, so the Apostle likens her to a great house which contains both precious and worthless vessels. Timothy's duty was plain. He must shun evil and exhibit on his own life 'the broad seal of Heaven'; and he must seek lovingly and patiently to win the errorists to repentance.

Cf. Dt. iv. 9, xi. 20.

Mt. xiii. 24-30.

14 Remind men of all this, solemnly charging them in the sight
of God to refrain from verbal disputation, a thing which
15 serves no useful end and tends to subvert the hearers. Do your
best to present yourself to God as sterling coin, a workman
who has no need to be ashamed of his right handling of the
16 Word of Truth. As for profane babblings, avoid them; for
17 they will make further progress in irreligion, and their talk
will keep eating like a cancer. Of this sort are Hymenæus and
18 Philetus. They have missed the mark in relation to the
truth, saying that resurrection is an accomplished experience;
and they are upsetting the faith of some.
19 Yet God's firm foundation stands fast, bearing this seal
'The Lord knows those who are His' and 'Let every one who
"names the Lord's name" depart from unrighteousness.'
20 In a great house there are not only gold and silver vessels but
also wooden and earthen, and some for honourable and others

Num. xvi. 5 LXX. Is. xxvi. 13.

[1] The doctrine of the Naasenes (Hippol. v. 3). Cf. Iren. II. xlviii. 2; Tert. *De Resurr. Carn.* 19.

21 for dishonourable use. If, then, one clear himself out from
the latter, he will be a vessel for honourable use, sanctified,
22 serviceable to the master, prepared for every good work. Fly
youthful desires, and pursue righteousness, faith, love, peaceful
fellowship with those who call on the Lord out of a clean heart.
23 But with foolish and uninstructed questionings have nothing
24 to do, knowing that they breed quarrels; and a slave of the
Lord must not quarrel but be gentle toward all, apt at teaching,
25 patient of ill,[1] in meekness instructing those who steel themselves against him,[2] in the hope that God may grant them
26 repentance issuing in full knowledge of the truth, and that,
coming to their sober senses, they may escape from the Devil's
snare and be captured by him to serve God's will.

A premonition of the approaching End.

Those defections from the truth were no surprise; for they seemed to the Apostle, sharing as he did the primitive expectation of the Lord's speedy return to judgment, preparations for the approaching consummation. He describes the abounding wickedness, dwelling especially on the malign machinations of the heretical teachers who, after the constant fashion of spiritualistic charlatans, found their readiest dupes in credulous and neurotic females. It is indeed a dark picture, and it is no wonder that it seemed to him prophetic of the end. In truth, however, iniquity always abounds, and it has appeared to devout souls in every generation as though the world were hastening to its doom. The antidote lies in remembrance of the past; and, not without inconsistency, the Apostle proceeds to refute his own eschatological inference by reminding Timothy that the situation was in nowise unprecedented. His Ephesian adversaries had their prototypes in the Egyptian magicians who had opposed Moses and who in Jewish legend bore the names of Jannes and Jambres; and they would be confounded like their predecessors.

iii. 1 But recognise this—that in the last days distressful
2 seasons will set in. For men will be lovers of self, lovers of
money, braggarts, swaggerers, calumniators, disobedient to
3 parents, unthankful, unholy, destitute of natural affection,
truceless, slanderers, uncontrolled, savage, no lovers of the
4 good, betrayers, reckless, swollen with windy pride, loving
5 pleasure more than God, with an outward form of religion

[1] *ἀνεξίκακος*, a medical term. Cf. Moulton and Milligan, *Voc.*

[2] Cf. Moulton and Milligan, *Voc.* under *ἀντιδιατίθημι*.

while they have denied its power. On these turn your back.
6 For to this sort belong those who sneak into houses and
captivate weak women heaped over with sins, the sport of
7 capricious desires, always learning and ever powerless to
8 reach a full knowledge of the Truth. And even as Jannes Cf. Ex. vii.
and Jambres[1] opposed Moses, so these also oppose the 11, 22.
Truth, men mentally debased, counterfeit coin in relation to
9 the Faith. However, they will make no further progress;
for their mentality will be exposed just as it happened with
the others.

A personal appeal.

There was no occasion for disquietude, and the Apostle introduces a personal appeal. It was nigh twenty years since Timothy had made his acquaintance, and throughout that long period the example of his father in Christ had been before his eyes. Among his childish memories were the persecutions which the Apostle had encountered in Galatia—at Antioch, Iconium, and his native town of Lystra—and the deliverances which had been vouchsafed him. Suffering was inevitable in Christ's service, and Timothy would not forget his master's example or belie his own early promise. These were dark days, and there was urgent and ever increasing need of faithful service. Timothy's difficulties were a challenge to his devotion, and it was accentuated by the prospect of the Apostle's death. Soon he would be gone and receive the crown of his long conflict, and then it would lie with Timothy to continue his work and win the same reward.

10 But you followed the course of my discipline, my conduct,
my purpose, my faith, my patience, my love, my endurance,
11 my persecutions, my sufferings—what was done to me at
Antioch, at Iconium, at Lystra; what persecutions I under-
12 went, and how the Lord rescued me from them all. Yes,
and all who wish to live religiously in Christ Jesus will be
13 persecuted. But evil men and magicians[2] will progress from
14 bad to worse, deceiving and deceived. But as for you, continue
in all that you learned and were assured of, knowing from

[1] The Rabbinical names of the Egyptian magicians. Cf. Wetstein. Jewish fables were employed by the Gnostic legend-mongers. Cf. *Evang. Nicod.* (*Gest. Pil.*), v.

[2] The successors of Jannes and Jambres. Like all the Gnostics (cf. Eus. *Hist. Eccl.* IV. 7), the Naasenes practised magic-incantations and exorcisms (cf. 1 Tim. iv. 1), and they found a fitting arena in Ephesus, the home of magic (cf. p. 228).

15 whom you learned it, and that since your infancy you have
known the Sacred Writings which have power to give you
the wisdom that issues in salvation through faith in Christ
16 Jesus. 'Every God-breathing scripture is also profitable in
connection with discipline, with refutation, with correction,
17 with instruction in righteousness, that the man of God may
be perfect, equipped for every good work.'[1]
iv. 1 I solemnly charge you in the sight of God and of Christ
Jesus who will soon judge living and dead, and by His Ap-
2 pearing and His Kingdom: proclaim the Word; be urgent in
season, out of season; refute, rebuke, exhort, always patient
3 in your teaching. For there will be a season when they will
not put up with the healthful Discipline, but, wanting to have
their ears tickled, will accumulate teachers to suit their own
4 desires, and from the Truth they will turn away their ears
5 and be turned aside to their fables. But as for you, keep
your sober senses in all circumstances; suffer hardship; do
6 the work of an evangelist; discharge your ministry. For
Cf. Phil. ii. 17. already is the drink-offering of my blood being poured forth,
7 and the season for my unloosing has arrived. I have faced
the honourable contest, I have finished the course, I have
8 kept the Faith; and now there is in store for me the crown
of righteousness which the Lord, the righteous Judge, will
award to me on that Day, and not only to me but also to all
who have loved His Appearing.

A darkened prospect.

This intimation of his certain and imminent martyrdom is significant. Hitherto the letter has been a message of counsel and encouragement to Timothy, contemplating his continuance at Ephesus and expressing the Apostle's longing to see him there again in the event of his release. (Cf. i. 4.) But it seems as though at this point tidings had reached the prisoner which quenched his lingering hope. His case

[1] A quotation from the Teacher's Manual (cf. p. 594). θεόπνευστος may be (1) like ἔμπνευστος, passive, 'breathed by God,' *divinitus inspirata* (Vulg.). Cf. Plut. *De Plac. Phil.* 904 F: τοὺς ὀνείρους τοὺς θεοπνεύστους. Pseud.-Phocyl. 121: τῆς δὲ θεοπνεύστου σοφίης. (2) Like ἄπνευστος, εὔπνευστος, active, 'breathing God.' Thus Marcus Eremita Ægyptius was ὁ θεόπνευστος ἀνήρ (Wetstein), 'breathing God' as a flower breathes its perfume (cf. 2 Cor. ii. 15). Hence, since everything about a holy man is holy, it was used of some belonging of a holy man. Cf. Nonn. *Paraphr.* I. 99: ἱμάντα θεοπνεύστοιο πεδίλου, 'the latchet of His God-breathing sandal.' So here. It was properly the sacred writers, ὑπὸ Πνεύματος Ἁγίου φερόμενοι (2 Pet. i. 21), that were 'God-breathing,' but just as the Lord's sandals were 'God-breathing,' so the sacred writings were 'God-breathing' too. The passive sense, 'every God-breathed scripture,' is inadmissible, since it is the Spirit, not the Scripture, that is the breath of God (cf. Jo. xx. 22).

had taken an adverse turn. Something had emerged, and whatever it may have been, it sealed his doom. He recognised that his condemnation was certain, and he now alters his instructions to Timothy. He would never return to Ephesus and see him there; yet he would fain see him again if only to bid him farewell. And so he charges him to leave Ephesus and hasten to Rome. There was no foreseeing how long his imprisonment might drag on ere he was brought to trial; and he directs Timothy to convey to him the belongings which he had left at Troas—his mantle, of which he was feeling the need as the days grew chillier, and his manuscripts and rolls of the Old Testament Scriptures which, as St. Chrysostom suggests, he desired to bequeath to his faithful friends—and also to bring with him John Mark whom, after their happy reconciliation during his former imprisonment at Rome, he had sent to Asia, and who was now labouring presumably at Ephesus.[1] The reason which he alleges is that in his desolation Mark's tendance would be helpful to him, and it was the more needful, since he was despatching his present attendant Tychicus to convey the latter to Ephesus; but doubtless there also was a gracious intention in the request. It was a final testimony that the old quarrel was buried in oblivion. He would fain die at peace with all men.

9, 10 Do your best to join me soon. For Demas abandoned me
for love of the present age, and went his way to Thessalonica.
11 Crescens went to Galatia,[2] Titus to Dalmatia. Luke alone
is with me. Bring Mark along with you; for he is service-
12 able in waiting upon me, and I am sending Tychicus[3] to
13 Ephesus. The mantle[4] which I left at Troas in the house
of Carpus, fetch when you come, and the books, especially
14 the parchments.[5] Alexander the coppersmith displayed

[1] Cf. p. 566. [2] Cf. p. 613.

[3] *ἀπέστειλα*, epistolary aorist. Cf. p. 219.

[4] *φελόνης* (*φαινόλης*), *pænula*, 'mantle.' Suidas: *χιτωνίσκος· οἱ δὲ παλαιοί, ἐφεστρίδα* ('wrapper'). The word signified also a portfolio for carrying books. Cf. Chrys.: *φελόνην ἐνταῦθα τὸ ἱμάτιον λέγει· τινὲς δέ φασι τὸ γλωσσόκομον ἔνθα τὰ βιβλία ἔκειτο.*

[5] The 'books' were probably documents of his own, written on papyrus, the common writing-material; while the 'parchments' were his precious rolls (*volumina*) of the O. T., written on vellum. Cf. Theodrt.: *μεμβράνας τὰ εἰλητὰ κέκληκεν· οὕτως γὰρ Ῥωμαῖοι καλοῦσιν τὰ δέρματα.*

Ps. lxii. 12; Prov. xxiv. 12. much rancour against me: 'the Lord will requite him
15 according to his works.' And against him be you too on
16 your guard; for he stoutly opposed our cause. At my first
defence no one supported me, but all abandoned me: may
17 it not be reckoned to their account! However, the Lord stood
by me and put power into me, that through me the message
might be fully proclaimed and all the Gentiles hear it; and
Ps. xxii. 21. 18 I was rescued 'from the lion's mouth.' The Lord will
deliver me from every evil work and bring me safe into
His Heavenly Kingdom. Glory to Him for ever and ever.
Amen.

Closing greetings. The letter closes, after the accustomed manner, with personal greetings, and even here the Apostle's disquietude intrudes. He sends greeting to his old friends Prisca and Aquila and to the family of good Onesiphorus; and then, with generous consideration, he pauses to do justice to an absent comrade. He has just described his forlorn condition by way of justifying his request that Timothy and Mark should hasten to him. Of all the companions who had set forth with him from Asia, only Luke remained. Tychicus indeed had also stood faithful, but he was the bearer of the letter to Ephesus and he would presently be gone. They had not all deserted him, and he has explained the absence of Crescens and Titus; but now he bethinks himself that he has made no mention of Erastus, and, lest it should be inferred that he too had proved recreant, he repairs the omission and explains that 'Erastus had stayed at Corinth.' And with a like purpose he mentions that Trophimus, another of his Ephesian followers, was absent inasmuch as he had fallen sick at Miletus. Then he reverts to his own urgent need. It was the autumn, and two or three weeks would elapse ere his summons reached Ephesus. Since navigation was dangerous after the autumnal solstice and was entirely suspended after the first week of November, there was no time to lose. And so he amends his injunction: 'Do your best to join me soon.' 'Do your best,' he says, 'to come ere winter.' And then, as though to prove that, little as they had availed him in his need, the Roman Christians were still true to him, he sends greetings not only from their leaders but from 'all the brothers.'

19 Greet Prisca and Aquila and the house of Onesiphorus.
20 Erastus remained at Corinth, and Trophimus I left at
Miletus, ill.
21 Do your best to come ere winter. Eubulus and Pudens
and Linus and Claudia and all the brothers greet you.
22 THE LORD BE WITH YOUR SPIRIT. GRACE BE WITH YOU
ALL.

THE APOSTLE'S MARTYRDOM

What sealed the Apostle's doom:

IT has appeared that in the course of the writing of his letter to Timothy the Apostle's case took an adverse turn. His successful defence at the preliminary examination had encouraged the anticipation that his formal trial would issue (Cf. i. 4.) in his acquittal; and when he began the letter he cherished the hope that ere long he would rejoin Timothy at Ephesus. (Cf. iv. 6-8.) But presently the prospect was overclouded. His hope vanished. He recognised that his doom was sealed, and he (Cf. iv. 9, 21.) penned an urgent entreaty that Timothy should hasten to Rome and be with him at the end. What was it that had happened so untowardly? Evidence is lacking, but there are two suggestions which are not without probability.

(1) His defiance of the decree of banishment.

At the precognition the Apostle had been arraigned on the old charge of seditious propagandism; and, though it was aggravated by the calumny that it was the Christians who had fired the city in the year 64, he had succeeded in demonstrating its unreasonableness. It was likely that, if he were brought to trial on that score, he would be acquitted; (Cf. iv. 14, 15.) and it would seem that his Jewish prosecutors, particularly Alexander the coppersmith, fearing lest their prey should escape, had resolved to concentrate on the circumstance that he had been expelled from Rome five and a half years previously and had now returned in defiance of the edict. Here he could offer no defence, and his condemnation was inevitable. This is indeed mere conjecture, yet there is reason for it; and it is this. Timothy, his companion during his first imprisonment, would be included in the edict of expulsion in March 62, and in bidding him hasten (Cf. iv. 15.) to Rome the Apostle warns him of the danger which he would run, since it was likely that Alexander would proceed against him also. Nor was the apprehension groundless. At all events some two years later the author of the anonymous Epistle to the Hebrews informs his readers that Timothy had been set at liberty, and it is a reasonable inference that he had reached Rome ere the end and had been arrested.[1] Luke ran the same risk, yet it does not appear that he was arrested; and the fact that Timothy was assailed by Jewish animosity would seem to prove how fearlessly, despite his constitutional timidity, he had supported his beloved master.

(2) The Emperor's displeasure.

Nor is this the only suggestion. At the precognition in autumn Nero had been absent in Greece; but presently some state crisis had arisen, and he had been hastily summoned back to Rome.[2] The case of a poor Jewish stranger would naturally have concerned him nothing, but an incident had occurred which touched him closely. St. Chrysostom relates that, probably during the interval between his arrival in the city and his arrest, Paul had encountered a beautiful concubine of the dissolute Emperor and had won her for Christ; and when she refused to resume the unhallowed alliance, the incensed tyrant wreaked his vengeance on the Apostle and had him sentenced to death.[3]

His sentence.

There is intrinsic probability in the story, nor would St. Chrysostom have lightly retailed a baseless fable; and it strikingly illustrates the sudden change in the Apostle's fortunes. The Emperor's displeasure sealed his doom. It would be toward the close of the year when he was brought into court, and he was sentenced to execution, not, like the Apostle Peter who, according to tradition, was tried and condemned on the self-same day, by the *servile supplicium* of crucifixion but, as became a Roman citizen, by decapitation.

It was a merciful ordinance of the Roman Senate that ten

[1] That precious scripture, the Epistle to the Hebrews, is certainly not Paul's work. Ancient opinion is thus stated by St. Jerome (*Catal. Script. Eccl.* under *Paulus Apostolus*): 'The Epistle addressed to the Hebrews is not believed, on account of the difference of style and language, to be his work but a work either of Barnabas, according to Tertullian, or of the Evangelist Luke, according to some, or of Clement afterward Bishop of the Roman Church, who, they say, arranged and adorned the opinions of Paul in his own language.' It was an acute and attractive suggestion of Luther that the author was Apollos, the learned and eloquent Jewish Christian of Alexandria.

[2] Cf. Lewin, 2055.

[3] Chrys. *Adv. Vitup. Vit. Monast.* I. iv.

His execution. days should elapse between the condemnation of a criminal and his execution in order that the Emperor, should he think fit, might grant him a free pardon [1] and though it was too often overridden by personal or political animosity, it was doubtless observed in the Apostle's case. He was conducted from the court and recommitted to his cell, and on the tenth day he was led forth to death. It was customary, especially when there was some likelihood of a popular demonstration, that an execution should take place outside the city; [2] and so it was ordered in the case of Paul, perhaps in view of the turbulence of his Jewish enemies. The scene of his execution, according to the constant testimony of tradition,[3] was a spot subsequently known as *Aquæ Salviæ* some two miles southward from the Ostian Gate. It was excellently suited for a public spectacle, being a hollow girt by low hills and thus forming a sort of natural amphitheatre. Thither he would be conducted by a detachment of the Prætorian Guard under the command of a centurion, and the procession would be followed by a noisy and insulting rabble. For a mile and a quarter the route lay along the Ostian Way, passing to the right just outside the Ostian Gate the conspicuous Pyramid of Caius Cestius Epulo; [4] and thence it diverged for three-quarters of a mile into the New Ardeatine Way, whence a lane leads down to *Aquæ Salviæ*. There his eyes were bound and his head laid on the block and severed by the headsman's axe.

Tre Fontane. This is the utmost that may be surely believed of the Apostle's martyrdom; and of all the devout imaginations of later days there is perhaps only one which is worthy of regard. In the valley of *Aquæ Salviæ* stand three churches, and one of these, named *San Paolo alle Tre Fontane*, occupies, it is affirmed, the very spot where he died.[5] The story is that, when his head was struck off, it rebounded thrice, and each time it smote the ground, a living fountain gushed forth possessing a healing virtue, whence the name *Aquæ Salviæ*, 'the Healing Waters.' And there is a heart of

[1] Cf. Suet. *Tib.* 75; Tac. *Ann.* III. 51. [2] Cf. Tac. *Hist.* IV. 11.

[3] Cf. *Act. Petr. et Paul.* 37: τὸ δὲ τοῦ ἁγίου Παύλου (σῶμα) εἰς τὴν Ὀστησίαν ὁδὸν ἀπὸ μιλίων δύο τῆς πόλεως.

[4] Cf. Baedeker, *Central Italy*, p. 329. [5] *Ibid.*, p. 448.

truth in the beautiful legend. Like the superscription on the Cross in Hebrew and Greek and Latin, the Three Fountains aptly symbolise the Apostle's Gospel of world-wide salvation.

His burial. There is an early and steadfast tradition that he was buried by the Ostian Way,[1] and the Church of San Paolo, on the site of a small church erected by the Emperor Constantine about a mile outside the Ostian Gate, marks his resting-place. The story is that after his execution his mutilated body was cast into the criminals' charnel-house, and a Roman convert, a lady named Lucina, sought it and bore it away and buried it in her own garden.[2] There beside the city of his desire lies his mortal body, awaiting the day when, according to his Gospel, it shall be raised immortal and clothed with incorruption, and his undimmed eyes behold the City of God, the realisation of his wistful dream.

[1] Cf. the Roman Presbyter Caius in Eus. *Hist. Eccl.* II. 25.

[2] Cf. Baedeker, *Central Italy*, pp. 445 f.

APPENDIX

I

PAULINE CHRONOLOGY

Saul's Birth at Tarsus . . . . A.D. 1

In the *Oratio Encomiastica in Principes Apostolorum Petrum et Paulum*, erroneously ascribed to Chrys., Paul's career is thus summarised : τριακονταπέντε ἐδούλευσε τῷ Κυρίῳ μετὰ πάσης προθυμίας· τελέσας δὲ τὸν ὑπὲρ τῆς εὐσεβείας δρόμον ἀνεπαύσατο ὡς ἐτῶν ἑξήκοντα ὄκτω, 'Thirty-five years he served the Lord with all eagerness ; and having finished his course in the cause of religion he went to his rest about sixty-eight years of age.' The precision and confidence of this statement attest it as a recognised tradition ; and if it be accepted, then, since he was executed toward the close of 67 (*vid. infra*), he was born about the year 1, five or six years later than our Lord (cf. *The Days of His Flesh*. pp. 11 f.), and converted about 33.

Martyrdom of Stephen . . . . . . April 33

From the activity of the Hellenist synagogues (cf. Ac. vi. 9) it is probable that it was during the paschal week, when the city was thronged with foreign worshippers, that Stephen was arrested. In 33 the Passover fell on April 2 (cf. Lewin, *Fasli Sacri*, p. 241).

Saul's Conversion . . . . . . summer of 33

The persecution in Jerusalem was sharp and short, and as soon as he had finished the work there Saul set out for Damascus (cf. Ac. viii. 3, ix. 1, 2). The thunder-storm (cf. ix. 3) suggests the heat of midsummer. Moreover, it would seem to have been summer-time when he returned to Jerusalem three years later, since all the Apostles except Peter were then absent from the city, probably on missions. They would not travel in the winter (cf. Mt. xxiv. 20).

Stay at Damascus . . . . summer 33—summer 36

A period of three years broken by a season of retirement in Arabia (Gal. i. 17, 18). Cf. Ac. ix. 23 ; ἡμέραι ἱκαναί—a vague phrase denoting generally a considerable time (cf. Ac. ix. 43, xviii. 18, xxvii. 7). Its use here of a period of three years is precisely paralleled by 1 Ki. ii. 38, 39: 'Shimei dwelt in Jerusalem many days (יָמִים רַבִּים). And it came to pass *at the end of three years*, etc.' The order of events here is (1) confession of Jesus in the synagogues of Damascus 'for some days' (Ac. ix. 19, 20); (2) retirement in Arabia (Gal. i. 17)—perhaps several months; (3) active propaganda in Damascus (Ac. ix. 22)—over two years.

FORTNIGHT'S VISIT TO JERUSALEM (Ac. ix. 26-30; Gal. i. 18, 19) . . . . summer 36

IN TARSUS AND SYRIA-CILICIA (Ac. ix. 30; Gal. i. 21) summer 36—summer 45

AGRIPPA'S PERSECUTION . . spring and early summer 44

Ac. xii. 1-23 is a digression explanatory of the situation presented in xi. 27-30. The persecution was in progress at Passover and terminated with Agrippa's sudden death during the celebration of the victorious return of the Emperor Claudius from Britain in spring 44 (cf. Jos. *Ant.* XIX. viii. 2). The tidings would take some time to reach Judæa, and it would be summer ere the celebration was held. Cf. Lewin, 1674.

ARRIVAL AT ANTIOCH OF FUGITIVE PROPHETS (Ac. xi. 27) late in 44

PREDICTION OF FAMINE (Ac. xi. 28) . . . spring 45

SAUL'S CALL TO ANTIOCH (Ac. xi. 25, 26) . summer 45

ELEEMOSYNARY EXPEDITION TO JERUSALEM (Ac. xi. 30; Gal. ii. 1) . . . . summer 46

The famine happened under the procurators Cuspius Fadus and Tiberius Alexander (cf. Jos. *Ant.* XX. v. 2); *i.e.*, it began while the former was still in office and continued after the latter's accession. The administration of Fadus began in 44, and Alexander's ended in 48. The dividing year is unrecorded, but if each held office for equal terms, then it was 46; and thus the period of the famine was 45-46. Cf. Lewin, p. lxix, 1701. Orosius indeed assigns the famine to the year 44 (vii. 6); but it appears that he has miscalculated the events of Claudius' reign and antedated them all by a year (cf. Ramsay, *St. Paul the Traveller*, p. 68). Further, if it was in the fourteenth year after his conversion that Paul paid his eleemosynary visit to Jerusalem (cf. Gal. ii. 1), then that visit fell in the summer of 46.

CONFERENCE AT JERUSALEM . . . late summer 46

It is assumed in the text that Gal. ii. 1-10 refers to Paul's second visit to Jerusalem (cf. Ac. xi. 29, 30, xii. 25). So Tert. *Contra Marc.* I. 20; Eus. *Chron. Pasch.*; Calv.;

Caspari, *Chron. and Geogr. Introd.*, 35; Ramsay, *St. Paul the Traveller*, pp. 51-60; Lake, *Earlier Epistles*, pp. 279-86. Other views, however, have been taken: 1. Irenæus (III. xiii. 3) connected Gal. ii. 1-10 with the third visit (cf. Ac. xv. 1-29), identifying the conference with the Council at Jerusalem. And this is the general opinion in modern times (Grot., Neand., Baur, Meyer, Conybeare and Howson, Farrar, Weizsäcker, Lightfoot). 2. Wieseler connected it with the fourth visit (cf. Ac. xviii. 22). 3. Epiphanius (XXVIII. 4) thought of the fifth visit (cf. Ac. xxi. 15 ff.), an opinion which no one shares. The choice lies between the second visit and the third; and the evidence for the former is conclusive. (1) Paul says that he 'went up in pursuance of a revelation' (Gal. ii. 2); and this can hardly be other than a reference to the prophecy of Agabus (cf. Ac. xi. 27-30). At the third visit he went up by the Church's appointment (cf. Ac. xv. 2). (2) κατ' ἰδίαν τοῖς δοκοῦσιν (Gal. ii. 2) implies a private conference and not an open discussion (cf. Ac. xv. 6, 22). (3) The argument in Gal. i. 17-ii. 10 is decisive. Paul maintains that he had received his Gospel from the Lord and not from the Twelve, and this he demonstrates by recounting his dealings with the latter. He specifies two interviews, one three years and the other fourteen after his conversion, at neither of which had they questioned his doctrine; and it would have been fatal to his argument had there actually been during the interval another interview (cf. Ac. xi. 29, 30) which he suppresses. Lightfoot pleads that it was legitimate for him to ignore the second visit since it fell, as he calculates, during Agrippa's persecution and the Apostles had fled from the city, adducing by way of evidence that the Antiochene bounty was delivered not to the Apostles but to the Elders (cf. Ac. xi. 30). But (*a*) 'the Elders' is a generic term for the leaders of the Church and may include the Apostles (cf. 1 Pet. v. 1). (*b*) A persecution which drove the Apostles from Jerusalem would have prevented the visit of the relief-party. In fact Agrippa's persecution had happened two years earlier. Nor (*c*) does it appear that the Apostles fled from it any more than from the fiercer persecution under Saul (cf. p. 46). It is indeed said that on his escape from prison Peter betook himself to Mary's house and then went εἰς ἕτερον τόπον' (Ac. xii. 17); but this need not mean 'to another *town*.' Rather 'to another *house*'—his own lodging in the city.

Unfortunately the chronological note 'then after an interval of fourteen years' (Gal. ii. 1)—*i.e.*, according to the ancient reckoning, thirteen full years—is indecisive, since it is questionable whether the starting-point of the calculation is the conversion in 33 or the previous visit in 36. On the former and more probable view the occasion was, as the foregoing evidence proves, the eleemosynary visit in 46 (Ac. xi. 29, 30); on the latter it would be the visit to the Council in 49 (cf. Ac. xv. 2).

SAUL'S VISION IN THE TEMPLE (Ac. xxii. 17-21) beginning of 47

Generally connected with the first visit to Jerusalem (cf. Ac. ix. 26-30), but this is plainly its proper place. (1) The first visit was terminated not by a divine vision but by a Jewish plot. (2) The command that Saul should hasten from Jerusalem in order that he might be sent to the Gentiles was fulfilled not by his retiral to Tarsus (cf. ix. 30), but by his despatch from Antioch on his first mission (cf. xiii. 1-3). Perhaps a confirmation is furnished by the textual variation in xii. 25. The situation there requires ὑπέστρεψαν ἐξ (A Syr^{sch} Sah Cop Arm Æth^{pp}) or ἀπὸ (DE Vulg.) Ἰερουσαλήμ, 'returned from Jerusalem'; but several important authorities (ℵBHLP Syr^{p} Æth^{rom}) give εἰς Ἰερουσαλήμ, 'to Jerusalem,' probably (cf. Ramsay, *St. Paul the Traveller*, pp. 63 f.) because the vision in the Temple was connected with xii. 25, and ὑπέστρεψαν ἐξ (ἀπὸ) Ἰερουσαλήμ was then assimilated to ὑποστρέψαντι εἰς Ἰερουσαλήμ (xxii. 17).

FIRST MISSION . . . spring 47—midsummer 49

THE DEPARTURE . . . about beginning of March 47

It fixes the *terminus a quo* and the *terminus ad quem* that they sailed direct from Seleuceia to Salamis (cf. Ac. xiii. 4, 5). (1) Navigation ceased during the winter. It became dangerous after the autumnal equinox and was suspended from Nov. 11 (cf. Veget. *De Re Milit.* v. 9) until Feb. 8 (Plin. *Nat. Hist.* II. 47). (2) On July 11 the Etesian Winds set in and blew unintermittently from N.W. until Sept. 14 (cf. Plin. *Nat. Hist.* II. 47), and during their prevalence westward-bound ships held northward and crept along the coast of Asia Minor by the aid of land-breezes and tides (cf. Strabo, 683). This was the course of the ship by which Paul sailed from Cæsarea in Aug. 59 on his voyage to Rome (cf. 491); and so also, according to *Act. Barn.* (xi-xiv), Barnabas and Mark on their second voyage to Cyprus (cf. Ac. xv. 39) coasted along to Anemurium in Cilicia and then struck across to Crommyon. As soon as a good harvest in March 47 was assured, the relief-party would be free to return to Antioch; and Paul would hasten to obey his call and set forth on his mission.

CYPRUS . . . . . March—close of June 47

PAMPHYLIA . . . . July 47

Pisidian Antioch . . beginning of Aug.—end of Oct. 47

Paul and Barnabas arrived here early in Aug. Ere they began their ministry some time elapsed, long enough for its becoming known that they were qualified to address the synagogue (cf. Ac. xiii. 14, 15)—probably about a fortnight. The rupture with the Jews (cf. vers. 44-47) would thus occur on the last Sabbath of Aug., and the subsequent diffusion of the Gospel throughout the Phrygian District (cf. ver. 49) involves a considerable time, quite two months.

Iconium . . . . . Nov. 47—early summer 48

Cf. Ac. xiv. 3: ἱκανὸν μὲν οὖν χρόνον διέτριψαν, 'they were away a considerable time.' The phrase implies a protracted period. Cf. p. 645.

Lystra . . . . . early summer—end of Aug. 48

The appearance of the Jewish grain-merchants (cf. p. 103) indicates the time of departure.

Derbe . . . . Sept. 48—midwinter

Return through Southern Galatia midwinter—spring 49

Departure from Pisidian Antioch . . . spring 49

They stayed to evangelise in the course of their journey through Pamphylia (cf. Ac. xiv. 25); and Paul, mindful of his previous experience in that malarial region, would set out in time to reach the coast and put to sea ere the heat of midsummer.

Departure from Attaleia . . . . June 49

Arrival at Syrian Antioch . . midsummer 49

Peter's Visit to Antioch and appearance of Judaist Propagandists . . . . . . close of 40

The historical position of Gal. ii. 11 ff. is much disputed. The decision turns mainly on two questions: (1) whether Gal. ii. 1-10 refers to the Council at Jerusalem (cf. Ac. xv. 1-29) or to a previous conference during the eleemosynary visit (cf. Ac. xi. 29, 30; p. 74); and (2) whether Gal. ii. 11 ff. pursues the chronological sequence so clearly indicated in the preceding narrative (cf. i. 18, 21, ii. 1) or introduces an illustrative incident which may have preceded vers. 1-10. Lightfoot, identifying Gal. ii. 1-10 with the Council and insisting on the continuance of chronological sequence, regards this visit of Peter to Antioch as subsequent to the Council and places it during the sojourn of Paul and Barnabas at Antioch after their return from Jerusalem (cf. Ac. xv. 30-40). It seems incredible, however, that Peter should have deserted the cause of Gentile Christianity immediately after his advocacy of it at the Council; and Lewin (1797) places the incident during Paul's stay at Antioch after his second mission (cf. Ac. xviii. 23, 24). Others, again, suppose that chronological sequence is abandoned at Gal. ii. 11, and, identifying vers. 1-10 with the Council, they regard the rencontre between Paul and Peter as having occurred not immediately before the Council but on the occasion of a visit of Peter to Antioch before the first mission of Paul and Barnabas, when he was, it is presumed, sent thither to inspect the original development of Gentile evangelisation (cf. Ac. xi. 26). This is apparently Ramsay's later opinion (cf. *Cities of St. Paul*, pp. 302 f.). The objection is that it supposes two distinct though precisely similar visits of Judaist propagandists to Antioch, one recorded by Paul (cf. Gal. ii. 12) and the other by Luke (cf. Ac. xv. 1). The identification of Paul's 'certain from James' with Luke's 'certain men' who 'came down from Judæa' claiming the authority of the Apostles and Elders at Jerusalem, *i.e.*, James and his colleagues (cf. Ac. xv. 1, 24), is reasonable if not inevitable; and it establishes the view of Lake (cf. *Earlier Epistles*, pp. 293 ff.), formerly shared by Ramsay (cf. *St. Paul the Traveller*, pp. 158 ff.; *Hist. Comm. on Gal.*, pp. 304 ff.), that the chronological sequence is maintained throughout Gal. ii.; that vers. 1-10 refer not to the Council but to a conference at the time of the famine; and that vers. 11 ff. relate to the controversy at Antioch which occasioned the Council at Jerusalem.

Council at Jerusalem . . . . . . early in 50

Second Mission . . . . . spring 50—May 53

Departure from Syrian Antioch . . probably Apr. 50

The 'confirmation of the churches' during the progress through the Province of Syria-Cilicia (cf. Ac. xv. 41) demands probably a full month, and the passage of the Taurus was impossible before the end of May (cf. p. 120).

Derbe . . . . June 50

Pisidian Antioch . . . . July 50

It was the danger of venturing into the valley of the Lycus during the heat of midsummer that deterred Paul from passing into the Province of Asia (cf. Ac. xvi. 6). Cf. p. 122.

Troas . . . . Aug. 50

Philippi . . . . Aug.—Dec. 50

Thessalonica . . . . Jan.—May 51

A considerable stay here is implied by (1) the three weeks' ministry in the synagogue and the subsequent evangelisation of the Gentile populace, and (2) the repeated receipt of relief from Philippi (cf. p. 137).

BERŒA . . . . May—July 51

ATHENS . . . . Aug. 51

Here Luke's summary narrative (Ac. xvii. 14, 15) is elucidated by Paul's statement (cf. 1 Th. iii. 1-6). According to the former it might seem as though Silas and Timothy, notwithstanding Paul's urgent message, did not rejoin him until he had left Athens and settled at Corinth (cf. xviii. 5); but neither is this likely nor is it a reasonable construction of the narrative. It is Luke's manner after intimating an intention to leave his readers to assume that it was carried out. Cf. his statement of Paul's purpose to reach Jerusalem in time for Pentecost (xx. 16). So also in his Gospel: contrast Lk. vii. 10 with Mt. viii. 13. It must therefore be assumed that Silas and Timothy responded to Paul's appeal and presently joined him at Athens. And this is attested by 1 Th. iii. 1. Luke mentions both Silas and Timothy, but Paul only Timothy since he is writing to the Thessalonians and Timothy was sent to them. The plurs. ηὐδοκήσαμεν, ἐπέμψαμεν (1 Th. iii. 1, 2) imply the presence of Silas at Athens. This, then, is the course of events: (1) Silas and Timothy left by Paul at Berœa and instructed to join him at Athens (Ac. xvii. 15). (2) Silas and Timothy with Paul at Athens (1 Th. iii. 1). (3) Timothy sent to Thessalonica (1 Th. iii. 1-5) and Silas probably to Philippi (Ac. xviii. 5; Phil. iv. 15). (4) Paul removes from Athens to Corinth (Ac. xviii. 1). (5) Silas and Timothy return to Paul at Corinth from Macedonia (Ac. xviii. 5)—the former from Thessalonica (1 Th. iii. 6) and the latter probably from Philippi (Phil. iv. 15).

Paul's stay at Athens can hardly have lasted less than a month in view of all that happened: (1) the return of the guides to Macedonia; (2) the journey of Silas and Timothy to Athens; (3) their conference with Paul and their departure again for Macedonia; (4) Paul's inspection of the city; (5) his discussions, evidently frequent (cf. imper. διελέγετο in Ac. xvii. 17), in synagogue and market-place; (6) his meeting with Stephanas; (7) his arraignment before the Court of the Areiopagos.

CORINTH . . . . . . Sept. 51—close of Feb. 53

The accession of Gallio to the proconsulship of Achaia (Ac. xviii. 12) is an historical landmark, and its date has been fixed by the discovery of a mutilated inscription at Delphi. This is a letter of the Emperor Claudius apparently confirming certain of the city's ancient privileges; and it is dated by his twenty-sixth *acclamatio imperatoria* ([αὐτοκράτωρ τ]ὸ κϛ′) and mentions Gallio, in official terms, as his 'friend and proconsul of Achaia' ([Λούκιος Ἰού]νιος Γαλλίων ὁ φ[ίλος] μου κα[ὶ ἀνθύ πατος [τῆς Ἀχαίας]). Hence the twenty-sixth *acclamatio* fell in the year of Gallio's proconsulship; and this is determined by two data. (1) An inscription in the Carian city of Cys puts in the same year Claudius' twelfth *tribunicia potestas* (δημαρχικὴ ἐξουσία), his fifth consulship, and his twenty-sixth *acclamatio* (αὐτοκράτορα τὸ εἰκοστὸν καὶ ἕκτον). (2) The *Arcus Aquæ Claudiæ* is dated by his twelfth *tribunicia potestas*, his fifth consulship, and his twenty-seventh *acclamatio*. The arch was dedicated Aug. 1, A.D. 52; and thus by comparison of the Carian inscription it appears that the twenty-seventh *acclamatio* immediately preceded that date. Gallio assumed his proconsulate during the Emperor's twelfth *tribunicia potestas* and his fifth consulship and just before his twenty-seventh *acclamatio*; *i.e.*, at the beginning of the proconsular year on July 1, 52. Cf. *P.E.F.Q. St.*, Jan. 1908, p. 5, Apr. 1908, pp. 163 f.; Ramsay, *Expositor*, May, 1909; Deissmann, *St. Paul*, Append. I.

Ac. xviii. 11 is neither retrospective, indicating the time which Paul had already spent at Corinth, nor prospective, indicating the period between the accession of Gallio and Paul's departure. Vers. 1-10 relate his settlement, and ver. 11 states the time he spent in the city from his arrival to his departure. He was arraigned before Gallio soon after the latter's accession, probably in Aug.; and thereafter he remained at Corinth ἡμέρας ἱκανάς—a vague phrase (cf. p. 645) denoting here some six months.

ARRIVAL OF SILAS AND TIMOTHY FROM BERŒA . Oct. 51

FIRST LETTER TO THE THESSALONIANS . . Oct. 51

SECOND LETTER TO THE THESSALONIANS . . Nov. 51

ACCESSION OF GALLIO . . . . . . July 1, 52

ARRAIGNMENT BEFORE GALLIO . . . . Aug. 52

DEPARTURE FROM CORINTH . towards close of Feb. 53

ARRIVAL AT JERUSALEM . . . . early May 53

The journey was protracted by (1) Paul's sickness at Cenchreæ (cf. p. 189) and (2) the stoppage at Ephesus (cf. Ac. xviii. 19-21), but he would easily reach Jerusalem in time for Pentecost (cf. Ac. xviii. 21 T. R.), which fell that year on May 12 (cf. Lewin, p. 301).

RETURN TO ANTIOCH . . . toward close of May 53

LETTER TO THE GALATIANS . . . . June 53

Paul paid three visits to Galatia: (1) from Aug. 47 to spring 49 in the course of his first Mission (cf. Ac. xiii. 14-xiv. 23), (2) in early summer 50 at the beginning of his second Mission (cf. Ac. xvi. 1-5), and (3) in autumn 53 at the outset of his third Mission (cf. Ac. xviii. 23); and his statement εὐηγγελισάμην ὑμῖν τὸ πρότερον (Gal. iv. 13) places the letter between (2) and (3). The simple πρότερον would mean merely 'formerly' (cf. 2 Cor. i. 15), but the art. marks a distinction between two conditions, either (1) a previous condition in contrast with the present (cf. Jo. vi. 62, ix. 8; 1 Tim. i. 13) or two past conditions. Had Paul been in Galatia when he said εὐηγγελισάμην ὑμῖν τὸ πρότερον, then τὸ πρότερον would have implied only one previous visit: 'I preached to you on the former occasion, the last time I was here'; but since he was writing *to Galatia*, it implies two previous visits: 'I preached to you on the former of the two occasions when I visited you.' Hence the letter was written before the third visit in autumn 53. This is the *terminus ad quem*; and it excludes both the opinions which prevailed among the Fathers. One, based on the fancy that the Apostle was a prisoner when he wrote (cf. iv. 20, vi. 17), is that the letter was written at Rome. Cf. subscript. in several MSS.: ἐγράφη ἀπὸ Ῥώμης. The other is that it was written at Ephesus, and it has been largely approved in modern times. It is tenable only on the impossible assumption that Paul wrote the letter not during his Ephesian ministry after his third visit to Galatia but during his brief stoppage at the Asian capital in the course of his voyage between Cenchreæ and Cæsarea (cf. Ac. xviii. 19-21). Again, the *terminus a quo* is the second visit in early summer 50; and this excludes Calvin's opinion (cf. comment on ii. 1), which is not without recent support, that, since Paul makes no appeal in his anti-Judaist argument to the Apostolic Decree, the letter must have been written before the Council of Jerusalem at the beginning of 50, perhaps in the course of his journey from Antioch to the Sacred Capital (cf. Ac. xv. 3). It has been assigned also, with extreme unlikelihood, to his sojourn at Athens (Aug. 51), and again to his first Corinthian ministry (Sept. 51—Feb. 53); but the probabilities point to his stay at Antioch in summer 53 between his second and third Missions and just before his third visit to Galatia. The evidence is twofold: (1) the certainty that he would speedily repair to Galatia in order to retrieve the situation (cf. iv. 20); (2) the linguistic affinity between the Galatian letter and those belonging to the third Mission (cf. Append. VII, pp. 688 ff.), especially—as Theod. Mops. observes in his preface—2 Cor. (cf. Gal. vi. 7 with 2 Cor. ix. 6; Gal. i. 6-9 with 2 Cor.

xi. 4; Gal. vi. 15 with 2 Cor. v. 17; Gal. iv. 17, 18 with 2 Cor. xi. 2; Gal. i. 10, v. 8 with 2 Cor. v. 11; Gal. i. 9, v. 21 with 2 Cor. xiii. 2; Gal. iii. 3 with 2 Cor. viii. 6; Gal. v. 15 with 2 Cor. xi. 20). And, further, it should be considered that Rom. is an elaboration of the argument hastily sketched in Gal. (cf. p. 373), and the urgent demand for an adequate exposition required the intervention of the least possible delay.

THIRD MISSION . . . . . . July 53—May 57

DEPARTURE FROM SYRIAN ANTIOCH . . . . July 53

GALATIA . . . . . Aug.—beginning of Oct. 53

EPHESUS (cf Ac. xix. 8, 10; xx. 31) . . Oct. 53—Jan. 56

FIRST LETTER TO CORINTH (LOST) . . . autumn 54

The evidence of the writing of this letter is the Apostle's reference to it (cf. 1 Cor. v. 9-11). Two fragments of it survive: (1) 1 Cor. vi. 12-20. This passage is a manifest interpolation, alien from the passage and marring the impressive close (vers. 9-11). And the repetition of iii. 16, vii. 23 in vi. 19, 20 is impossible in the same letter. Moreover, when it is recognised that vii-xvi deals with a letter which had just arrived from Corinth in reply to the Apostle's previous letter of remonstrance and which submitted to him a series of questions suggested by that previous letter, the significance of various cross-references appears. Thus (i) vi. 13 occasioned the question about 'things sacrificed to idols' (viii-xi. 1); (ii) vi. 14 occasioned the question about the resurrection of the body (xv. 35); and (iii) vi. 20 occasioned the question about slavery (vii. 21-24). (2) 2 Cor. vi. 14-vii. 1. This also is plainly an interpolation. Observe how vi. 13 links with vii. 2. Again, the Corinthians' wonderment at 2 Cor. vi. 14 (in previous letter) occasioned 1 Cor. vii. 12-14 (in the Apostle's reply).

This letter must have been written in autumn 54. When Paul was writing the first part (i-vi) of the ensuing letter (our '1 Cor.'), the Passover of 55, which fell that year on March 30 (cf. Lewin, p. 306), was approaching (cf. 1 Cor. v. 6-8); and between the two letters there was a considerable interval. Paul expected an answer to his first letter, and when none arrived, he was at length moved to write another by the evil report of 'the people of Chloe' (cf. 1 Cor. i. 11).

SECOND LETTER TO CORINTH (OUR '1 COR.') begun Feb. 55

Paul contemplated its delivery before Passover (cf. v. 6-8).

ARRIVAL AT EPHESUS OF CORINTHIAN DEPUTIES (1 Cor. xvi. 17) Feb. 55

In the early part of the letter (i-vi. 11) Paul proceeds upon the report of 'the people of Chloe'; at vii. 1 he starts answering a letter just to hand from Corinth.

THE SECOND LETTER DESPATCHED TO CORINTH . June 55

Since Paul intimates his intention of 'remaining at Ephesus until Pentecost,' *i.e.*, in the year 56, the letter must have been despatched after Pentecost 55, which fell that year on May 20 (cf. Lewin, p. 306). The composition of the latter part of the letter would occupy a considerable time, involving as it did conference with the Corinthian delegates and careful consideration of the questions presented.

PAUL'S HASTY VISIT TO CORINTH . . . autumn 55

The evidence of this otherwise unrecorded episode is twofold: (1) In his stern letter (2 Cor. x-xiii. 10) he refers to the visit which he had in contemplation and which he actually paid (cf. Ac. xx. 2, 3), as his *third* visit to Corinth (cf. xii. 14, xiii. 1), mentioning also a *second* visit which he had paid and reiterating a threat of disciplinary procedure which he had then intimated in the event of continued obduracy (cf. xiii. 2). (2) In his glad letter (2 Cor. i-ix, xiii. 11-14) after the trouble was ended he refers to a painful visit which he had paid to Corinth—an experience which he had determined never to repeat (cf. ii. 1).

This visit would involve hardly a month's absence from Ephesus. The wind at that season was N.W. (cf. p. 648), and the ship would easily fetch Cenchreæ in a week. The return, with the wind on the quarter, would be more expeditious.

STERN LETTER TO CORINTH (CONVEYED BY TITUS) toward close of 55

This letter Paul expressly mentions in the subsequent glad letter (cf. 2 Cor. ii. 2-4, vii. 8); and there is strong reason for recognising 2 Cor. x-xiii. 10 as the substance of it. 1. Our '2 Cor.' is plainly composite: it breaks in two between ix. 15 and x. 1. The first portion is a joyful and affectionate congratulation of the Corinthians on their repentance and reformation; the second an indignant and unmeasured invective against their obduracy and insolence. 2. The two portions are related by a nexus of cross-references. (1) In iii. 1 Paul protests that some personal apology which he has made is not a resumption of the odious business of 'self-commendation': of this he has already had enough, and it is no longer necessary. His meaning, otherwise inexplicable, appears when it is recognised that he is here referring to his elaborate 'self-commendation' in the previous stern letter (cf. x. 7-xii. 10). (2) In xii. 20-xiii. 3 he intimates his determination to deal severely with the impenitent Corinthians when next he visited them and his distaste for the painful duty; and in i. 23-ii. 1 he explains that it was this distaste that had kept him from visiting them sooner: he had stayed away in the hope that they would repent and thus render severity unnecessary. Cf. also ii. 3 with xiii. 10 and ii. 9 with x. 6.

There is a suggestive passage in St. Clement of Rome's Epistle to Corinthians (xlvii) in the last decade of I C. Referring to 1 Cor. i. 10-17, he says: 'Take up the letter (τὴν ἐπιστολήν) of the blessed Paul the Apostle: what did he write to you at the beginning of the Gospel?' The natural inference is that Clement knew only *one* letter of Paul to the Corinthians—our '1 Cor.'; and this is confirmed by the circumstance that he never quotes from or alludes to our '2 Cor.' The fact would seem to be that only '1 Cor.,' that elaborate discussion of universally interesting questions, was at the outset generally circulated in the Church; but by and by, in justice to the Corinthians, the Apostle's glad letter of congratulation (2 Cor. i-ix, xiii. 11-14) was published, all the more readily that it had, by his desire (cf. i. 1), been originally communicated to the neighbouring churches in the Province of Achaia. Many references in the two letters were obscure to strangers, and, in order to elucidate these, fragments of the rest of the correspondence were interpolated—two passages of the first letter (1 Cor. vi. 12-20; 2 Cor. vi. 14-vii. 1) and the bulk of the third (2 Cor. x-xiii. 10).

RIOT AT EPHESUS AND FLIGHT OF PAUL . . Jan. 56

TROAS . . . . . . till early summer 56

MACEDONIA . . early summer—beginning of Dec. 56

GLAD LETTER TO CORINTH (2 Cor. i-ix, xiii. 11-14) Sept. 56

It seems (cf. v. 1) that Paul wrote at the joyous season of the Feast of Tabernacles, which fell that year on Sept. 13 (cf. Lewin, p. 307)

CORINTH (Ac. xx. 3) . . early Dec. 56—early March 57

Here the encyclical on Justification by Faith ('the Epistle to the Romans').

DEPARTURE FROM CORINTH . . . early March 57

Evidently Paul's first intention was to reach Jerusalem in time for Passover, which fell that year on Apr. 7 (cf. Lewin, p. 311).

PHILIPPI (Ac. xx. 6) . . . . Passover 57

The paschal season extended from sunset (when, according to Jewish reckoning, the day began) Apr. 6 to sunset Apr. 14.

TROAS . . . . Apr. 19-25, 57

Being in haste to keep their appointment at Troas (cf. Ac. xx. 5) they would set out from Philippi immediately on the conclusion of the Feast. The passage from Neapolis to Troas occupied four full days (cf. Ac. xx. 6 : ἄχρι ἡμερῶν πέντε, where Cod. Bez. (D) has πεμπταῖοι, 'on the fifth day') ; and they stayed at Troas seven days, reckoning from the day of their arrival.

TROAS TO ASSOS (cf. Ac. xx. 7, 11) . Monday, Apr. 26, 57

ASSOS TO MITYLENE . . . . Tuesday, Apr. 27, 57

MITYLENE TO CHIOS . . . . Wednesday, Apr. 28, 57

CHIOS TO TROGYLLIUM . . . Thursday, Apr. 29, 57

TROGYLLIUM TO MILETUS . . . Friday, Apr. 30, 57

INTERVIEW WITH EPHESIAN ELDERS
night of Saturday, May 1, 57

The Elders would arrive at Miletus on the evening of May 1, and it appears that the interview took place by night since at its close 'they escorted him to the ship' (Ac. xx. 38), which sailed with the morning breeze.

MILETUS TO COS . . . . Sunday, May 2, 57

COS TO RHODES . . . . Monday, May 3, 57

JERUSALEM . . . . eve of Pentecost, May 27, 57

Pentecost fell this year on May 28 (cf. Lewin, p. 311).

TRIAL BEFORE SANHEDRIN . . . . May 31, 57

ARRIVAL AT CÆSAREA . . . . . June 2, 57

TRIAL BEFORE FELIX . . . . . June 7, 57

Twelve days elapsed between Paul's arrival at Jerusalem and his trial at Cæsarea (cf. Ac. xxiv. 11), and they are probably computed thus: (1) the day of his arrival at Jerusalem (xxi. 17)—May 27 ; (2) the day of the meeting of Presbytery (vers. 18-25)—May 28 ; (3) the day when he presented himself in the Temple with the four Nazirites (ver. 26)—May 29 ; (4) the day of purgation and the riot (ver. 27-xxii. 29)—May 30 ; (5) the day of his trial before the Sanhedrin (xxii. 30-xxiii. 11)—May 31 ; (6) the day of the conspiracy to assassinate him and his conveyance from Jerusalem (vers. 12-31)—June 1 ; (7) the day of his arrival at Cæsarea (vers. 32-35)—June 2; (8-12) five days of waiting for his accusers (xxiv. 1)—June 3-7.

IMPRISONMENT AT CÆSAREA FOR TWO FULL YEARS (Ac. xxiv. 27) June 57—July 59

His imprisonment terminated on the recall of Felix and the accession of Festus. The external evidence of the date is uncertain, but it points to 58 at the earliest and 60 at the latest (cf. Schürer, I. ii. pp. 182 ff.). From the narrative of the Book of Acts it appears to have been the year 59, and Festus would, in due course, assume office on July 1.

TRIAL BEFORE FESTUS . . about the middle of July 59

EXAMINATION BEFORE AGRIPPA . about the close of July 59

After his accession on July 1 Festus stayed three days at Cæsarea and then visited Jerusalem (cf. Ac. xxv. 1). The upward journey would take two days, his visit lasted eight or ten (cf. ver. 6), and the return to Cæsarea would take two more. The day after his return Paul was arraigned before him (cf. ver. 6). After an interval of 'some days' (cf. ver. 13), perhaps two or three, Agrippa arrived at Cæsarea. His stay lasted 'a good many days,' πλείους ἡμέρας (ver. 14; cf. xxi. 10), probably a full week; and it was in the course of it, probably toward the close, that Paul made his defence before him (cf. vers. 22, 23).

EMBARKATION FOR ROME . . . . . . Aug. 59

AT FAIR HAVENS, CRETE . . . . . early in Oct. 59

The Fast (Ac. xxvii. 9), *i.e.*, the Day of Atonement (cf. Lev. xvi. 29, 30), fell in the year 59 on Oct. 5, five days before the Feast of Tabernacles (Oct. 10). Cf. Lewin, p. 318. They left Fair Havens about the middle of Oct., sailed slowly westward till the gale broke, then made the ship snug and drifted for a fortnight ere discovering land (cf. xxvii. 27).

SHIPWRECK ON MELITA . . . beginning of Nov. 59

DEPARTURE FROM MELITA . . . . . . Feb. 8, 60

On the resumption of navigation (cf. p. 648) after three months on the island (cf. Ac. xxviii. 11).

ARRIVAL AT PUTEOLI . . . . . about Feb. 18, 60

The course of some 100 miles from Melita to Syracuse would be accomplished in twenty-four hours; at Syracuse they stayed three days; thence it would take two or three days to beat up to Rhegium, where they stayed some twenty-four hours; the run of about 200 miles from Rhegium to

Puteoli with a fair wind took some twenty-four hours (cf. xxviii. 13): in all, some nine days.

Departure from Puteoli (cf. Ac. xxviii. 14) about Feb. 25, 60

Arrival at Rome . . . . first week of March 60

From Puteoli to Rome along the Appian Way from Sinuessa was about 130 miles' march.

First Roman Imprisonment (cf. Ac. xxviii. 30) March 60—March 62

Arrival of Epaphroditus from Philippi midsummer 60

Letter to Philippi . . . . . . Nov. 60

The Apostle was a prisoner when he wrote this letter (cf. i. 12-14, 17), and the imprisonment in question is certainly, according to ancient tradition, the first at Rome and not, according to Paulus and a few others, the earlier imprisonment at Cæsarea (June 57—July 59). On the latter view ἐν ὅλῳ τῷ πραιτωρίῳ (i. 13) would refer to 'the Prætorium of Herod' (cf. Ac. xxiii. 35), the official residence of the Procurator. But οἱ ἐκ τῆς Καίσαρος οἰκίας (iv. 22) plainly indicates Rome. Nor is it without significance that it is in the Philippian letter that the conception of the Church as the *Civitas Dei* first appears in the Apostle's thought (cf. p. 512). The ideal was inspired by the spectacle of the Imperial City.

Arrival of Tychicus from Ephesus toward the close of 61

Encyclical to the Churches of Asia ('Epistle to Ephesians')
Letters to Colossæ and Philemon } despatched about beginning of 62

These three letters form a distinct group. Eph. and Col. were conveyed by the same messenger, Tychicus (cf. Eph. vi. 21; Col. iv. 7), and Phm. is linked to them by the circumstance that Onesimus accompanied Tychicus (cf. Col. iv. 9; Phm. 10-12). The Apostle was a prisoner when he wrote all three (cf. Eph. iii. 1, iv. 1; Col. iv. 18; Phm. 1, 9, 10, 13). Ancient tradition assigns the group to the Roman imprisonment, but not a few moderns (including Meyer and Bernhard Weiss) have referred them to the imprisonment at Cæsarea, chiefly on the twofold ground (1) that the fugitive Onesimus could more easily have fled to Cæsarea then to distant Rome, and (2) that if the letters had been despatched from Rome, Tychicus and Onesimus would have travelled first to Ephesus *en route* for Colossæ, and then the Apostle must have mentioned Onesimus in the Ephesian letter. But (1) Rome offered a safer refuge for the runaway than the provincial town of Cæsarea, and, though more remote, it was in fact more easily accessible whether by ship from Ephesus or by the overland route along the Egnatian Way; and (2) Eph., being an encyclical, lacks all personal references. Moreover, their imperial conception of the Church (cf. p. 533) suggests that Eph. and Col., like Phil., were written at Rome. They were written after Phil. when the Apostle's imprisonment was nearing its end. His trial had been fixed, and he was confident of the issue (cf. Phm. 22). His acquittal was no longer, as when he wrote Phil. (cf. i. 20-26, ii. 24) a question but a certainty.

TRIAL AND ACQUITTAL . . . . . . March 62

AT EPHESUS . . . . Apr. 62

IN MACEDONIA . . . . till close of 62

AT COLOSSÆ . . . . . . early in 63 till June

FIRST LETTER TO TIMOTHY . . . . early in 63

PROGRESS THROUGH SOUTHERN GALATIA . late summer 63

AT SYRIAN ANTIOCH . . . . winter 63-64

MISSION TO GAUL AND SPAIN . . spring 64—spring 66

EVANGELISATION OF CRETE . . . summer of 66

LETTER TO TITUS . . . . . . late autumn 66

Written probably from Corinth on the eve of Paul's departure for Nicopolis (cf. iii. 12).

AT NICOPOLIS . . . . winter 66-67

DEPARTURE ON WESTWARD MISSION . . . spring 67

ARRIVAL AT ROME . . . . . . late summer 67

ARREST AND PRECOGNITION . . . . . Sept. 67

SECOND LETTER TO TIMOTHY not later than close of Sept. 67

The letter was written during the Apostle's imprisonment between his precognition and his trial (cf. iv. 16, 17), and he urges Timothy to make haste and join him at Rome ere winter (cf. iv. 9, 21), *i.e.*, before the suspension of navigation on Nov. 11 (cf. p. 648). Since it would take some six weeks for the letter to reach Ephesus and Timothy to make the voyage to Rome, the letter must have been written by the close of Sept. at the latest. The overland route from Ephesus to Rome took about twice as long as the direct voyage; and Paul's solicitude lest Timothy should miss the last maritime connection shows that he contemplated an early martyrdom.

Trial and Execution Ten Days Later

toward the close of Nov. 67

According to St. Jerome (*Catal. Script. Eccl.*) the Apostle was martyred in the fourteenth year of Nero, *i.e.*, between Oct. 13, 67, and June 9, 68, since Nero reigned from Oct. 13, 54, till June 9, 68 (cf. Lewin, 1802 f., 2066). According to Epiphanius (*Hær.* XXVII. 6), in the twelfth year of Nero (ἐπὶ δωδεκάτῳ ἔτει Νέρωνος); according to Eusebius (*Chron.*), in the thirteenth year. 66 is the year accepted by the ecclesiastical calendar, which commemorates the martyrdom on June 29, following here the anonymous *Martyrium Pauli* prefixed to the works of Œcumenius. The chronology of the *Martyrium*, however, is palpably erroneous; and June 29 is inconsistent with the Apostle's datum (cf. 2 Tim. iv. 9, 21).

II

THE NARRATIVES OF SAUL'S CONVERSION

THERE are three narratives of Saul's conversion in the Book of Acts. The first the historian's (ix. 3-9); and the second and third are his own—the former occurring in his speech to the mob from the stairway of the Castle at Jerusalem (xxii. 6-11), and the latter in his address to Agrippa at Cæsarea (xxvi. 12-18). And these exhibit two apparent divergences.

1. In ix. 4 and xxii. 7 it is said that after the blaze of light Saul fell to the earth, whereas in xxvi. 14 it is pointedly stated that they all—he and his attendants—fell. The fact is that the whole company fell prostrate, but, whereas his attendants quickly recovered from their panic and arose, Saul lay still, engaged with the vision which was hidden from them. When all was over, he —not 'arose' but—'was raised' (ἠγέρθη) by them (ix. 8).

2. In ix. 7 it is said that the attendants 'stood mute, hearing the voice, but beholding no man'; while in xxii. 9 it is said: 'they beheld the light, but they did not hear the voice of Him that talked to me.' This seems a manifest contradiction; and if it were real, it would be equally serious and surprising. It would not merely cast discredit on the veracity of the story, but would convict the historian of crass carelessness. It is inconceivable that so obvious a discrepancy should have escaped so skilful a writer. His justification has been attempted by appealing to a grammatical distinction. In ix. 7 ἀκούειν takes the gen. (τῆς φωνῆς), while in xxii. 9 it takes the accus. (τὴν φωνήν); and the distinction is that ἀκούειν τὴν φωνήν signifies *to hear the voice and understand what is said*, whereas ἀκούειν τῆς φωνῆς is *to hear the sound of the voice as a mere inarticulate noise without distinguishing the words or understanding the sense.* Cf. Grotius: 'Sonum confuse audientes, non autem intelligentes verba.' Bengel: 'Audiebat vocem solem, non vocem cum verbis.' The distinction, however, is not strictly observed. Cf. Acts xi. 7; xxii. 7; Mk. xiv. 64, where in each case it would require the

accus. A simple and satisfactory explanation of the apparent discrepancy is furnished by Chrysostom, who understands that the attendants heard Saul's voice (ix. 7), but they did not hear the Lord's voice (xxii. 9). They did not hear the Lord's question, but they heard Saul's answer, and they wondered at the one-sided conversation, as it appeared to them. 'The voice' in ix. 7 does not necessarily refer to 'the voice' already mentioned in ver. 4 (Blass), since then in ver. xxii. 9 there would, in view of ver. 7, have been no need to define 'the voice' as 'the voice of Him that talked to me.'

III

PAUL'S MALADY

WHAT this may have been is and probably must remain problematic. All the valid evidence is furnished by two references of the Apostle. Writing to the Galatians in the year 53, he recalls the circumstances of his first appearance among them six years previously (cf. Gal. iv. 13-15); and here three facts emerge. 1. The occasion of his visit was 'a physical infirmity.' He had not intended visiting them just then, but an illness had compelled him. 2. The malady was not merely distressing to himself but offensive to those about him. It was 'a trial to them'; and he gratefully acknowledges how they had conquered their natural aversion. 3. It affected his sight, and had evoked their special sympathy: 'if possible, they would have dug out their eyes and given them to him.'

Jerome presents four opinions apparently current in his day. 1. The Apostle's 'infirmity' was the rudimentary teaching (*carnalis mei sermonis annuntiatio*) which he had at the outset been obliged to address to the Galatians as babes unfit for strong meat (*quasi parvulis vobis atque lactentibus per infirmitatem carnis vestræ*). 2. The insignificance of his personal appearance which might have led them to despise his message. 3. A sickness from which he was suffering when he came among them and which, according to tradition, was severe headache (*tradunt eum gravissimum capitis dolorem sæpe perpessum*). Cf. Tert. *De Pudic.* 13: 'dolorem, ut aiunt, auriculæ vel capitis.' 4. The insults and persecutions which the enemies of the Gospel inflicted upon him at the beginning of his Galatian ministry. So Chrys., Theod. Mops., Aug. (*Expos. Epist. ad Gal.* 37).

Whatever the trouble may have been, it was no temporary affliction; for he refers to it eight years later (cf. 2 Cor. xii. 7) and shows how it had clung to him during the interval and how he had recognised in it a precious use. He styles it here σκόλοψ τῇ σαρκί, and the primary question is the significance of σκόλοψ.

It properly denoted 'a stake' (*stipes, sudes*), especially the sharp stake which, in the horrible torture of impalement (σκόλοψις), was driven through the length of the victim's body, like a spit through a fish, till it emerged from his mouth. Cf. Lipsius, *De Cruce*, vi; Sen. *De Consol. ad Marc.* xx; *Epist.* xiv. It is, however, incredible that the Apostle should have likened his infirmity, whatever it may have been, to this awful agony. That would have been a gross exaggeration. Nor is it necessary to impute it to him, since in later Greek σκόλοψ denoted merely a large 'thorn.' Cf. Æsop. *Fab.* 334 (Halm), where for τὸν σκόλοπα Babrius (122) has τὴν ἄκανθαν. And this is the meaning of the word in LXX. Cf. Num. xxxiii. 55; Ez. xxviii. 24; Hos. ii. 6.

What, then, does the Apostle mean when he says that 'there was given him a thorn for his flesh'? An enormous array of opinions is presented by Poole (*Synops. Crit.*), but these fall under three types. 1. 'Some bodily infirmity.' This is the earliest definition (cf. Iren. v. iii. 1). Presently, however, the infirmity, as we have seen, was specified as headache. 2. Chrys. rejects the tradition of headache (κεφαλαλγία), and here as in Gal. finds a reference to the Apostle's persecutions. 3. Misled by Vulg. *stimulus carnis meæ*, the mediæval monastics supposed that it was the solicitation of carnal desire. Cf. Bern. *De Grad. Humil.* (*prim. grad.*). And this is the Roman Catholic interpretation. Cf. Corn. a Lap.: 'Videtur communis fidelium sensus, qui hinc libidinis tentationem stimulum carnis vocant.'

On the Apostle's own testimony his infirmity was a physical malady; and perhaps this is the utmost certainty attainable. It is regrettable that Lightfoot (*Gal.*, pp. 186 ff.) should have approved the unfortunate theory that, like Julius Cæsar, Mohammed, Cromwell, and Napoleon, Paul was an epileptic (cf. Ramsay's discussion in *Teaching of Paul*, pp. 306 ff.). It is a warning against rash speculation; nevertheless the very antiquity of the 'headache' tradition entitles it to consideration; and what is recorded of the Apostle's malady—especially the circumstances of his first seizure and its frequent recurrence—is strongly suggestive of malarial fever. 'Every one,' says Ramsay in his authoritative and persuasive discussion (*Hist. Comm. on Gal.*, pp. 422 ff.), 'who is familiar with the effect of the fevers that infest especially the south coasts of Asia Minor, but are found everywhere in the country, knows that they come in recurring attacks, which prostrate the sufferer for the time, and then, after exhausting themselves, pass off, leaving him very weak; that a common remedy familiar to all is change to the higher lands; and that, whenever any one who has once suffered has his strength taxed, physically or mentally, the old enemy prostrates him afresh, and makes him for a time incapable of any work. Apart from the weakness and ague, the most trying and painful accompaniment is severe headache.'

IV

LUKE AND ANTIOCH

THE tradition is that Luke was a native of Antioch. Cf. Eus. *Hist. Eccl.* III. 4: Λουκᾶς δὲ τὸ μὲν γένος ὢν τῶν ἀπ' Ἀντιοχείας τὴν δὲ ἐπιστήμην ἰατρὸς τὰ πλεῖστα συγγεγονὼς τῷ Παύλῳ. Hieronym. *Script Eccl.*: 'Lucas medicus Antiochensis, ut ejus scripta indicant, Græci sermonis non ignarus fuit, sectator Apostoli Pauli et omnis peregrinationis ejus comes.' It has from an early date been generally assumed that by Antioch was meant the famous Syrian capital (cf. Hieronym., *Comment. in Matt. Præfat.*: 'Lucas medicus, natione Syrus Antiochensis'); and hence much doubt has arisen.

The tradition has either been entirely discredited, as by Meyer, and ascribed to a confusion of Luke with Lucius, the prophet of Syrian Antioch (cf. Ac. xiii. 1), or explained away, as by Ramsay (cf. *St. Paul the Traveller*, p. 389; *Luke the Physician*, pp. 65 ff.), who finds something singular in the phrase of Eusebius 'being according to birth of those from Antioch,' and maintains that 'this curious and awkward expression is obviously chosen in order to avoid the statement that Luke was an Antiochian; and it amounts to an assertion that Luke was not an Antiochian, but belonged to a family that had a connection with Antioch.' Ramsay's theory is that he was a Macedonian and belonged to Philippi. He appears, on the evidence of the first personal narration, in Paul's company at Troas (cf. Ac. xvi. 10), and he was, Ramsay thinks, the 'man of Macedonia' who appealed to the Apostle 'Come over and help us' (*St. Paul the Traveller*, pp. 200 ff.). But indeed there is nothing either curious or awkward in the language of Eusebius. He might have written 'Luke being by race an Antiochene' (τὸ μὲν γένος ὢν Ἀντιοχεύς), but Antioch had furnished other notable converts, and therefore he wrote 'being in respect of his race one of the Antiochene group.'

There is, however, good reason for doubting the tradition if Syrian Antioch be intended; for there is not the slightest evidence in the Book of Acts that Luke was ever connected with that city, excepting only a curious variant in xi. 28 where Cod. Bez. (D), supported by Vet. It. (cf. Aug. *De Serm. Dom. in Mont.* II. 57), has ἦν δὲ πολλὴ ἀγαλλίασις· συνεστραμμένων δὲ ἡμῶν ἔφη εἷς ἐξ αὐτῶν ὀνόματι Ἄγαβος σημαίνων, 'And there was much rejoicing; and when we were assembled, one of them named Agabus spake signifying.' This implies that the historian Luke was a member of the Church at Syrian Antioch in the year 44, but it is doubtless the emendation of a copyist who shared the idea that Syrian Antioch was Luke's home. Since, however, in its earliest form as it appears in Eusebius the tradition simply avers that he was an Antiochene, it may very well be Pisidian Antioch that is intended; and this possibility is substantiated by the sacred narrative.

(1) Observe the fulness and manifest verisimilitude of the account of Paul's first appearance in Pisidian Antioch (xiii. 14-52), especially the report of his discourse in the synagogue. It is unmistakably the report of a hearer and one who had been impressed deeply. One evidence is the distinctively Pauline doctrine (cf. vers. 38, 39); and even more significant is the preface (vers. 16): 'And Paul stood up, and beckoning with the hand said.' There are two peculiarities here. First, the Jewish manner was that a preacher should sit while he addressed his audience (cf. *The Days of His Flesh*, p. 213), but Paul, as befitted the Apostle of the Gentiles, adopted the fashion of a Greek orator (cf. Ac. xvii. 22). Again, 'beckoning with the hand' was a rhetorical habit of the Apostle, designed to arrest attention at the outset (cf. xxi. 40; xxvi. 1). Here also the eye-witness appears. Luke was present in the synagogue, and the scene lived in his memory. It may be that he took down the discourse in shorthand; for this is a very ancient art, having been practised in Greece at least as early as the fourth century. At all events Diogenes Laertius (II. 48) tells how Xenophon, the 'hearer of Socrates' (ἀκροατὴς Σωκράτους), 'took shorthand notes of what he said (ὑποσημειωσάμενος τὰ λεγόμενα) and published them under the title of *Memoirs*.' The shorthand writers were termed σημειογράφοι, ὀξυγράφοι, or ταχυγράφοι, in Latin *notarii*. The invention of the art was ascribed to Ennius, and it was extensively practised. Thus Plutarch (*Cat. Min.* xxiii.) explains how it came about that Cato the Younger's speech at the trial of the Catilinarian conspirators was, alone of all his speeches, preserved: 'Cicero the Consul had beforehand instructed specially swift writers in signs

which had the force of many letters in little short marks, and introduced them into various parts of the Senate House.' Socrates Scholasticus (*Eccl. Hist.* VI. iv.) says that some of Chrysostom's brilliant Homilies were 'published by himself, while others were taken down while he spoke by shorthand writers'; and this explains the numerous impromptus which they exhibit, as when he rebukes the congregation for letting themselves be distracted from his discourse by watching an acolyte lighting the church lamps. Cf. Ausonius, *Epigr.* cxlvi; Becker, *Gallus*, p. 33; Bingham, *Antiq.* XIV. iv. 29; Milligan, *N. T. Documents*, pp. 241 ff. Peculiarly interesting in this connection is *Oxyrh. Pap.* 724.

(2) On their return journey Paul and Barnabas visited Antioch and counselled their converts (cf. xiv. 21-23); and in reporting their exhortations the historian includes himself among the hearers by employing the first personal pronoun: they 'confirmed the souls of the disciples, exhorting to continuance in the Faith, and that through many tribulations *we* must enter into the Kingdom of God.' This may indeed be taken as an abrupt transition from *oratio obliqua* to *oratio recta* (cf. Moulton's Winer, p. 725), but it is more naturally regarded as the first of the '*we* passages.'

(3) When he visited Pisidian Antioch in the course of his second mission, Paul intended to proceed westward into the Province of Asia, but he was providentially prevented, probably by a recurrence of his malady, and travelled northward, uncertain where he was called to labour. At Troas the question was decided by the call to pass over to Europe. Luke was with him at that momentous crisis (cf. xvi. 10), and it is reasonable to suppose that he had accompanied the ailing Apostle from Antioch, or perhaps, since the brief record of the northward wandering is in the third person (vers. 7, 8), had followed him thence and joined him at Troas.

(4) It is further significant that in his narrative of the Apostle's movements through Southern Galatia Luke displays a local intimacy which stamps him as a native. An apt instance is Ac. xiv. 6, where, relating the flight of Paul and Barnabas from Iconium, he says that 'they fled unto the cities of Lycaonia, Lystra and Derbe, and the surrounding District.' Iconium belonged officially to the Lycaonian District, and therefore it was, no less than Lystra and Derbe, 'a city of Lycaonia,' and when they quitted the town, they did not flee into the Lycaonian

District: they were in that District already. This is true according to the imperial nomenclature; but Iconium had formerly belonged to Phrygia, and its people clung to the old connection and still reckoned themselves Phrygians. And thus Luke's language here betrays his intimacy with local usage and his sympathy with local sentiment. He was himself a Phrygian.

Hence it appears that the sacred narrative associates Luke with Pisidian Antioch and points to the conclusion that, when the primitive tradition makes him an Antiochene, it means Pisidian Antioch. This city was important in the apostolic period, but it quickly decayed and sank into obscurity; and hence it was natural that centuries later, when Antioch was mentioned without definition, it should be supposed that the famous Syrian capital was intended.

V

THE DECREE OF THE COUNCIL AT JERUSALEM

THE authorities exhibit a radical divergence in the text both of the motion of James and of the Council's resolution. 1. The motion (Ac. xv. 20): (1) ℵCEHLP, Vulg., Chrys.: *τῶν ἀλισγημάτων τῶν εἰδώλων καὶ τῆς πορνείας καὶ τοῦ* (AB om. *τοῦ*) *πνικτοῦ καὶ τοῦ αἵματος*, 'the pollutions of idols and fornication and what is strangled and blood.' (2) Cod. Bez. (D), Iren. (III. xii. 17), Ambrstr. (on Gal. ii. 1, 2) omit *καὶ τοῦ πνικτοῦ*, 'and what is strangled.' 2. The decree (ver. 29): (1) ℵ*A*BC, Sah., Cop., Vulg., Clem. Alex. (*Pædag.* II. vii. 56), Orig. (*In Ep. ad Rom. Comment.* II. 13, IX. 28; *Contra Cels.* VIII. 29): *εἰδωλοθύτων καὶ αἵματος καὶ πνικτῶν* (ℵ[c]A[2]EHLP *πνικτοῦ*) *καὶ πορνείας*, 'things sacrificed to idols and blood and things strangled (what is strangled) and fornication.' (2) Cod. Bez. (D), Iren., Tert. (*De Pud.* 12), Cypr. (*Test. adv. Jud.* 119), Ambrstr. omit *καὶ πνικτῶν*, 'and things strangled.'

The situation is thus that the Alexandrian and the Western authorities are ranged against each other; and the difference between them is that, according to the former, the prohibition was fourfold—(1) things sacrificed to idols, (2) blood, (3) things strangled, and (4) fornication; whereas, according to the latter, it was threefold—(1) things sacrificed to idols, (2) blood, and (3) fornication. Moreover, at the close of ver. 20 and in ver. 29 after *πορνείας* the Western authorities generally—the one important exception being Tertullian—insert the Golden Rule, negatively expressed: *καὶ ὅσα μὴ θέλουσιν* (*θέλετε*) *ἑαυτοῖς γίνεσθαι, ἑτέροις μὴ ποιεῖν*. And after *πράξετε* (ver. 29) Cod. Bez. (D), Iren., Tert. add *φερόμενοι ἐν τῷ Ἁγίῳ Πνεύματι*, 'being borne along in the Holy Spirit' (cf. 2 Pet. i. 21). The question is, Which of these versions of the decree is authentic? There are two possibilities: either that the clause *καὶ τοῦ πνικτοῦ* (*τῶν πνικτῶν*) in the Alexandrian is a marginal gloss interpolated in the text, or that it is genuine and has been omitted from the Western text; and the evidence decisively favours the former alternative.

1. It is true that the Alexandrian reading is supported by the great uncials; but it should be considered that the earliest of

these dates only from the 4th cent., and the Western reading is confirmed by Irenæus (2nd cent.) and Tertullian (early 3rd cent.). Nor is there lacking textual evidence that the Alexandrian clause καὶ τοῦ πνικτοῦ is a gloss. (1) The variant καὶ πνικτοῦ in ver. 20 suggests that the simple πνικτοῦ was entered in the margin over against αἵματος, explaining the latter in terms of the Mosaic precept (Lev. xvii. 10-16). Presently it crept into the text and καὶ was prefixed to make it an article in the enumeration. Afterwards τοῦ was added to bring it into conformity with the other clauses. Here the interpolation is seen in progress. (2) Though elsewhere Origen quotes the fourfold Alexandrian prohibition, in one instance (*In Matt. Comment. Ser.* 10, surviving only in a Latin translation) he quotes, not indeed the Western, but a threefold prohibition—*immolatum et suffocatum et fornicationem,* 'what is sacrificed and what is strangled and fornication.' Here πνικτοῦ holds the place of αἵματος in the Western threefold enumeration, suggesting that in some Alexandrian texts the gloss was not interpolated but substituted. And indeed this was a more reasonable procedure, since on the Levitical interpretation αἵματος and πνικτοῦ are synonymous, both alike denoting the eating of flesh which retains the blood.

2. On the assumption that the Western text is authentic the genesis of the Alexandrian is apparent. According to the Western three restrictions were imposed on the Gentile converts, and all three were ethical, not ceremonial. 'Things sacrificed to idols' denoted the flesh of victims which had been offered in pagan temples and of which only certain portions were consumed on the altars; and what is here contemplated is, as appears from the controversy which afterwards arose in the Corinthian Church (cf. 1 Cor. viii), the countenance which a Christian lent to idolatry and its attendant immoralities by participating in a pagan banquet, particularly when it was celebrated in an idol-temple (cf. p. 269). Thus the prohibition of 'things sacrificed to idols' or 'the pollutions of idols' is not a food-law but an ethical precept. And similarly with the prohibition of 'blood,' αἷμα has here its frequent signification (cf. Lev. xvii. 4; Num. xxxv. 27; Ps. li. 14; Mt. xxiii. 30; Rev. vi. 10) of 'murder,' *homicidium* (Tert. Cf. Aug. *Contra Faust. Manich.* xxxii. 13: 'id est, ne quidquam ederent carnis, cujus sanguis non est effusus. Quod alii non sic intelligunt, sed a sanguine præceptum esse abstinendum, ne quis homicidio se contaminet.'); and so neither is the prohibition of blood a food-law. What is forbidden is not the

eating but the *shedding* of blood. The Alexandrian corruption of the text originated in a natural failure to perceive the consistently ethical intention of the decree. It began with a narrow interpretation of 'things sacrificed to idols'; and the situation is illustrated by the subsequent controversy at Corinth. The flesh of the numerous temple-victims furnished the city-market, and the more scrupulous sort of Christians, with the decree of the Council in view, regarded it as unclean. Paul dealt with this scruple, and defined the prohibition of 'things sacrificed to idols' as applying only to participation in the sacrifice. Once the prohibition of 'things sacrificed to idols' had been misconstrued as a food-law, it was inevitable that the prohibition of 'blood' should be likewise misconstrued and taken to mean not the shedding but the eating of blood; and it was so defined by the marginal gloss πνικτοῦ, 'what is strangled,' which by and by crept into the text.

Thus the Alexandrian text was a natural and indeed inevitable corruption of the Western. Cf. Ambrstr.: 'Denique tria hæc mandata ab apostolis et senioribus data reperiuntur, quæ ignorant leges Romanæ, id est, ut abstineant se ab idololatria, et sanguine, sicut Noe, et fornicatione. Quæ sophistæ Græcorum non intelligentes, scientes tamen a sanguine abstinendum, adulterarunt Scripturam, quartum mandatum addentes, et a suffocato observandum.' On the other hand, it is an untenable supposition that the Western text is a corruption of the Alexandrian, prompted by dislike of the food-restrictions. And that for this reason, that the prohibition of eating blood actually prevailed and was scrupulously observed in the West, particularly in Gaul and North Africa. Thus in the letter which the Churches of Lyons and Vienne addressed to Asia and Phrygia in 172, and which was probably written by Irenæus, it is told how the female martyr Biblias answered the persecutors' charge that the Christians indulged in 'Thyestean banquets.' 'How,' she said, 'could such persons eat children, when they are not permitted to eat the blood even of brute beasts?' (Cf. Eus. *Hist. Eccl.* v. I.) Similarly, according to Tertullian (*Apol.* 9; cf. *De Spect.* 13; *De Monogam.* 5; *De Jejun.* 4, 15), the Christians were forbidden to eat blood, and therefore they abstained from the flesh of animals which had been strangled or died naturally (*suffocatis et morticinis*). Hence so little were the Westerns likely to be offended by food-regulations that they would rather have been inclined by their actual practice to approve of these; and their retention of the threefold text constitutes a strong evidence of its authenticity. It would appear that there was a disposition among them to adopt the ceremonial interpretation; and the addition of the Golden Rule and the words 'borne along in the Holy Spirit' was doubtless designed to safeguard the ethical and spiritual interpretation.

3. According to the Western text the decree of the Council was a courageous decision such as the crisis demanded, recognising the new order and making a clean sweep of the ancient and outworn ceremonies. But according to the Alexandrian text it was a faltering compromise, meeting the Gentile converts half-way, releasing them from the main obligations of the Mosaic Law, particularly the rite of Circumcision, but requiring that they should propitiate Jewish sentiment by submitting to certain food-restrictions. Such a decision would have been at once futile and mischievous. It would have contented neither party, since no avoidance of unclean meats would have atoned in Jewish eyes for neglect of the supreme rite of Circumcision; while the food-restrictions would have seemed to the Gentile converts ridiculous and vexatious, and they would speedily have been ignored. 'The Apostles,' says St. Augustine (*Contra Faust. Manich.* xxxii. 13), 'seem to me to have chosen for the time an easy thing in nowise burdensome to observe, that therein Gentiles and Israelities withal might observe something in common. But that time being past, what Christian now observes this rule, not to touch thrushes or tinier birds unless their blood has been poured out, nor to eat a hare if it has been knocked on the head and not killed by a bleeding wound? And the few who still perhaps dread touching those things, are ridiculed by the rest; so firmly held in this matter are all men's minds by that judgment of the Truth: "Not that which entereth into your mouth, defileth you, but that which proceedeth out" (Mt. xv. 11).' The compromise would have been futile. At the best it would have established a short-lived *modus vivendi*; and while it continued, it would have operated mischievously, making a cleavage in the Church and creating a caste-distinction. The presupposition was that the Jewish Christians should continue to observe the Mosaic Law in its entirety; but a concession was granted to the weakness of the Gentile Christians. They were required to observe only 'the necessary things,' and thus they were recognised as an inferior order. And it would be amazing had a Christian Council reckoned among the 'things necessary' to salvation a scrupulosity which our Lord had so emphatically condemned.

VI

THE SACRAMENT OF BAPTISM

I. The Mode.—Baptism (βαπτισμός, βάπτισμα) is the Greek rendering of the Hebrew טְבִילָה which was employed of the Jewish ceremonial ablutions, especially the purificatory bath—the Baptism of Proselytes (cf. Edersheim, *Life and Times of Jesus the Messiah,* Appendix XII ; Schürer, II. ii. pp. 319 ff.)—administered to converts from heathenism on their admission to the Commonwealth of Israel. The verb טָבַל signified ' immerse ' or ' dip.' Cf. 2 Ki. v. 14 : ' Then went he down, and *dipped himself* (יִטְבֹּל) seven times in Jordan.' Here the Septuagint have ἐβαπτίσατο, and βαπτίζειν also signified 'immerse.' It was used, for example, of a ship sinking in the sea. Cf. Æsop. *Fab.* 370 (Halm) : τῆς νεὼς κινδυνευούσης βαπτίζεσθαι. Jos. *Vit.* 3 : βαπτισθέντος γὰρ ἡμῶν τοῦ πλοίου κατὰ μέσον τὸν Ἀδρίαν.

Immersion was thus the proper Jewish mode, but it was found not only difficult where water was scanty but in certain cases actually dangerous. It is told that in the days of R. Joshua ben Levi the Galileans represented that the chill was harmful to their women and occasioned sterility (cf. Lightfoot, *Hor. Heb.* on Mt. iii. 6) ; and among the Christians at all events a modification was certainly adopted in the administration of the Sacrament. They retained the method of immersion, but two others were recognised and practised in the primitive Church. These were effusion or pouring (ἔκχυσις, *effusio*) and aspersion or sprinkling (ῥαντισμός, *aspersio*). The evidence appears on the pages of the New Testament, and it is this—that the sacred writers not merely make distinct allusion to all the three modes but unfold the symbolic significance of each.

1. St. Paul plainly had the mode of immersion in view when to the charge that his doctrine of Justification by Faith apart from Works involved antinomianism he opposed the idea of a mystic union of believers with Christ (cf. Rom. vi. 3, 4 ; Col. ii. 12). Faith identifies us with Him at each stage of His redemptive

career—His Death, His Burial, His Resurrection, and His Ascension. And this is symbolised by our immersion in the baptismal water: we die with Him, are buried with Him, are raised with Him, and live with Him.

This idea was afterwards quaintly elaborated. The fish (ἰχθύς) was the commonest of all the numerous symbols in vogue among the early Christians. It denoted Christ, inasmuch as the letters of ἰχθύς are the initials of Ἰησοῦς Χριστὸς Θεοῦ Υἱὸς Σωτήρ, 'Jesus Christ God's Son Saviour.' The Lord had called His disciples to be 'fishers of men,' catching them in the Gospel-net and drawing them out of the world's restless sea; and so believers were termed 'fishes.' Cf. these lines in Clement of Alexandria's hymn at the close of the *Pædagogus*:

ἁλιεῦ μερόπων
τῶν σωζομένων,
πελάγους κακίας
ἰχθῦς ἁγνοὺς
κύματος ἐχθροῦ
γλυκερᾷ ζωῇ δελεάζων.

'Fisher of mortals, whom Thou dost save
Out of the ocean's strife,
Luring pure fish from the angry wave
With the sweet bait of life.'

The idea was naturally associated with Baptism—the immersion of the fishes in the water and their drawing forth, their 'catching for life' (cf. Lk. v. 10). 'We little fishes,' says Tertullian (*De Bapt.* 1), 'according to our Fish, Jesus Christ, are born in the water' ('Nos pisciculi secundum ἰχθὺν nostrum, Jesum Christum, in aqua nascimur').

2. The mode of effusion also appears in the New Testament, and that in a singularly impressive fashion. John the Baptist declared that his Baptism with water unto repentance was prophetic of a nobler Baptism—the Messiah's Baptism with the Holy Spirit and with fire (cf. Mt. iii. 11); and the Lord reiterated the promise at His Ascension (cf. Ac. i. 5). And how was it fulfilled? On the Day of Pentecost 'there appeared unto them tongues parting asunder, like as of fire; and it sat upon each one of them. And they were all filled with the Holy Spirit' (Ac. ii. 3, 4). That was the promised Baptism; and it is presently defined as an 'outpouring' or 'effusion' (vers. 16, 17, 33: ἐκχεῶ, ἐξέχεεν). Cf. Tit. iii. 4-6. It could not have been thus designated unless effusion had been a recognised mode of administration; and the symbolic value of this mode lies in its proclamation of the essential truth that the grace of the Sacrament is an operation of the Holy Spirit.

3. Aspersion too was a recognised mode of administration. Cf. Heb. x. 22: 'Let us draw near with a true heart in fulness of faith, having our hearts sprinkled (ῥεραντισμένοι τὰς καρδίας) from an evil conscience, and our body washed with pure water.' Here are both the symbol of Baptism (' our body washed with pure water') and its spiritual counterpart (' our hearts sprinkled from an evil conscience'). The language is derived from Ez. xxxvi. 25, 26, where Jerome comments thus: 'I restored them to their pristine glory, so that, when they believed and turned from their error, I might pour forth upon them the clean water of saving Baptism and cleanse them from all their abominations; and might give them a new heart to believe in the Son of God, and a new spirit. And it should be considered that the new heart and the new spirit are given through effusion and sprinkling of water (*per effusionem et aspersionem aquæ*).' The closing words indicate that effusion and aspersion were regarded as practically identical, and from this and other passages (cf. Aug. *Quæst. in Num.* xxxiii; *Contra Adversar. Leg. et Proph.* II. 23) it appears that in the time of Jerome and Augustine effusion or aspersion was the prevailing mode of administration. An interesting corroboration is furnished by the textual variations in two passages. (1) Mk. vii. 4: 'When they come from the market-place, except they *wash themselves*, they eat not.' Here the MSS. vary between βαπτίσωνται, 'baptise (*i.e.*, 'dip' or 'immerse') themselves,' and ῥαντίσωνται, 'sprinkle themselves.' (2) Rev. xix. 13, where A.V. has 'clothed with a vesture *dipt* in blood,' and R.V. 'arrayed in a garment *sprinkled* with blood.' These renderings represent different readings. Some MSS. have βεβαμμένον, 'baptised' or 'dipped,' and others περιρεραμμένον or ῥεραντισμένον, 'sprinkled.' The plain inference is that βαπτίζειν, 'baptise,' and ῥαντίζειν, 'sprinkle,' had come to be employed as synonymous terms.

The conclusion from all this evidence is that in the Apostolic Church the Sacrament of Baptism was administered after three modes—Immersion or Dipping, Effusion or Pouring, and Aspersion or Sprinkling. (Cf. 1 Cor. x. 2, where Aspersion and Immersion appear side by side.) Each was recognised as legitimate, and the choice was determined by considerations of convenience and suitability. This is borne out by the article on Baptism in that primitive directory, *The Teaching of the Twelve Apostles* (vii): 'Concerning Baptism: thus baptise. After all this preliminary instruction baptise into the name of the Father and the Son and the Holy Spirit in living (*i.e.*, 'running') water. And if thou hast not living water, baptise into other water; and if thou canst not do it in cold water (*i.e.*, in cases of delicacy), do it in warm. And if thou hast neither, pour forth (ἔκχεον) water on the head thrice in the name of Father and Son and Holy Spirit.'

II. The Subjects.—The question here is whether the grace of Baptism be limited to persons of mature understanding, capable of personal faith, or extends to the children of the faithful, though still unconscious babes. It may seem at the first glance as though the testimony of the New Testament were decisive, since the command is 'Believe, and be baptised' (cf. Ac. ii. 38, 41). But it should be considered that Christianity was then at the outset of its career. The message was a new thing in the world, and converts both Jewish and pagan were baptised on profession of 'repentance toward God and faith toward our Lord Jesus Christ' (Ac. xx. 21). So it happens still on mission fields, and the conditions in apostolic days were analogous. Moreover, the Apostles recognised that the promise was not to their converts alone but to their converts' children (cf. Ac. ii. 37-39); and it is repeatedly recorded that they baptised not only their converts but their converts' households (cf. xvi. 14, 15; 29-34), plainly implying that the faith of the head of the house availed vicariously for his family (cf. 1 Cor. vii. 14). And this inference is surely attested.

1. According to Paul Baptism is 'the Circumcision of Christ' (Col. ii. 11, 12). It is the seal of God's New Covenant with Christ and His Church as Circumcision was the seal of the Old Covenant with Abraham and his seed after him (cf. Rom. iv. 11). The New Covenant is not less but larger, wider and more benignant than the Old; and as the children of faithful Israelites were comprehended in the Old Covenant and every male received the seal of Circumcision, so the children of believers are comprehended in the New and receive the seal of Baptism.

2. Infant Baptism was early practised, and Origen expressly and repeatedly affirms that it was derived from the Apostles (cf. *Ad Rom. Comment.* v. 9; *In Lev. Hom.* viii. 3; *In Luc. Hom.* xiv). Its legitimacy went unchallenged until post-Reformation days, and the objection came of over-emphasis of the Lutheran doctrine of Justification by Faith. It is indeed by faith that we are saved; but, as the Pauline doctrine of Imputation and the scientific law of Heredity proclaim, the efficacy of faith is vicarious

as well as personal. Christian nurture avails much. The nature which he inherits and the atmosphere which he breathes make a momentous difference to a child; and the Christian Sacrament of Baptism recognises this. As a matter of fact the children of believing parents share the blessings of the Covenant of Grace; and since they are actually in the Covenant, they receive its seal.

3. It is frequently objected to the practice of Infant Baptism that, so far from being a primitive usage, it is a late outgrowth of the doctrine of Baptismal Regeneration. The Sacrament was conceived as not merely sealing but conferring grace; and therefore its administration was extended to infants, since they were doomed on the score of Original Sin, and must perish everlastingly if they died unbaptised. This, however, is a false reading of history. The idea of the regenerating efficacy of Baptism appeared at a very early date, and it invested post-baptismal sin with a peculiar heinousness, since it was nothing less than a desecration of the Holy Spirit's grace, and not only was it fatal to the sinner but it involved his sponsors in grave liability. So heavy a responsibility, it was felt, should not be lightly incurred; and during the Middle Ages it was customary for warriors, when on their conversion to the Christian Faith they received the Sacrament of Baptism, to exempt their right arms from immersion in 'the laver of regeneration,' that they might thus continue without sacrilege to work bloodshed and violence. But in earlier and less superstitious days a different device was adopted. It was the withholding of Baptism from infants and the postponement of the administration until they had passed the perilous period of youth with its passions and inexperience. This was advocated as early as the close of the second century. 'The delaying of Baptism,' argues Tertullian (*De Bapt.* 18), 'is more advantageous, especially in the case of little children. For what need is there that danger should be thrust upon the sponsors also, in that it is possible that they may both themselves fail of their promises by dying and be foiled by the issue of the child's evil disposition? The Lord indeed says (Mt. xix. 14): "Forbid them not to come unto Me." Let them come, then, when they grow up; let them come when they learn, when they are taught whither they are coming; let them be made Christians when they can know Christ.'

Thus it appears that Infant Baptism was the Church's practice down to the time of Tertullian, and its disuse was an innovation dictated by the notion of Baptismal Regeneration. Thenceforward the custom prevailed of postponing the administration until the attainment of maturity and often indeed until the approach of death. It was, for example, in the year 306 that the Emperor Constantine was converted, but it was not until his last illness in 335 that he submitted to the sacred ordinance (cf. Gibbon, *Decline and Fall*, chap. xx). The pious Emperor Valentinian II. in like manner delayed his Baptism, meaning to receive it in due season; but the hand of an assassin cut short his life, and he died unbaptised to the exceeding distress of his relatives, whom Ambrose consoled in a fine discourse, assuring them that the Emperor's desire for the Sacrament would be accepted by God as equivalent to its observance (Ambros. *De Obit. Valent. Consol.*). There is also the case of Augustine. He was three and thirty ere he was baptised (*Confess.* ix. 6); and he relates that once during his early childhood he fell dangerously ill, and his mother Monnica was minded to have the Sacrament administered to him forthwith; but she was restrained by the dread of his incurring the guilt of post-baptismal sin should he recover. And so it came to pass that he went so long unbaptised, 'because after that washing there would be greater and more perilous guilt in the defilement of transgressions' (*Confess.* i. 11). Cf. *Reliq. Baxter.* I. ii. 6: 'I found in all Antiquity, that though Infant Baptism was held lawful by the Church, yet some with *Tertullian* and *Nazianzen*, thought it most convenient to make no haste, and the rest left the time of Baptism to every ones liberty, and forced none to be baptized: Insomuch as not only *Constantine, Theodosius,* and such others as were converted at Years of Discretion, but *Augustine* and many such as were the Children of Christian Parents (one or both) did defer their Baptism much longer than I think they should have done. So that in the Primitive Church some were Baptized in Infancy, and some at ripe Age, and some a little before their Death; and none were forced, but all left free; and the only Penalty (among men) of their delay was, that so long they were without the Priviledges of the Church, and were numbred but with the *Catechumens*, or *Expectants*.'

VII

VERBAL PECULIARITIES IN THE PAULINE LETTERS

I

The Epistles to the Thessalonians

1. In 1 Th. and nowhere else in Pauline Epistles:—

αἰφνίδιος v. 3. ἀληθῶς ii. 13. ἀμέμπτως* ii. 10, iii. 13, v. 23. ἀναμένω* i. 10. ἀπάντησις iv. 17. ἀπορφανίζω* ii. 17. ἀρχάγγελος iv. 6. ἀσφάλεια v. 3. ἄτακτος* v. 14. γαστήρ v. 3 (also in quot. Tit. i. 12). εἴσοδος i. 9, ii. 1. ἐκδιώκω ii. 15. ἐνορκίζω* v. 27. ἐξηχέομαι* i. 8. ἡσυχάζω iv. 11. θεοδίδακτος* iv. 9. καταξιόομαι i. 5. κέλευσμα* iv. 16. κολακία* ii. 5. ὀλιγόψυχος* v. 14. ὁλόκληρος v. 23. ὁλοτελής* v. 23. ὁμείρομαι* ii. 8. ὁσίως ii. 10. παραμυθέομαι ii. 11, v. 14. περιλείπομαι* iv. 15, 17. προπάσχω ii. 10. σαίνομαι* iii. 3. συμφυλέτης* ii. 14. τοιγαροῦν iv. 8. τροφός* ii. 7. ὑβρίζω ii. 2. ὑπερβαίνω iv. 6. ὑπερεκπερισσῶς* v. 13. φλόξ* i. 8. ὠδίν v. 3.

2. In 2 Th. and nowhere else in Pauline Epistles:—

ἀναιρέω ii. 8. ἀποστασία ii. 3. ἀπακτέω* iii. 7. ἀτάκτως* iii. 6, 11. ἄτοπος iii. 2. δίκη i. 9. ἔνδειγμα* i. 5. ἐνδοξάζεσθαι* i. 10, 12. ἐνκαυχάομαι* i. 4. ἐπισυναγωγή ii. 1. θροέομαι ii. 2. καλοποιέω* iii. 13. μιμέομαι iii. 7, 9. περιεργάζομαι* iii. 11. σαλεύω ii. 2. σέβασμα ii. 4. σημειόομαι* iii. 14. τίνω* i. 9. ὑπεραυξάνω* i. 3.

3. In 1 and 2 Th. and nowhere else in Pauline Epistles:—

κατευθύνω 1 Th. iii. 11, 2 Th. iii. 5 (only other N. T. instance *Benedictus*, Lk. i. 79).

* Nowhere else in N. T.

II

Period of Judaist Controversy

1. In Rom. and nowhere else in Pauline Epistles :—

ἄβυσσος x. 7 (quot.). ἀγριέλαιος* xi. 17, 24. ἀδύνατος viii. 3, xv. 1. ἀΐδιος i. 20. αἰνέω xv. 11 (quot.). ἄκακος xvi. 18. ἀκροατής ii. 13. ἀλάλητος* viii. 26. ἀμετανόητος* ii. 5. ἄμμος ix. 27 (quot.). ἀνάγω x. 7. ἀναζάω vii. 9. ἀναλογία* xii. 6. ἀναπολόγητος* i. 20, ii. 1. ἀνελεήμων* i. 31. ἀνεξεραύνητος* xi. 33. ἄνθραξ* xii. 20 (quot.). ἀνόμως* ii. 12. ἀνοχή* ii. 4, iii. 26. ἀνταπόδομα x. 9 (quot.). ἀνταποκρίνομαι ix. 20. ἀντιστρατεύομαι* vii. 23. ἀντιτάσσομαι xiii. 2. ἀπειθέω ii. 8, x. 21, xi. 30, 31, xv. 31. ἀπέναντι iii. 18 (quot.). ἀποβολή xi. 15. ἀποστυγέω* xii. 9. ἀποτομία* xi. 22. ἀρά* iii. 14 (quot.). ἀριθμός ix. 27 (quot.). ἀσθένημα* xv. 1. ἄσπις* iii. 13 (quot.). ἀσύνετος i. 21, 31, x. 19 (quot.). ἀσύνθετος* i. 31. ἀσχημοσύνη i. 27. ἀτιμάζω i. 24, ii. 23. ἀφαιρέω xi. 27 (quot.) ἀφικνέομαι* xvi. 19. ἀχρεόομαι* iii 12 (quot.). βδελύσσομαι ii. 22. βούλημα ix. 19. γέμω iii. 14 (quot.). γνωστός i. 19. δεῦρο i. 13. διαγγέλλω ix. 17. διαπορεύομαι xv. 24. διαταγή xiii. 2. δικαιοκρισία* ii 5. δικαίωμα i. 32, ii. 26, v. 16, 18, viii. 4. δολιόω* iii. 13 (quot.). δοῦλος (adj.)* v. 19 *bis*. δώρημα v. 16. ἐγκαλέω viii. 33. ἑκατονταετής* iv. 19. ἐκζητέω iii. 11 (quot.). ἐκκαίομαι* i. 27. ἐκκλάομαι* xi. 17, 19, 20. ἐκκλίνω iii. 12 (quot.), xvi. 17. ἐκπετάννυμι* xi. 21 (quot.). ἐκχύννομαι v. 5. ἐλαία xi. 17, 24. ἐμπίμπλημι xv. 24. ἐμφανής x. 20 (quot.). ἔνδικος iii. 8. ἐνκεντρίζω* xi. 17, 19, 23, 24. ἐντυγχάνω viii. 27, 34, xi. 2. ἐπαναμιμνήσκω* xv. 15. ἐπαναπαύομαι ii. 17. ἐπικαλύπτειν* iv. 17 (quot.). ἐπιπίπτω xv. 3. ἐπιποθία* xv. 23. ἐπίσημος xvi. 7. ἐπιτυγχάνω xi. 7. ἐπιφέρω iii. 5. ἐπονομάζομαι* ii. 17. ἑρπετόν i. 23. ἐφευρετής* i. 30. ζέω xii. 11. ἥκω xi. 26 (quot.). ἤτοι* vi. 16. θεάομαι xv. 24. θειότης* i. 20. θεοστυγης* i. 30. θήρα* xi. 9 (quot.). ἱεροσυλέω* ii. 22. ἱερουργέω* xv. 16. ἱλαρότης* xii. 8. ἱλαστήριον iii. 25. ἰός iii. 13 (quot.). καθήκω i. 28. καθοράω* i. 20. καινότης* vi. 4, vii. 6. κακοήθεια* i. 29. καλλιέλαιος* xi. 24. κατάγω x. 6. κατακαυχάομαι xi. 18 *bis*. κατάκριμα* v. 16, 18, viii. 1. κατάλαλος* i. 30. κατανοέω iv. 19. κατάνυξις* xi. 8 (quot.). καταράομαι xii. 14. κατασκάπτω* xi. 3 (quot.). κατηγορέω ii. 15. κεραμεύς xi. 21. κλάδος xi. 16, 17,

* Nowhere else in N. T.

18, 19, 21. κοίτη ix. 10, xiii. 13. κύκλῳ xv. 19. λάρυγξ* iii. 13 (quot.). λατρεία ix. 4, xii. 1. λάχανον xiv. 2. λεῖμμα* xi. 5. λειτουργέω xv. 27. λογικός xii. 1. λόγιον iii. 2. λογισμός ii. 15. ματαιόομαι* i. 21. μέμφομαι ix. 19. μεστός i. 29, xv. 14. μεταλλάσσω* i. 25, 26. μεταξύ ii. 15. μήπω ix. 11. μήτρα iv. 19. μοιχαλίς vii. 3 *bis*. μοιχεύω ii. 22, xiii. 9. μόλις v. 7. νικάω iii. 4 (quot.), xii. 21 *bis*. νομοθεσία* ix. 4. ὁδηγός ii. 19. οἰκέτης xiv. 4. οἰκουμένη x. 18 (quot.). ὁμοθυμαδόν xv. 6. ὁμοιόω ix. 29 (quot.). ὀξύς iii. 15. ὄρεξις* i. 27. ὁρίζω i. 4. ὀφείλημα iv. 4. παιδευτής ii. 20. παλαιότης* vii. 6. παράκειμαι* vii. 18, 21. πάρεσις* iii. 25. πέρας x. 18 (quot.). πετεινόν i. 23. πηλός ix. 21. πιότης, xi. 17. πιπράσκω vii. 14. πλάσμα* ix. 20. ποιητής ii. 13. που iv. 19. πρόβατον viii. 36 (quot.). προγίνομαι* iii. 25. προγινώσκω viii. 29, xi. 2. προδίδωμι* xi. 35 (quot.). προέχομαι* iii. 9. προηγέομαι* xii. 10. πρόθυμος i. 15. πρόνοια xiii. 14. προπάτωρ* iv. 1. προσκόπτω ix. 32, xiv. 21. πρόσλημψις* xi. 15. προστάτις* xvi. 2. προφητικός* xvi. 26. πταίω xi. 11. σαβαώθ ix. 29 (quot.). σεβάζομαι* i. 25. σκληρότης* ii. 5. σκληρύνω ix. 18. σκοτίζομαι i. 21, xi. 10 (quot.). στεναγμός viii. 26. συγγενής ix. 3, xvi. 7, 11, 21. σύμβουλος* xi. 34 (quot.). σύμφυτος* vi. 5. συναγωνίζομαι* xv. 30. συναναπαύομαι* xv. 32. συναντιλαμβάνομαι viii. 26. συνδοξάζω* viii. 17. συνήδομαι* vii. 22. συνκάμπτω* xi. 10 (quot.). συνμαρτυρέω* ii. 15, viii. 16, ix. 1. συνπαρακαλέομαι* i. 12. συνστενάζω* viii. 22. συνσχηματίζομαι xii. 2. συντελέω ix. 28 (quot.). συντέμνω* ix. 28 (quot.). συντρίβω xvi. 20. σύντριμμα* iii. 16 (quot.). σύνφημι* vii. 16. συνωδίνω* viii. 22. σφαγή* viii. 36 (quot.). ταλαιπωρία iii. 16 (quot.). ταλαίπωρος vii. 24. τάφος iii. 13 (quot.). τετράπους i. 23. τολμηροτέρως* xv. 15. τράχηλος xvi. 4. τυφλός ii. 19. ὕπανδρος* vii. 2. ὑπερεντυγχάνω* viii. 26. ὑπερνικάω* viii. 37. ὑπερφρονέω* xii. 3. ὕπνος xiii. 11. ὑπόδικος* iii. 19. ὑπόλειμμα* ix. 27 (quot.). ὑπολείπομαι* xi. 3 (quot.). φάσκω i. 22. φιλοξενία xii. 13. φιλόστοργος* xii. 10. φονεύω xiii. 9 (quot.). φόνος i. 29. φόρος xiii. 6, 7. φρόνημα viii. 6, 7, 27. φύραμα ix. 21, xi. 16 (also in proverb 1 Cor. v. 6, Gal. v. 9). φυσικός i. 26, 27. χρηματίζω, vii. 3. χρηματισμός* xi. 4. χρηστολογία* xvi. 18. ψεῦσμα* iii. 17. ψιθυριστής* i. 30. ὡραῖος x. 15 (quot.). ὡσεί vi. 13. ὠφελεία iii. 1.

2. In 1 Cor. and nowhere else in Pauline Epistles :—

ἄγαμος* vii. 8, 11, 32, 34. ἀγενής* i. 28. ἀγνωσία xv. 34. ἀγοράζω vi. 20, vii. 23, 30. ἀδάπανος* ix. 18. ἄδηλος xi. 8. ἀδήλως*

* Nowhere else in N. T.

ix. 26. ἄζυμος v. 7, 8. αἴνιγμα* xiii. 12. ἀκατακάλυπτος* xi. 5, 13. ἀκολουθέω x. 4. ἀκρασία vii. 5. ἄκων* ix. 17. ἀλαλάζω xiii. 1. ἀμέριμνος vii. 32. ἀμετακίνητος* xv. 58. ἀμπελών ix. 7. ἀνά vi. 5, xiv. 27. ἀνακρίνω ii. 14, 15 *bis*, iv. 3 *bis*, ix. 3, x. 25, 27, xiv. 24. ἀνάμνησις xi. 24, 25 (quot. from Evangelic Tradition). ἀνάξιος* vi. 2. ἀναξίως* xi. 27. ἀνδρίζομαι* xvi. 13. ἀντίλημψις* xii. 28. ἀπάγω xii. 2. ἀπελεύθερος* vii. 22. ἀπερισπάστως* vii. 35. ἀπόδειξις* ii. 4. ἀπολούω vi. 11. ἀποφέρω xvi. 3. ἀργύριον iii. 12. ἀροτριάω ix. 10. ἅρπαξ v. 10, 11, vi. 10. ἄρρωστος xi. 30. ἀρχιτέκτων* iii. 10. ἀστατέω* iv. 11. ἀστήρ xv. 41. ἀσχημονέω* vii. 36, xiii. 5. ἀσχήμων* xii. 23. ἄτιμος iv. 10, xii. 23. ἄτομος* xv. 22. αὐλέομαι xiv. 7. αὐλός* xiv. 7. αὔριον xv. 32 (quot.). ἄφωνος xii. 2, xiv. 10. ἄψυχος* xiv. 7. βιωτικός vi. 3, 4. βρόχος* vii. 35. γάλα iii. 2. γαμίζω vii. 38. γεώργιον* iii. 9. γογγύζω x. 10. γραμματεύς i. 20. γυμνιτεύω* iv. 11. δειπνέω xi. 25. δή vi. 20. διαίρεσις* xii. 4, 5, 6. διαιρέω xii. 11. διδακτός ii. 13. διερμηνευτής (v. l.)* xiv. 28. διερμηνεύω xii. 30, xiv. 5, 13, 27. διόπερ* viii. 13, x. 14. διψάω iv. 11 (also in quot. Rom. xii. 20). δουλαγωγέω* ix. 27. δράσσομαι* iii. 19 (quot.). δυσφημέω* iv. 13. δώδεκα (οἱ) xv. 5. ἐάω x. 13. ἐγκρατεύομαι* vii. 9, ix. 25. εἰδώλιον* viii. 10. εἰδωλόθυτος viii. 1, 4, 7, 10, x. 19. εἰσακούω xiv. 21 (quot.). ἔκβασις x. 13. ἐκδέχομαι xi. 33, xvi. 11. ἐκκοπή (v. l. ἐγκοπή)* ix. 12. ἐκνήφω* xv. 34. ἐκπειράζω x. 9. ἔκτρωμα* xv. 8. ἐλεεινός xv. 19. ἐνέργημα* xii. 6, 10. ἔννομος ix. 21. ἔνοχος xi. 27. ἐντροπή* vi. 5, xv. 34. ἐξαίρω* v. 13 (quot.). ἐξεγείρω vi. 14 (also in quot. Rom. ix. 17). ἐξουσιάζω vi. 12, vii. 4 *bis*. ἑορτάζω* v. 8. ἐπάνω xv. 6. ἐπερωτάω xiv. 35 (also in quot. Rom. x. 20). ἐπιβάλλω vii. 35. ἐπιθανάτιος* iv. 19. ἐπιθυμητής* x. 6. ἐπίκειμαι ix. 16. ἐπισπάομαι* vii. 18. ἔρημος x. 5 (also in quot. Gal. iv. 27). ἑρμηνία* xii. 10, xiv. 26. ἔσοπτρον xiii. 12. ἑτερόγλωσσος* xiv. 21 (quot.). εὐγενής i. 26. εὐκαιρέω xvi. 12. εὐπάρεδρος* vii. 35. εὔσημος* xiv. 9. εὐσχημοσύνη* xii. 23. εὐσχήμων vii. 35, xii. 24. ἦθος* xv. 33 (quot.). ἠχέω* xiii. 1. θάπτω xv. 4. θηριομαχέω* xv. 32. ἴαμα* xii. 9, 28, 30. ἱερόθυτος* x. 28. ἱερόν ix. 13. ἵνα τί x. 29. ἰχθύς xv. 39. καίω xiii. 3. καλάμη* iii. 12. καλύπτω iv. 3. κατακαίω iii. 15. κατακαλύπτομαι* xi. 6 *bis*, 7. καταμένω (*v.* l.) xvi. 6. καταστρώννυμι* x. 5. καταχράομαι* vii. 31, ix. 18. κείρω xi. 6 *bis*. κέντρον xv. 55 and 56 (quot.). κημόω* ix. 9 (quot.). κιθάρα xiv. 7. κιθαρίζω xiv. 7. κινδυνεύω xv. 30. κλάω x. 16, xi. 24 *bis*. κόκκος xv. 37. κομάω*

* Nowhere else in N. T.

xi. 14, 15. κόμη* xi. 15. κορέννυμι iv. 8. κριτήριον vi. 2, 4. κτῆνος xv. 39. κυβέρνησις* xii. 28. κύμβαλον* xiii. 1. κυριακός xi. 20. λογία* xvi. 1, 2. λοιδορέω iv. 12. λοίδορος* v. 11, vi. 10. λύσις* vii. 27. μαίνομαι xiv. 23. μάκελλον* x. 25. μαλακός vi. 9. μαράνα θά (μαρὰν ἀθά)* xvi. 22. μέθυσος* v. 11, vi. 10. μείζων xii. 31, xiii. 13, xiv. 5 (also in quot. Rom. ix. 12). μέλει vii. 21, ix. 9. μετέχω ix. 10, 12, x. 17, 21, 30. μηνύω x. 28. μήτιγε* vi. 3. μοιχός vi. 9. μολύνω viii. 7. μυρίος iv. 15, xiv. 19. μωρία* i. 18, 21, 23, ii. 14, iii. 19. νή* xv. 31. νηπιάζω* xiv. 20. νῖκος* xv. 54, 55, 57 (quots.). ξυράομαι xi. 5, 6. ὀλοθρευτής* x. 10. ὅλως v. 1, vi. 7, xv. 29. ὁμιλία* xv. 33 (quot.). ὁσάκις xi. 25. ὄσφρησις* xii. 17. οὐαί ix. 16. οὐδέποτε xiii. 8. οὖς xii. 16 (also in quots. ii. 19, Rom. xi. 8). ὄφελος xv. 32. παιδίον xiv. 20. παίζω* x. 7 (quot.). πανταχοῦ iv. 17. παράγω vii. 31. παραμυθία* xiv. 3. παρεδρεύω* ix. 13. πάροδος* xvi. 7. παροξύνομαι xiii. 5. πάσχα v. 7. πειθός* ii. 4. πεντηκοστή xvi. 8. περιάγω ix. 5. περιβόλαιον* xi. 15 (also in quot. Heb. i. 12). περικάθαρμα* iv. 13. περιτίθημι xii. 23. περίψημα* iv. 13. περπερεύομαι* xiii. 14. πέτρα x. 4 *bis* (also in quot. Rom. ix. 33). πιάζω xi. 32. πλεῖστος xiv. 27. πνευματικῶς ii. 13 (v. l.), 14. ποιμαίνω ix. 7. ποίμνη ix. 7 *bis*. πόλεμος xiv. 8. πόμα x. 4. πορνεύω vi. 18, x. 8. πόρνη vi. 15, 16. ποτήριον x. 16, 21, xi. 25, 26, 27, 28. ποτίζω iii. 2, 6, 7, 8, xii. 13 (also in quot. Rom. xii. 20). προσκυνέω xiv. 25. προφητεύω xi. 4, 5, xiii. 9, xiv. 1, 3, 4, 5, 24, 31, 39. πτηνός* xv. 39. πυκτεύω* ix. 26. πωλέω x. 25. ῥάβδος iv. 21. ῥιπή* xv. 52. σαλπίζω xv. 52. σελήνη xv. 41. σῖτος xv. 37. στάδιον ('racecourse')* ix. 24. συμβαίνω x. 11. σύμφορος* vii. 35, x. 33. σύμφωνος* vii. 5. συνάγω v. 4. συγγνώμη* vii. 6. σύνοιδα iv. 4. συνέρχομαι xi. 17, 18, 20, 33, 34, xiv. 23, 26. συνετός i. 19 (quot.). συνζητητής* i. 20. συνήθεια viii. 7, xi. 16. συνκεράννυμι xii. 24. συνμερίζομαι* ix. 13. συνστέλλω vii. 29. σχίσμα i. 10, xi. 18, xii. 25. σχολάζω vii. 5. τάγμα* xv. 23. τήρησις vii. 19. τίμιος iii. 12. τοίνυν ix. 26. τράπεζα x. 21 (also in quot. Rom. xi. 9). τυπικῶς* x. 11. τύπτειν viii. 12. ὑπέρακμος* vii. 36. ὑπηρέτης iv. 1. ὑπόστασις ix. 4, xi. 17. ὑπωπιάζω ix. 27. φιλόνεικος* xi. 16. φρήν* xiv. 20 *bis*. φυτεύω iii. 6, 7, 8, ix. 7. χαλκός xiii. 1. χοϊκός* xv. 47, 48, 49. χόρτος iii. 12. χρηστεύομαι* xiii. 4. ψευδομάρτυς xv. 15. ψυχικός ii. 14, xv. 44 *bis*, 46. ψῦχος xi. 26. ψωμίζω* xiii. 3 (also in quot. Rom. xii. 20). ὡσπερεί* xv. 8.

3. In 2 Cor. and nowhere else in Pauline Epistles:—

ἀβαρής* xi. 9. ἀγανάκτησις* vii. 11. ἁγιότης v. 12. ἁγνότης*

* Nowhere else in N. T.

vi. 6, xi. 3. ἀγρυπνία* vi. 5, xi. 27. ἁδρότης* viii. 20. ἀεί iv. 11, vi. 10 (also in quot. Tit. i. 12). ἀλλ' ἤ i. 13. ἄμετρος* x. 13, 15. ἀναγγέλλω vii. 7 (also in quot. Rom. xv. 21). ἀνακαλύπτω* iii. 14, 18. ἀνεκδιήγητος* ix. 15. ἀπαρασκεύαστος* ix. 4. ἀπεῖπον* iv. 2. ἀπόκριμα* i. 9. ἀποτάσσομαι ii. 13. ἀριστερός vi. 7. ἁρμόζομαι* xi. 2. ἄρρητος* xii. 4. ἀρχαῖος v. 17. ἄρχω iii. 1 (also in quot. Rom. xv. 12). ἀτενίζω iii. 7, 13. αὐγάζω* iv. 4. αὐθαίρετος* viii. 3, 17. ἀφροσύνη xi. 1, 17, 21. βαρύς (quot. of Corinthian criticism) x. 10. Βελίαρ* vi. 15. βοηθέω vi. 2 (quot.). βουλεύομαι i. 17. βυθός* xi. 25. γένημα ix. 10. δαπανάω xii. 15. δίψος* xi. 27. δολόω* iv. 2. δότης* ix. 7 (quot.). δυσφημία* vi. 8. ἐθνάρχης* xi. 32. εἰσδέχομαι* vi. 17 (quot.). ἐκδαπανάομαι* xii. 15. ἐκδημέω* v. 6, 8, 9. ἐκδύω v. 4. ἐκφοβέω* x. 9. ἐλαττονέω* viii. 15 (quot.). ἐλαφρία* i. 17. ἐλαφρός iv. 17. ἐνγράφομαι iii. 2, 3. ἐνδημέω* v. 6, 8, 9. ἐνκρίνω* x. 12. ἐνπεριπατέω* vi. 16 (quot.). ἐντυπόω* iii. 7. ἐξαπορέομαι* i. 8, iv. 8. ἐξίστημι v. 13. ἐπακούω* vi. 2 (quot.). ἐπενδύομαι* v. 2, 4. ἐπιεικία x. 1. ἐπιπόθησις* vii. 7, 11. ἐπισκηνόω* xii. 9. ἐπίστασις xi. 28. ἐπιτιμία* ii. 6. ἐρημία xi. 26. ἔσωθεν vii. 5. ἑτεροζυγέω* vi. 14. ἑτοίμως xii. 14. εὐφημία* vi. 8. εὐφραίνω ii. 2 (also in quots. Rom. xv. 10, Gal. iv. 27). ἐφικνέομαι* x. 13, 14. ἡδέως xi. 19, xii. 9, 15. ἡνίκα* iii. 15, 16. ἡττάομαι xii. 13. θαρρέω v. 6, 8, vii. 16, x. 1, 2. θαῦμα xi. 14. θυγάτηρ v. 18 (quot.). θυρίς xi. 33. ἱκανότης* iii. 5. ἱλαρός* ix. 7 (quot.). καθαίρεσις* x. 4, 8, xiii. 10. καθαιρέω x. 5. καθώσπερ iii. 18. κάλυμμα* iii. 13 (quot.), 14, 15, 16. καπηλεύω* ii. 17. καταβάλλω iv. 9. καταβαρέω* xii. 16. κατάκρισις* iii. 9, vii. 3. καταλαλία xii. 20. καταναρκάω* xi. 9, xii. 13, 14. καταπίνω ii. 7, v. 4 (also in quot. 1 Cor. xv. 54). κατάρτισις* xiii. 9. κατοπτρίζομαι* iii. 18. λάμπω iv. 6. λῃστής xi. 26. λιθάζω xi. 25. λίθινος iii. 3. μέλαν iii. 3. μέριμνα xi. 28. μεταμέλομαι vii. 8. μετανοέω xii. 21. μετοχή* vi. 14. μετρέω x. 12. μικρόν xi. 1, 16. μολυσμός* vii. 1. μωμάομαι* vi. 3, viii. 20. νηστεία vi. 5, xi. 27. νυχθήμερον* xi. 25. ὁδοιπορία xi. 26. ὀδυρμός* vii. 7 (also in quot. Mt. ii. 18). οἰκητήριον v. 2. ὀπτασία xii. 1. ὀχύρωμα* x. 4. πάλαι xii. 19. πανοῦργος* xii. 16. παντοκράτωρ vi. 18 (quot.). παράδεισος xii. 4. παραυτίκα* iv. 17. παραφρονέω* xi. 23. παρεκτός xi. 28. παρέρχομαι v. 17. πένης* ix. 9 (quot.). περιαιρέω iii. 16. περίσσευμα viii. 13, 14. πέρυσι* viii. 10, ix. 2. πλάξ iii. 3. πλατύνω vi. 11, 13. πληγή vi. 5, xi. 23. πληθύνω ix. 10. ποταμός xi. 26. προαιρέομαι* ix. 7. προαμαρτάνω* xii. 21, xiii. 2. προενάρχομαι* viii. 6, 10.

* Nowhere else in N. T.

προέρχομαι ix. 5. προθυμία viii. 11, 12, 19, ix. 2. προκαταρτίζω* ix. 5. πρόκειμαι viii. 12. προσαναπληρόω* ix. 12, xi. 9. πρόσκαιρος iv. 18. προσκοπή* vi. 3. πτωχεία viii. 2, 9. πτωχεύω* viii. 9. ῥαβδίζω xi. 25. σαργάνη* xi. 33. σήμερον iii. 14, 15 (also in quot. Rom. xi. 8). σκῆνος* v. 1, 4. σκόλοψ* xii. 7. σκορπίζω ix. 9 (quot.). σπόρος ix. 10. σπουδαῖος* viii. 17, 22. στενοχωρέομαι* iv. 8, vi. 12. στρατιά x. 4. συλάω* xi. 8. συμφώνησις* vi. 15. συναποστέλλω* xii. 18. συνέκδημος viii. 19. συνκατάθεσις* vi. 16. συνοχή ii. 4. συνπέμπω* viii. 18, 22. συνυπουργέω* i. 11. συστατικός* iii. 1. τεῖχος xi. 33. τηλικοῦτος i. 10. τρίς xi. 25, xii. 8. τυφλόω iv. 4. ὕβρις xii. 10. ὕπερ* xi. 23. ὑπερβαλλόντως* xi. 23. ὑπερέκεινα* x. 16. ὑπερεκτείνω* x. 14. ὑπερλίαν* xi. 5, xii. 11. ὑψόω xi. 7. φειδομένως* ix. 6 (proverb). φθόγγος* x. 10 (also in quot. Rom. x. 18). φυλακή vi. 5, xi. 23. φυσίωσις* xii. 20. φωτισμός* iv. 4. χαλάω xi. 33. χειροτονέω viii. 19. χορηγέω ix. 10. χρίω i. 21. χωρέω vii. 2. ψευδαπόστολος* xi. 13. ψιθυρισμός* xii. 20.

4. In Gal. and nowhere else in Pauline Epistles :—

Ἄγαρ* iv. 24, 25. ἀκυρόω iii. 17. ἀλληγορέω* iv. 24. ἀναστατόω v. 12. ἀνατίθεμαι ii. 2. ἀνέρχομαι i. 17, 18. ἄνωθεν iv. 9. ἀποκόπτω v. 12. ἆρα ii. 17. βασκαίνω* iii. 1. βοάω iv. 27 (quot.). δάκνω* v. 15. διαμένω ii. 5. ἐγκράτεια v. 23. ἐθνικῶς* ii. 14. εἴκω* ii. 5. ἐκβάλλω iv. 30 (quot.). ἐκλύομαι vi. 9. ἐκπτύω* iv. 14. ἐμμένω iii. 10. ἐνευλογέομαι iii. 8 (quot.). ἐνιαυτός iv. 10. ἐξαιρέω i. 4. ἐξαποστέλλω iv. 4, 6. ἐξορύσσω iv. 15. ἐπιδιατάσσομαι* iii. 15. ἐπικατάρατος* iii. 10 (quot.), 13 (quot.). ἐπίτροπος iv. 2. εὐθέως i. 16. εὐπροσωπέω* vi. 12. ἴδε v. 2. ἰουδαΐζω* ii. 14. ἰουδαϊκῶς* ii. 14. ἰουδαϊσμός* i. 13, 14. ἱστορέω* i. 18. καταγινώσκω ii. 11. κατάρα iii. 10, 13. κατασκοπέω* ii. 4. κενόδοξος* v. 26. κρεμάννυμι iii. 13 (quot.). μεταστρέφω i. 7. μετατίθημι i. 6. μήν iv. 10. μορφόομαι* iv. 19. μυκτηρίζομαι* vi. 7. ὅμοιος v. 2. ὀρθοποδέω* ii. 14. παιδίσκη iv. 22, 23, 30 *bis* (quot.), 31. παρατηρέω iv. 10. παρείσακτος* ii. 4. πατρικός* i. 14. πεισμονή* v. 8. πηλίκος vi. 11. πορθέω i. 13, 23. προεῖδον iii. 8. προευαγγελίζομαι* iii. 8. προθεσμία* iv. 2, προκαλέομαι* v. 26. προκυρόομαι* iii. 17. προσανατίθεμαι* i. 16, ii. 6. προστίθημι iii. 19. ῥήγνυμι iv. 27 (quot.). στεῖρος iv. 27 (quot.). στίγμα* iv. 17. συνηλικιώτης* i. 14. συνπαραλαμβάνω ii. 1. συνστοιχέω* iv. 25. συνυποκρίνομαι* ii. 13. ταράσσω i. 7, v. 10. τεκνίον (v. l.) iv. 19. τίκτω iv. 27 (quot.). ὑποστέλλω

* Nowhere else in N. T.

ii. 12. ὑποστρέφω i. 17. φαρμακία v. 20. φθονέω v. 26. φορτίον vi. 5. φρεναπατάω* vi. 3. ὠδίνω iv. 19, 27 (quot.).

5. In two or more of the group and nowhere else in Pauline Epistles :—

Ἀββᾶ Rom. viii. 15, Gal. iv. 6. Ἀβραάμ Rom. iv. 1, 2, 3 (quot.), 9, 12, 13, 16, ix. 7, xi. 1, 2 Cor. xi. 22, Gal. iii. 6, 7, 8, 9, 14, 16, 18, 29. ἄδικος Rom. iii. 5, 1 Cor. vi. 1, 9. αἵρεσις 1 Cor. xi. 19, Gal. v. 20. ἀκαταστασία 1 Cor. xiv. 33, 2 Cor. vi. 5, xii. 20. ἀλλάσσειν Rom. i. 23, 1 Cor. xv. 51, 52, Gal. iv. 20. ἁμάρτημα Rom. iii. 25, 1 Cor. vi. 18. ἀμεταμέλητος* Rom. xi. 29, 2 Cor. vii. 10. ἀναγκάζω 2 Cor. xii. 11, Gal ii. 3, 14, vi. 12. ἀνάθεμα Rom. ix. 3, 1 Cor. xii. 3, xvi. 22, Gal. i. 8, 9. ἀνθρώπινος Rom. vi. 19. 1 Cor. ii. 13, iv. 3, x. 13. ἀντιμισθία* Rom. i. 27, 2 Cor vi. 13. ἀπέρχομαι Rom. xv. 28, Gal. i. 17. ἀπολογέομαι Rom. ii. 15, 2 Cor. xii. 19. ἀπορέω 2 Cor. iv. 8, Gal. iv. 20. ἀποστολή Rom. i. 5, 1 Cor. ix. 2, Gal. ii. 8. ἄρσην Rom. i. 27 *bis*, Gal. iii. 28. ἀφίημι Rom. i. 27, iv. 7 (quot.), 1 Cor. vii. 11, 12, 13. ἀφορίζω Rom. i. 1, 2 Cor. vi. 17, Gal. i. 15, ii. 12. βαπτίζω Rom. vi. 3 *bis*, 1 Cor. i. 13, 14, 15, 16, 17, x. 2, xii. 13, xv. 29 *bis*, Gal. iii. 27. βαστάζω Rom. xi. 18, xv. 1, Gal v. 10, vi. 2, 5, 17. βέβαιος Rom. iv. 16, 2 Cor. i. 7. βῆμα Rom. iv. 10, 2 Cor. v. 10. γυμνός 1 Cor. xv. 37, 2 Cor. v. 3. γυμνότης Rom. viii. 35, 2 Cor. xi. 27. δέρω 1 Cor. ix. 26, 2 Cor. xi. 20. δῆλος 1 Cor. xv. 27, Gal. iii. 11. διακρίνω Rom. iv. 20, xiv. 23, 1 Cor. iv. 7, vi. 5, xi. 29, 31, xiv. 29. διάκρισις Rom. xiv. 1, 1 Cor. xii. 10. διαστολή* Rom. iii. 22, x. 12, 1 Cor. xiv. 7. διέρχομαι Rom. v. 12, 1 Cor. x. 1, xvi. 5, 2 Cor. i. 16. διχοστασία* Rom. xvi. 17, Gal. v. 20. δουλεία Rom. viii. 15, 21, Gal. iv. 24, v. 1. δυνατέω* Rom. xiv. 4, 2 Cor. ix. 8, xiii. 3. εἰλικρινία* 1 Cor. v. 8, 2 Cor. i. 12, ii. 27. εἰσέρχομαι Rom. v. 12, xi. 25, 1 Cor. xiv. 23, 24. ἐκδικέω Rom. xii. 19, 2 Cor. x. 6. ἐκκλείω* Rom. iii. 27, Gal. iv. 17. ἐκκόπτω Rom. xi. 22, 23, 2 Cor. xi. 12. ἐκπίπτω Rom. ix. 6, Gal. v. 4. ἑκών* Rom. viii. 20, 1 Cor. ix. 17. ἐλευθερία Rom. viii. 21, 1 Cor. x. 29, 2 Cor. iii. 17, Gal. ii. 4, vi. 13. ἐλευθερόω Rom. vi. 18, 22, viii. 2, 21, Gal. v. 1. ἕνεκεν Rom. viii. 36 (quot.), xiv. 20, 2 Cor. iii. 10, vii. 12. ἔξεστιν 1 Cor. vi. 12, x. 23, 2 Cor. xii. 4. ἐπαινέω Rom. xv. 11, 1 Cor. xi. 2, 17, 22. ἐπεί Rom. iii. 6, xi. 6, 22, 1 Cor. v. 10, vii. 14, xiv. 12, 16, xv. 29, 2 Cor. xi. 18, xiii. 3. ἐραυνάω Rom. viii. 27, 1 Cor. ii. 10. εὐοδόομαι Rom. i. 10, 1 Cor. xvi. 2. εὐπρόσδεκτος Rom. xv. 16, 31, 2 Cor. vi. 2 (quot.), viii. 12. εὔχομαι Rom. ix. 3, 2 Cor. xiii. 7, 9. ἐφάπαξ Rom. vi. 10, 1 Cor. xv. 6. ἕως (prep.) 1 Cor. i. 8, iv. 13,

* Nowhere else in N. T.

viii. 7, xv. 6, xvi. 8, 2 Cor. i. 13, iii. 15, xii. 2 (also in quots. Rom. iii. 12, xi. 8). ζηλόω 1 Cor. xii. 31, xiii. 4, xiv. 1, 39, 2 Cor. xi. 2, Gal. iv. 17, 18. ζυμή 1 Cor. v. 6, 7, 8, Gal. v. 9. ζυμόω 1 Cor. v. 6 = Gal. v. 9 (proverb). ζωοποιέω Rom. iv. 17, viii. 11, 1 Cor. xv. 22, 36, 45, 2 Cor. iii. 6, Gal. iii. 21. ἥσσων* 1 Cor. xi. 17, 2 Cor. xii. 15. ἥττημα* Rom. xi. 12, 1 Cor. vi. 7. θάλασσα 1 Cor. x. 1, 2, 2 Cor. xi. 26 (also in quot. Rom. ix. 27). θανατόω Rom. vii. 4, viii. 13, 36 (quot.), 2 Cor. vi. 9. θερίζω 1 Cor. ix. 11, 2 Cor. ix. 6, Gal. vi. 7, 8, 9. θῆλυς Rom. i. 26, 27, Gal. iii. 28. θησαυρίζω Rom. ii. 5, 1 Cor. xvi. 2, 2 Cor. xii. 14. θνητός* Rom. vi. 12, viii. 11, 1 Cor. xv. 53, 2 Cor. iv. 11, v. 4. θυσιαστήριον Rom. xi. 3, 1 Cor. ix. 13, x. 18. ἰδιώτης 1 Cor. xiv. 16, 23, 24, 2 Cor. xi. 6. ἰδού 1 Cor. xv. 51, 2 Cor. v. 17, vi. 2, 9, vii. 11, xii. 14, Gal. i. 20 (also in quot. Rom. ix. 33). Ἰσραηλείτης Rom. ix. 4, xi. 1, 2 Cor. xi. 22. ἰσχυρός 1 Cor. i. 25, 27, iv. 10, x. 22, 2 Cor. x. 10. ἴχνος Rom. iv. 12, 2 Cor. xii. 18. καθό Rom. viii. 26, 2 Cor. viii. 12. κἄν 1 Cor. xiii. 2 *bis*, 3 *ter* (v. l.), 2 Cor. xi. 16. κανών* 2 Cor. x. 13, 15, 16, Gal. vi. 16. καταδουλόω* 2 Cor. xi. 20, Gal. ii. 4. καταισχύνω Rom. v. 5, ix. 33, x. 11, 1 Cor. i. 27 *bis*, xi. 4, 5, 22, 2 Cor. vii. 14, ix. 4. κατακρίνω Rom. ii. 1, viii. 3, 34, xiv. 23, 1 Cor. xi. 32. καταλλαγή* Rom. v. 11, xi. 15, 2 Cor. v. 18, 19. καταλλάσσω* Rom. v. 10 *bis*, 1 Cor. vii. 11, 2 Cor. v. 18, 19, 20. καταλύω Rom. xiv. 20, 2 Cor v. 1, Gal. ii. 18. κατέναντι Rom. iv. 17, 2 Cor. ii. 17, xii. 19. κατεσθίω 2 Cor. xi. 20, Gal. v. 15. κατηχέω Rom. ii. 18, 1 Cor. xiv. 9, Gal. vi. 6. κίνδυνος* Rom. viii. 35, 2 Cor. xi. 26. κληρονομέω 1 Cor. vi. 9, 10, xv. 50 *bis*, Gal. iv. 30 (quot.), v. 21. κλητός Rom. i. 1, 6, 7, viii. 28, 1 Cor. i. 1, 2, 24. κλίμα* Rom. xv. 23, 2 Cor. xi. 10, Gal. i. 21. κολαφίζω 1 Cor. iv. 11, 2 Cor. xii. 7. κολλάομαι Rom. xii. 9, 1 Cor. vi. 16, 17. κράζω Rom. viii. 15, ix. 27, Gal. iv. 6. κρέας* Rom. xiv. 21, 1 Cor. viii. 13. κρυπτός Rom. ii. 16, 29, 1 Cor. iv. 5, xiv. 25, 2 Cor. iv. 2. κυρόω* 2 Cor. ii. 8, Gal. iii. 15. κῶμος Rom. xiii. 13, Gal. v. 21. λίθος 1 Cor. iii. 12, 2 Cor. iii. 7 (also in quot. Rom. ix. 32, 33). λιμός Rom. viii. 35, 2 Cor. xi. 27. μακαρισμός* Rom. iv. 6, 9, Gal. iv. 15. μέθη Rom. xiii. 13, Gal. v. 21. μερίζω Rom. xii. 3, 1 Cor. i. 13, vii. 17, 34, 2 Cor. x. 13. μεταμορφόομαι Rom. xii. 2, 2 Cor. iii. 18. μικρός 1 Cor. v. 6, Gal. v. 9. μωραίνω Rom. i. 22, 1 Cor. i. 20. νέκρωσις* Rom. iv. 19, 2 Cor. iv. 10. ξύλον 1 Cor. iii. 12, Gal. iii. 13. ὁμοίως Rom. i. 27, 1 Cor. vii. 3, 4, 22. ὅμως 1 Cor. xiv. 7, Gal. iii. 15. ὅπλον Rom. vi. 13, xiii. 12, 2 Cor. vi. 7, x. 4. ὄρος 1 Cor. xiii. 2 (proverb), Gal. iv. 24, 25. οὐθείς 1 Cor. xiii. 2,

* Nowhere else in N. T.

3, 2 Cor. xi. 8. ὀφειλέτης Rom. i. 14, viii. 12, xv. 27, Gal. v. 3. ὀφειλή Rom. xiii. 7, 1 Cor. vii. 3. ὄφελον 1 Cor. iv. 8, 2 Cor. xi. 1, Gal. v. 12. ὄφις 1 Cor. x. 9, 2 Cor. xi. 3 ὀψώνιον Rom. vi. 23, 1 Cor. ix. 7, 2 Cor. xi. 8. παιδαγωγός* 1 Cor. iv. 15, Gal. iii. 24, 25. πάντως Rom. iii. 9, 1 Cor. v. 10, ix. 10, 22, xvi. 12. παραβάτης Rom. ii. 25, 27, Gal. ii. 18. παραζηλόω* Rom. x. 19, xi. 11, 14, 1 Cor. x. 22. παρακοή Rom. v. 19, 2 Cor. x. 6. παρασκευάζω 1 Cor. xiv. 8, 2 Cor. ix. 2, 3. παρεισέρχομαι* Rom. v. 20, Gal. ii. 4. παρθένος 1 Cor. vii. 25, 28, 34, 36, 37, 38, 2 Cor. xi. 2. πενθέω 1 Cor. v. 2, 2 Cor. xii. 21. περισσεία Rom. v. 17, 2 Cor. viii. 2, x. 15. περισσός Rom. iii. 1, 1 Cor. xii. 23, 24, xv. 10, 2 Cor. ii. 7, ix. 1, x. 8. πίνω Rom. xiv. 21, 1 Cor. ix. 4, x. 4, 7 (quot.), 21, 31, xi. 22, 25, 26, 27, 28, 29, xv. 32 (quot.). πίπτω Rom. xi. 11, 22, xiv. 4, 1 Cor. x. 8, 12, xiii. 8, xiv. 25. πλουτίζω* 1 Cor. i. 5, 2 Cor. vi. 10. ix. 11. ποῖος Rom. iii. 27, 1 Cor. xv. 35. ποῦ Rom. iii. 27, 1 Cor. i. 20, xii. 17, 19, xv. 55 (quot.), Gal. iv. 15. προεπαγγέλλομαι* Rom. i. 2, 2 Cor. ix. 5. προερῶ Rom. ix. 29, 2 Cor. vii. 3, xiii. 2. Gal. i. 9. προλαμβάνω 1 Cor. xi. 21, Gal. vi. 1. πρόσκομμα Rom, ix. 32, 33 (quot.), xiv. 13, 20, 1 Cor. viii. 9. πτωχός Rom. xv. 26. 2 Cor. vi. 10, Gal. ii. 10, iv. 9. πωρόω Rom. xi. 7, 2 Cor. iii. 14. σαρκικός 1 Cor. iii. 3 *bis*, ix. 11, 2 Cor. i. 12, x. 4. σάρκινος Rom. vii. 14, 1 Cor. iii. 1, 2 Cor. iii. 3. σιγάω Rom. xvi. 25, 1 Cor. xiv. 28, 30, 34. σκανδαλίζω Rom. xiv. 21, 1 Cor. viii. 13 *bis*, 2 Cor. xi. 29. σκάνδαλον Rom. ix. 33 (quot.), xi. 9 (quot.), xiv. 13, xvi. 17. 1 Cor. i. 23, Gal. v. 11. σπείρω 1 Cor. ix. 11, xv. 36, 37, 42, 43, 44, 2 Cor. ix. 6 *bis*, 10, Gal. vi. 7, 8 *bis*. σπουδή Rom. xii. 8, 11, 2 Cor. vii. 11, 12, viii. 7, 8, 16. σταυρόω 1 Cor. i. 13, 23, ii. 2, 8, 2 Cor. xiii. 4, Gal. iii. 1, v. 24, vi. 14. στενάζω Rom. viii. 23, 2 Cor. v. 2, 4. στενοχωρία* Rom. ii. 9, viii. 35, 2 Cor. vi. 4, xii. 20. συμφέρω 1 Cor. vi. 12, x. 23, xii. 7, 2 Cor. viii. 10, xii. 1. συναπάγομαι Rom. xii. 16, Gal. ii. 13. συνεργέω Rom. viii. 28, 1 Cor. xvi. 16, 2 Cor. vi. 1. συνεσθίω 1 Cor. v. 11, Gal. ii. 12. συνευδοκέω Rom. i. 32, 1 Cor vii. 12, 13. συνκλείω Rom. xi. 32, Gal. iii. 22, 23. συνκρίνω* 1 Cor. ii. 13, 2 Cor. x. 12. συνπάσχω* Rom. viii. 17, 1 Cor. xii. 26. συνσταυρόω Rom. vi. 6, Gal. ii. 20. ταπεινός Rom. xii. 16, 2 Cor. vii. 6, x. 1. τάσσω Rom. xiii. 1, 1 Cor. xvi. 15. τοσοῦτος 1 Cor. xiv. 10, Gal. iii. 4. τοὐναντίον 2 Cor. ii. 7, Gal. ii. 7. τρίτον 1 Cor. xii. 28, 2 Cor. xii. 14, xiii. 1. τρίτος 1 Cor. xv. 4, 2 Cor. xii. 2. ὑμέτερος Rom. xi. 31, 1 Cor. xv. 31, xvi. 17, 2 Cor. viii. 8, Gal. vi. 13. ὑπερβολή* Rom. vii. 13, 1 Cor. xii. 31, 2 Cor. i. 8, iv. 7, 17, xii. 7, Gal. i. 13. ὑπερπερισσεύω* Rom. v. 20, 2 Cor.

* Nowhere else in N. T.

vii. 4. ὕψωμα* Rom. viii. 39, 2 Cor. x. 5. φανέρωσις* 1 Cor. xii. 7, 2 Cor. iv. 2. φείδομαι Rom. viii. 32, xi. 21, 1 Cor. vii. 28, 2 Cor. i. 23, xii. 6, xiii. 2. φημί Rom. iii. 18, 1 Cor. vi. 16, vii. 29, x. 15, 19, xv. 50, 2 Cor. x. 10. φθαρτός Rom. i. 23, 1 Cor. ix. 25, xv. 53, 54. φορέω Rom. xiii. 4, 1 Cor. xv. 49. φράσσω Rom. iii. 19, 2 Cor. xi. 10. φρόνιμος Rom. xi. 25, xii. 16, 1 Cor. iv. 10, x. 15, 2 Cor. xi. 19. χεῖλος Rom. iii. 13 (quot.), 1 Cor. xiv. 21 (quot.). χρῄζω Rom. xvi. 2, 2 Cor. iii. 1. ψευδάδελφος* 2 Cor. xi. 26. Gal. ii. 4. ὠφελέω Rom. ii. 25, 1 Cor. xiii. 3, xiv. 6, Gal. v. 2.

III

The Prison Epistles

1. In Phil. and nowhere else in Pauline Epistles:—

ἁγνῶς* i. 17. ἀδημονέω ii. 26. αἴσθησις* i. 9. αἴτημα iv. 6. ἀκαιρέομαι* iv. 10. ἄλυπος* ii. 28. ἀναθάλλω* iv. 10. ἀναλύω i. 23. ἀποβαίνω i. 19. ἀπουσία* ii. 12. ἀρετή iv. 8. ἁρπαγμός* ii. 6. ἀσφαλής iii. 1. αὐτάρκης* iv. 11. ἀφοράω ii. 23. βεβαίωσις i. 7. βίβλος iv. 3. γνησίως* ii. 20. δόσις iv. 15. εἰλικρινής i. 10. ἔντιμος ii. 29. ἐξανάστασις* iii. 11. ἐξαυτῆς ii. 23. ἐπεκτείνομαι* iii. 13. ἐπιλανθάνομαι iii. 13. ἐπιπόθητος* iv. 1. ἑτέρως* iii. 15. εὔφημος* iv. 8. εὐψυχέω* ii. 19. ζημία iii. 7, 8. ἴσος ii. 6. ἰσόψυχος* ii. 20. καίπερ iii. 4. κατατομή* iii. 2. καταχθόνιος* ii. 10. κενοδοξία* ii. 3. κύων iii. 2. λῆμψις* iv. 15. μεγάλως* iv. 10. μορφή ii. 6, 7. μυέομαι* iv. 12. οἶμαι i. 17. ὀκταήμερος* iii. 5. παραβολεύομαι* ii. 30. παραμύθιον* ii. 1. παραπλήσιον* ii. 27. πολίτευμα* iii. 20. πολιτεύομαι i. 27. πραιτώριον i. 13. πτύρομαι* i. 28. σκολιός ii. 15. σκύβαλον* iii. 8. συλλαμβάνω iv. 3. συμμορφίζομαι* iii. 10. συναθλέω* i. 27, iv. 3. σύνζυγος* iv. 3. συνμιμητής* iii. 17. σύνψυχος* ii. 2. ταπείνωσις iii. 21. τελειόω iii. 12. ὑπερυψόω* ii. 9. ὑστέρησις iv. 11. Φαρισαῖος iii. 5. φωστήρ ii. 15. χορτάζω iv. 12.

2. In Eph. and nowhere else in Pauline Epistles:—

ἀγνοία iv. 18. ἀγρυπνέω vi. 18. ἄθεος* ii. 12. αἰσχρότης* v. 4. αἰχμαλωσία iv. 8 (quot.). αἰχμαλωτεύω* iv. 8 (quot.). ἀκρογωνιαῖος ii. 20. ἀμφότεροι ii. 14, 16, 18. ἀνανεόομαι* iv. 23. ἀνίημι vi. 9. ἄνοιξις* vi. 19. ἀπαλγέομαι* iv. 19. ἀπειλή vi. 19. ἄσοφος* v. 15. βέλος* vi. 16. δῶρον ii. 8. ἐκπορεύομαι iv. 29.

* Nowhere else in N. T.

ἐκτρέφω* v. 29, iv. 4. ἑνότης* iv. 3, 13. ἐξισχύω* iii. 18. ἐπέρχομαι ii. 17. ἐπιδύω* iv. 26. ἐπιφαύσκω* v. 14 (quot. from hymn). ἐπουράνια (τά)* i. 3, 20, ii. 6, iii. 10, vi. 12. ἐργασία iv. 19. ἑτοιμασία* vi. 15. εὖ vi. 3 (quot.). εὔνοια* vi. 7. εὔσπλαγχνος iv. 32. εὐτραπελία* v. 4. ἡλικία iv. 13. θυρεός* vi. 16. καταβολή i. 4. καταρτισμός* iv. 12. κατοικητήριον ii. 22. κατώτερος* iv. 19 (quot.). κληρόομαι* i. 11. κλυδωνίζομαι* iv. 14. κοσμοκράτωρ* vi. 12. κραυγή iv. 31. κρυφῇ* v. 12. κυβία* iv. 14. μακράν ii. 13, 17. μακροχρόνιος* vi. 3 (quot.). μέγεθος* i. 19. μεθοδία* iv. 14, vi. 11. μεσότοιχον* ii. 14. μῆκος iii. 18. μωρολογία* v. 4. ὀργίζομαι iv. 26 (quot.). ὁσιότης iv. 24 (only other N. T. instance *Benedictus*, Lk. i. 75). ὀσφύς vi. 14. πάλη* vi. 12. πανοπλία vi. 11. πάροικος ii. 19. παροργισμός* iv. 26. πατριά iii. 15. περιζώννυμι vi. 14. πλάτος iii. 18. ποιμήν iv. 11. πολιτεία ii. 12. πολυποίκιλος* iii. 10. προελπίζω* i. 12. προσκαρτέρησις* vi. 18. προσκολλάομαι v. 31 (quot.). ῥυτίς* v. 27. σαπρός iv. 29. σκοτόομαι iv. 18. σπίλος v. 27. συναρμολογέω* ii. 21, iv. 16. συνκαθίζω ii. 6. συνμέτοχος* iii. 6, v. 7. συνοικοδομέω* ii. 22. συνπολίτης* ii. 19. σύνσωμος* iii. 6. σωτήριον (noun)* vi. 17. ὕδωρ v. 26. ὑπεράνω i. 21, iv. 10. ὑποδέομαι vi. 15. ὕψος iii. 18, iv. 8 (quot.). φραγμός ii. 14. φρόνησις i. 8. χαριτόω i. 6. χειροποίητος ii. 11.

3. In Col. and nowhere else in Pauline Epistles :—

ἀθυμέω* iii. 21. αἰσχρολογία* iii. 8. ἅλας iv. 6. ἀνεψιός* iv. 10. ἀνταναπληρόω* i. 24. ἀνταπόδοσις* iii. 24. ἀπεκδύομαι* ii. 15, iii. 9. ἀπέκδυσις* ii. 11. ἀποκρίνομαι iv. 6. ἀπόκρυφος ii. 3. ἀπόχρησις* ii. 22. ἀρεσκία* i. 10. ἀρτύω iv. 6. ἀφειδία* ii. 23. βραβεύω* iii. 15. γεύομαι ii. 21. δειγματίζω ii. 15. δογματίζομαι* ii. 20. ἐθελοθρησκία* ii. 23. εἰρηνοποιέω* i. 20. ἐμβατεύω* ii. 18. ἔνταλμα* ii. 22 (also in quot. Mt. xv. 9=Mk. vii. 7). ἐξαλείφω ii. 14. ἑορτή ii. 16. εὐχάριστος* iii. 15. θεότης* ii. 9. θιγγάνω ii. 21. θρησκεία ii. 18. θρόνος i. 16. ἰατρός iv. 14. καταβραβεύω* ii. 18. κλῆρος i. 12. μετακινέω* i. 23. μομφή* iii. 13. νεομηνία* ii. 16. ὁρατός* i. 16. παραλογίζομαι ii. 4. παρηγορία* iv. 11. πιθανολογία* ii. 4. πικραίνω iii. 19. πλησμονή* ii. 23. πόνος iv. 13. προακούω* i. 5. προσηλόω* ii. 14. πρωτεύω* i. 18. σκιά ii. 17. Σκύθης* iii. 11. στερέωμα* ii. 5. συλαγωγέω* ii. 8. σύνδουλος i. 7, iv. 7. σωματικῶς* ii. 9. τελειότης iii. 14. ὑπεναντίος ii. 14. φιλοσοφία* ii. 8. χειρόγραφον* ii. 14.

* Nowhere else in N. T.

4. In Eph. and Col. and nowhere else in Pauline Epistles:—

ᾄδω Eph. v. 19, Col. iii. 16. ἀνθρωπάρεσκος* Eph. vi. 6, Col. iii. 22. ἀπαλλοτριόομαι* Eph. ii. 12, iv. 18, Col. i. 21. ἀποκαταλλάσσω* Eph. ii. 16, Col. i. 20, 21. αὔξησις* Eph. iv. 16, Col. ii. 19. ἄφεσις Eph. i. 7, Col. i. 14. ἁφή* Eph. iv. 16, Col. ii. 19. διάνοια Eph. ii. 3, iv. 18, Col. i. 21. δόγμα Eph. ii. 15, Col. ii. 14. δυναμόω Eph. vi. 10, Col. i. 11. θεμελιόω Eph. iii. 18, Col. i. 23. κατενώπιον Eph. i. 4, Col. i. 22. κατοικέω Eph. iii. 17, Col. i. 19, ii. 9. κυριότης Eph. i. 21, Col. i. 16. ὀφθαλμοδουλία* Eph. vi. 6, Col. iii. 22. ῥιζόομαι* Eph. iii. 18, Col. ii. 7. σύνδεσμος Eph. iv. 3, Col. ii. 19, iii. 14. συνζωοποιέω* Eph. ii. 15, Col. ii. 13. ὕμνος* Eph. v. 19, Col. iii. 16. ᾠδή Eph. v. 19, Col. iii. 16.

5. In Phm. and nowhere else in Pauline Epistles:—

ἀναπέμπω 11. ἀποτίνω* 19. ἄχρηστος* 11. ἑκούσιος* 14. ἐπιτάσσω 8. ξενία 22. ὀνίναμαι* 20. προσοφείλω* 19.

6. In two or all of the group (Phil., Eph.-Col., Phm.) and nowhere else in Pauline Epistles:—

ἄμωμος Phil. ii. 15, Eph. i. 4, v. 27, Col. i. 22. ἀνήκω* Eph. v. 4, Col. iii. 18, Phm. 8. γενεά Phil. ii. 15, Eph. iii. 5, 21, Col. i. 26. ἐπιχορηγία* Phil. i. 19, Eph. iv. 16. συνκοινωνέω Phil. iv. 14, Eph. v. 11. συνστρατιώτης* Phil. ii. 25, Phm. 2. ταπεινοφροσύνη Phil. ii. 3, Eph. iv. 2, Col. ii. 18, 23, iii. 12.

IV

The Pastoral Epistles

1. In 1 Tim. and nowhere else in Pauline Epistles:—

ἁγνεία* iv. 12, v. 2. ἀδηλότης* vi. 17. αἰδώς* ii. 9. ἄλλως v. 25. ἀμοιβή* v. 4. ἀνδραποδιστής* i. 10. ἀνεπίλημπτος* iii. 2, v. 7, vi. 14. ἀντίθεσις* vi. 20. ἀντιλαμβάνομαι† vi. 2. ἀντίλυτρον* ii. 6. ἀπέραντος* i. 4. ἀπόβλητος* iv. 4. ἀπόδεκτος* ii. 3, v. 4. ἀποδοχή* i. 15, iv. 9. ἀποθησαυρίζω* vi. 19. ἀπόλαυσις§ vi. 17. ἀποπλανάω vi. 10. ἀπρόσιτος* vi. 6. ἀργός v. 13 *bis* (also in quot. Tit. i. 12). αὐθεντέω* ii. 12. ἀφιλάργυρος§ iii. 3. βαθμός* iii. 13. βλαβερός* vi. 9. βραδύνω iii. 15. βυθίζω† vi. 9. γραώδης* iv. 7. γυμνάζω iv. 7. γυμνασία* iv. 8. διαπαρατριβή* vi 5 διατροφή* vi. 8. δίλογος* iii. 8. διώκτης*

* Nowhere else in N. T.

† Elsewhere in N. T. only in Luke (Gospel and Acts).

§ Elsewhere in N. T. only in Heb.

i. 13. δυνάστης† vi. 15. ἑδραίωμα* iii. 15. εἰσφέρω vi. 7. ἔκγονος* v. 4. ἐκζήτησις* i. 4. ἐκφέρω vi. 7. ἐλάσσων v. 9 (also in quot. Rom. ix. 2). ἐμπίπτω iii. 6, 7, vi. 9. ἔντευξις* ii. 1, iv. 5. ἐντρέφομαι* iv. 6. ἐπακολουθέω v. 10, 24. ἐπαρκέω* v. 10, 16 *bis*. ἐπιλαμβάνομαι vi. 12, 19. ἐπιμελέομαι† iii. 5. ἐπίορκος* i. 10. ἐπιπλήσσω* v. 1. ἐπισκοπή iii. 1. ἐπίσταμαι iv. 4. ἐπιτίθημι v. 22. ἑτεροδιδασκαλέω* i. 3, vi. 3. εὐεργεσία† vi. 2. εὐμετάδοτος* vi. 18. εὐσεβέω† v. 4. ζωογονέω† vi. 13. ἤρεμος* ii. 2. ἡσύχιος ii. 2. θεοσέβεια* ii. 10. θνήσκω v. 6. ἱματισμός† ii. 9. καταλέγομαι* v. 9. καταστολή* ii. 9. καταστρηνιάω* v. 11. καυστηριάζομαι* iv. 2. κοινωνικός* vi. 18. κόσμιος* ii. 9, iii. 2. κοσμίως* ii. 9. κτίσμα iv. 4. λογομαχία* vi. 4. λοιδορία v. 14. μαργαρίτης ii. 9. ματαιολογία* i. 6. μελετάω* iv. 15 (also in quot. Ac. iv. 25). μετάλημψις* iv. 3. μητρολῴης* i. 9. μονόομαι* v. 5. νεότης iv. 12. νεόφυτος* iii. 6. νίπτω v. 10. νομοδιδάσκαλος† i. 7. νοσέω* vi. 4. ξενοδοχέω* v. 10. οἰκοδεσποτέω* v. 14. ὁμολογουμένως* iii. 16. ὀρέγομαι§ iii. 1, vi. 10. παραδέχομαι v. 19. πατρολῴης* i. 9. περίεργος† v. 13. περιέρχομαι v. 13. περιπείρω* vi. 10. περιποιέομαι† iii. 13. πλέγμα* ii. 9. πολυτελής ii. 9. πορισμός* vi. 5, 6. πραϋπαθία* vi. 11. πρεσβυτέριον† iv. 14. πρόδηλος§ v. 24, 25. πρόκριμα* v. 21. πρόσκλισις* v. 21. προσμένω i. 3, v. 5. πυκνός† v. 23. ῥητῶς* iv. 1. σκέπασμα* vi. 8. σπαταλάω v. 6. στόμαχος* v. 23. σωματικός† iv. 8. σωφροσύνη† ii. 9. τάχειον (v.l.) iii. 14. τεκνογονέω* v. 14. τεκνογονία* ii. 15. τεκνοτροφέω* v. 10. τιμάω v. 3 (also in quot. Eph. vi. 2). ὑδροποτέω* v. 23. ὑπερπλεονάζω* i. 14. ὑπόνοια* vi. 4. ὕστερος iv. 1. ὑψηλοφρονέω* vi. 17. φιλαργυρία* vi. 10. φλύαρος* v. 13. ψευδολόγος* iv. 2. ψευδώνυμος* vi. 20.

2. In 2 Tim. and nowhere else in Pauline Epistles:—

ἀθλέω* ii. 5. ἀκαίρως* iv. 2. ἀκρατής* iii. 3. ἀναζωπυρέω* i. 6. ἀνάλυσις* iv. 6. ἀνανήφω* ii. 26. ἀναψύχω* i. 16. ἀνεξίκακος* ii. 24. ἀνεπαίσχυντος* ii. 15. ἀνήμερος* iii. 3. ἄνοια† iii. 9. ἀντιδιατίθεμαι* ii. 25. ἀπαίδευτος* ii. 23. ἀποτρέπομαι* iii. 5. ἀπρόσιτος* vi. 16. ἀργύρεος ii. 20. ἄρτιος* iii. 17. ἄσπονδος* iii. 3. ἀφιλάγαθος* iii. 3. ἀχάριστος† iii. 2. βέλτιον i. 18. βρέφος iii. 15. γάγγραινα* ii. 17. γεωργός ii. 6. γόης* iii. 13. γυναικάριον* iii. 6. δειλία* i. 7. δρόμος† iv. 7 (cf. Ac. xx. 24). ἔκδηλος* iii. 9. ἐλεγμός* iii. 16. ἐμπλέκω ii. 4.

* Nowhere else in N. T.

† Elsewhere in N. T. only in Luke (Gospel and Acts).

§ Elsewhere in N. T. only in Heb.

ἐνδύνω* iii. 6. ἐξαρτίζω† iii. 17. ἐπανόρθωσις* iii. 16. ἐπισωρεύω* iv. 3. ἐπιτιμάω iv. 2. ζωγρέω† ii. 26. ζωογονέω† vi. 13. ἤπιος* ii. 24 (also v. l. 1 Th. ii. 7). θεόπνευστος* iii. 16. κακοπαθέω ii. 9. κακοῦργος† ii. 9. καταστροφή ii. 14. καταφθείρω* iii. 8. κνήθω* iv. 3. κριτής iv. 8. λέων iv. 17. λίαν iv. 15. λογομαχέω* ii. 14. μάμμη* i. 5. μάχομαι ii. 24. μεμβράνα* iv. 13. μέντοι ii. 19. μήποτε ii. 25. νεωτερικός* ii. 22. νομή ii. 17. ξύλινος ii. 20. ὀρθοτομέω* ii. 15. πιστόομαι* iii. 14. πραγματία ii. 4. προδότης† iii. 4. προπετής† iii. 4. σοφίζω iii. 15. στερεός ii. 19. στεφανόω§ ii. 5. στρατιώτης ii. 3. στρατολογέω* ii. 4. συνκακοπαθέω* i. 8, ii. 3. σωρεύω* iii. 6 (also in quot. Rom. xii. 20). σωφρονισμός* i. 7. ὑπόμνησις i. 5. φελόνης* iv. 13. φιλάργυρος† iii. 2. φίλαυτος* iii. 2. φιλήδονος* iii. 4. φιλόθεος* iii. 4. χαλεπός iii. 1. χαλκεύς* iv. 14. χρήσιμος* ii. 14. χρύσεος ii. 20.

In Tit. and nowhere else in Pauline Epistles:—

αἱρετικός* iii. 10. ἀκατάγνωστος* ii. 8. ἀντιλέγω i. 9, ii. 9 (also in quot. Rom. x. 21). ἀνωφελής§ iii. 9. αὐθάδης i. 7. αὐτοκατάκριτος* iii. 11. ἀφθορία* ii. 7. ἀψευδής* i. 2. βδελυκτός* i. 16. ἐγκρατής* i. 8. ἐκστρέφομαι* iii. 11. ἐπιδιορθόω* i. 5. ἐπιστομίζω* i. 11. ἐπιφαίνω† ii. 11, iii. 4. ἡδονή iii. 3. θηρίον i. 12 (quot.). ἱεροπρεπής* ii. 3. Ἰουδαϊκός* i. 14. καλοδιδάσκαλος* ii. 3. κατάστημα* ii. 3. κοσμικός§ ii. 12. λείπω i. 5, iii. 13. λυτρόομαι ii. 14. ματαιολόγος* i. 10. μιαίνω i. 15. νομικός iii. 9, 13. νοσφίζομαι† ii. 10. οἰκουργός* ii. 5. ὀργίλος* i. 7. παλινγενεσία iii. 5. πειθαρχέω† iii. 1. περιούσιος* ii. 14 (quot.). περιφρονέω* ii. 15. πρεσβῦτις* ii. 3. στυγητός* iii. 3. σωτήριος* ii. 11. σωφρονίζω* ii. 4. σωφρόνως* ii. 12. ὑγιής ii. 8. φιλάγαθος* i. 8. φίλανδρος* ii. 4. φιλανθρωπία† iii. 4. φιλότεκνος* ii. 4. φρεναπάτης* i. 10. φροντίζω* iii. 6.

4. In two or all of the group and nowhere else in Pauline Epistles:—

αἰσχροκερδής* 1 Tim. iii. 8, Tit. i. 7. ἄμαχος* 1 Tim. iii. 3, Tit. iii. 2. ἀνατρέπω 2 Tim. ii. 18, Tit. i. 11. ἀνόσιος* 1 Tim. i. 9. 2 Tim. iii. 2. ἀνυπότακτος§ 1 Tim. i. 9, Tit. i. 6, 10. ἀπολείπω 2 Tim. iv. 13, 20, Tit. i. 5. ἀρνέομαι 1 Tim. v. 8, 2 Tim. ii. 12, 13 (quot. from hymn), Tit. i. 16, ii. 12. ἀστοχέω* 1 Tim. i. 6, vi. 21, 2 Tim. ii. 18. βέβηλος§ 1 Tim. i. 9, iv. 7, vi. 20, 2 Tim. ii. 16.

* Nowhere else in N. T.
† Elsewhere in N. T. only in Luke (Gospel and Acts).
§ Elsewhere in N. T. only in Heb.

βίος 1 Tim. ii. 2, 2 Tim. ii. 4. *βλάσφημος* 1 Tim. i. 13, 2 Tim. iii. 2. *γενεαλογία** 1 Tim. i. 4, Tit. iii. 9. *δεσπότης* 1 Tim. vi. 1, 2, 2 Tim. ii. 21, Tit. ii. 9. *διαβεβαιόομαι** 1 Tim. i. 7, Tit. iii. 8. *διάγω** 1 Tim. ii. 2, Tit. iii. 3. *διδακτικός** 1 Tim. iii. 2, 2 Tim. ii. 24. *ἐκτρέπομαι*§ 1 Tim. i. 6, v. 15, vi. 20, 2 Tim. iv. 4. *ἐπίθεσις* 1 Tim. iv. 14, 2 Tim. i. 6. *εὐσέβεια* 1 Tim. ii. 2, iii. 16, iv. 7, 8, vi. 3, 5, 6, 11, 2 Tim. iii. 5, Tit. i. 1. *εὐσεβῶς** 2 Tim. iii. 12, Tit. ii. 12. *ζήτησις* 1 Tim. vi. 4, 2 Tim. ii. 23, Tit. iii. 9. *κατηγορία* 1 Tim. v. 19, Tit. i. 6. *κενοφωνία** 1 Tim. vi. 20, 2 Tim. ii. 16. *κῆρυξ* 1 Tim. ii. 7, 2 Tim. i. 11. *κοσμέω* 1 Tim. ii. 9, Tit. ii. 10. *μαρτυρία* 1 Tim. iii. 7, Tit. i. 13. *μῦθος* 1 Tim. i. 4, iv. 7, 2 Tim. iv. 4, Tit. i. 14. *νηφάλιος** 1 Tim. iii. 2, 11, Tit. ii. 2. *νομίμως** 1 Tim. i. 8, 2 Tim. ii. 5. *ὅσιος* 1 Tim. ii. 8, Tit. i. 8. *παραθήκη** 1 Tim. vi. 20, 2 Tim. i. 12, 14. *παραιτέομαι* 1 Tim. iv. 7, v. 11, 2 Tim. ii. 23, Tit. iii. 10. *παρακολουθέω* 1 Tim. iv. 6, 2 Tim. iii. 10. *πάροινος** 1 Tim. iii. 3, Tit. i. 7. *περιίστημι* 2 Tim. ii. 16, Tit. iii. 9. *πλήκτης** 1 Tim. iii. 3, Tit. i. 7. *ποικίλος* 2 Tim. iii. 6, Tit. iii. 3. *πρεσβύτερος* 1 Tim. v. 1, 2, 17, 19, Tit. i. 5. *προγόνος** 1 Tim. v. 4, 2 Tim. i. 3. *προσέχω* 1 Tim. i. 4, iii. 8, iv. 1, 13, vi. 3, Tit. i. 14. *σεμνότης** 1 Tim. ii. 2, iii. 4, Tit. ii. 7. *σώφρων** 1 Tim. iii. 2, Tit. i. 8, ii. 2, 5. *τυφόομαι** 1 Tim. iii. 6, vi. 4, 2 Tim. iii. 4. *ὑγιαίνω* 1 Tim. i. 10, vi. 3, 2 Tim. i. 13, iv. 3, Tit. i. 9, 13, ii. 1, 2. *ὑπομιμνήσκω* 2 Tim. ii. 14, Tit. iii. 1. *ὑποτύπωσις** 1 Tim. i. 16, 2 Tim. i. 13. *φιλόξενος* 1 Tim. iii. 2, Tit. i. 8. *χείρων* 1 Tim. v. 8, 2 Tim. iii. 13. *ὠφέλιμος** 1 Tim. iv. 8, 2 Tim. iii. 16, Tit. iii. 8.

* Nowhere else in N. T.
† Elsewhere in N. T. only in Luke (Gospel and Acts).
§ Elsewhere in N. T. only in Heb.

INDEX

I.—NAMES AND SUBJECTS

ACHAICUS, 259, 261.
Acts, an unfinished work, 584.
Adada, 106.
Adoption, 209, 419 f.
Adria, 497.
Æons, 524, 592.
Agabus, 72, 466.
'Ages,' 153.
Agrippa I, 71 f.
Agrippa II, 486 ff.
Agrippina, 503 f.
Alexander of Ephesus, 342.
—— the coppersmith, 624.
—— the Great, 7.
Alexandria, 4.
Allegorising, Gnostic, 592 f.
—— Rabbinical, 27.
Altars to unknown gods, 11.
Amanuensis, 154 f.
Ambrose and Theodosius, 326.
Amphipolis, 135.
Ananias of Damascus, 55.
—— the High Priest, 475, 481.
Anastasis, 144.
Angaria, 166.
Angelic mediators, 524, 531, 550, 592.
Angelolatry, 550.
Angels, 206, 284.
Animal body, 319.
Animal-worship, 382.
Anthropomorphites, 317.
Antichrist, 171 ff.
Antinomianism, 153, 161, 195, 201, 214, 238, 293, 411, 517.
Antioch, Pisidian, 89 f.
—— Syrian, 65 ff.
Antiochene subsidy, 73.
Antiochus Epiphanes, 172, 181.
Appeal to the Emperor, 485.
Apocryphal Gospels, 593.
Apollonia, 135.
Apollos, 228, 240, 323, 615 f., 621.
Apostasy, 181.
Apostle, large use of, 60.
Apostleship of Paul challenged, 195, 197 ff., 272 ff.
Apostolic Fathers and Pastorals, 587 f.
Apphia, 568.
Aquæ Salviæ, 640.
Aquila and Prisca, 151, 189 f., 228, 324, 343.
Arabia, 56 f.
Aratus, 18, 24.
Archippus, 568.
Archons, 97 f.
Areiopagos, 144.
Aristarchus, 137, 342, 491, 522.
Aristobulus, 456.
Arria, 491.
Artemas, 621.
Asceticism, 235, 447 ff., 551 f., 559 f., 604.
Asiarchs, 225, 342.
Assassins, 473.
Astral body, 319.
Astrology, 84 f.
Attaleia, 87, 106.
Attendant, 79.
Augustan Cohort, 490.
Autobiography, Paul's spiritual, 414 ff.
Autonomy of the Jews in religion, 45.

BAPTISM for the dead, 314 f.
Barjesus, 85.
Barnabas, 59 f., 69 f., 73, 81, 116 ff., 118.
Bernice, 486.
Berœa, 139.
Bestiarii, 254.
'Bishop,' 463, 589 ff.
Body and flesh, 318 f., 418.
Body essentially evil, 235.
Body of Christ (the Church), 291, 442.
Brigandage, 9, 89, 90.
Burial of Paul, 641.
Burning of Rome, 612, 625.
Burrus, 503.

CARPUS, 624.
Castra Peregrinorum, 490, 502.
Casuistry, 390.
Catechists, 218.
Catholic custom, 286, 310.

Cenchreæ, 189.
Cerinthus, 524, 525.
Chanina, R., 32.
'Chief Shepherd,' 590.
Chloe, 238.
'Christ Jesus': 'Jesus Christ,' 379, 629 f.
Christian, the name, 67 f.
Church, growth in Paul's conception, 533 f.
—— modelled on Synagogue, 605.
—— the Body of Christ, 291, 531.
—— the Commonwealth of God, 512, 533.
—— the Living Temple, 534.
—— the Pillar of the Truth, 603 f.
Cilician Gates, 104, 120, 223.
Circumcision, 109, 391.
Civitas Dei, 512, 518, 533.
Classical quotations, 24.
Clauda, 494.
Claudius' expulsion of Jews from Rome, 131, 151.
Claudius Lysias, 472.
Clemens Romanus, 585, 587.
Clement, 519.
Collection for poor at Jerusalem, 223, 234, 321 f., 344, 366.
Colleges, Rabbinical, 26.
Colossæ, 546.
Colossians, letter to the, 555 ff.
Common Greek, 7 f.
Communism, 36 f.
Conference at Jerusalem, 74 f.
Corinth, 149 ff., 188.
—— parties at, 240.
Corinthians, first letter to (1 Cor. vi. 12-20; 2 Cor. vi. 14-vii. 1), 236 f.
—— second letter to (1 Cor.), 242 ff.
—— third letter to (2 Cor. x-xiii. 10), 327 ff.
—— fourth letter to (2 Cor. 1-ix, xiii. 11-14), 346 ff.
Cornelius, 112.
Corn-ships, 492.
Council at Jerusalem, 111 ff.
Couriers, 167.
Covenant, Old and New, 354 ff.
Cremation, 316.
Crescens, 624.
Crete, 613 f.
Crispus, 168.
Cyprus, 81 ff.

DALMATIA, 612, 624.
Damaris, 148.
Damascus, 49 ff.
Darwin, 306.
Deacon, 39, 589, 603.
Deaconess, 189, 603.
Death and sin, 403 ff.
Decree of Council at Jerusalem, 113.
Deity of Christ, 161, 426, 451 f., 464.
Delation, 384 f.
Demas, 522, 624 f., 635.
Demetrius, the silversmith, 341.
Democratic constitution of Apostolic Church, 39, 81, 111, 114, 605.
'Deposit,' 593 f., 628.
Derbe, 104, 120.
Descensus ad Inferos, 539.
Dionysius the Areopagite, 147.
'Discipline,' 593.
Discipline of offenders, 216.
Disembodiment, 359 ff.
Dispersion, 3 ff.
Divine right of kings, 444.
Divorce, 262.
'Dogs,' 516.
Dreams, 54 f., 125.
Drusilla, 480, 482.

'EARNEST,' 349.
Earthly body, 319.
Egnatian Way, 9.
Elder, 463, 589 f., 603, 605.
Elders of Ephesus at Miletus, 462 ff.
Election, 426 f.
Elymas, 85.
Empire, Roman, 8 ff.
Epænetus, 191.
Epaphras, 546, 566.
Epaphroditus, 507 ff., 516.
'Ephesian Letters,' 228.
'Ephesians, Epistle to the,' 528 ff.
Ephesus, 225 ff.
Epictetus, 548, 570.
Epicureans, 143.
Epimenides, 11, 24, 618.
Episcopos, 590, 605.
Erastus of Ephesus, 260, 623 f.
Erskine of Linlathen, 301 ff.
Essenes, 37, 447, 549 ff.
Ethereal body, 52, 319.
Euodia, 518.
Eunice, 100.
Euraquilo (Euroclydon), 493.
Eutychus, 461.
Evil eye, 203.
'Examination,' 252 f., 425.
Execution of Paul, 640.
Exorcism, 231 ff.
Exposure of children, 386.

'FABLES,' 592.
Fair Havens, 492 f.
'Faithful words,' 594.
Famine, 72 f.
'Fashion,' 513.

Fatherhood, the Heavenly Archetype of, 537.
'Fear of the Lord,' 361.
Feasts in idol-temples, 269.
Felix, 480 ff.
Festus, 484 ff.
Flesh and spirit, 214, 418.
'Form,' 513.
Fortunatus, 259, 261.
Fortune-teller, 130.
'Forty stripes save one,' 334.
Francis of Assisi, 336.
'Fruit of the spirit,' 215.
'Fulness,' 524, 531.

GAIUS of Corinth, 168, 372.
—— of Derbe, 104, 224, 342, 371.
Galatia, 89 f., 223 f.
Galatians, letter to the, 195 ff.
Gallia Cisalpina, mission to, 612 f., 624.
Gallio, 185 f.
Gamaliel, 28 f.
Gaoler of Philippi, 133 f.
Gates of Cilicia, 104, 120, 223.
'Genealogies,' 592.
Gentile converts, low morality of, 161, 195, 214, 517, 540.
—— hostility to the Gospel worldly, not religious, 130, 341.
Gentiles and the Law, 108 ff.
—— first evangelised at Antioch, 69.
Gibbon, 11.
Gnosticism, 523 ff.
Gnostics (the name), 525.
God-fearers, 12 f.
Gods of heathendom, 270 f.
Gospel a treasonable propaganda, 131, 138, 174.
Grafting, 438.
Greek colonisation, 3.
—— conquests, 7.
—— Common, 7 f.

HADRIAN to his soul, 360.
Hagar, 211.
Haggadah, 27.
Halachah, 27.
'Harrowing of Hell,' 539.
Headship of Christ, 531.
Heathendom, corruption of, 383 ff.
Heavenly body, 319.
'Heavenly regions,' 524.
Heavens, the Seven, 335.
Hebrews, 38.
—— Epistle to the, 639.
Helena, Queen of Abdiene, 73.
Helius, 625.
Hellenists, 5, 38.
Heresy in Asia, 523 ff.
Hermes, 101.
Hermogenes, 623, 629.
Herod Agrippa I, 71 f.
—— —— II, 486 ff.
Hierapolis, 548.
High Priest, Paul's encounter with, 475 f.
Hillel, 28.
'House of Interpretation,' 26.
'House of the Book,' 22.
Huns, 176.
Husbands and wives, 542 f., 564.
Hymenæus, 631.
Hymns, quotations from primitive, 161, 410 f., 542, 595, 604, 630.

ICONIUM, 96 f.
Idolatry, 382.
Idols, food sacrificed to, 269 ff.
'Image of God,' 513 f., 556.
Immortality, quarrel between Sadducees and Pharisees, 476 f.
Imputation, 313, 402 f., 436.
Inarticulate language, 306.
Incarnation, 514, 525, 538.
Informers, 384 f.
Insanity, reverence for, 130.
Intellectuals, 244 ff., 249.
Irresponsibility of God, 428.
Irvingites, 300 ff.
Islam, 176.
Isthmian Games, 150, 275.

JAMES, the Lord's brother, 60, 108, 112 f.
—— the son of Zebedee, 72.
Jannes and Jambres, 632 f.
Jason, 136 f.
'Jesus Christ': 'Christ Jesus,' 379, 629 f.
Jesus Justus, 523.
'Jew,' 389.
Jewish Gnosticism, 549 ff.
—— monotheism, attraction of, 12.
Jews, contempt for, 5.
—— expelled from Rome, 131, 151.
—— first addressed, 83, 380 f., 502 f.
John Mark. *See* Mark.
John the Baptist's disciples, 228 ff.
Judaists, 74 f., 108 ff., 194 ff., 260, 329 ff., 372 f., 506, 516 f.
Judas Barsabbas, 114, 116.
Julian, 67.
Julius the centurion, 491 ff.
Justin Martyr, 11.
Justus (Titius), 168.

KINGS, divine right of, 444.
Kiss, 166, 464.

LANGUAGE, universal, 7 f.
Languages and tongues, 296 ff.
Laodiceia, 546 f.
Law, double signification, 396.
—— given by angels, 206.
—— Paul's attitude to the, 120, 193, 413 ff.
—— study of the, 26.
—— taught by rote to children, 23.
Lawyer, 26, 622.
Laying on of hands, 605.
Letters, conveyance of, 166 f.
Letter-writing, 154 f.
Libertinism, 235.
Liberty, Christian, 272 ff.
Linus, 588.
Litigation, 242, 258.
Lois, 100.
'Lord,' title of heathen deities and Emperor, 271.
'Lords' and 'masters,' 588.
Love-feast, 37, 286.
Love, praise of, 293 ff.
Lucina, 641.
Lucius of Cyrene, 80.
Luke, 90 f., 105, 123, 125, 135, 344, 368, 491, 522, 584, 595 f.,
Lycus valley, 546 ff., 598.
Lydia, 128 f.
Lysias, 472.
Lystra, 99 f.

MACEDONIA, 125.
Macedonian poverty, 366.
Magic, Ephesian, 228, 231, 633.
Maimonides, 22, 30.
Malady, Paul's, 87, 122, 149, 189.
Malaria, 87.
Malea, 149.
Manaen, 80.
Manual of Christian teaching, 412, 594.
Marcus Aurelius, 410.
Marginalia, 245, 334, 389, 401, 609, 610.
Mark, 79, 88, 117, 522, 566, 635.
Marriage, 30, 262, 543.
Mary of Ephesus, 457.
'Masters' and 'lords,' 588.
Masters and slaves, 543, 564.
Matter essentially evil, 524, 549.
Medical terms, 56, 70, 161, 491, 499, 589, 610.
Melita (Malta), 496, 498.
Menander, 24.
Mercenariness, 608, 609 f.
Midrash, 26 f.
Miletus, 462.
Millennium, 154, 300.
Ministries in the Church, 292.
Miraculous gifts, 35 f.
Mishnah, 23.
Mixed marriages, 263 f.
Mnason, 467.
Muratorian, Canon, 585.
Mysteries, Greek, 276 f.
'Mystery,' 320, 440, 529, 536.

NAASENES, 524, 548.
Names, Jews' double, 21.
Nannacus, 96.
Narcissus, 456.
Natural affection, 386.
Navigation, season for, 648.
Nazirite vow, 190, 472.
Neapolis, 126.
Neopythagoreanism, 448.
Nephew of Paul, 478.
Nero, 503 ff., 625, 639.
—— *redivivus*, 174 f.
Nicolaitans, 526.
Nicolaus, 39, 526.
Nicopolis, 615 f., 622.
Nympha, 566.

OATHS, absolution from, 485.
Onesimus, 545 f.
Onesiphorus, 626, 629.
Ophiorymè, 548.
Ophites, 524, 548.
Oral tradition, 80, 218, 287.
Orders of primitive ministry, 463, 589, 605.
Ordination, 605.
Overseer, 589 ff., 603.

PAGAN RELIGION, decay of, 10 f.
Pamphylia, 86 f.
'Panoply of God,' 543 f.
Paphos, 84.
Papyrus, 155.
Paradise, 335.
Parents and children, 543, 564.
Paronomasia, 517.
Parties at Corinth, 241 f.
Pastoral Epistles, 579 ff.
Pastors, 539.
Paul, the name, 21.
'Pedagogue,' 206 f.
Pentecost, 4.
Pentecostal Brethren, 302.
Peregrini, 490.
Perga, 87, 106.
Persecution a furtherance of the Gospel, 65.
—— the first, 45 ff.
—— Herod Agrippa I's, 71 f.

Persecution in Macedonia, 141.
Peter at Antioch, 108 ff.
—— at the Council, 112.
Pharisaism, 32.
Pharisees, 20 f., 32.
Philemon, 545, 568.
—— letter to, 574 ff.
Philetus, 631.
Philip, 39 f., 466.
Philippi, 126 f.
Philippian generosity, 137, 142, 152, 273, 508, 520.
Philippians, letter to the, 510 ff.
Philosophers, 143 f.
Phœbe, 189.
Phœnix, 493.
Phrygian slave, 545.
Phygelus, 623, 629.
'Pillars,' 199.
Piracy, 9.
Plausibility, charge of, 197, 213, 362.
Pleroma, 524.
Plot to assassinate Paul, 459, 477 f.
Politarchs, 136.
Pompey's deportation of Jewish captives, 3.
—— desecration of the Temple, 172.
Pope as Antichrist, 176.
Poppæa Sabina, 505.
Potter and clay, 428, 430 f.
Precognition, 252 f., 625.
Presbyter, 463, 589 ff., 603, 605.
Presbytery, 605.
Prisca, Priscilla, 151.
Prison at Philippi, 132 f.
Progress of Gospel after Crucifixion, 35 f.
Prophecy and tongues, 302 f.
Prophet, 72, 292, 535.
Prophetess, 310.
Prophets, Essene, 551.
—— of the Cevennes, 299 f.
Proselytism, 6.
Proverbs, 48, 65, 149, 150, 184, 213, 218, 251, 253, 276, 293, 370, 384, 475, 532, 545, 572, 608, 614.
Providential interposition, 122.
Publius, 499.
Puteoli, 500.
Ptolemais, 466.

Quinquennium Neronis, 504.

Rab, *Rabbi*, *Rabban*, 26.
Rabbinism of Paul, 27, 204.
Rabbis and trade, 24 f.
'Reading,' 536, 605.
Reception, 37, 288.
Reconciliation, 362, 402.
Reformation as the Apostasy, 177.
Reformers as precursors of Antichrist, 177.
Remuneration, 273 ff., 325, 338.
'Restraint,' 'Restrainer,' 173.
Resurrection, 144, 311 ff.
—— Gnostic doctrine of, 631.
Riot of Ephesus, 342 f.
—— Jerusalem, 472 f.
Rock, the stricken, 277.
Roman Citizenship, 20, 132, 474.
—— Empire, 8 ff.
—— Law, 10, 173 f.
—— Peace, 9.
—— Roads, 9.
'Romans, Epistle to the,' 378 ff.
Rome, burning of, 612, 625.
—— early introduction of Christianity, 151, 506.
Rulers, obedience to, 444 f.

SABINUS, 625.
Sacramental security, 276 ff.
Sacrilege, 389 f.
Salamis, 83.
Sanhedrin, 475 f.
Sarcasm of Paul, 327.
Saul, Paul's Jewish name, 21.
Scurrility of the Antiochenes, 67.
Second Advent, 35, 136 f., 138, 153, 170 ff., 300, 632.
'Seed,' 204 f.
Seneca, 185, 503, 571.
Septuagint, 22.
Sergius Paulus, 84.
Seven Heavens, 335.
Seven, the, 39.
Shammai, 28.
Shekinah, 277, 337 f., 426.
Ships, 492.
Shorthand, 668 f.
Silas (Silvanus), 114, 118, 142, 152.
Simon Magus, 524.
'Slave of Christ,' 265.
Slavery, 569 ff., 609.
Socrates, 144.
Sosthenes, 187, 243.
Sovereignty of Christ, 531.
—— God, 427.
Spain, mission to, 612 f.
Spirit and flesh, 214, 418.
Spiritual body, 319.
—— gifts, 289 ff.
'Spiritual marriage,' 266 f.
Spirituals, 238, 289.
Stephanas, 148, 259, 261, 324.
Stephen, 39 ff.
Stoic, 24, 143.
Suicide, 385.
Sun-worship, Essene, 553.
Supper, Lord's, 286 ff.

Symeon Niger, 80.
Syncretism, 12.
Syntyche, 518.
Syria-Cilicia, 61 f., 119 f.
Syrtis, 494.

Tarsus, 17 ff.
Taurus, 89, 106.
Taxes, 445 f.
Teacher, 80, 218, 292, 593.
Temple of Artemis, 226 f.
Temples, plunder of heathen, 389.
Tent-making, 25.
Tertius, 378.
Tertullus, 481.
'Testimonies,' 229, 394.
Theatre, 342.
Theodore of Mopsuestia, 586.
Thessalonica, 135 f.
Thessalonians, first letter to the, 154 ff.
—— second letter to the, 179 ff.
'Thorn for the flesh,' 337, 664 f.
Tigellinus, 625.
Timothy, 100, 121, 142, 152, 167, 191, 260, 323, 325, 597 ff., 638 f.
—— first letter to, 599 ff.
—— second letter to, 627 ff.
Titius Justus, 168.
Titus, with eleemosynary expedition, 73 f.
—— question of his circumcision, 74 f.
—— accompanies third mission, 223 f.
—— first mission to Corinth, 234, 338.
—— second mission to Corinth, 340, 345.
—— third mission to Corinth, 366.
—— joins Paul at Antioch, 611.
—— accompanies him on his last journey, 623.
—— letter to, 617 ff.
Tongues, 295 ff.
Trade, 24 f.
Tradition, Evangelic, 80, 218, 287, 593 f.
Tre Fontane, 640.
Tripartite nature of man, 166, 249.
Triumph (Roman), 352.
Troas, 124, 344, 624.
Trogyllium, 462.
Trophimus, 371 f., 472, 623.
Tresly, Council of, 154.
Tryphæna, 457.
Tryphosa, 457.
Tychicus, 371 f., 522, 621, 635.
Tyrannos, 231.

Union with Christ, 201, 216, 409, 418, 532, 563.
'Universal Bishop,' 176.
Unknown gods, 11, 143.
Unwritten Law, 389.

Varro, 10.
Vegetarianism, 448.
Veil, 282 ff.
Ventriloquist, 130.
Viper, 497, 499.
Virginity, 266 f.
'Voices,' 298.
Vows, absolution from, 485.

Way, the, 47.
'West, the boundary of the,' 585.
Widows, 606.
Women and Jewish religion, 6.
Women in Macedonia, 128.
—— their position in the Church, 282 ff., 310, 602.
'Works of the flesh,' 215.

Xenophanes, 10.

Zealots, 444.
Zenas, 616, 621.
Zeus, 101.

II.—GREEK WORDS AND PHRASES

ἀββᾶ, 209
ἄβυσσος, 433
ἀγαθός, 402
ἄγαμος, 31
Ἄγαρ, 211
ἀγνοεῖν, 163
ἀγοραῖος, 138
ἀδημονεῖν, 515
ἀδιάλειπτος, 425
Ἀδρίας, 497
αἰών, 153, 524
αἰώνιος, 180
ἀκρογωνιαῖος, 534
ἀλαζονία, 384
ἀληθεύειν, 211
ἅλς, 565
ἀνάγνωσις, 536
ἀνακόπτειν, 213
ἀνακρίνειν, 252 f.
ἀνάστασις ἐκ νεκρῶν, ἀνάστασις τῶν νεκρῶν, 518
ἀναστατοῦν, 214
ἀνεξίκακος, 632
ἀνεψιός, 79
ἀντιδιατίθημι, 632
ἀντίθεσις, 611
ἀπαντᾶν, 130
ἀπ' ἀρχῆς, 183
ἀπεκδύεσθαι, 561
ἀπέχειν, 521, 575
ἀπόκριμα, 347
ἀρέσκειν, 418
ἁρπαγμός, 514
ἀρραβών, 349
ἀρτέμων, 497
ἀρχιποίμην, 590
ἀσχημονεῖν, 269
ἀτενίζειν, 70
ἄτοπος, 183
αὐθάδης, 618
αὐτάρκεια, 24, 370
ἄφεσις, 396
ἀφθαρσία, 545
ἀφθορία, 619
ἀφορίζειν, 21
ἀφορμή, 215
ἄφρων, 318

Βάαλ (ἡ), 435
βαπτίζειν, 675
βάρβαρος, 380, 497
βασκαίνειν, 203
Βελίαρ, 237
βιωτικός, 259

γαμίζειν, 268
γενεαλογία, 592
γνήσιε σύνζυγε, 519
γνῶσις, 290, 517

δειγματίζειν, 561
δεισιδαίμων, 145
δεσπότης, 588
διάκονος, 463
διδασκαλία, 593
διέρχεσθαι, 83
διθάλασσος, 497
δίκαιος, 402
δικαίωμα, 407
δοκιμάζειν, 165
δοκιμάζειν τὰ διαφέροντα, 390, 510
δολοῦν, 357
δόσις καὶ λῆμψις, 521
δυνατὰ τῷ Θεῷ, 328
δωρεά, 407

εἶδος, 165
εἰλικρινία, 354
ἐκδέχεσθαι, 288
ἐκ πίστεως εἰς πίστιν, 381
ἔκστασις, 76
ἔκτρωμα, 312
ἔκχυσις, 675
ἐμβατεύειν, 562
ἐνεργεῖν, 159
ἐνκόπτειν, 213
ἐν ὀλίγῳ, 489
ἐν πρώτοις, 312
ἐν Χριστῷ, 202
ἐξαρτίζειν, 594
ἐπιεικές, ἐπιεικία, 520
ἐπιθανάτιος, 254
ἐπιμελεία, 491
ἐπισκηνοῦν, 338
ἐπίσκοπος, 463
ἐπιστολαί, 322, 507
ἐπισυναγωγή, 182
ἐπίτροπος, 208
ἐπιφαίνειν, 594
ἐπιφάνεια, 182
ἐπιχορηγεῖν, 203
ἐπουράνια (τά), 557
Ἐσσαῖοι, 551
ἔσοπτρον, 295
ἐσταυρωμένος, 203
ἔσχηκα, 347
ἑτεροζυγεῖν, 236
εὐρακύλων, 493
εὐτραπελία, 541
ἐφ' ᾧ, 403
ἕως τέλους, 348

ζωογονεῖν, 610

ἡλικία, 540

θεόπνευστος, 634
θεοστυγής, 384
θηριομαχεῖν, 315
θριαμβεύειν, 353

ἰδιώτης, 307
ἱερόθυτον, 281
Ἰησοῦς Χριστός, Χριστὸς Ἰησοῦς, 379, 629 f.
ἱκαναὶ ἡμέραι, 645
ἱλαστήριον, 396
ἵνα τί, 281
ἱστορεῖν, 59

κάθαρμα, 254
καθορᾶν, 383
καλῶς ποιεῖν, 521
καπηλεύειν, 354
καταβραβεύειν, 562
καταναρκᾶν, 331
καταρτίζειν, 161
κατέχειν, 383
κατέχον (τό), 174
κατηχεῖν, 390
κατοπτρίζεσθαι, 356

καυστηριάζεσθαι, 589
κοιμᾶσθαι, 163, 288, 405 f.
κοσμοκράτορες, 544
κτίσις, 220
κύριος, 271, 588

λαλεῖν, λέγειν, 394
λογικός, 442
λόγιον, 392
λόγιος, 228

μάμμη, 100
μαραναθά, 325
μαρτύριον τοῦ Θεοῦ, 247
μεσόστοιχον τοῦ φραγμοῦ, 534
μετασχηματίζειν, 253, 514
μετατίθεσθαι, 196
μὴ γένοιτο, 202
μολύνειν, 237
μορφή, 514
μόρφωσις, 390
μυστήριον, 320
μωρολογία, 565

νήπιος, 208
νομικός, 622

ξενία, 502
ξύλον, 132

οἰκονόμος, 208
οἱ πολλοί, 407
ὁλόκληρος, 166
ὁλοτελής, 166
ὀψώνια, 413

παιδαγωγός, 206 f.
παραβιάζεσθαι, 129
παραθήκη, 593
παράκλησις, 60
πάρεσις, 396
πατριά, 537
περικάθαρμα, 254
περίψημα, 254
πιστεύειν, 156
πλήρωμα, 524
πληροφορεῖν, 399
πνευματικός, 289
ποιμένες, 539
πρεσβύτης, 575
πρεσβύτερος, 463
προγράφειν, 203
προέχεσθαι, 394
προσαγωγή, 400
προσευχή, 127
προστάτις, 189
προσωποληψία, 199
πρόσωπον, 347
πρότερον(τό), 653
πρῶτος(ὁ), 499
πρῶτος λόγος, 584
Πύθων, 130
πυρά, 499
πυρετοί, 499
πωροῦν, 356

ῥαντισμός, 675

σαρκικός, 249
σάρκινος, 249
σκανδαλίζειν, 272
σκάνδαλον τοῦ σταυροῦ, 214
σκεῦος, 161
σκόλοψ, 664 f.
σκύβαλον, 518
σοφία, 84, 290, 530
σπεῖρα Σεβαστή, 490
σπερμολόγος, 143
στέγειν) 160, 294
στίγμα, 220
στοιχεῖν, 217
στοιχεῖον, 208, 561
στοργή, 386
συγγενής, 458
συναντιλαμβάνεσθαι, 421
συνείδησις, 24
συνέκδημος, 342
σύνεσις, 84
συνκρίνειν, 248
σύνοιδα ἐμαυτῷ, 253
σύντροφος, 80
σχῆμα, 253, 514
σῶμα ('slave'), 410
Σωτὴρ Θεός, 595

τεκνογονία, 602
τέλειος, 248
τέλος, 278, 433
τὸ κατ' ἐμέ, 380
τύπος, 412

ὕβρις, 384
ὑγιαίνειν, ὑγιής, 589
ὑδροποτεῖν, 609
υἱοθεσία, 209
Υἱὸς τοῦ Θεοῦ, 56
Υἱὸς τῆς ἀγάπης αὐτοῦ, 556
ὑπαντᾶν, 130
ὑπάρχειν, 200, 514
ὑπέρακμος, 268 f.
ὑπερηφανία, 384
ὑπηρέτης, 79
ὑποκριτής, 110
ὑπόστασις, 332
ὑπωπιάζειν, 276

φελόνης, 635
φημι, 268
φθόνος φόνος, 384
φιλανθρωπία, 498, 595
φρονεῖν, 418
φρόνησις, 530
φωνή, 298

χάρισμα, 289, 413
χειροτονεῖν, 105
χρηματίζειν, 67
χριστέμπορος, 157

ψυχικός, 249, 319 f.

δόξα τῷ Θεῷ πάντων ἕνεκα. ἀμήν.